Prentice Hall Study Guide

American Diploma Project℠ Algebra I End-of-Course Exam

A. Rose Primiani, Ed.D. / William Caroscio

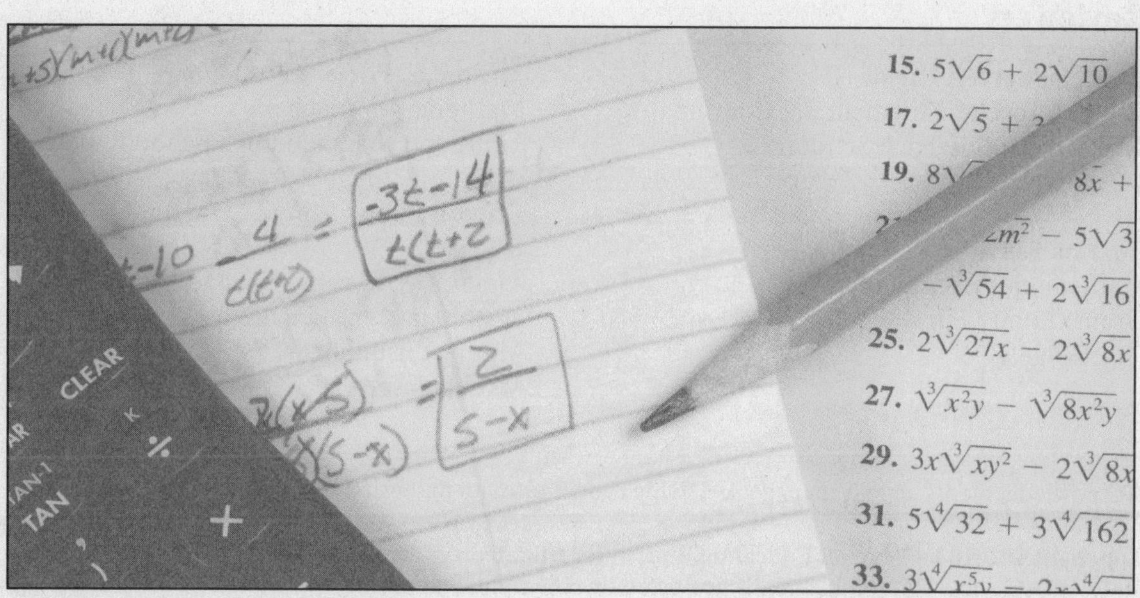

Order Information

Send orders to:
PEARSON CUSTOMER SERVICE
P.O. BOX 2500
LEBANON, IN 46052-3009
or
CALL TOLL FREE 1-800-848-9500
(8:00 A.M.-6:00 P.M. EST)

- Orders can be placed via phone

PEARSON

Authors

A. Rose Primiani, Ed.D. (1939–2009), was a former Director of Mathematics and Computer Education for District 10, Bronx, NYC, and a Supervisor of Mathematics K–12 for the Yonkers Public Schools, NY. She was also an adjunct professor at Manhattan College, Mercy College, CUNY, and Fordham University. Dr. Primiani was a Curriculum and Instructional Materials Consultant for Pearson Publishers, School Division. She consulted extensively on mathematics curriculum development and effective instructional practices and was involved in correlating other states' curriculum to Pearson middle school and high school mathematics texts; including those of New Jersey, Ohio, Maryland, and New York.

William Caroscio has over 35 years of experience in mathematics education. This experience includes middle school, high school, and college teaching experience. Mr. Caroscio is past president of the Association of Mathematics Teachers of New York State and the New York State Mathematics Supervisor Association. He is a member of AMTNYS, NYSAMS, NCTM, MAA, NCSM, NYSMATYC, and AMATYC. Mr. Caroscio is a National Instructor in the T3 (Teachers Teaching with Technology) program. He has conducted sessions and workshops at the local, state, and national levels. Mr. Caroscio has served as an item writer for the NYS Education Department assessment committees, as a member of the Commissioner's Committee on the New Mathematics Standards, and the Geometry Committee, writing sample tasks for the new standards.

Reviewers

Jean Henderson Larson
Algebra Teacher/Instructional Coordinator
Westerly Middle/High School
Westerly, RI

Charma Linville
Mathematics Consultant
Grant County High School
Dry Ridge, KY

Mickey E. Porter
Mathematics Teacher
Thurgood Marshall High School
Academic Magnet Academy
Dayton Public Schools, Dayton OH

Jamal K. Wakeem MA, MAT
Mathematics Curriculum Coordinator
Math Consultant
Mechanicsburg, PA

Acknowledgements appear on page A–1, which constitutes an extension of this copyright page.

ISBN-13: 978-0-13-368419-3
ISBN-10: 0-13-368419-9

1 2 3 4 5 6 7 8 9 13 12 11 10 09

TABLE OF CONTENTS

Chapter 3 Linear Equations and Inequalities in Two Variables

Chapter 5 Polynomials and Factoring

Chapter 6 Quadratic Equations and Functions

Chapter 7 Rational and Radical Expressions and Equations

Chapter 8 Probability

Chapter 9 Data Analysis

Algebra I End-of-Course Exam

Students are competing with students from other states as well as from around the world. It is the goal of the American Diploma Project (ADP℠) to better prepare you for today's challenges in the classroom and beyond.

DISCLAIMER: Some of the information below has been taken in part from the ADP℠ Algebra I Achieve Web site. American Diploma Project is a service mark of Achieve, Inc., which was not involved in the production of, and does not endorse, this project.

A consortium of states (Hawaii, Kentucky, Maryland, Minnesota, New Jersey, North Carolina, Ohio, and Pennsylvania) formed a group to develop common standards and content for an End-of-Course Exam in Algebra I. The Algebra I standards are vertically aligned with the Algebra II End-of-Course Exam. The content standards that are now being used for ADP Algebra I can be found at http://www.achieve.org/files/ADPAlgebraIEOCExamStandardsupdated102108.pdf.

This book is designed to help you become familiar with the content and structure of the exam. Included in this book are review lessons of material that may help you with the exam. This review will measure your level of understanding of the content and help you develop the organizational tools to solve questions in-depth, correctly, and logically.

Each lesson in this book will:

- address one or more specific content standards developed for Algebra I.
- include definitions, formulas, and examples that include full explanations.
- provide end-of-lesson and end-of-chapter practice exercise tests to prepare for the Algebra I Exam.

Exam Purposes

The purposes behind developing a common Algebra I End-of-Course Exam were:

1. ***To improve classroom instruction—and ensure consistency within and across states.*** The standards and exam will provide teachers with an opportunity to develop lessons and curricula that feature the most important concepts and skills.
2. ***To help determine if students are ready to do college-level coursework.*** The exam measures skills students need to enter and succeed in first-year mathematics courses. This assessment should help high schools better prepare their students for college.
3. ***To compare student scores and progress among states.*** By developing common standards and a common test, educators will be able to better assess students' knowledge. This also allows educators to refine content areas and continue to make adjustments in order to improve students' learning in Algebra I content.

INTRODUCTION

About the ADP℠ Algebra I End-of-Course Exam

The Algebra I End-of-Course Exam will consist of Algebra I skills and concepts, which will be taken by students across all participating states. The Algebra I Exam will cover a range of algebraic topics that are typically taught in an Algebra I course, including:

1. Operations on Numbers and Expressions	25%
2. Linear Relationships	35%
3. Non-Linear Relationships	20%
4. Data, Statistics, and Probability	20%

The Exam is divided into two parts. Part I does *not* allow the use of calculators. Part II *does* allow calculator use. Each part is 45–60 minutes long. However, additional time may be allowed if needed to complete the test.

The Exam consists of a total of forty-seven questions
• Forty multiple-choice questions (1 point each)
• Five short-answer questions (2 points each)
• Two extended-response questions (4 points each)

Test-Taking Tips

1. Bring pencils, erasers, a ruler, and a calculator to the exam area. Multiple-choice answer sheet bubbles must be filled in using a pencil.
2. Show your work in the exam booklet in the assigned white area under the corresponding question. Include tables, graphs, and diagrams where required. Partial credit will be awarded on correct representation of the answer.

The following are general guidelines for constructed-response items on the Algebra I End-of-Course Exam. These guidelines are to help you understand what is expected of your responses on these items.

Multiple-Choice Items, General Guidelines

1. Read the test instructions before you start answering the questions.
2. Read questions and options carefully to understand what is being asked before you answer the question.
3. Answer all questions and do not leave any blanks. By guessing you have a 25% chance of getting the correct answer.
4. Immediately cross out answers that cannot be correct. Also use estimation when appropriate to narrow down the answer choices.
5. If a question is consuming more time than you anticipated, mark the question, skip it, and return to it later. REMEMBER TO SKIP the answer location (bubble) on the answer sheet.
6. Perform all computations on the exam booklet.
7. Use a calculator (when allowed) for square roots, decimals, and other computations.
8. Fill in the correct corresponding bubble on the answer sheet.
9. Check to see if your answer is reasonable.

Constructed-Response Items, General Guidelines

1. A response consists of the answer to the item, as well as any information requested of you. When you are asked to show or explain your work, justify your answer, or explain your reasoning, you also receive credit for a correct strategy or justification, in addition to credit for a correct answer. It is possible to receive credit for one without the other.
2. When an item requires you to show or explain a strategy, a response of *I plugged it into my calculator* or an equivalent response does not earn credit for the strategy. You must explain how the calculator was used, either by indicating key entries or describing the calculation process to earn credit for the strategy.
3. When using a guess-and-check method, you must show more than one trial to earn credit for the strategy.
4. When an item, or part of an item, refers to only one particular unit of measure (inches, degrees Celsius, and so on) throughout the entire item or part, the response to that item or part does not need to restate the unit in the answer to earn credit. Also, if the question is phrased in terms of a particular unit, the answer will be considered to be in that measurement. However, in a case where multiple units of measure are referenced in the item or the unit of measurement would change in your answer (for example, feet to feet squared), your response must give the appropriate units (or change of units) to earn credit for the answer.
5. When an item gives specific instructions about the format of the answer, you must respond to the item in the format that is asked for to earn credit for the answer. For example:
   - Round to the correct decimal place, when specified.
   - Label axes and scales in graphs (including a scale of 1) when required.
   - Give an equation if an equation is asked for, not an expression.

Calculator Use

For purposes of the Algebra I End-of-Course Exam, you are expected to have access to a calculator for the second of the two testing sessions, and use of a graphing calculator is strongly recommended. Scientific or four-function calculators are permitted but not recommended because they do not have graphing capabilities. Use the calculator to which you are accustomed to using. Note that not all items in the calculator session of the exam require the use of a calculator. For more information on calculator use, see the Using a Calculator section of this book.

Sample Test Items

The following items have been provided to give you an idea of the types of items you might see on the Algebra I End-of-Course Exam. For these purposes only, items are grouped as calculator or non-calculator, as well as by item type—multiple-choice (MC), short-answer (SA), or extended-response (ER). Note that the amount of workspace provided will indicate if an item is a short-answer (two-point, one-half page) or extended-response (four-point, full page) item.

Items may appear differently on the ADP[SM] Algebra I Exam.

Non-Calculator Items

1 Consider the equation below.

$$x(3x - 2) = 0$$

Solve for x.

A. $\{0\}$

B. $\left\{\frac{2}{3}\right\}$

C. $\left\{0, \frac{2}{3}\right\}$

D. [null]

2 Rewrite $\frac{5^{-3} \cdot 2^4}{2^{-2} \cdot 5^2}$ as a fraction having only positive exponents.

A. $\frac{2^6}{5^5}$

B. $\frac{2^8}{5^6}$

C. $\frac{5^5}{2^6}$

D. $\frac{2^2}{5}$

3 Which of the following equations is parallel to the line given by the equation $y = 3x + 7$?

A. $y = \frac{1}{3}x + 4$

B. $y = -\frac{1}{3}x - 7$

C. $y = 3x - 4$

D. $y = -3x$

Extended Response

4 Let $f(x) = x^2 + x + c$.

Part A For what value of c will $f(x)$ have exactly one real root? Show or explain your work.

Part B Using one of the values for c that you found in Part A, determine the roots of $f(x)$. Show or explain your work.

Calculator Items

Multiple Choice

5 What is the solution set of $|x - 1| = 3$?

A. $\{-1, 1\}$

B. $\{-2, 4\}$

C. $\{-2\}$

D. $\{4\}$

6 What is the solution to $x - 6 \leq 4$?

A. $x = 10$

B. $x < 10$

C. $x \leq 10$

D. $x \leq -2$

7 Which of the following graphs represents the inequality $x - 2y > 6$?

A.

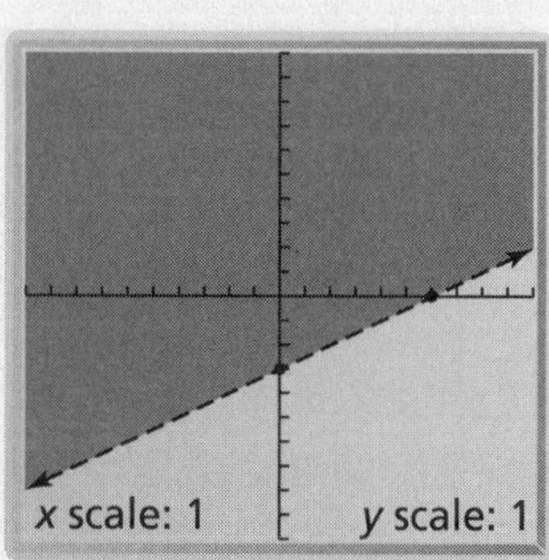

B.

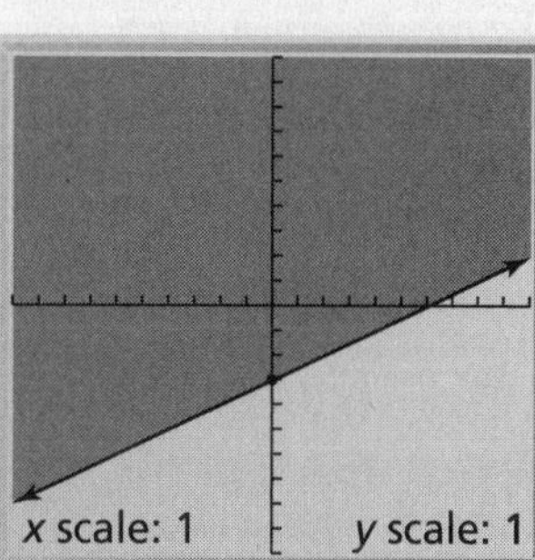

C.

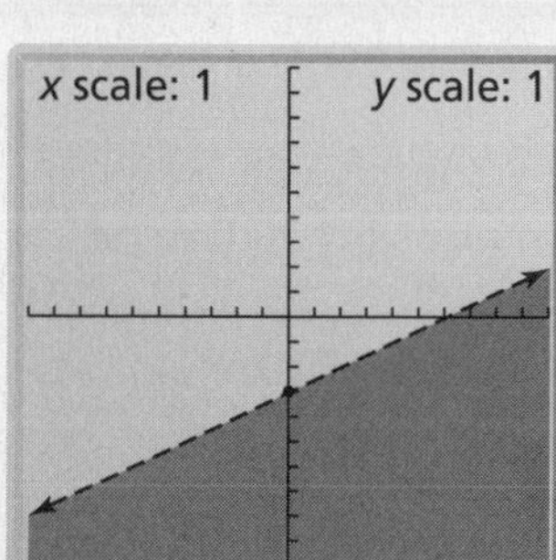

D.

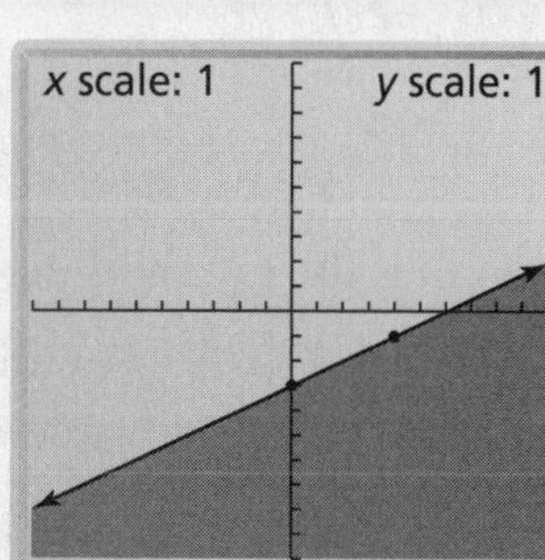

8 Consider the diagram below.

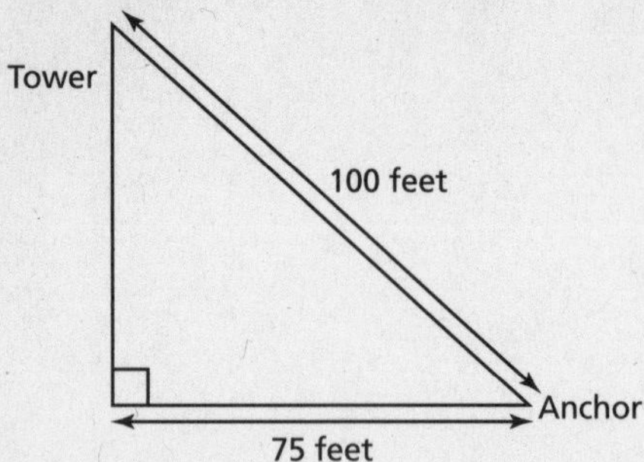

A wire is anchored to the ground 75 feet from a tower. The wire is 100 feet long from the point where it is anchored to the ground to the top of the tower. The tower forms a right angle with the ground. Approximately how tall is the tower?

A. 13 feet

B. 66 feet

C. 125 feet

D. 4,375 feet

Short Response

9 Simplify the expression $\sqrt{\frac{20}{5y^3}}$. Show or explain your work.

10 Consider the quadratic function graphed in the figure below.

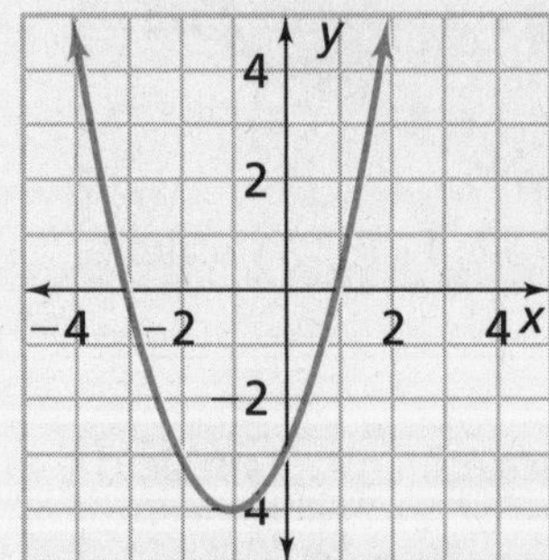

Write an equation that describes the graph of the function. Explain your reasoning.

11 A car has an original value of $20,000. The value decreases at a rate of 18% each year.

Part A Write a function where $f(x)$ represents the value of the car in dollars and x represents years.

Part B What is the value of the car after 5 years? Show or explain your work.

Answers and Solutions

1 Sample Solution: In order for this equation to be true, then either $x = 0$ or $3x - 2 = 0$. When x is 0 or $\frac{2}{3}$, the equation is equal to 0. Therefore, the solution to this equation is $\{0, \frac{2}{3}\}$.
Correct Answer: C

$x(3x - 2) = 0$
$x = 0$ or $3x - 2 = 0$
$x = 0$ or $x = \frac{2}{3}$

2 Sample Solution: To rewrite this expression, rewrite negative exponents in the numerator as positive exponents in the denominator and negative exponents in the denominator as positive exponents in the numerator.
Correct Answer: A

$\frac{5^{-3} \cdot 2^4}{2^{-2} \cdot 5^2} = \frac{2^2 \cdot 2^4}{5^3 \cdot 5^2}$
$\frac{2^6}{5^5}$

3 Sample Solution: The key to this problem is to recognize that parallel lines have equal slopes. The slope of the line given by an equation in the form $y = mx + b$ is m. Any line given by the equation $y = 3x + b$ will be parallel to the given line.
Correct Answer: C

Find the equation of the line with slope $m = 3$.

4 Sample Solution: Part A The function $f(x) = x^2 + x + c$ has exactly one real root when the discriminant, $b^2 - 4ac$, is zero.

Correct Answer: $c = \frac{1}{4}$

Part B Let $c = \frac{1}{4}$ and use it to determine the zero for the resulting function.

Correct Answer: $-\frac{1}{2}$

$b^2 - 4ac = 1 - 4c$
$1 - 4c = 0$
$c = \frac{1}{4}$

$$\frac{-1 \pm \sqrt{(1)^2 - 4(1)\left(\frac{1}{4}\right)}}{(2)(1)}$$
$$= \frac{-1 \pm \sqrt{0}}{2}$$
$$= \frac{-1}{2}$$

5 Sample Solution: The solution to this absolute value equation is $x = -2$ *or* $x = 4$. Both solutions satisfy the original equation when checked.
Correct Answer: B

$|x - 1| = 3$
$x - 1 = 3$, or
$x - 1 = -3$
$x = 4$ or $x = -2$

6 Sample Solution: The solution to this inequality is $x \leq 10$. A test point will verify the solution.
Correct Answer: C

$x - 6 \leq 4$
$x - 6 + 6 \leq 4 + 6$
$x \leq 10$

7 **Sample Solution:** Begin by rewriting the inequality to solve for y. Graph the inequality as though it were an equation. Since the inequality uses a ">", draw the line using a dashed line. This boundary line divides the plane into two regions. Test one point that is not on the boundary line to decide which side of the line to shade.
Correct Answer: C

$x - 2y > 6$
$-2y > -x + 6$
$y < \frac{1}{2}x - 3$
Test (0,0)
$0 < -3$ *False*

8 **Sample Solution:** You can use the Pythagorean Theorem to find the height of the tower. Round your answer to the nearest foot.
Correct Answer: B

x = height of tower
$75^2 + x^2 = 100^2$
$x = \sqrt{100^2 - 75^2}$

9 **Sample Solution:** In a simplified radical expression, no denominator contains a radical. Remember to rationalize the denominator.

Correct Answer: $\frac{2\sqrt{y}}{y^2}$

$$\sqrt{\frac{20}{5y^3}} = \frac{\sqrt{4}}{\sqrt{y^3}}$$
$$= \frac{2}{\sqrt{y^2 \cdot y}} = \frac{2}{y\sqrt{y}} \cdot \frac{\sqrt{y}}{\sqrt{y}}$$
$$= \frac{2\sqrt{y}}{y\sqrt{y^2}} = \frac{2\sqrt{y}}{y^2}$$

10 **Sample Solution:** To find the equation of the function, first locate the points where the graph crosses the x-axis. The graph crosses the x-axis when $x = -3$ and $x = 1$.

The equation of the parabola will be of the form $(x - h)(x - k)$, where h and k are the roots. To find the equation, expand the equation $(x + 3)(x - 1)$.
Correct Answer: $y = x^2 + 2x - 3$

$y = (x + 3)(x - 1)$
$y = x^2 + 3x - x - 3$
$y = x^2 + 2x - 3$

11 **Sample Solution: Part A** You may simply know that this situation can be modeled by a function of the form $f(x) = ab^x$, where a represents the starting value, b represents the decay factor, and x indicates the time.
Correct Answer: $f(x) = 20{,}000(0.82)^x$

Part B Evaluate $f(5)$.
Substitute 5 for x and solve.
Correct Answer: $7,414.80

$f(5) = 20{,}000(0.82)^5$
$= 7{,}414.8$

The Role of Calculators in Algebra I

The ADP℠ calculator policy states "**The use of a graphing calculator is highly recommended,** although not required." When used appropriately, a graphing calculator provides the user with a new set of algorithms for problem solving. The ADP℠ Algebra I Exam is designed so that some, but not all, of the questions on the calculator portion of the test require the use of a calculator. The Achieve ADP℠ calculator policy states that "It is important for students learn to assess for themselves whether or not a calculator would be helpful. Students should be able to solve test problems in multiple ways, with and without a calculator."

As you work through this text, you should consider solution methods that can be implemented on a graphing calculator. Often these solutions and the ability to work with the data provide insight that would otherwise be overlooked.

Numeration

The large screen on a graphing calculator is helpful. You can see both the expression and the answer displayed on the screen at the same time.

Note

When you enter an operation without first entering a value, the calculator will perform the operation on the previous answer.

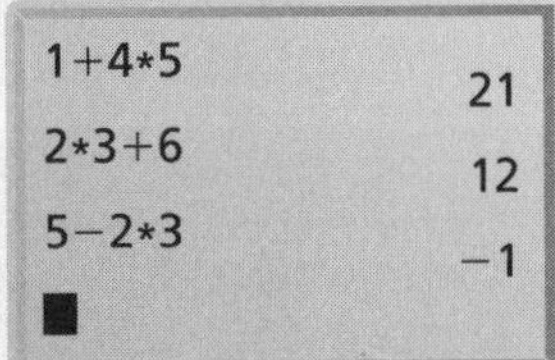

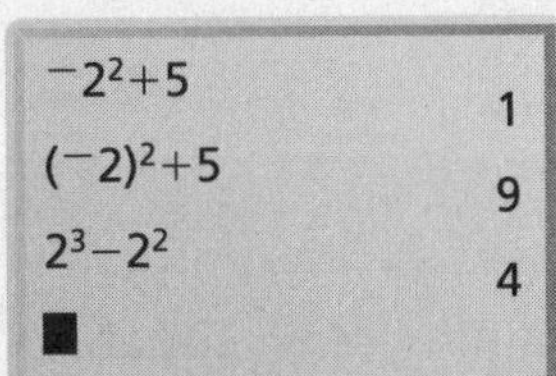

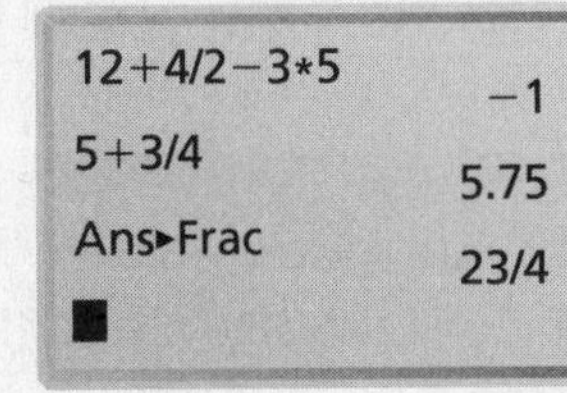

In the display at the right above, the result is shown as a fraction by using MATH 1: ▷ Frac. In this case, 5.75 is displayed as a fraction.

1555999*3888666
6.050760407E12

Your calculator can display results in scientific notation. The product of two large numbers is shown at the right. This result is the same as $6.050760407 \times 10^{12}$. The symbol **E** represents multiplying by 10 and the number following the symbol is the exponent. Numbers can also be entered into the calculator in scientific notation by typing 2nd , which is **EE**. If you want the result displayed in scientific notation, choose Sci in the MODE menu. From the display at the right below, you can read that $(2.5 \times 10^4)(3.7 \times 10^2) = 9.25 \times 10^6$.

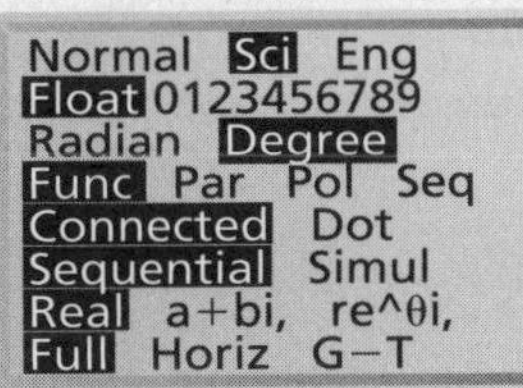

2.5E4*3.7E2
9250000
2.5E4*3.7E2
9.25E6

USING A CALCULATOR

Evaluating algebraic expressions

Using STO▸, you can evaluate an expression like $a^2 - ab$, given $a = 2$ and $b = -3$. In the figure below, you can see how to combine these instructions onto one line by using a colon between the statements.

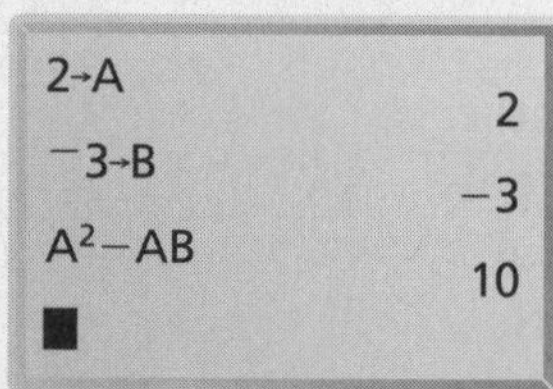


```
2→A:⁻3→B:A²−AB
                10
■
```

Informal logic

Logical statements such as those below can be investigated by using the 2nd MATH, or **TEST**, feature of the calculator. Consider these statements.

$$5 = 3 + 2 \text{ and } 5 = 10 \div 2 \qquad 5 = 3 \times 2 \text{ and } 5 = 10 \div 2$$

```
5=3+2  and 5=10/2
                 1
5=3*2  and 5=10/2
                 0
```

The screen at the right shows the results of testing the truth of these statements. The display shows the following as truth values.

True: 1 *False*: 0

Testing equality of radical expressions

When simplifying a radical expression such as $\sqrt{24}$, you can check to see if $\sqrt{24} = 2\sqrt{6}$ by using **TEST**. You can also check the validity of an equation. The statement below is false.

```
√(24)=2√(6)
           1
√(48)=4√(3)
           1
√(18)=6√(3)
           0
■
```

$$2\sqrt{5} + 3\sqrt{5} = 5\sqrt{10}$$

The calculator confirms this by displaying 0. However, the following statement is true.

$$2\sqrt{5} + 3\sqrt{5} = 5\sqrt{5}$$

```
2√(5)+3√(5)=5√(1
0)
                 0
2√(5)+3√(5)=5√(5
)
                 1
■
```

The calculator confirms this by displaying 1.

Used in this way, the calculator enables you to verify answers worked out with paper and pencil.

Logical tests can also be performed to check for the correct factorization of algebraic expressions. This checking procedure can often help you identify errors before you proceed with the remainder of a problem. Notice that in the second example below, a result of zero would indicate that the result is incorrect, allowing the opportunity to correct the answer.

```
X²+5X+6=(X+2)(X+
3)
                 1
```

```
X²−9=(x−3)(X−3)
                 0
■
```

Linear functions and equations

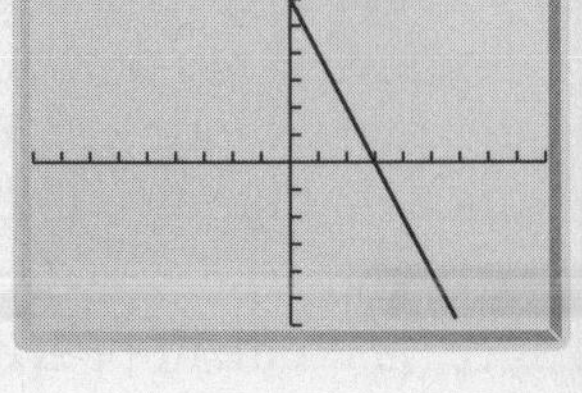

Suppose that you want to graph $4x + 2y = 12$. First solve for y.

$$y = -2x + 6$$

Enter $-2x + 6$ into the function list Y= . Press the GRAPH button, and you will see a display like the one at the right.

If you want to solve $-2x + 6 = 0$, you can use the graph of $y = -2x + 6$ and a solving routine to find where the graph intersects the x-axis. Press 2nd TRACE **CALC.** You will see the menu below. From it, select **2: zero.** Enter a *left bound*, *right bound*, and *guess*. The exact solution will be displayed.

CALCULATE
1: value
2: zero
3: minimum
4: maximum
5: intersect
6: dy/dx
7: ∫f(x)dx

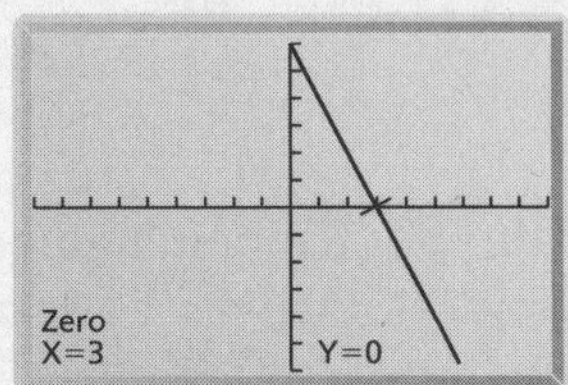

This equation could also be solved by using the Solver feature of the calculator. In the MATH menu, choose item **0: Solver.** Notice that the equation you wish to solve must be set equal to zero. Enter the equation as shown in the figure below. Press ENTER to see the Solver screen. To solve for the variable, press ALPHA ENTER, which is the SOLVE command. It is important to note that the Solver has not determined the solution until the black square (■) appears in front of the variable you are solving for and the check sum **left – rt = 0** appears.

EQUATION SOLVER
eqn:0=−2X+6■

−2X+6=0
X=10
bound=(−1E99, 1...

−2X+6=0
■X=3
bound=(−1E99, 1...
■left−rt=0

Friendly window

WINDOW
Xmin=−9.4
Xmax=9.4
Xscl=1
Ymin=−6.2
Ymax=6.2
Yscl=1
Xres=■

When using a graphing calculator, it is important to have graphical representations displayed accurately. Perpendicular lines should look perpendicular, circles should look like circles, and so on. With most graphing calculators, graphic accuracy can be accomplished by setting a "friendly window." One such window is shown at the right. This window establishes a "nice" value for the change in x and also takes the screen aspect ratio into account. When the calculator graphs a function, it creates a table of values beginning with x-min and ending with x-max. You want the increments to be "nice." By setting the Xmin = −9.4 and Xmax = 9.4, whenever the numerator is a multiple of 94, the increment in x will be 0.2. By maintaining a ratio of approximately $\frac{3}{2}$ for x to y, the screen is "squared," meaning that perpendicular lines will look perpendicular, and so on.

USING A CALCULATOR

If you are to interpret graphical information visually, it is important that you can set windows that take into account these two important ideas, "nice" Δx and square window. These two features are shown in the following graphs. Notice that the two lines look perpendicular. You can also trace the graph of one of these lines by hitting the TRACE key. Notice that the points reflect the "nice" increment of $\Delta x = 0.2$.

Enter the expressions.

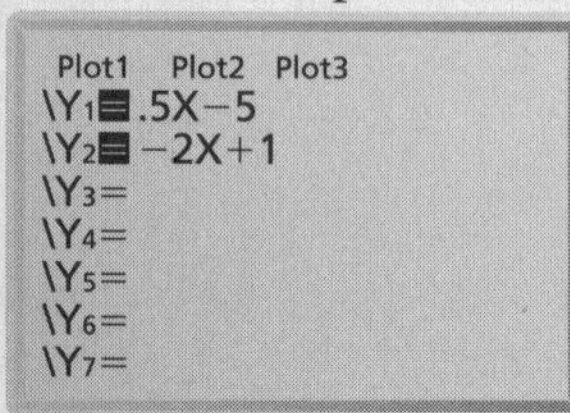

Draw the graphs.

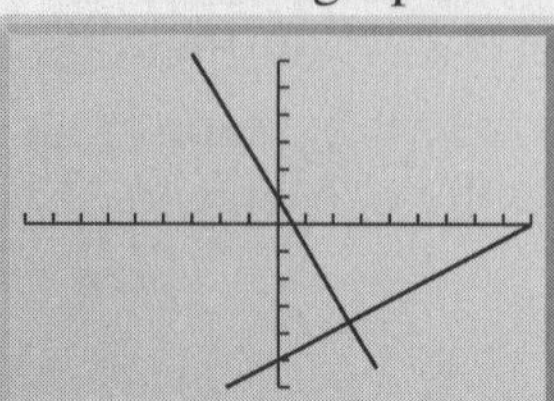

Use tracing.

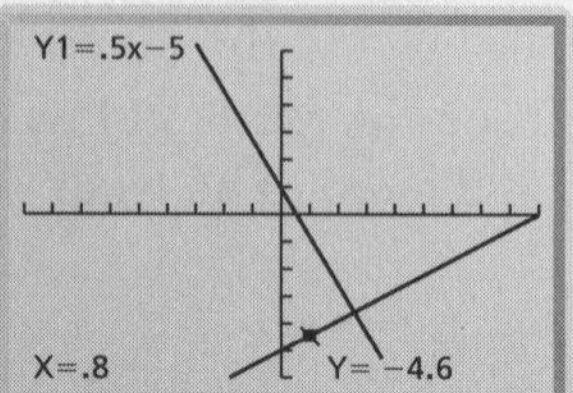

You can use calculator features under the ZOOM menu, namely **4: ZDecimal** and **5: ZSquare**, to get a "friendly window." However, by setting the window manually, you will better understand the numerical features of the calculator you are using. Whichever graphing calculator you choose to use, you will find it helpful to determine the appropriate settings for establishing a "friendly window."

Solving systems of equations and inequalities

Suppose that you are given the system of equations at the right. You can find a solution to such a system in a variety of ways. You can use a graphing approach, or you can use a matrix approach.

$$\begin{cases} x - y = -1 \\ x + 2y = 6 \end{cases}$$

Use the **CALC** feature by pressing 2nd TRACE. Selecting menu option **5: intersect** requires three inputs; *first curve*, *second curve*, and *guess*. After you enter a guess, the solution is displayed. In the **HOME** screen at the right below, the results can be displayed as fractions.

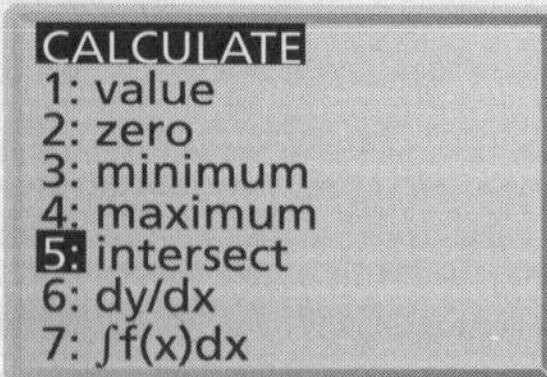

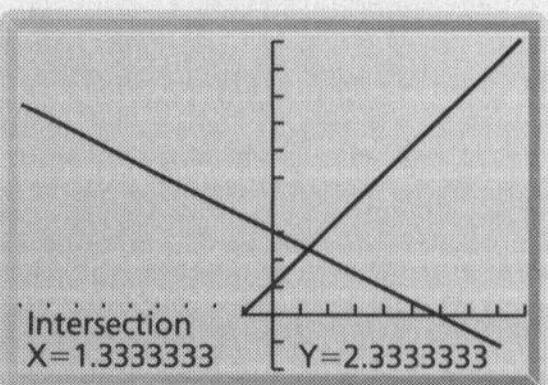

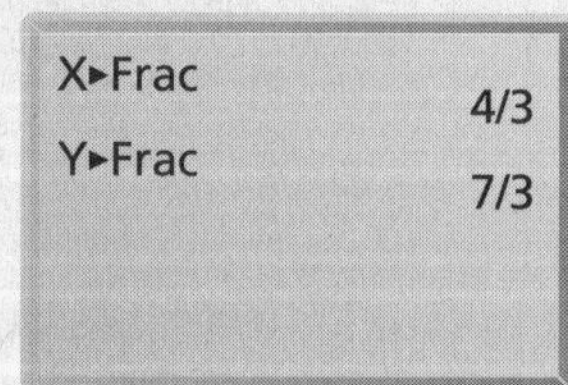

The solution to the system is $x = \frac{4}{3}$ and $y = \frac{7}{3}$, or $\left(\frac{4}{3}, \frac{7}{3}\right)$.

The system $\begin{cases} x - y = -1 \\ x + 2y = 6 \end{cases}$, or $\begin{cases} y = x + 1 \\ y = -\frac{1}{2}x + 3 \end{cases}$, is related to $x + 1 = -\frac{1}{2}x + 3$.

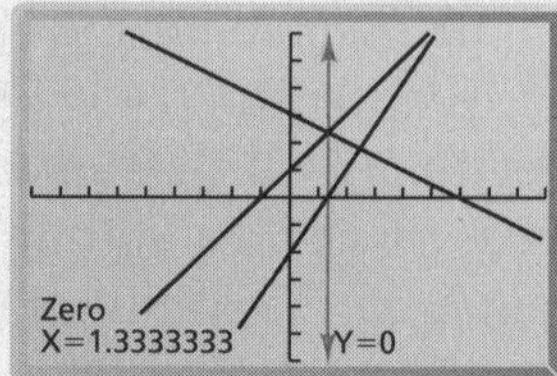

With technology, the solution $\left(\frac{4}{3}, \frac{7}{3}\right)$ can be compared to the result of solving the equation $x + 1 = -\frac{1}{2}x + 3$, which you can write as $\frac{3}{2}x - 2 = 0$. Graphing this line with the system provides a visualization that allows for the comparison of these graphs. The point of intersection for the system occurs at the same x-value at which the single equation has a solution.

Solving a system of inequalities using the calculator is similar to solving the system of equations graphically. The system $y < -\frac{1}{2}x + 3$ and $y \geq x + 1$ is entered in the Y= menu as shown below, and then the style icon in front of **Y1** and **Y2** is changed to the appropriate *shade above* or *shade below* icon. The region in which the shaded areas intersect is the solution set. It is important to state whether or not the line is part of the solution. Some calculators do not allow the line **Y1** to be drawn as a "dashed" line.

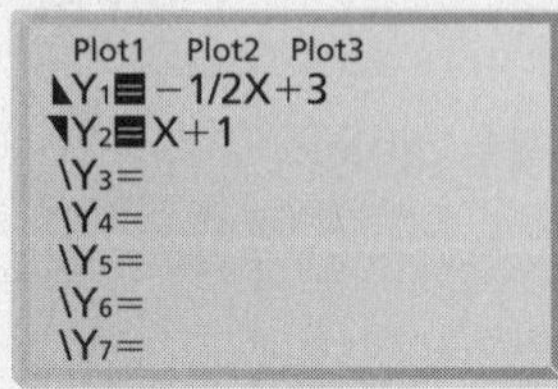

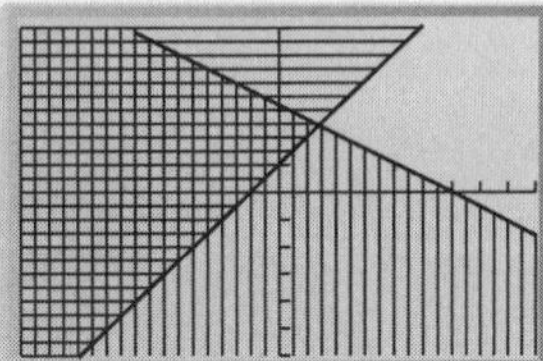

Quadratic functions and equations

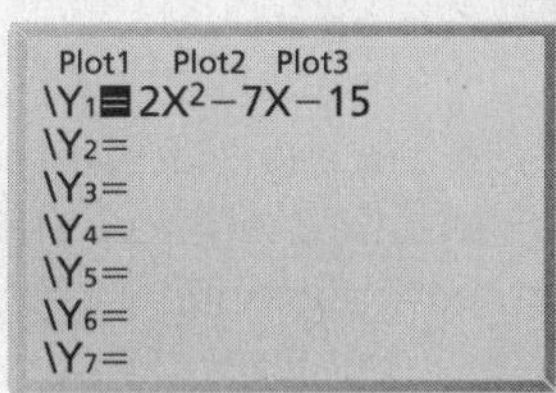

When you are solving a quadratic equation such as $2x^2 - 7x - 15 = 0$, a graphical solution is easily implemented by using the calculator. Use the graphing calculator to display the graph of $y = 2x^2 - 7x - 15$. The equation is entered in Y= and the **CALC** menu is accessed by pressing 2nd TRACE. Each root is found separately by entering a *left bound*, *right bound*, and *guess*. Shown below are the window settings, the graph, and the solutions for this quadratic equation.

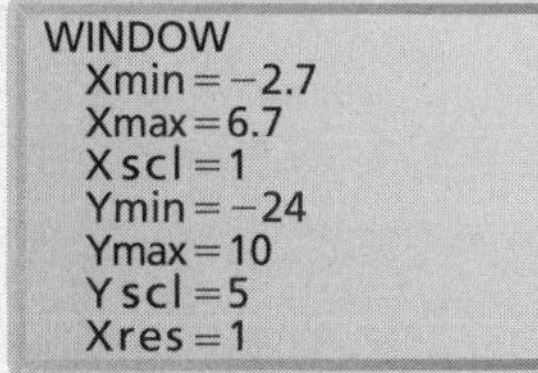

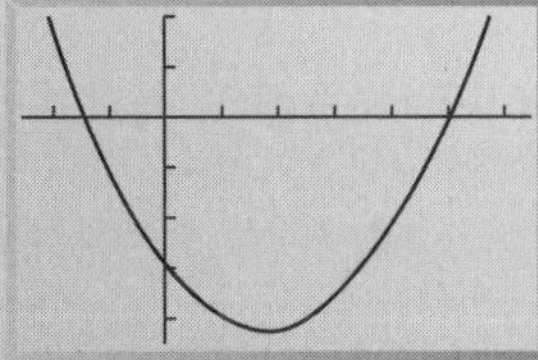

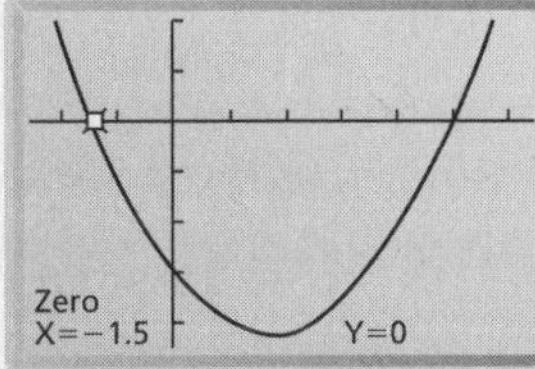

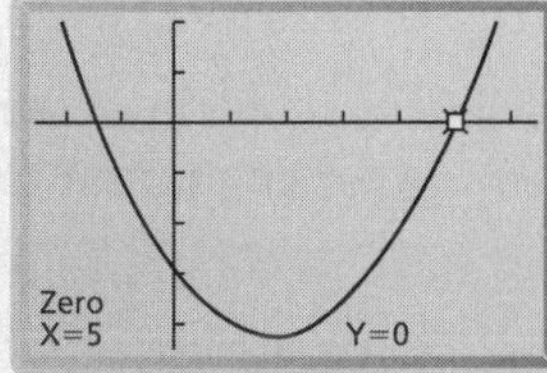

The graph of a quadratic function can also be helpful when trying to factor a quadratic expression. For example, when factoring $3x^2 + x - 24$, it is helpful to know the roots. You can find the roots using the graph, as shown below.

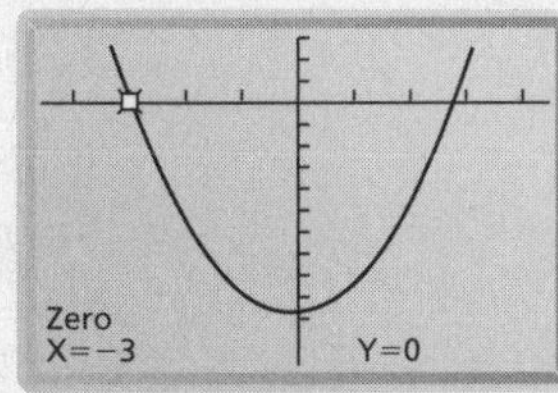

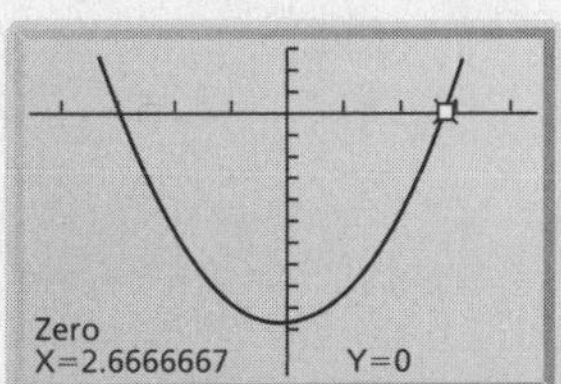

$x = -3$ or $x = 2\frac{2}{3}$

$x + 3 = 0$ or $3x - 8 = 0$

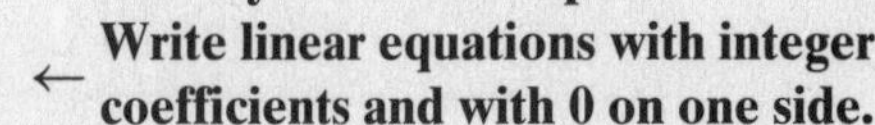

USING A CALCULATOR

Write the product of the linear expressions, $(x + 3)(3x - 8)$. Therefore, $3x^2 + x - 24 = (x + 3)(3x - 8)$.

The calculator can help create a table of values for an expression like $x^2 - x - 6$. This is helpful when you are graphing by traditional methods using paper and pencil. Enter the equation in the Y= menu. Then the values are entered into 2nd WINDOW, **TBLSET**. Finally, press 2nd GRAPH, **TABLE**, to display the table of values. By using the calculator in this way, you can often eliminate careless mistakes in creating a table of values.

```
Plot1 Plot2 Plot3
\Y1=X²-X-6
\Y2=
\Y3=
\Y4=
\Y5=
\Y6=
\Y7=
```

Enter $x^2 - x - 6$.

```
Plot1 Plot2 Plot3
\Y1=X²-X-6
\Y2=
\Y3=
\Y4=
\Y5=
\Y6=
\Y7=
```

Set the lowest value for x.

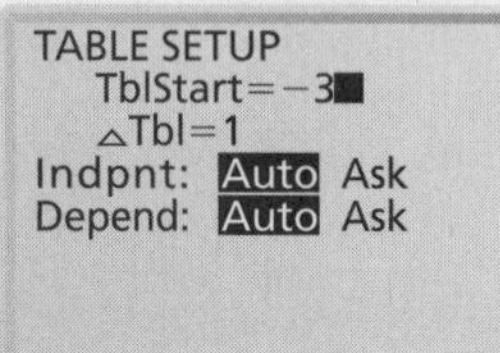

Display the table.

X	Y1
-3	6
-2	0
-1	-4
0	-6
1	-6
2	-4
3	0

X=-3

You can also determine the nature of the roots of a quadratic equation by looking at its graph.
The graph touches the x-axis once: double root.
The graph crosses the x-axis twice: two real roots.
The graph never touches the x-axis: no real roots.

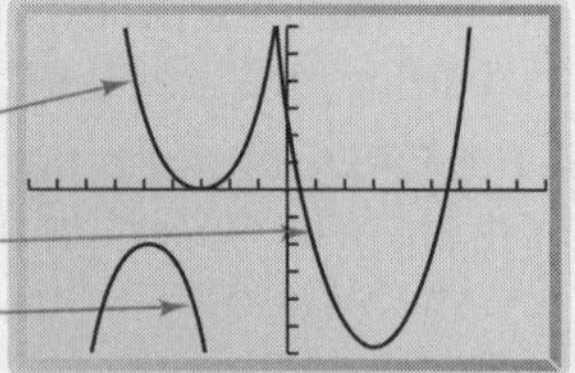

Permutations and Combinations

Like a scientific calculator, the graphing calculator can evaluate an expression involving permutations and combinations.

permutations: ${}_nP_r$ combinations: ${}_nC_r$

These features are located in the MATH menu under **PRB.** When evaluating an expression like ${}_{10}P_6$, enter 10 on the home screen first, and then press and select MATH **PRB 2: nPr**, enter 6, and finally press ENTER. The result can be verified by entering the factorial form of the expression, $\frac{10!}{(10-6)!}$, or $\frac{10!}{4!}$.

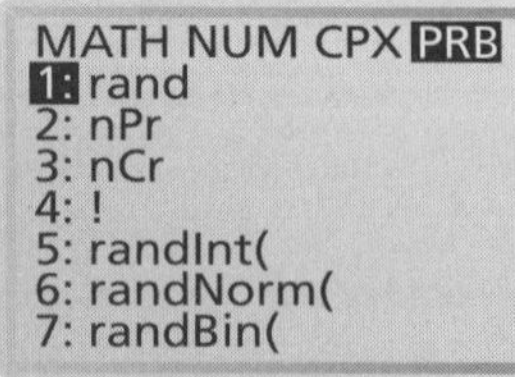


```
10 nPr 6
                151200
10!/4!
                151200
```

Statistics

Statistical data can be entered from the home screen by using the STO▸ key and listing the data as a set. The screen at the left below shows a set of test scores entered into list one, **L1**. Enter **{** and **}** by typing 2nd (and 2nd). Press the ENTER key to store this list. When this is done, the set of scores is echoed back as shown in the display at the right below.

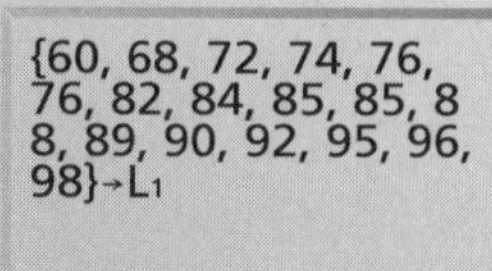

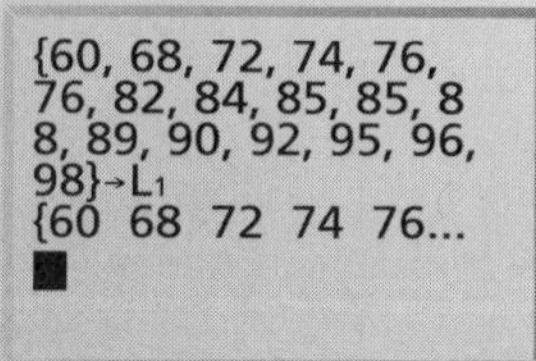

Now these data can be examined by performing one-variable statistical analysis. Pressing STAT will access the statistics menu shown below. Selecting **1: Edit** . . . displays the data as a list **L1**. Pressing STAT again and ▸ shows the **CALC** menu for statistics.

```
EDIT CALC TESTS
1: Edit...
2: SortA(
3: SortD(
4: ClrList
5: SetUpEditor
```

```
L1     L2      L3    2
60     ------  ------
68
72
74
76
76
82
L2(1)=
```

```
EDIT CALC TESTS
1: 1–Var Stats
2: 2–Var Stats
3: Med–Med
4: LinReg(ax+b)
5: QuadReg
6: CubicReg
7↓QuartReg
```

Selecting **1** now places the command on the home screen. Press 2nd **1**. You will see the screen at the left below. Press ENTER to view the middle display below. The arrow to the left of $n = 17$ tells you that there is more information to be shown. Holding down the ▾ key, you can scroll through the other items resulting in the screen at the right below. The mean, $\overline{x}$; median, Med; the first quartile, Q_1; and third quartile, Q_3, are easily identified. (Some information shown here is beyond the scope of this book.)

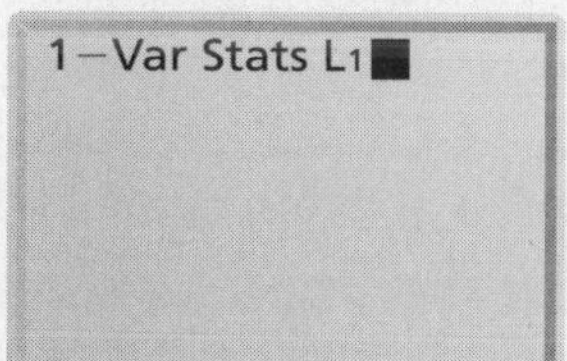


```
1–Var Stats
 x̄=82.94117647
 Σx=1410
 Σx²=118740
 Sx=10.58578403
 σx=10.26971898
↓n=17
```

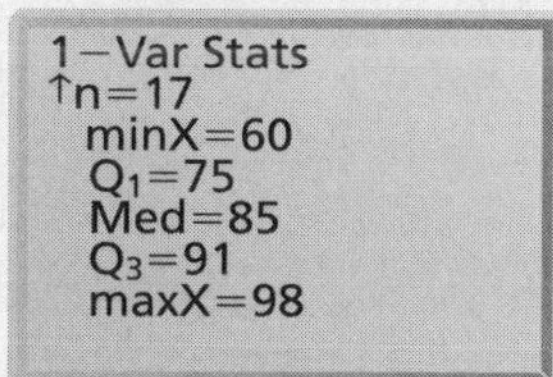

A graphical representation of a data set that includes the Min, Q_1, Med, Q_3, and Max is called a box plot. The box plot for the set of test scores is shown to the right. You graph the box plot by typing 2nd Y= to display the **STAT PLOTS** screen. Select plot **1**, turn on box plot, use **L1** as the **Xlist**, and **Freq = 1**.

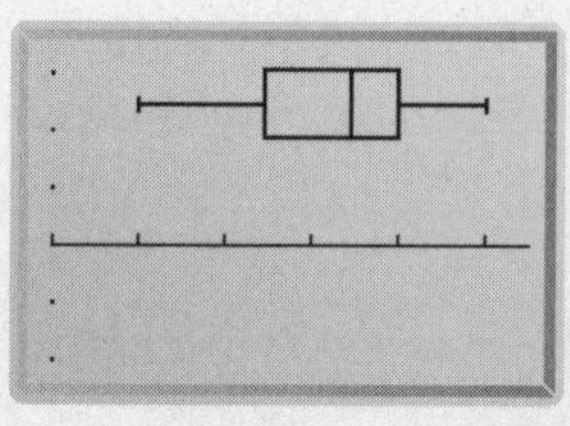

USING A CALCULATOR

These data can also be graphed in a histogram in a similar fashion. From the **STAT PLOTS** screen, select plot **2**, select histogram, use **L1** as the **Xlist**, and **Freq = 1**. Using the same window settings as shown above, you can make the histogram. If the two plots are left on together, both will be displayed at the same time.

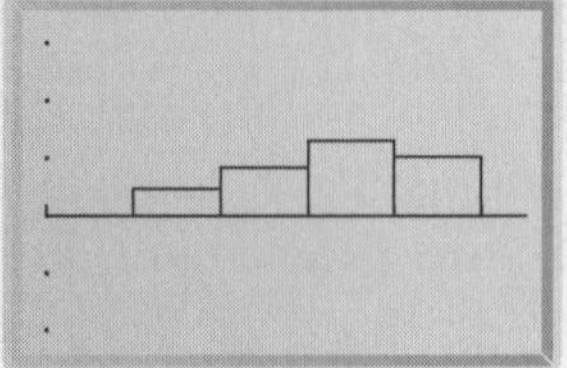

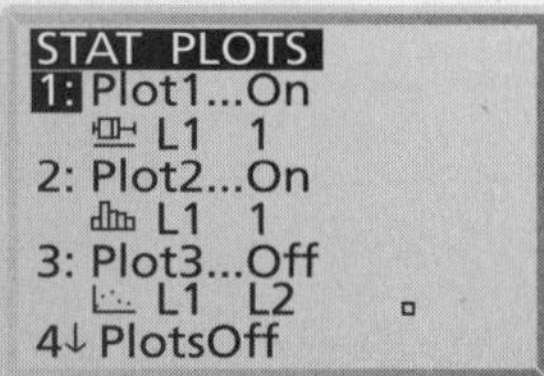

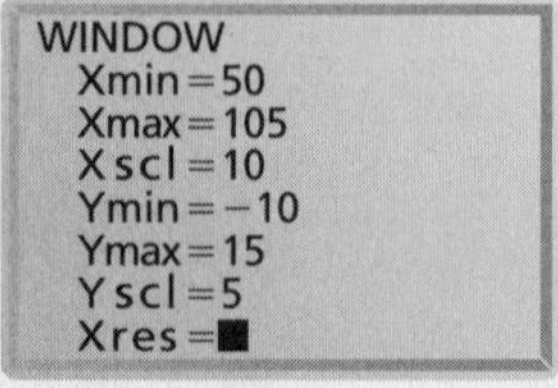

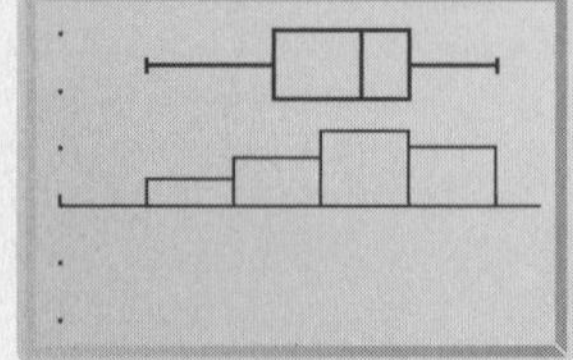

If you want to compare scores already analyzed to a second set of scores, perhaps in science, a scatter plot can be used to visualize these two sets of data. The second set of data, 58, 70, 75, 68, 75, 72, 80, 88, 85, 89, 84, 90, 85, 96, 96, 92, 95, is entered in **L2.** In the **STAT PLOTS** screen, select plot **1** and scatter plot.

The **Xlist** is **L1** and the **Ylist** is **L2**. The displays are shown below.

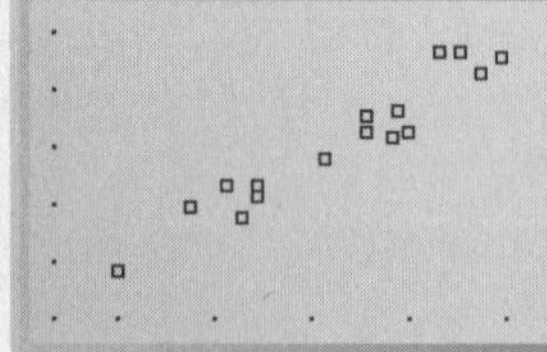

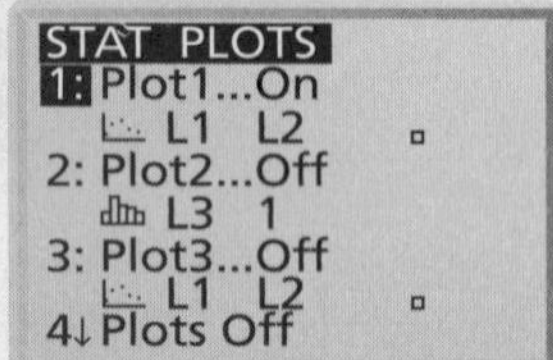

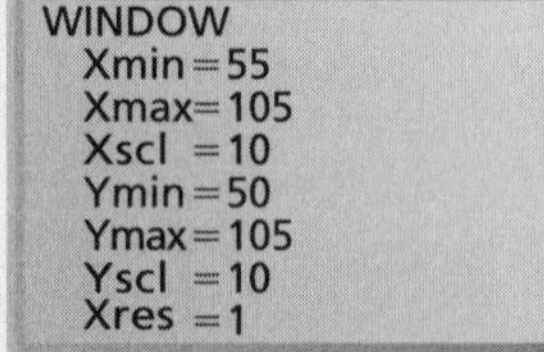

To get an estimate for trend line, press STAT ▶ **CALC** and arrow down to item **D: Manual-Fit**. The cursor appears on the graph with the coordinates showing. Move the cursor to the first point on your estimated line and press ENTER. Then move to a second point and press ENTER again. Now you can change the values of the slope and y-intercept until you have the best estimate for the trend line.

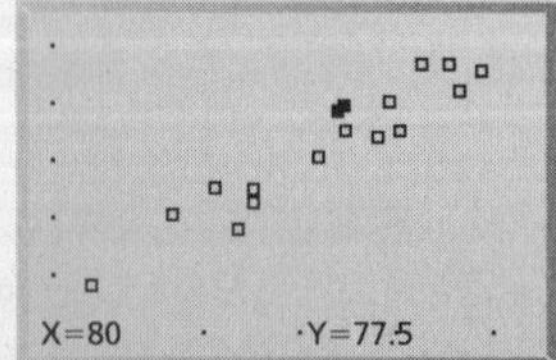

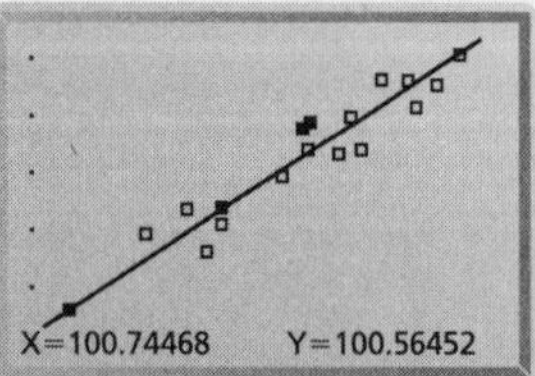

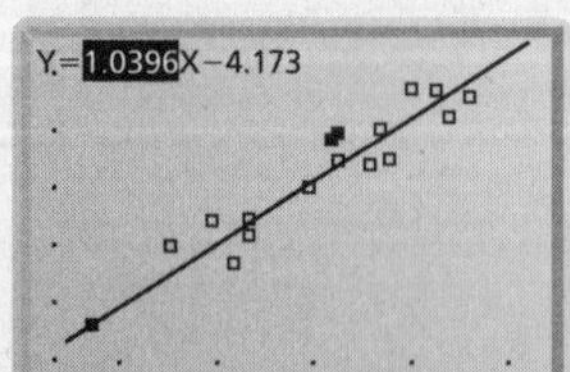

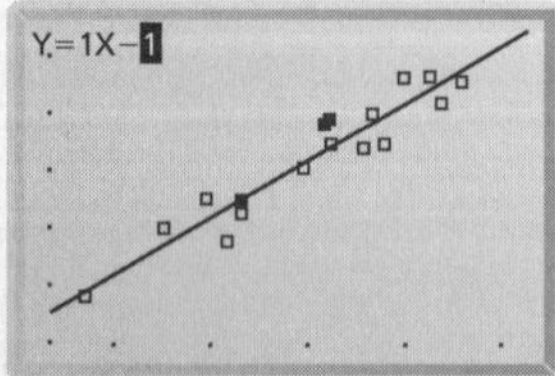

To determine the Least Squares Line of Best Fit, press and select STAT ▶ **CALC** and arrow down to item **4: LinReg(ax + b)**. These choices result in the screen display shown at the right.

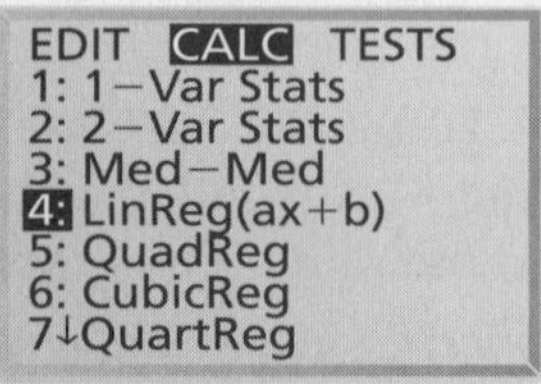

In order to see the screen including the values of r^2 and r, the correlation coefficient, you must press 2nd **0,** which displays the **CATALOG,** and toggle down ▼ until you come to **DiagnosticOn.** From the display, you can read the slope of the line of best fit as approximately 0.99 and the y-intercept of the line as approximately -0.12. The correlation coefficient is approximately 0.95, indicating a very high positive correlation.

```
LinReg
 y=ax+b
 a=.9929133858
 b=-.1181102362
 r²=.9069092385
 r=.9523178243
```

The equation of the line can be placed in a Y= location when making the selection from the home screen by indicating the desired location after the **4: LinReg(ax+b)** menu choice. This is shown at the right. Now when the graph is displayed by pressing GRAPH, both the scatter plot and the least-square regression (line of best fit) line are displayed.

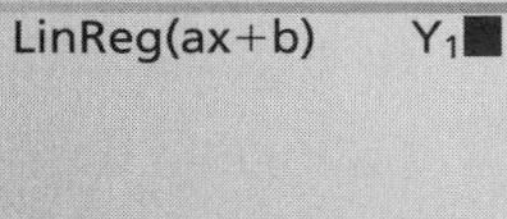

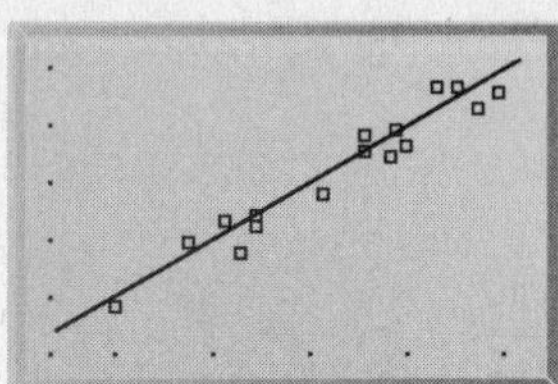

This line is referred to as the line of best fit and can be used to extrapolate and interpolate the data.

Solver and formula evaluation

In the MATH menu, **0: Solver** is the Solver. This feature can be used to solve an equation that has 0 on one side for any one of the variables in the equation if the values of the other variables are known.

For example, the volume of a right circular cylinder is given by $V = \pi r^2 h$. This formula can be set equal to zero by subtracting V from each side, resulting in $0 = \pi r^2 h - V$. You can see this below.

```
EQUATION SOLVER
eqn:0=πR²H-V
```

$$V = \pi r^2 h$$
$$V - V = \pi r^2 h - V$$
$$0 = \pi r^2 h - V$$

Given a value for the volume and the radius, you can use the solver to determine the height of the cylinder. Suppose that the volume of a certain cylinder is 100 cm^3 and that the radius of the base is 5 cm. What would the height of the cylinder be? Enter V and R. Move the cursor to H as shown. Press ALPHA ENTER for **SOLVE.** The ■ to the left of H indicates that H has been found.

```
πR²H-V=0
 R=5
 H=0
 V=100
 bound={-1E99, 1...
```

```
πR²H-V=0
 R=5
■H=1.2732395447...
 V=100
 bound={-1E99, 1...
■left-rt=0
```

The solver can be used to find V, given R and H. Enter R and H as shown. Press and select ALPHA ENTER for **SOLVE** when the cursor is at the desired variable. One display shows the volume of a cylinder with radius 5 and height 5. The other display shows the volume of a cylinder with radius 2 and height 4.

```
πR²H-V=θ
 R=5
 H=5
■V=392.69908169...
 bound={-1E99, 1...
■left-rt=0
```

```
πR²H-V=θ
 R=2
 H=4
■V=50.265482457...
 bound={-1E99, 1...
■left-rt=0
```

Diagnostic Test: ADP℠ Algebra I

Name ______________________ Date __________

Diagnostic Test 1: Chapter 1

Real Numbers and Algebraic Expressions

Choose the letter preceding the word or expression that best completes the statement or answers the question.

1 Which statement best describes the number 8?

A. Eight is a composite number.

B. Eight is a prime number.

C. Eight is divisible by 3.

D. Eight is a factor of 2.

2 Evaluate $-1\frac{3}{4} + \left(-2\frac{1}{8}\right)$.

A. $-3\frac{1}{3}$ **C.** $-3\frac{7}{8}$

B. $-1\frac{1}{2}$ **D.** $-3\frac{1}{2}$

3 If n is a number, translate the phrase "6 less than n."

A. $6 < n$ **C.** $n - 6$

B. $n < 6$ **D.** $6 - n$

4 Which expression names an integer?

A. $\frac{2}{6}$ **C.** $0.\overline{3}$

B. $\frac{-6}{2}$ **D.** 0.333

5 Which point on the number line has the greatest absolute value?

A B C D
−7 −6 −5 −4 −3 −2 −1 0 1 2 3 4 5

A. A **C.** C

B. B **D.** D

6 Find the 5th term of the sequence 33, 27, 21, . . .

A. 5

B. 9

C. 15

D. 45

7 The number $\sqrt{107}$ is between

A. 26 and 28.

B. 53 and 54.

C. 100 and 110.

D. 10 and 11.

8 Which of the following is an example of the Associative Property of Multiplication?

A. $a(bc) = (ab)c$

B. $a(bc) = (bc)a$

C. $a(bc) = (ab) + (ac)$

D. $a(bc) = (ab)(ac)$

9 If $a = -2$, then $2a^2 - 5a + 6$ equals

A. 4. **C.** −12.

B. 8. **D.** 24.

10 Rewrite 4.5×10^6 in standard form.

A. 45,000,000

B. 4,500,000

C. 0.0000045

D. 0.00000045

Name ______________________________ Date __________

Diagnostic Test 2: Chapter 2

Linear Equations and Inequalities in One Variable

Choose the letter preceding the word or expression that best completes the statement or answers the question.

1 If $a = b$, then $b = a$ illustrates which property?

A. the reflexive property

B. the symmetric property

C. the transitive property

D. the addition property

2 Find a if $8a - 23 = 4a + 45$.

A. 68 **C.** 22

B. 17 **D.** 6.75

3 Which number is not a solution of $2(k - 6) \leq -2$?

A. -1 **C.** 5

B. 0 **D.** 6

4 Solve $|2p + 4| = 10$.

A. $p = 3$ **C.** $p = -7$

B. $p = 3$ and -7 **D.** $p = -3$ and 7

5 Find the solution set of the inequality $42 > -3x$.

A. $x < -14$ **C.** $x > 14$

B. $x > -14$ **D.** $x < 14$

6 $C = \frac{5}{9}(F - 32)$, where C is the temperature in degrees Celsius and F is the temperature in degrees Fahrenheit. Solve the formula for F.

A. $F = \frac{9}{5}C + 32$ **C.** $F - 32 = \frac{5}{9}C$

B. $F = \frac{9}{5}(C + 32)$ **D.** $F + 32 = \frac{5}{9}C$

7 Solve for c.

$$\frac{c + 4}{12} = \frac{c + 2}{10}$$

A. $c = 1$ **C.** $c = 8$

B. $c = -1$ **D.** $c = -8$

8 Jim and Susan mow lawns. The ratio that compares the amount of time each works is 8:5. They were paid \$65 for their work. How much did Susan earn if she worked more than Jim?

A. \$25 **C.** \$30

B. \$45 **D.** \$40

In Exercises 9–10, use the following problem situation.

Students raised \$800 for a ski trip. The cost of the bus for the trip will be \$350. The bus holds 40 students. The cost for each student's lift ticket is \$25.

9 If 40 students wish to attend, how much more money must be collected to pay for the entire trip?

A. \$550 **C.** \$1000

B. \$800 **D.** \$1350

10 If no additional money is collected, what is the maximum number of students who can go on the trip?

A. 23 students **C.** 18 students

B. 20 students **D.** 15 students

Name ______________________________ Date __________

Diagnostic Test 3: Chapter 3

Linear Equations and Inequalities in Two Variables

Choose the letter preceding the word or expression that best completes the statement or answers the question.

1 The slope of the line passing through the points $(3, -2)$ and $(7, 2)$ is

A. 0.

B. 1.

C. undefined.

D. -1.

2 If the slope of a line is *zero*, then the line is

A. rising left to right.

B. falling left to right.

C. horizontal.

D. vertical.

3 Which of the following is not a function?

A.

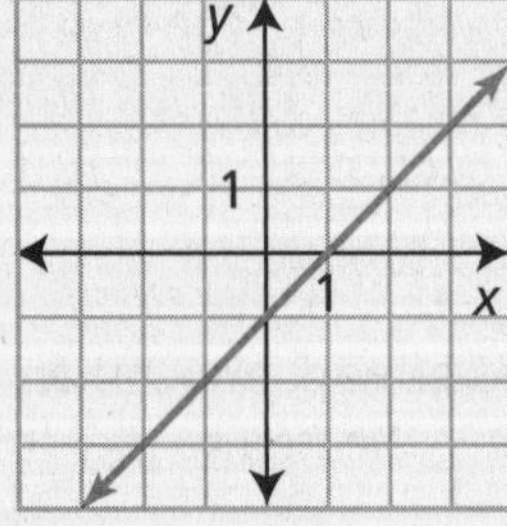

C.

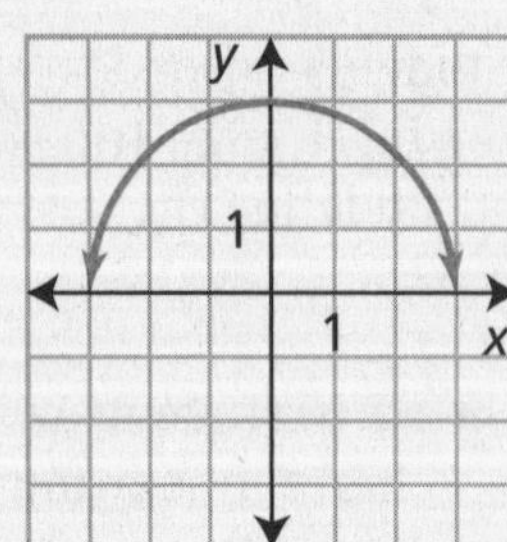

B.

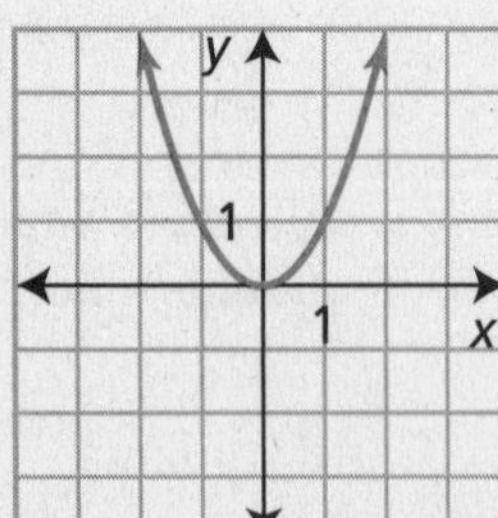

D.

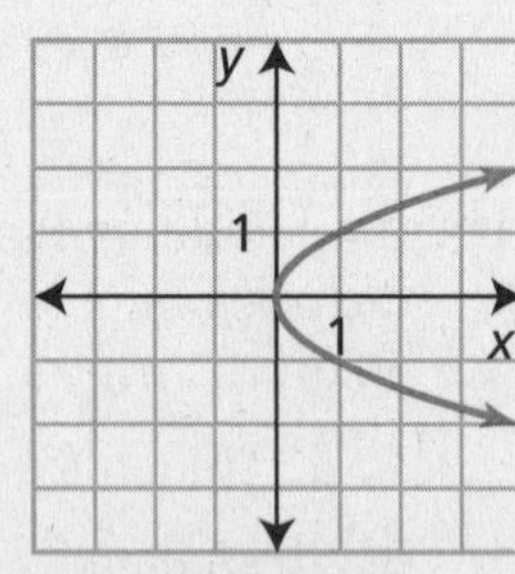

4 Determine the range value of the function $f(x) = \frac{3}{4}x - 11$ when $x = 8$.

A. $\frac{9}{4}$ **C.** $-\frac{9}{4}$

B. -5 **D.** $\frac{3}{4}$

5 Which equation does not represent a function?

A. $x = 4$ **C.** $y = 4$

B. $y = x$ **D.** $-4 = y$

6 What is the slope of a line perpendicular to $y = 4x + 3$?

A. 4 **B.** -4 **C.** $\frac{1}{4}$ **D.** $-\frac{1}{4}$

7 The equation of a line with a slope of 3 and a *y*-intercept of -8 is which of the following?

A. $y = -8x + 3$ **C.** $y = 3x + 8$

B. $y = 3x - 8$ **D.** $y = 3x - (-8)$

8 The equation $y = |x - 2| + 5$ is which translation of the absolute value function?

A. left two up five

B. right two down five

C. left two down five

D. right two up five

9 The solution to the system of equations $3x + 2y = 12$ and $x - 2y = 12$ is

A. $(6, -3)$. **C.** $(3, 6)$.

B. $(-3, 6)$. **D.** $(6, 3)$.

ALGEBRA I

Name ______________________________ Date __________

Diagnostic Test 4: Chapter 4

More About Exponents and Exponential Functions

Choose the letter preceding the word or expression that best completes the statement or answers the question.

1 Which of the following is equivalent to $(3a^2b^3)^3$?

A. $3a^6b^9$

B. $27a^6b^9$

C. $3a^5b^6$

D. $27a^5b^6$

2 The product of 5.4×10^3 and 6.2×10^5 written in scientific notation is

A. 11.6×10^8.

B. 33.48×10^{15}.

C. 33.48×10^8.

D. 3.348×10^9.

3 Which of the following is equivalent to $\left(\frac{a^2}{b^{-2}}\right)^3\left(\frac{ab^{-3}}{a^2}\right)$ when written in simplest form with all positive exponents?

A. a^5b^3

B. $\frac{a^5}{b^3}$

C. $\frac{1}{a^5b^3}$

D. $\frac{a}{b}$

4 Which of the following is not an exponential function?

A. $y = 3^x$

B. $y = 2(5^x)$

C. $y = x^3$

D. $y = \left(\frac{1}{4}\right)^x$

5 If $a \neq 0$ and $y = a^x$, what value of x will result in a value of 1 for y?

A. $x = 1$

B. $x = -1$

C. $x = 0$

D. $x = a$

6 The function $y = a(b^x)$ will represent exponential growth when

A. $a < 0$ and $b > 1$.

B. $a < 0$ and $b < 1$.

C. $a > 0$ and $b > 1$.

D. $a > 0$ and $b < 1$.

7 The graphs of every exponential function of the form $y = k^x$ have a point in common. What is that point?

A. $(1, 1)$

B. $(0, 1)$

C. $(1, 0)$

D. $(0, 0)$

8 If \$10,000 is invested at 6% interest compounded annually, the value of the investment can be represented by which of the following functions?

A. $y = 10{,}000(1.06)^x$

B. $y = 10{,}600^x$

C. $y = 10{,}000(6)^x$

D. $y = 10{,}000(0.94)^x$

9 The half-life of a certain substance is two days. If you have 200 grams of the substance, how much is left after 10 days?

A. 200 g

B. 100 g

C. 6.25 g

D. 0 g

Name ______________________________ Date __________

Diagnostic Test 5: Chapter 5

Polynomials and Factoring

Choose the letter preceding the word or expression that best completes the statement or answers the question.

1 Simplify the expression $\frac{5y^3 + 35y^2 - 25y}{5y}$.

A. $5y^3 + 35y - 30y$

B. $y^3 - 7y - 5y$

C. $5y^2 + 35y - 30$

D. $y^2 + 7y - 5$

2 Factor the expression $4x^2 - 36$.

A. $4(x - 3)(x + 3)$

B. $(4x - 9)(4x + 9)$

C. $(x - 6)(x + 6)$

D. $(4x - 9)(x + 4)$

3 Factor $a^2 + 7a + 12$.

A. $(a + 2)(a + 6)$

B. $(a - 2)(a + 6)$

C. $(a + 3)(a + 4)$

D. $(a - 3)(a - 4)$

4 Simplify the following expression.
$(-10n^5 - 30n^4 + 10n^3 - 20n^2) \div 10n^2$

A. $n^3 + 3n^2 - n + 2$

B. $-n^3 - 3n^2 + n - 2$

C. $-n^4 - 3n^3 + n^2 - 2n$

D. $n^4 + 3n^3 + n^2 + 2n$

5 Find the product of $(y + 8)(y - 1)$.

A. $y^2 + 9y - 9$ **C.** $y^2 - 7y - 8$

B. $y^2 + 7y - 8$ **D.** $y^2 + 9y - 8$

6 Factor completely. $3x^2 - 12x + 9$

A. $3(x + 1)(x + 3)$

B. $(3x - 9)(x - 1)$

C. $(3x - 3)(x - 3)$

D. $3(x - 1)(x - 3)$

7 Simplify the following expression.
$(4b^2 - 6b + 9) - (5b^2 + 8b + 6)$

A. $-b^2 - 14b + 3$

B. $-b^2 + 2b + 15$

C. $9b^2 + 2b + 15$

D. $b^2 + 14b - 3$

In Exercises 8–9, find the product of the algebraic expressions.

8 $(2x^3y^2)(-2x^2y)(-x^4)$

A. $4x^{10}y^4$ **C.** $4x^9y^3$

B. $-2x^9y^3$ **D.** $-4x^{10}y^4$

9 $5m^2n\,(3mn^2 - mn + n)$

A. $8m^2n^3 + 6m^2n^2 + 6n$

B. $15m^3n^3 + 5m^3n^2 + 5m^2n^2$

C. $8m^2n^2 + 4mn + 6n^2$

D. $15m^3n^3 - 5m^3n^2 + 5m^2n^2$

10 Simplify $(c - d)^2$.

A. $c^2 - d^2$ **C.** $c^2 - d^2$

B. $c^2 - 2cd + d^2$ **D.** $c^2 + 2cd + d^2$

Name ____________________ Date ________

Diagnostic Test 6: Chapter 6

Quadratic Equations and Functions

Choose the letter preceding the word or expression that best completes the statement or answers the question.

1 Which of the following is the solution(s) to the equation $k^2 = 36$?

A. $k = 6$

B. $k = 18$

C. $k = \pm 6$

D. $k = 4$ and $k = 9$

2 For which value of b will the equation $x^2 = b$ have irrational roots?

A. $b = 25$ **C.** $b = 10$

B. $b = -9$ **D.** $b = 0$

3 The product of two consecutive positive integers is 240. What is the sum of the two integers?

A. 15 **C.** 240

B. 31 **D.** 16

4 Which of the following does not have a maximum?

A. $y = x^2 + 3x + 5$

B. $y = -4x^2 - 3x - 7$

C. $y = 5x + 7 - 3x^2$

D. $y = -x^2$

5 Which of the following are the coordinates of the vertex of the parabola whose equation is $y = x^2 - 4x + 5$?

A. $(0, 0)$ **C.** $(2, 1)$

B. $(1, 2)$ **D.** $(-4, 5)$

6 Which of the following is an equation of a circle?

A. $x^2 = y + 3$

B. $x^2 + y^2 = 3$

C. $y^2 = x + 3$

D. $x^2 - y^2 = 3$

7 What are the solutions of the equation $x^2 - 4x - 12 = 0$?

A. $(-2, 6)$

B. $(-3, 4)$

C. $(-4, 3)$

D. $(-6, 2)$

8 If the roots of a quadratic equation are $x = 2$ and $x = 5$, which of the following are possible factors of the quadratic?

A. $(x + 2)$ and $(x + 5)$

B. $(x - 2)$ and $(x - 5)$

C. $(x + 2)$ and $(x - 5)$

D. $(x - 2)$ and $(x + 5)$

9 The formula for the area of a circle is πr^2. What is the radius of a circle that has an area of 49π?

A. 7

B. 7π

C. $7\sqrt{\pi}$

D. 49

Name ______________________________ Date __________

Diagnostic Test 7: Chapter 7

Rational and Radical Expressions and Equations

Choose the letter preceding the word or expression that best completes the statement or answers the question.

1 For what value of n will the rational expression $\frac{4}{n+3}$ be undefined?

A. 3 **C.** 0
B. -3 **D.** 4

2 Simplify $\frac{x^2 - y^2}{x^2 - 2xy + y^2}$.

A. $\frac{x-y}{x+y}$ **C.** $\frac{x+y}{x-y}$
B. -1 **D.** 0

3 Multiply $\frac{a-2}{3a+9} \cdot \frac{2a+6}{2a-4}$.

A. $\frac{1}{3}$ **C.** $\frac{4}{6}$
B. $\frac{a-2}{a+3}$ **D.** $\frac{a+3}{a-2}$

4 Divide $\frac{4}{m^2 - 25} \div \frac{8}{m^2 + 10m + 25}$.

A. $\frac{2}{m-5}$
B. $\frac{2(m+5)}{m-5}$
C. $\frac{m+5}{2(m-5)}$
D. $\frac{10m-1}{2}$

5 For what value(s) of m in Exercise 4 is the expression undefined?

A. $25, -25$ **C.** 0
B. -5 **D.** $5, -5$

6 What is the least common denominator of $\frac{q}{q^2 - 1}$ and $\frac{-2}{q-1}$?

A. $(q-1)(q^2-1)$
B. $(q-1)$
C. (q^2-1)
D. $(q+1)$

7 Simplify $\frac{3p}{2p-8} - \frac{12}{p-4}$.

A. $\frac{3p-24}{2p-8}$ **C.** $\frac{3p}{p-4}$
B. $\frac{3}{2}$ **D.** $\frac{6}{p-4}$

8 Solve $\frac{2}{3x} + \frac{3}{4} = 1$.

A. $\frac{8}{3}$ **C.** $\frac{5}{12}$
B. 8 **D.** 1

9 Simplify $3\sqrt{3} + \sqrt{45} + \sqrt{12}$.

A. $8\sqrt{3}$ **C.** $8\sqrt{15}$
B. $8\sqrt{5}$ **D.** $5\sqrt{3} + 3\sqrt{5}$

10 Solve $\sqrt{2-y} = y$.

A. $\{-1, 2\}$
B. no solution
C. $\{1\}$
D. $\{-1, -2\}$

Name ______________________ Date __________

Diagnostic Test 8: Chapter 8

Probability

Choose the letter preceding the word or expression that best completes the statement or answers the question.

1 A die is rolled. Which has the same probability as P(prime)?

A. P(greater than 4)

B. P(1 or 6)

C. P(odd)

D. P(multiple of 3)

2 In how many ways can the letters in the word **MATH** be arranged?

A. 4 **C.** 12

B. 6 **D.** 24

3 A bag contains 3 red and 5 blue marbles. What is the probability that if two marbles are selected *without replacement* they will both be blue?

A. $\frac{5}{8} + \frac{4}{8}$ **C.** $\frac{5}{8} + \frac{4}{7}$

B. $\frac{5}{8} \cdot \frac{4}{8}$ **D.** $\frac{5}{8} \cdot \frac{4}{7}$

4 If $P(A \text{ and } B) = 0$, then the events A and B are

A. impossible. **C.** mutually exclusive.

B. dependent. **D.** random.

5 A bag contains 10 balls numbered 1 through 10. Three balls are selected at random. How many different groups of 3 balls could be chosen?

A. 6

B. 10

C. 120

D. 720

6 How many six letter "words" can be made by using the letters in *butter*?

A. 360 **C.** 720

B. 120 **D.** 36

7 The $P(E) = \frac{5}{8}$. What is the probability that event E does not occur?

A. $\frac{5}{8}$ **C.** $\frac{8}{8}$

B. $\frac{3}{8}$ **D.** $\frac{0}{8}$

8 If A and B are independent, then

A. $P(A \text{ and } B) = P(A) + P(B)$.

B. $P(A \text{ and } B) = P(A) + P(B) - P(A \text{ or } B)$.

C. $P(A \text{ and } B) = P(A) - P(B)$.

D. $P(A \text{ and } B) = P(A) \cdot P(B)$.

9 Jacob is choosing 3 CDs out of his collection of 10 CDs to take on a trip. How many combinations are possible?

A. 3

B. 30

C. 120

D. 720

10 A bag contains red and green marbles. The probability of picking a red marble from a bag is $\frac{2}{9}$. If the bag contains 27 marbles, how many green marbles are there in the bag?

A. 6 **C.** 21

B. 7 **D.** 27

Name ______________________ Date __________

Diagnostic Test 9: Chapter 9

Data Analysis

Choose the letter preceding the word or expression that best completes the statement or answers the question.

1 What is the range of the data set {12, 14, 21, 23, 32, 41, 42, 43}?

A. 23

B. 26

C. 31

D. 42

2 When gathering data for a survey, you should make every attempt to avoid which of the following?

A. random samples

B. long questions

C. measures of central tendency

D. bias

3 What is the median of the data set {50, 55, 62, 66, 78, 82, 82}?

A. 67.857 **C.** 82

B. 66 **D.** 78

4 A set of data has a mean of 70. If 5 is added to each value in the set, what will the new mean will be?

A. less than 70

B. 75

C. 70

D. The new mean cannot be determined.

5 Another name for the mean is

A. average. **C.** range.

B. median. **D.** most.

6 Which of the following statements about the following data set is true? {9, 12, 19, 12, 2, 24, 17, 30}

A. The mode is 12. **C.** The range is 12.

B. The median is 12. **D.** The mean is 12.

7 What type of correlation is shown in the graph below?

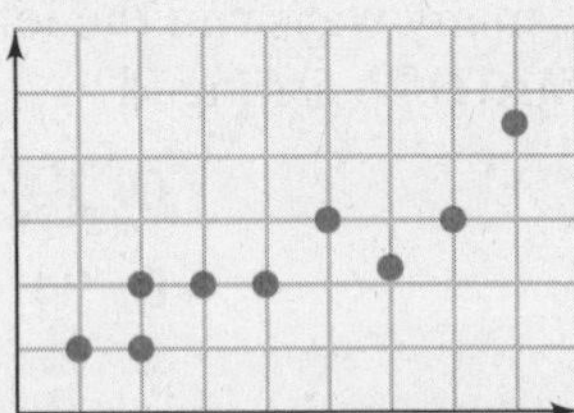

A. negative **C.** positive

B. no correlation **D.** scatter plot

8 When making a prediction from a scatter plot, which of the following should be used?

A. trend line

B. correlation coefficient

C. guess

D. statistics line

9 Paula's average score on 4 quizzes is 17. If she wants to increase her average score to 18, what score must she receive on the next quiz?

A. 18

B. 22

C. 68

D. 90

1 Real Numbers and Algebraic Expressions

Discovering Arizona

Arizona Meteor Crater

Sometime between 5,000 and 50,000 years ago, a meteorite approximately 80 feet in diameter struck the earth 19 miles west of Winslow, Arizona. The impact resulted in a bowl-shaped crater 4,000 feet in diameter and over 600 feet deep.

This crater is the best-preserved impact crater on the planet. However, the crater's extraterrestrial origin was disputed for many years.

At the beginning of the twentieth century, there were two theories explaining the creation of the crater. According to one theory, an impact of a meteor created the crater. A competing theory explained that the crater was caused by a volcanic explosion.

It was not until 1960 that enough evidence had been collected to prove that the crater was indeed caused by a meteor.

1.1 Real Numbers

ADP℠ Standards

O1.a Reason with real numbers

The set of **natural numbers,** or **counting numbers,** consists of the numbers that you use when you count.

$$N = \{1, 2, 3, 4, 5, 6\ldots\} \text{ or } N = \{x \mid x \text{ is a counting number}\}$$

When 0 is an element, the new set is the set of **whole numbers**.

$$W = \{0, 1, 2, 3, 4, 5, 6\ldots\} \text{ or } W = \{x \mid x \text{ is a whole number}\}$$

The set of whole numbers and their **opposites** is called the set of **integers**.

$$Z = \{\ldots, -3, -2, -1, 0, 1, 2, 3\ldots\} \text{ or } Z = \{x \mid x \text{ is an integer}\}$$

The set of **rational numbers** consists of all numbers that can be expressed in the form $\frac{a}{b}$, where a and b are integers and $b \neq 0$.

Any repeating or terminating decimal can be written as a fraction. Some decimals do not terminate or repeat. **Nonterminating, nonrepeating** decimals are **irrational numbers.**

If we try to find the square root of a nonperfect square, we will get only an approximation. Square roots of numbers that are not perfect squares are irrational. The resulting root will be a nonterminating, nonrepeating decimal.

Some examples of irrational numbers are:

a) $0.01010011101111\ldots$

b) $\pi = 3.14159\ldots$

c) $\sqrt{3} = 1.732\ldots$

The **rational numbers** and the **irrational numbers** together make up the set of **real numbers.** The diagram at the right shows how the real numbers and its subsets are related.

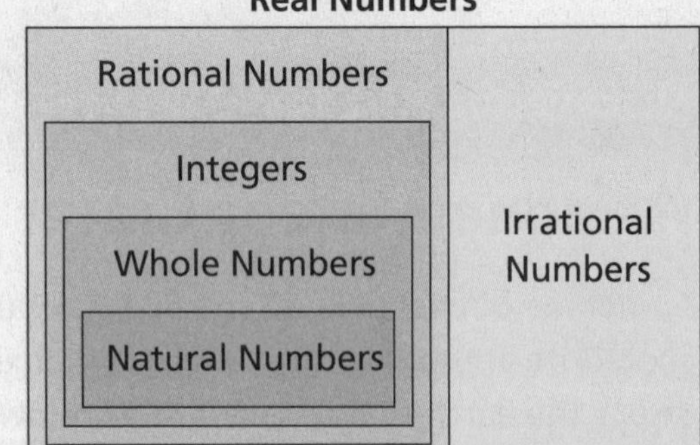

EXAMPLE 1 **Recognizing irrational numbers**

Which of the following is an irrational number?

A. 5.209 **B.** $5.\overline{209}$ **C.** 5.209090909 . . . **D.** 5.2090090009 . . .

▪ SOLUTION

Choice A is a terminating decimal; therefore, it is rational.
Choice B and C are nonterminating but are repeating; therefore, they are rational.
Choice D is a nonterminating, nonrepeating decimal; therefore, it is irrational.

The correct choice is D.

The set of rational numbers and the set of irrational numbers make up the set of real numbers.

There is a *one-to-one correspondence* between the set of real numbers and the points on a **number line.**

The point that corresponds to a real number is called the **graph of the number.** The number line below shows the graphs of $-2\frac{3}{4}$, -1.6, $\sqrt{2}$, 2, and π.

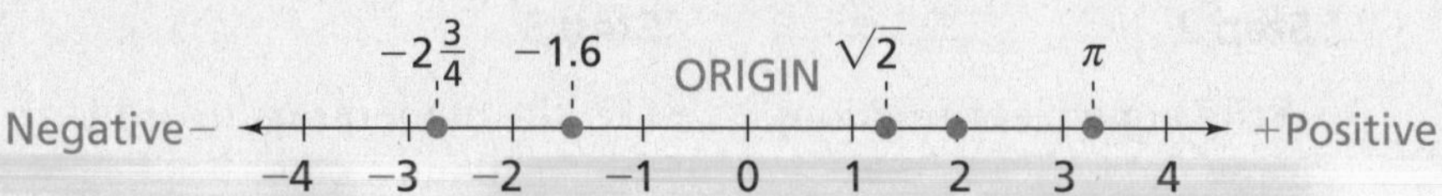

> **Note**
>
> If $a < b$ or $a > b$, then $a \neq b$ (a is not equal to b). Also, if $a < b$ or $a = b$, then $a \leq b$ (a is less than or equal to b) and if $a > b$ or $a = b$, then $a \geq b$ (a is greater than or equal to b).

You can use a number line to *compare* numbers. Given real numbers a and b, exactly one of the following is true.

a is less than b		a is equal to b		a is greater than b
$a < b$	or	$a = b$	or	$a > b$

EXAMPLE 2 **Using a number line to compare**

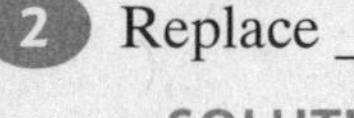

2 Replace __?__ with <, >, or = to make a true statement: 1 __?__ −3

■ **SOLUTION**

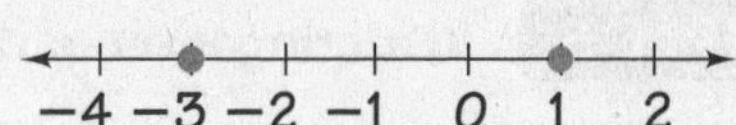

Draw a number line like the one at the right. The graph of 1 is to the right of the graph of −3. Therefore, $1 > -3$.

To place a set of three or more decimals in increasing or decreasing *order*, you can use the method in Example 2.

EXAMPLE 3 **Ordering a set of decimals**

3 Write these decimals in order from least to greatest: 1.04, −14, −1.4, 0.104

■ **SOLUTION**

Step 1	**Step 2**	**Step 3**
Write the numbers with the decimal points lined up.	Annex zeros so that each has the same number of decimal places.	Order the numbers as if they were integers.
1.04	1.040	−14.000
−14.	−14.000	−1.400
−1.4	−1.400	0.104
0.104	0.104	1.040

From least to greatest, the numbers are −14, −1.4, 0.104, 1.04.

To order a set of fractions, you may need to write equivalent fractions using the least common denominator. The **least common denominator,** or **LCD,** of a set of fractions is the **least common multiple (LCM)** of all the denominators.

EXAMPLE 4 Ordering a set of fractions

4 Write these fractions in order from least to greatest: $\frac{3}{4}, \frac{5}{6}, \frac{11}{15}$

■ **SOLUTION**

Step 1

Find the least common denominator (LCD).

$\frac{3}{4}, \frac{5}{6}, \frac{11}{15}$

The LCM of 4, 6, and 15 is 60.

Step 2

Write equivalent fractions, using the LCD.

$\frac{3}{4} = \frac{3 \times 15}{4 \times 15} = \frac{45}{60}$

$\frac{5}{6} = \frac{5 \times 10}{6 \times 10} = \frac{50}{60}$

$\frac{11}{15} = \frac{11 \times 4}{15 \times 4} = \frac{44}{60}$

Step 3

Use the numerators to order the fractions.

$44 < 45 < 50$

$\frac{44}{60} < \frac{45}{60} < \frac{50}{60}$

$\frac{11}{15} < \frac{3}{4} < \frac{5}{6}$

Written in order from least to greatest, the fractions are $\frac{11}{15}, \frac{3}{4}, \frac{5}{6}$.

Note

$a < b < c$ means that "a is less than b and b is less than c" or "b is between a and c."

You can use a calculator to order a set of numbers that includes both fractions and decimals.

EXAMPLE 5 Ordering a set of decimals and fractions

5 Write these numbers in order from least to greatest:

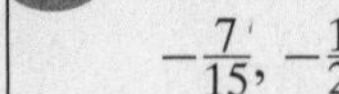

$-\frac{7}{15}, -\frac{11}{24}, -\frac{9}{20}, -0.4512$

■ **SOLUTION**

The fraction $\frac{a}{b}$ means $a \div b$. Use a calculator to perform the divisions.

$-\frac{7}{15}$ → (−) 7 ÷ 15 ENTER −.4666666667 → −0.4666666667

$-\frac{11}{24}$ →  11  24 ENTER −.4583333333 → −0.4583333333

$-\frac{9}{20}$ →  9 ÷ 20 ENTER −.45 → −0.4500000000

−0.4512 → −0.4512000000

Written in order from least to greatest, the numbers are $-\frac{7}{15}, -\frac{11}{24}, -0.4512, -\frac{9}{20}$.

Practice

Choose the letter preceding the word or expression that best completes the statement or answers the question.

1 Which number is not an integer?

A. −9

B. 0

C. $\frac{3}{15}$

D. $\frac{8}{2}$

2 Which of the following is a true statement?

A. −3 is a whole number.

B. $\sqrt{9}$ is an irrational number.

C. 0 is a natural number.

D. $\frac{1}{3}$ is a rational number.

3 Which expression represents an irrational number?

A. 0.040404...

B. $1.\overline{01001}$

C. 0.7070070007...

D. $\sqrt{2} - \sqrt{2}$

4 Which of the following statements is false?

A. All real numbers are rational numbers.

B. Every integer is a rational number.

C. All natural numbers are integers.

D. Every whole number is a real number.

5 Which number is not greater than -5?

A. $5\frac{1}{2}$

B. 0

C. $-\frac{5}{2}$

D. $-5\frac{1}{2}$

6 Which statement is true?

A. $\frac{1}{4} < \frac{1}{3}$

B. $-\frac{1}{2} > -\frac{1}{4}$

C. $-\frac{1}{4} > \frac{1}{3}$

D. $\frac{1}{2} < -\frac{1}{3}$

7 Which number is between -2.5 and $-2\frac{3}{5}$?

A. $-2\frac{2}{5}$

B. $-2.\overline{3}$

C. $-2.\overline{5}$

D. 0

8 Which number is less than -3.2?

A. -5

B. $-3\frac{1}{5}$

C. 0

D. $3\frac{1}{5}$

9 Which number is between -1.6 and $1\frac{1}{3}$?

A. -1.7

B. $-1.\overline{3}$

C. 1.6

D. 1.7

In Exercises 10–13, show that each expression represents a rational number.

10 $4\frac{1}{8}$

11 0.42

12 0.222...

13 0

In Exercises 14–23, replace each ? with <, >, or = to make a true statement.

14 -100 ? 4

15 -2 ? -35

16 6.01 ? -6.1

17 -8.98 ? -8.94

18 $\frac{7}{12}$? $\frac{11}{18}$

19 $1\frac{1}{5}$? $1\frac{1}{6}$

20 $-2\frac{3}{4}$? $-2\frac{7}{8}$

21 $2\frac{5}{11}$? 2.45

22 -0.23 ? $-\frac{2}{9}$

23 $\frac{14}{25}$? $0.5\overline{6}$

In Exercises 24–29, write each set of numbers in order from least to greatest.

24 $\frac{9}{5}, \frac{5}{3}, \frac{17}{10}$

25 $-\frac{5}{6}, -\frac{13}{15}, -\frac{8}{9}$

26 $-3.7, -10, 0, -5, 1, -2$

27 $-1.1, -1.01, -1.101, -0.1001$

28 $\frac{1}{20}, 0.5, \frac{2}{5}, \frac{5}{9}, 0.505$

29 $-\frac{9}{2}, -4.3, -4\frac{1}{3}, 4.\overline{3}, -4\frac{3}{100}$

In Exercises 30–35, give an example to illustrate the type of number described and explain your answer.

30 a whole number that is not a natural number

31 a real number that is not rational

32 a rational number that is not an integer

33 an integer that is not a whole number

34 a rational number that is not a natural number

35 a real number that is not an integer

1.2 Real Number Operations

ADP℠ Standards

O1.a Reason with real numbers

The **absolute value** of a number is its distance from zero on a number line. The symbol for the absolute value of a number n is $|n|$.

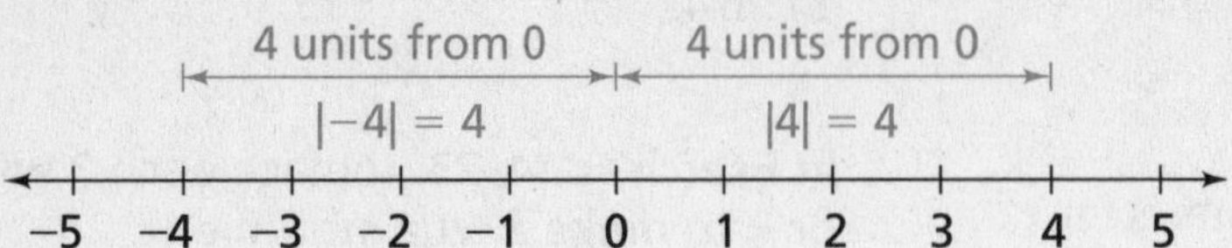

Opposites are two numbers that are the same distance from zero on a number line, but on opposite sides of zero. The opposite of a number n is written as $-n$.

−4 is the opposite of 4. 4 is the opposite of −4.

The concept of absolute value is used in establishing rules for basic operations with signed numbers.

The absolute value of 0 is 0.

$$|0| = 0$$

The opposite of 0 is 0.

$$-0 = 0$$

Note

Recall that in addition, the numbers you are adding are called **addends** and the result of the addition is called the **sum.**

Adding Integers

- To add two numbers with like signs, add their absolute values. The sum has the same sign as both addends.
- To add two numbers with unlike signs, subtract the lesser absolute value from the greater absolute value. The sum has the same sign as the addend with the greater absolute value.

EXAMPLES 1 through 4 **Adding integers**

1 7 + 9

SOLUTION

|7| → 7 ← Both addends
|9| → + 9 are *positive.*
16

7 + 9 = 16 ← The sum is *positive.*

2 −8 + (−6)

SOLUTION

|−8| → 8 ← Both addends
|−6| → + 6 are *negative.*
14

−8 + (−6) = −14 ← The sum is *negative.*

3 −12 + 5

SOLUTION

|−12| → 12 ← *Negative* addend
|5| → 5 has the greater absolute value.

12 − 5 = 7

−12 + 5 = −7 ← The sum is *negative.*

4 −6 + 15

SOLUTION

|15| → 15 ← *Positive* addend
|−6| → 6 has the greater absolute value.

15 − 6 = 9

−6 + 15 = 9 ← The sum is *positive.*

Subtracting Integers

- To subtract a signed number, add its opposite.

Note

When you subtract two numbers, the result is called the **difference.**

Using this rule, you can rewrite any subtraction $a - b$ as $a + (-b)$. Then you proceed by following the rules for adding signed numbers.

EXAMPLES 5 through 7 Subtracting integers

5 $-7 - (-21)$

■ **SOLUTION**

$-7 - (-21)$
$-7 + 21$
14

6 $-9 - 18$

■ **SOLUTION**

$-9 - 18$
$-9 + (-18)$
-27

7 $2 - 14$

■ **SOLUTION**

$2 - 14$
$2 + (-14)$
-12

The rules for adding and subtracting signed numbers can also be applied to decimals.

EXAMPLES 8 and 9 Adding and subtracting decimals

8 $-0.23 + (-0.083) + (-9.5)$

■ **SOLUTION**

-0.230 ← Line up the decimal points. Annex zeros so that each addend has the same number of decimal places.
-0.083
-9.500
-9.813

9 $34 - 2.75$

■ **SOLUTION**

34.00 ← In a whole number, the decimal point follows the ones' place.
$-\ 2.75$
31.25

You must also use the rules for adding and subtracting signed numbers with fractions.

Go Online PearsonSchool.com
Visit: PearsonSchool.com
Web Code: ayp-0046

EXAMPLES 10 and 11 Adding and subtracting fractions

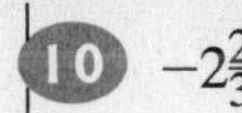

10 $-2\frac{2}{3} + \left(-4\frac{2}{3}\right)$

■ **SOLUTION**

$-2\frac{2}{3} + \left(-4\frac{2}{3}\right)$

$-\frac{8}{3} + \left(-\frac{14}{3}\right)$ ← Rewrite the mixed numbers as fractions.

$\frac{-8 + (-14)}{3}$ ← Write the sum of the numerators over the common denominator.

$\frac{-22}{3}$

$-7\frac{1}{3}$

11 $\frac{1}{5} - \frac{5}{8}$

■ **SOLUTION**

$\frac{1}{5} - \frac{5}{8}$

$\frac{1}{5} + \left(-\frac{5}{8}\right)$ ← Rewrite the subtraction as an addition.

$\frac{8}{40} + \left(-\frac{25}{40}\right)$ ← The LCD is 40.

$\frac{8 + (-25)}{40}$

$\frac{-17}{40} = -\frac{17}{40}$

The procedure for multiplication of signed numbers is related to the procedure for division. The rules for both operations can be summarized as follows.

Multiplying and Dividing Integers

- To multiply or divide two numbers with like signs, multiply or divide their absolute values. The product or quotient is positive.
- To multiply or divide two numbers with unlike signs, multiply or divide their absolute values. The product or quotient is negative.

EXAMPLES 12 and 13 **Multiplying and dividing integers**

12 $(-12) \times (-6)$

■ SOLUTION

$(-12) \times (-6)$ ← **The numbers have like signs.**

$12 \times 6 = 72$ ← $|-12| = 12$ **and** $|-6| = 6$

$(-12) \times (-6) = 72$ ← **The product is *positive.***

13 $-72 \div 9$

■ SOLUTION

$-72 \div 9$ ← **The numbers have unlike signs.**

$72 \div 9 = 8$ ← $|-72| = 72$ **and** $|9| = 9$

$-72 \div 9 = -8$ ← **The quotient is *negative.***

Although you do not need to align the decimals before multiplying, you must be careful to place the decimal in the answer correctly.

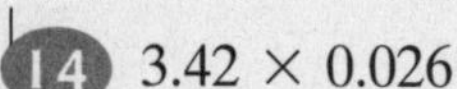

EXAMPLES 14 and 15 **Multiplying decimals**

14 3.42×0.026

■ SOLUTION

- Multiply as with whole numbers.
- Count the *total* decimal places in the factors.
- Give the product that number of decimal places.
- Insert zeros as placeholders where necessary.

```
   3.42   ←      2 decimal places
× 0.026   ←  +   3 decimal places
   2052
   684
0.08892   ←      5 decimal places
```

15 $(-0.32)(12.5)$

■ SOLUTION

- The decimals have unlike signs.
- Multiply the absolute values of the decimals.
- Count the *total* decimal places in the factors.
- Place the decimal in the product accordingly.

```
(−0.32) (12.5)
          0.32
        × 12.5
           160
           64
          32
         4.000
```

- The product is *negative.* Therefore, $(-0.32)(12.5) = -4$.

Remember that to divide by a decimal, you change the divisor into a whole number by moving the decimal all the way to the right. To keep the value of the original division problem, you need to move the decimal in the dividend the same number of places to the right. The remaining steps are reviewed in the following example.

EXAMPLES 16 and 17 Dividing decimals

 $1.452 \div 0.24$

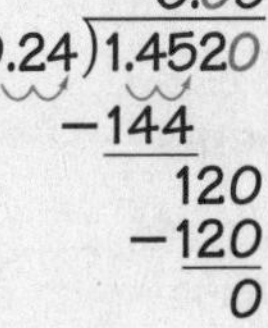

■ **SOLUTION**

- In the *divisor,* move the decimal point right to make it a whole number.
- In the *dividend,* move the decimal point the same number of places to the right.
- Divide as with whole numbers.
- Place the decimal point in the quotient above the decimal point in the dividend.
- Insert zeros as placeholders where necessary.

17 $12.35 \div -0.125$

$$\begin{array}{r} 98.8 \\ 0.125\overline{)12.3500} \\ -1125 \\ \hline 1100 \\ -1000 \\ \hline 1000 \\ -1000 \\ \hline 0 \end{array}$$

■ **SOLUTION**

- The decimals have unlike signs.
- Divide the absolute values of the decimals.
- Insert zeros as placeholders where necessary.
- The quotient is *negative*. Therefore, $12.35 \div -0.125 = 98.8$.

Again, you must apply the rules for multiplying and dividing signed numbers when finding the products and quotients of fractions.

EXAMPLES 18 and 19 Multiplying and dividing fractions

 $\left(-1\frac{1}{2}\right)\left(1\frac{7}{9}\right)$

■ **SOLUTION**

- Multiply the numerators.
- Multiply the denominators.
- Simplify the result.

$\left(-1\frac{1}{2}\right)\left(1\frac{7}{9}\right)$

$-\frac{3}{2} \times \frac{16}{9}$ ← **Rewrite the mixed numbers as fractions.**

$\frac{-3 \times 16}{2 \times 9}$

$\frac{-48}{18} = -\frac{8}{3} = -2\frac{2}{3}$

 $-\frac{3}{4} \div (-3)$

■ **SOLUTION**

- Multiply the dividend by the reciprocal of the divisor.
- Simplify the result.

$-\frac{3}{4} \div (-3)$

$-\frac{3}{4} \times -\frac{1}{3}$ ← **The reciprocal of -3 is $-\frac{1}{3}$.**

$\frac{3}{12} = \frac{1}{4}$

The following are *field properties* of real numbers. These properties govern the operations of addition and multiplication.

Field Properties of Real Numbers
Let *a, b,* and *c* represent real numbers.

Property	Addition	Multiplication
Closure	$a + b$ is a unique real number.	$a \cdot b$ is a unique real number.
Commutative	$a + b = b + a$	$a \cdot b = b \cdot a$
Associative	$a + b + c = (a + b) + c$ $= a + (b + c)$	$a \cdot b \cdot c = (a \cdot b) \cdot c$ $= a \cdot (b \cdot c)$
Identity	$a + 0 = a$ and $0 + a = a$ The **additive identity** is 0.	$a \cdot 1 = a$ and $1 \cdot a = a$ The **multiplicative identity** is 1.
Inverse	For every real number a, there is a unique real number $-a$ such that $a + (-a) = 0$ and $-a + a = 0$; $-a$ is the **additive inverse** of a, or the **opposite** of a.	For every nonzero real number a, there is a unique real number $\frac{1}{a}$ such that $a \cdot \frac{1}{a} = 1$ and $\frac{1}{a} \cdot a = 1$; $\frac{1}{a}$ is the **multiplicative inverse** of a, or the **reciprocal** of a.
Distributive	$a \cdot (b + c) = a \cdot b + a \cdot c$ and $(b + c) \cdot a = b \cdot a + c \cdot a$	

EXAMPLES 20 through 22 **Using properties of real numbers**

Simplify each expression.

20 $-19 + 24 + (-11)$

SOLUTION

$$\begin{aligned} -19 + 24 + (-11) &= 24 + (-19) + (-11) \\ &= 24 + [(-19) + (-11)] \\ &= 24 + (-30) \\ &= -6 \end{aligned}$$

← Use the Associative and Commutative Properties of Addition to change the order and group the negative numbers.

21 $12 \times 25 \times \frac{1}{12}$

SOLUTION

$$\begin{aligned} 12 \times 25 \times \tfrac{1}{12} &= \left[12 \times \tfrac{1}{12}\right] \times 25 \\ &= 1 \times 25 \\ &= 25 \end{aligned}$$

← Use the Associative and Commutative Properties of Multiplication.
← Use the Multiplicative Inverse Property.
← Use the Multiplicative IdentityProperty.

22 $36 \cdot \left(0.01 + \frac{1}{3}\right)$

SOLUTION

$$\begin{aligned} 36 \cdot \left(0.01 + \tfrac{1}{3}\right) &= 36 \cdot 0.01 + 36 \cdot \tfrac{1}{3} && \leftarrow \text{Use the Distributive Property.} \\ &= 0.36 + 12 && \leftarrow \text{Find the products.} \\ &= 12.36 && \leftarrow \text{Find the sum.} \end{aligned}$$

Practice

Choose the letter preceding the word or expression that best completes the statement or answers the question.

1 Which sum is a negative number?

A. $\frac{1}{2} + \left(-\frac{3}{4}\right) + \frac{3}{4}$ **C.** $-\frac{1}{2} + \left(-\frac{3}{4}\right) + \frac{1}{2}$

B. $\frac{1}{2} + \frac{3}{4} + \left(-\frac{1}{2}\right)$ **D.** $-\frac{1}{2} + \frac{3}{4} + \frac{1}{2}$

2 Which is true of $\left(-1\frac{1}{2}\right)\left(-3\frac{1}{3}\right)$?

A. The product is negative.

B. The product is positive and less than 1.

C. The product is positive and greater than 6.

D. The product is a whole number.

3 Which expression is *not* equivalent to $-6.25 \div 2.5$?

A. $-62.5 \div 25$ **C.** $-625 \div 25$

B. $-0.625 \div 0.25$ **D.** $-6250 \div 2500$

4 Which statement about inverses is false?

A. Every real number has a reciprocal.

B. Every real number has an additive inverse.

C. The sum of a number and its additive inverse is 0.

D. The product of a number and its reciprocal is 1.

5 Which statement is true?

A. $|-8| = -|8|$ **C.** $-|-8| = -(-8)$

B. $|-8| = -(-8)$ **D.** $-|-8| = |-(-8)|$

In Exercises 6–18, simplify each expression.

6 $-9 + (-5)$ **7** $-0.15 + 0.75$

8 $\frac{7}{8} + \left(-\frac{1}{6}\right)$ **9** $12 - 19$

10 $124.7 - 56.79$ **11** $\left(-\frac{3}{5}\right) - \frac{9}{10}$

12 $15 \times (-8)$ **13** $(-1.3)(5.6)$

14 $\frac{1}{9} \times \frac{3}{8}$ **15** $14 \div (-7)$

16 $-57 \div 2.4$ **17** $-\frac{7}{20} \div \left(-\frac{3}{7}\right)$

18 $|22.7 - 173|$

In Exercises 19–24, write the name of the property that is illustrated by each statement.

19 $8(5) = 5(8)$

20 $-3.008 + 3.008 = 0$

21 $6(10 + 5) = 6(10) + 6(5)$

22 $1 \cdot (6 - 0.02) = (6 - 0.02)$

23 $(8 + 3) + 4 = 4 + (8 + 3)$

24 $(6 \cdot 5) \cdot 4 = 6 \cdot (5 \cdot 4)$

In Exercises 25–27, simplify each expression.

25 $|-9|$ **26** $-|-4|$ **27** $-(-2)$

In Exercises 28–29, replace each __?__ with <, >, or = to make a true statement.

28 $|-5|$ __?__ $|5|$ **29** $-|1|$ __?__ $|-1|$

In Exercises 30–33, $T = \{x \mid x \text{ is an odd whole number}\}$ and $T \subset W$.

30 Is T closed under addition? Explain.

31 What is the additive identity of T?

32 What is T'?

33 Is T commutative under addition? Explain your reasoning.

1.3 Exponents, Square Roots, and the Order of Operations

ADP℠ Standards

O1.a Reason with real numbers

O1.c Apply laws of exponents

You can write $3 \cdot 3 \cdot 3 \cdot 3 \cdot 3 \cdot 3$ in **exponential form** as 3^6. In this expression, 3 is the **base** and 6 is the **exponent.** It is read as "three to the sixth power." Because $3^6 = 729$, the number 729 is called *the sixth power of three.*

$$\underbrace{3 \cdot 3 \cdot 3 \cdot 3 \cdot 3 \cdot 3}_{6 \text{ factors}} = \overset{\text{exponent}}{3^6} = 729 \leftarrow \text{6th power of 3}$$

(3 is the base)

It is also possible for an exponent to be 0 or a negative integer.

- For any nonzero number a, $a^0 = 1$.
- For any nonzero number a and any integer n, $a^{-n} = \frac{1}{a^n}$.

EXAMPLES 1 through 3 **Simplifying exponential expressions**

Simplify each expression.

1 5^4

■ **SOLUTION**

$5^4 = 5 \cdot 5 \cdot 5 \cdot 5 = 625$

2 372^0

■ **SOLUTION**

$372^0 = 1$

3 2^{-3}

■ **SOLUTION**

$2^{-3} = \frac{1}{2^3} = \frac{1}{2 \cdot 2 \cdot 2} = \frac{1}{8}$

Exponents are used to write very large and very small positive numbers in *scientific notation.* A number written in **scientific notation** has two factors.

The first factor is a number that is at least 1, but is less than 10. → $a \times 10^n$ ← **The second factor is an integer power of 10, expressed in exponential form.**

Go Online
PearsonSchool.com
Visit: PearsonSchool.com
Web Code: ayp-0243

You can use what you know about scientific notation to convert a number in standard form to scientific notation.

EXAMPLES 4 through 7 **Converting numbers in standard form and scientific notation**

Write each number in standard form.

4 7.4×10^5 ■ **SOLUTION** The exponent is 5. Move the decimal point 5 places *to the right.*

$7.4 \times 10^5 = 7.4 \times 100{,}000 = 740{,}000$

5 4.43×10^{-6} ■ **SOLUTION** The exponent is −6. Move the decimal point 6 places *to the left.*

$4.43 \times 10^{-6} = 4.43 \times 0.000001 = 0.00000443$

Write each number in scientific notation.

6 32,500,000 ■ **SOLUTION** $\underbrace{32{,}500{,}000}_{7 \text{ places}} = 3.25 \times 10{,}000{,}000 = 3.25 \times 10^7$

7 0.0068 ■ **SOLUTION** $\underbrace{0.0068}_{3 \text{ places}} = 6.8 \times 0.001 = 6.8 \times 10^{-3}$

For any real number a, finding the value of a^2 is called **squaring** the number.

$4^2 = 16 \rightarrow$ 4 squared is equal to 16. $\rightarrow$ The square of 4 is 16.

$(-4)^2 = 16 \rightarrow$ -4 squared is equal to 16. $\rightarrow$ The square of -4 is 16.

If $a^2 = b$, then a is called a **square root** of b. The *radical sign* $\sqrt{}$ indicates a square root. The expression under the radical sign is called the **radicand.** An expression that contains a radical sign is called a **radical expression.**

Every positive real number b has two square roots. The expression $\sqrt{b}$ indicates its positive square root, called the **principal square root.** The expression $-\sqrt{b}$ indicates its negative square root.

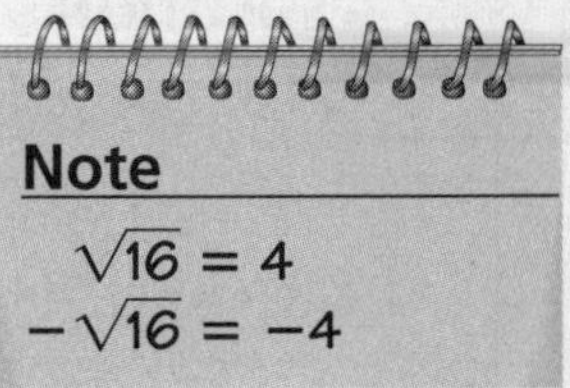

Rational numbers such as 25 and 0.01 are called **perfect squares** because their square roots are rational numbers.

$\sqrt{25} = 5$ and $-\sqrt{25} = -5$ $\qquad$ $\sqrt{0.01} = 0.1$ and $-\sqrt{0.01} = -0.1$

If a rational number is not a perfect square, then its square roots are irrational numbers. This means that their decimal representations are nonterminating, nonrepeating decimals. Therefore, you cannot write exact decimal values. However, it is possible to find an *approximation*.

EXAMPLE 8 **Locating square roots between consecutive integers**

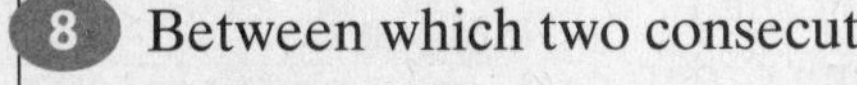

8 Between which two consecutive integers is $\sqrt{42}$?

▪ SOLUTION 1

$\sqrt{36} < \sqrt{42} < \sqrt{49}$ ← **42 is between the perfect-square integers 36 and 49.**

$6 < \sqrt{42} < 7$

Therefore, $\sqrt{42}$ is between 6 and 7.

▪ SOLUTION 2

You can also use a calculator to find an approximation of a radical expression.

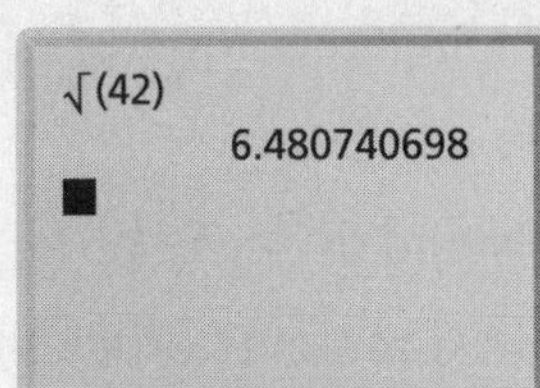

Therefore, $\sqrt{42}$ is between 6 and 7.

Sometimes your approximation needs to be more precise. You may be asked to determine which whole number is closest to a root.

EXAMPLE 9 **Approximating square roots to the nearest whole number**

9 What is $\sqrt{132}$ to the nearest whole number?

▪ SOLUTION

$11 < \sqrt{132} < 12$ ← **$\sqrt{132}$ is between 11 and 12.**

Is it closer to 11 or 12?

$11^2 = 121; 132 - 121 = 11$

$12^2 = 144; 144 - 132 = 12$

Therefore, $\sqrt{132} \approx 11$.

Note

The symbol ≈ is read "is approximately equal to."

You can also use a calculator to find a more exact approximation of a square root. A calculator gives an estimate of the square root of a nonsquare, rational number.

Note

To round a decimal: Look at the digit to the right of the place to which you are rounding.

- If it is less than 5, round down.
- If it is greater than or equal to 5, round up.

EXAMPLES 10 and 11 **Approximating irrational square roots**

10 Approximate $\sqrt{4.3}$ to the nearest hundredth.

■ SOLUTION

$\sqrt{4.3}$ → [√] 4.3 [ENTER]

→ 2.073644135 ← 3 is less than 5, so round down. Drop the digits to the right of 7.

Therefore, $\sqrt{4.3} \approx 2.07$.

11 Approximate $-\sqrt{10.8}$ to the nearest hundredth.

■ SOLUTION

$-\sqrt{10.8}$ → [(-)] [√] 10.8 [ENTER]

→ -3.286335345 ← 6 is greater than 5, so round up. Add 1 to 8. Drop the digits to the right of 8.

Therefore, $-\sqrt{10.8} \approx -3.29$.

Many expressions involve two or more operations. When simplifying such expressions, it is important to perform the operations in the following order.

Note

Grouping symbols:

parentheses	( )
brackets	[ ]
braces	{ }
fraction bar	—
absolute-value bars	| |
radical sign	√

Order of Operations

1. Perform any operation(s) within grouping symbols.
2. Simplify all powers.
3. Multiply and divide in order from left to right.
4. Add and subtract in order from left to right.

Go Online PearsonSchool.com

Visit: PearsonSchool.com
Web Code: ayp-0142

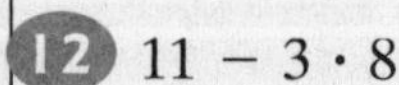

EXAMPLES 12 and 13 **Applying the order of operations**

Simplify each expression.

12 $11 - 3 \cdot 8$

■ SOLUTION

$11 - 3 \cdot 8$ ← Multiply first.
$11 - 24$ ← Then subtract.
-13

13 $3(5 + 4^2) \div 7 - 7$

■ SOLUTION

$3(5 + 4^2) \div 7 - 7$ ← Simplify 4^2.
$3(5 + 16) \div 7 - 7$ ← Add within the parentheses.
$3(21) \div 7 - 7$ ← Multiply 3(21).
$63 \div 7 - 7$ ← Divide $63 \div 7$.
$9 - 7$ ← Subtract.
2

By using the order of operations, you know that you will always come up with same answer when solving mathematical statements. For example, you know that the statement

$$5 + 2 \times 7 = 19$$

is true, but the statement

$$5 + 2 \times 7 = 49$$

is false because of the order of operations.

However, sometimes you will be asked to decide whether a statement is true or false without using the order of operations. For example, think about the following statement:

All square roots are irrational.

Is this statement true or false?

If you can find even one counterexample, you have proven the statement is false. A **counterexample** is one case that makes a statement false.

For example, $\sqrt{4} = 2$. Since 2 is a rational number, it is a counterexample that shows the statement *All square roots are irrational* is not true. Again, all you need to do is find **one** counterexample to show that a statement is false.

Note that while you need only one counterexample to prove that a statement is false, a single example **does not** prove that a statement is true. For example, $\sqrt{3}$ is a square root that is an irrational number, but this example does not prove that the statement *All square roots are irrational* is true.

EXAMPLES 14 and 15 Finding counterexamples

Find a counterexample for each situation.

14 Jani sees the statement $x < 1$. She tells her friend that x must be 0 or a negative number. Find a counterexample that shows Jani's conclusion is false.

■ SOLUTION

The value of x could be a fraction. If $x = \frac{1}{2}$, then $x < 1$. The number $\frac{1}{2}$ is a counterexample that shows Jani's conclusion is false.

15 Andre wrote the statement $-1 < x < 1$. Then he made the claim that x must be a rational number. Find a counterexample that shows Brian's claim is false.

■ SOLUTION

At first glance, the statement appears to be true. Possible values for x include proper fractions and the integer 0, all of which are rational numbers.

Now consider irrational numbers. What do you know about irrational numbers? An irrational number has a nonterminating and nonrepeating decimal part. Can you write a decimal less than 1 that neither ends nor repeats?

0.1011011101111011111... The pattern will never end or repeat. Its value is greater than -1 and less than 1. This counterexample proves that Brian's claim is false.

Note

Values that often produce counterexamples include 0, 1, fractions, negative values, and square roots.

Examples and counterexamples allow us to establish facts about rational and irrational numbers and the rules and properties that govern them.

EXAMPLES 16 and 17 Drawing conclusions about real numbers

16 Manuel needs to solve $(9 + 12)^2$.

Using the Distributive Property, he knows that $2(3 + 4) = 2(3) + 2(4)$. He wonders whether the Distributive Property can be used with exponents.

Does $(9 + 12)^2 = 9^2 + 12^2$?

■ **SOLUTION**

Work the expressions separately.

$(9 + 12)^2$		$9^2 + 12^2$	
$= 21^2$	← **Add first.**	$81 + 144$	← **Square each addend.**
$= 441$	← **Square the sum.**	$= 225$	← **Find the sum.**

Since the two expressions do not have the same value, they are not equal.

From this example, you can conclude that you cannot use the Distributive Property with exponents in this way.

17 Lynn says that if she has two positive numbers, *a* and *b,* then the square root of their sum is equal to the sum of their square roots. Is Lynn's claim true or false?

■ **SOLUTION**

First, write out Lynn's claim in a mathematical sentence. Lynn says that the following is true:

$$\sqrt{a + b} = \sqrt{a} + \sqrt{b}$$

Pick two numbers that are perfect squares, for example, let $a = 16$ and $b = 9$. Substitute these values into the equation.

$$\sqrt{a + b} = \sqrt{a} + \sqrt{b}$$

$$\sqrt{16 + 9} = \sqrt{16} + \sqrt{9} \quad \leftarrow \textbf{Substitute.}$$

$$\sqrt{25} = 4 + 3 \quad \leftarrow \textbf{Simplify.}$$

$$5 \neq 7$$

The equation is false. The numbers 16 and 9 are counterexamples that prove Lynn's statement *The square root of their sum is equal to the sum of their square roots* is false.

Using examples and counterexamples to draw conclusions or disprove statements is a powerful test-taking skill. From time to time, you may have trouble remembering a rule you have learned. By trying an example with numbers that are easy to work with, you may avoid making mistakes by applying rules in error.

Remember, however, that while a single counterexample shows that a statement is false, a single example that shows that a statement is true **does not** mean the statement is **always** true.

Practice

Choose the letter preceding the word or expression that best completes the statement or answers the question.

1 Which expression is equivalent to 3^{-4}?

A. $3(-4)$ B. $\frac{1}{3^4}$ C. $|3^4|$ D. $\frac{1}{3 \cdot 4}$

2 Which number is equivalent to 8.72×10^{-4}?

A. 0.000872 C. 0.0872

B. 0.00872 D. 87,200

3 Which expression represents 32.45 in scientific notation?

A. $3 \times 10^1 + 2 \times 10^0 + 4 \times 10^{-1} + 5 \times 10^{-2}$

B. 3.245×10^1

C. 3.245×10^{-1}

D. 3.245×10^{-2}

4 Which symbol makes a true statement when placed in the blank below?

0.38×10^{-2} __?__ 0.38×10^{-3}

A. $<$ B. $>$ C. $=$ D. $\leq$

5 Which is not a perfect square?

A. $\frac{1}{4}$ B. $\frac{28}{63}$ C. $\frac{18}{2}$ D. $\frac{32}{48}$

6 Between which two consecutive integers does $-\sqrt{20}$ lie?

A. 4 and 5 C. -5 and -3

B. -5 and -4 D. -21 and -19

7 To simplify $15 + 5(12 \div 4)$, first calculate

A. $15 + 5$. C. $12 \div 4$.

B. $5(12)$. D. $5 \div 4$.

8 Which set of numbers has been placed in order from least to greatest?

A. $-\sqrt{7.2}, -2.\overline{7}, -2\frac{1}{7}$

B. $-2\frac{1}{7}, -2.\overline{7}, -\sqrt{7.2}$

C. $-2.\overline{7}, -\sqrt{7.2}, -2\frac{1}{7}$

D. $-2.\overline{7}, -2\frac{1}{7}, -\sqrt{7.2}$

In Exercises 9–12, simplify each expression.

9 11^2 **10** 2^7 **11** 5^0 **12** 9^1

In Exercises 13–16, write each number in standard form.

13 8×10^3 **14** 8×10^{-3}

15 3.1×10^{-5} **16** 9.2×10^7

In Exercises 17–22, write each number in scientific notation.

17 4,000,000 **18** 0.000004

19 34.09 **20** 0.205

21 65,000,000 **22** 0.0099

In Exercises 23–26, simplify each expression.

23 $\sqrt{64}$ **24** $-\sqrt{400}$ **25** $-\sqrt{1.44}$ **26** $\sqrt{0.09}$

In Exercises 27–30, name the two consecutive integers between which each number lies.

27 $\sqrt{30}$ **28** $-\sqrt{75}$ **29** $\sqrt{14.9}$ **30** $-\sqrt{32.2}$

In Exercises 31–36, use a calculator to approximate to the nearest hundredth.

31 $\sqrt{3}$ **32** $-\sqrt{24}$ **33** $-\sqrt{4.9}$

34 $\sqrt{85.2}$ **35** $\sqrt{0.95}$ **36** $\sqrt{0.2}$

In Exercises 37–42, simplify each expression.

37 $15 - 8 \times 4$ **38** $-4 + 32 \div 4 - 2$

39 $(-2 + 6)^2 \div 2$ **40** $16 - 2^2 \times 8 + 16$

41 $[2(6 - 5) + 8] - 2^3$ **42** $2^2 \cdot 3^1 \cdot 5^2 \cdot 11^1$

In Exercises 43 and 44, write a counterexample to show each conclusion is false.

43 The square of any rational number is always greater than the number.

44 For any real number a, $(2a)^2 > 2a^2$.

In Exercises 45–46, solve the following problems. Clearly explain your reasoning and show all necessary work.

45 Insert one pair of grouping symbols into $4 \times 3 + 12 \div 3$ to create an expression that is equivalent to 8.

46 Write $3 \times 10^0, 3 \times 10^2, 3 \times 10^{-2}$, and 3×10^{-5} from least to greatest.

1.4 Arithmetic and Geometric Sequences

ADP℠ Standards

O1.c Apply laws of exponents

L1.a Represent linear relationships

N1.b Distinguish between function types

A number pattern is called an **arithmetic sequence** when each **term** of the sequence differs by a fixed number, called the **common difference.**

Go Online PearsonSchool.com

Visit: PearsonSchool.com

Web Code: ayp-0201

EXAMPLES 1 and 2 Finding the common difference of a sequence

Find the common difference and determine the next three terms of the sequence

1 $-9, -4, 1, 6, \ldots$

■ **SOLUTION**

To find the common difference, find the difference between consecutive terms.

$$-4 - (-9) = 5$$
$$1 - (-4) = 5$$
$$6 - 1 = 5$$

The common difference is **5**.

Add 5 to the fourth term to find the fifth term, add 5 to the fifth term to find the sixth, and so on. So the next three terms of the sequence are **11, 16, 21.**

2 $11, 4, -3, -10$

■ **SOLUTION**

To find the common difference, find the difference between consecutive terms.

$$4 - 11 = -7$$
$$-3 - 4 = -7$$
$$-10 - (-3) = -7$$

The common difference is **−7.**

Add −7 to the fourth term to find the fifth term, add −7 to the fifth term to find the sixth, and so on. So the next three terms of the sequence are **−17, −24, −31.**

a_1 represents the first term of a sequence, a_2 the second term, a_3 the third, and so on to the nth term a_n. You can find any term of an arithmetic sequence by using the common difference d and the first term a_1 of the sequence.

In the sequence 6, 10, 14, 18, . . . , the 1st term a_1 is 6 and each consecutive term is found by the formula $a_n = 6 + (n - 1)4$ where n represents the number of the term in the sequence.

The *n*th Term of an Arithmetic Sequence

The nth term in an arithmetic sequence $\boldsymbol{a_n}$, where $\boldsymbol{a_1}$ is the first term and $\boldsymbol{d}$ is the common difference is

$$\boldsymbol{a_n = a_1 + (n - 1)d}$$

EXAMPLES 3 and 4 Finding the terms of an arithmetic sequence

3 Find the 9th term of the sequence 29, 26, 23, ...

■ **SOLUTION**

$$a_n = a_1 + (n - 1)d$$
$$a_9 = 29 + (9 - 1)(-3) \leftarrow a_1 = 29 \text{ and } d = -3.$$
$$a_9 = 29 + (-24)$$
$$a_9 = 5$$

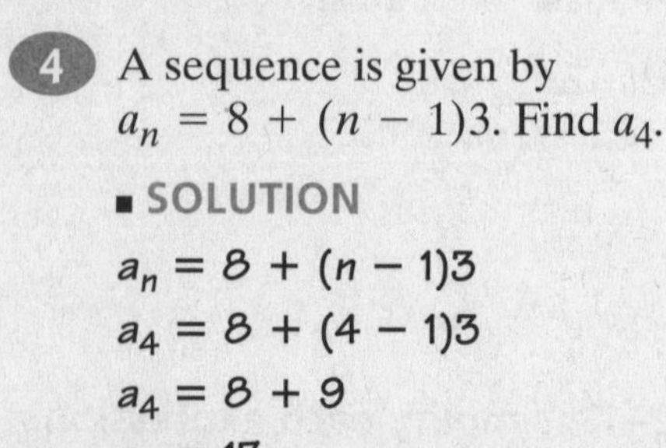

4 A sequence is given by $a_n = 8 + (n - 1)3$. Find a_4.

■ **SOLUTION**

$$a_n = 8 + (n - 1)3$$
$$a_4 = 8 + (4 - 1)3$$
$$a_4 = 8 + 9$$
$$a_4 = 17$$

You can also find the equation that represents the nth term of an arithmetic sequence. Once you have found this equation you can find the value of any term of the sequence.

EXAMPLE 5 **Finding the equation for the *n*th term of an arithmetic sequence**

5 Write the equation that represents the nth term of the sequence 12, 17, 22, 27, . . .

■ **SOLUTION**

Step 1

Identify a_1.
$a_1 = 12$

Step 2

Find d.
$17 - 12 = 5, 22 - 17 = 5, 27 - 22 = 5$
$d = 5$

Step 3

Use the formula $a_n = a_1 + (n - 1)d$ to write the equation for the nth term.
$a_n = 12 + (n - 1)5$

Another type of number sequence is a **geometric sequence.** This quotient is constant between consecutive terms of a geometric sequence and is called the **common ratio *r*.** You can find the common ratio by dividing any term of the sequence by the preceding term.

EXAMPLES 6 and 7 **Finding the common ratio of a geometric sequence**

Find the common ratio and the next two terms of each of the following geometric sequences.

6 4, 12, 36, . . .

■ **SOLUTION**

Find the common ratio

$$\frac{12}{4} = 3$$

The common ratio is 3.
The next two terms are $36(3) = 108$ and $108(3) = 324$.

7 9, 3, 1, . . .

■ **SOLUTION**

Find the common ratio

$$\frac{3}{9} = \frac{1}{3}$$

The common ratio is $\frac{1}{3}$.
The next 2 terms are $1(\frac{1}{3}) = \frac{1}{3}$ and $\frac{1}{3}(\frac{1}{3}) = \frac{1}{9}$.

The nth Term of a Geometric Sequence

The nth term in a geometric sequence a_n where a_1 is the first term and r is the common ratio is

$$a_n = a_1 r^{n-1}$$

Visit: PearsonSchool.com
Web Code: ayp-0255

EXAMPLES 8 and 9 — Finding the terms of a geometric sequence

8 Find the 6th term of the sequence 7, 14, 28, . . .

■ SOLUTION

$$\begin{aligned} a_n &= a_1 r^{n-1} && \leftarrow n = 6. \\ a_6 &= a_1 r^{6-1} && \leftarrow a_1 = 7 \text{ and } r = 2. \\ &= 7(2)^{6-1} \\ &= 7(2)^5 \\ &= 224 \end{aligned}$$

The 6th term of the sequence is 224.

9 Find the 8th term of the sequence 4, 20, 100, . . .

■ SOLUTION

$$\begin{aligned} a_n &= a_1 r^{n-1} \\ a_8 &= a_1 r^{8-1} \\ &= 4(5)^{8-1} \\ &= 4(5)^7 \\ &= 312{,}500 \end{aligned}$$

The 8th term of the sequence is 312,500.

Likewise, you can write an equation for the nth term of a given geometric sequence by determining the value of the common ratio, r.

EXAMPLE 10 — Finding the equation for the nth term of a geometric sequence

10 Write an equation for the nth term of the sequence 10, 7.5, 5.625, . . .

■ SOLUTION

Step 1

Identify a_1.

$a_1 = 10$

Step 2

Find the common ratio, r.

$\frac{7.5}{10} = \frac{5.625}{7.5} = \frac{3}{4}$

Step 3

Use the equation $a_n = a_1 r^{n-1}$ to write the equation for the nth term.

$$a_n = 10\left(\tfrac{3}{4}\right)^{n-1}$$

You can also use geometric sequences to solve real-world problems.

EXAMPLE 11 — Using geometric sequences to solve real-world problems

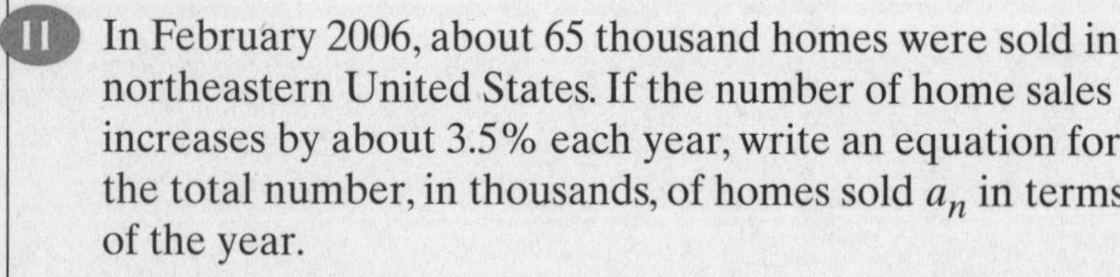

11 In February 2006, about 65 thousand homes were sold in northeastern United States. If the number of home sales increases by about 3.5% each year, write an equation for the total number, in thousands, of homes sold a_n in terms of the year.

■ SOLUTION

Let $a_1 = 65$ and $r = 1 + 3.5\% = 1.035$, then $a_n = 65(1.035)^{n-1}$

Practice

Choose the letter preceding the word or expression that best completes the statement or answers the question

1 Which set of numbers extends the pattern 27, 9, 3, 1, . . .?

A. 3, 9, 27
C. $3, \frac{1}{3}, \frac{1}{27}$
B. $\frac{1}{3}, \frac{1}{9}, \frac{1}{27}$
D. $\frac{1}{3}, \frac{1}{12}, \frac{1}{36}$

2 Which equation can be used to find the next number in the pattern 4, 8, 16, 32, 64, . . .?

A. $a_n = 4^{n-1}$
C. $a_n = 4(2)^{n-1}$
B. $a_n = 4(2n)$
D. $a_n = 4(n^2)$

3 What is the 8th term of the sequence 48, 24, 12, 6, . . .?

A. 0.375
C. 0.25
B. 0.75
D. 1.5

4 What is 7th term of the sequence $a_n = -9 + (n - 1)0.5$?

A. −6.5
C. −7
B. −6
D. −5.5

In Exercises 5–8, determine whether each sequence is arithmetic or geometric.

5 −6, 0, 6, 12, . . .

6 2, 6, 18, 54, . . .

7 $4, 2, 1, \frac{1}{2}, \ldots$

8 13, 6, −1, −8, . . .

In Exercises 9–12, find the 7th and 10th term of each sequence.

9 $a_n = 2 + (n - 1)3$

10 $a_n = -5 + (n - 1)7$

11 $a_n = 9 + (n - 1)(-6)$

12 $a_n = 0.5 + (n - 1)3$

In Exercises 13–16, find the 3rd and 5th term of each sequence.

13 $a_n = 5(3)^{n-1}$

14 $a_n = -2(5)^{n-1}$

15 $a_n = 5(-3)^{n-1}$

16 $a_n = -5(3)^{n-1}$

In Exercises 17–20, find the common difference in each sequence and then find the next two terms in each sequence.

17 −5, −10, −15, . . .

18 0.7, 1.4, 2.1, . . .

19 12, 8, 4, 0, . . .

20 0.5, 0.25, 0, . . .

In Exercises 21–24, find the common ratio in each sequence and then find the next two terms.

21 18, 9, 4.5, . . .

22 2, 12, 72, . . .

23 9, −36, 144, . . .

24 9, 12, 16, . . .

In Exercises 25–32, write an equation for the *n*th term of the sequence.

25 7, 14, 21, 28, . . .

26 3, 9, 27, 81, . . .

27 $-252, -42, -7, -\frac{7}{6}, \ldots$

28 5, 2, −1, −4, . . .

29 4, 9, 14, 19, . . .

30 3, 12, 48, 192, . . .

31 −8, −4, −2, −1, . . .

32 10, 8, 6, 4, . . .

1.5 Variables and Variable Expressions

ADP℠ Standards

02.b Operate with polynomial expressions

A **variable** is a letter that represents a number. An expression that contains at least one variable is called a **variable expression** or an **algebraic expression.** A variable expression has one or more *terms*. A **term** is a number, a variable, or a product of numbers and variables.

variable expression → $7x^2y + \frac{1}{2}xy + x - 5$

4 terms

When working with variable expressions, you often use the following basic principle.

Note

A product involving a variable is often written without an operation symbol or parentheses.
$m \cdot n$ is written mn.
$3 \cdot x$ is written $3x$.

Substitution Principle

If $a = b$, then a may be replaced by b in any expression.

The set of numbers that a variable may represent is called the **replacement set,** or **domain,** of the variable. Each number in the replacement set is a **value** of the variable. To **evaluate a variable expression,** you replace each variable with one of its values and simplify the numerical expression that results.

Go Online
PearsonSchool.com

Visit: PearsonSchool.com
Web Code: ayp-0002

EXAMPLES 1 through 3 **Evaluating variable expressions**

Evaluate each expression for $x = 10$ and $y = -7$.

1 $3x - 4y$ ■ **SOLUTION**

$3x - 4y$
$3(10) - 4(-7)$ ← **Replace x with 10 and y with −7.**
$30 - (-28)$ ← **Multiply first.**
$30 + 28$ ← **Rewrite the subtraction as an addition.**
58 ← **Add.**

2 $(x + y)^2$ ■ **SOLUTION**

$(x + y)^2$
$(10 + [-7])^2$ ← **Replace x with 10 and y with −7.**
3^2 ← **Add inside the parentheses first.**
9 ← **Simplify the power.**

3 $5xy^2$ ■ **SOLUTION**

$5xy^2$
$5(10)(-7)^2$ ← **Replace x with 10 and y with −7.**
$5(10)(49)$ ← **Simplify the power first.**
$2{,}450$ ← **Multiply.**

To **simplify a variable expression,** you must perform as many of the indicated operations as possible. The Distributive Property is frequently used to do this.

EXAMPLE 4 **Simplifying an indicated multiplication**

Go Online
PearsonSchool.com
Visit: PearsonSchool.com
Web Code: ayp-0795

4 Simplify $-4(k - 6)$.

■ SOLUTION

$-4(k - 6)$

$-4(k + [-6])$ ← Rewrite the subtraction as addition.

$(-4) \cdot k + (-4) \cdot (-6)$ ← Apply the Distributive Property.

$-4k + 24$ ← Simplify each term.

In a variable expression, **like terms** are terms that have exactly the same variable part. The numerical part of a term that contains variables is the **coefficient,** or **numerical coefficient,** of the term. The Distributive Property allows you to simplify an expression by adding the coefficients of like terms. This process is called *combining like terms*.

Note

Examples of Like Terms
$4n$ and $-6n$
pq and $2pq$
1 and -5

Examples of Unlike Terms
$4n$ and $-6n^2$
pq and $2pr$
x and -5

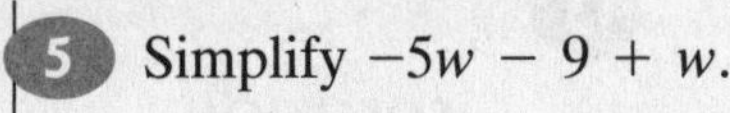

EXAMPLES 5 and 6 **Combining like terms**

5 Simplify $-5w - 9 + w$.

■ SOLUTION

$-5w - 9 + w$

$[-5w + w] - 9$ ← Change the order. Group like terms.

$[-5w + 1w] - 9$ ← Rewrite w as $1w$.

$-4w - 9$ ← Combine like terms by adding the coefficients of w.

6 Simplify $6c^2 - 8c - 4c^2 - 2c$.

■ SOLUTION

$6c^2 - 8c - 4c^2 - 2c$

$6c^2 + (-8c) + (-4c^2) + (-2c)$ ← Write the subtractions as additions.

$[6c^2 + (-4c^2)] + [(-8c) + (-2c)]$ ← Change the order. Group like terms.

$2c^2 + -10c$ ← Add the coefficients of c^2 and of c.

$2c^2 - 10c$

It often is helpful to use a numerical or variable expression to represent a real-life situation. To do this, you must be able to translate words and phrases into symbols. The following table shows some common translations.

English Phrase	Mathematical Expression
m plus n, the sum of m and n, m increased by n, n more than m	$m + n$
m minus n, the difference when n is subtracted from m, m decreased by n, n less than m, n fewer than m	$m - n$
m times n, the product of m and n	mn, $m \times n$, $m \cdot n$, $(m)(n)$
m divided by n, the quotient when m is divided by n	$m \div n$, $\frac{m}{n}$

EXAMPLES 7 through 10 Translating phrases into variable expressions

Write each phrase as a variable expression.

7 five less than a number s ■ **SOLUTION** $s - 5$

8 three times a number z, increased by 4 ■ **SOLUTION** $3z + 4$

9 seven times the sum of a number p and 25 ■ **SOLUTION** $7(p + 25)$

10 the square of a number a, divided by nine ■ **SOLUTION** $a^2 \div 9$, or $\frac{a^2}{9}$

You may also be asked to translate an algebraic expression into words.

Note

Translations may vary.

EXAMPLES 11 through 13 Translating algebraic expressions into English phrases

Translate the algebraic expressions into English phrases.

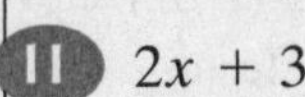

11 $2x + 3y$

■ **SOLUTION**

the sum of twice a number and 3 times a different number

12 $-4(a + b)$

■ **SOLUTION**

-4 times the sum of a and b

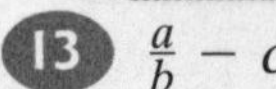

13 $\frac{a}{b} - c$

■ **SOLUTION**

c subtracted from the quotient of a and b

Translating word phrases into arithmetic and algebraic expressions can be helpful when setting up and solving application problems.

Note

even numbers:

$\ldots, -4, -2, 0, 2, 4, \ldots$

odd numbers:

$\ldots, -5, -3, -1, 1, 3, \ldots$

Both differ by 2.

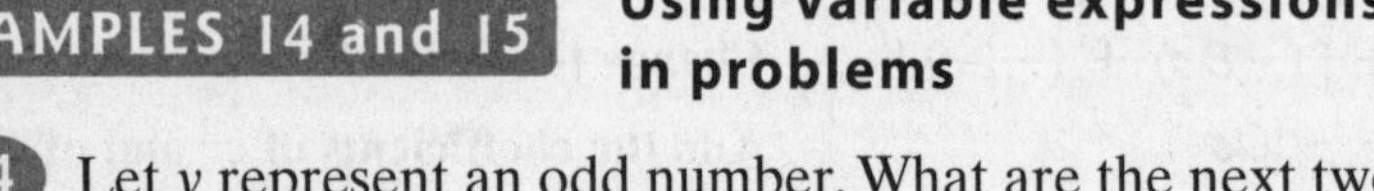

EXAMPLES 14 and 15 Using variable expressions in problems

14 Let y represent an odd number. What are the next two odd numbers?

■ **SOLUTION**

$y + 2$ and $y + 4$

15 Sam started hiking on a trail at 6:00 A.M. His sister Lisa began hiking the same trail at 8:00 A.M. Sam has now been hiking for h hours. Which expression represents the number of hours that Lisa has been hiking?

A. $h + 2$ **B.** $h - 2$ **C.** $h + 8$ **D.** $h - 6$

■ **SOLUTION**

Lisa started two hours after Sam, so she has been hiking two fewer hours. *Two fewer than a number h* is translated into symbols as $h - 2$.

The correct choice is *B*.

Practice

Choose the letter preceding the word or expression that best completes the statement or answers the question.

1 Which expression results from substituting 5 for m and -6 for n in $-3m - 9n$?

A. $3(-6) - 9(5)$ **C.** $-3(-6) - 9(-6)$

B. $-3(5) - 9(5)$ **D.** $-3(5) - 9(-6)$

2 Which number is the value of $\frac{k-p}{p-k}$ for $k = -6$ and $p = 6$?

A. -12 **B.** -1 **C.** 0 **D.** 1

3 If $a = -2$, then $3a^2 - 4a + 6$ equals

A. 2 **B.** 5 **C.** 10 **D.** 26

4 Which are a pair of like terms?

A. $5x$ and $7y$ **C.** $5x$ and $7x$

B. $5x$ and $7x^2$ **D.** $-5x$ and $-5y$

5 Which expression is not equivalent to $-5n + 9 - 2n$?

A. $-5n - 2n + 9$ **C.** $-5n + 2n - 9$

B. $9 - 5n - 2n$ **D.** $9 + (-5n - 2n)$

6 Which expression represents the phrase "a number x less a number y"?

A. $x < y$ **C.** $x - y$

B. $y - x$ **D.** $y < x$

7 If $d + 2$ is an even integer, which is the next greater even integer?

A. d **B.** $d + 3$ **C.** $d + 4$ **D.** $2d$

8 For which value of z is the following true?

$$z < \sqrt{z+1} < 1$$

A. -1 **B.** 1 **C.** 2 **D.** 3

In Exercises 9–13, evaluate each expression for the given value(s) of the variable(s).

9 $3s - 5$; $s = -5$

10 $q^2 + 9q$; $q = -3$

11 $\frac{j+k}{2}$; $j = 5$ and $k = 6$

12 $rs - r$; $r = 2$ and $s = -3$

13 $3a^2 - 4b$; $a = -2$ and $b = 0$

In Exercises 14–21, simplify each expression.

14 $2(a + b)$ **15** $-5(r - s)$

16 $8(6 - p)$ **17** $-3(x + 12)$

18 $(c + 5)(6)$ **19** $(v - 7)(-11)$

20 $-6n + 20n$ **21** $3t - (-15t)$

In Exercises 22–27, write each phrase as a variable expression.

22 eight more than a number t

23 a number c decreased by seventeen

24 the quotient when the square root of a number n is divided by two

25 twice the sum of a number y and nine

26 twelve less than the product of a number m and its opposite

27 the quotient when the sum of a number a and a number b is divided by their product

In Exercises 28–30, translate the algebraic expressions into English phrases.

28 $(abc)^3$ **29** $\sqrt{\frac{3a^2}{5b^4}}$ **30** $(7 - 2x)(-3y)$

In Exercises 31–33, solve the following problems. Clearly show all necessary work.

31 If $-2n - 4$ represents an even integer, write an expression to represent the next lesser even integer.

32 If n is an integer, which of the following expressions always represents an odd integer? Show your work.

$$n - 2, n - 1, n, 2n + 1, n + 2$$

33 Mel began studying at 6:45 P.M., and Tim began at 6:15 P.M. Let m represent the number of minutes Mel has been studying. Write an expression to represent the number of minutes Tim has been studying.

Chapter 1 Preparing for the ADP℠ Algebra 1 Exam

DIRECTIONS FOR QUESTIONS 1–28: For each of the questions below, select the answer choice that is best for each case.

1 Which statement represents the relationship between the set of integers and the set of rational numbers?

A. All integers are rational numbers.

B. All rational numbers are integers.

C. Some integers are rational numbers and others are not.

D. No numbers are in both sets.

2 Which of the following equations is an example of the Distributive Property of Multiplication over Addition?

A. $7 + ab = ab + 7$

B. $5(x + y) = 5x + 5y$

C. $ax + b = b + ax$

D. $(a)0 = 0(a) = 0$

3 Which number has the greatest value?

A. $1\frac{2}{3}$ **B.** $\sqrt{2}$

C. 1.7 **D.** $\frac{3}{2}$

4 Evaluate the expression $-|x + y|$ for $x = 3$ and $y = -10$.

A. 13 **B.** −13

C. 7 **D.** −7

5 Simplify $3^2 - (25 \div 5 \cdot 2) + 4^3$.

A. 70.5 **B.** 8

C. 67.5 **D.** 63

6 Find the 7th term of the sequence −2, 1, 4, ...

A. −2 **B.** 16

C. 2.5 **D.** 4

7 Which statement illustrates the Associative Property of Multiplication?

A. $2 \cdot (3 \cdot 4) = (3 \cdot 4) \cdot 2$

B. $2 \cdot (3 \cdot 4) = (2 \cdot 3) \cdot 4$

C. $2 \cdot (3 \cdot 4) = (2 \cdot 3) \cdot (2 \cdot 4)$

D. $2 \cdot (3 \cdot 4) = (2 + 3) \cdot (2 + 4)$

8 If $a \neq 0$ and the product of x and $-a$ is 1, then

A. $x = 1$. **B.** $x = a$.

C. $x = 1 + a$. **D.** $x = -\frac{1}{a}$.

9 Which expression is equivalent to 6.4 − 8.2?

A. $|8.2 - 6.4|$ **B.** $8.2 - 6.4$

C. $-(8.2 - 6.4)$ **D.** $6.4 - (-8.2)$

10 The number $\sqrt{83}$ is between

A. 9 and 10. **B.** 41 and 42.

C. 10 and 20. **D.** 80 and 90.

11 Which expression is not equivalent to $-\frac{1}{2}(3 + 2)$?

A. $(3 + 2)(-0.5)$ **B.** $-\frac{3 + 2}{2}$

C. $-\frac{1}{2}(3) + 2$ **D.** $-\frac{5}{2}$

In Exercises 12–19, simplify each expression.

12 $(-4)^3$

A. −12 **B.** −64

C. 64 **D.** 12

13 7^0

A. 1 **B.** 0

C. 7 **D.** $\frac{1}{7}$

14 3^{-5}

A. 15 **B.** −243 **C.** $\frac{1}{243}$ **D.** $-\frac{1}{15}$

15 $-\sqrt{225}$

A. 15 **B.** −15 **C.** −225 **D.** 25

16 $\sqrt{1.21}$

A. 1 **B.** 11 **C.** 60.5 **D.** 1.1

17 $-\sqrt{\frac{1}{9}}$

A. $-\frac{1}{9}$ **B.** −3 **C.** $-\frac{1}{3}$ **D.** $\frac{1}{9}$

18 $0.32 \div (-8)$

A. 0.4 **B.** −0.04

C. 0.24 **D.** 8.32

19 $-12.8 + 17$

A. −29.8 **B.** 4.2

C. 29.8 **D.** −4.2

20 Ari bought twelve CDs that each cost *d* dollars. Write an expression to represent the total cost in dollars of the CDs.

A. $12 + d$ **B.** $\frac{d}{12}$

C. $12d$ **D.** $12 + d + 100$

21 Given that $a = 3b$, simplify $a - 3b$.

A. $6b$ **B.** $3ab$

C. $3 - ab$ **D.** 0

22 If $z = -2$, what is the value of the square of z divided by the sum of twice z and 3?

A. $-\frac{4}{3}$ **B.** −4

C. $\frac{4}{7}$ **D.** 4

23 If $2n - 1$ represents an odd integer, which of the following expressions represents the next greater odd integer?

A. $2n + 2$ **B.** $2n - 3$

C. $2n$ **D.** $2n + 1$

In Exercises 24–26, evaluate each expression for the given values of the variable.

24 $g(h + 9)^2$; $g = -10$ and $h = 8$

A. −2890

B. 5041

C. 8

D. −64

25 xy^2z; $x = -4$, $y = -1$, and $z = 5$

A. 20 **B.** −80

C. −20 **D.** 100

26 $(a + b)(c - 4)$; $a = -2$, $b = -1$, and $c = 0$

A. 4 **B.** 12

C. −4 **D.** 0

27 Write 7.011×10^{-4} in standard notation.

A. 0.0007011 **B.** 70,110

C. 0.7011 **D.** 701.1

28 Which of the following reasons explains why the following solution is incorrect?

$$\frac{(2 + 5)}{(3 + 5)} = \left(\frac{2}{3}\right) + 1 = 1\frac{2}{3}$$

A. The commutative property does not apply to division.

B. The fraction bar is a grouping symbol so you must add before you divide.

C. The fraction does not always equal the value 1.

D. The method only works if you cross multiply first.

DIRECTIONS FOR 29–31: Solve each problem. Show your work or provide an explanation for your answer.

29 The employees of a company contribute d dollars to charity. The company matches the contribution with an equal amount, and the total is shared equally among c charities.

Write an expression to represent the dollar amount received by each charity.

How much does each charity receive if the employees contributed \$280.75 and there are 3 charities? Show all your work or provide an explanation for your answer.

30 The distance from the sun to Earth is approximately 9.3×10^7 miles and the distance from the sun to Mars is approximately 1.4×10^8 miles. Write the given distances in standard form.

Use these distances to approximate the distance from Earth to Mars via the sun.

31 The following table shows how many miles George ran each day during the week.

Mon.	Tues.	Wed.	Thurs.	Fri.
3	4.5	$3\frac{3}{4}$	2	$4\frac{1}{3}$

On what day did George run the farthest?

Write the distance he ran on Wednesday as a terminating decimal.

How many miles did he run in total for the week?

2 Linear Equations and Inequalities in One Variable

Discovering Arkansas

Silent Hattie

Hattie Ophelia Caraway (1878–1950) was the first woman elected to the United States Senate.

Her husband, Thaddeus Caraway, represented Arkansas in the Senate from 1920 until his death in November 1931. Hattie was appointed to fill his seat in the Senate until a special election could be held. Hattie won that election, and she was re-elected to the Senate in 1932 and 1938.

Hattie Caraway earned the nickname "Silent Hattie" because she spoke so infrequently. Despite such restraint, "Silent Hattie" achieved notable success in the U.S. Senate. She was the first woman to serve as the Senate's presiding officer, and she was the first woman to serve as a committee chair. She served a total of 13 years in the Senate.

2.1 Solving Linear Equations in One Variable

ADP℠ Standards

L2.a Solve linear equations and inequalities
L2.b Solve equations involving absolute value
L2.e Model linear equations and inequalities
N2.e Solve literal equations

An **equation** is a statement that sets two mathematical expressions equal.

When both sides of an equation are numerical expressions, the equation is a closed statement. This means the equation can be assigned a truth value.

$6 + 4 = 10$ *true* $7 - 2 = 6$ *false*

If an equation is neither true nor false, the equation is an **open sentence.** When variables are present in an equation, the **solution** is unknown. The set of numbers that you use to represent the variable(s) is called the **replacement set.** The **solution set** is found when any value(s) for the variable from the replacement set makes the equation a **true statement.**

Note

The equation $n + 4 = 12$ is an example of an open sentence.

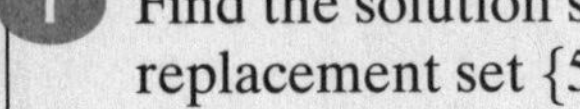

EXAMPLES 1 and 2 **Finding the solution of an equation from a replacement set**

1 Find the solution set of the equation $x + 4 = 13$, given the replacement set {5, 6, 7, 8, 9}.

■ **SOLUTION**

Substitute the values from the replacement set for x into the equation.

Let $x = 5$; is $5 + 4 = 13$? *No*

Let $x = 6$; is $6 + 4 = 13$? *No*

Let $x = 7$; is $7 + 4 = 13$? *No*

Let $x = 8$; is $8 + 4 = 13$? *No*

Let $x = 9$; is $9 + 4 = 13$? *Yes*

Therefore, **{9} is the solution set or solution for $x + 4 = 13$.**

2 Find the solution set of the equation $3x - 6 = 12$, given the replacement set {5, 6, 7, 11, 13}.

■ **SOLUTION**

Substitute the values from the replacement set into the equation.

Let $x = 5$; is $3(5) - 6 = 12$? *No*

Let $x = 6$; is $3(6) - 6 = 12$? *Yes*

Let $x = 7$; is $3(7) - 6 = 12$? *No*

Let $x = 11$; is $3(11) - 6 = 12$? *No*

Let $x = 13$; is $3(13) - 6 = 12$? *No*

Therefore, **{6} is the solution set or solution for $3x - 6 = 12$.**

If you multiply all of the terms of the equation from Example 1 by 2, will $2x + 8 = 26$ still have a solution of $x = 9$?

Does $2(9) + 8 = 26$? Yes; $18 + 8 = 26$.

Equations that have the same solution set are called **equivalent equations.** In general, solving an equation is a process of writing a set of equivalent equations until you *isolate* the variable on one side. To find these equivalent equations, you must apply the following *properties of equality*.

Properties of Equality

Let a, b, and c represent real numbers.

Reflexive Property	$a = a$
Symmetric Property	If $a = b$, then $b = a$.
Transitive Property	If $a = b$ and $b = c$, then $a = c$.
Addition Property	If $a = b$, then $a + c = b + c$.
Subtraction Property	If $a = b$, then $a - c = b - c$.
Multiplication Property	If $a = b$, then $ac = bc$.
Division Property	If $a = b$ and $c \neq 0$, then $\frac{a}{c} = \frac{b}{c}$.

To determine which property of equality to apply, you use *inverse operations*. Addition can "undo" subtraction, and subtraction can "undo" addition. Addition and subtraction are considered inverse operations. By similar reasoning, multiplication and division are inverse operations.

EXAMPLES 3 through 6 Solving equations by using one property of equality

Solve each equation.

3 $n - 6 = 9$

■ SOLUTION

Use the addition property of equality.

$$n - 6 = 9$$
$$n - 6 + 6 = 9 + 6$$
$$n = 15$$

← **To isolate *n*, *add* 6 to each side.**

Check: $n - 6 = 9 \rightarrow 15 - 6 = 9$ ✔

4 $y + 12 = 5$

■ SOLUTION

Use the subtraction property of equality.

$$y + 12 = 5$$
$$y + 12 - 12 = 5 - 12$$
$$y = -7$$

← **To isolate *y*, *subtract* 12 from each side.**

Check: $y + 12 = 5 \rightarrow -7 + 12 = 5$ ✔

5 $\frac{x}{-4} = 8$

■ SOLUTION

Use the multiplication property of equality.

$$\frac{x}{-4} = 8$$
$$-4\left(\frac{x}{-4}\right) = -4(8)$$
$$x = -32$$

← **To isolate *x*, *multiply* each side by −4.**

Check: $\frac{x}{-4} = 8 \rightarrow \frac{-32}{-4} = 8$ ✔

6 $-35 = -5r$

■ SOLUTION

Use the division property of equality.

$$-35 = -5r$$
$$\frac{-35}{-5} = \frac{-5r}{-5}$$
$$7 = r$$

← **To isolate *r*, *divide* each side by −5.**

Check: $-35 = -5r \rightarrow -35 = -5(7)$ ✔

You may need to apply more than one property of equality to solve an equation.

Note

If the variable is negative, such as $-x$, $-y\ldots$, then you can multiply both sides of the equation by -1 to make the variable positive. The variable in the solution of an equation must always be positive.

EXAMPLES 7 and 8 **Solving equations by using two properties of equality**

Solve each equation.

7 $4z + 28 = 5$

■ **SOLUTION**

$$4z + 28 = 5$$
$$4z + 28 - 28 = 5 - 28$$
$$4z = -23$$
$$\frac{4z}{4} = \frac{-23}{4}$$
$$z = -5.75$$

Check: $4z + 28 = 5$

$\rightarrow 4(-5.75) + 28 = 5$ ✔

8 $6 = -4 - k$

■ **SOLUTION**

$$6 = -4 - k$$
$$6 + 4 = -4 - k + 4$$
$$10 = -k$$
$$(-1)10 = (-1)(-k) \leftarrow$$ Recall that $-k = -1k$.
$$-10 = k$$

Check: $6 = -4 - k$

$\rightarrow 6 = -4 - (-10)$ ✔

Sometimes the first step in solving an equation is using the distributive property to simplify one or both sides.

Note

To check a solution, substitute it for the variable in the original equation. If the resulting statement is true, you have found a solution.

EXAMPLE 9 **Using the distributive property before solving**

9 Solve $-3(m + 3) = 16$.

■ **SOLUTION**

$$-3(m + 3) = 16$$
$$-3m - 9 = 16 \quad \leftarrow$$ **Use the distributive property to simplify the left side.**
$$-3m - 9 + 9 = 16 + 9$$
$$-3m = 25$$
$$\frac{-3m}{-3} = \frac{25}{-3}$$
$$m = -\frac{25}{3}$$

Check: $-3(m + 3) = 16 \rightarrow -3(-\frac{25}{3} + 3) = 16$ ✔

You must combine all like terms on one or both sides of an equation before solving an equation.

EXAMPLE 10 **Combining like terms before solving**

10 Solve $99 - 4s - 6s = -1$.

■ **SOLUTION**

$$99 - 4s - 6s = -1 \quad \leftarrow$$ **$-4s$ and $-6s$ are like terms.**
$$99 - 10s = -1$$
$$99 - 10s - 99 = -1 - 99 \quad \leftarrow$$ **Subtract 99 from both sides.**
$$-10s = -100$$
$$\frac{-10s}{-10} = \frac{-100}{-10} \quad \leftarrow$$ **Divide by -10 on both sides.**
$$s = 10$$

Check: $99 - 4s - 6s = -1 \rightarrow 99 - 4(10) - 6(10) = -1$ ✔

Sometimes there are variable terms on both sides of an equation.

EXAMPLE 11 **Solving equations with variable terms on both sides**

11 Solve $-5 - \frac{1}{2}g = 4 + \frac{1}{4}g$.

■ **SOLUTION**

$$-5 - \tfrac{1}{2}g = 4 + \tfrac{1}{4}g$$
$$-5 - \tfrac{1}{2}g + \tfrac{1}{2}g = 4 + \tfrac{1}{4}g + \tfrac{1}{2}g \quad \leftarrow \text{Add } \tfrac{1}{2}g \text{ to each side.}$$
$$-5 = 4 + \tfrac{3}{4}g$$
$$-5 - 4 = 4 + \tfrac{3}{4}g - 4 \quad \leftarrow \text{Subtract 4 from both sides.}$$
$$-9 = \tfrac{3}{4}g$$
$$\tfrac{4}{3}(-9) = \tfrac{4}{3}(\tfrac{3}{4}g) \quad \leftarrow \text{Multiply each side by } \tfrac{4}{3}.$$
$$-12 = g$$

Check: $-5 - \frac{1}{2}g = 4 + \frac{1}{4}g \rightarrow -5 - \frac{1}{2}(-12) = 4 + \frac{1}{4}(-12)$ ✔

Note

If the variable term is isolated and the coefficient is a fraction, multiply both sides of the equation by the reciprocal of the fraction.

Some equations are true for all values of the variable. An equation like this is called an **identity,** and its solution set is the set of all real numbers. Other equations are true for no value of the variable, and they have no solution.

EXAMPLES 12 and 13 **Solving equations that are identities or that have no solution**

Solve each equation.

12 $-7t + 9 = 1 - 7t$

■ **SOLUTION**

$$-7t + 9 = 1 - 7t$$
$$-7t + 9 + 7t = 1 - 7t + 7t$$
$$9 = 1$$

The equation $9 = 1$ is a false statement. The equation has no solution.

13 $3(q + 5) = 3q + 15$

■ **SOLUTION**

$$3(q + 5) = 3q + 15$$
$$3q + 15 = 3q + 15$$

The equation $3q + 15 = 3q + 15$ is true for any value of q, so it is an identity. The solution set is the set of all real numbers.

A **literal equation** is an equation that contains two or more variables. You can use the properties of equality to solve for one variable *in terms of* the others.

EXAMPLE 14 **Solving a literal equation for one of its variables**

14 Given that $2a + b = c$, which equation expresses a in terms of b and c?

A. $a = -\frac{1}{2}b + c$ **B.** $a = -\frac{1}{2}b - c$ **C.** $a = -\frac{1}{2}(b + c)$ **D.** $a = \frac{1}{2}(c - b)$

■ **SOLUTION**

$$2a + b = c$$
$$2a = c - b \quad \leftarrow \text{Subtract } b \text{ from each side.}$$
$$a = \frac{c - b}{2} = \tfrac{1}{2}(c - b) \quad \leftarrow \text{Divide each side by 2.}$$

The correct choice is *D*.

A **formula** is a literal equation in which each variable represents a specific quantity. The formula describes the relationship between the quantities. Often a formula is given in one form and you need to *transform* it to an equivalent form.

Go Online
PearsonSchool.com
Visit: PearsonSchool.com
Web Code: ayp-0886

EXAMPLE 15 **Transforming formulas**

15 The formula $F = \frac{9}{5}C + 32$ gives the temperature F in degrees Fahrenheit in terms of a given temperature C in degrees Celsius. Write a formula for C in terms of F.

■ **SOLUTION**

$$F = \frac{9}{5}C + 32$$

$$F - 32 = \frac{9}{5}C \quad \leftarrow \text{Subtract 32 from each side.}$$

$$\frac{5}{9}(F - 32) = C, \text{ or } C = \frac{5}{9}(F - 32) \quad \leftarrow \text{Multiply each side by } \frac{5}{9}.$$

When an equation involves absolute value, you can use a number line and the definition of absolute value to solve. If $|x| = 3$, then the value of x can be any integer exactly 3 units from zero on the number line. You can count these units to the left or to the right of zero. Therefore, $x = 3$ or $x = -3$.

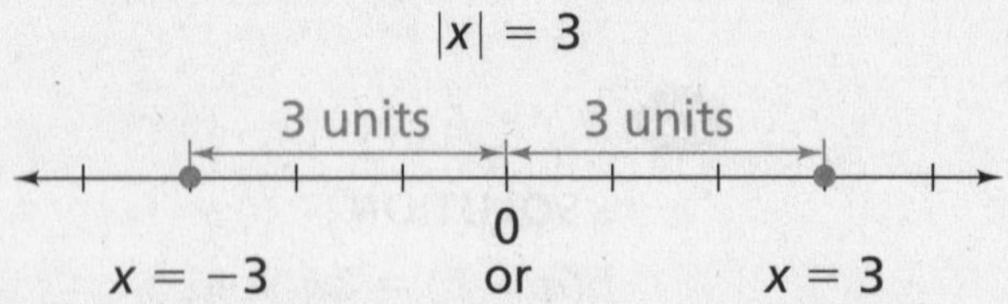

Note

The absolute value of a number is its distance from 0 on a number line.

The absolute value of zero is zero.

This example leads to the following algebraic generalization.

Absolute Value Equations

Let $|x| = a$.

If $a > 0$, then $x = a$ or $x = -a$.	If $a = 0$, then $x = 0$.	If $a < 0$, then there is no solution.

Go Online
PearsonSchool.com
Visit: PearsonSchool.com
Web Code: ayp-0489

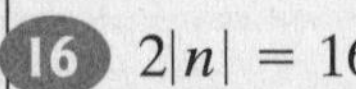

EXAMPLES 16 through 18 **Solving absolute value equations**

Solve each equation.

16 $2|n| = 16$

■ **SOLUTION**

$2|n| = 16$

$|n| = 8$

$n = 8$ or $n = -8$

17 $|b| - 7 = 3$

■ **SOLUTION**

$|b| - 7 = 3$

$|b| = 10$

$b = 10$ or $b = -10$

18 $|t - 2| = 5$

■ **SOLUTION**

$|t - 2| = 5$

$t - 2 = 5$ or $t - 2 = -5$

$t = 7$ or $t = -3$

Practice

Choose the letter preceding the word or expression that best completes the statement or answers the question.

1 Which is the solution to $\frac{2a-1}{3} = 7$?

A. $5\frac{1}{3}$ **B.** 11 **C.** 12 **D.** 21

2 In which equation is it possible to isolate the variable by first subtracting 3 from each side and then multiplying each side by 4?

A. $4x + 3 = 7$ **C.** $4x - 3 = 7$

B. $\frac{1}{4}x + 3 = 7$ **D.** $\frac{1}{4}x - 3 = 7$

3 If $2c - d = c - 2d$, then $c =$

A. 0 **B.** 1 **C.** d **D.** $-d$

4 Which equation is equivalent to $6(m + 5) = -6$?

A. $4 + 2(m + 3) = 28$

B. $\frac{m}{4} = -2.25$

C. $2(m + 6) - 4 = 26$

D. $\frac{m}{2} + 4 = 1$

5 Which is equivalent to $|2d + 6| = 18$?

A. $2d = 12$

B. $2d = 12$ or $2d = -12$

C. $2d = 12$ or $2d = 24$

D. $2d = 12$ or $2d = -24$

6 Which equation has no solution?

A. $|p - 1| = 5$

B. $7 = |p + 3|$

C. $|p| - 3 = -8$

D. $|8 - 2p| = 6$

In Exercises 7–23, solve each equation. Check your solution(s). If there is no solution, so state.

7 $b - 13 = 24$ **8** $j + 8 = 7$

9 $-x + 12 = -9$ **10** $10 = 3 - m$

11 $\frac{d}{5} = -20$ **12** $-45 = -3h$

13 $14 = -\frac{2}{3}k$ **14** $4z + 5 = -25$

15 $4(z + 5) = -25$ **16** $0.4(s + 4) = 4.8$

17 $\frac{1}{4}(p + 8) = 12$ **18** $n + 9n + 7 = -41$

19 $6g + 1 = -3g - 8$ **20** $1 + 2(y + 4) = 29$

21 $5 = 6h + 5(h - 5)$

22 $4(x - 1) - 2x = 2x - 4$

23 $6(q - 4) - 3(q - 2) = 12$

In Exercises 24–29, solve each equation for the given variable.

24 $a + b = c; b$ **25** $2p - q = r; p$

26 $2(p - q) = r; p$ **27** $xy = z; y$

28 $I = prt; p$ **29** $r = \frac{d}{t}; t$

In Exercises 30–33, solve each equation. Check your solution(s).

30 $|z| = 11$ **31** $5|k| = 24$

32 $|n| - 3 = -6$ **33** $3|b - 2| = 4$

In Exercises 34–35, solve the problem. Clearly show all necessary work.

34 Sean says that the equation $s + 3 = s - 3$ has no solution. Is Sean's statement correct? Explain your answer.

35 Daneesha says that the equation $3t = -3t$ has no solution. Is Daneesha's statement correct? Explain your answer.

2.2 Problems Involving Linear Equations in One Variable

ADP℠ Standards

L2.e Model linear equations and inequalities

Just as you can translate verbal phrases into mathematical expressions, you can translate English sentences into mathematical statements. This means that you can use an equation to model and solve a problem.

In general, before solving a problem you should assign a variable to the unknown and translate the problem into a mathematical equation. After you have solved the equation for the variable, label the solution according to the question asked. To check whether the solution is correct, apply the problem statement to the solution.

Visit: PearsonSchool.com
Web Code: ayp-0066

EXAMPLES 1 through 3 **Using equations and formulas to model and solve problems**

1 Wendy has 14 coins. Some are quarters and some are nickels. The total value of the coins is \$1.70. How many quarters does Wendy have?

■ **SOLUTION**

Let q represent the number of quarters. Then $14 - q$ is the number of nickels.

Step 1 Translate the words into an equation.

value of quarters in cents	plus	value of nickels in cents	is	170 cents
↓	↓	↓	↓	↓
$25q$	$+$	$5(14 - q)$	$=$	170

Step 2 Solve the equation.

$$25q + 5(14 - q) = 170$$
$$20q + 70 = 170$$
$$20q = 100$$
$$q = 5$$

Wendy has five quarters.

2 The sum of three consecutive integers is 99. Find the three integers.

■ **SOLUTION**

Step 1 Assign the variable and write the equation.

$x = $ 1st integer,
$x + 1 = $ 2nd integer,
$x + 2 = $ 3rd integer.

So, $x + (x + 1) + (x + 2) = 99$
or $3x + 3 = 99$

Step 2 Solve the equation.

$$3x + 3 = 99$$
$$3x = 96$$
$$x = 32$$

Therefore, the three integers are $x = 32$, $x + 1 = 33$, $x + 2 = 34$.

Note

Consecutive integers always increase by 1, so if x represents an integer, then $x + 1$ represents the next *consecutive* integer.

3 Mr. Redbird is driving at an average speed of 60 miles per hour. How far can he drive in 4.5 hours?

■ **SOLUTION**

Step 1 Apply the formula $d = rt$, where d represents distance, r represents rate, and t represents time.

$$d = r \times t$$
↓ ↓ ↓
$$d = 60 \times 4.5$$

Step 2 Solve the equation.

$$d = 60 \times 4.5$$
$$d = 270$$

Mr. Redbird can drive 270 miles in 4.5 hours.

You can use formulas to solve problems that involve perimeter.

EXAMPLE 4 **Using formulas to solve problems**

 Ben builds a fence around a rectangular garden. The perimeter of the garden is 64 ft. The width is 12 ft less than the length. Find the dimensions of the garden.

■ **SOLUTION**

Step 1 Apply the formula for the perimeter of a rectangle.

$p = 2l + 2w$

$p = 64$

$w = l - 12$

Step 2 Substitute and solve.

$64 = 2l + 2(l - 12)$

$64 = 2l + 2l - 24$

$64 = 4l - 24$

$88 = 4l$

$22 = \text{length}$

Step 3 Find both dimensions.

If the **length is 22 ft,** and the width is 12 ft less than the length, then the **width is 10 ft.**

Practice

Choose the letter preceding the word or expression that best completes the statement or answers the question.

1 The total value of some nickels and dimes is \$2.20. There are 36 coins in all. which equation gives the number of dimes, d?

A. $10d + 5d = 220$

B. $10d + 5(d - 36) = 220$

C. $10d + 5(36 - d) = 220$

D. $10d + 5(36 - d) = 2.20$

2 The formula $A = lw$ gives the area A of a rectangle with length l and width w. What is the width in feet of a rectangle with length 8 feet and area 14 square feet?

A. 112 **B.** 22 **C.** 6 **D.** 1.75

3 If the number represented by $x - 5$ is an odd integer, which expression represents the next greatest odd integer?

A. $x - 7$ **B.** $x - 4$ **C.** $x - 3$ **D.** $x - 6$

4 Half of the money collected for a show was donated to charity. Tickets for a show cost \$100 per pair. The charity collected \$3500. How many tickets were sold?

A. 140 **B.** 700 **C.** 350 **D.** 70

5 Find four consecutive integers whose sum is 138.

A. 68, 69, 70, 71 **C.** 33, 34, 35, 36

B. 38, 39, 40, 41 **D.** 35, 36, 37, 38

6 A computer programmer charges \$30 for an initial consultation and \$35 per hour for programming. Write an expression for her total charge for h hours of work.

A. $(30 + 35)^h$ **C.** $35 + 30h$

B. $30 + 35h$ **D.** $65h$

In Exercises 7–9, solve the problem.

7 Complementary angles have a sum of 90°. The sum of the measure of an angle and 5 times its complement is 298. What is the measure of the angle?

8 A train traveling at the rate of 90 miles per hour (mi/hr) leaves New York City. Two hours later, another train traveling at the rate of 120 mi/hr also leaves New York City on a parallel track. How long will it take the faster train to catch up to the slower train?

9 Five times a number n is three less than twice n. Find n.

2.3 Ratio and Rates

ADP℠ Standards

O1.b Use ratios, rates, and proportions

A **ratio** is a comparison of two numbers. You can write a ratio in these ways: *a* to *b*, *a* : *b*, or $\frac{a}{b}$. A ratio that is expressed as a fraction is generally written in lowest terms. If the ratio involves units of measure, you must ensure that the units are the same.

EXAMPLES 1 and 2 Writing ratios in lowest terms

Write each ratio as a fraction in lowest terms.

1 240 freshmen to 200 sophomores

■ **SOLUTION**

$$\frac{\text{freshmen} \rightarrow 240}{\text{sophomores} \rightarrow 200} = \frac{240 \div 40}{200 \div 40} = \frac{6}{5}$$

2 40 inches to 6 feet

■ **SOLUTION**

$$\frac{\text{inches} \rightarrow 40}{\text{inches} \rightarrow 72} = \frac{40 \div 8}{72 \div 8} = \frac{5}{9} \leftarrow$$ **Rewrite 6 feet as 72 inches.**

A **continued ratio,** or **extended ratio,** relates more than two numbers.

EXAMPLE 3 Using continued ratios to solve problems

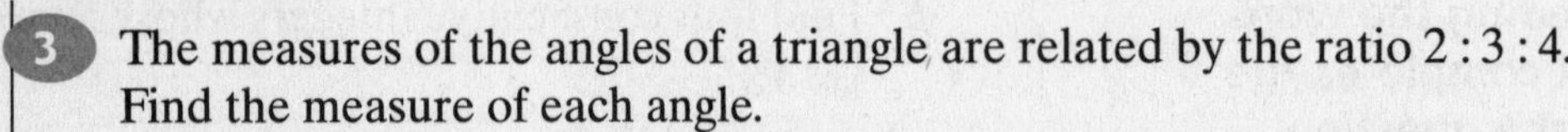

3 The measures of the angles of a triangle are related by the ratio 2 : 3 : 4. Find the measure of each angle.

■ **SOLUTION**

The ratio 2 : 3 : 4 is equivalent to $2x : 3x : 4x$. Write an equation using $2x$, $3x$, and $4x$ to represent the measures of the angles.

$$2x + 3x + 4x = 180 \quad \leftarrow \text{The sum of the measures of the angles is } 180°.$$
$$9x = 180$$
$$x = 20$$

The measures of the angles are 2(20°), 3(20°), and 4(20°), or ***40°, 60°, and 80°.***

A ratio that compares different types of measures is called a **rate.** A **unit rate** is a rate per one unit of a given measure.

Visit: PearsonSchool.com
Web Code: ayp-0891

EXAMPLES 4 and 5 Using unit rates to solve problems

4 Three cans of peas cost \$2. Write the unit cost per can of peas.

■ **SOLUTION**

$$\frac{\text{dollars} \rightarrow 2}{\text{cans} \rightarrow 3} = \frac{2 \div 3}{3 \div 3} = \frac{0.6666\ldots}{1} \leftarrow$$ **Divide both numerator and denominator by 3 to obtain a denominator equal to 1.**

The exact unit cost is ***$\$0.6\overline{6}$ per can.***

5 A 13-ounce box of cereal costs \$3.99, and a 16-ounce box of cereal costs \$5.19. Which is the better buy? Round to the nearest cent.

■ **SOLUTION**

$\frac{3.99}{13} \approx \$0.31/\text{oz}$ ← **Cost per ounce of 13-ounce box of cereal**

$\frac{5.19}{16} \approx \$0.32/\text{oz}$ ← **Cost per ounce of 16-ounce box of cereal**

The better buy is the ***13-ounce box because $\$0.31 < \$0.32$.***

You can use the simple interest formula to solve problems involving interest rates.

Go Online
PearsonSchool.com
Visit: PearsonSchool.com
Web Code: ayp-0070

EXAMPLE 6 **Solving interest rate problems**

6 Ariane has invested $500 in an account that earns simple interest at an annual rate of 4%. Assuming that Ariane makes no withdrawals or additional deposits, how long will it take for this money to earn $50 in interest?

■ **SOLUTION**

Step 1 Apply the simple interest formula $I = prt$, where I is the amount of interest, p is the amount invested, r is the annual interest rate, and t is the time in years.

$$\begin{array}{ccccccc} I & = & p & \times & r & \times & t \\ \downarrow & & \downarrow & & \downarrow & & \downarrow \\ 50 & = & 500 & \times & 0.04 & \times & t \end{array}$$

It will take 2.5 years to earn $50 in interest.

Step 2 Solve the equation.

$50 = 500 \times 0.04 \times t$

$50 = 20t$

$2.5 = t$

Practice

Choose the letter preceding the word or expression that best completes the statement or answers the question.

1 Which ratio is equivalent to $\frac{7}{9}$?

A. $\frac{6}{8}$ **B.** $\frac{21}{27}$ **C.** $\frac{14}{20}$ **D.** $\frac{14}{16}$

2 A soccer team won 18 games and lost 6 games. What is the ratio of the team's wins to the total games played?

A. 3 to 1 **C.** 4 to 3

B. 1 to 4 **D.** 3 to 4

3 A small company made a $900 profit one year. The two partners split the profit, using a ratio of 2 to 3. What was each partner's share?

A. $180 and $720 **C.** $360 and $540

B. $450 and $450 **D.** $300 and $600

4 Which of the following jars of peanut butter represents the lowest unit cost?

A. a 10-ounce jar for $2.36

B. a 12-ounce jar for $2.52

C. a 16-ounce jar for $2.64

D. a 20-ounce jar for $3.50

5 A total of 175 people are on a jogging trail. Of these people, 125 are running and 50 are walking. What is the ratio of runners to walkers?

A. $\frac{2}{5}$ **C.** $\frac{5}{2}$

B. $\frac{5}{7}$ **D.** $\frac{2}{7}$

6 Sammy rides his bike 14 miles in $3\frac{1}{2}$ hrs. What is his average speed?

A. 4 mi/hr **C.** 12 mi/hr

B. $3\frac{1}{2}$ mi/3 hr **D.** 0.25 mi/hr

7 The lengths of the sides of a triangle are related by the ratio 3 : 4 : 5. Which set of measures could be the lengths of the sides?

A. 6 ft, 7 ft, 8 ft

B. 6 ft, 8 ft, 10 ft

C. 9 ft, 12 ft, 20 ft

D. 9 ft, 16 ft, 25 ft

2.4 Proportion and Percents

ADP℠ Standards

O1.b Use ratios, rates, and proportions

A **proportion** is a statement that two ratios are equal. You can write a proportion in different ways, as shown in the note below. The numbers that form a proportion are called the **terms of the proportion.** There is a special relationship between the terms, called the *cross products property.* For example,

$$\frac{3}{7} = \frac{15}{35}$$

$$3 \cdot 35 = 7 \cdot 15$$

$$105 = 105$$

Cross Products Property of Proportions

For real numbers *a, b, c,* and *d,* where $b \neq 0$ and $d \neq 0$, if $\frac{a}{b} = \frac{c}{d}$, then $ad = bc$.

Note

Ways to Write a Proportion

a is to *b* as *c* is to *d*

$a : b = c : d$

$\frac{a}{b} = \frac{c}{d}$

In $\frac{a}{b} = \frac{c}{d}$, *a* and *d* are called the **extremes** of the proportion and *b* and *c* are called the **means.** So the cross products property is sometimes stated as follows.

In a proportion, the product of the means equals the product of the extremes.

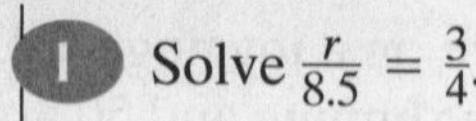

EXAMPLE 1 **Using cross products to solve a proportion**

1 Solve $\frac{r}{8.5} = \frac{3}{4}$.

■ SOLUTION

$\frac{r}{8.5} = \frac{3}{4}$

$r(4) = (8.5)(3)$ ← Write the cross products.

$4r = 25.5$ ← Simplify each side.

$r = 6.375$ ← Divide each side by 4.

You can use a proportion to solve problems involving ratios.

EXAMPLE 2 **Using a proportion to solve problems**

2 The scale of a map is 1 inch : 24 miles. What map distance represents 75 miles?

■ SOLUTION

Step 1 Write a proportion.

map distance in inches → $\frac{1}{24} = \frac{n}{75}$ ← Let *n* represent the unknown map distance.
actual distance in miles →

Step 2 Solve the proportion.

$\frac{1}{24} = \frac{n}{75}$

$1 \cdot 75 = 24 \cdot n$ ← Write the cross products.

$3.125 = n$ ← Divide each side by 24.

The map distance is 3.125 inches, or $3\frac{1}{8}$ inches.

If two triangles have angles of equal measure, then they are similar and their corresponding sides are proportional.

Visit: PearsonSchool.com
Web Code: ayp-0830

EXAMPLE 3 **Using proportions to solve similar-triangle problems**

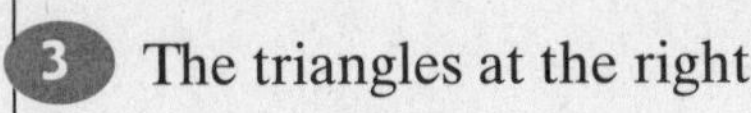

3 The triangles at the right are similar. Find *KM*.

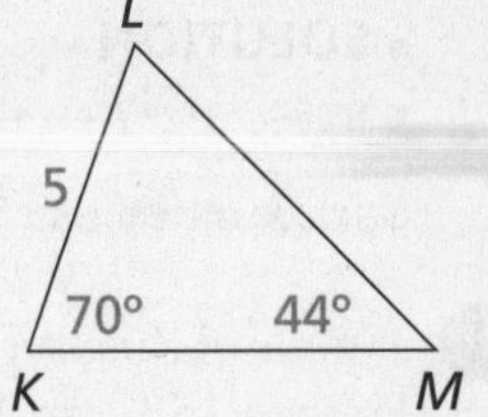

■ **SOLUTION**

Write and solve a proportion.

$$\frac{KL}{AB} = \frac{KM}{AC}$$

$$\frac{5}{4} = \frac{KM}{5}$$

$4(KM) = 5(5)$ ← **The cross products are equal.**

$KM = 6.25$

Therefore, $KM = 6.25$.

You can also use proportions to solve percent problems.

EXAMPLES 4 through 7 **Solving percent problems**

Note

The word percent means "per 100," "out of 100," or "divided by 100." The symbol for percent is %.

4 What is 16% of 23?

■ **SOLUTION**

$$\frac{16}{100} = \frac{x}{23}$$

$23 \cdot 16 = 100x$

$$\frac{368}{100} = x$$

$x = 3.68$

5 15 is what percent of 90?

■ **SOLUTION**

$$\frac{15}{90} = \frac{x}{100}$$

$90x = 1500$

$$x = \frac{1500}{90}$$

$x = 16\frac{2}{3}$ Thus, 15 is $16\frac{2}{3}$% of 90.

6 75 is 25% of what number?

■ **SOLUTION**

$$\frac{75}{x} = \frac{25}{100}$$

$25x = 7500$

$x = 300$

7 35% of 18 is what number?

■ **SOLUTION**

$$\frac{35}{100} = \frac{x}{18}$$

$100x = 35 \cdot 18$

$x = 6.3$

You can use equations to solve problems involving percent. The following are three basic types of percent problems and their solutions.

What is 25% of 10?
↓ ↓ ↓ ↓ ↓
$n = 25\% \times 10$
$n = 0.25 \times 10$
$n = 2.5$
So 25% of 10 is 2.5.

80 is 40% of what number?
↓ ↓ ↓ ↓ ↓
$80 = 0.4 \times n$
$\frac{80}{0.4} = n$
$n = 80 \div 0.4 = 200$
So 80 is 40% of 200.

75 is what percent of 62.5?
↓ ↓ ↓ ↓ ↓
$75 = n \times 62.5$
$\frac{75}{62.5} = n$
$n = 1.2 = 120\%$
So 75 is 120% of 62.5.

You can use percent equations to solve real-life problems.

EXAMPLES 8 through 10 **Using percent equations to solve real-life problems**

8 Carlos works at a computer store. He earns a 4% commission on all of his sales. What amount must he sell to earn a commission of $200?

▪ **SOLUTION**

$200 is 4% of what amount? → $\$200 = 0.04n \rightarrow n = \$200 \div 0.04 = \$5000$

Carlos must sell $5000 worth of goods to earn a $200 commission.

9 Jane and Susan go to dinner. The cost of the dinner is $45.60 and they leave a 15% tip. What is the total cost of the dinner, including the tip?

▪ **SOLUTION**

Step 1 What is 15% of $45.60? → $n = 0.15(\$45.60) \rightarrow n = \$6.84$

Step 2 Add the tip to the price of the dinner. $\$6.84 + \$45.60 = \$52.44$

The total cost of the dinner is $52.44.

10 Carlos purchases a sweater on sale for 30% off. The original price of the sweater is $54. How much does Carlos spend on the sweater?

▪ **SOLUTION**

Step 1 What is 30% of $54? → $x = 0.30(\$54) \rightarrow x = \$16.20$

Step 2 Subtract the savings from the original price. $\$54 - \$16.20 = \$37.80$

The purchase price of the sweater is $37.80.

A **percent of change** is the percent something increases or decreases from an original amount.

$$\textbf{percent of increase} = \frac{\text{new amount} - \text{original amount}}{\text{original amount}} \qquad \textbf{percent of decrease} = \frac{\text{original amount} - \text{new amount}}{\text{original amount}}$$

EXAMPLES 11 and 12 **Solving problems involving percent of change**

11 There were 75 members of the Drama Club last year, but there are only 65 members this year. What is the percent of decrease?

▪ **SOLUTION**

Let p represent the percent of decrease.

$$p = \frac{75 - 65}{75} \leftarrow \frac{\text{original} - \text{new}}{\text{original}}$$

$$p = \frac{10}{75} = 0.13333\ldots = 13\tfrac{1}{3}\%$$

The percent of decrease is $13\frac{1}{3}\%$.

12 Sam's employer has promised him a 20% pay increase. He presently earns $5 per hour. What will be his new hourly pay after the increase?

▪ **SOLUTION**

Let n represent the new hourly pay.

$$20\% = \frac{n - 5}{5} \leftarrow \frac{\text{new} - \text{original}}{\text{original}}$$

$$5(20\%) = n - 5$$

$$1 = n - 5$$

$$6 = n$$

Sam's new pay will be $6 per hour.

Practice

Choose the letter preceding the word or expression that best completes the statement or answers the question.

1 What percent of 42 is equal to 35% of 120?

A. 50% **B.** 75% **C.** 100% **D.** 120%

2 Which of these questions can be modeled by the equation $72 = 0.18n$?

A. 72 is what percent of 18?

B. 72 is 18 percent of what number?

C. 18 is what percent of 72?

D. What number is 18 percent of 72?

3 Which is a true statement?

A. $\frac{16}{5} = \frac{12}{9}$ **C.** $\frac{16}{5} = \frac{28.8}{9}$

B. $\frac{16}{5} = \frac{20}{9}$ **D.** $\frac{16}{5} = \frac{139}{9}$

4 There were 420 students in the senior class last year. This year's senior class has 378 students. Which statement is false?

A. The percent of decrease in the size of the class is 10%.

B. This year there are 10% fewer students in the senior class than there were last year.

C. The size of the senior class increased by 10% from last year to this year.

D. This year's class is 90% of the size of last year's class.

5 The scale of a map is 1 in. : 50 mi. How many miles correspond to a map distance of 3.25 in.?

A. 150 mi **C.** 62.5 mi

B. 162.5 mi **D.** 200 mi

6 Solve the proportion $\frac{54}{8} = \frac{r}{6}$.

A. 72 **B.** 40.5 **C.** 324 **D.** 48

In Exercises 7–9, answer the question by solving a percent equation.

7 What percent of 50 is 36?

8 12% of what number is 15?

9 What is 150% of 8?

In Exercises 10–13, find the percent of change from the first quantity to the second. Describe it as a percent of *increase* or *decrease*.

10 16 pounds
20 pounds

11 50 inches
36 inches

12 \$13.98
\$9.32

13 1.6 meters
4 meters

In Exercises 14–15, solve each proportion.

14 $\frac{m}{2} = \frac{56}{16}$

15 $\frac{51}{21} = \frac{z}{7}$

In Exercises 16–22, solve the problem. Clearly show all necessary work.

16 John plans to save 15% of his salary each week. His weekly salary is \$700. What amount does he plan to save each week?

17 The marked price of a CD is \$12.75. In addition, there is a state sales tax of 4% of the price. What is the total cost of the CD?

18 A retailer buys T-shirts from a supplier for \$6 each and sells each T-shirt for \$13.50. What is the percent of increase in the price?

19 A copy machine can print 125 pages in 3 minutes. How many minutes will it take for this machine to print 800 pages?

20 Tamara buys a \$23 blouse on sale for 20% off. How much did Tamara spend on the blouse?

21 80% of the students at Rally High participate in a pep rally. If there are 1800 students in the school, how many participate in the pep rally?

22 A food inspector weighs 50 cans of soup taken at random from a shipment of 3,000 cans. She finds that 4 out of the 50 cans are underweight. Based on this sample, how many cans in the shipment can the inspector expect to be underweight?

2.5 Solving Linear Inequalities in One Variable

ADP℠ Standards

L2.a Solve linear equations and inequalities

An **inequality** is a statement that consists of two mathematical expressions joined by an inequality symbol. The expressions are called the **sides of the inequality.**

Just as with equations, both sides of an inequality may be numerical expressions. In such a case, the inequality is a closed statement and can be assigned a truth value.

$5 + (-9) < 0$ *true* $\qquad$ $5 + (-9) > 0$ *false*

When at least one side of an inequality is a variable expression, the inequality is an open statement. To solve the inequality, you must find its solution set. When the, replacement set of the variable is the set of all real numbers, the inequality may have infinitely many solutions. For example, given the inequality $x < 3$, each of the following replacements for x results in a true statement.

$-17 < 3$ $\qquad$ $-5.4 < 3$ $\qquad$ $0 < 3$ $\qquad$ $\frac{1}{2} < 3$ $\qquad$ $2{,}999 < 3$

In fact, any number to the left of 3 on a number line is a solution to $x < 3$. Clearly it would be impossible to list all these solutions. For this reason, a number line is used to draw the *graph of the inequality*. The **graph of an inequality** consists of the graphs of all its solutions.

Note

Inequality Symbols
$<$ is less than
$\leq$ is less than or equal to
$>$ is greater than
$\geq$ is greater than or equal to
$\neq$ is not equal to

EXAMPLES 1 through 5 **Graphing an inequality**

Graph each inequality on a number line.

1 $x < 3$ ■ **SOLUTION** Graph all real numbers to the left of 3.

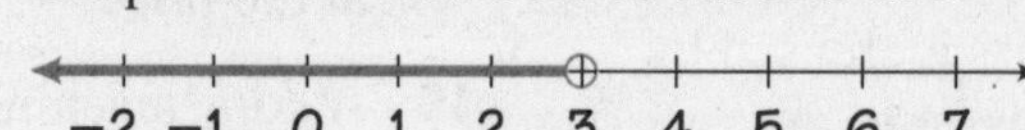

← **Use an open dot to indicate that 3 is *not* a solution.**

2 $x > 3$ ■ **SOLUTION** Graph all real numbers to the right of 3.

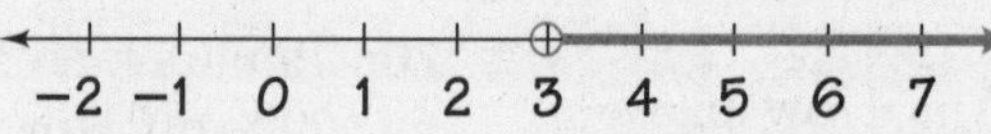

3 $x \leq 3$ ■ **SOLUTION** Graph 3 and all real numbers to its left.

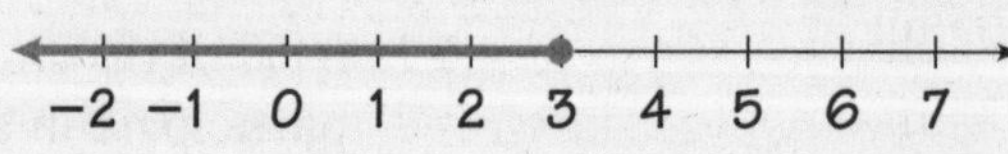

← **Use a closed dot to indicate that 3 *is* a solution.**

4 $x \geq 3$ ■ **SOLUTION** Graph 3 and all real numbers to its right.

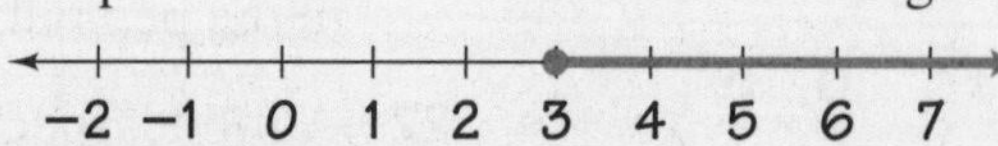

5 $x \neq 3$ ■ **SOLUTION** Graph all real numbers except 3.

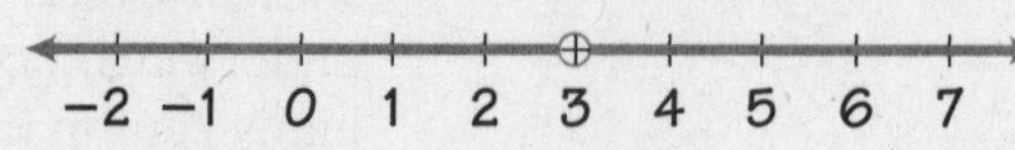

Inequalities that have the same solution set are called **equivalent inequalities.** Solving an inequality is a process of writing equivalent inequalities until you isolate the variable. To do this, you apply the following *properties of inequality.*

Properties of Inequality

Let a, b, and c represent real numbers.

Addition Property

If $a < b$, then $a + c < b + c$.

If $a > b$, then $a + c > b + c$.

Subtraction Property

If $a < b$, then $a - c < b - c$.

If $a > b$, then $a - c > b - c$.

Multiplication Property

If $a < b$ and $c > 0$, then $ac < bc$.

If $a < b$ and $c < 0$, then $ac > bc$.

If $a > b$ and $c > 0$, then $ac > bc$.

If $a > b$ and $c < 0$, then $ac < bc$.

Division Property

If $a < b$ and $c > 0$, then $\frac{a}{c} < \frac{b}{c}$.

If $a < b$ and $c < 0$, then $\frac{a}{c} > \frac{b}{c}$.

If $a > b$ and $c > 0$, then $\frac{a}{c} > \frac{b}{c}$.

If $a > b$ and $c < 0$, then $\frac{a}{c} < \frac{b}{c}$.

Transitive Property

If $a < b$ and $b < c$, then $a < c$.

If $a > b$ and $b > c$, then $a > c$.

Note

For each property of inequality, a true statement also results if $<$ is replaced by $\leq$ and if $>$ is replaced by $\geq$.

Adding or subtracting the same number from each side of an inequality results in an equivalent inequality. To apply the addition and subtraction properties, use inverse operations: addition and subtraction.

Note

If a is greater than b, it is also true that b is less than a. So $a > b$ is equivalent to $b < a$.

EXAMPLES 6 and 7 — Solving inequalities by using addition or subtraction

Solve each inequality and graph it on a number line.

 $b + 7 \leq 4$

SOLUTION

$b + 7 \leq 4$

$b + 7 - 7 \leq 4 - 7$ ← Subtract 7 from each side.

$b \leq -3$

All numbers less than or equal to -3 are solutions.

−6 −5 −4 −3 −2 −1 0 1

7 $-5 < n - 3$

SOLUTION

$-5 < n - 3$

$-5 + 3 < n - 3 + 3$ ← Add 3 to each side.

$-2 < n$

$n > -2$

All numbers greater than -2 are solutions.

−5 −4 −3 −2 −1 0 1 2

It is impossible to check every solution to inequalities like those in Examples 6 and 7. However, you can usually detect an error by checking one number from each region of the graph. For example, here is how you might verify that $n > -2$ is a reasonable solution to $-5 < n - 3$.

You should obtain a *true* statement when you replace n with any number greater than -2.

Try -1: $-5 < n - 3 \rightarrow -5 < -1 - 3$ *true*

You should obtain a *false* statement when you replace n with any number less than -2.

Try -3: $-5 < n - 3 \rightarrow -5 < -3 - 3$ *false*

If you multiply or divide each side of an inequality by the same positive number, the inequality symbol stays the same. If you multiply or divide each side by the same negative number, the inequality symbol is reversed.

EXAMPLES 8 and 9 Solving inequalities by using multiplication or division

Solve each inequality and graph it on a number line.

8 $\frac{a}{4} < -1$

■ **SOLUTION**

$\frac{a}{4} < -1$

$4\left(\frac{a}{4}\right) < 4(-1)$ ←

$a < -4$

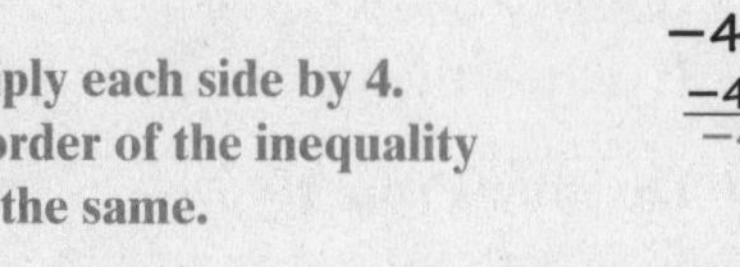

All numbers less than -4 are solutions.

−7 −6 −5 −4 −3 −2 −1 0

9 $-4w \leq 20$

■ **SOLUTION**

$-4w \leq 20$

$\frac{-4w}{-4} \geq \frac{20}{-4}$ ← Divide each side by -4. Reverse the order of the inequality.

$w \geq -5$

All numbers greater than or equal to -5 are solutions.

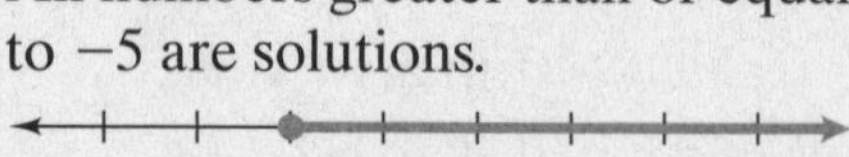

You may need to apply the properties of equality several times to isolate the variable and solve the inequality.

Visit: PearsonSchool.com
Web Code: ayp-0180

EXAMPLE 10 Solving an inequality in multiple steps

10 Solve the inequality $-2(p - 5) \leq -5$ and graph it on a number line.

$-2(p - 5) \leq -5$

$-2p + 10 \leq -5$ ← Use the distributive property to simplify the left side.

$-2p \leq -15$ ← Subtract 10 from each side.

$p \geq 7.5$ ← Divide each side by -2. Reverse the order of the inequality.

All numbers greater than or equal to 7.5 are solutions. The graph is shown at the right.

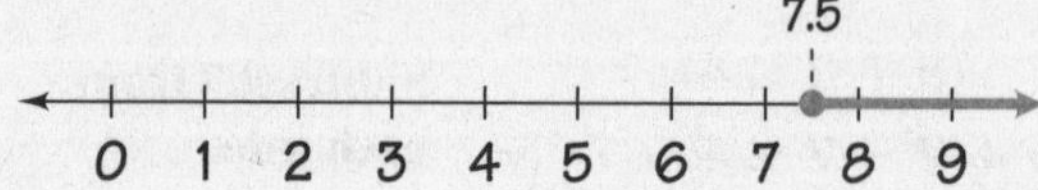

■ **SOLUTION 2**

Another method for solving inequalities is to use a graphing calculator.

- In the Y= screen, enter −2(X − 5) as Y1 and −5 as Y2.
- Choose WINDOW settings that will show where the lines intersect.
- Press GRAPH.
- Using intersect in the CALC menu, find the intersection of the lines.

The intersection is X = 7.5, Y = −5. So when $p = 7.5$, $-2(p - 5) = -5$.
You also see that when $p > 7.5$, $-2(p - 5) < -5$. Therefore, $p \geq 7.5$ is correct.

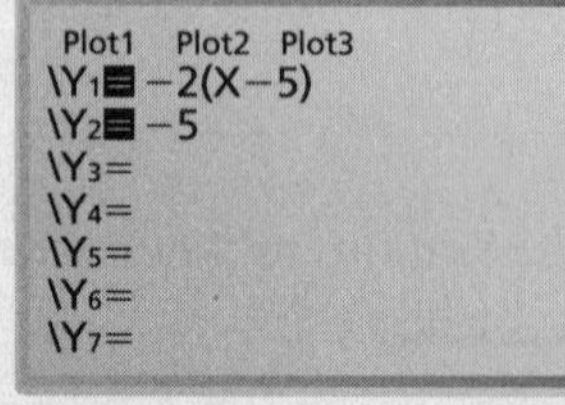

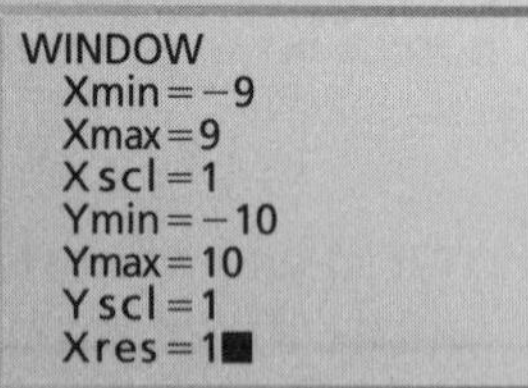

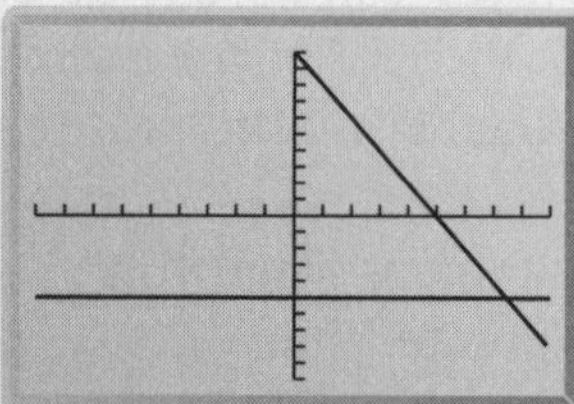

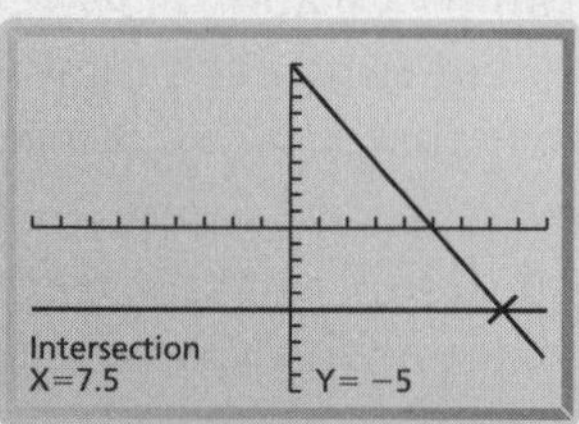

Two inequalities joined by the word *and* or the word *or* form a **compound inequality.**

$h > -2$ and $h < 4$

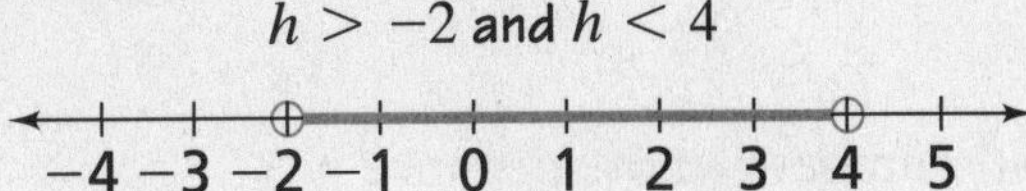

The word *and* signals a conjunction. The solutions are all numbers that are solutions of *both* inequalities.

$j < -2$ or $j > 4$

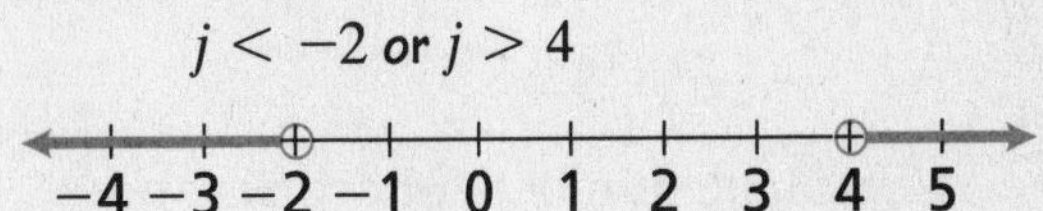

The word *or* signals a disjunction. The solutions are all numbers that are solutions of *either* inequality.

EXAMPLE 12 **Solving a compound inequality**

Go Online
PearsonSchool.com
Visit: PearsonSchool.com
Web Code: ayp-0182

12 Solve $-3 < 2 - b \le 1$ and graph it on a number line.

■ SOLUTION

Write two inequalities joined by *and*. Then solve each inequality.

$$-3 < 2 - b \le 1$$

$-3 < 2 - b$	and	$2 - b \le 1$	
$-3 - 2 < 2 - b - 2$		$2 - b - 2 \le 1 - 2$	← Subtract 2 from each side.
$-5 < -b$		$-b \le -1$	← Recall that $-b = -1b$.
$-1(-5) > -1(-b)$		$-1(-b) \ge -1(-1)$	← Multiply each side by -1.
$5 > b$	and	$b \ge 1$	Reverse the order.

$$5 > b \ge 1$$
$$1 \le b < 5$$

All numbers greater than or equal to 1 and less than 5 are solutions. The graph is at the right.

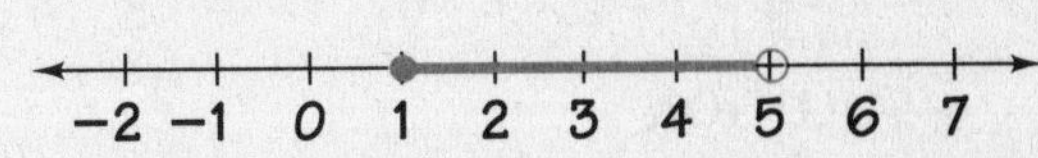

Just as with equations, some inequalities have no solution. For other inequalities, the solution set is the set of all real numbers.

$$2(y - 3) > 2y + 8$$
$$2y - 6 > 2y + 8$$
$$-6 > 8 \quad \textit{false}$$

The inequality has no solution.

$$5t + 1 \ge 6t - 1 - t$$
$$5t + 1 \ge 5t - 1$$
$$1 \ge -1 \quad \textit{true}$$

All real numbers are solutions.

Usually the replacement set for the variable in an inequality is the set of all real numbers. In some cases, however, the replacement set is restricted.

EXAMPLE 13 **Solving an inequality given a restricted replacement set**

Note

Three dots (...) on a graph indicate that the pattern continues without end.

13 Given the set of integers as the replacement set for z, solve the following inequality. $2z < -1$ or $z + 3 > 5$

■ SOLUTION

$2z < -1$	or	$z + 3 > 5$
$\frac{2z}{2} < \frac{-1}{2}$		$z + 3 - 3 > 5 - 3$
$z < -0.5$	or	$z > 2$

All *integers* less than -0.5 or greater than 2 are solutions. The graph is at the right.

... −3 −2 −1 0 1 2 3 4 5 ...

When an inequality involves an absolute value, you can use a number line and the definition of absolute value to locate its solutions.

$|x| < 3$

Graph all numbers whose distance from zero is less than 3 units.

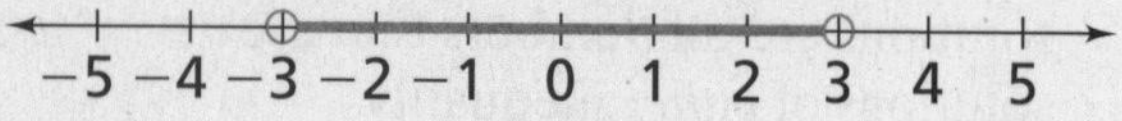

$x > -3$ and $x < 3$

$|x| > 3$

Graph all numbers whose distance from zero is greater than 3 units.

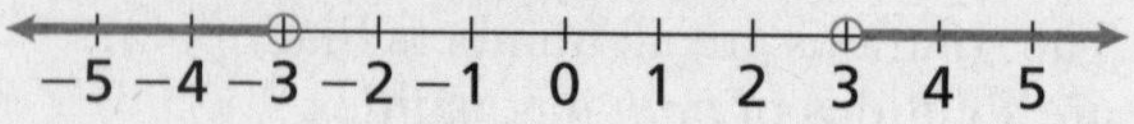

$x < -3$ or $x > 3$

These examples lead to the following algebraic generalization.

Absolute Value Inequalities

If $a > 0$ and $|x| < a$, then $x > -a$ and $x < a$.

If $a > 0$ and $|x| > a$, then $x < -a$ or $x > a$.

Go Online
PearsonSchool.com
Visit: PearsonSchool.com
Web Code: ayp-0185

EXAMPLE 14 **Solving absolute value inequalities**

14 Which is the graph of $|v + 3| + 1 < 2$?

A.
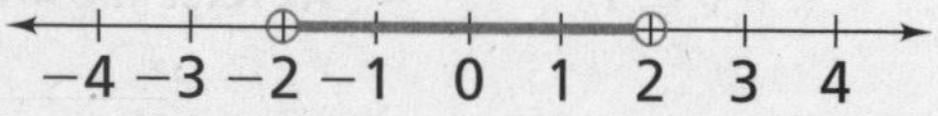

C.
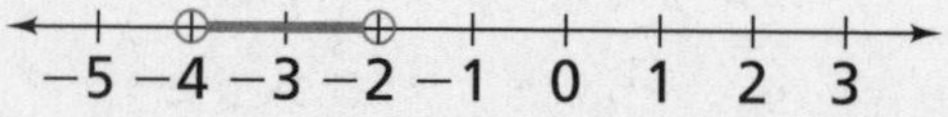

B.
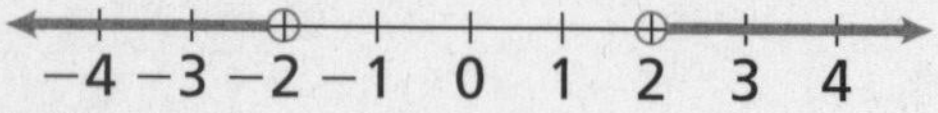

D.
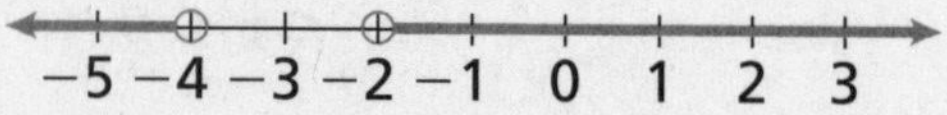

■ SOLUTION

$|v + 3| + 1 < 2$ ← **Isolate the absolute value expression.**

$|v + 3| < 1$ ← **Write the equivalent compound inequality.**

$v + 3 > -1$	and	$v + 3 < 1$
$v + 3 - 3 > -1 - 3$		$v + 3 - 3 < 1 - 3$
$v > -4$	and	$v < -2$

All numbers greater than −4 and less than −2 are solutions. The correct choice is C.

Practice

Choose the letter preceding the word or expression that best completes the statement or answers the question.

1 Given $-4t < 28$, which step can be used to obtain the equivalent inequality $t > -7$?

A. Divide each side by −4.

B. Multiply each side by 4.

C. Add 4 to each side.

D. Subtract −4 from each side.

2 Which is not equivalent to $-3x < 15$?

A. $-x < 5$

B. $-5 < x$

C. $x < -5$

D. $5 > -x$

3 Which inequality is graphed below?

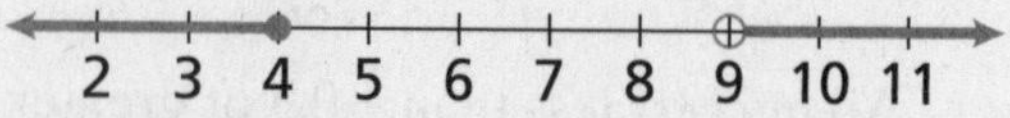

A. $4 < b \leq 9$

B. $4 \leq b < 9$

C. $b \geq 4$ or $b < 9$

D. $b \leq 4$ or $b > 9$

4 Which inequality is not equivalent to $-3 \le k < 5$?

A. $5 < k \le -3$ C. $-3 \le k$ and $k < 5$

B. $5 > k \ge -3$ D. $k < 5$ and $k \ge -3$

5 Which inequality represents all of the solutions to $-3m + 8 \ge -13$?

A. $m \le \frac{5}{3}$ C. $m \ge 7$

B. $m \le 7$ D. $m \le -7$

6 Suppose that m, n, r, and s are positive numbers, with $\frac{m}{n} < 1$ and $\frac{r}{s} > 1$. Which statement is always true?

A. $\frac{m}{n} \cdot \frac{r}{s} < 1$ C. $\frac{m}{n} + \frac{r}{s} < 1$

B. $\frac{m}{n} \cdot \frac{r}{s} > 1$ D. $\frac{m}{n} + \frac{r}{s} > 1$

In Exercises 7–10, write an inequality that each graph could represent.

7 −4 −3 −2 −1 0 1 2 3 4

8 −4 −3 −2 −1 0 1 2 3 4

9 −3 −2 −1 0 1 2 3 4 5

10 −1 0 1 2 3 4 5 6 7

In Exercises 11–18, graph each inequality on a number line.

11 $c > 5$ 12 $-2 > k$

13 $r < -1$ or $r \ge 3$ 14 $-7 < m < -2.5$

15 $x < 5$ and $x > 3$ 16 $g \ge 8$ or $g \le -4$

17 $p \le 12$ and $p \ge 1$ 18 $-5 \le b \le 2$

In Exercises 19–29, solve each inequality and graph it on a number line.

19 $n - 3 > -11$ 20 $-8x \ge -16$

21 $\frac{a}{6} \le -3$ 22 $-y < 4$

23 $\frac{1}{3}w \ge 1$ 24 $3f - 12 \le 15$

25 $45 > 3(6 - z)$

26 $5n + 3 - 4n < -5 - 3n$

27 $5 - 2(4 - c) \le 9 - c$

28 $4d < -8$ or $6 < 2d$

29 $5 < x + 4 \le 8$

In Exercises 30–33, given the set of integers as the replacement set, solve each inequality and graph it on a number line.

30 $0 < a + 4 < 3$

31 $n - 6 \ge 4$

32 $s + 2 \le -2$ or $-2s \le -2$

33 $-2r \le 9$ and $7 > 3r$

In Exercises 34–37, solve each inequality and graph it on a number line.

34 $|w| \le 4.5$ 35 $|h| > 2$

36 $|3c - 6| \ge 3$ 37 $|4t + 2| + 1 < 7$

In Exercises 38–39, solve the problem. Clearly show all necessary work.

38 Are there any integers that satisfy the following inequality? If so, what are they?

$0 \le 2c \le 9$ and $-4 < 3c - 5 < 13$

39 Is the statement below *true* or *false*? Explain your response.

The inequalities $2q + 5 \le 3$ and $q > 0$ taken together have no solution.

2.6 Problems Involving Linear Inequalities in One Variable

ADP℠ Standards

L2.a Solve linear equations and inequalities

When a verbal problem includes a verb such as *is, are, will be, were,* or *equals,* you often can translate it into an equation. The table below summarizes some ways to tell when an appropriate translation of a problem is an *inequality.*

English Sentence	Mathematical Statement
p is greater than q, p is more than q	$p > q$
p is greater than or equal to q, p is no less than q, p is at least q	$p \geq q$
p is less than q, p is fewer than q	$p < q$
p is less than or equal to q, p is no more than q, p is at most q	$p \leq q$
q is greater than p and less than r, q is between p and r	$p < q < r$
q is greater than or equal to p and less than or equal to r, q is between p and r inclusive	$p \leq q \leq r$

EXAMPLES 1 and 2 **Translating and solving inequality problems**

Go Online PearsonSchool.com
Visit: PearsonSchool.com
Web Code: ayp-0507

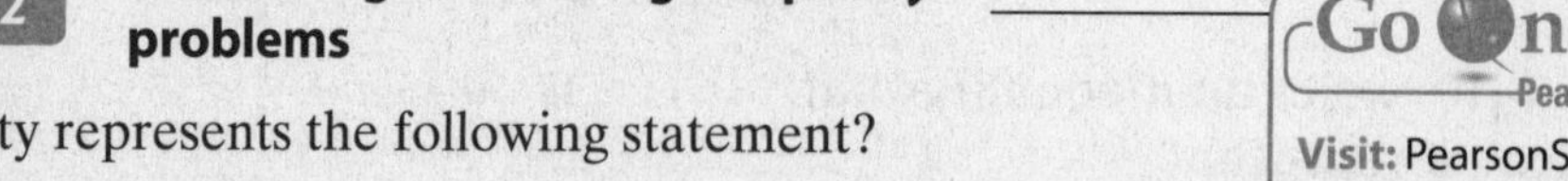

1 Which inequality represents the following statement?

Five less than a number y is at most twenty.

A. $y - 5 < 20$ **B.** $y - 5 \leq 20$ **C.** $y - 5 \geq 20$ **D.** $5 < y < 20$

■ SOLUTION

Examine the choices and eliminate those that are inappropriate.

In **D,** $5 < y < 20$ describes a number y between 5 and 20. *Eliminate choice* ***D.***

In **C,** the symbol $\geq$ means that $y - 5$ is 20 or more. *Eliminate choice* ***C.***

In **A,** the symbol $<$ means that $y - 5$ cannot equal 20. *Eliminate choice* ***A.***

The remaining choice is **B.** Work backward to verify the translation.

$y - 5$	$\leq$	20
↓	↓	↓
five less than a number y	is at most	twenty

The correct choice is B.

2 A real number c increased by six is more than four times c. Identify all possible values of c.

■ SOLUTION

Step 1 Translate the words into an inequality.

a number c increased by six	is more than	four times c
↓	↓	↓
$c + 6$	$>$	$4c$

Step 2 Solve the inequality.

$$c + 6 > 4c$$
$$6 > 3c$$
$$2 > c$$

All real numbers less than 2 can be values of c.

When you use an inequality to model a real-life problem, it is important to consider replacement sets. For instance, consider this situation.

The temperature t on Tuesday ranged from 25°F to 35°F, inclusive.

Temperature is a continuous measure. Therefore, the replacement set for t is the set of all real numbers, and the graph of the temperatures is the graph of all real-number solutions to $25 \leq t \leq 35$.

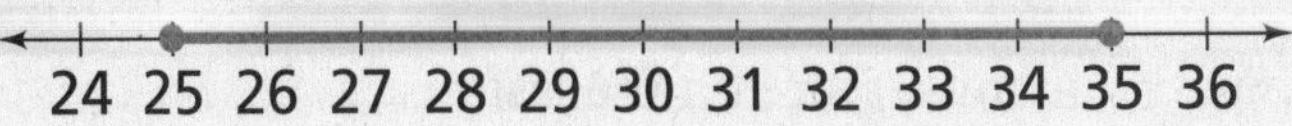

Now consider this situation.

The number n of students in a homeroom is between 25 and 35, inclusive.

The numbers of students in the homerooms form a discrete set of data. In this case, the replacement set for n is the set of whole numbers. So the graph is the graph of all whole-number solutions to $25 \leq n \leq 35$.

Note

The graph of a set of data that is **continuous** has no breaks in it. The set of real numbers would be a continuous graph.

The graph of a set of data that is **discrete** consists of points that are not connected. The set of integers would be an example of a discrete graph.

EXAMPLES 3 and 4 **Using an inequality to solve a real-life problem**

3 Nancy earns $6.50 per hour. How many hours must she work to earn $130?

■ SOLUTION

Let h represent the number of hours Nancy must work. Then $6.50h$, or $6.5h$, represents the amount in dollars that she earns in h hours.

Step 1 Translate the words into an inequality.

amount earned in dollars	is at least	130
↓	↓	↓
$6.5h$	$\geq$	130

Step 2 Solve the inequality.

$$6.5h \geq 130$$
$$h \geq 20$$

Nancy must work at least 20 hours.

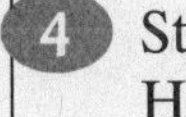
4 Stan has $55. He wants to buy a belt that costs $14 and some T-shirts that cost $9 each. How many T-shirts can he buy?

■ SOLUTION

Let n represent the number of T-shirts. Then $9n$ represents the cost in dollars of the T-shirts.

Step 1 Translate the words into an inequality.

cost of belt in dollars	plus	cost of T-shirts in dollars	is no more than	55
↓	↓	↓	↓	↓
14	+	$9n$	$\leq$	55

Step 2 Solve the inequality.

$$14 + 9n \leq 55$$
$$9n \leq 41$$
$$n \leq 4.\overline{5}$$

Stan can buy any whole number of T-shirts that is less than or equal to $4.\overline{5}$.
Stan can buy 0, 1, 2, 3, or 4 T-shirts.

You can use a combined inequality to find a range of possible values.

EXAMPLE 5 Using a combined inequality to solve a real-life problem

5 To get a grade of A for the semester, you must earn between 540 and 600 points inclusive. Before the last test, you have a total of 503 points. How many points must you earn on the last test in order to get a grade of A for the semester?

■ SOLUTION

Let p represent the number of points you must score on the last test. Then $503 + p$ represents your total points for the semester.

$$540 \leq 503 + p \leq 600$$

$$540 \leq 503 + p \quad \text{and} \quad 503 + p \leq 600$$

$$37 \leq p \quad \text{and} \quad p \leq 97$$

$$37 \leq p \leq 97$$

Your number of points on the last test must be between 37 and 97 inclusive.

Although formulas are equations, you may need to use a formula when solving a problem involving inequality.

Note

Perimeter of a rectangle = 2 × length + 2 × width

$P = 2l + 2w$

EXAMPLE 6 Using formulas when solving inequality problems

6 Rosalita has 68 feet of fencing. She wants to use it to fence the perimeter of a rectangular garden so that it is 5 feet longer than it is wide. What is the greatest possible width for her garden?

■ SOLUTION

Let w represent the width of the garden. Then $w + 5$ represents the length.

$$2(w + 5) + 2w \leq 68$$

$$2w + 10 + 2w \leq 68$$

$$4w + 10 \leq 68$$

$$4w \leq 58$$

$$w \leq 14.5$$

The greatest possible width for the garden is 14.5 feet.

Practice

Choose the letter preceding the word or expression that best completes the statement or answers the question.

1 Which could not be modeled by $n \leq 2$?

A. A number n is not more than two.

B. A number n is not less than two.

C. A number n is less than or equal to two.

D. A number n is not greater than two.

2 Which describes all numbers r that are at most 5 units from zero on a number line?

A. $|r| < 5$

B. $|r| \leq 5$

C. $|r| > 5$

D. $|r| \geq 5$

3 Today's high temperature of 54°F was more than 20°F above T, the normal high temperature. Which inequality can be used to represent this situation?

A. $20 < T < 54$ **C.** $54 > 20 - T$

B. $54 > 20 + T$ **D.** $T - 20 > 54$

4 The perimeter P of an equilateral triangle is given by the formula $P = 3s$, where s is the length of one side. In a certain equilateral triangle, the length of each side is a whole number of inches, and the perimeter is less than 15 inches. Which describes all possible values of s?

A. $s < 5$

B. $s \leq 4$

C. $s = 1, s = 2, s = 3$, or $s = 4$

D. $s = 1, s = 2, s = 3, s = 4$, or $s = 5$

5 A bag contains some red marbles and some blue marbles. There are fewer than 63 marbles in all. The ratio of red marbles to blue marbles is 5 to 3. If b represents the number of blue marbles, which inequality represents this situation?

A. $b + \frac{3}{5}b < 63$ **C.** $b + \frac{5}{3}b \leq 63$

B. $b + \frac{3}{5}b \leq 63$ **D.** $b + \frac{5}{3}b < 63$

In Exercises 6–18, solve the problem. Clearly show all necessary work.

6 Ten more than 3 times a real number j is greater than negative 31. What are the possible values of j?

7 Twice the sum of a whole number w and 5 is at most 15. What are all possible values of w?

8 Find all sets of three consecutive odd whole numbers whose sum is less than 45.

9 The cost of a gallon container of orange juice is $3.50. What is the maximum number of containers you can buy for $15?

10 To rent a car for one day, you must pay a base fee of $19.50. There is an additional charge of $.25 for each mile that you drive. You want to spend no more than $50 for the one-day rental. What is the greatest number of miles you can drive?

11 Jane is a salesperson at an automobile dealership. Each week she earns a base pay of $200, plus an 8% commission on her sales during the week. What must be the amount of her sales in one week if she wants her total earnings for the week to be at least $400?

12 A restaurant waiter earns a weekly base pay of $100, plus an average tip of $5 for each table served. In a five-day work week, how many tables must be served on average per day for the waiter to earn at least $450?

13 Ernest's job is to load shipping crates with cartons of merchandise. The weight of an empty shipping crate is 150 pounds. How many 35-pound cartons can Ernest load into a crate if the total weight of the crate and cartons may not exceed 850 pounds?

14 The perimeter of any triangle is the sum of the lengths of its sides. The lengths of the three sides of a certain triangle, in inches, are consecutive integers. The perimeter does not exceed 48 inches. What are all the possible measures for the longest side of this triangle?

15 The length and width of a rectangle are consecutive integers. The perimeter of this rectangle is at most 60 meters. What are the possible measures for the shorter side of this rectangle?

16 The Art Club is sponsoring a four-day art show. Their goal is for the average daily attendance to be between 100 and 120, inclusive. The attendance for the first three days of the show is 100, 105, and 91. What must be the attendance on the fourth day in order for the club to achieve its goal?

17 Two partners in a business share all profits in the ratio 4 to 5. They expect their profits for next month to be at least $1800 but no more than $3600. What amount of money might each partner expect to receive next month?

18 The formula $C = \frac{5}{9}(F - 32)$ gives the temperature C in degrees Celsius in terms of F degrees Fahrenheit. The temperature of a certain substance ranges from 20°C to 25°C inclusive. Find the corresponding range of temperatures in degrees Fahrenheit.

Chapter 2 Preparing for the ADP[SM] Algebra I Exam

DIRECTIONS FOR QUESTIONS 1–22: For each of the questions below, select the answer choice that is best for each case.

1 If $3(x + 2) = -12$, then $x =$

A. -6 **B.** -2 **C.** 2 **D.** 6

2 If $-2d + 5 = -31$, then $3d - 9 =$

A. -63 **B.** -54 **C.** 18 **D.** 45

3 If $-4t + 4 + 2a = 3a - 12 - 5t$, then $t =$

A. $a - 3$ **B.** $-a + 3$

C. $a - 16$ **D.** $a - 8$

4 Last week a company's income was \$530. From this, \$50 was withheld for expenses. The rest was shared by two partners in the ratio 3 to 5. How much did each receive?

A. \$180 and \$300

B. \$198.75 and \$331.25

C. \$72.50 and \$457.50

D. \$217.50 and \$362.50

5 Each situation below gives an original amount followed by a new amount. Which illustrates the greatest percent of increase?

A. 230 pencils; 253 pencils

B. 12 gallons; 15 gallons

C. 18 miles; 21 miles

D. \$12; \$3

6 The total value of a collection of 34 nickels and quarters is at least \$3.60. Let n represent the number of nickels. Which inequality models this situation?

A. $5n + 25(n - 34) \geq 360$

B. $5n + 25(34 - n) \geq 360$

C. $5n + 25(n - 34) \geq 3.60$

D. $5n + 25(34 - n) < 3.60$

7 A 14-ounce solution is made of water, salt, and sugar in the ratio 12 to 1 to 1. Which statement is false?

A. If x represents the number of ounces of sugar, then $12x + x + x = 14$.

B. Water, salt, and sugar are equal in amount.

C. The solution contains 12 ounces of water and 1 ounce each of salt and sugar.

D. The amount of water is 12 times the amount of salt.

8 If $|d| - 9 = 45$, then $d =$

A. 54 or -54 **B.** 54 or 36

C. 6 or -6 **D.** 36 or -36

9 What number is 110% of 19?

A. 29 **B.** 2.09 **C.** 17.3 **D.** 20.9

10 Which of the following is the ratio of 2 pounds to 48 ounces expressed as a fraction in lowest terms?

A. $\frac{1}{24}$ **B.** $\frac{1}{2}$ **C.** $\frac{2}{3}$ **D.** $\frac{1}{3}$

11 Solve the proportion $\frac{5.4}{8} = \frac{t}{6}$.

A. $t = 4.05$ **B.** $t = 3.4$

C. $t = 1.43$ **D.** $t = 7.2$

12 Solve the inequality $15c - 4 \leq 12c + 5$.

A. $c \geq 3$ **B.** $c \leq \frac{1}{3}$

C. $c \leq 3$ **D.** $c > \frac{1}{3}$

13 Which of the following includes all possible solutions of the inequality $-2 \leq -2m < 10$?

A. $1 \leq m < 5$ **B.** $m \geq 1$

C. $-5 > m$ **D.** $-5 < m \leq 1$

ALGEBRA I

14 Which is the graph of the solution set of the inequality $p \leq -1.5$?

A. 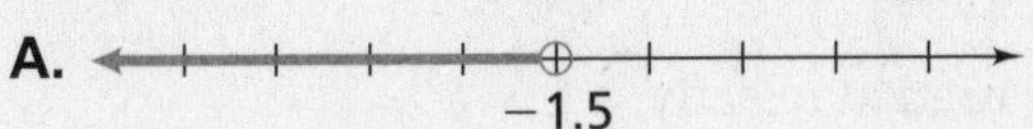

B. −1.5

C. −1.5

D. −1.5

15 The graph matches the solution set of which of the following inequalities?

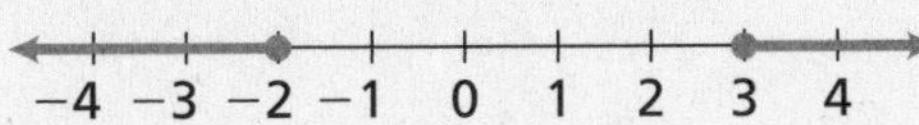

A. $|4a - 2| \geq 10$

B. $|5a + 6| \leq -4$

C. $|a| > 3$

D. $|3a + 4| > 13$

16 The graph matches the solution set of which of the following inequalities?

−24 −23 −22 −21 −20 −19 −18 −17

A. $-23 \leq k \leq -18$

B. $-23 \geq k \geq -18$

C. $-19 < k + 4 < -14$

D. $-19 \geq k + 4 \geq -14$

17 Which of the following represents the set of all integers between −4 and 10 as a single inequality?

A. $-4 < x < 10$

B. $x < 10$

C. $x > -4$

D. $-4 > x > 10$

18 Which statement describes the set of all integers that satisfy $3(n - 5) \geq 20$ and $n \leq 12$?

A. {11.6, 11.7, . . ., 12}

B. all integers between 11.67 and 12

C. no solution

D. {12}

19 The ratio of right-handed students to left-handed students in a grade is 11 : 2. There are 38 left-handed students in this class. How many right-handed students are there?

A. 7 **B.** 209

C. 47 **D.** 437

20 Greg bought a television on sale for $336. The regular price was $420. What was the percent of decrease in the price?

A. 80% **B.** 20%

C. 25% **D.** 16%

21 The formula for calculating simple interest is $I = prt$, where I is the amount of interest, p is the amount invested, r is the annual rate of interest, and t is the time in years. Suppose that you invested $1200 for a period of six years and earned $396 simple interest. What was the annual rate of interest?

A. 0.055% **B.** 18%

C. 0.55% **D.** 5.5%

22 At Roosevelt High School, 12% of the students belong to the Drama Club. There are 66 students in the Drama Club. How many students are in the school altogether?

A. 550 **B.** 616

C. 792 **D.** 8

DIRECTIONS FOR 23–25: Solve each problem. Show your work or provide an explanation for your answer.

23 A car left point X at noon, traveling along a straight road at exactly 60 miles per hour. It arrived at point Y at 1:00 P.M. on the same day. When this car was at point M, halfway between X and Y, a second car traveling at exactly 45 miles per hour left point X and traveled toward point Y along the same road.

What is the distance in miles from point X to point M? At what time did the second car reach point Y?

How far had the second car traveled when the first car reached point Y?

How long will it take the second car to travel from point X to point Y

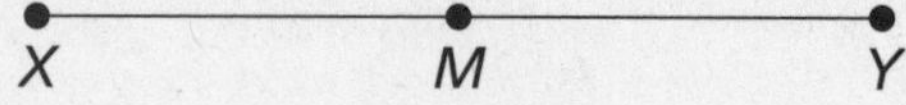

24 The perimeter of any triangle is the sum of the lengths of its sides. The lengths of the sides of a certain triangle, in feet, are consecutive even integers. The perimeter of this triangle is between 10 feet and 24 feet inclusive.

Write three expressions that represent the lengths of the sides of the triangle.

Write an inequality to describe the possible measures of the perimeter of the triangle.

Solve the inequality. List all possible lengths for the longest side of the triangle.

25 A furniture store is having its annual spring sale. All furniture is on sale for 15% off. Janet purchases a sofa and receives an additional 10% off of the sale price. The original price of the sofa is \$600.

What is the price of the sofa before the additional 10% discount?

How much more does Janet save with the additional 10% discount?

Is the final sale price of the sofa the same as the price if the sale is 25% off the price of the sofa? Explain your reasoning.

3 Linear Equations and Inequalities in Two Variables

Discovering Hawaii

Kamehameha the Great

Kamehameha founded a dynasty that ruled the Hawaiian Islands for more than 100 years. The island of Hawaii was ruled by King Kalaniopuu. Upon Kalaniopuu's death in 1782, Hawaii was divided between his son, Kiwalao, and his nephew, Kamehameha. Through a series of conquests and peaceful negotiations, Kamehameha succeeded in uniting all of the Hawaiian Islands in 1810.

Kamehameha protected the rights of the common people and promoted trade with Europeans and Americans. He maintained Hawaii's independence during a time when European nations explored and colonized the region.

Kamehameha died in 1819. Today, he is remembered and honored as "Kamehameha the Great."

3.1 Lines in the Coordinate Plane

ADP℠ Standards

L1.b Analyze linear functions

L1.d Model problems using linear functions

The **coordinate axes system** is created by two intersecting number lines, one **horizontal axis** called the ***x*-axis** and one **vertical axis** called the ***y*-axis.** The intersection point is called the **origin.** The axes system divides the plane into points on the axes and into four regions called **quadrants.** Points in the plane are named by using a capital letter and an **ordered pair, *P* (*a*, *b*).** Point *P* has **abscissa,** or ***x*-coordinate,** *a*, and **ordinate,** or ***y*-coordinate,** *b*. Point $F(2, -4)$ has abscissa 2 and ordinate -4. Point *F* is in the fourth quadrant.

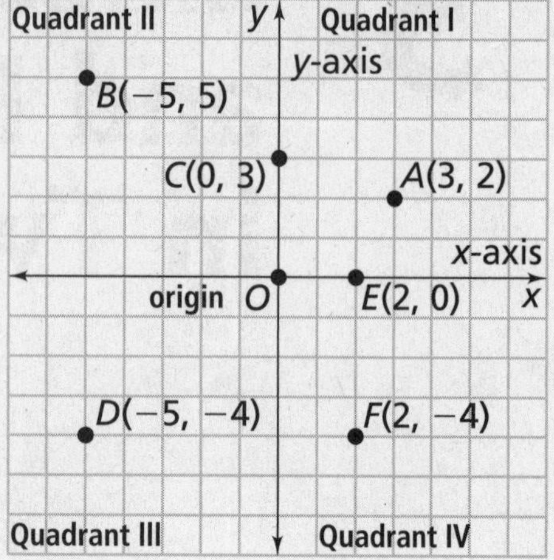

Just as the graph of a real number is the point on the number line representing that number, the **graph of an ordered pair** (a, b) of real numbers *a* and *b* is the point *P* in the coordinate plane whose *x*-coordinate is *a* and whose *y*-coordinate is *b*. As shown at the right, the ordered pairs $(-5, 5)$ and $(0, 3)$ are represented by points $B(-5, 5)$ and $C(0, 3)$, respectively.

EXAMPLES 1 and 2 **Working with points in the coordinate plane**

1 Which is true of all points in the second quadrant?

A. positive *x*-coordinate; positive *y*-coordinate

B. negative *x*-coordinate; negative *y*-coordinate

C. negative *x*-coordinate; positive *y*-coordinate

D. positive *x*-coordinate; negative *y*-coordinate

SOLUTION

To locate a point in the second quadrant, go left from the origin, and then go up.

go left: negative *x*-coordinate
go up: positive *y*-coordinate
The correct choice is C.

2 Which point lies in the third quadrant?

A. $P(0, -5)$ **B.** $Q(-5, -11)$ **C.** $R(-5, 0)$ **D.** $T(-5, 11)$

SOLUTION

Points in the third quadrant have a negative *x*-coordinate and a negative *y*-coordinate. The correct choice is B.

$Q(-5, -11) \rightarrow$ Quadrant III

Two points in the coordinate plane determine a line. The ratio of the vertical change to the horizontal change is the measure of the **slope of the line,** and the letter ***m*** is used to represent this measure. The horizontal change from point *A* to *B* is 5 units and the vertical change from *A* to *B* is 4 units.

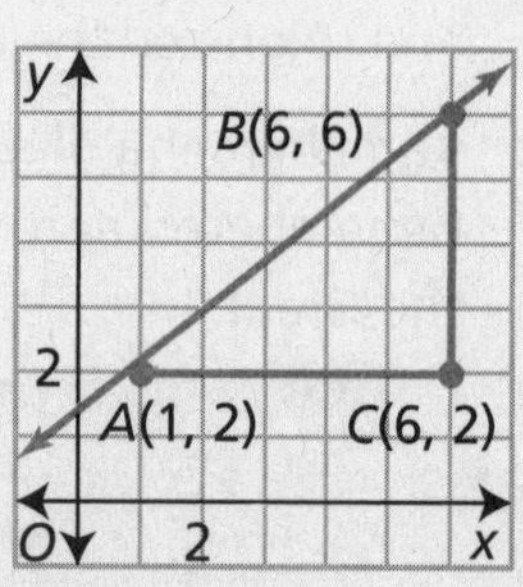

Slope of a Line

For any two points in the plane $P(x_1, y_1)$ and $Q(x_2, y_2)$ the slope can be represented in the following ways.

$$\text{slope} = m = \frac{\text{vertical change}}{\text{horizontal change}} = \frac{\text{rise}}{\text{run}} = \frac{\Delta y}{\Delta x} = \frac{y_1 - y_2}{x_1 - x_2} = \frac{y_2 - y_1}{x_2 - x_1}$$

These diagrams illustrate a line with positive slope, line *m;* a line with negative slope, line *n;* and a line with 0 slope, line *z*.

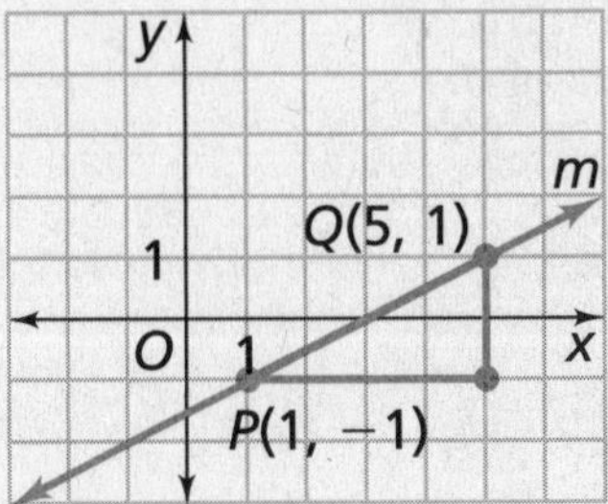

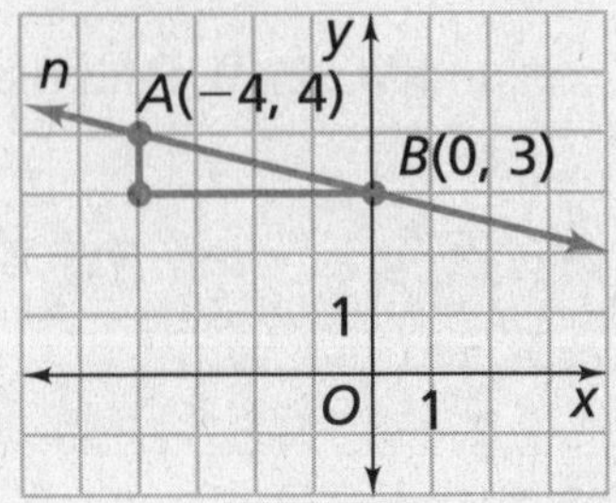

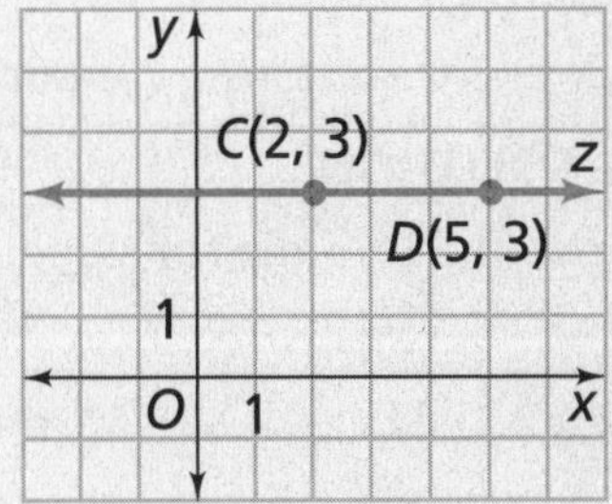

If the line is horizontal, then the vertical change $y_1 - y_2$, or rise, is equal to zero and the slope of the line is zero.

$$m = \frac{2 - 2}{1 - (-3)} = \frac{0}{4} = 0$$

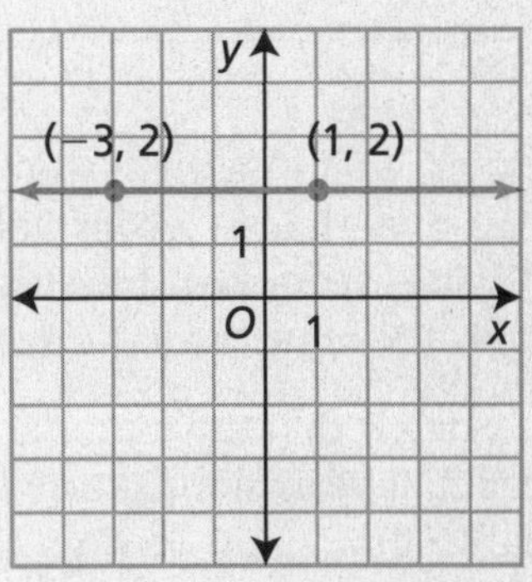

If the line is vertical, then the horizontal change, or run, is zero. A ratio is undefined when the denominator is zero and the numerator is nonzero. Therefore, **a vertical line has no slope.**

$$m = \frac{2 - 5}{1 - 1} = \frac{-3}{0} = \text{undefined}$$

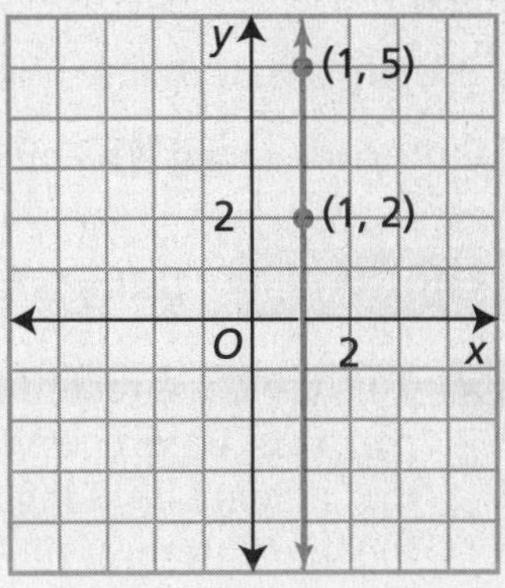

EXAMPLES 3 through 5 **Calculating the slope of a line**

Find the slope of the line containing the given points.

3 $P(1, -1)$ and $Q(5, 1)$

■ **SOLUTION**

$m = \frac{1 - (-1)}{5 - 1} = \frac{2}{4} = \frac{1}{2}$

4 $A(-4, 4)$ and $B(0, 3)$

■ **SOLUTION**

$m = \frac{3 - 4}{0 - (-4)} = -\frac{1}{4}$

5 $C(2, 3)$ and $D(5, 3)$

■ **SOLUTION**

$m = \frac{3 - 3}{5 - 2} = 0$

You can use what you know about slope to analyze and solve problems involving slopes of lines.

EXAMPLES 6 and 7 Solving problems that involve slope

6 Which describes the slope of the line containing $W(-1, 5)$ and $Z(4, 5)$?

A. positive **B.** negative **C.** 0 **D.** does not exist

▪ SOLUTION

The y-coordinates of W and Z are equal; therefore, the line is horizontal. The correct choice is C.

7 A line with slope $\frac{1}{3}$ contains $R(3, n)$ and $S(-2, 2)$. Find the value of n.

▪ SOLUTION

Use the formula for slope. $\frac{1}{3} = \frac{2-n}{-2-3}$ ← $m = \frac{y_2 - y_1}{x_2 - x_1}$

$$\frac{1}{3} = \frac{2-n}{-5}$$

$$n = \frac{11}{3}$$

The diagram at the right shows the distance a certain motorist travels over time at a constant speed. Notice that after 2 hours of driving, the motorist has traveled 130 miles. After 4 hours of driving, the motorist has traveled 260 miles.

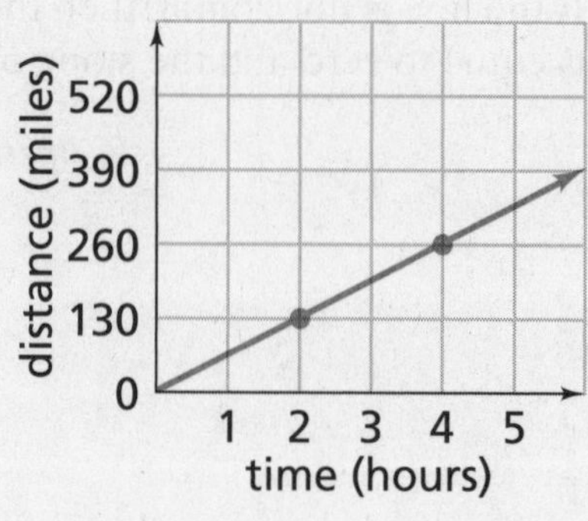

You can say that the motorist's speed is the ratio of the dependent variable, distance traveled, to the independent variable, time spent driving. This is an example of *rate of change.* You can calculate rate of change by finding the slope of the line.

$$\text{speed(rate of change)} = \frac{\text{change in distance}}{\text{change in time}} = \frac{260 - 130}{4 - 2} = 65$$

The motorist's speed is 65 miles per hour.

EXAMPLE 8 Using rate of change with data

8 This table is a record of plant height over a period of time. Graph the data. Assuming that all data lie along a line, find the slope of the line. Interpret the slope.

day	1	2	3	4	5	6
height (inches)	1.0	1.5	2.0	2.5	3.0	3.5

▪ SOLUTION

Record days on the horizontal axis and height on the vertical axis. Choose any two points from the data set. Use the formula for slope.

day 2: height 1.5 inches day 6: height 3.5 inches

$$\frac{\text{difference in height}}{\text{difference in days}} = \frac{3.5 - 1.5}{6 - 2} = \frac{1}{2}$$

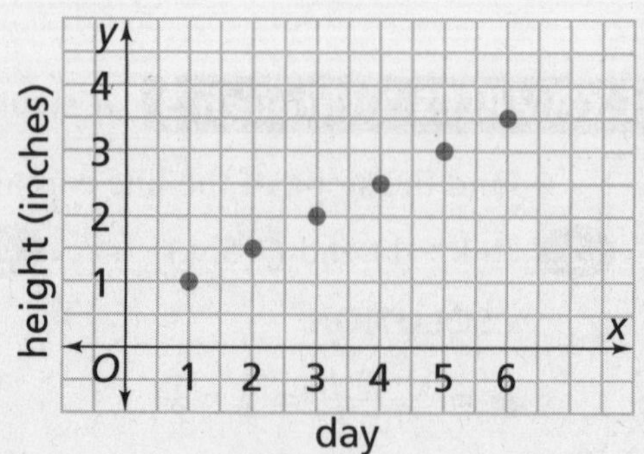

Each day, plant height increased 0.5 inch.

Practice

Choose the letter preceding the word or expression that best completes the statement or answers the question.

1 Which statement best describes a line with positive slope?

A. From left to right, the line falls.

B. From left to right, the line rises.

C. The line is parallel to the x-axis.

D. The line is parallel to the y-axis.

2 Which line has negative slope?

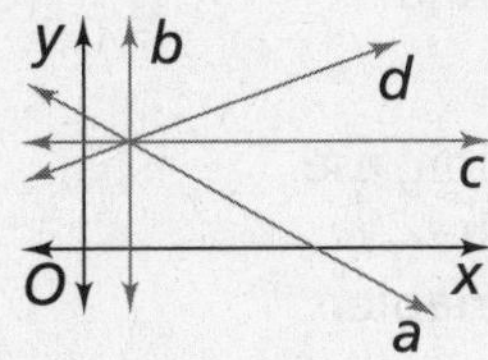

A. a B. b C. c D. d

3 The slope of the line containing $G(-7, 4)$ and $H(6, -2)$ is

A. $\frac{6}{13}$ B. $-\frac{13}{6}$ C. $-\frac{6}{13}$ D. $\frac{13}{6}$

4 Which ordered pairs represent X, Y, and Z?

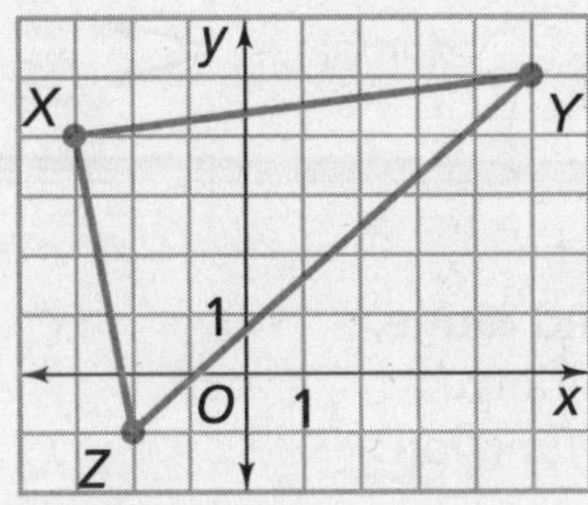

A. $X(-3, 3), Y(5, 4)$, and $Z(-2, -2)$

B. $X(5, 5), Y(-3, 4)$, and $Z(-2, -1)$

C. $X(-3, 4), Y(5, 5)$, and $Z(-2, 1)$

D. $X(-3, 4), Y(5, 5)$, and $Z(-2, -1)$

In Exercises 5–6, identify the figure determined by joining the points in the order given.

5 $A(-3, -5), B(3, 5)$, and $C(10, -5)$

6 $C(0, 5), D(-6, 0), E(0, -5)$ and $F(6, 0)$

In Exercises 7–13, find the slope of the line containing each pair of points. If the line has no slope, so state.

7 $A(-3, -5), B(3, 5)$ 8 $X(3, -7), Y(-5, 11)$

9 $K(0, 5), L(3, 0)$ 10 $P(4, 7), Q(4, -7)$

11 $C(0, 5), D(0, -6)$ 12 $R(-3, -3), S(3, 3)$

13 $U(-0.5, 0.6), V(-2.5, 1.4)$

In Exercises 14–19, point $P(x, y)$ has coordinates $x = -3$ and $y = 4$. Give the coordinates of each point.

14 $A(-x, -y)$ 15 $B(x, -y)$

16 $C(-x, y)$ 17 $P(-2x, 3y)$

18 $Q(x + 5, y - 3)$ 19 $F(-3x, y + 2.5)$

In Exercises 20–22, solve the problem. Clearly show all necessary work.

20 A line has slope -2 and contains $P(3, 4)$ and $Q(-4, a)$. Find the value of a.

21 Use this table to find the rate of change of distance (in miles) over time.

hour	1	2	3	4	5	6
distance	54	108	162	216	270	324

22 Which line is steeper, a line with slope 0.4 or a line with slope 0.6? Explain.

3.2 Relations and Functions

ADP[SM] Standards

L1.a Represent linear relationships

A student earns \$4.50 per hour as a baby sitter. She is paid for a whole number of hours of work and works up to 6 hours at a time. The sitter can represent the relationship between time worked and money earned in a table, a list, an equation or rule, or a graph.

hours h	1	2	3	4	5	6
wage w	\$4.50	\$9.00	\$13.50	\$18.00	\$22.50	\$27.00

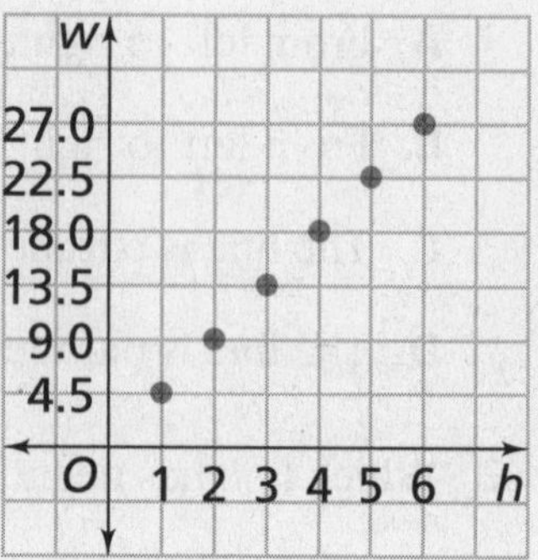

$$\{(1, 4.50), (2, 9.00), (3, 13.50), (4, 18.00), (5, 22.50), (6, 27.00)\}$$

$$w = 4.5h$$

The relationship between hours worked and wages is an example of a *function.* A **function** is a relationship in which every member of one set, the **domain,** is assigned exactly one member of a second set, the **range.** Members of the range of a function are also called **values of a function.** If the function is defined by an equation, you *evaluate the function* to find its values.

An equation can represent a function. To write an equation as a function, use function notation. The notation $f(x)$ is read "f of x." The variable x is the **independent variable,** and the variable y or $f(x)$ is the **dependent variable.**

Equation: $y = 3x + 15$ Equation: $f(x) = 3x + 15$

EXAMPLE 1 **Recognizing functions**

1 Which list does not represent a function?

A. $\{(1, 2), (3, 4), (5, 7), (7, 5)\}$

B. $\{(-2, 4), (0, 0), (1, 1), (2, 4)\}$

C. $\{(0, -3), (-2, 0), (7.5, 8.9), (-0.002, -0.002)\}$

D. $\{(1, 1), (4, 2), (9, 3), (4, -2), (49, 7), (100, 10)\}$

▪ **SOLUTION**

In choice **D,** 4 is paired with 2 and with −2. So the list in choice D does not represent a function.

domain 4 → 2 range, → −2

A **relation** is any correspondence between two sets, the **domain** and **range,** without requiring that each domain member be assigned only one range member. These *mapping diagrams* show the difference between a function and a relation.

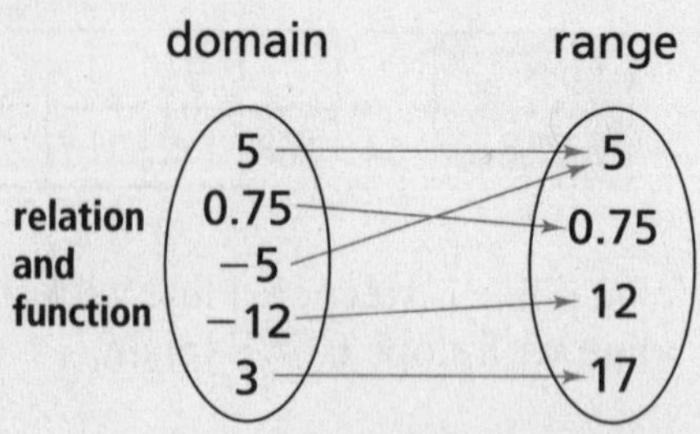

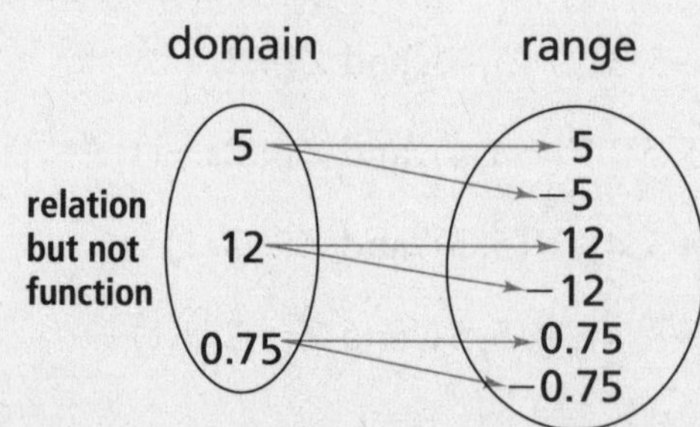

The domain and range of a function can be given using a list, interval notation, or a written description. You find the domain of a function by identifying all of the possible x-values of the function. You find the range of a function by identifying all of the possible y-values of the function.

Go Online
PearsonSchool.com
Visit: PearsonSchool.com
Web Code: ayp-0495

EXAMPLES 2 and 3 **Finding the domain and range of a function**

Find the domain and range of each function.

2 $\{(1, 5), (2, 10), (3, 15), (4, 20), (5, 25), (6, 30)\}$

■ SOLUTION

domain: first members in the ordered pairs
range: second members in the ordered pairs

domain: {1, 2, 3, 4, 5, 6}
range: {5, 10, 15, 20, 25, 30}

3 $f(x) = x^2 + 2$

■ SOLUTION

For any real number x, $x^2 \geq 0$. Thus, $x^2 + 2$ is always 2 or more.

domain: all real numbers
range: all real numbers 2 or more

The *vertical-line test* can help you determine whether a graph represents a function. If the graph does represent a function, you can use the graph to find the domain and range. The graph at the right does not represent a function because it does not pass the vertical-line test.

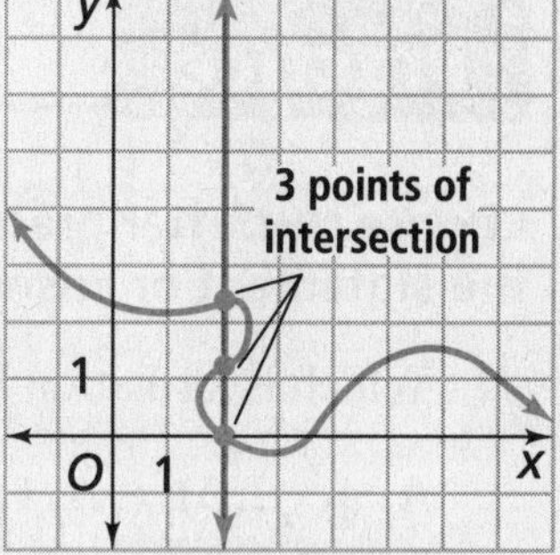

Vertical-Line Test

If every vertical line that intersects a graph does so in exactly one point, then the graph represents a function.

EXAMPLES 4 and 5 **Using graphs and the vertical-line test**

Does the graph represent a function? If it does, what are the domain and range?

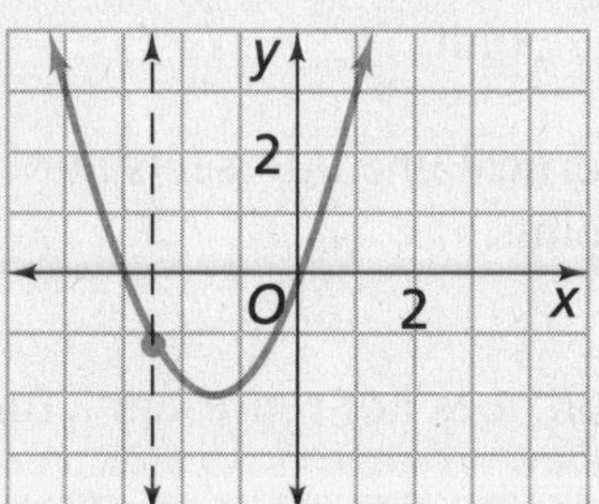

■ SOLUTION

Every vertical line intersects the graph in exactly one point. **The graph represents a function.**

domain: all real numbers
range: all real numbers −2 or more

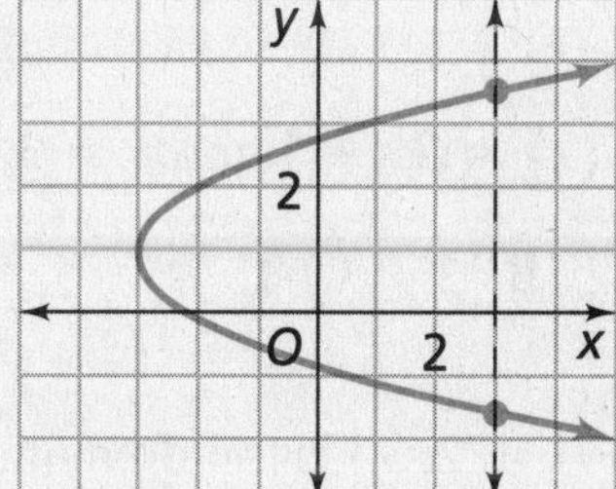

■ SOLUTION

Every vertical line with x-coordinate more than -3 intersects the graph in two points. For example, the line $x = 3$ intersects the graph in two points.

The graph does not represent a function.

You can use what you know to recognize relations and functions given in different representations, such as a list, table, graph, or equation.

EXAMPLE 6 **Recognizing a relation from different representations**

6 Which represents a relation that is not a function?

A. $\{(0, 0), (0, 7), (6, 6), (6, -6)\}$

B.

domain	range
−3	0
5	10
7	−5.4

C. $f(x) = -3.5x + 7$

D. 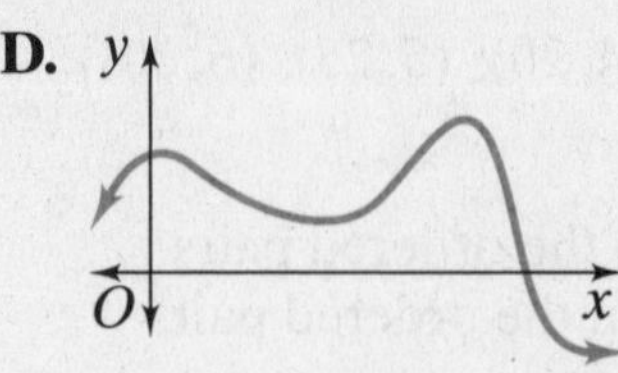

■ SOLUTION

In choice **A,** the domain values 0 and 6 are each assigned two range values. The list in choice **A** is a relation but not a function. The correct choice is A.

Practice

Choose the letter preceding the word or expression that best completes the statement or answers the question.

1 Which is a relation but not a function?

A. $\{(-2, 3), (-1, 1), (0, 7), (2, 3), (3, 2)\}$

B. $\{(2, 3), (3, 4), (5, 7), (1, 2), (9, 9)\}$

C. $\{(-2, 4), (2, 3), (5, 6), (-2, 6)\}$

D. $\{(-1, -1), (-2, -2), (-3, -3), (4, 4)\}$

2 Given $f(x) = 3x + 1$ and $x = 3$, find $f(x)$.

A. 1 **B.** 3 **C.** 9 **D.** 10

3 If $\{-3, -1, 1, 2, 3\}$ is the domain, what is the range of $f(x) = x^2 - x$?

A. $\{-3, -1, 1, 2,\}$

B. $\{0, 2, 6, 12\}$

C. $\{1, 4, 9\}$

D. $\{-3, -2, -1, 1\}$

4 A graph passes the vertical-line test if

A. every vertical line intersects it at exactly one point.

B. every vertical line intersects it at two points.

C. every vertical line intersects it at more than one point.

D. every vertical line intersects at two or more points.

5 Which graph does not represent a function?

A. 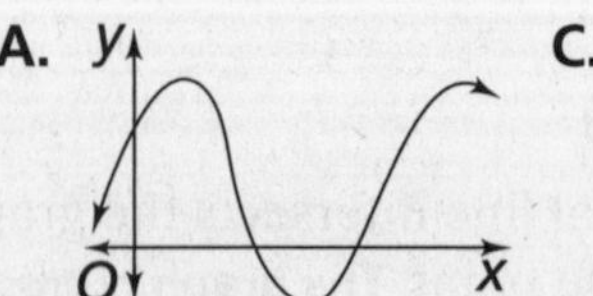

C. 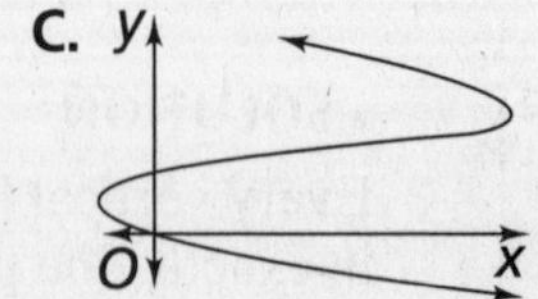

B. 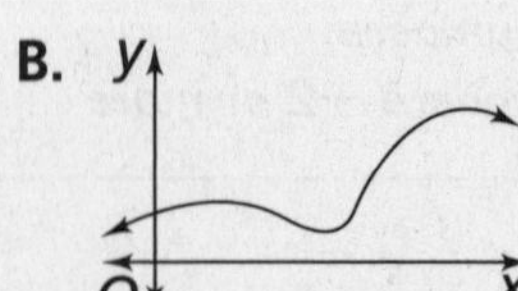

D. 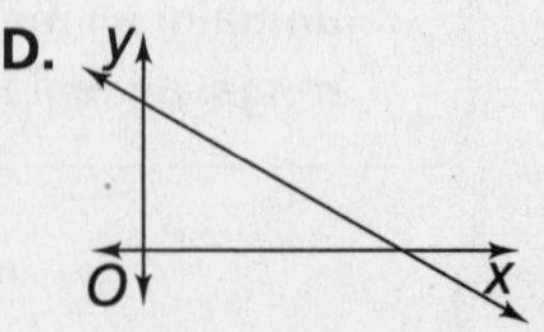

6 Which equation represents the verbal description of this function?

To change length f in feet to length I in inches, multiply f by 12.

A. $f = 12I$ **C.** $I = 12f$

B. $I = \frac{12}{f}$ **D.** $f = \frac{12}{I}$

7 The values of the independent variable for a function are also known as the

A. values.

B. domain.

C. range.

D. coordinates.

8 Given the function rule $g(x) = 2x - 1$, what is the value of $g(3)$?

A. 3 **C.** 5

B. 9 **D.** 10

9 $A = \{(1, 4), (4, 7), (3, 7), (5, 9), (9, 2)\}$. Which of the following statements is **not** true?

A. The domain of A is $\{1, 4, 3, 5, 7, 9\}$.

B. A is a function.

C. The range of A is $\{4, 7, 9, 2\}$.

D. A is a relation.

10 Which of the following lines has an undefined slope?

A. a line containing the points $(3, -4)$ and $(-4, 3)$

B. a line containing the points $(2, 1)$ and $(-2, -3)$

C. a horizontal line through the point $(3, 4)$

D. a vertical line through the point $(-1, 5)$

11 Determine whether the following graph represents a function.

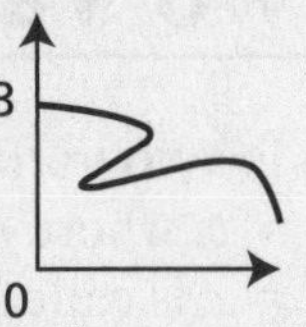

In Exercises 12–16, write a formula for the relation described and give its domain and range.

12 To convert a length in inches i to centimeters c, multiply by 2.54.

13 The Coach USA Center seats 3200 fans. Tickets sell for $9. The number of seats sold, s, determines the gross take G.

14 Your grade G on a test worth 80 points is the number of points you earned e divided by 0.8.

15 The points you score p in basketball is 2 times the number of field goals f you make.

16 The area A of a square is the length of its side s multiplied by itself.

In Exercises 17–25, graph the function by using a table of values and state its domain and range.

17 $f(x) = 2x - 1$

18 $f(x) = |x| - 1$

19 y is the quotient of some number and 3.

20 $f(x) = -5x + 7$

21 $4x + 3y = 12$

22 $f(x) = x$

23 $f(x) = |x + 1|$

24 y is the sum of 3 times x and 4.

25 $f(x) = |x| - 5$

3.3 Linear Equations in Two Variables

ADP℠ Standards

L1.b Analyze linear functions

L1.d Model problems using linear functions

N2.a Solve literal equations

A **linear equation in two variables** is any equation that can be written in the form $ax + by = c$, where a, b, and c are real numbers and $a, b \neq 0$. The equation $ax + by = c$ is called the **standard form** of a linear equation in two variables.

Examples:
$$y = 2x + 1$$
$$-3x + 2y = 6$$

A **solution to an equation in two variables** is any ordered pair (x, y) that makes the equation true.

The **graph of an equation in two variables** is the set of all points in the coordinate plane that correspond to solutions to the equation.

Graph of a Linear Equation in Two Variables

The graph of an equation of the form $ax + by = c$, where a, b, and c are real numbers and $a, b \neq 0$, is a line.

- A ***y*-intercept** of a graph is the y-coordinate of any point where the graph crosses the y-axis.
- An ***x*-intercept** of a graph is the x-coordinate of any point where the graph crosses the x-axis.

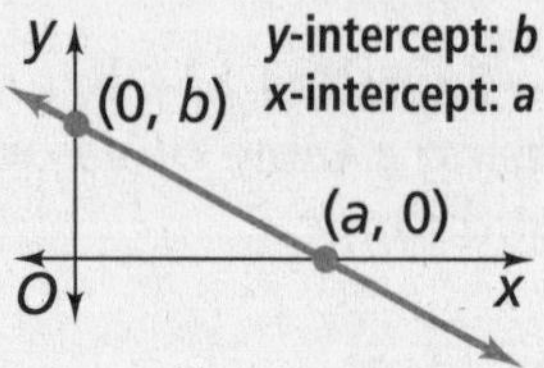

A linear equation in two variables can be written in **slope-intercept form,** $y = mx + b$, for real numbers m and b. The slope is m and the y-intercept is b.

EXAMPLE 1 **Writing a linear equation in two variables in slope-intercept form**

1 Write $5x - 3y = 15$ in slope-intercept form. What are the slope and y-intercept?

■ SOLUTION

$$5x - 3y = 15$$
$$y = \frac{5}{3}x + (-5), \text{ or } y = \frac{5}{3}x - 5 \leftarrow \textbf{Slope-intercept form}$$

The slope is $\frac{5}{3}$ and the y-intercept is -5.

You can use a table of solutions to graph an equation in two variables. You can also graph a line by plotting the y-intercept and using the definition of slope $= \frac{\text{rise}}{\text{run}}$ to plot additional points of the line.

EXAMPLES 2 and 3 Graphing linear equations in two variables

 Graph $y = 2x + 1$.

▪ SOLUTION

Use a table of values

Graph the points.

x	y
−1	2(−1) + 1 = −1
0	2(0) + 1 = 1
1	2(1) + 1 = 3

 Graph $y = -\frac{2}{3}x + 3$.

▪ SOLUTION

Use slope $-\frac{2}{3}$ and y-intercept 3.

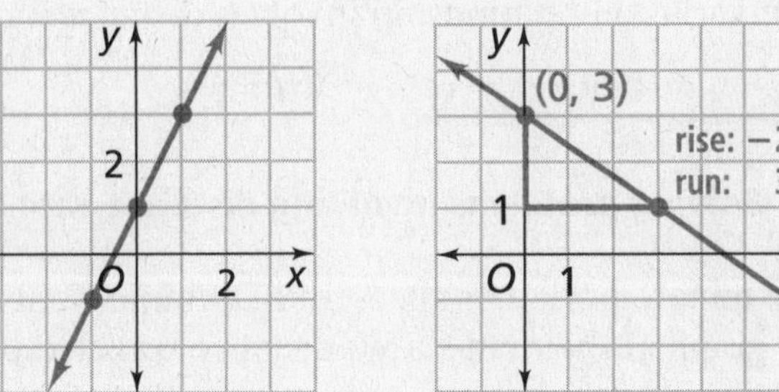

If a or b is zero in the equation $ax + b = c$, the resulting line is horizontal or vertical respectively. Recall that line AB is horizontal; therefore, its slope is zero. $y = (0)x + 2$ or $y = 2$ is the equation of the line.

Line BC is vertical and has no slope; therefore, the slope-intercept form is of no help in writing the equation. Every point on this line has an x-value of 4; therefore, the equation of the line is $x = 4$.

Equations of **vertical lines** are of the form $\boldsymbol{x = k}$ and **horizontal lines** are $\boldsymbol{y = k}$.

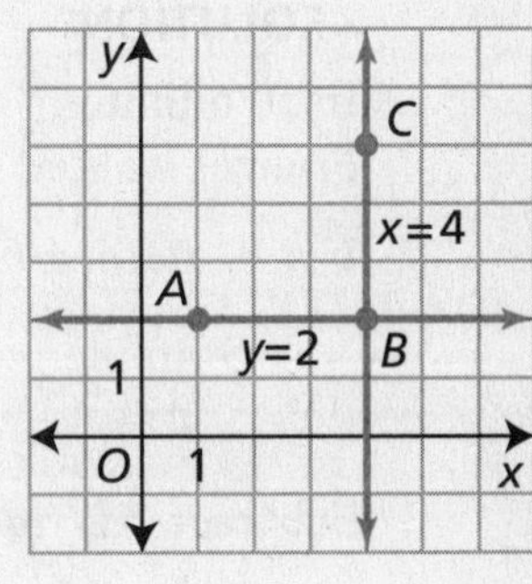

EXAMPLE 4 Graphing a linear equation in two variables from standard form

 Graph $-3x + 2y = 6$, using any method.

▪ SOLUTION 1

using the intercepts of the graph

If $x = 0$, then $2y = 6$. So, $(0, 3)$ is a solution.

If $y = 0$, then $-3x = 6$. So, $(-2, 0)$ is a solution.

Graph $(0, 3)$ and $(-2, 0)$. Draw the line.

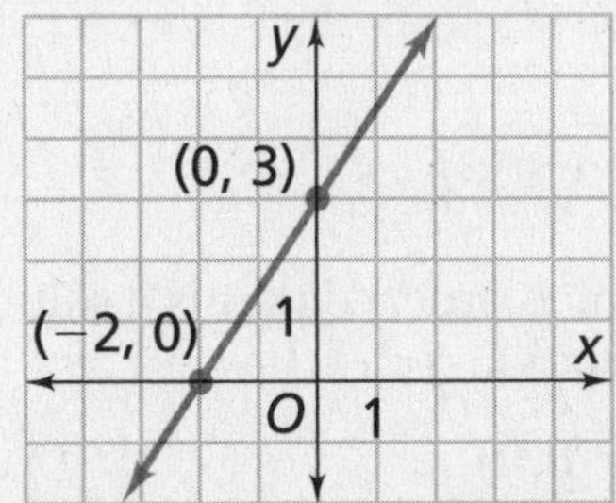

▪ SOLUTION 2

solving for y in terms of x

If $-3x + 2y = 6$, then $y = \frac{3}{2}x + 3$.

Plot the y-intercept $(0, 3)$.

Use the slope $= \frac{3}{2} = \frac{\text{rise}}{\text{run}}$ to plot additional points of the line. Draw the line.

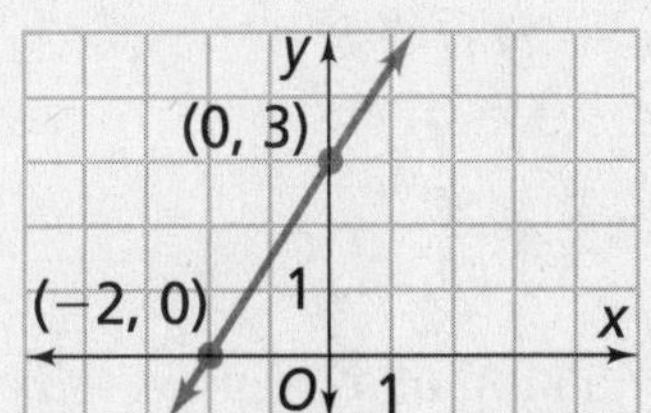

The amount of sales tax paid on a purchase depends on the value of the purchase. You can say that one variable, amount of purchase, is the **independent variable,** and a second variable, amount of tax, is the **dependent variable.** The amount of tax *varies directly* with amount of purchase.

In general, if the value of one variable y is found by multiplying the value of a second variable x by a constant nonzero real number k, the **constant of variation,** then the relationship is called a **direct variation.**

Go Online PearsonSchool.com
Visit: PearsonSchool.com
Web Code: ayp-0169

If $y = kx$, where $k \neq 0$, then y varies directly with x.

An important direct-variation relationship involves distance, rate, and time.

distance d = rate r × time t

EXAMPLE 5 **Solving problems involving distance, rate, and time**

5 During a 50-minute period, Frances and Dominic went out for a walk. The graph at the right shows distance traveled over time for each walker. In miles per hour, how much faster did Dominic walk than Frances?

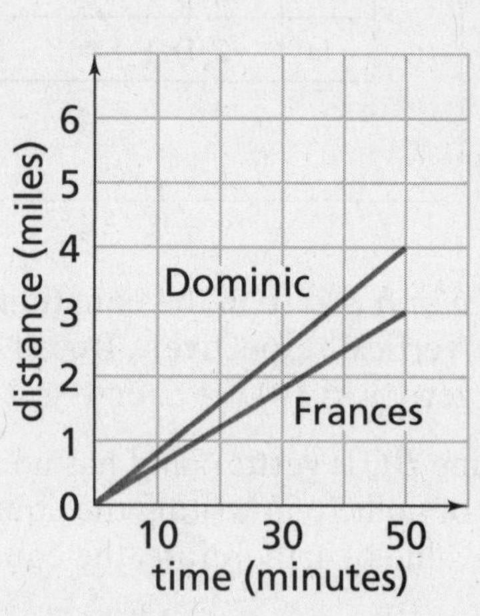

▪ SOLUTION

In 50 minutes, $\frac{5}{6}$ of an hour, Dominic walked 4 miles and Frances walked 3 miles.

If $d = rt$, then $r = \frac{d}{t}$.

Dominic: $r = \frac{4}{\frac{5}{6}} = 4.8$ Frances: $r = \frac{3}{\frac{5}{6}} = 3.6$

Subtract 3.6 from 4.8. Dominic walked 1.2 miles per hour faster than Frances.

Practice

Choose the letter preceding the word or expression that best completes the statement or answers the question.

1 Which of the following is not the equation of a line?

A. $y = 4$

B. $3x + 2y = 7$

C. $y = x^2 - 6$

D. $x = -5$

2 The equation of a line is $y = 3x - 7$. What is the y-intercept of the line?

A. 3 **C.** 7

B. 4 **D.** −7

3 Which equation represents variables that are directly related?

A. $y = 2x + 3$

B. $F = 1.8C + 32$

C. $zw = 6$

D. $y = 3f$

4 Which ordered pair is a solution to the equation $5x - 3y = 9$?

A. (0, 0) **C.** (5, 5)

B. (3, 2) **D.** (2, 3)

In Exercises 5–8, the equation $F = \frac{9}{5}C + 32$ relates temperature in degrees Fahrenheit (F) to degrees Celsius (C). Rewrite this equation as a function C in terms of F. Use the appropriate equation to calculate, to the nearest tenth, the corresponding temperature for each of the following.

5 $9°C$

6 $-20°C$

7 $0°F$

8 $95°F$

In Exercises 9–11, evaluate each function for the given member of the domain.

9 $y = \frac{2}{3}x + 9; x = -6$

10 $y = 1 - x^2; x = -3$

11 $y = \frac{2}{3}x - \frac{1}{2}; x = -6$

In Exercises 12–15, find the domain and range.

12 $y = 0.6x + 9$

13 $y = -0.25x$

14 $y = 1 - x^2$

15 $y = x^2 - 1$

In Exercises 16–27, graph each equation.

16 $y = -2x + 3$ **17** $y = 3x - 5$

18 $y = 2x - 1$ **19** $y = -3x$

20 $y = -\frac{1}{3}x - 2$ **21** $y = \frac{1}{2}x$

22 $-2x + y = 1$ **23** $x - y = 4$

24 $x + 3y = 3$ **25** $x + 2y = 2$

26 $-x + 2y = 3$ **27** $2x - 3y = 2$

28 During a 40-minute period, Dana and Li went out for a walk. The graph below shows distance traveled over time for each walker. In miles per hour, how much faster did Dana walk than Li?

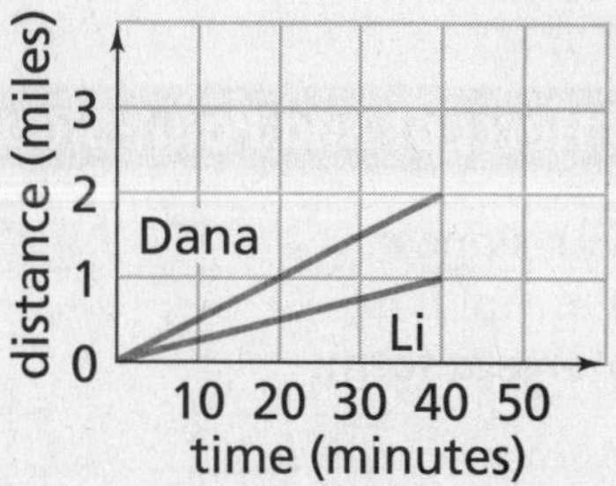

29 Marissa has $1.20 in nickels and dimes. Write an equation that represents this situation using n for the number of nickels and d for the number of dimes.

30 The sales tax in a certain area is 5%, or 5 cents on the dollar. Write an equation to represent the amount a of tax in terms of the cost c of a purchase.

31 Hank has $2.45 in nickels and dimes. Write an equation that represents this situation where n is the number of nickels and d is the number of dimes.

32 At a certain theater, an adult's ticket costs $9 and a child's ticket costs $5. The manager counted the receipts one night and determined that $2,250 was taken in. Write an equation to represent this situation, using a to represent the number of adults and c to represent the number of children.

33 A collection of 185 marbles consists of only red marbles, blue marbles, and 35 yellow marbles. Write an equation in r and b to represent the situation. List three possible solutions to the equation.

34 A choir sold fruit as represented below. Write an equation to represent this situation.

5-pound box	10-pound box	Total
f boxes	*t* boxes	200 pounds

Determine two possible numbers of cartons of 5-pound boxes and 10-pound boxes that satisfy the given conditions.

3.4 Writing Equations for Lines

ADP℠ Standards

L1.b Analyze linear functions

Given sufficient information about a line in the coordinate plane, you can write a linear equation in two variables to represent it. Stated below are important forms for an equation of a line.

Slope-Intercept and Point-Slope Forms

A line with slope m and y-intercept b has **slope-intercept form:**

$$y = mx + b$$

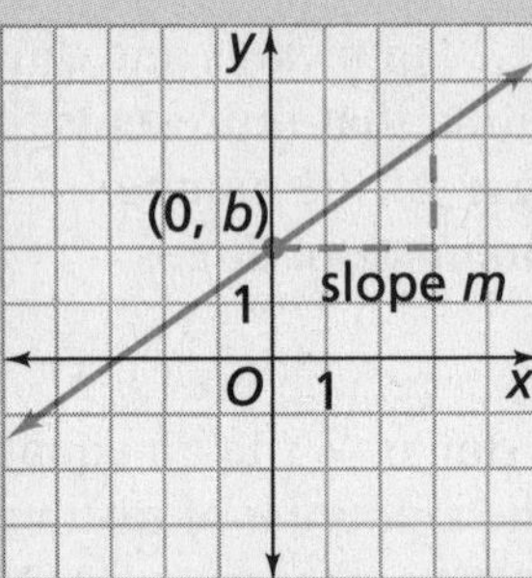

A line with slope m and containing $P(x_1, y_1)$ has **point-slope form:**

$$y - y_1 = m(x - x_1)$$

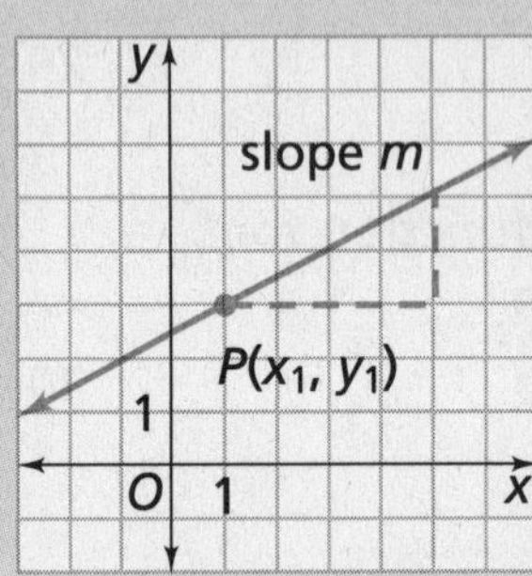

Visit: PearsonSchool.com
Web Code: ayp-0208
ayp-0215

Any vertical line containing $P(x_1, y_1)$ has equation $x = x_1$. For example, if a vertical line contains the point $(5, 2)$, an equation for that line is $x = 5$.

Any horizontal line containing $P(x_1, y_1)$ has equation $y = y_1$. For example, if a horizontal line contains the point $(4, -8)$, an equation for that line is $y = -8$.

EXAMPLES 1 and 2 Using slope and y-intercept to identify an equation for a line

1 Write an equation that represents the line with a slope of $-\frac{4}{5}$ and a y-intercept of 3.

■ **SOLUTION**

Use the slope-intercept form.

$$y = mx + b.$$
$$y = -\tfrac{4}{5}x + 3 \quad \leftarrow \text{Replace } m \text{ with } -\tfrac{4}{5} \text{ and } b \text{ with 3.}$$

2 Which equation represents the line at the right?

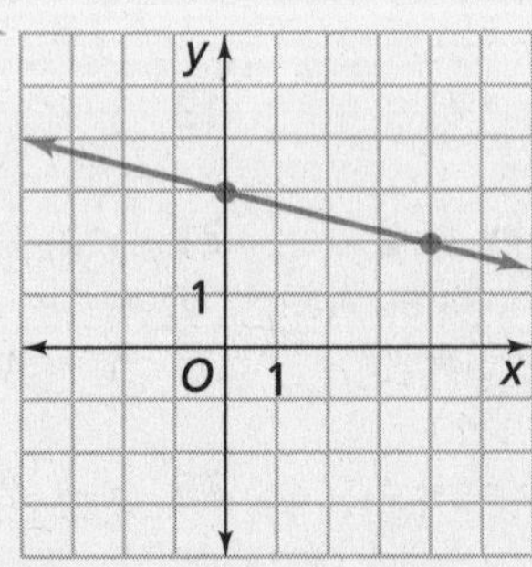

A. $y = \frac{1}{4}x + 3$ **C.** $y = \frac{1}{4}x - 3$

B. $y = -\frac{1}{4}x + 3$ **D.** $y = -2x + 3$

■ **SOLUTION**

The y-intercept is 3. The slope of the line is $-\frac{1}{4}$. Using the slope-intercept form, the correct choice is B.

When you are given the slope and a point on a line, you can use the point-slope form to write an equation for that line.

Go Online PearsonSchool.com
Visit: PearsonSchool.com
Web Code: ayp-0214

EXAMPLES 3 through 5 **Writing an equation for a line by using slope and a point on the line**

Write an equation in slope-intercept form for each line, if possible.

3 the line with slope $\frac{3}{4}$ and containing $P(2, -3)$

■ **SOLUTION**

$y - (-3) = \frac{3}{4}(x - 2)$

$y = \frac{3}{4}x - 4.5$

4 the line with slope 0 and containing $P(2, -3)$

■ **SOLUTION**

Because the slope is 0, the line is horizontal.

$y = -3$

5 the line with no slope and containing $P(2, -3)$

■ **SOLUTION**

Because there is no slope, the line is vertical.

$x = 2$

You can also use the point-slope form to find an equation of a line through two specific points. The point-slope form requires that you first find the slope. Recall that slope $= m = \frac{y_2 - y_1}{x_2 - x_1}$. You can write an equation of a line in slope-intercept or standard form.

EXAMPLES 6 through 9 **Writing an equation for a line given two points**

Write an equation for

6 the line containing $L(-5, -6)$ and $M(3, -6)$.

■ **SOLUTION**

The y-coordinates of L and M are equal. The line is horizontal.

$y = -6$

7 the line containing $R(4.2, -6)$ and $S(4.2, 9)$.

■ **SOLUTION**

The x-coordinates of R and S are equal. The line is vertical.

$x = 4.2$

8 the line containing $A(-5, -6)$ and $B(3, 8)$.

■ **SOLUTION**

First determine the slope.

$m = \frac{y_2 - y_1}{x_2 - x_1} = \frac{-6 - 8}{-5 - 3}$

$= \frac{-14}{-8} = \frac{7}{4}$

Using the point $B(3, 8)$ and the point-slope form results in:

$y - 8 = \frac{7}{4}(x - 3)$

$y - \frac{32}{4} = \frac{7}{4}x - \frac{21}{4}$

$y = \frac{7}{4}x + 2.75$

9 $\overleftrightarrow{DG}$ containing $D(2, 3)$ and $G(8, 11)$ in standard form.

■ **SOLUTION**

First determine the slope.

$m = \frac{y_2 - y_1}{x_2 - x_1} = \frac{11 - 3}{8 - 2} = \frac{8}{6}$

Using the point $D(2, 3)$ and the point-slope form results in:

$y - 3 = \frac{4}{3}(x - 2)$

$3y - 9 = 4x - 8$

$-4x + 3y = 1$

The standard form for the equation is $-4x + 3y = 1$.

Use what you know to solve problems involving points on a line.

EXAMPLES 10 and 11 **Solving problems about points on a line**

10 The point $Z(3, w)$ is on the graph of $y = 2x + 5$. The value of w is

A. -1 **B.** $w - 5$ **C.** 11 **D.** $2w + 5$

■ SOLUTION

If $x = 3$ and $y = w$, then $w = 2(3) + 5$; that is, $w = 11$
The correct choice is C.

11 Which point lies on the line containing $P(-3, -1)$ and $Q(5, 6)$?

A. $A(-3, 0)$ **B.** $B(21, 19)$ **C.** $C(21, 20)$ **D.** $D(-3, -2)$

■ SOLUTION

$m = \frac{6 - (-1)}{5 - (-3)} = \frac{7}{8}$ ← **Determine the slope.**

$y = \frac{7}{8}(x - 5) + 6$ ← **Write an equation for the line containing P and Q.**

Because $\frac{7}{8}(21 - 5) + 6 = 20$, the correct choice is C.

Two lines in a plane either intersect or do not intersect. If the lines never intersect, they are **parallel.** If the lines intersect at a right angle, the lines are **perpendicular.**

l: $y - \frac{1}{2}x + 3$ n: $y = \frac{1}{2}x - 1$

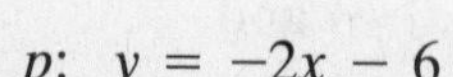

p: $y = -2x - 6$ q: $y = \frac{1}{2}x - 1$

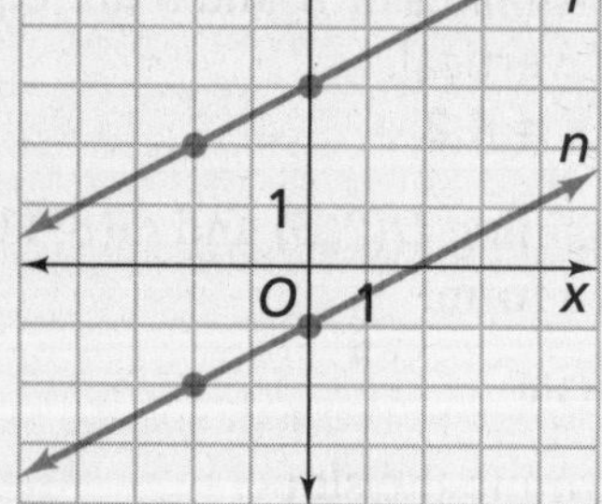

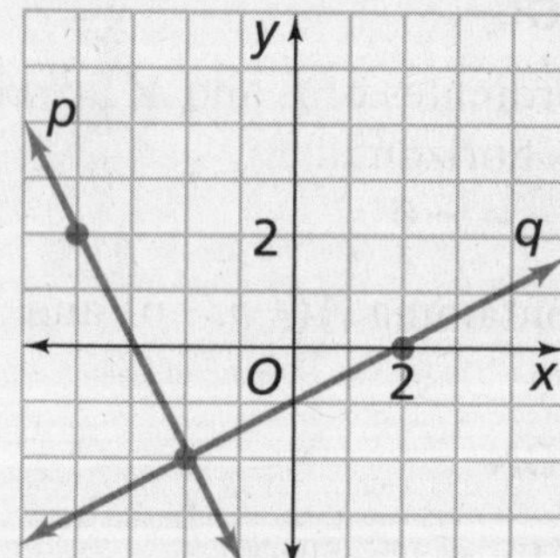

slope of l: $\frac{1}{2}$ slope of n: $\frac{1}{2}$

The lines are **parallel lines.**
The **slopes** of these lines are **equal.**

slope of p: -2 slope of q: $\frac{1}{2}$ Note: $-2 \cdot \frac{1}{2} = -1$

The lines are **perpendicular lines.**
The slopes are **negative reciprocals** of each other.

Parallel and Perpendicular Lines

- Two lines with slopes m_1 and m_2 are parallel if and only if $m_1 = m_2$.
(Any two vertical or horizontal lines are parallel.)
- Two lines with slopes m_1 and m_2 are perpendicular if and only if $m_1 m_2 = -1$.
(Every vertical line is perpendicular to every horizontal line.)

EXAMPLES 12 and 13 Identifying a line parallel to another line

12 Which line is parallel to the graph of $5x - 6y = 2$?

A. the line with slope $-\frac{5}{6}$ and y-intercept $-\frac{1}{3}$ **C.** the line with slope $-\frac{6}{5}$ and y-intercept $-\frac{1}{3}$

B. the line with slope $\frac{5}{6}$ and y-intercept 3 **D.** the line with slope $\frac{6}{5}$ and y-intercept 3

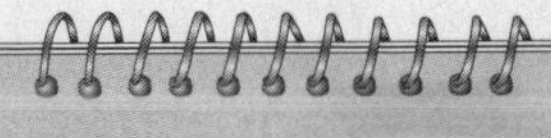

Note

To see whether two distinct nonvertical lines are parallel, check to see whether:

- slopes are equal;
- y-intercepts are unequal.

■ SOLUTION

Write $5x - 6y = 2$ in slope-intercept form.

$$5x - 6y = 2$$
$$-6y = -5x + 2$$
$$y = \frac{5}{6}x - \frac{1}{3}$$

A line parallel to the graph of $5x - 6y = 2$ must have slope $\frac{5}{6}$.
Therefore, eliminate choices **A, C,** and **D.**
The correct choice is B.

13 Which line is parallel to $3x + 4y = 12$?

A.

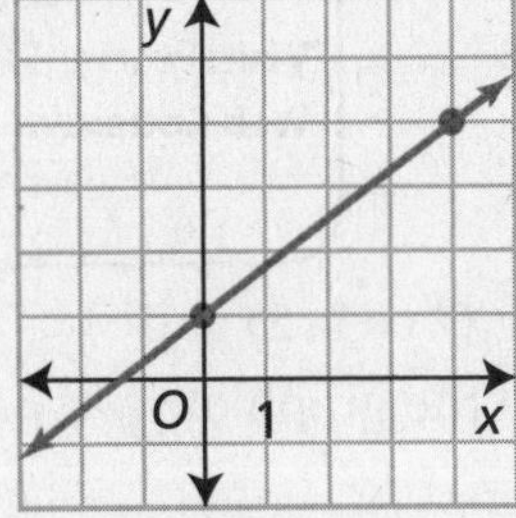

C.

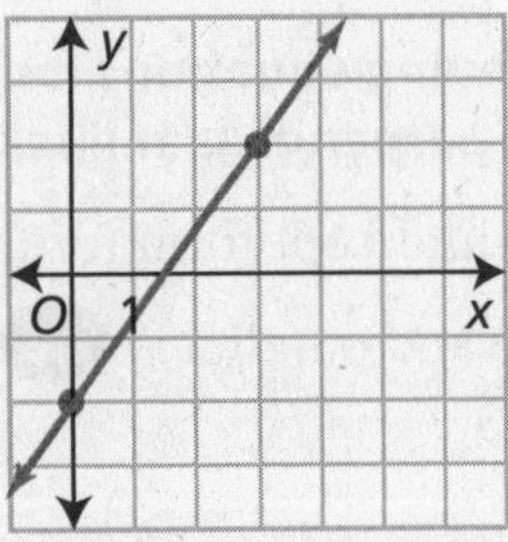

B.

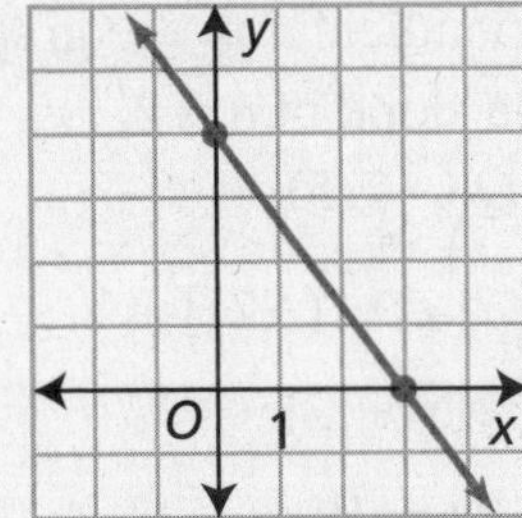

D.

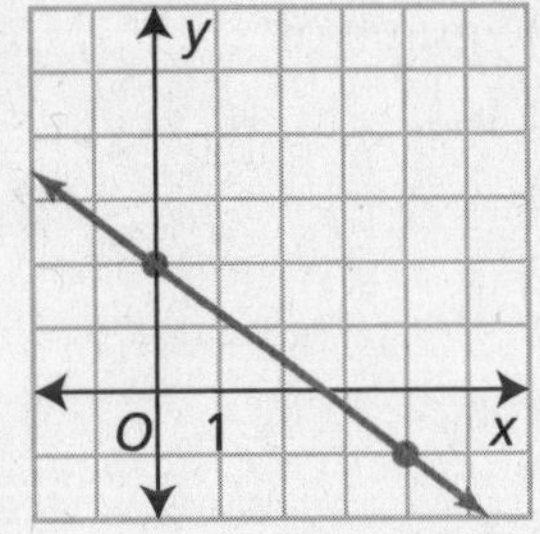

■ SOLUTION

Write $3x + 4y = 12$ in slope-intercept form.

$$y = -\frac{3}{4}x + 3$$

A line parallel to $3x + 4y = 12$ must have slope $-\frac{3}{4}$.
Therefore, eliminate choices **A** and **C** since the slopes are positive.
Find the slope of the line in choice **B.**

$$m = \frac{0 - 4}{3 - 0} = -\frac{4}{3}$$

The slope is not equal to $-\frac{3}{4}$; eliminate choice **B.**
Verify the slope of the line in choice **D.**

$$m = \frac{2 - (-1)}{0 - 4} = -\frac{3}{4}$$

The slope is equal to $-\frac{3}{4}$; the correct choice is D.

You can also use slope to identify perpendicular lines.

EXAMPLE 14 Identifying a line perpendicular to a given line

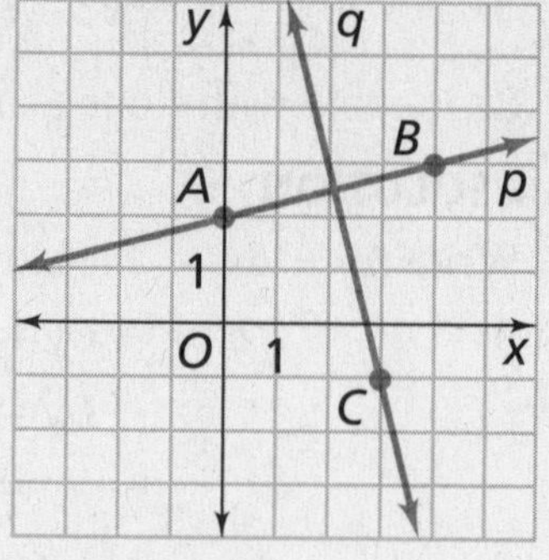

14 Which equation represents line q perpendicular to line p?

A. $-x + 4y = -2$ **C.** $-x + 4y = -7$

B. $4x + y = 11$ **D.** $4x + y = 2$

▪ **SOLUTION**

Write each equation in slope-intercept form.

A. $y = \frac{1}{4}x - \frac{1}{2}$ **C.** $y = \frac{1}{4}x - \frac{7}{4}$

B. $y = -4x + 11$ **D.** $y = -4x + 2$

Because the slope of p is $\frac{1}{4}$, the slope of q is -4. Eliminate choices **A** and **C.** $C(3,-1)$ does not satisfy the equation in choice **D.** The correct choice is B.

You can find an equation of a line parallel or perpendicular to a given line.

Go Online PearsonSchool.com
Visit: PearsonSchool.com
Web Code: ayp-0218
ayp-0220

EXAMPLES 15 and 16 Finding equations for parallel or perpendicular lines

Find an equation in slope-intercept form for the specified line.

15 line z containing $P\,(4, -3)$ and parallel to the graph of $y = \frac{1}{2}x + 3$

▪ **SOLUTION**

Because z is parallel to the graph of $y = \frac{1}{2}x + 3$, the slope of z is $\frac{1}{2}$.
Also, z contains $P\,(4, -3)$.

$$y - (-3) = \frac{1}{2}(x - 4)$$
$$y = \frac{1}{2}x - 5$$

16 line n containing $Q\,(-2, 5)$ and perpendicular to the graph of $y = -\frac{1}{2}x + 5$

▪ **SOLUTION**

Because n is perpendicular to the graph of $y = -\frac{1}{2}x + 5$, the slope of n is 2.
Also, n contains $Q\,(-2, 5)$.

$$y - 5 = 2[x - (-2)]$$
$$y - 5 = 2(x + 2)$$
$$y = 2x + 9$$

Practice

Choose the letter preceding the word or expression that best completes the statement or answers the question.

1 What is the slope of a line parallel to a line with slope -2?

A. 2 **B.** -2 **C.** $\frac{1}{2}$ **D.** $-\frac{1}{2}$

2 What is the slope of a line perpendicular to a line with slope -2?

A. 2 **C.** $\frac{1}{2}$

B. -2 **D.** $-\frac{1}{2}$

3 Which describes the relationship between two distinct nonvertical parallel lines?

A. equal slopes; unequal y-intercepts

B. unequal slopes; unequal y-intercepts

C. equal slopes; equal y-intercepts

D. unequal slopes; equal y-intercepts

4 Find the slope of a line perpendicular to line p.

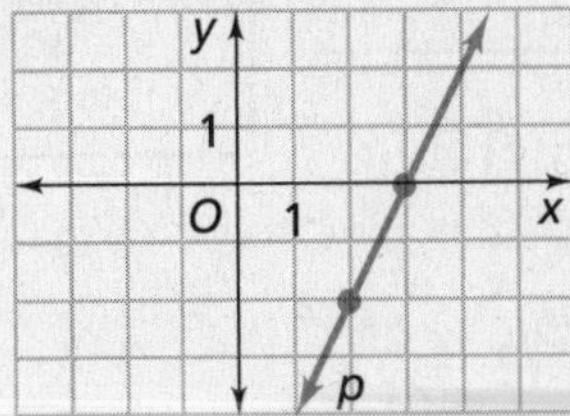

A. 2 **B.** 0.5 **C.** −2 **D.** −0.5

5 Which equation represents the line with slope −3 and y-intercept −7?

A. $y = -3x + 7$ **C.** $y = -3x - 7$

B. $y = -7x + 3$ **D.** $y = 7x - 3$

6 What is the slope of a line parallel to m?

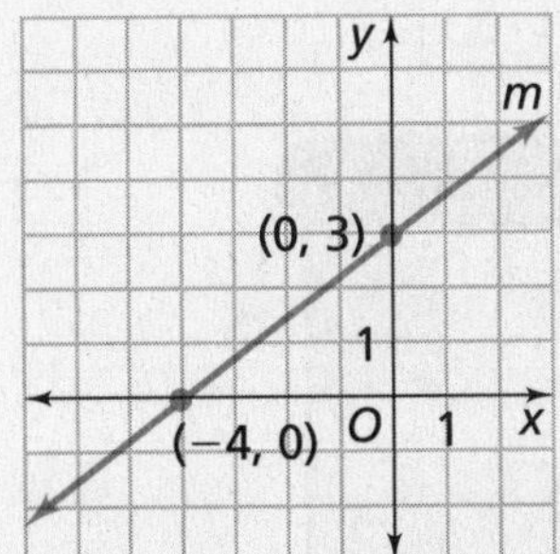

A. $-\frac{4}{3}$ **B.** $\frac{4}{3}$ **C.** $-\frac{3}{4}$ **D.** 0.75

7 Which equation could not represent a line parallel to the graph of $y = -2.5x + 1$?

A. $y = -2.5x + 3$ **C.** $y = -2.5x - 1$

B. $y = 2.5x + 1$ **D.** $y = -2.5x$

In Exercises 8–16, write an equation in slope-intercept form for the specified line, where possible.

8 the line containing A (0, 7) and B (7, 0)

9 the line containing C (3, −7) and D (−3, 5)

10 slope: 2; containing P (4, 5)

11 slope: −0.6; containing Z (−1, 1)

12 slope: 0; y-intercept −7

13 no slope; x-intercept −11

14 containing H (2, 2) and parallel to the graph of $y = x - 3$

15 containing A (−2, −2) and parallel to the graph of $y = 2x - 1$

16 containing M (1, 4) and perpendicular to the graph of $y = -\frac{2}{3}x + 5$

In Exercises 17–22, solve the problem. Clearly show all necessary work.

17 What are the coordinates of the point where the line containing K (−3, 5) and L (5, −4) crosses the y-axis?

18 Is the relationship between y and x linear? Explain your answer.

x	0	4	8	12
y	2	5	8	11

19 Write an equation in standard form for this graph.

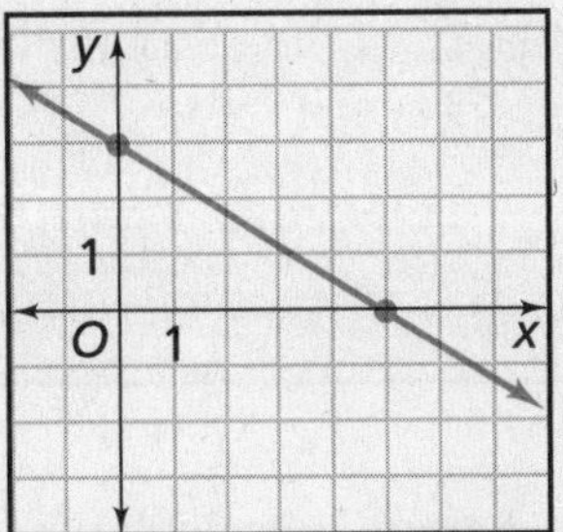

20 A student can work at a job that pays \$4 an hour for 25 hours to earn \$100 or can work at a second job that pays \$5 per hour for 20 hours to earn \$100. If the student spends time at each job, find two other amounts of time at each job needed to earn \$100. Show your work.

21 Is S (93, 83) on the line containing P (−3, −1) and Q (5, 6)? Justify your response.

22 Is K (−90, −232) on the line shown below?

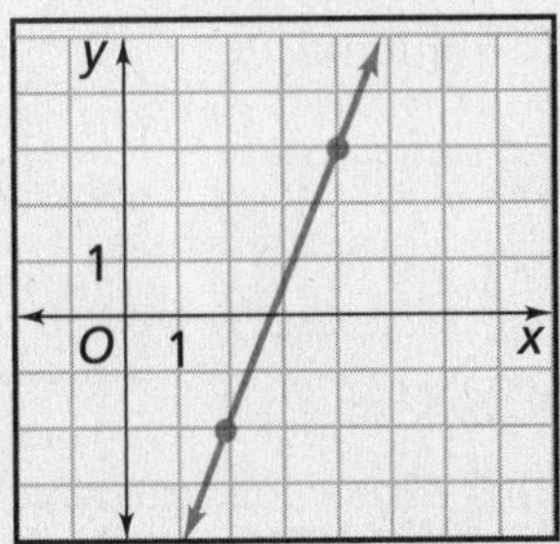

3.5 Graphs of Absolute Value Functions

ADP℠ Standards

L1.c Graph linear absolute value functions

You have learned that the **absolute value** of a number is its distance from zero on a number line. The definition of the absolute value is

$$abs(x) = |x| = \begin{cases} x \text{ if } x \geq 0 \\ -x \text{ if } x < 0 \end{cases} \quad or \quad abs(x) = |x| = \begin{cases} x \text{ if } x \text{ is positive or zero} \\ \text{the opposite of } x \text{ if } x \text{ is negative} \end{cases}$$

The shape of the graph of the absolute value function $y = |x|$ is a **V.** The vertex of the absolute value function is the point where the function changes direction. The table gives certain values of the absolute value function.

If you look at the table of values for this function, you will see that if x is negative, y is the opposite of x and if x is positive, y is equal to x.

The coefficient of the absolute value term determines the shape of the graph.

x	y
−3	3
−2	2
−1	1
0	0
1	1
2	2
3	3

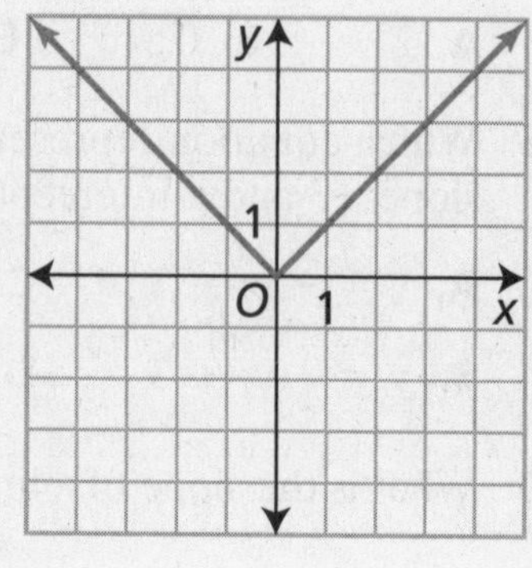

Shapes of Absolute Value Graphs

If the cofficient of the absolute value term of the function is positive, the **V** points down; if the coefficient is negative, the **V** points up.

- If $y = a|x|$, the graph is narrower.
- If $y = \frac{1}{a}|x|$, the graph is wider.

You can use a graphing calculator to graph the $y = abs(x)$ function by entering it into the function list, selecting an appropriate window, and pressing the GRAPH key.

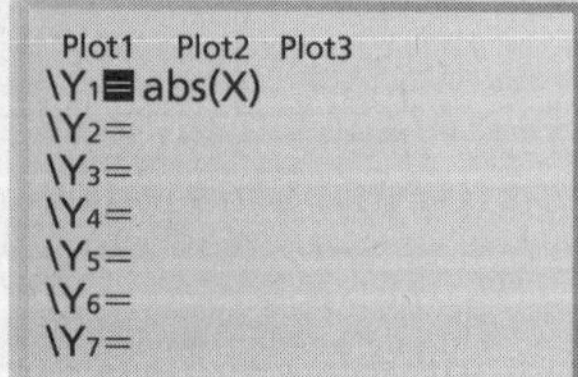

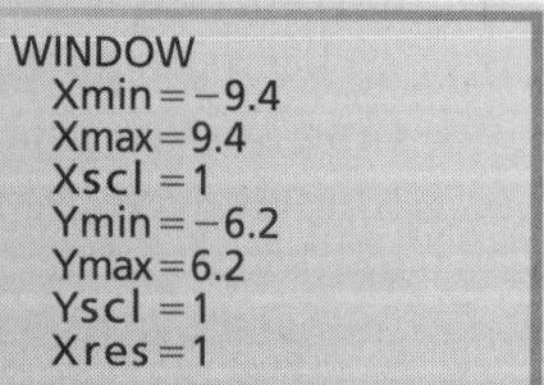

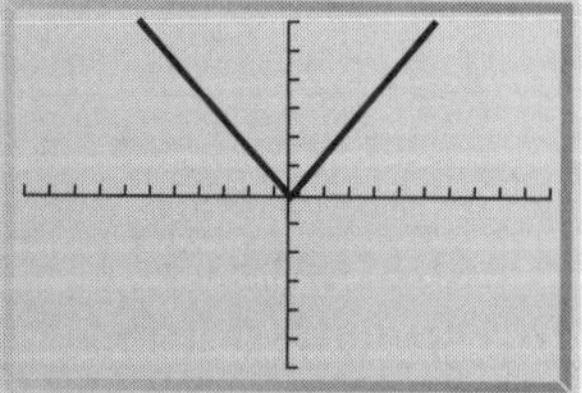

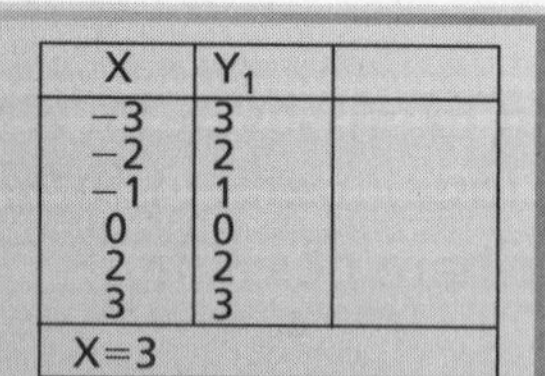

X	Y_1	
−3	3	
−2	2	
−1	1	
0	0	
2	2	
3	3	
X=3		

The absolute value functions $y = -|x|$, $y = 3|x|$, and $y = \frac{1}{3}|x|$ graphed below show how the shape of the graph changes with the value of the coefficient of the absolute value term.

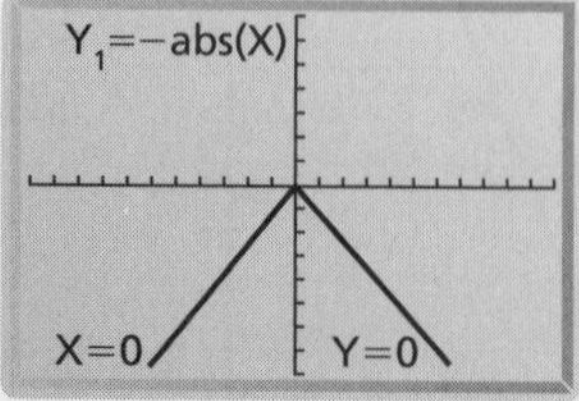

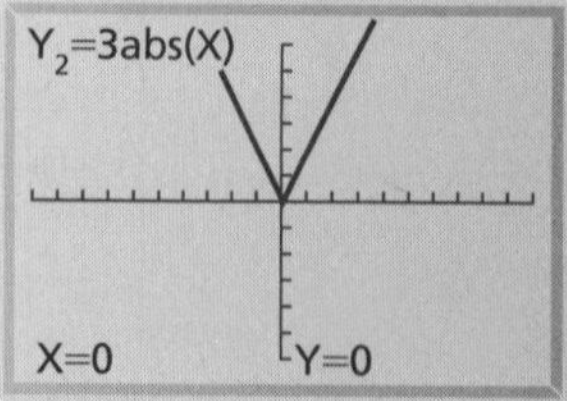

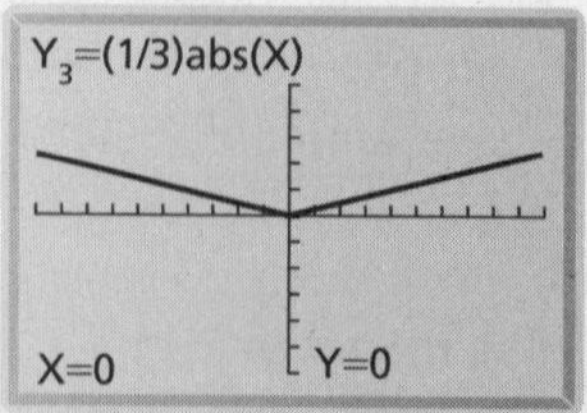

The vertex of the absolute value function is the point where the function changes direction.

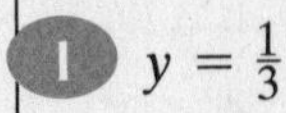

EXAMPLES 1 and 2 **Graphing absolute value functions**

Visit: PearsonSchool.com
Web Code: ayp-0130

Use a table to construct the graph of the function.

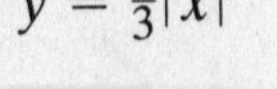

1 $y = \frac{1}{3}|x|$

■ **SOLUTION**

x	y
-3	1
-2	$\frac{2}{3}$
-1	$\frac{1}{3}$
0	0
1	$\frac{1}{3}$
2	$\frac{2}{3}$
3	1

2 $y = -2|x|$

■ **SOLUTION**

x	y
-3	-6
-2	-4
-1	-2
0	0
1	-2
2	-4
3	-6

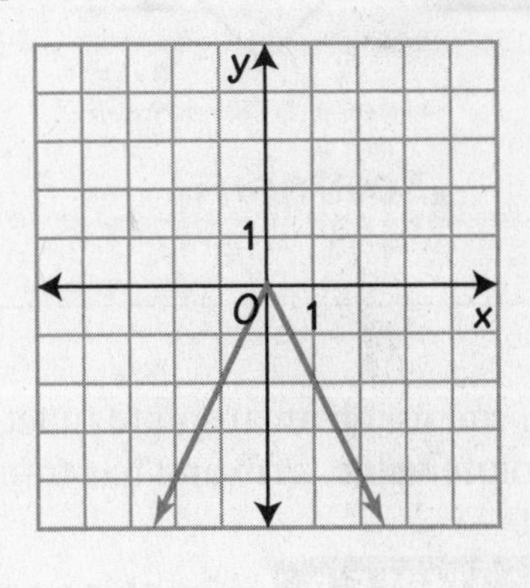

A **translation** is a shift of a graph vertically, horizontally, or both. The translated graph is the same size and shape as the original but is in a different position in the plane.

Go Online
PearsonSchool.com

Visit: PearsonSchool.com
Web Code: ayp-0225
ayp-0226

Graphs of Absolute Value Functions

- If $y = |x + a|$, the graph translates a units to the left.
- If $y = |x - a|$, the graph translates a units to the right.
- If $y = |x| + a$, the graph translates a units up.
- If $y = |x| - a$, the graph translates a units down.

EXAMPLES 3 through 5 **Graphing absolute value functions**

Graph the following functions on a calculator.

3 $y = |x + 3|$

■ **SOLUTION**

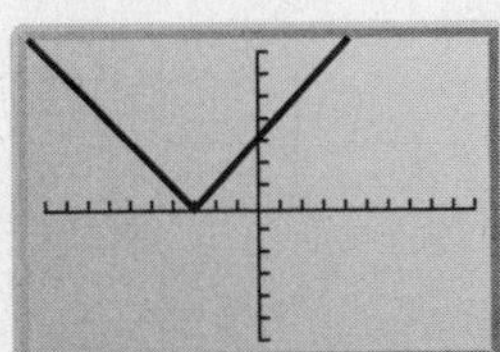

4 $y = |x - 3|$

■ **SOLUTION**

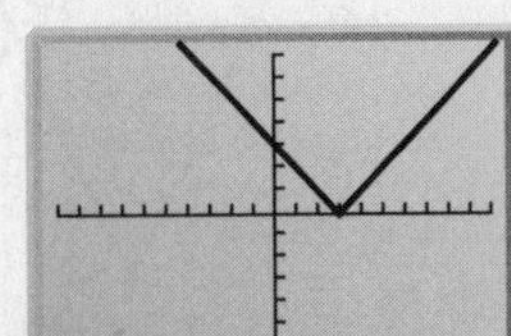

5 $y = |x| + 3$

■ **SOLUTION**

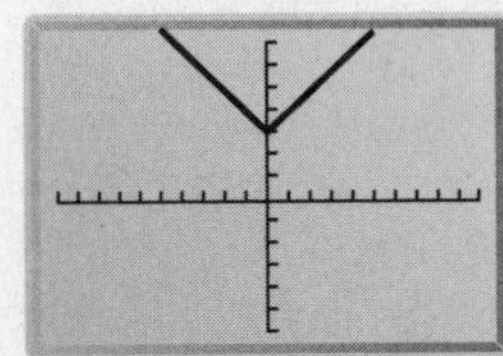

You can also write an equation of an absolute value function from its graph.

EXAMPLES 6 through 8 **Writing an equation of an absolute value function from its graph**

Write an equation for each translation of $y = |x|$ shown below.

6

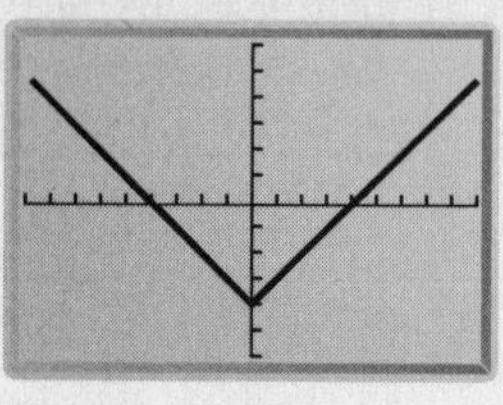

■ **SOLUTION**

$y = |x| - 4$

7

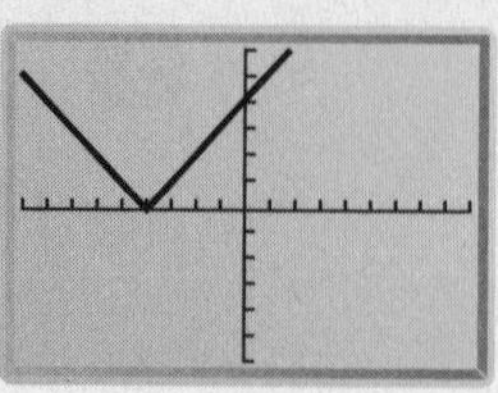

■ **SOLUTION**

$y = |x + 4|$

8

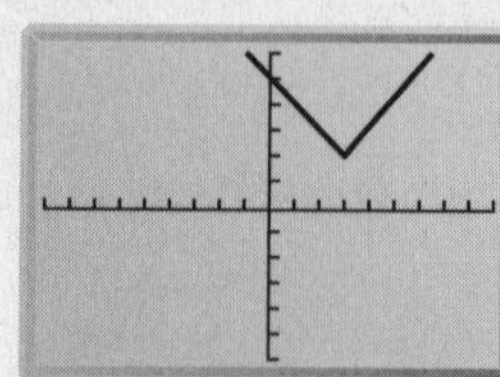

■ **SOLUTION**

$y = |x - 3| + 2$

You can graph an absolute function that has a constant coefficient in the absolute value term and has translations one step at a time.

EXAMPLE 9 **Graphing an absolute value function in multiple steps**

9 Graph the function $y = 2|x + 1| - 4$.

■ **SOLUTION**

Step 1

Graph the function $y = |x + 1|$. This is a translation of the graph of $y = |x|$ to the left 1 unit.

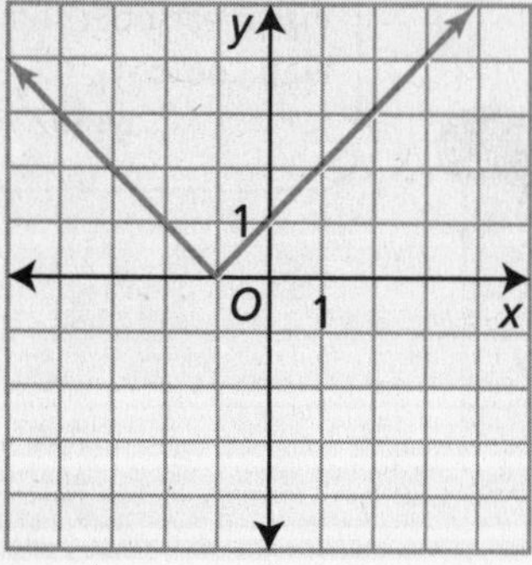

Step 2

Graph the function $y = 2|x + 1|$. Because the coefficient 2 is greater than 1, the graph is narrower. The table shows several values of the function.

x	y
−3	4
−2	2
−1	0
0	2
1	4

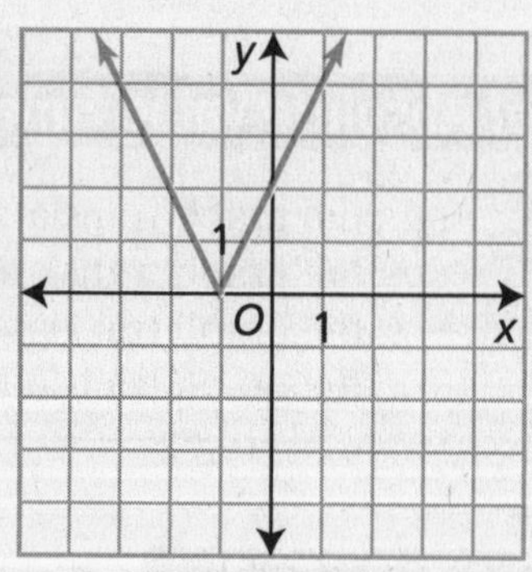

Step 3

Finally, graph $y = 2|x + 1| - 4$. This is a translation of the graph in Step 2 down 4 units.

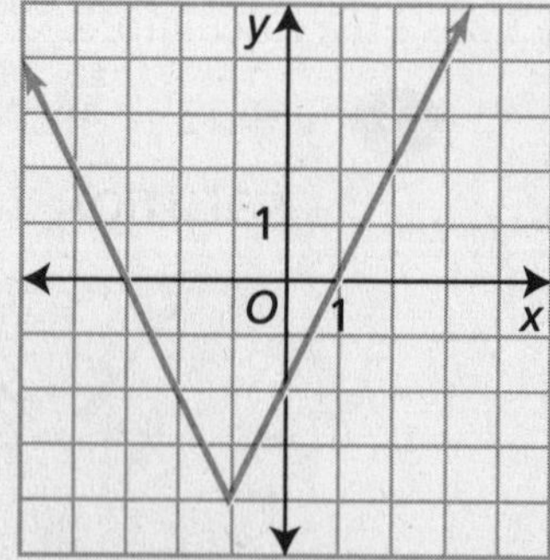

Practice

Choose the letter preceding the word or expression that best completes the statement or answers the question.

In Exercises 1–2, use the graph below.

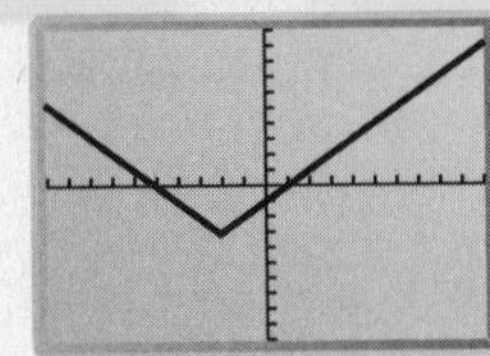

1 Which statement best describes the translation of $y = |x|$ shown in the graph above?

A. 2 units up, 3 units left

B. 2 units left, 3 units down

C. 2 units down, 3 units left

D. 2 units right, 3 units right

2 Which equation represents the graph?

A. $y = |x + 2| - 3$

B. $y = |x + 3| - 2$

C. $y = |x - 2| + 3$

D. $y = |x - 3| + 2$

3 Which of the following has a vertex of (4, 0)?

A. $y = |x| + 4$ C. $y = |x + 4|$

B. $y = |x| - 4$ D. $y = |x - 4|$

4 Which equation has a graph that is narrower than $y = \frac{9}{2}|x|$?

A. $y = 2|x|$ C. $y = |x|$

B. $y = 9|x|$ D. $y = \frac{2}{9}|x|$

5 Which equation has a graph that opens downwards?

A. $y = |x - 3|$ C. $y = |x| - 3$

B. $y = |-x| + 3$ D. $y = -|x| + 3$

In Exercises 6–13, graph each function and state its vertex.

6 $y = |x| + 2$ 7 $y = |x - 2|$

8 $y = |x| - 5$ 9 $y = |x - 1| + 3$

10 $y = -|x| + 1$ 11 $y = 4|x|$

12 $y = -|x - 3|$ 13 $y = -\frac{1}{2}|x|$

In Exercises 14–19, write an equation for each translation of $y = |x|$.

14 9 units up

15 6 units down

16 right 9 units

17 left 0.5 units

18

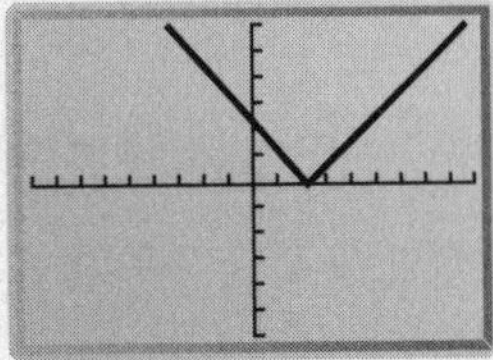

19

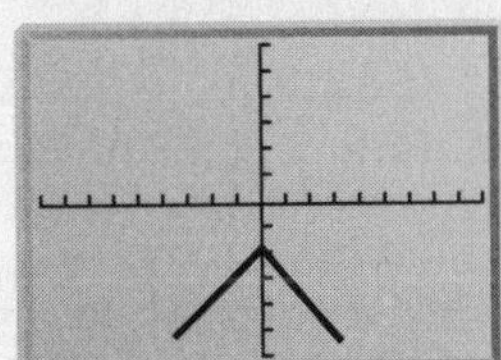

In Exercises 20–22, solve the problem. Clearly show all necessary work.

20 Describe the translation that shifts the graph of $y = |x + 1|$ to a graph that has a vertex at (3, 4).

21 Find the equations of two absolute values graphs which have a y-intercept of 3.

22 Describe the values of x such that the graph of $y = |x - 3|$ is the same as the graph of $y = x - 3$.

3.6 Systems of Linear Equations

ADP[SM] Standards

L2.d Solve systems of linear equations

L2.e Model linear equations and inequalities

A **system of equations in two variables** is a set of equations in the same two variables as illustrated at the right. You can use a single brace { to indicate that a collection of equations is a system.

$$\begin{cases} x + y = 30 \\ x - y = 8 \end{cases}$$

EXAMPLES 1 and 2 Recognizing and representing a situation as a system of equations

1 The sum of two numbers x and y is 26. Twice x minus y equals 16. Which system could not represent this situation?

A. $\begin{cases} x + y = 26 \\ 2x - y = 16 \end{cases}$ **B.** $\begin{cases} 2x - y = 16 \\ x + y = 26 \end{cases}$ **C.** $\begin{cases} 26 = x + y \\ 16 = 2x - y \end{cases}$ **D.** $\begin{cases} x + y = 16 \\ 2x - y = 26 \end{cases}$

■ **SOLUTION**

The sum of two numbers is 26. $x + y = 26$

Twice x minus y equals 16. $2x - y = 16$

Only choice **D** does not contain these equations. The correct choice is D.

2 Club members at the Queen Video Store pay \$24 to be members and pay \$4 for each video rental. Those who are not members rent videos for \$5.50 each. Represent total expense in terms of videos rented as a system of equations.

■ **SOLUTION**

Let n represent the number of videos rented. Let c represent total cost.

Member expense c: $4n + 24$ $c = 4n + 24$

Nonmember expense c: $5.5n$ $c = 5.5n$

$$\begin{cases} c = 4n + 24 \\ c = 5.5n \end{cases}$$

A **solution to a system of equations** in two variables x and y is any ordered pair (x, y) that makes each equation in the system true.

EXAMPLE 3 Verifying a solution to a system of equations

3 Which ordered pair (a, b) is a solution to $\begin{cases} a + 2b = 12 \\ 2a - 3b = -25 \end{cases}$?

A. (7, −2) **B.** (−2, 7) **C.** (4, 4) **D.** (−8, 3)

■ **SOLUTION**

Test each ordered pair in each equation.

A. (7, −2) $\begin{cases} 7 + 2(-2) \neq 12 \\ 2(7) - 3(-2) \neq -25 \end{cases}$ ✗

B. (−2, 7) $\begin{cases} -2 + 2(7) = 12 \\ 2(-2) - 3(7) = -25 \end{cases}$ ✔

C. (4, 4) $\begin{cases} 4 + 2(4) = 12 \\ 2(4) - 3(4) \neq -25 \end{cases}$ ✗

D. (−8, 3) $\begin{cases} -8 + 2(3) \neq 12 \\ 2(-8) - 3(3) = -25 \end{cases}$ ✗

The correct choice is B.

By graphing each equation in a system of equations, you can approximate the coordinates of any solution.

EXAMPLE 4 Recognizing estimates of solutions to a system of equations

Which best represents the coordinates of the point of intersection of these lines?

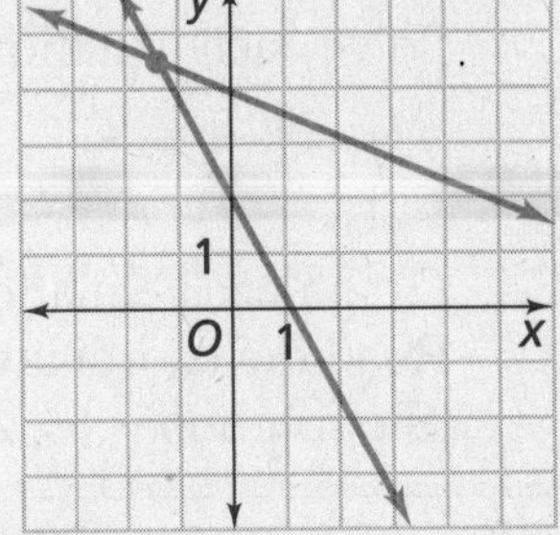

A. x is between -2 and -1.
y is between 3 and 4.

B. $x = -1.25$
$y = 4.\overline{3}$

C. x is between -3 and -2.
y is between 4 and 5.

D. x is between -2 and -1.
y is between 4 and 5.

■ **SOLUTION**

The x-coordinate is more than 1 unit but less than 2 units left of the origin.
The y-coordinate is more than 4 units but less than 5 units above the origin.
No further claim can be made of the solution. The correct choice is D.

You can use a graphing calculator to find more accurate solutions to systems of equations.

EXAMPLE 5 Finding a solution to a system of equations by graphing

Solve the system $\begin{cases} y = 2x + 3 \\ y = -3x - 1 \end{cases}$.

■ **SOLUTION**

- Enter $y = 2x + 3$ and $y = -3x - 1$ into the function list.
- Set an appropriate window.
- Press 2nd CALC #5Intersect.
- Choose the functions in response to the prompts.
- Enter a guess.
- The solution is displayed

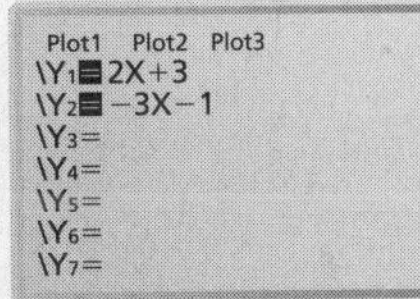

WINDOW
Xmin=−4.7
Xmax=4.7
Xscl=1
Ymin=−3.1
Ymax=3.1
Yscl=1
Xres=1

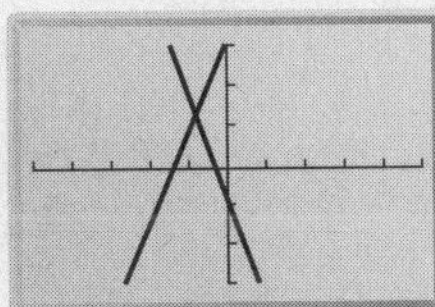

CALCULATE
1: value
2: zero
3: minimum
4: maximum
5: intersect
6: dy/dx
7: ∫f(x)dx

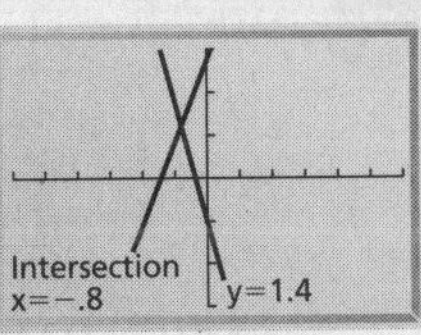

The solution is $(-0.8, 1.4)$.

You may have a system of equations in which y is not written in terms of x. To solve by graphing, first solve each equation for y.

$$\begin{cases} x + y = 8 \\ x - 2y = 2 \end{cases}$$

$x + y = 8$
$y = -x + 8$

$x - 2y = 2$
$y = 0.5x - 1$

EXAMPLE 6 Solving systems by solving for the same variable

6 Solve $\begin{cases} x + y = 8 \\ x - 2y = 2 \end{cases}$ graphically.

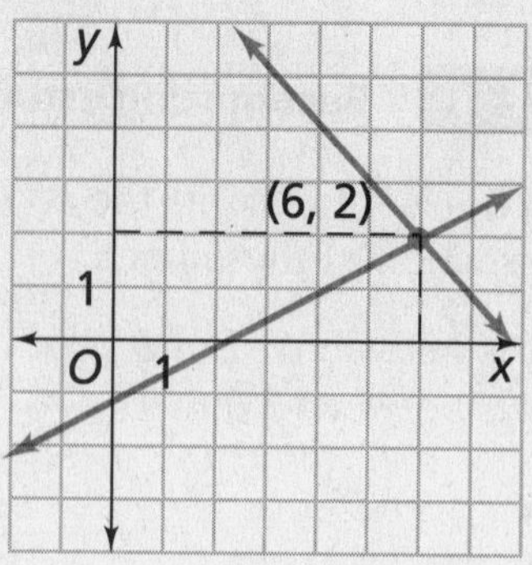

■ **SOLUTION**

Solve each equation for y in terms of x.

$$\begin{cases} x + y = 8 \\ x - 2y = 2 \end{cases} \rightarrow \begin{cases} y = -x + 8 \\ y = \frac{1}{2}x - 1 \end{cases}$$

Graph each equation on the same coordinate plane.
Read the coordinates of the point of intersection.
The solution is (6, 2), or $x = 6$ and $y = 2$.

Not every pair of equations in the same two variables has a solution.

- If the system has exactly one solution, it is called **independent.**

$$\begin{cases} y = x - 2 \\ y = -2x + 10 \end{cases}$$

- If the graphs of the equations are **distinct** and **intersect,** then the system is independent.

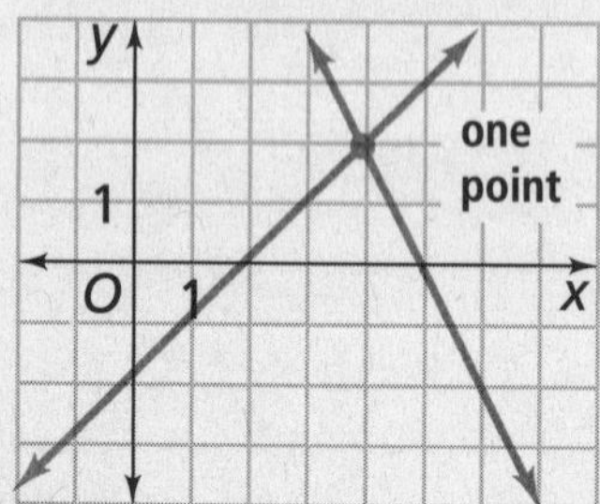

- If the system has infinitely many solutions, it is called **dependent.**

$$\begin{cases} y = x - 2 \\ x - y = 2 \end{cases}$$

- If the graphs of the equations **coincide,** then the system is dependent.

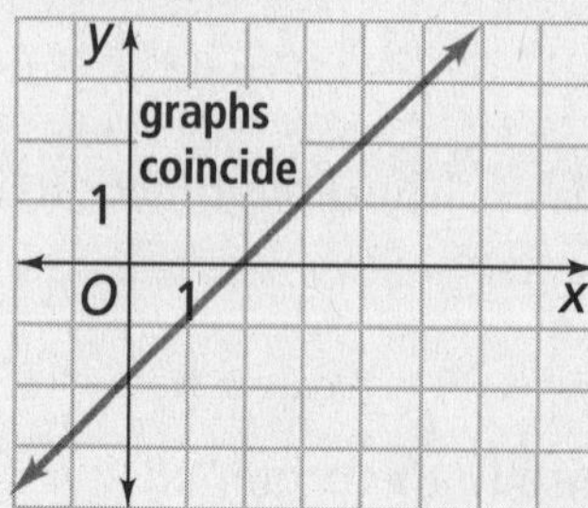

- If the system has no solution, it is called **inconsistent.**

$$\begin{cases} y = -x + 2 \\ y = -x \end{cases}$$

- If the graphs of the equations are parallel lines, then the system is inconsistent.

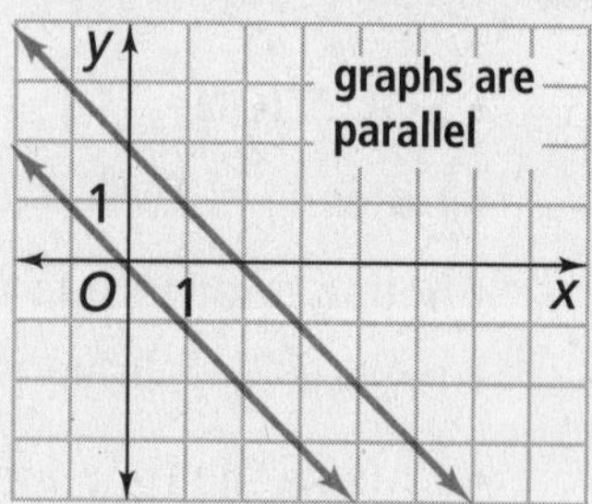

EXAMPLE 7 Identifying independent, dependent, and inconsistent systems

7 Which system of equations is independent?

A. $\begin{cases} x + y = 4 \\ 2x + y = 6 \end{cases}$ **B.** $\begin{cases} 2x + y = 4 \\ 2x + y = 9 \end{cases}$ **C.** $\begin{cases} x - y = 2 \\ 3x - 3y = 6 \end{cases}$ **D.** $\begin{cases} x - y = 0 \\ 3x - 3y = 0 \end{cases}$

■ **SOLUTION**

In each system, solve for y. Read slope and y-intercept.

A. $\begin{cases} y = -1x + 4 \\ y = -2x + 6 \end{cases}$ **B.** $\begin{cases} y = -2x + 4 \\ y = -2x + 9 \end{cases}$ **C.** $\begin{cases} y = -1x - 2 \\ y = -1x - 2 \end{cases}$ **D.** $\begin{cases} y = 1x \\ y = 1x \end{cases}$

The graphs in choice **A** have unequal slopes and unequal y-intercepts. The graphs intersect in exactly one point.
The correct choice is A.

Visit: PearsonSchool.com
Web Code: ayp-0510

Practice

Choose the letter preceding the word or expression that best completes the statement or answers the question.

1 Which ordered pair is the solution to $\begin{cases} 2x - 5y = -11 \\ 2x - y = 1 \end{cases}$?

A. $(-8, -1)$ **C.** $(3, 2)$

B. $(3, 5)$ **D.** $(2, 3)$

2 Which best describes the solution to the system whose graphs are shown here?

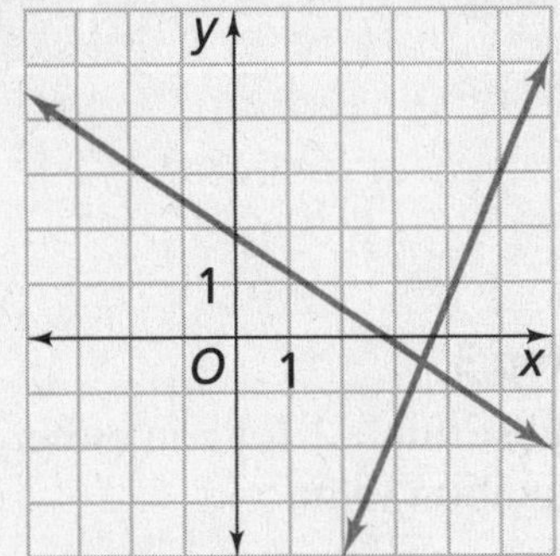

A. x is between 3 and 4; y is between 0 and 1.

B. x is between 3 and 4; y is between 0 and -1.

C. x is between -4 and -3; y is between 0 and 1.

D. x is between -4 and -3; y is between 0 and -1.

3 Which best describes $\begin{cases} y = 2x - 5 \\ y = 2x - 13 \end{cases}$?

A. No solution; the slopes are equal and the y-intercepts are unequal.

B. One solution; the slopes are equal and the y-intercepts are unequal.

C. Two solutions; the slopes are equal and the y-intercepts are unequal.

D. Infinite solutions; the slopes are equal and the y-intercepts are equal.

In Exercises 4–7, use graphs of the equations in each system to find the coordinates of any point of intersection.

4 $\begin{cases} x + y = 4 \\ -2x + y = 1 \end{cases}$ 5 $\begin{cases} y = 2x + 5 \\ y = 1 \end{cases}$

6 $\begin{cases} y = 3x + 1 \\ y = 4x + 2 \end{cases}$ 7 $\begin{cases} -7x + 5y = 10 \\ -2x + 5y = -15 \end{cases}$

In Exercises 8–11, represent each situation as a system of two equations in two variables. Identify the variables.

8 The larger of two numbers decreased by the smaller is 5. Twice the smaller number increased by the larger number is 41.

9 The Health Gym charges \$50 plus \$20 per month for membership. Chyna's Health Club charges \$80 plus \$15 per month for membership.

10 Kisha has \$1.75 in nickels and dimes. She has 23 coins in all.

11 One number is twice another number. Their sum is 21.

In Exercises 12–16, solve the problem. Clearly show all necessary work.

12 Graph the equations in the system $\begin{cases} x + y = 7 \\ 3x - y = 7 \end{cases}$. Find consecutive integers between which the x- and y-coordinates of the solution lie.

13 What are the coordinates of the solution to the system whose graph is shown here?

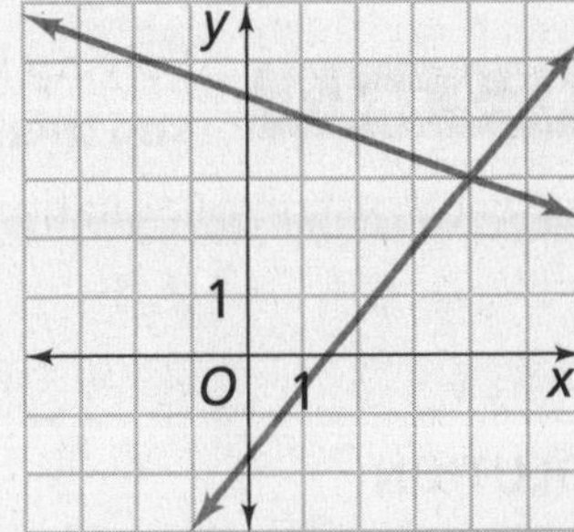

14 Is the system $\begin{cases} y = -2.5x - 3 \\ y = 2.2x - 10 \end{cases}$ independent, dependent, or inconsistent? Explain.

15 Is the system $\begin{cases} y = 3x + 5 \\ 4y = 12x + 20 \end{cases}$ independent, dependent, or inconsistent? Explain.

16 Graph $y = 1.5x - 1$, $x = 4$, and $y = -2$ on the same coordinate plane. Find the area of the triangle enclosed by the graphs.

3.7 Solving Systems of Equations

ADP℠ Standards

L2.d Solve systems of linear equations

L2.e Model linear equations and inequalities

In the system of equations at the right, y is given in terms of x in each equation. Although you can solve this system graphically, there is an algebraic method you can use. It is called the **substitution method.**

$$\begin{cases} y = -x + 4 \\ y = 2x + 7 \end{cases}$$

When you use the substitution method, you transform a pair of equations in two variables into one equation in one variable.

If $y = -x + 4$ and $y = 2x + 7$, then $-x + 4 = 2x + 7$.

The solution to $-x + 4 = 2x + 7$ gives the value of x. The following example shows how to continue to get the complete solution.

Note

The Transitive Property of Equality states the following: If $a = b$ and $b = c$, then $a = c$.

EXAMPLE 1 **Solving by simple substitution**

1 Solve $\begin{cases} y = -x + 4 \\ y = 2x + 7 \end{cases}$ by substitution.

■ SOLUTION

Step 1

Equate the expressions for y.

$-x + 4 = 2x + 7$

Step 2

Solve $-x + 4 = 2x + 7$.

$-x + 4 = 2x + 7$

$x = -1$

Step 3

Substitute -1 for x in either equation to find y.

$y = -(-1) + 4$

$= 5$

The solution to the system is $(-1, 5)$.

Check: $\begin{cases} -(-1) + 4 = 5 \checkmark \\ 2(-1) + 7 = 5 \checkmark \end{cases}$

Sometimes you must first solve one of the equations for a specific value before you can use the substitution method.

Go Online PearsonSchool.com

Visit: PearsonSchool.com

Web Code: ayp-0231

EXAMPLES 2 and 3 **Solving by isolating one variable and then using substitution**

Solve each system of equations by substitution.

2 $\begin{cases} x + y = 7 \\ y = 2x - 3 \end{cases}$

■ SOLUTION

$x + (2x - 3) = 7$

$3x - 3 = 7$

$x = \frac{10}{3}$

If $\frac{10}{3} + y = 7$, $y = \frac{11}{3}$. Solution: $\left(\frac{10}{3}, \frac{11}{3}\right)$

Check: $\begin{cases} \frac{10}{3} + \frac{11}{3} = \frac{21}{3} = 7 \checkmark \\ 2\left(\frac{10}{3}\right) - 3 = \frac{20}{3} - \frac{9}{3} = \frac{11}{3} \checkmark \end{cases}$

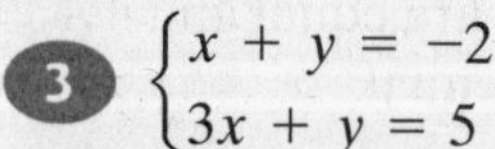

3 $\begin{cases} x + y = -2 \\ 3x + y = 5 \end{cases}$

■ SOLUTION

Solve $3x + y = 5$ for y. $y = -3x + 5$.

$x + (-3x + 5) = -2$

$-2x + 5 = -2$

$x = \frac{7}{2}$

If $\frac{7}{2} + y = -2$, $y = -\frac{11}{2}$. Solution: $\left(\frac{7}{2}, -\frac{11}{2}\right)$

Check: $\begin{cases} \frac{7}{2} + \left(-\frac{11}{2}\right) = -\frac{4}{2} = -2 \checkmark \\ 3\left(\frac{7}{2}\right) + \left(-\frac{11}{2}\right) = \frac{21}{2} - \frac{11}{2} = \frac{10}{2} = 5 \checkmark \end{cases}$

You can use the substitution method to solve problems involving systems of equations.

EXAMPLES 4 and 5 Using substitution to solve problems

4 Which system of equations has no solution?

A. $\begin{cases} y = x - 3 \\ 2x - 3y = 5 \end{cases}$ **B.** $\begin{cases} y = -5x - 3 \\ 2x - 2y = 5 \end{cases}$ **C.** $\begin{cases} y = x - 2.5 \\ 2x - 2y = -5 \end{cases}$ **D.** $\begin{cases} y = x - 3 \\ 2x - 2y = 5 \end{cases}$

■ **SOLUTION**

In choice **D,** $2x - 2(x - 3) = 5$. So, $6 = 5$. Choice D has no solution.

5 Angela has 30 nickels and dimes totaling \$2.40. How many of each has she?

■ **SOLUTION**

Let n and d represent the number of nickels and dimes, respectively.

In all, she has 30 coins. → $n + d = 30$

In pennies, total worth is 240 cents. → $5n + 10d = 240$

Note

The value of all the nickels is $5n$ cents and the dimes are worth $10d$ cents.

Use substitution to eliminate d from $5n + 10d = 240$.

$$5n + 10(30 - n) = 240 \quad \rightarrow \text{ because } d = 30 - n$$
$$-5n = -60$$
$$n = 12$$

Therefore, $d = 30 - 12 = 18$. So, Angela has 12 nickels and 18 dimes.

The **addition-multiplication method,** or **elimination method,** is a useful solution method if the variables in a system have coefficients other than 1. Use the properties of equality to make an **equivalent system,** a system that has the same solution set.

To make an equivalent system you multiply each term of an equation by a value that results in coefficients of matching terms that are opposites of each other.

In the system of equations below, you would multiply both sides of the second equation by -2.

$$\begin{cases} 4x + 2y = 7 \\ 2x + 5y = 4 \end{cases} \longrightarrow \begin{cases} 4x + 2y = 7 \\ -4x - 10y = -8 \end{cases}$$

EXAMPLE 6 Identifying equivalent systems of equations

6 Which system of equations is equivalent to $\begin{cases} -3x - 5y = -3 \\ 5x - 15y = 7 \end{cases}$?

A. $\begin{cases} -6x - 10y = -3 \\ 5x - 15y = 7 \end{cases}$ **B.** $\begin{cases} -3x - 5y = -2 \\ 5x - 15y = 7 \end{cases}$ **C.** $\begin{cases} -9x - 15y = -9 \\ 5x - 15y = 7 \end{cases}$ **D.** $\begin{cases} 6x - 10y = -6 \\ 5x - 15y = 7 \end{cases}$

■ **SOLUTION**

The system in choice C is equivalent to the given system.

$3(-3x - 5y) = -9x - 15y$ and $3(-3) = -9$ ✔

In the following example, the coefficients of each of the x-terms are opposites. When you add the terms of an equation, the x-term will be eliminated. Then you solve a simple one-variable equation.

Visit: PearsonSchool.com
Web Code: ayp-0233

EXAMPLE 7 **Solving a system with coefficients of one variable being opposites**

Solve $\begin{cases} -2x + 7y = 11 \\ 2x - 5y = -1 \end{cases}$ using the addition-multiplication method.

■ SOLUTION

Step 1 Use the Addition Property of Equality.

$$\begin{array}{rcr} -2x + 7y & = & 11 \\ +\ 2x - 5y & = & +\ -1 \\ \hline 2y & = & 10 \end{array}$$

$$y = 5$$

Step 2 If $y = 5$, then $-2x + 7(5) = 11$. So, $x = 12$.

The solution is $(12, 5)$.

You can carefully consider the equations of a system to determine which equation to rewrite.

Go Online
PearsonSchool.com
Visit: PearsonSchool.com
Web Code: ayp-0234

EXAMPLE 8 **Using addition and one multiplier to solve a system**

Solve $\begin{cases} 4a + 2b = 7 \\ 2a + 5b = 4 \end{cases}$ by using addition and multiplication.

■ SOLUTION

Step 1 Multiply each side of $2a + 5b = 4$ by -2.

$$-4a - 10b = -8$$

Step 2 Add.

$$\begin{array}{rcr} 4a + 2b & = & 7 \\ + -4a - 10b & = & + -8 \\ \hline -8b & = & -1 \end{array}$$

$$b = \frac{1}{8}$$

Step 3 If $b = \frac{1}{8}$, then

$$2a + 5\left(\frac{1}{8}\right) = 4.$$

$$a = \frac{27}{16}$$

The solution to the system is $\left(\frac{27}{16}, \frac{1}{8}\right)$.

Sometimes you need to use the Multiplication Property of Equality twice to solve a system of equations.

EXAMPLE 9 Using addition and two multipliers to solve a system

9 Solve $\begin{cases} 2x + 3y = 15 \\ 5x - 2y = -29 \end{cases}$ by using the addition-multiplication method.

■ **SOLUTION 1**

Solve by eliminating y.

$$\begin{cases} 2x + 3y = 15 \\ 5x - 2y = -29 \end{cases} \rightarrow \begin{cases} 2(2x + 3y) = 2(15) \\ 3(5x - 2y) = 3(-29) \end{cases} \rightarrow \begin{array}{rcr} 4x + 6y & = & 30 \\ +15x - 6y & = & +-87 \\ \hline 19x & = & -57 \end{array}$$

Therefore, $x = -3$. Substitute -3 for x in one of the given equations.

$$2(-3) + 3y = 15$$
$$y = 7$$

So, the solution is $(-3, 7)$.

■ **SOLUTION 2**

Solve by eliminating x.

$$\begin{cases} 2x + 3y = 15 \\ 5x - 2y = -29 \end{cases} \rightarrow \begin{cases} 5(2x + 3y) = 5(15) \\ -2(5x - 2y) = -2(-29) \end{cases} \rightarrow \begin{array}{rcr} 10x + 15y & = & 75 \\ -10x + 4y & = & +58 \\ \hline 19y & = & 133 \end{array}$$

Therefore, $y = 7$. Substitute 7 for y in one of the given equations.

$$5x - 2(7) = -29$$
$$x = -3$$

You find the same solution $(-3, 7)$ whether you eliminate x or y.

Check: $\begin{cases} 2(-3) + 3(7) = -6 + 21 = 15 \checkmark \\ 5(-3) - 2(7) = -15 - 14 = -29 \checkmark \end{cases}$

You can write a system of equations to solve many problems that involve two equations in two variables.

EXAMPLE 10 Writing a system of equations to solve a real-world problem

10 Bowling costs \$2.25 a game and video games cost \$0.50 each. Gianna bowls x games, plays y video games, and spends \$7.00. Ricardo bowls y games, plays x video games, and spends \$13.25. Write a system of equations that can be used to find how many of each game they play.

■ **SOLUTION**

The equation $2.25x + 0.50y = 7$ represents how Gianna spends her money and the equation $0.50x + 2.25y = 13.25$ represents how Ricardo spends his. Therefore, you can solve the following system of equations to find the number of each game they play.

$$\begin{cases} 2.25x + 0.50y = 7 \\ 0.50x + 2.25y = 13.25 \end{cases}$$

You can use a system of equations to solve problems that describe two equations.

EXAMPLE 11 Using the addition-multiplication method

11 Twice one integer plus 3 times a second integer equals 9. Five times the first integer plus 4 times the second integer equals 5. What are the numbers?

■ SOLUTION

Step 1 Write a system of equations.

Twice one integer m plus 3 times a second integer n equals 9. $\rightarrow 2m + 3n = 9$

Five times the first integer m plus 4 times the second integer n equals 5. $\rightarrow 5m + 4n = 5$

Step 2 Solve the system of equations.

Multiply by 5.
Multiply by -2.

$$\begin{cases} 2m + 3n = 9 \\ 5m + 4n = 5 \end{cases} \rightarrow \begin{cases} 10m + 15n = 45 \\ -10m - 8n = -10 \end{cases} \rightarrow \begin{array}{rr} 10m + 15n = & 45 \\ + -10m - 8n = & + -10 \\ \hline 7n = & 35 \end{array}$$

Therefore, $n = 5$. Substitute 5 for n in $2m + 3n = 9$ to find m.

$$2m + 3(5) = 9$$
$$m = -3$$

Step 3 Answer the question. The first number is -3. The second number is 5.

Check: $\begin{cases} 2(-3) + 3(5) = -6 + 15 = 9 \checkmark \\ 5(-3) + 4(5) = -15 + 20 = 5 \checkmark \end{cases}$

Practice

Choose the letter preceding the word or expression that best completes the statement or answers the question.

1 Which ordered pair (a, b) is the solution to $\begin{cases} b = 3.5a \\ b = 2a - 3 \end{cases}$?

A. (0, 0) **C.** (2, −3.5)
B. (2, −8) **D.** (−2, −7)

2 A line segment 15 inches long is separated into two smaller segments. The length y of the longer segment is 3 inches more than twice the length x of the shorter segment. Which system cannot represent this situation?

A. $\begin{cases} x + y = 15 \\ y = 2x + 3 \end{cases}$ **C.** $\begin{cases} x + y = 15 \\ x = 2y + 3 \end{cases}$

B. $\begin{cases} y = 2x + 3 \\ x + y = 15 \end{cases}$ **D.** $\begin{cases} y = 15 - x \\ y = 2x + 3 \end{cases}$

3 Which system of equations represents this situation?

Nikki has 20 dimes and quarters in all. Their total value is \$3.80.

Let d represent the number of dimes and q represent the number of quarters.

A. $\begin{cases} d + q = 20 \\ 25q + 10d = 3.80 \end{cases}$

B. $\begin{cases} d + q = 20 \\ d + q = 3.80 \end{cases}$

C. $\begin{cases} d + q = 20 \\ 10d + 25q = 3.80 \end{cases}$

D. $\begin{cases} d + q = 20 \\ 0.1d + 0.25q = 3.80 \end{cases}$

4 Which system of equations has the same solution as $\begin{cases} 5x - 3y = 24 \\ 2x - 7y = 11 \end{cases}$?

A. $\begin{cases} 10x - 6y = 48 \\ 2x - 7y = 11 \end{cases}$

B. $\begin{cases} 5x - 3y = 48 \\ 2x - 7y = 11 \end{cases}$

C. $\begin{cases} 10x - 6y = 24 \\ 2x - 7y = 11 \end{cases}$

D. $\begin{cases} 5x - 3y = 24 \\ 10x - 35y = 11 \end{cases}$

In Exercises 5–12, solve each system of equations.

5 $\begin{cases} x = 2y - 3 \\ 2x - 3y = -5 \end{cases}$

6 $\begin{cases} y = 4 - 4x \\ 3x + y = 5 \end{cases}$

7 $\begin{cases} x = 3y + 5 \\ y = 2x + 1 \end{cases}$

8 $\begin{cases} 2x + 3y = 0 \\ -2x + 5y = 8 \end{cases}$

9 $\begin{cases} 3x - 7y = 13 \\ 6x + 5y = 7 \end{cases}$

10 $\begin{cases} 2x + 3y = 21 \\ 5x - 2y = -14 \end{cases}$

11 $\begin{cases} 2x = y + 12 \\ 3x + 2y = -3 \end{cases}$

12 $\begin{cases} 5x = 4y + 15 \\ 6y = 3x - 9 \end{cases}$

In Exercises 13–20, use a system of equations to solve each problem.

13 The larger of two supplementary angles is 15° more than twice the measure of the smaller angle. Find each angle measure.

14 Top Tunes sells CDs for a single price and sells tapes for a single price. Bianna bought 3 CDs and 2 tapes for \$58. Ramon bought 1 CD and 4 tapes for \$46. Determine the selling price for 1 CD and for 1 tape.

15 The sum of two numbers is 70. The difference of the these numbers is 24. What are the numbers?

16 Tickets for the school play sell for \$3 for a student and \$5 for an adult. One night, 595 people bought tickets. The school took in \$1951. How many adult tickets and how many student tickets were sold?

17 There are 250 students in the freshman class. The number of girls is 20 fewer than twice the number of boys. How many boys and how many girls are in the class?

18 The length of a rectangular flower garden is 6 feet more than three times the width. The perimeter of the garden is 32 feet. What is the area of the garden?

19 Stefan has a collection of nickels, dimes, and quarters. In all, he has 24 coins. Seven of the coins are quarters. The total value of the collection is \$2.90. How many nickels and how many dimes does he have?

20 Delila has \$1200 in a savings account and in a checking account. The ratio of money in savings to money in checking is 3 to 2. Use a system of equations to find how much money is in each account.

In Exercises 21–25, solve the problem. Clearly show all necessary work.

21 For what value of k will the system of equations below have no solution? Explain.

$$\begin{cases} 2x - 4y = 6 \\ kx - 4y = 9 \end{cases}$$

22 The graphs of $kx + 2y = 2$ and $2x + hy = 10$ intersect at $(2, -2)$. Find h and k.

23 What are the coordinates of the point where the graphs of the equations below intersect?

$$3x - 5y = 4 \text{ and } 4x + 7y = 19$$

24 Find the measures in degrees of the angles indicated by x and y. The measure of angle y is 15 degrees more than 3 times the measure of angle x.

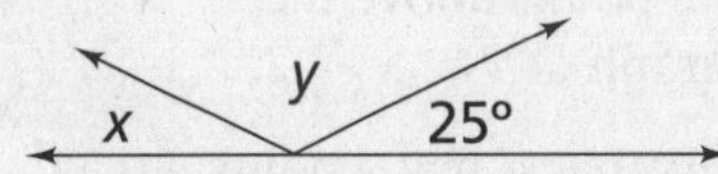

25 Find k such that the graphs of $y = 3x + 4$ and $y = kx - 5$ do not intersect.

3.8 Linear Inequalities in Two Variables

ADP℠ Standards

L2.c Graph two-variable linear inequalities

L2.e Model linear equations and inequalities

On a number line, the graph of $x \geq 3$ is a closed ray. In the coordinate plane, the graph of $x \geq 3$ is a **closed half-plane.** The graph of $x > 3$ is an **open half-plane.**

−3 −2 −1 0 1 2 3 4 5

The **boundary** of the graph is the line separating it from the rest of the plane.

- If the inequality contains $\leq$ or $\geq$, the boundary is part of the solution.

  $\leq$ or $\geq$ solid line

- If the inequality contains $>$ or $<$, the boundary is not part of the solution.

  $>$ or $<$ dashed line

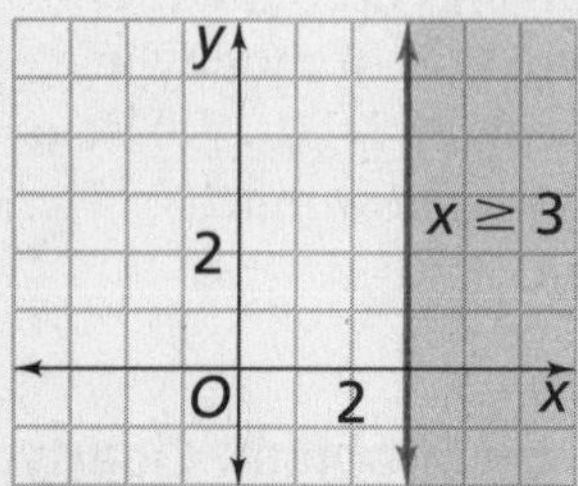

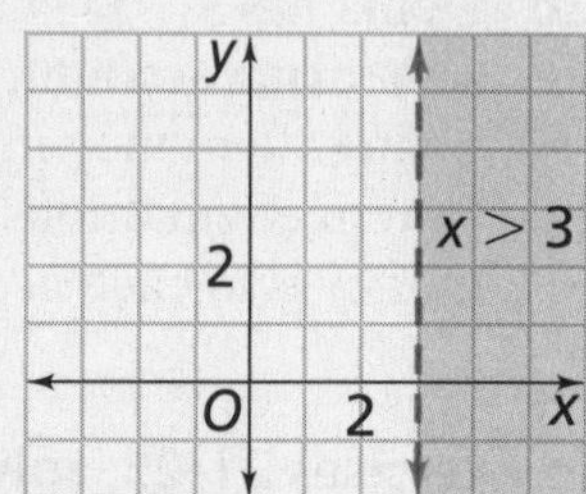

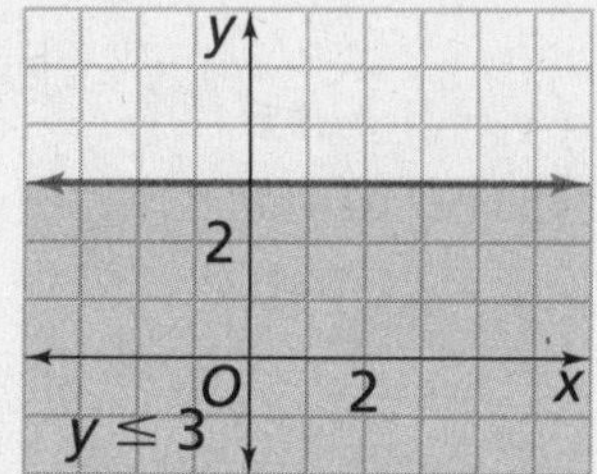

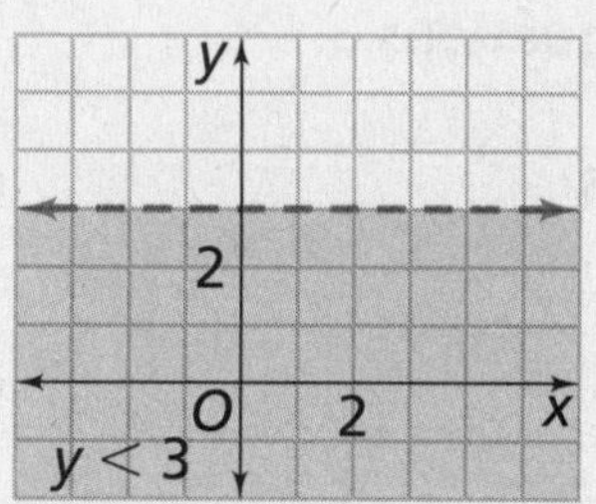

A **linear inequality in two variables** x and y is any inequality that can be written in one of these forms:

$$ax + by \geq c \qquad ax + by > c \qquad ax + by \leq c \qquad ax + by < c,$$

where a, b, and c are real numbers and not both a and b equal 0. A **solution to an inequality in two variables** is any ordered pair that makes the inequality true. The **graph of an inequality in two variables** is the set of the graphs of all solutions.

EXAMPLES 1 and 2 Graphing a linear inequality in two variables

Graph each linear inequality in two variables.

1 $y > x - 2$

■ SOLUTION

Graph $y = x - 2$ with a dashed line because the given inequality involves $>$. The solution region is all points above the graph of $y = x - 2$.

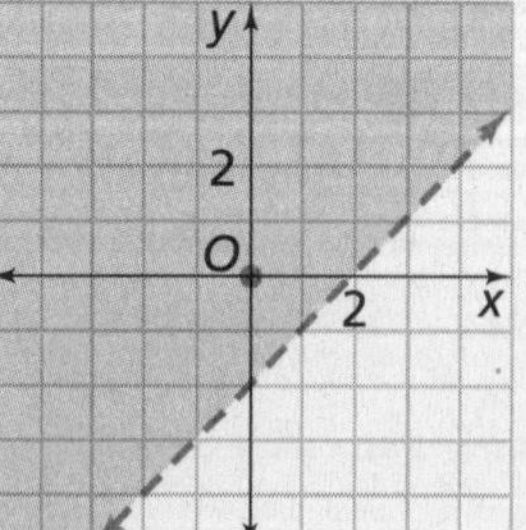

To check, test a point in the plane. For example, (0, 0) satisfies $y > x - 2$. So, it is in the solution region.

2 $y \leq -2x - 2$

■ SOLUTION

Graph $y = -2x - 2$ with a solid line because the given inequality involves $\leq$. The solution region is all points on or below the graph of $y = -2x - 2$.

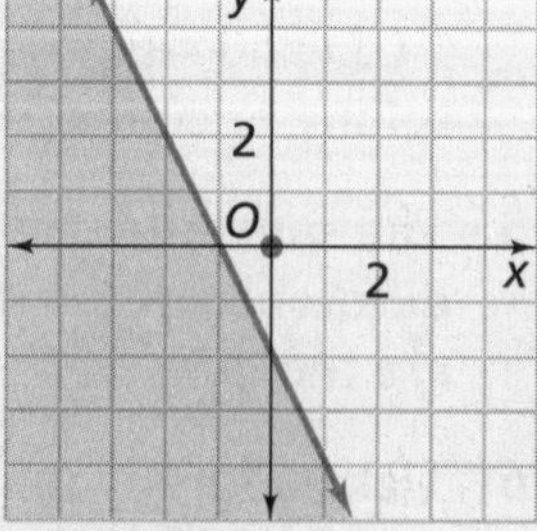

To check, test a point in the plane. For example, (0, 0) does not satisfy $y \leq -2x - 2$. So, it is not in the solution region.

Sometimes it is easier to solve the inequality for y before graphing.

EXAMPLES 3 and 4 Graphing a linear inequality in which y is not isolated

Graph each linear inequality in two variables.

3 $2x + 3y < 9$

■ **SOLUTION**

Solve for y. $y < -\frac{2}{3}x + 3$

Graph $y = -\frac{2}{3}x + 3$ with a dashed line. Shade the region below the line.

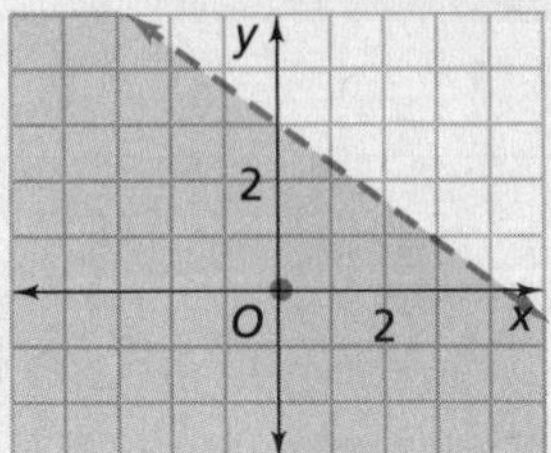

Because $(0, 0)$ satisfies $2x + 3y < 9$, the solution contains the origin.

4 $2x - 3y \geq 9$

■ **SOLUTION**

Solve for y. $y \leq \frac{2}{3}x - 3$

Graph $y = \frac{2}{3}x - 3$ with a solid line. Shade the line and the region below the line.

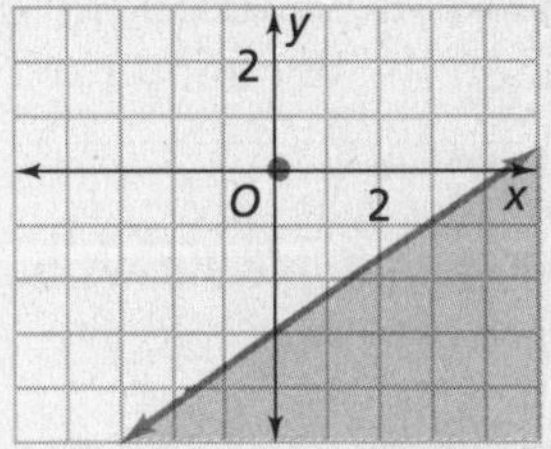

Because $(0, 0)$ does not satisfy $2x - 3y \geq 9$, the solution does not contain the origin.

A **system of inequalities in two variables** is a set of inequalities in those variables as illustrated below. A **solution to a system of inequalities** is any ordered pair that makes all of the inequalities in the system true.

$$\begin{cases} y \geq -x + 2 \\ x \geq 0 \\ y \geq 0 \end{cases}$$

EXAMPLE 5 Recognizing the correct solution region for a system

Which system of inequalities represents the solution region shown here?

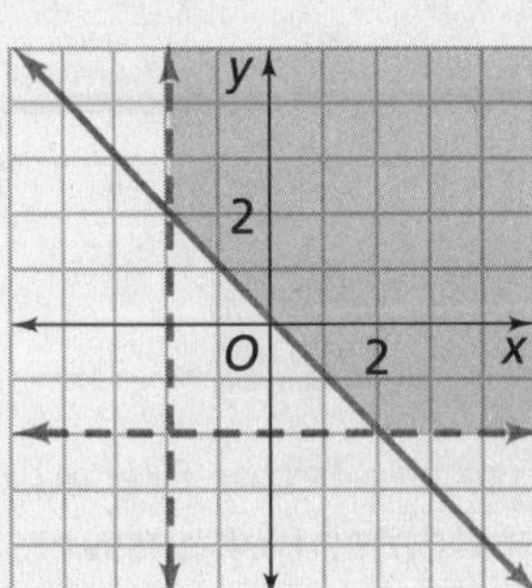

A. $\begin{cases} y \geq -x \\ x > -2 \\ y > -2 \end{cases}$ **B.** $\begin{cases} y \geq -x \\ x > -2 \\ y < -2 \end{cases}$ **C.** $\begin{cases} y \geq -x \\ x < -2 \\ y < -2 \end{cases}$ **D.** $\begin{cases} y \geq -x \\ x < -2 \\ y > -2 \end{cases}$

■ **SOLUTION**

The shaded region lies entirely to the right of $x = -2$ and above $y = -2$. Only choice **A** meets all these conditions. The correct choice is A.

A system of linear inequalities can also consist of a pair of inequalities in two variables.

EXAMPLE 6 Graphing systems of linear inequalities

Go Online
PearsonSchool.com
Visit: PearsonSchool.com
Web Code: ayp-0238

 Graph this system of linear inequalities. $\begin{cases} 2x + 3y \leq 6 \\ -5x + 2y > -4 \end{cases}$

■ **SOLUTION**

Solve for y. $\begin{cases} y \leq -\frac{2}{3}x + 2 \\ y > \frac{5}{2}x - 2 \end{cases}$

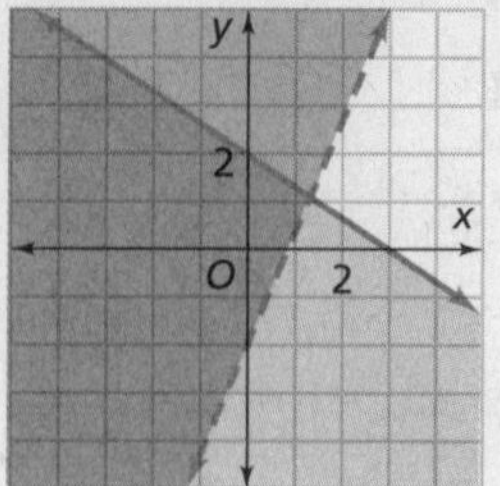

Graph $y = -\frac{2}{3}x + 2$ with a solid line, and graph $y = \frac{5}{2}x - 2$ with a dashed line.

Shade below the graph of $y = -\frac{2}{3}x + 2$.

Shade above the graph of $y = \frac{5}{2}x - 2$.

Shade the common region.

The following example shows how you can use a system of inequalities to solve a real-world problem.

Visit: PearsonSchool.com
Web Code: ayp-0239

EXAMPLE 7 Solving a real-world problem by using a system of inequalities

 A gardener wants to use at least 40 feet and no more than 120 feet of fencing to enclose a rectangular garden. The length is equal to or greater than its width. What possible dimensions may the garden have if dimensions are multiples of 10 feet?

■ **SOLUTION**

Let L represent length in feet and W represent width in feet. Graph the solution to the system at the right. Mark points whose coordinates are multiples of 10. Keep in mind that length and width must be positive.

$$\begin{cases} 2L + 2W \geq 40 \\ 2L + 2W \leq 120 \\ L \geq W \end{cases}$$

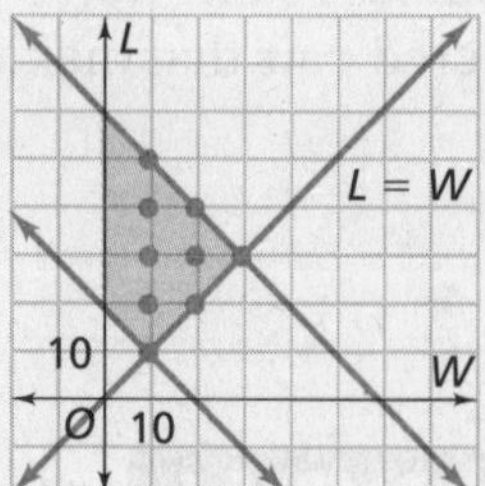

Make a table listing ordered pairs that satisfy all conditions.

Width	10	10	10	10	10	20	20	20	30
Length	10	20	30	40	50	20	30	40	30

Practice

Choose the letter preceding the word or expression that best completes the statement or answers the question.

1 A rectangular garden is to have a perimeter no more than 66 feet. The length of the garden is to be at least twice the width. Which dimensions satisfy these conditions?

A. length 20 feet and width 20 feet
B. length 40 feet and width 20 feet
C. length 30 feet and width 10 feet
D. length 20 feet and width 8 feet

2 Sheila has nickels and dimes but not more than 25 coins. The value of the coins is between \$2.00 and \$3.00. Which combination of coins is not possible?

A. 6 nickels and 18 dimes
B. 8 nickels and 10 dimes
C. 7 nickels and 18 dimes
D. 1 nickel and 21 dimes

3 Which is a solution to $\begin{cases} y \leq 3x + 5 \\ y \geq -x - 5 \end{cases}$?

A. $x = 0, y = 5$ **C.** $x = 4, y = -10$

B. $x = -3, y = -7$ **D.** $x = 0, y = -6$

4 Which system has the shaded region as its solution?

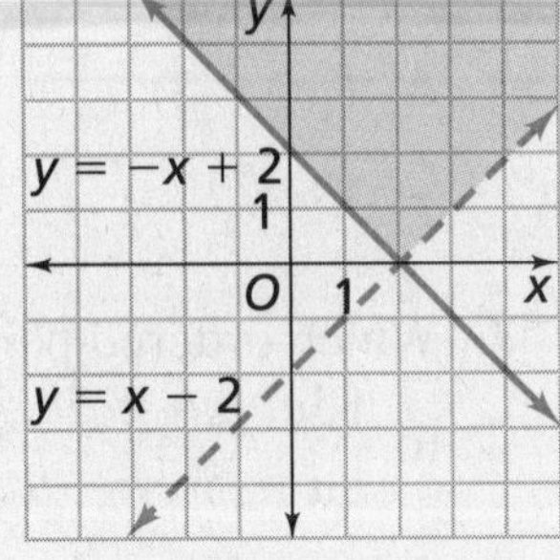

A. $\begin{cases} y > -x + 2 \\ y \geq x - 2 \end{cases}$

B. $\begin{cases} y \geq -x + 2 \\ y \geq x - 2 \end{cases}$

C. $\begin{cases} y \leq -x + 2 \\ y > x - 2 \end{cases}$

D. $\begin{cases} y \geq -x + 2 \\ y > x - 2 \end{cases}$

5 Which accurately describes the solution region for $y \leq -4x + 11$?

A. all points on or below the graph of $y = -4x + 11$

B. all points on or above the graph of $y = -4x + 11$

C. all points below but not on the graph of $y = -4x + 11$

D. all points above but not on the graph of $y = -4x + 11$

6 Which point is in the shaded region?

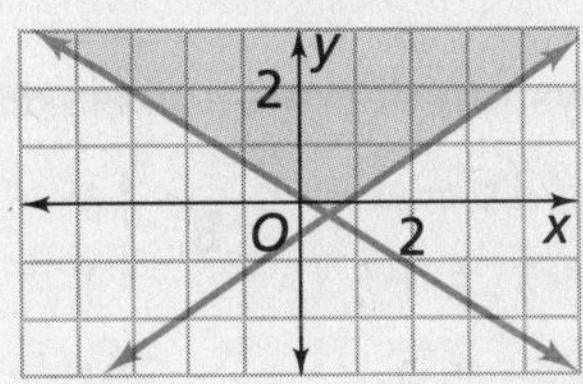

A. $(-99, 0)$ **C.** $(-99, -99)$

B. $(1, 99)$ **D.** $(99, -99)$

7 Which inequality symbol will make the solution region all points above but not on the graph of $y = 13x + 9$?

y ____ $13x + 9$

A. $\leq$ **B.** $\geq$ **C.** $<$ **D.** $>$

8 The length of a board in feet is between 14 and 16. The board is cut into two unequal pieces. Which pair of lengths is possible?

A. 7 and 6 **C.** 7 and 8

B. 7.5 and 7.5 **D.** 9 and 8

In Exercises 9–16, graph each linear inequality in two variables.

9 $y > x$ **10** $y \leq x$

11 $y \geq 2x - 3$ **12** $y \leq -x + 4$

13 $2x + y < 3$ **14** $2x + 3y \geq 6$

15 $x - 2y > -1$ **16** $2x + 5y < 10$

In Exercises 17–20, graph each system of linear inequalities in two variables.

17 $\begin{cases} y \leq x + 2 \\ y \geq x - 2 \end{cases}$ **18** $\begin{cases} y \geq 3 \\ y > x \end{cases}$

19 $\begin{cases} y \leq 3x + 2 \\ y < -2x + 1 \end{cases}$ **20** $\begin{cases} y < \frac{3}{5}x + 4 \\ -3x + 5y \geq -5 \end{cases}$

In Exercises 21–24, solve the problem. Clearly show all necessary work.

21 Today Jessica and Melissa are having a birthday. Both girls are at least 9 years old but not older than 16. If Melissa is 2 years older than Jessica, how old can they be? Show your work.

22 The sum of two positive integers is at most 5. What could the integers be if they are unequal? Show your work and explain your reasoning.

23 Graph the solution to $y \geq x$, $y \leq 3$, and $y \geq -2x + 1.5$. Describe the solution region.

24 Jeremy is thinking of two positive integers. He says that their sum is less than 6 and both numbers are at least 2. What could the numbers be? Show your work and explain your reasoning.

Chapter 3 Preparing for the ADP℠ Algebra I Exam

DIRECTIONS FOR QUESTIONS 1–20: For each of the questions below, select the answer choice that is best for each case.

1 Which is the slope of the line containing $P(-5, 6)$ and $Q(3, -1)$?

A. $-\frac{8}{7}$ **B.** $-\frac{7}{8}$

C. $\frac{7}{2}$ **D.** $\frac{5}{2}$

2 Which is true of all points in the third quadrant?

A. positive x-coordinate; positive y-coordinate

B. negative x-coordinate; negative y-coordinate

C. negative x-coordinate; positive y-coordinate

D. positive x-coordinate; negative y-coordinate

3 Which of the following is **not** a value in the range of the function $\{(-2, 4), (0, -4), (1, -2), (3, 14)\}$?

A. 1 **B.** −2

C. 14 **D.** −4

4 If $y = \frac{2}{3}x - 4$ and $x = 15$, find y.

A. 6 **B.** 26

C. 14 **D.** $\frac{37}{2}$

5 Which of the following is the equation in slope-intercept form for the line containing $P(4, 1)$ with slope $\frac{3}{4}$?

A. $y = \frac{3}{4}x + 1$ **B.** $y = \frac{3}{4}x - 2$

C. $y = \frac{3}{4}x - \frac{13}{4}$ **D.** $y = \frac{3}{4}x + 4$

6 Which point lies along the line containing $P(-1, 2)$ and $Q(2, -4)$?

A. $(-1, -2)$ **B.** $(1, 2)$

C. $(6, 12)$ **D.** $(2, -4)$

7 Which ordered pair (a, b) is a solution to $\begin{cases} 3a + b = 5 \\ a - 5b = -9 \end{cases}$?

A. $(4, -7)$ **B.** $(1, 2)$

C. $(3, -4)$ **D.** $(-4, 1)$

8 The sum of two numbers x and y is 49. Twice one number less 14 is the other number. Which system could **not** represent this situation?

A. $\begin{cases} x + y = 49 \\ 14 - 2x = 49 \end{cases}$

B. $\begin{cases} x + y = 49 \\ 2x - 14 = y \end{cases}$

C. $\begin{cases} 49 = x + y \\ y = 2x - 14 \end{cases}$

D. $\begin{cases} 2x - 14 = y \\ x + y = 49 \end{cases}$

9 Which system of equations is dependent?

A. $\begin{cases} y = 3x - 2 \\ y = x + 1 \end{cases}$ **B.** $\begin{cases} y = x - 1 \\ y - 1 = x \end{cases}$

C. $\begin{cases} x + y = 5 \\ y = x + 5 \end{cases}$ **D.** $\begin{cases} y = \frac{2}{5}x - 4 \\ 5y = 2x - 20 \end{cases}$

10 Which system of equations has no solution?

A. $\begin{cases} y = x + 4 \\ 3x - 2y = 10 \end{cases}$ **B.** $\begin{cases} y = -3x - 5 \\ 2x - 2y = 50 \end{cases}$

C. $\begin{cases} y = x - 2 \\ 3x + 3y = 12 \end{cases}$ **D.** $\begin{cases} y = x - 4 \\ 3x - 3y = 15 \end{cases}$

11 Which accurately describes the solution region for the graph of $y \geq \frac{2}{3}x + 5$?

A. all points on or below the graph of $y \geq \frac{2}{3}x + 5$

B. all points on or above the graph of $y \geq \frac{2}{3}x + 5$

C. all points below but not on the graph of $y \geq \frac{2}{3}x + 5$

D. all points above but not on the graph of $y \geq \frac{2}{3}x + 5$

12 Brian and Lauren are at least 20 years old but not older than 30. If Lauren is 8 years younger than Brian, what could their ages be?

A. 23 and 27

B. 18 and 26

C. 20 and 27

D. 21 and 29

13 The vertex of $y + 3 = |x + 2|$ is

A. (2, 3).

B. (−2, 3).

C. (−2, −3).

D. (2, −3).

14 Which is the slope of a line perpendicular to the graph of $y = \frac{5}{4}x + 8$?

A. −0.8

B. 0.8

C. 1.25

D. −1.25

15 A collection of dimes and quarters has a value of $4.60. The number of dimes is d and the number of quarters is q. Which equation represents this situation?

A. $10d + 25q = 4.60$

B. $25d + 10q = 460$

C. $1.0d + 2.5q = 4.60$

D. $0.1d + 0.25q = 4.60$

16 What is the x-intercept of $y = 2x - 12$?

A. −12

B. −6

C. 2

D. 6

17 Which of the following describes the translation that shifts the graph of $y = |x - 2|$ to a graph that has a vertex of (−2, −3)?

A. $y = |x + 2| - 3$

B. $y = |x - 2| + 3$

C. $y = |x + 3| - 2$

D. $y = |x - 3| + 2$

18 Which is an equation of a vertical line?

A. $y = 7$

B. $x = 3y$

C. $y = -5x$

D. $x = 2$

19 Which inequality symbol will make the solution region consist of all points below but not on the graph of $y = 7x - 3$?

A. ≤

B. ≥

C. <

D. >

20 Which ordered pair (x, y) is the solution to this system?

$$\begin{cases} y = -2x + 7 \\ 2x + 5y = 19 \end{cases}$$

A. (1, 5)

B. (−3, 5)

C. (2, 3)

D. (3, 2)

DIRECTIONS FOR 21–23: Solve each problem and show your work or provide an explanation for your answer.

21 A line passes through the point (1, 3) and has a slope of 4. Write an equation for the line.

Find the equation of the line that is perpendicular to the first line and passes through (1, 3).

22 The following table shows the distance a car has traveled for given times.

Time (hr)	0	2	3	5	6	8
Distance (miles)	0	80	120	200	240	320

Write an equation that gives the distance traveled of the car given time.

Do distance and time vary directly, indirectly, or neither?

23 A box contains a combination of dimes and quarters.

Write a system of inequalities to describe the possible combinations if there are at most 50 coins in the box and between \$7.00 and \$9.00.

Graph the system of inequalities.

If there are 25 quarters in the box, what is the least number of dimes that could be in the box? Describe how this is reflected in the graph.

4 More About Exponents and Exponential Functions

ALGEBRA I

Discovering Ohio

The Bell of the *Cortland*

On June 20, 1868, the 170-foot ship *Cortland,* loaded with iron ore and sailing for Cleveland, collided with the paddlewheel ship *Morning Star.*

While the location of the wreck was known for many years, the identity of the wreck as the *Cortland* was not proven until August 22, 2006. On that day, divers from the Cleveland Underwater Explorers, in cooperation with the Great Lakes Historical Society and the Ohio Department of Natural Resources, recovered the bell from the wreck. The bell confirmed that the shipwreck was that of the *Cortland*.

The bell is now on display at the Inland Seas Maritime Museum in Vermillion, Ohio. The Museum hopes the display of the *Cortland's* bell educates Ohio citizens about Ohio's rich maritime history.

4.1 Properties of Exponents

ADP℠ Standards

O1.c Apply laws of exponents

O2.a Use algebraic exponential expressions

The exponential expression a^n is read as "a to the nth power." In this expression, a is the **base** and n is the **exponent.** The number represented by a^n is called *the nth power of a.*

When n is a positive integer, you can interpret a^n as follows.

$$a^n = \underbrace{a \cdot a \cdot a \cdot \ldots \cdot a}_{n \text{ factors}}$$

Note

Notice that you can add exponents only when the bases are the same.

Now observe how this interpretation can help you simplify products such as the following.

$p^5 \cdot p^3 = (p \cdot p \cdot p \cdot p \cdot p) \cdot (p \cdot p \cdot p) = p^8$ ← **Notice that 5 + 3 = 8.**

$(q^2)^3 = (q^2)(q^2)(q^2) = (q \cdot q) \cdot (q \cdot q) \cdot (q \cdot q) = q^6$ ← **Notice that 2 · 3 = 6.**

$(rs)^4 = (r \cdot s)(r \cdot s)(r \cdot s)(r \cdot s) = (r \cdot r \cdot r \cdot r)(s \cdot s \cdot s \cdot s) = r^4s^4$

These examples are generalized in the following properties of exponents.

Multiplication Properties of Exponents

Let m and n represent integers and a and b represent nonzero real numbers.

Product of Powers Property	**Power of a Power Property**	**Power of a Product Property**
$a^m \cdot a^n = a^{m+n}$	$(a^m)^n = a^{mn}$	$(ab)^m = a^m b^m$

You can use the multiplication properties of exponents to simplify the following exponential expressions.

Go Online PearsonSchool.com
Visit: PearsonSchool.com
Web Code: ayp-0250

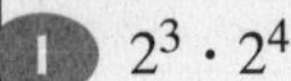

EXAMPLES 1 through 7 **Using the multiplication properties of exponents**

Simplify each expression. Write answers using positive exponents.

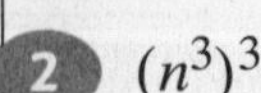

1 $2^3 \cdot 2^4$ ■ **SOLUTION** $2^3 \cdot 2^4 = 2^{3+4} = 2^7 = 128$

2 $(n^3)^3$ ■ **SOLUTION** $(n^3)^3 = n^{3 \cdot 3} = n^9$

3 $(-2x)^3$ ■ **SOLUTION** $(-2x)^3 = (-2)^3x^3 = -8x^3$

4 $(yz^4)^2$ ■ **SOLUTION** $(yz^4)^2 = (y^1z^4)^2 = (y^1)^2(z^4)^2 = y^{1 \cdot 2}z^{4 \cdot 2} = y^2z^8$

5 $(pq)^3 \cdot (pq)^5$ ■ **SOLUTION** $(pq)^3 \cdot (pq)^5 = (pq)^{3+5} = (pq)^8 = p^8q^8$

6 $(-3s^3t^2)^4$ ■ **SOLUTION** $(-3s^3t^2)^4 = (-3)^4(s^3)^4(t^2)^4 = 81s^{3 \cdot 4}t^{2 \cdot 4} = 81s^{12}t^8$

7 $(df)^2(gh)^5$ ■ **SOLUTION** $(df)^2(gh)^5 = d^2f^2g^5h^5$

Notice that in order to apply the product property of exponents, you add exponents when you are multiplying powers of like bases. In some numerical expressions, however, you can apply this property if the given bases are not alike but can be changed to like bases.

EXAMPLE 8 **Applying the product property of exponents to a numerical expression**

8 Which is equivalent to $3^5 \cdot 9^4$?

A. 3^{11} **B.** 3^{13} **C.** 27^9 **D.** 27^{20}

■ SOLUTION

The bases of the factors are not alike; however, 9 can be written as an exponent with a base of 3. $9 = 3^2$

Rewrite the expression, substituting 3^2 for 9; $3^5 \cdot 9^4 = 3^5 \cdot (3^2)^4 = 3^5 \cdot 3^8 = 3^{13}$

The correct choice is B.

When you understand the multiplication properties of exponents, you can multiply terms by using the following procedure.

Multiplying Terms

Step 1 Multiply the coefficients, using the rules for multiplying signed numbers.

Step 2 Multiply the variable factors, using the multiplication properties of exponents.

Step 3 Write the product of the results from Steps 1 and 2.

EXAMPLES 9 and 10 **Multiplying terms**

Go Online PearsonSchool.com
Visit: PearsonSchool.com
Web Code: ayp-0248

Simplify each expression. Write answers using positive exponents.

9 $(3a^2)(5a^4)$

■ SOLUTION

$(3a^2)(5a^4)$
$= 3 \cdot 5 \cdot a^2 \cdot a^4$
$= 15 \cdot a^2 \cdot a^4$
$= 15 \cdot a^{2+4}$
$= 15a^6$

10 $(2rs^3)(5r^3s)^2$

■ SOLUTION

$(2rs^3)(5r^3s)^2$
$= (2r^1s^3)(5^1r^3s^1)^2$
$= (2r^1s^3)(5^2r^6s^2)$
$= 2 \cdot 5^2 \cdot r^1 \cdot r^6 \cdot s^3 \cdot s^2$
$= 50 \cdot r^{1+6} \cdot s^{3+2}$
$= 50r^7s^5$

Now examine these quotients involving exponents.

$$\frac{x^9}{x^2} = \frac{\cancel{x}_1 \cdot \cancel{x}_1 \cdot x \cdot x \cdot x \cdot x \cdot x \cdot x \cdot x}{\cancel{x}_1 \cdot \cancel{x}_1} = \frac{x^7}{1} = x^7 \leftarrow \textbf{Notice that } 9 - 2 = 7.$$

$$\left(\frac{v}{w}\right)^5 = \frac{v}{w} \cdot \frac{v}{w} \cdot \frac{v}{w} \cdot \frac{v}{w} \cdot \frac{v}{w} = \frac{v \cdot v \cdot v \cdot v \cdot v}{w \cdot w \cdot w \cdot w \cdot w} = \frac{v^5}{w^5}$$

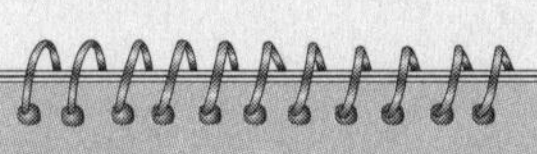

Note

A quotient involving exponents is also called a **ratio of powers.**

The results of the divisions on the preceding page are generalized in the following properties of exponents.

Division Properties of Exponents

Let m and n represent integers and a and b represent nonzero real numbers.

Quotient of Powers Property

$$\frac{a^m}{a^n} = a^{m-n}$$

Power of a Quotient Property

$$\left(\frac{a}{b}\right)^m = \frac{a^m}{b^m}$$

You can now divide terms by using the following procedure.

Dividing Terms

Step 1 Divide the coefficients, using the rules for dividing signed numbers.

Step 2 Divide the variable factors, using the division properties of exponents.

Step 3 Write the product of the results from Steps 1 and 2.

EXAMPLES 11 through 14 Dividing terms

Simplify each expression. Write each answer using positive exponents.

11 $\frac{5^6}{5^3}$ ■ **SOLUTION** $\frac{5^6}{5^3} = 5^{6-3} = 5^3$

12 $\left(\frac{2}{z^3}\right)^2$ ■ **SOLUTION** $\left(\frac{2}{z^3}\right)^2 = \frac{2^2}{(z^3)^2} = \frac{4}{z^6}$

13 $\frac{6r^8}{3r^2}$ ■ **SOLUTION** $\frac{6r^8}{3r^2} = 2r^{8-2} = 2r^6$

14 $\frac{32m^5n^3}{2^3m^4n^2}$ ■ **SOLUTION** $\frac{32m^5n^3}{2^3m^4n^2} = \frac{2^5m^5n^3}{2^3m^4n^2} = 2^{5-3}m^{5-4}n^{3-2} = 2^2m^1n^1 = 4mn$

Practice

Choose the letter preceding the word or expression that best completes the statement or answers the question.

1 Which is equivalent to r^4s^8?

A. $(rs)^{12}$

B. $(r^4s^4)^2$

C. $(rs^2)^4$

D. $r^4 + s^4 + s^4$

2 Which expression is equivalent to $\frac{4^{12}}{2^6}$?

A. 2^6

B. 2^4

C. 4^8

D. 2^{18}

3 Which is not equivalent to $(-w)^2$?

A. $-w^2$ **C.** w^2

B. $w \cdot w$ **D.** $(-w)(-w)$

4 Which is the product of pr^3 and p^2q^2r?

A. $p^3q^2r^4$ **C.** $p^3q^2r^3$

B. $p^5q^2r^4$ **D.** $\frac{r^2}{pq^2}$

5 Which is not equivalent to n^4?

A. $n^2 \cdot n^2$ **C.** $\frac{n^4}{n}$

B. $(n^2)^2$ **D.** $\frac{1}{n^{-4}}$

6 If $a = -2$ and $b = 3$, find the value of $\frac{a^2b^3}{a^3b^2}$.

A. $-\frac{3}{2}$ **C.** $-\frac{2}{3}$

B. $\frac{3}{2}$ **D.** $\frac{2}{3}$

7 The expression $[(2a)(2b)]^2$ is equivalent to

A. $4a^2b^2$. **C.** $8a^2b^2$.

B. $16ab^2$. **D.** $16a^2b^2$.

8 Which is the quotient of $18gh^3k^5$ and $20g^6hk^3$?

A. $\frac{10g^5}{9h^2k^2}$ **C.** $\frac{9h^2k^2}{10g^5}$

B. $\frac{9g^5h^2}{10k^2}$ **D.** $\frac{10h^2k^2}{9g^5}$

9 Evaluate $(6^4)(3^5)$.

A. 39 **C.** 1,539

B. 314,928 **D.** 360

10 Which is the product of $(4a^3b^2)^3$ and $(2ab)^3$?

A. $512a^{12}b^9$ **C.** $512a^{10}b^9$

B. $72a^9b^8$ **D.** $18a^9b^9$

11 If $g^x \cdot g^3 = g^{12}$, find x.

A. $x = 4$ **C.** $x = 36$

B. $x = 15$ **D.** $x = 9$

12 If $\left(\frac{r^8}{r^x}\right)^2 = r^{16}$, find x.

A. $x = 4$ **C.** $x = 0$

B. $x = 1$ **D.** $x = 12$

In Exercises 13–15, simplify each expression.

13 $3^3 \cdot 3^2$ **14** $\frac{5^4}{5^7}$ **15** $\left(-\frac{1}{2}\right)^3$

In Exercises 16–30, simplify each expression. Write answers using positive exponents.

16 $(-5r^2s^2)(-3r^2s)$ **17** $(12x^2y)(4x^5)(-2z)$

18 $(-3a^3b^2c)^3$ **19** $(x^2y^2)^2(xy^3)^4$

20 $\frac{p^6q^{10}}{p^3q^8}$ **21** $\frac{3v^2w^4}{9vw^3}$

22 $\left(\frac{3a}{7b}\right)^2$ **23** $\left(\frac{x^3}{y^7}\right)^2$

24 $\left(\frac{-2ab}{c}\right)^2$ **25** $\left(\frac{-2y^5}{3x^3}\right)^3$

26 $\left(\frac{c^3d^3}{c^2}\right)^3$ **27** $\frac{(5ab^4)^2}{5ab^4}$

28 $\frac{(3y^2)(2y^3)}{3y^4}$ **29** $\frac{(-4n^5)(2n^3)}{2n^4}$

30 $\frac{(9x^2y)(3x^3y^2)}{-27x^5y}$

In Exercises 31–36, find the value of x that makes each statement true. Assume that no base is equal to zero.

31 $r^x \cdot r^2 = r^6$ **32** $(r^x)^2 = r^6$

33 $r^x \cdot r^2 = 1$ **34** $(r^x)^2 = 1$

35 $\frac{r^2}{r^x} = r^6$ **36** $\left(\frac{r}{r^x}\right)^2 = r^6$

In Exercises 37–38, solve the problem. Clearly show all necessary work.

37 Are -5^2 and $(-5)^2$ equivalent expressions? Explain your answer.

38 Given that m and n are integers and x is a nonzero real number, is it true that $(x^m)^n = (x^n)^m$? Justify your answer.

4.2 Zero and Negative Exponents

ADP℠ Standards

O1.c Apply laws of exponents

O2.a Use algebraic exponential expressions

You can use the division property of exponents to develop a rule for negative exponents. Recall that $\frac{b^m}{b^n} = b^{m-n}$. If n is greater than m, then $m - n$ is negative. The problem below shows how you can simplify a ratio of powers when the degree of the numerator is less than the degree of the denominator.

$$\frac{s^3}{s^5} = \frac{s \cdot s \cdot s}{s \cdot s \cdot s \cdot s \cdot s} = \frac{\cancel{s} \cdot \cancel{s} \cdot \cancel{s}}{\cancel{s} \cdot \cancel{s} \cdot \cancel{s} \cdot s \cdot s} = \frac{1}{s \cdot s} = \frac{1}{s^2}\text{; therefore, } \frac{1}{s^2} = s^{-2}$$

Likewise, $\frac{s^3}{s^5} = s^{3-5} = s^{-2}$.

Visit: PearsonSchool.com
Web Code: ayp-0039

EXAMPLES 1 through 3 **Using the division property of exponents**

Simplify the following expressions using the division property of exponents.

1 $\frac{5^2}{5^6}$ ■ **SOLUTION** $\frac{5^2}{5^6} = 5^{2-6} = 5^{-4} = \frac{1}{5^4} = \frac{1}{625}$

2 $\frac{12m^3n^5}{4m^7n^3}$ ■ **SOLUTION** $\frac{12m^3n^5}{4m^7n^3} = 3m^{3-7}n^{5-3} = 3m^{-4}n^2 = \frac{3n^2}{m^4}$

3 $\frac{15rs^5}{-3r^3s^{-2}}$ ■ **SOLUTION** $\frac{15rs^5}{-3r^3s^{-2}} = -5r^{1-3}s^{5-(-2)} = -5r^{-2}s^{5+2} = -5r^{-2}s^7 = \frac{-5s^7}{r^2}$

If the degree of the numerator is equal to the degree of the denominator, the division property will result in an exponent of zero.

$\frac{5^3}{5^3} = 5^{3-3} = 5^0$. Similarly, $\frac{5^3}{5^3} = \frac{125}{125} = 1$. Therefore, $\frac{5^3}{5^3} = 5^0 = 1$.

Note

For any real number x, $x^1 = x$. For any non zero real number x. $x^0 = 1$. For any non zero real number x and any integer n, $x^{-n} = \frac{1}{x^n}$.

EXAMPLES 4 through 7 **Simplifying expressions with exponents equal to zero**

Simplify each of the following exponential expressions.

4 $(fg^3)^0$

■ **SOLUTION**

$(fg^3)^0 = f^0g^{(3)(0)} = (1)(1) = 1$

5 $x^0y^3z^2$

■ **SOLUTION**

$x^0y^3z^2 = (1)(y^3)(z^2)$
$= y^3z^2$

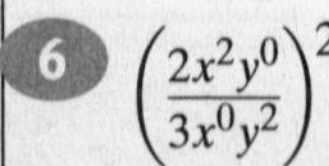

6 $\left(\frac{2x^2y^0}{3x^0y^2}\right)^2$

■ **SOLUTION**

$$\left(\frac{2x^2y^0}{3x^0y^2}\right)^2 = \frac{2^2x^{(2)(2)}y^{(0)(2)}}{3^2x^{(0)(2)}y^{(2)(2)}} = \frac{4x^4y^0}{9x^0y^4} = \frac{4x^4}{9y^4}$$

7 $\frac{16a^0b^3}{2a^4}$

■ **SOLUTION**

$$\frac{16a^0b^3}{2a^4} = 8a^{0-4}b^3 = 8a^{-4}b^3 = \frac{8b^3}{a^4}$$

You can use all of the rules of exponents to simplify exponential expressions.

EXAMPLES 8 through 10 Simplifying exponential expressions

Simplify each expression. Write each answer using positive exponents.

8 $(v^{-2}w^3)^{-2}$

■ **SOLUTION** $(v^{-2}w^3)^{-2} = (v^{-2})^{-2}(w^3)^{-2}$

$= v^{(-2)(-2)}w^{(3)(-2)} = v^4w^{-6} = \frac{v^4}{w^6}$

9 $\left(\frac{2z^3r^{-2}}{3zr^4}\right)^3$

■ **SOLUTION** $\left(\frac{2z^3r^{-2}}{3zr^4}\right)^3 = \frac{2^3z^{(3)(3)}r^{(-2)(3)}}{3^3z^{(1)(3)}r^{(4)(3)}} = \frac{8z^9r^{-6}}{27z^3r^{12}} = \frac{8z^6}{27r^{18}}$

10 $\frac{-36a^0b^3}{9a^5b}$

■ **SOLUTION** $\frac{-36a^0b^3}{9a^5b} = -4a^{0-5}b^{3-1} = -4a^{-5}b^2 = \frac{-4b^2}{a^5}$

Recall that a number written in scientific notation has the following form.

The first factor is a number that is at least 1, but is less than 10. $\rightarrow a \times 10^n \leftarrow$ **The second factor is an integer power of 10, expressed in exponential form.**

The properties of exponents can be used when performing operations on numbers written in scientific notation.

Go Online
PearsonSchool.com
Visit: PearsonSchool.com
Web Code: ayp-0940

EXAMPLES 11 through 13 Multiplying and dividing with numbers in scientific notation

Simplify each expression. Write answers in scientific notation.

11 $5000 \times (1.39 \times 10^{-8})$

■ **SOLUTION**

$5000 \times (1.39 \times 10^{-8})$
$= (5 \times 10^3) \times (1.39 \times 10^{-8})$
$= (5 \times 1.39) \times (10^3 \times 10^{-8})$
$= 6.95 \times (10^3 \times 10^{-8})$
$= 6.95 \times 10^{3+(-8)}$
$= 6.95 \times 10^{-5}$

12 $(6 \times 10^4)^2$

■ **SOLUTION**

$(6 \times 10^4)^2$
$= (6)^2 \times (10^4)^2$
$= 36 \times (10^4)^2$
$= 36 \times 10^{4 \cdot 2}$
$= 36 \times 10^8$
$= 3.6 \times 10^1 \times 10^8$
$= 3.6 \times 10^9$

13 $\frac{1.29 \times 10^{-2}}{4 \times 10^{-9}}$

■ **SOLUTION**

$\frac{1.29 \times 10^{-2}}{4 \times 10^{-9}}$
$= \frac{1.29}{4} \times \frac{10^{-2}}{10^{-9}}$
$= 0.3225 \times \frac{10^{-2}}{10^{-9}}$
$= 0.3225 \times 10^{-2-(-9)}$
$= 0.3225 \times 10^7$
$= 3.225 \times 10^{-1} \times 10^7$
$= 3.225 \times 10^6$

Most calculators display numbers written in scientific notation without the base *10* showing. The symbol *E* represents multiplying by 10, and the number following is the exponent. For example, if the calculator displays 5.68 E −8, that represents the number 5.68×10^{-8} or 0.0000000568.

The solutions to the example problems above performed on a calculator are displayed in the accompanying figure.

```
5000*(1.396E-8)
            6.95E-5
(6E4)2
              3.6E9
(1.29E-2)/(4E-9)
            3.225E6
■
```

Practice

Choose the letter preceding the word or expression that best completes the statement or answers the question.

1 Which is a true statement?

A. $\frac{z^6}{z^2} = z^3$

B. $\frac{z^3}{z^5} = \frac{1}{z^{-2}}$

C. $\frac{z^0}{z^{-3}} = z^3$

D. $\frac{z^{-4}}{z^2} = z^{-2}$

2 Simplify the expression $\frac{k^4l^2}{k^{-3}l^6}$.

A. kl^4

B. k^7l^4

C. $\frac{k^7}{l^4}$

D. $\frac{k}{l^4}$

3 Which is equivalent to $\frac{8.125 \times 10^{-8}}{3.25 \times 10^3}$?

A. 2.5×10^{-11}

B. 4.875×10^{-11}

C. 2.5×10^{-5}

D. 4.875×10^{-5}

4 Which is the proper way to write $(3.62 \times 10^{-3})^2$ in standard form?

A. 0.0000131044 **C.** 0.000000362

B. 13,104,400,000 **D.** 36,200,000

5 What value of x will make the equation $\frac{6^6}{6^x} = 1$ true?

A. 0 **B.** −6 **C.** 1 **D.** 6

6 What value of x will make the equation $\frac{r^3s^7}{r^xs^2} = r^7s^5$ true?

A. 4 **B.** 2 **C.** −4 **D.** −2

7 If the length of one side of a cube is denoted by x, the volume of the cube would be denoted as which of the following?

A. $3x$ **B.** 3^x **C.** x^3 **D.** $(3x)^3$

8 If the length of one side of a rectangular garden is denoted by l and the width is 4 units shorter than the length, the area of the garden would be denoted as which of the following?

A. $l - 4$ **C.** $l(l + 4)$

B. $(l - 4)^2$ **D.** $l^2 - 4l$

9 If $k = 3.2 \times 10^{-4}$, what is the value of $3k^2$?

A. 3.072×10^{-7}

B. 9.216×10^{-7}

C. 30,720,000

D. 0.0000003072

10 If $b = 1.8 \times 10^5$, what is the value of $2b^2$?

A. 3.6×10^7 **C.** 12.96×10^{10}

B. 6.48×10^{10} **D.** 3.6×10^{10}

Solve the following problems. Clearly show all necessary work.

11 The planet Earth is approximated by a sphere with a radius of 6.4×10^6 meters. Use the formula $S = 4\pi r^2$ to approximate the surface area of the Earth.

12 If the area of a rectangle is represented by $60a^2b^5$ and its width is represented by $12ab$, express the length of the rectangle in terms of a and b.

13 The national debt was approximately 8.5 trillion dollars in August of 2006. At that time, the population of the United States was 300 million. If the debt were divided equally among all of the people in the United States, how much would each person owe?

In Exercises 14–30, simplify each expression. Write each answer using positive exponents.

14 $b^{-4} \cdot b^{-3} \cdot b^5$

15 $k^{-7} \cdot (k^2)^5$

16 $(m^{-3}n^4)^{-4}$

17 $(2^3a^5)^2(16a^{-5})$

18 $2^3 \cdot 7^4 \cdot 2^{-3} \cdot 7^{-4}$

19 $\frac{a^2b^2}{a^3b^2}$

20 $\frac{15c^8d^3}{-3c^{10}d^{-2}}$

21 $\left(\frac{c^3d^3}{c^2}\right)^4$

22 $\left(\frac{-2x^3y^{-3}}{x^2y^5}\right)^3$

23 $\frac{(-3n^{-5})(4n^3)}{(2n^{-2})}$

24 $\left(\frac{s^3t^{-5}}{s^{-1}t^{-4}}\right)^2$

25 $\frac{(2a^3)^{-2}(3a^4b^0)}{6a^{-2}}$

26 $(4g^3h^3)^{-4}(-2gh)^3$

27 $(m^2)^{-4}(m^2n^3)^2$

28 $\frac{r^3s^{-1}}{r^2s^6}$

29 $\frac{3j^{-3}k^{-5}}{2j^{-5}k^{-3}}$

30 $\left(\frac{a^{-2}b^{-1}}{a^{-5}b^3}\right)^{-3}$

In Exercises 31–36, simplify each expression. Write each answer in scientific notation.

31 $(2.6 \times 10^{-9})(3 \times 10^2)$

32 $12{,}000 \times (6.5 \times 10^{-11})$

33 $(3 \times 10^{-4})^2$

34 $(1.6 \times 10^4)^3$

35 $\frac{4.8 \times 10^8}{7.5 \times 10^2}$

36 $\frac{2.43 \times 10^{-9}}{7.5 \times 10^{-10}}$

In Exercises 37–39, solve the problem. Clearly show all necessary work.

37 There are approximately 6.02×10^{23} molecules in one mole of a substance. How many molecules are in 5,000 moles?

38 When the planet Mars is closest to Earth, the distance between Earth and Mars is about 3.38×10^7 miles. Suppose that you were to travel this distance at an average speed of 60 miles per hour. How many years would it take to travel to Mars?

39 In 1998, municipalities in the United States recovered about 7×10^{10} pounds of waste paper. The population of the United States in 1998 was about 2.7×10^8. How many pounds of waste paper were recovered per person? Round your answer to the nearest pound.

4.3 Exponential Functions

ADP℠ Standards

N1.b Distinguish between function types

Many teenagers would like to persuade their parents to pay them an allowance in the following way. One cent (1¢) is paid on the first day of the month and doubled each successive day. The table shows the amount to be paid each day for the month of February.

Day	x	Amount	Day	x	Amount
1	0	$.01	15	14	$163.84
2	1	$.02	16	15	$327.68
3	2	$.04	17	16	$655.36
4	3	$.08	18	17	$1,310.72
5	4	$.16	19	18	$2,621.44
6	5	$.32	20	19	$5,242.88
7	6	$.64	21	20	$10,485.76
8	7	$1.28	22	21	$20,971.52
9	8	$2.56	23	22	$41,943.04
10	9	$5.12	24	23	$83,886.08
11	10	$10.24	25	24	$167,772.16
12	11	$20.48	26	25	$335,544.32
13	12	$40.96	27	26	$671,088.64
14	13	$81.92	28	27	$1,342,177.28

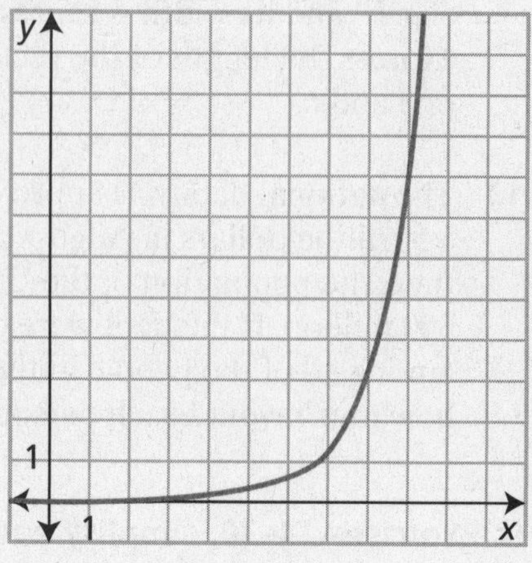

The amount due on the last day is over one million dollars, and it all started with just one penny!

The equation that determines the amount paid each day is $y = 0.01(2^x)$. The graph of this function is shown in the diagram above. This type of function is known as an **exponential function.**

Exponential Functions

An exponential function is of the form $y = a \cdot b^x$ where a is nonzero, $b > 0, b \neq 1$, and x is a real number.

Go Online PearsonSchool.com

Visit: PearsonSchool.com

Web Code: ayp-0131

EXAMPLE 1 Graphing exponential functions from a table

1 Use the table to graph the exponential function.

x	y
−2	0.04
−1	0.2
0	1
1	5
2	25

■ **SOLUTION**

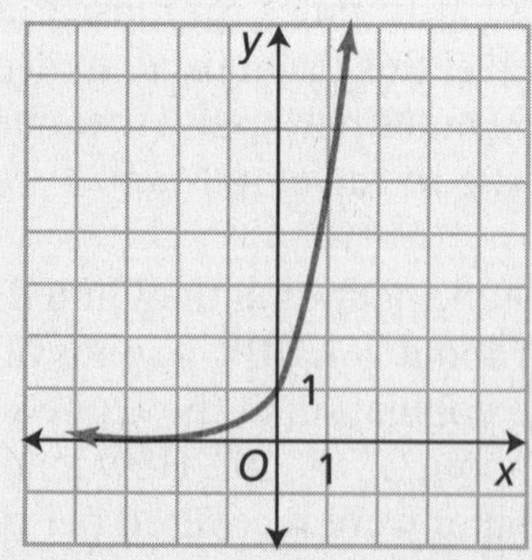

Note

The graph of an exponential function will never go below the x-axis.

Examples of the exponential functions $y = 2^x$, $y = 3^x$, and $y = 5^x$ and their graphs are shown below.

x	2^x	3^x	5^x
-1	$2^{-1} = \frac{1}{2}$	$3^{-1} = \frac{1}{3}$	$5^{-1} = \frac{1}{5}$
0	$2^0 = 1$	$3^0 = 1$	$5^0 = 1$
1	$2^1 = 2$	$3^1 = 3$	$5^1 = 5$
2	$2^2 = 4$	$3^2 = 9$	$5^2 = 25$
3	$2^3 = 8$	$3^3 = 27$	$5^3 = 125$

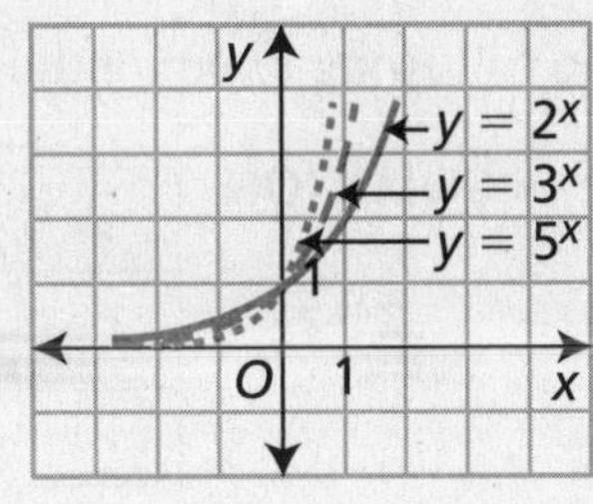

Notice that the point $(0, 1)$ is the y-intercept for each of these graphs. Also notice that none of these graphs crosses the x-axis. There is no value of x for which y will be negative.

Go Online
PearsonSchool.com
Visit: PearsonSchool.com
Web Code: ayp-0257

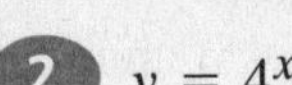

EXAMPLES 2 and 3 **Evaluating exponential functions**

Evaluate the following functions for $x = \{-2, -1, 0, 1, 2\}$. As the values of x increase, determine whether the values of the function increase or decrease.

2 $y = 4^x$

■ **SOLUTION**

x	4^x
-2	$4^{-2} = \frac{1}{4^2} = \frac{1}{16}$
-1	$4^{-1} = \frac{1}{4}$
0	$4^0 = 1$
1	$4^1 = 4$
2	$4^2 = 16$

Increase

3 $y = \left(\frac{1}{3}\right)^x$

■ **SOLUTION**

x	$\left(\frac{1}{3}\right)^x$
-2	$\left(\frac{1}{3}\right)^{-2} = \frac{1^{-1}}{3^{-2}} = \frac{\frac{1}{1^2}}{\frac{1}{3^2}} = \frac{1}{1^2} \cdot \frac{3^2}{1} = \frac{9}{1} = 9$
-1	$\left(\frac{1}{3}\right)^{-1} = \frac{1^{-1}}{3^{-1}} = \frac{\frac{1}{1}}{\frac{1}{3}} = \frac{1}{1} \cdot \frac{3}{1} = \frac{3}{1} = 3$
0	$\left(\frac{1}{3}\right)^0 = 1$
1	$\left(\frac{1}{3}\right)^1 = \frac{1^1}{3^1} = \frac{1}{3}$
2	$\left(\frac{1}{3}\right)^2 = \frac{1^2}{3^2} = \frac{1}{9}$

Decrease

You can use a chart of values to graph exponential functions.

Go Online
PearsonSchool.com
Visit: PearsonSchool.com
Web Code: ayp-0258

EXAMPLES 4 and 5 Graphing exponential functions

Graph the following exponential functions.

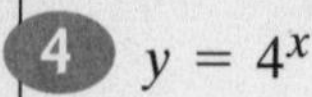

4 $y = 4^x$ ■ **SOLUTION**

x	4^x
-2	$4^{-2} = \frac{1}{16}$
-1	$4^{-1} = \frac{1}{4}$
0	$4^0 = 1$
1	$4^1 = 4$
2	$4^2 = 16$
3	$4^3 = 64$

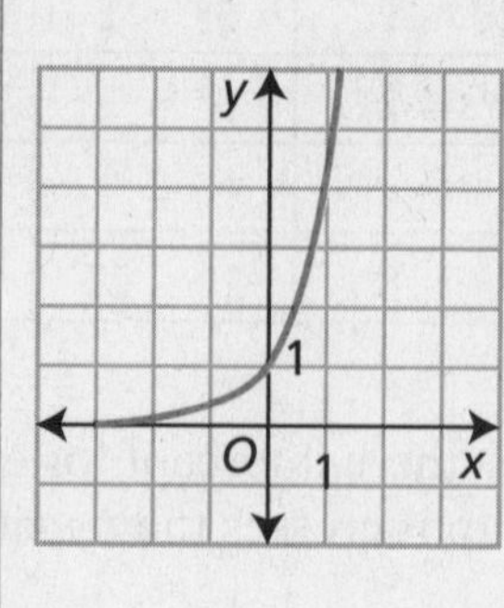

Notice that the curve of the function $y = 4^x$ rises from left to right.

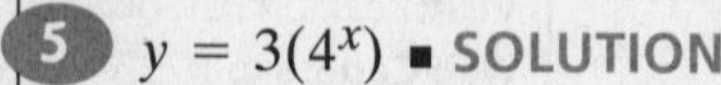

5 $y = 3(4^x)$ ■ **SOLUTION**

x	$3(4^x)$
-2	$3(4^{-2}) = \frac{3}{16}$
-1	$3(4^{-1}) = \frac{3}{4}$
0	$3(4^0) = 3$
1	$3(4^1) = 12$
2	$3(4^2) = 48$
3	$3(4^3) = 192$

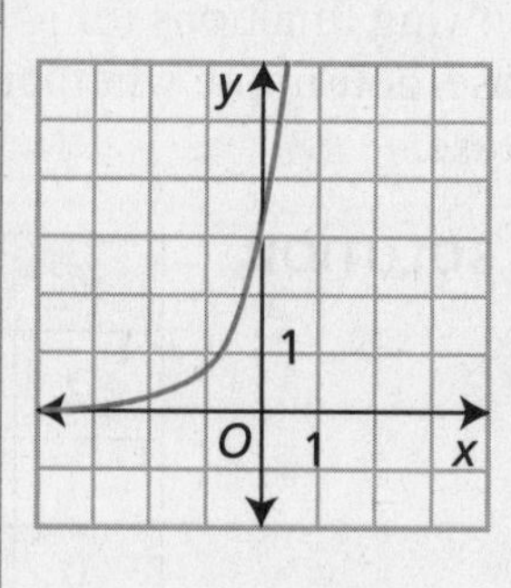

Notice that changing the function $y = 4^x$ to $y = 3(4^x)$ changes the y-intercept from 1 to 3. The steepness of the function's curve also increases.

Observe what happens when you graph an exponential function with a base that is less than 1.

EXAMPLE 6 Graphing exponential functions with a base that is less than 1

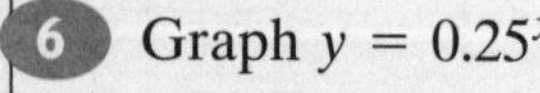

6 Graph $y = 0.25^x$

■ **SOLUTION**

x	0.25^x
-2	$0.25^{-2} = 16$
-1	$0.25^{-1} = 4$
0	$0.25^0 = 1$
1	$0.25^1 = 0.25$
2	$0.25^2 = \frac{1}{16}$
3	$0.25^3 = \frac{1}{64}$

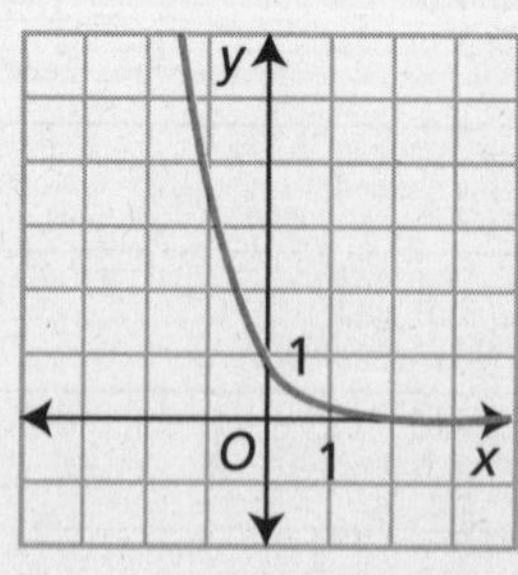

Notice that when the base is less than 1, the function's curve decreases from left to right.

Practice

Choose the letter preceding the word or expression that best completes the statement or answers the question.

1 Where does the function cross the x-axis?

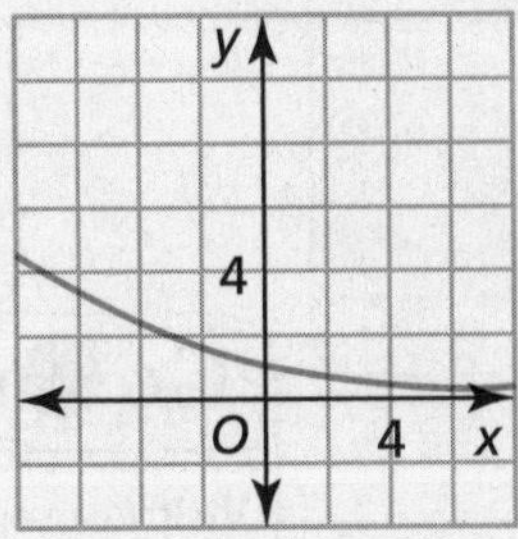

A. $y = 1$ **C.** $x = 0$

B. $x = 1$ **D.** never

2 Where does the function cross the y-axis?

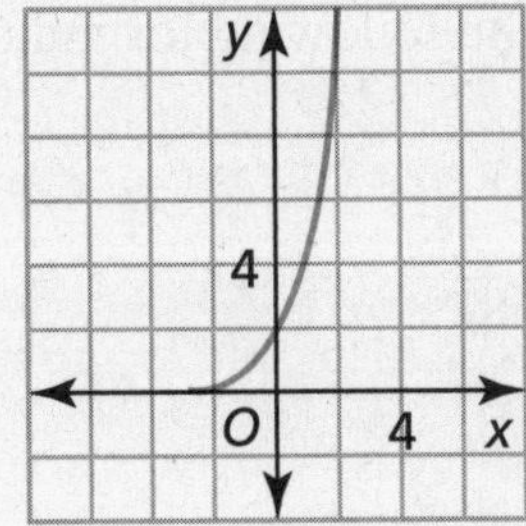

A. $y = 0$ **C.** $x = 2$

B. $y = 2$ **D.** never

3 Which of the following is not an exponential function?

A. $y = 0.2(8^x)$ **C.** $y = 4x^2$

B. $y = \left(\frac{1}{4}\right)^x + 2$ **D.** $y = 2^x$

In Exercises 4–6, solve the problem. Clearly show all necessary work.

4 When an exponential function has a base that is >1, does its graph rise or fall from left to right? Explain.

5 When an exponential function has a base that is <1, does its graph rise or fall from left to right? Explain.

6 Does the graph of an exponential function have an x-intercept? Explain.

In Exercises 7–9, evaluate each function for $x = \{-2, -1, 0, 1, 2, 3\}$. As the values for x increase, determine whether the values of the function increase or decrease.

7 $y = 2.5^x$ **8** $f(x) = 5(4^x)$ **9** $y = \left(\frac{2}{3}\right)^x$

In Exercises 10–13, find the y-intercept and determine whether the function is increasing or decreasing.

10 $y = \left(\frac{1}{2}\right)^x$ **11** $y = 2^x$

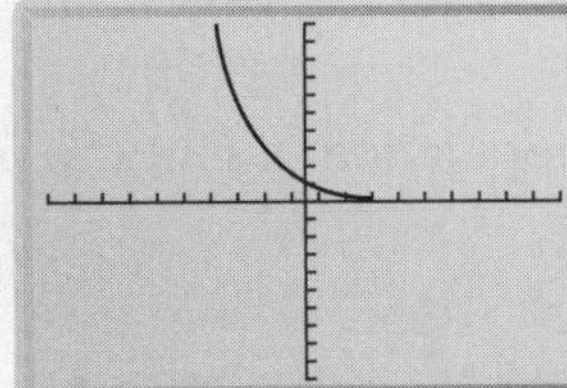

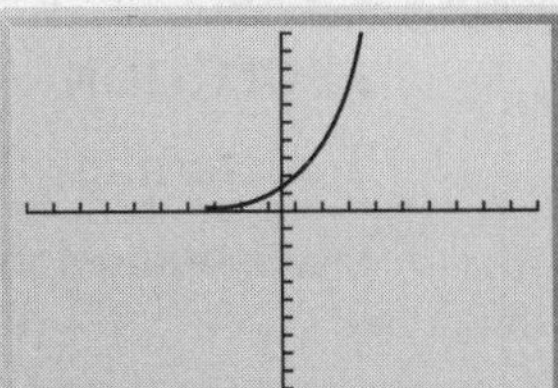

12 $y = -(2^x)$ **13** $y = 5(2^x)$

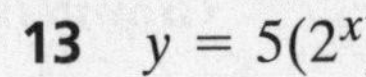

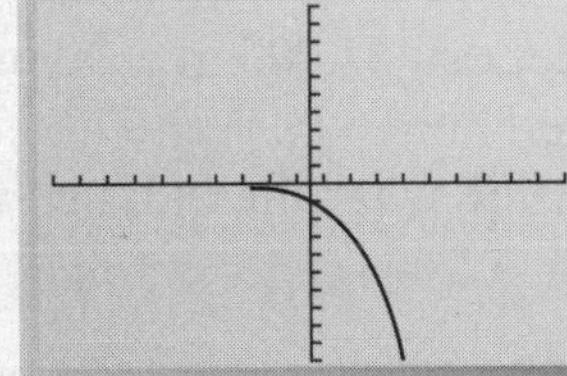

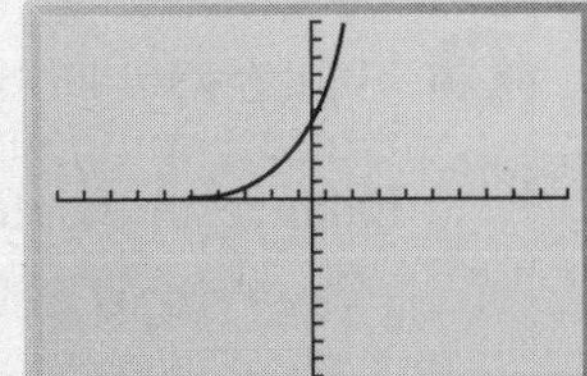

In Exercises 14–20, evaluate each function for $x = \{-2, -1, 0, 1, 2\}$.

14 $y = 2^x$ **15** $y = 0.5^x$

16 $y = 2(3^x)$ **17** $y = \left(\frac{1}{3}\right)^x$

18 $f(x) = 0.4^x$ **19** $f(x) = -\left(\frac{3}{4}\right)^x$

20 $f(x) = -5^x$

4.4 Exponential Growth and Decay

ADP℠ Standards

N1.b Distinguish between function types

Recall that an exponential function is of the form $y = a \cdot b^x$ where a is nonzero, $b > 0$, $b \neq 1$, and x is a real number. If the value of a is positive and the value of b is greater than 1, this function models growth.

Exponential Growth

Exponential growth can be modeled by the function

$$y = a \cdot b^x \text{ with } a > 0 \text{ and } b > 1.$$

a = the starting amount when $x = 0$.
b = is the growth factor and is greater than one.
x is the exponent.

Visit: PearsonSchool.com
Web Code: ayp-0260

EXAMPLES 1 and 2 **Solving problems involving exponential growth**

1 If the population of Ontario County, New York, was 102,500 in 2003 and has been increasing at an average rate of 2.2% per year, find the projected population of the county in 2010.

■ SOLUTION

To determine the population of Ontario County, we can use the following formula.

Current population ↓

$P = 102{,}500(1.022)^x$ → Number of years since 2003

↑ Growth rate

$P = 102{,}500(1.022)^7 = 1.193658612 \cdot 10^5 \approx 119{,}366$ people

2 Suppose that you deposit \$1,000 in a savings account that pays 5.6% interest compounded annually. Write an equation to model the account balance, and determine what the balance will be after 4 years.

■ SOLUTION

$A = \$1{,}000(1.056)^t$

$A = \$1{,}000(1.056)^t = \$1{,}000(1.056)^4 = \$1{,}243.528298 \approx \$1{,}243.53$

A function in the form $y = a \cdot b^x$ where a is greater than zero and b is between zero and one models exponential decay.

Exponential Decay

Exponential decay can be modeled by the function

$$y = a \cdot b^x \text{ with } a > 0 \text{ and } 0 < b < 1.$$

a = the starting amount when $x = 0$.
b = is the decay factor and is between zero and one.
x is the exponent.

The radioactive half-life of a substance is the length of time it takes for one half of the substance to decay.

EXAMPLE 3 **Solving problems involving half-life with exponential decay**

3 Radioactive iodine is used to treat some medical conditions. The half-life of iodine-131 is 8 days. A doctor administers a 12-unit treatment to a patient. How much iodine-131 is left in the patient after 24 days?

▪ **SOLUTION**

In 24 days, there are three 8-day half-lives.
After one half-life, there are 6 units.
After the second half-life, there are 3 units.
Finally, after the third half-life, there are 1.5 units.

This result can also be obtained in the following way:
$y = 12(0.5)^3 = 1.5$

Note

When a quantity is decreased by 10%, the result is 90% of the original quantity. When thinking of the decay factor, think of 100% minus the percent by which the quantity is decreasing.

You can also use exponential decay to model a decrease in population.

EXAMPLES 4 and 5 **Solving problems involving population decrease with exponential decay**

4 An antidote is introduced into a colony of bacteria that contains 1 million bacteria. If the antidote reduces the population by 25% every hour, what is the population after 24 hours?

▪ **SOLUTION**

$1{,}000{,}000$ ← This is the initial bacteria population.
$1 - 0.25 = 0.75$ ← This is the decay factor.
$1{,}000{,}000(0.75)^x$ ← This equation models the declining population.
$1{,}000{,}000(0.75)^{24}$ ← This equation models the population after 24 hours.
$1{,}000{,}000(0.75)^{24} = 1{,}003.3912$ ← This is the population after 24 hours.
$\approx 1{,}003$

5 In 2000, the population of Someplace was 702,000 people. The population decreases about 1.7% per year. Predict the population of Someplace in 2010.

▪ **SOLUTION**

$702{,}000$ ← This is the initial number of people.
$1 - 0.017 = 0.983$ ← This is the decay factor.
$y = 702{,}000(0.983)^x$ ← This equation models the population since 2000.
$y = 702{,}000(0.983)^x$
$= 702{,}000(0.983)^{10}$
$= 591{,}387.70$
$\approx 591{,}388$ ← This is the projected population in 2010.

You can determine the equation of a function given a set of data.

EXAMPLE 6 **Determining a function that models given data**

6 The data from the table are shown in the accompanying scatter plot. Write an equation to model the data.

x	y
−1	12
0	6
1	3
2	1.5
3	0.75
4	0.375
5	0.1875

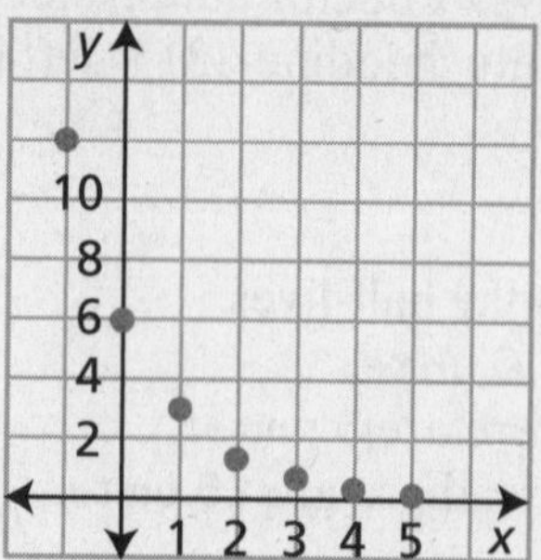

■ **SOLUTION**

The graph of the data suggests an exponential model. Test for a common ratio.

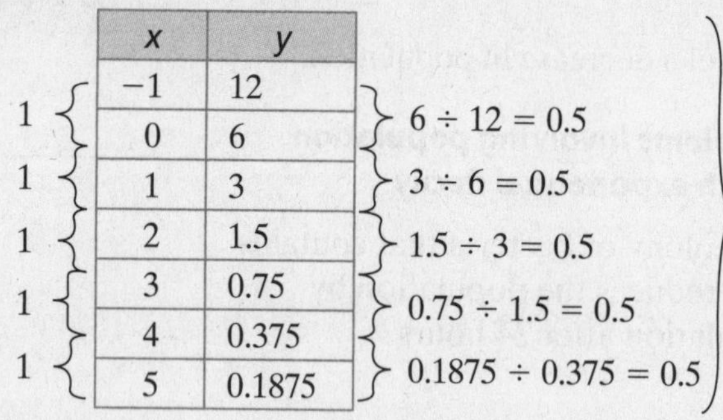

x	y
−1	12
0	6
1	3
2	1.5
3	0.75
4	0.375
5	0.1875

The common ratio is 0.5.

The initial value $y = 6$ when $x = 0$ determines the value of a. The common ratio determines the decay factor. *Therefore, the equation that models this data is* $y = 6\left(\frac{1}{2}\right)^x = 6(0.5)^x$.

Practice

Choose the letter preceding the word or expression that best completes the statement or answers the question.

1 Which of the following is an exponential growth function with an initial amount of 2?

A. $y = 5 \cdot 4^x$

B. $g(x) = \frac{1}{2}(3)^x$

C. $y = 2\left(\frac{4}{3}\right)^x$

D. $f(t) = \frac{3}{4}\left(\frac{2}{3}\right)^t$

In Exercises 2–6, use the following information.

Suppose that the population of a city is 75,000 and is growing 2.5% per year.

2 What is the initial amount a?

3 What is the growth factor b?

4 What do you multiply 75,000 by to find the population after one year?

5 Write an equation to find the population after x years.

6 Use the equation to predict the population after 25 years.

In Exercises 7–10, use the following information.

Suppose that the population of a large city was 8,000,000 six years ago, but since then it has been declining at an average rate of 1.75% per year.

7 What is the initial amount a?

8 What is the decay factor b?

9 Write an equation to find the population after x years.

10 Use the equation to predict the population after 6 years.

11 The value of a new car decreases exponentially at a rate of 15% per year. A new car has an inital value of $24,000. What is the value of the car after 5 years?

In Exercises 12–17, identify the functions as *linear, exponential,* or *neither*.

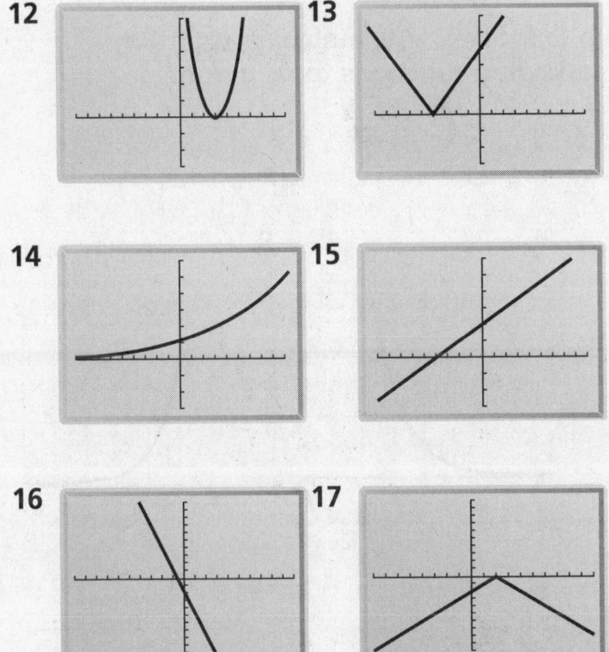

In Exercises 18–25, solve the problem. Clearly show all necessary work.

18 Write an exponential equation to represent the growth of an account with a $4,000 principal that earns a rate of 4.5% compounded annually.

19 Determine whether the data in the accompanying table represent a linear, absolute value, or exponential function. Explain your reasoning.

x	y
1	3
2	9
3	27
4	81

20 If the half-life of a certain compound is eight hours, how many half-lives occur in a two-day period?

21 The half-life of a certain substance is four days. If you have 100 grams of the substance, how much of it will remain after twelve days?

22 Suppose that a town had a population of 1,250 people in 2001. Over the next five years, however, the population decreased at an average rate of 1.3% per year. At this rate, what will be the town's population in the year 2010?

23 A common bacteria grows at a rate described by the function $B(t) = (3)^t$ where t is number of hours. How many bacteria are expected to have grown after 7 hours?

24 The amount in grams of a radioactive substance is given by the function $y = 50(1.7)^{-0.3t}$ where t is time in years. Find the number of grams of the substance after 20 years.

25 New vehicles lose value at a rate of 18.5% per year. Write an equation to calculate the value of a vehicle with an original value of $21,000 after t years.

Chapter 4 Preparing for the ADP℠ Algebra I Exam

DIRECTIONS FOR QUESTIONS 1–20: For each of the questions below, select the answer choice that is best for each case.

1 Which of the following statements is true?

A. Any number raised to the zero power is zero.

B. Any number raised to a negative power is a negative number.

C. The product of two powers with the same base equals the base raised to the sum of the powers.

D. The quotient of two powers with the same base equals the base raised to the quotient of the powers.

2 Determine the value of $\frac{-5x^3y^5}{15x^{-7}y^5z^{-2}}$ when $x = -1$, $y = 5$, and $z = 3$.

A. 29 **B.** -3 **C.** 21 **D.** 0

3 Determine the value of $\frac{-6a^{-2}bc^6}{24a^3c^{-4}}$ when $a = 2$, $b = 4$, and $c = -1$.

A. -32 **B.** $\frac{1}{2}$

C. -2 **D.** $-\frac{1}{32}$

4 Which of the following best describes the graph below?

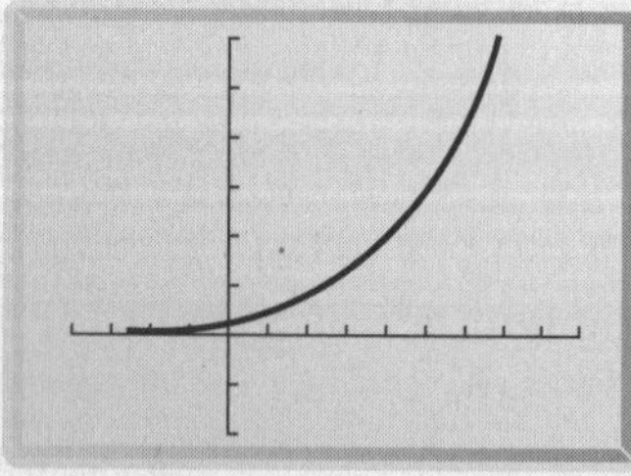

A. Linear growth

B. Exponential growth

C. Exponential decay

D. Quadratic growth

5 Which of the following is an exponential decay function with an initial amount of 2?

A. $y = 5 \cdot 4^x$ **B.** $g(x) = \frac{1}{2}(3)^x$

C. $y = 2(0.75)^x$ **D.** $f(t) = \frac{3}{4}\left(\frac{2}{3}\right)^t$

6 The amount in grams of a radioactive substance is given by the function $y = 50(1.7)^{-0.3t}$ where t is time in years. Find the number of grams of the substance after 20 years.

A. -510 g

B. 2.07 g

C. 8.3 g

D. 203.5 g

In Exercises 7–10, match each of the following functions to its graph.

7 $y = \left(\frac{1}{4}\right)^x$ **8** $y = -2(4^x)$

9 $y = 3^x$ **10** $y = -(6^x)$

A.

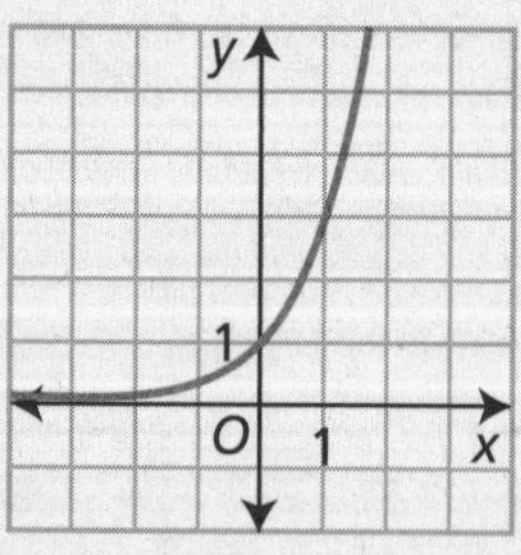

B.

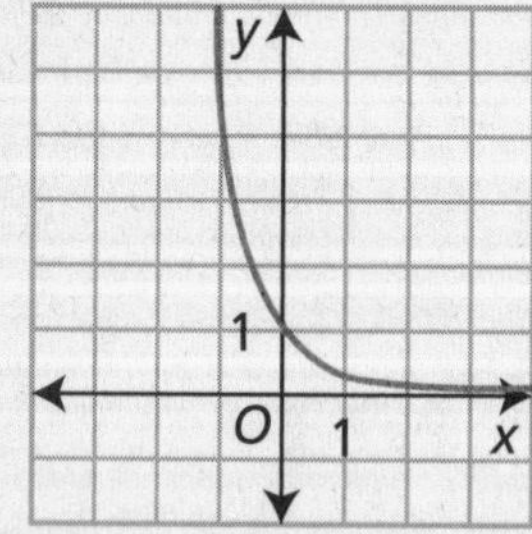

C.

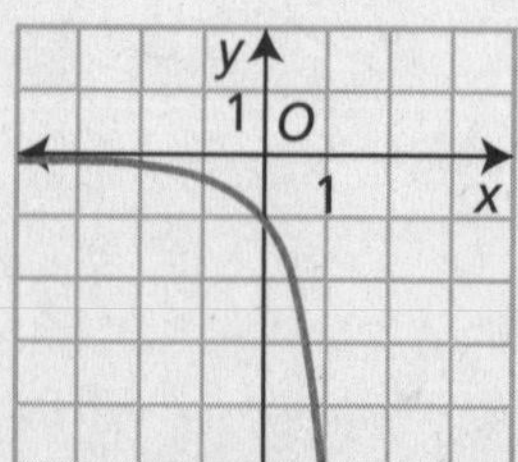

D.

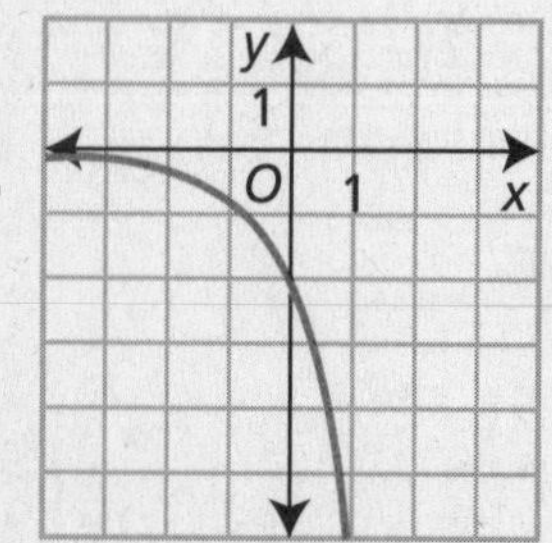

11 Which of the following is **not** an exponential function?

A. $5^x - 3$

B. $3\left(\frac{5}{2}\right)^x$

C. $5x^3$

D. $(0.25)^x$

12 Which exponential equation represents exponential decay?

A. $y = 0.5(1.5)^x$

B. $y = 1.5(3)^x$

C. $y = \frac{7}{2}(2)^x$

D. $y = 3\left(\frac{2}{7}\right)^x$

In Exercises 13–18, simplify each expression.

13 $(-3)^{-3}$

A. 27

B. $-\frac{1}{27}$

C. $-\frac{1}{9}$

D. $\frac{1}{27}$

14 $\frac{9a^2b^{-3}}{18a^5b^{-5}}$

A. $2a^3b^8$

B. $\frac{a^7}{2b^8}$

C. $\frac{-9}{a^3b^2}$

D. $\frac{b^2}{2a^3}$

15 $(z^3s^{-5}q^2)^0$

A. 1

B. zsq

C. $\frac{z^3q^2}{s^5}$

D. 0

16 $(2wz^2)(3wz^3)^2$

A. $18w^2z^{12}$

B. $18w^3z^8$

C. $36w^4z^{10}$

D. $12w^3z^7$

17 Which is equivalent to $\frac{1.92 \times 10^5}{2 \times 10^{-4}}$?

A. -0.08×10^1

B. 0.096×10^0

C. 0.96×10^9

D. 9.6×10^{-9}

18 Which is equivalent to $2000(1.27 \times 10^0)$?

A. 2540×10^1

B. 0.00254×10^0

C. 2.54×10^3

D. 2.54×10^{-3}

In Exercises 19–20, use the following information.

20% of a particular medicine is absorbed by the bloodstream every hour. A patient takes a 40-milligram dose of this medicine at 9 A.M.

19 Which function describes the amount of medicine absorbed in the bloodstream after x hours?

A. $y = 20(40)^x$

B. $\frac{1}{32}$

C. $y = 40(0.8)^x$

D. $y = 40(0.2)^x$

20 How many milligrams of medicine has been absorbed in the bloodstream by 2 P.M.?

A. 13.11 mg

B. 160 mg

C. 0.0128 mg

D. 4,000 mg

DIRECTIONS FOR 21–23: Solve each problem. Show your work or provide an explanation for your answer.

21 In a recent election, Candidate A received 62,040,610 votes, Candidate B received 59,028,111 votes, and other candidates received 1,224,611 votes.

Express the number of votes received by Candidate A in scientific notation.

Express the number of votes received by Candidate B in scientific notation.

Express the number of votes received by Candidate A as a percentage of total votes in scientific notation.

Express the number of votes received by Candidate B as a percentage of total votes in scientific notation.

22 Suppose that you deposit $750 in a savings account that pays 4.8% interest compounded annually.

Identify the initial amount.

Identify the growth factor.

Write an exponential growth equation that models the interest earned on the savings account.

Assuming no withdrawals or additional deposits, what is the balance after six years?

23 Determine whether the data in the accompanying table represent a linear, absolute value, or exponential function. Explain your reasoning.

x	y
1	3
2	9
3	27
4	81

5 Polynomials and Factoring

Discovering North Carolina

Physiography

North Carolina cuts across three distinct geographical regions of the eastern United States: the Coastal Plain, the Piedmont, and the Appalachian Mountains.

The Coastal Plain extends 120–140 miles inland from the coast of the Atlantic Ocean. The Coastal Plain makes up nearly one-half of the state.

The Piedmont refers to a stretch of land between New Jersey in the north and Alabama in the south. In North Carolina, the Piedmont is a low plateau with an elevation between 300 feet and 1,800 feet. This region consists of forested, rolling hills crisscrossed by many rivers.

The Blue Ridge Mountains rise sharply from the western edge of the Piedmont, with some peaks exceeding an elevation of 6,000 feet.

5.1 Addition and Subtraction of Polynomials

ADP℠ Standards

O2.b Operate with polynomial expressions

A single-term algebraic expression is called a **monomial.** A monomial is the product of real numbers and variables with nonnegative exponents.

EXAMPLE 1 **Recognizing monomials**

1 Which of the following are monomials?

A. $-3abc$ **B.** $\frac{4}{x}$ **C.** $-2r^2s$ **D.** $\frac{2}{3x}$ **E.** xy^{-2}

▪ **SOLUTION**

$-3abc$ and $-2r^2s$ are monomials. $\frac{4}{x}$, $\frac{2}{3x}$, and xy^{-2} are not because each has an unknown value in the denominator.

Note

No monomial may have a variable in the denominator because it may result in values for which the expression is undefined.

Recall that the number in front of the variable, or numerical factor, is called the **numerical coefficient** of the term, or **coefficient.**

Expression	Coefficient
$3x^2$	3
$-4y$	-4
$-\frac{5c}{6}$	$-\frac{5}{6}$

If no coefficient is indicated, then it is understood to be 1. For example, abc^2 has a numerical coefficient of 1.

Terms that have the same variable factors are **like terms.** Monomials with the same like terms can be combined.

EXAMPLES 2 and 3 **Combining monomials**

2 Can the terms $7x^3y^2$ and $-3x^3y^2$ be combined? Explain why or why not and describe the resulting expression.

▪ **SOLUTION**

$7x^3y^2$ and $-3x^3y^2$ can be combined because x^3 and y^2 are the same in both monomials. We apply the rule for addition of signed numbers on the coefficients and attach the variable expressions. So $7x^3y^2$ and $-3x^3y^2$ become $(7 - 3)x^3y^2$, or the monomial $4x^3y^2$.

3 Can the terms $2xy$ and y be combined?

▪ **SOLUTION**

The monomials $2xy$ and y cannot be combined because one monomial has x and y as its variables and the second monomial has only y. Therefore, the monomials are not like terms. The resulting expression will remain $2xy + y$.

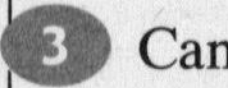

A **polynomial** is a monomial or a sum of monomials. Each of the monomials is a term of the polynomial. To write a polynomial in its simplest form, you must combine any like terms.

EXAMPLES 4 and 5 Simplifying a polynomial

4 Simplify $3a - 2ab + 4a$.

■ **SOLUTION**

$3a - 2ab + 4a$

$[3a + 4a] - 2ab$ ← Group like terms.

$7a - 2ab$ ← Add the coefficients of a.

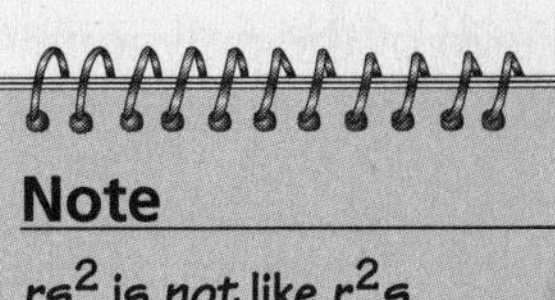

Note

rs^2 *is not like* r^2s.

5 Simplify $5r^2s + 10rs^2 - 8r^2s$.

■ **SOLUTION**

$5r^2s + 10rs^2 - 8r^2s$

$[5r^2s - 8r^2s] + 10rs^2$ ← Group like terms.

$-3r^2s + 10rs^2$ ← Subtract the coefficients of r^2s.

A polynomial in one variable is written in *descending order* when the powers of the variable decrease from left to right. It is written in *ascending order* when the powers of the variable increase from left to right. When a polynomial in one variable has no like terms, and the terms are written in descending order, the polynomial is said to be in **standard form.**

EXAMPLE 6 Writing a polynomial in standard form

6 Write $-8 + 4x^2 + 5 - 3x^2 + 2x$ in standard form.

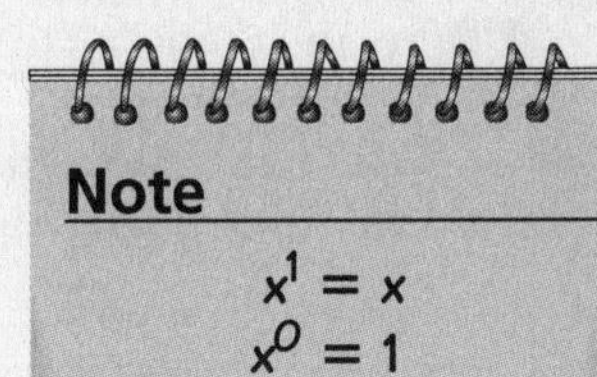

Note

$x^1 = x$

$x^0 = 1$

■ **SOLUTION**

$-8 + 4x^2 + 5 - 3x^2 + 2x$

$(-8 + 5) + (4x^2 - 3x^2) + 2x$ ← Group like terms.

$-3 + 1x^2 + 2x$ ← Simplify.

$x^2 + 2x - 3$ ← Use descending order: $x^2 + 2x^1 - 3x^0$

You can classify some polynomials by their number of terms. Polynomials with one, two, or three terms have special names.

Classifying Polynomials by Number of Terms		
Number of Terms	**Classification**	**Examples**
one	monomial	m, n^5, xy, $-5ab^2$, r^2st^3, 9
two	binomial	$3x + 4y$, $jk - 3$, $a^2 + 7a$, $p^3qr - 5p^2q^4$
three	trinomial	$r + s - t$, $-4x^2 + 8xy - 5y^2$, $a^2 + 2a - 6$

EXAMPLE 7 Classifying polynomials by number of terms

7 Classify $4x + 7$ as a monomial, binomial, or trinomial.

■ **SOLUTION**

$4x + 7$ has 2 terms; therefore, it is a **binomial.**

If a term of a polynomial has just one variable, the **degree of the term** is the exponent of the variable. A term that has no variable part is called a **constant term,** or simply a **constant.** The degree of a constant term is 0.

$$10k^4 \rightarrow \text{The degree is } 4.$$
$$-2t = -2t^1 \rightarrow \text{The degree is } 1.$$
$$6 = 6x^0 \rightarrow \text{The degree is } 0.$$

The **degree of a polynomial** is the greatest degree of any of its terms after it has been simplified. The term with the greatest degree is called the **leading term** of the polynomial. The coefficient of the leading term is called the **leading coefficient.**

Identifying the degree provides another means for classifying polynomials.

Note

When the term of a polynomial has more than one variable, the degree of the term is the sum of the exponents of the variables of the leading term.

$5x^4y^2 \rightarrow$ The degree is 6.

Classifying Polynomials by Degree

Degree of Polynomial	Classification	Examples
one	linear	x, $-6d$, $5s - 3$, $7 + 8y$
two	quadratic	x^2, $3m^2$, $9z^2 + 3z$, $k - k^2$, $4 - 2g + 6g^2$
three	cubic	x^3, $-8b^3 + 5b$, $4b^3 - b^2 + 7b + 6$

EXAMPLES 8 and 9 **Classifying polynomials by number of term and degree**

Go Online PearsonSchool.com
Visit: PearsonSchool.com
Web Code: ayp-0263

8 Which phrase best describes $-z^3 + 3z^2 - 2z - 3z^2$?

A. cubic trinomial
B. quadratic trinomial
C. cubic monomial
D. cubic binomial

■ SOLUTION

First simplify the polynomial.

$$-z^3 + 3z^2 - 2z - 3z^2$$
$$-z^3 + (3z^2 - 3z^2) - 2z$$
$$-z^3 + 0 - 2z$$
$$-z^3 - 2z$$

The simplified polynomial has two terms, so it is a *binomial.*
The greatest degree of any of its terms is 3, so it is *cubic.*
The correct choice is D.

9 Which phrase best describes $9x^2y + 3x^2 - 2x^2y - 5xy^2 - 4x^2$

A. quadratic binomial
B. quadratic trinomial
C. cubic binomial
D. cubic trinomial

■ SOLUTION

First simplify the polynomial.

$$9x^2y + 3x^2 - 2x^2y - 5xy^2 - 4x^2$$
$$-5xy^2 + (9x^2y - 2x^2y) + (3x^2 - 4x^2)$$
$$-5xy^2 + 7x^2y - x^2$$

The simplified polynomial has 3 terms, so it is a *trinomial.*
The greatest degree of any of its terms is 3, so it is *cubic.*
The correct choice is D.

To find a sum of polynomials, you add the like terms from all the polynomials. You can do this using either a horizontal or vertical format.

Go Online
PearsonSchool.com
Visit: PearsonSchool.com
Web Code: ayp-0135

EXAMPLES 10 and 11 **Adding polynomials**

Simplify each expression.

10 $(3x + x^2 - x^3) + (4x^3 + 2x^2 + 5x)$

■ **SOLUTION 1**

Group like terms.
Then add their coefficients.

$(3x + x^2 - x^3) + (4x^3 + 2x^2 + 5x)$
$= (-x^3 + 4x^3) + (x^2 + 2x^2) + (3x + 5x)$
$= 3x^3 + 3x^2 + 8x$

■ **SOLUTION 2**

Line up like terms in columns.
Then add their coefficients.

$$\begin{array}{r} -x^3 + x^2 + 3x \\ +\ 4x^3 + 2x^2 + 5x \\ \hline 3x^3 + 3x^2 + 8x \end{array}$$

11 $(3n^2 - 2n) + (-5n^3 + n^2) + (2n - 5)$

■ **SOLUTION 1**

$(3n^2 - 2n) + (-5n^3 + n^2) + (2n - 5)$
$= -5n^3 + (3n^2 + n^2) + (-2n + 2n) - 5$
$= -5n^3 + 4n^2 - 5$

■ **SOLUTION 2**

$$\begin{array}{rrrr} & 3n^2 & -\ 2n & \\ -5n^3 + & n^2 & & \\ + & & 2n & -\ 5 \\ \hline -5n^3 + & 4n^2 & & -5 \end{array}$$

To subtract one polynomial from another, you add the opposite, or additive inverse. In order to do this, it will be helpful to first review the procedure for finding the additive inverse of a polynomial.

EXAMPLE 12 **Finding the additive inverse of a polynomial**

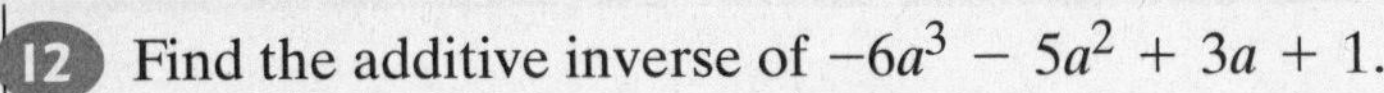

12 Find the additive inverse of $-6a^3 - 5a^2 + 3a + 1$.

■ **SOLUTION**

The sum of a number and its additive inverse is 0.
Find the polynomial that gives a sum of 0 when added to $-6a^3 - 5a^2 + 3a + 1$.

$$\begin{array}{r} -6a^3 - 5a^2 + 3a + 1 \\ +\ \qquad ? \qquad \\ \hline 0 \end{array} \quad \rightarrow \quad \begin{array}{r} -6a^3 - 5a^2 + 3a + 1 \\ +\ 6a^3 + 5a^2 - 3a - 1 \\ \hline 0 \end{array}$$

← **Write the opposite of each term.**

So the additive inverse of $-6a^3 - 5a^2 + 3a + 1$ is $6a^3 + 5a^2 - 3a - 1$.

You can find the additive inverse of a polynomial by finding the additive inverse of each term.

Opposites of Sums and Differences

For all real numbers a and b: $-(a + b) = -a + (-b) = -a - b$

$-(a - b) = -a + b$

Just as with addition, you can find a difference of polynomials using either a horizontal or vertical format.

Go Online
PearsonSchool.com
Visit: PearsonSchool.com
Web Code: ayp-0136

EXAMPLES 13 and 14 Subtracting polynomials

13 Simplify $(3c^2 - 8c + 4) - (7 + c^2 - 8c)$.

■ SOLUTION 1

Change the subtraction to addition. Then write the opposite of each term of the polynomial being subtracted. Finally, combine like terms.

$$\begin{aligned}&(3c^2 - 8c + 4) - (7 + c^2 - 8c)\\&= (3c^2 - 8c + 4) + (-7 - c^2 + 8c)\\&= (3c^2 - c^2) + (-8c + 8c) + (4 - 7)\\&= 2c^2 - 3\end{aligned}$$

■ SOLUTION 2

Line up like terms in columns. Write the opposite of each term of the polynomial being subtracted. Finally, combine like terms.

$$\begin{array}{rrrr} & 3c^2 & - 8c & + 4 \\ + & -c^2 & + 8c & - 7 \\ \hline & 2c^2 & & -3 \end{array}$$

14 Simplify the result when $(5d^2 - 2d^3 + 3)$ is subtracted from $(d^2 + 8 - 5d)$.

■ SOLUTION 1

Subtract horizontally.

$$\begin{aligned}&(d^2 + 8 - 5d) - (5d^2 - 2d^3 + 3)\\&= (d^2 + 8 - 5d) + (-5d^2 + 2d^3 - 3)\\&= 2d^3 + (d^2 - 5d^2) - 5d + (8 - 3)\\&= 2d^3 - 4d^2 - 5d + 5\end{aligned}$$

■ SOLUTION 2

Subtract vertically.

$$\begin{array}{rrrrr} & & d^2 & - 5d & + 8 \\ + & 2d^3 & - 5d^2 & & - 3 \\ \hline & 2d^3 & - 4d^2 & - 5d & + 5 \end{array}$$

Practice

Choose the letter preceding the word or expression that best completes the statement or answers the question.

1 Which best describes $-3x^2 + 3 - x + 3x^2$?

A. quadratic expression with four terms

B. linear binomial

C. polynomial with degree 2

D. not a polynomial

2 Which is a quadratic binomial when written in simplest form?

A. $(-z^2 + 3z) + (-z^2 - 3z)$

B. $(-z^2 + 3z) + (z^2 - 3z)$

C. $(-z^2 - 3z) + (-z^2 - 3z)$

D. $(-z^2 + 3z) + (z^2 + 3z)$

3 Which polynomial added to $3d^2 - 3d + 1$ will result in a sum of 0?

A. $-3d^2 - 3d + 1$

B. $-3d^2 + 3d + 1$

C. $-3d^2 + 3d - 1$

D. $3d^2 - 3d + 1$

4 What is the result when $2c^2 - 3c + 6$ is subtracted from $c^2 + c - 2$?

A. $c^2 - 4c + 8$

B. $-c^2 - 2c + 4$

C. $c^2 + 4c + 8$

D. $-c^2 + 4c - 8$

5 The perimeter of a polygon is the sum of the lengths of its sides. Which does not represent the perimeter of the polygon below?

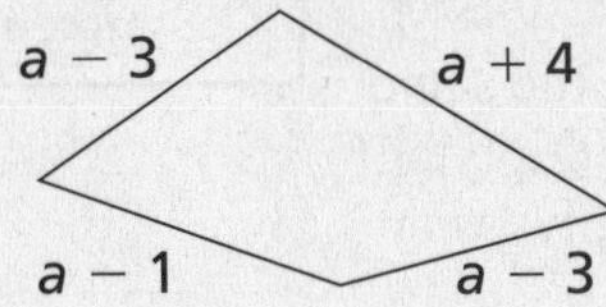

A. $(a - 3) + (a - 3) + (a - 1) + (a + 4)$

B. $2(a - 3) + (a - 1) + (a + 4)$

C. $4a + 3$

D. $4a - 3$

In Exercises 6–9, simplify each expression.

6 $yz^3 + 2y^3z - 4yz^3 - y^3z$

7 $5m^2n^2 - 4mn^2 - 9m^2n + 7mn^2$

8 $-4a^2b^2 + 3ab - a^3b - 8ba$

9 $2c^2d - 6d - 7d + 3cd^2 + c^4$

In Exercises 10–15, write each polynomial in standard form.

10 $y^2 - 7y - 3y^3$

11 $4b^3 + 1 - b + 9b^2$

12 $3x^2 - 2x + 5x - 6x^3$

13 $v^2 + v - 3v^3 - v^2$

14 $-7q^2 + 2q + 3q^2 - 2q + 5q^2$

15 $4w - 3w^2 + 7w^3 - w^3 - 7$

In Exercises 16–21, classify each polynomial by its degree and by its number of terms.

16 $3d^2$ **17** $y^2 - 3y - 7$

18 $-g - 4g^3 + 5g$ **19** $5d + 9$

20 $2m^2 + 3m^3 - 2m - 5m^2$

21 $b^3 - 2b - b^3 - 2b$

In Exercises 22–37, simplify each expression. Write answers in standard form.

22 $(n^3 + 8n^2 + 6n) + (8n^3 + 2n^2 - 6n)$

23 $(5s^2 + 7s - 11) + (4 + s - 5s^2)$

24 $(x^4 + x - 2) + (2x^4 + x^3 - 5)$

25 $(3a + 4a^3 - 8) + (a^2 + 2a - 7)$

26 $(3y^3 + 8y - 3) + (2y - 5y^2)$

27 $(-4r^3 + 2r - 3r^2 + 1) + (2r^3 - 5r + 1)$

28 $(5h^2 + 4h + 8) - (3h^2 + h + 3)$

29 $(-7z^3 + 2z - 7) - (2z^3 - z - 3)$

30 $(3c^2 + 4c - 6) - (3c - 8 + 5c^2)$

31 $(-a^2 - 3 + 7a) - (2a^3 - 7a)$

32 $(n^3 + n^2) - (2n^3 + 3n^2 - 2n)$

33 $(-2w^3 - 9 + 8w) - (2w^4 + 6w^3 - 11w^2)$

34 $(x^2 + 5) + (3x + 8) + (5x^2 + 3x)$

35 $(5j^2 + 3j) + (j^2 + 4j + 4) - (2j - 3)$

36 $(-5p^3 + 6p) - (2p^3 + 8p^2) + (6p + 2p^3)$

37 $(2z^2 - 4) - (z^2 - 4) - (-3z^2 - 2)$

In Exercises 38–42, solve the problem. Clearly show all necessary work.

38 Find the difference when $x^2 + 8 - 2x$ is subtracted from $2x - 10x^2 + 7$.

39 Is $2x^{-3} + x^2 + x - 4$ a polynomial? Explain your answer.

40 The perimeter of a polygon is the sum of the lengths of its sides. Write a simplified expression for the perimeter of this polygon.

m + n
2m + 3
4m − 2
3m + 15

41 The perimeter of the polygon below can be represented by the expression $12t - 5$. Write a simplified expression for the length of the side that is not labeled.

4t + 10
2t + 5
3t − 4

42 Is the sum of two binomials always a binomial? Explain your answer.

5.2 Multiplication and Division with Polynomials

ADP℠ Standards

O2.b Operate with polynomial expressions

Recall that a polynomial is simply the sum of monomials; therefore, the same rules that apply for multiplication of monomials also apply when multiplying a polynomial by a monomial. Use the distributive property to multiply every term of the polynomial by the monomial.

EXAMPLES 1 through 3 **Multiplying a polynomial by a monomial: one variable**

Simplify each expression.

1 $3(5z - 6)$

■ SOLUTION

$3(5z - 6)$ — Use the distributive property.
$3(5z) - 3(6)$ ←
$15z - 3(6)$ ← Simplify $3(5z)$.
$15z - 18$ ← Simplify $3(6)$.

2 $-7a(-2a + 9)$

■ SOLUTION

$-7a(-2a + 9)$
$(-7a)(-2a) + (-7a)(9)$
$14a^2 + (-63a)$
$14a^2 - 63a$

3 $2xy(-3x + 2y - 4)$

■ SOLUTION

$2xy(-3x + 2y - 4)$
$2xy(-3x) + 2xy(2y) - 2xy(4)$
$-6x^2y + 4xy^2 - 8xy$

Sometimes you must multiply polynomials before solving an equation.

Visit: PearsonSchool.com
Web Code: ayp-0269

EXAMPLES 4 and 5 **Multiplying polynomials in equation solving**

4 Solve $(3b^2 + 2b - 1) - 3b(b + 5) = 12$.

■ SOLUTION

$(3b^2 + 2b - 1) - 3b(b + 5) = 12$
$(3b^2 + 2b - 1) + (-3b)(b + 5) = 12$ ← Rewrite the subtraction as addition.
$(3b^2 + 2b - 1) + (-3b)(b) + (-3b)(5) = 12$ ← Apply the distributive property.
$(3b^2 + 2b - 1) + (-3b^2) + (-15b) = 12$ ← Simplify $(-3b)(b)$ and $(-3b)(5)$.
$[3b^2 + (-3b^2)] + [2b + (-15b)] - 1 = 12$ ← Combine like terms.
$-13b - 1 = 12$ ← Solve.
$-13b = 13$
$b = -1$

5 Solve $3(2m^2 + 5) = 3m(2m + 7) - 3m - 3$.

■ SOLUTION

$3(2m^2 + 5) = 3m(2m + 7) - 3m - 3$
$3(2m^2) + 3(5) = 3m(2m) + 3m(7) - 3m - 3$ ← Apply the distributive property.
$6m^2 + 15 = 6m^2 + 21m - 3m - 3$ ← Simplify.
$6m^2 + 15 = 6m^2 + 18m - 3$ ← Combine like terms.
$6m^2 - 6m^2 + 15 = 6m^2 - 6m^2 + 18m - 3$ ← Solve.
$15 + 3 = 18m - 3 + 3$
$18 = 18m$
$1 = m$

To multiply a polynomial by a binomial, you must apply the distributive property more than once. You begin by distributing the first term in the binomial factor to each term in the polynomial, and then you distribute the second term in the binomial factor to each term in the polynomial.

Go Online
PearsonSchool.com
Visit: PearsonSchool.com
Web Code: ayp-0270

EXAMPLES 6 and 7 Multiplying by a binomial

Simplify each expression.

6 $(2y - 3)(y + 2)$

■ SOLUTION 1

Multiply horizontally.

$$\begin{array}{ll} (2y - 3)(y + 2) & \\ (2y - 3)y + (2y - 3)2 & \leftarrow \text{Distribute } (2y - 3). \\ 2y^2 - 3y + (2y - 3)2 & \leftarrow \text{Simplify } (2y - 3)y. \\ 2y^2 - 3y + 4y - 6 & \leftarrow \text{Simplify } (2y - 3)2. \\ 2y^2 + y - 6 & \leftarrow \text{Combine like terms.} \end{array}$$

■ SOLUTION 2

Multiply vertically.

$$\begin{array}{rrrl} & 2y & - 3 & \\ \times & y & + 2 & \\ \hline & 4y & - 6 & \leftarrow \text{Multiply } 2(2y - 3). \\ 2y^2 & - 3y & & \leftarrow \text{Multiply } y(2y - 3). \\ \hline 2y^2 & + y & - 6 & \leftarrow \text{Combine like terms.} \end{array}$$

7 $(n + 4)(2n^2 - 3n + 3)$

■ SOLUTION 1

Multiply horizontally.

$$\begin{array}{c} (n + 4)(2n^2 - 3n + 3) \\ n(2n^2 - 3n + 3) + 4(2n^2 - 3n + 3) \\ 2n^3 - 3n^2 + 3n + 4(2n^2 - 3n + 3) \\ 2n^3 - 3n^2 + 3n + 8n^2 - 12n + 12 \\ 2n^3 + 5n^2 - 9n + 12 \end{array}$$

■ SOLUTION 2

Multiply vertically.

$$\begin{array}{rrrr} & 2n^2 & - 3n & + 3 \\ \times & & n & + 4 \\ \hline & 8n^2 & - 12n & + 12 \\ 2n^3 & - 3n^2 & + 3n & \\ \hline 2n^3 & + 5n^2 & - 9n & + 12 \end{array}$$

You may also need to multiply polynomials before you can simplify an algebraic expression.

Go Online
PearsonSchool.com
Visit: PearsonSchool.com
Web Code: ayp-0939

EXAMPLE 8 Using multiplication to simplify a polynomial

8 Simplify the expression $(b^2 + 2b - 1) - (b - 5)(b + 6)$.

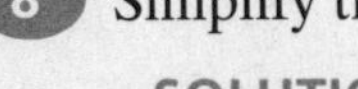
■ SOLUTION

$$\begin{array}{ll} (b^2 + 2b - 1) - (b - 5)(b + 6) & \\ (b^2 + 2b - 1) - [(b - 5)b + (b - 5)6] & \leftarrow \text{Distribute } (b - 5). \\ (b^2 + 2b - 1) - [b^2 - 5b + (b - 5)6] & \leftarrow \text{Simplify } (b - 5)b. \\ (b^2 + 2b - 1) - [b^2 - 5b + 6b - 30] & \leftarrow \text{Simplify } (b - 5)6. \\ (b^2 + 2b - 1) - [b^2 + b - 30] & \leftarrow \text{Combine like terms } -5b \text{ and } 6b. \\ (b^2 + 2b - 1) - b^2 - b + 30 & \leftarrow \text{Distribute } -1. \\ b + 29 & \leftarrow \text{Combine like terms.} \end{array}$$

When you use the Distributive Property to multiply binomials. You can use the letters in the word FOIL to help you remember which terms of two binomials are multiplied.

> **Note**
>
> FOIL can only be used to multiply two binomials.

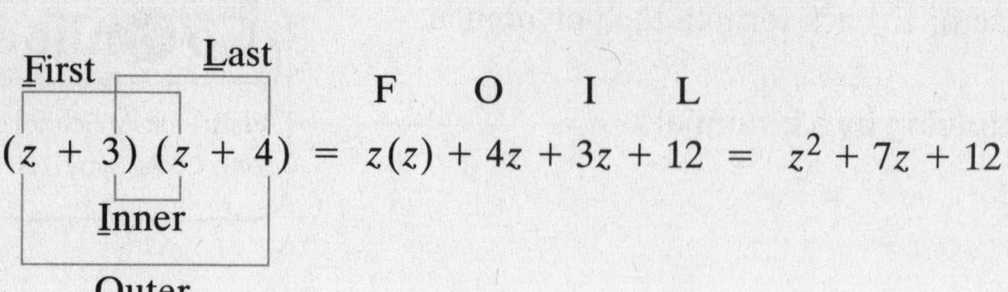

A special product, called a **perfect square trinomial,** results when a binomial is squared. Another pattern emerges, called the **difference of two squares,** when you multiply the sum of two terms by the difference of the same two terms. Look for the patterns in the following examples.

> **Go Online** PearsonSchool.com
> Visit: PearsonSchool.com
> Web Code: ayp-0271

EXAMPLES 9 and 10 **Squaring a binomial**

Simplify each expression.

9 $(c + 4)^2 = (c + 4)(c + 4)$

■ **SOLUTION**

$c^2 + 4c + 4c + 4^2$

$c^2 + 2(4c) + 4^2$

$c^2 + 8c + 16$

10 $(m + 5)(m - 5)$

■ **SOLUTION**

$m^2 + (-5m) + 5m + 5(-5)$

$m^2 + 0m + (-25)$

$m^2 - 25$

These patterns are often generalized as follows.

Squaring Patterns of Binomials

For all real numbers a and b: $(a + b)^2 = a^2 + 2ab + b^2$

$(a - b)^2 = a^2 - 2ab + b^2$

$(a + b)(a - b) = a^2 - b^2$

The same rules that apply for division of monomials will apply for division of a polynomial by a monomial. Every term of the polynomial in the numerator will be divided by the monomial in the denominator.

For all real numbers a and b and all nonzero real numbers c,

$$\frac{a + b}{c} = \frac{a}{c} + \frac{b}{c} \quad \text{and} \quad \frac{a - b}{c} = \frac{a}{c} - \frac{b}{c}.$$

$$\frac{2 + 5}{9} = \frac{2}{9} + \frac{5}{9} = \frac{7}{9} \quad \text{and} \quad \frac{8 - 3}{7} = \frac{8}{7} - \frac{3}{7} = \frac{5}{7}$$

EXAMPLES 11 and 12 **Dividing a polynomial by a monomial**

Go Online PearsonSchool.com
Visit: PearsonSchool.com
Web Code: ayp-0331

Simplify each expression.

11 $\frac{8a^2 - 12a}{4a}$

▪ **SOLUTION**

$\frac{8a^2 - 12a}{4a}$

$\frac{8a^2}{4a} - \frac{12a}{4a}$ ← Divide each term by $4a$.

$2a - 3$

12 $\frac{16yz^2 - 8y^2z + 10yz}{-2yz}$

▪ **SOLUTION**

$\frac{16yz^2 - 8y^2z + 10yz}{-2yz}$

$\frac{16yz^2}{-2yz} - \frac{8y^2z}{-2yz} + \frac{10yz}{-2yz}$ ← Divide each term by $-2yz$.

$-8z - (-4y) + (-5)$

$-8z + 4y - 5$

Practice

Choose the letter preceding the word or expression that best completes the statement or answers the question.

1 The expression $(s - 3)^2$ is equivalent to

A. $s^2 + 9$. **C.** $s^2 + 6s + 9$.
B. $s^2 - 9$. **D.** $s^2 - 6s + 9$.

2 What is the product of $4g^3 + 4g^2 + 2g$ and $2g$?

A. $2g^2 + 2g$ **C.** $8g^2 + 8g + 4$
B. $2g^2 + 2g + 1$ **D.** $8g^4 + 8g^3 + 4g^2$

3 Which is equivalent to $23^2 - 13^2$?

A. 10^2 **C.** 36^2
B. 10×36 **D.** $2(23 - 13)$

4 Which is the value of $\frac{6a^4 - 2a^3 - 2a^2}{2a^2}$ when $a = -2$?

A. 13 **B.** 9 **C.** 0 **D.** −11

5 Simplify $(5z - 9) - 4(-2z - 3)$.

A. $13z - 3$ **C.** $13z + 3$
B. $-3z + 21$ **D.** $3z - 8$

6 $4y^2 - 12y + 9$ is the perfect square of which binomial?

A. $(-2y + 3)$ **C.** $(y - 3)$
B. $(-2y - 3)$ **D.** $(2y + 3)$

In Exercises 7–21, simplify each expression.

7 $6(4a - 2)$ **8** $(8v - 3)(-5v)$

9 $(2y + 3)(y - 2)$ **10** $(2t - 5)(5t - 2)$

11 $(3w + 7)(2w - 5)$ **12** $(2d + 4)^2$

13 $(-3q - 4)^2$ **14** $(v + 9)(v - 9)$

15 $\frac{6k^2 + 15k}{3k}$

16 $(a^2b^2 + ab - 4)(-2a)$

17 $-5p^2(p^2 + 2p + 1)$

18 $(x^2 + 3x - 2)(x + 3)$

19 $(2n - 7)(n^2 - n + 3)$

20 $\frac{2w^3 + 6w^2 - 5w}{-2w}$

21 $\frac{15z^4 - 25z^3 - 20z^2}{5z^2}$

In Exercises 22–24, solve each equation.

22 $2(3n + 2) = 5n - 4$

23 $8w - 5(2w + 7) = 2w - 9$

24 Mark says that $(m + n)^2$ and $m^2 + n^2$ are equivalent expressions. Do you agree or disagree? Explain.

5.3 Factoring Polynomials

ADP℠ Standards

O2.c Factor simple polynomial expressions

When multiplying monomials, you write a simplified expression for their product. The reverse of this process is called *factoring the monomial.*

To **factor** a monomial, you start with the simplified expression and find a multiplication equivalent of it. For instance, using whole number coefficients, there are five ways to factor $9x^2$. These are shown at the right. From these factorizations, you arrive at the following list of factors.

factors of $9x^2$: $1, 3, 9, x, 3x, 9x, x^2, 3x^2, 9x^2$

$9x^2 = 1 \cdot 9x^2$
$9x^2 = 3 \cdot 3x^2$
$9x^2 = 9 \cdot x^2$
$9x^2 = x \cdot 9x$
$9x^2 = 3x \cdot 3x$

The **greatest common factor (GCF)** of two or more monomials is the product of the greatest common factor of their numerical coefficients and the greatest common factor of their variable parts.

EXAMPLE 1 **Finding the GCF of monomials**

1 Find the GCF of $12x^3$, $30x^2$, and $42x$.

■ **SOLUTION**

Step 1

Write the factored form of each monomial.
Circle the factors common to all the monomials.

$12x^3 = (2) \cdot 2 \cdot (3) \cdot (x) \cdot x \cdot x$
$30x^2 = (2) \cdot (3) \cdot 5 \cdot (x) \cdot x$
$42x = (2) \cdot (3) \cdot 7 \cdot (x)$

Step 2

Multiply the circled factors.
$2 \cdot 3 \cdot x = 6x$

The GCF of $12x^3$, $30x^2$, and $42x$ is $6x$.

When the terms of a polynomial have a GCF other than 1, you can factor the polynomial by using the distributive property.

EXAMPLES 2 and 3 **Common monomial factoring with a numerical GCF**

Factor each expression using the GCF of the terms.

2 $3a + 6$ ■ **SOLUTION**
$3a + 6$ ← The GCF of $3a$ and 6 is 3.
$3a + 3(2)$ ← Rewrite each term as a product.
$3(a + 2)$ ← Apply the distributive property.

3 $8x^2 - 12y + 20$ ■ **SOLUTION**
$8x^2 - 12y + 20$ ← The GCF of $8x^2$, $12y$, and 20 is 4.
$4(2x^2) - 4(3y) + 4(5)$ ← Rewrite each term as a product.
$4(2x^2 - 3y + 5)$ ← Apply the distributive property.

In Example 3, notice that it is also possible to factor $8x^2 - 12y + 20$ as $2(4x^2 - 6y + 10)$. However, the GCF was not used in this factoring. As a result, $4x^2 - 6y + 10$ can be factored further as $2(2x^2 - 3y + 5)$. This means that $2(4x^2 - 6y + 10)$ is considered only a *partial* factorization.

In general, your goal is to factor polynomials *completely*. A polynomial is factored completely when it is expressed as a product of one or more polynomials that cannot be factored further.

EXAMPLES 4 through 6 — Common monomial factoring with a variable expression as the GCF

Factor each expression completely.

4 $6r^4 + 9r^2 + 4r$

■ **SOLUTION**

$6r^4 + 9r^2 + 4r$ ← **The GCF of $6r^4$, $9r^2$, and $4r$ is r.**

$r(6r^3) + r(9r) + r(4)$

$r(6r^3 + 9r + 4)$

5 $4mn - 10m$

■ **SOLUTION**

$4mn - 10m$ ← **The GCF of $4mn$ and $10m$ is $2m$.**

$2m(2n) - 2m(5)$

$2m(2n - 5)$

6 $8a^3b^2 + 16a^2b^2 - 4ab$

■ **SOLUTION**

$8a^3b^2 + 16a^2b^2 - 4ab$ ← **The GCF of $8a^3b^2$, $16a^2b^2$, and $4ab$ is $4ab$.**

$4ab(2a^2b) + 4ab(4ab) - 4ab(1)$

$4ab(2a^2b + 4ab - 1)$

Many trinomials are the product of two binomial factors. The general formula for these trinomials is $ax^2 + bx + c$, where c is a constant term. Look at the products in the following table.

Factors		Quadratic Term		Linear Term		Constant Term
$(x + 2)(x + 5) = x^2 + 5x + 2x + 10 =$		x^2	+	$7x$	+	10
$(x - 3)(x - 1) = x^2 - 1x - 3x + 3 =$		x^2	−	$4x$	+	3
$(x + 6)(x - 4) = x^2 - 4x + 6x - 24 =$		x^2	+	$2x$	−	24
$(x - 8)(x + 7) = x^2 + 7x - 8x - 56 =$		x^2	−	x	−	56

Notice that the terms of the trinomials are related to the terms of their binomial factors. The constant term is the product of the last terms of the factors. The coefficient of the linear term is the sum of the last terms of the factors. You can use these relationships to factor many quadratic trinomials.

Go Online
PearsonSchool.com
Visit: PearsonSchool.com
Web Code: ayp-0274

EXAMPLES 7 and 8 — Factoring trinomials of the form $ax^2 + bx + c$ where $a = 1$ and $a > 0$

Factor each expression completely.

7 $h^2 + 8h + 15$

■ **SOLUTION**

Look for factors of 15 whose sum is 8.

Factors of 15	Sum of Factors
1, 15	16
3, 5	8

← **Both factors must be positive.**

The numbers 3 and 5 have product of 15 and a sum of 8.
So $h^2 + 8h + 15 = (h + 3)(h + 5)$.

8 $y^2 - 10y + 16$

■ **SOLUTION**

Look for factors of 16 whose sum is −10.

Factors of 16	Sum of Factors
−1, −16	−17
−2, −8	−10
−4, −4	−8

← **Both factors must be negative.**

The numbers −2 and −8 have a product of 16 and a sum of −10.
So $y^2 - 10y + 16 = (y - 2)(y - 8)$.

If every term of a quadratic trinomial is positive, then the second term of each binomial will be positive. If the second term of the trinomial is negative and the last term is positive, then the second term of each binomial will be negative.

If the second term of a trinomial is positive and the third term is negative, then each binomial will be opposite in sign and the sign of the number with the largest absolute value will be positive. If the second and third terms of a trinomial are negative, then each binomial will be opposite in sign and the sign of the number with the largest absolute value will be negative.

EXAMPLES 9 and 10 **Factoring trinomials of the form $ax^2 + bx + c$ where $c < 0$**

Factor each expression completely.

9 $n^2 + 3n - 10$

SOLUTION

Look for factors of -10 with sum 3.

Factors	Sum
$-1, 10$	9
$1, -10$	-9
$-2, 5$	3
$2, -5$	-3

← **The factors must have opposite signs.**

The numbers -2 and 5 have a product of -10 and a sum of 3.

So $n^2 + 3n - 10 = (n - 2)(n + 5)$.

10 $n^2 - 3n - 10$

SOLUTION

Look for factors of -10 with sum -3.

Factors	Sum
$-1, 10$	9
$1, -10$	-9
$-2, 5$	3
$2, -5$	-3

← **The factors must have opposite signs.**

The numbers 2 and -5 have a product of -10 and a sum of -3.

So $n^2 - 3n - 10 = (n + 2)(n - 5)$.

Sometimes you must factor a trinomial of the form $ax^2 + bx + c$ when a is a whole number greater than 1. In these cases you must consider not only the factors of the constant c, but also the factors of the leading coefficient a.

EXAMPLE 11 **Factoring trinomials of the form $ax^2 + bx + c$ where $a > 1$**

11 Factor the expression $2w^2 - w - 6$.

SOLUTION

Step 1

List the factors of the leading coefficient, which is 2:

1 and 2

List the factors of the constant, which is -6:

1 and -6
-1 and 6
2 and -3
-2 and 3

Step 2

Use the factors from Step 1 to write pairs of binomial factors. Look for $-1w$ as the middle term.

$(1w + 1)(2w - 6) \rightarrow -6w + 2w = -4w$
$(1w - 6)(2w + 1) \rightarrow 1w + (-12w) = -11w$
$(1w - 1)(2w + 6) \rightarrow 6w + (-2w) = 4w$
$(1w + 6)(2w - 1) \rightarrow -1w + 12w = 11w$
$(1w + 2)(2w - 3) \rightarrow -3w + 4w = 1w$
$(1w - 3)(2w + 2) \rightarrow 2w + (-6w) = -4w$
$(1w + 3)(2w - 2) \rightarrow -2w + 6w = 4w$
$(1w - 2)(2w + 3) \rightarrow 3w + (-4w) = -1w$ ✔

So $2w^2 - w - 6 = (w - 2)(2w + 3)$.

Recall that squares of sums and differences result in perfect square trinomials.

For all real numbers a and b: $(a + b)^2 = a^2 + 2ab + b^2$

$$(a - b)^2 = a^2 - 2ab + b^2$$

You can use what you know about the squares of sums and differences to factor perfect square trinomials. The steps are described below.

To Factor a Perfect Square Trinomial

- Find the square root of the first and last terms.
- If the sign of the middle term is positive then the second term of the factor is positive.
- If the sign of the middle term is negative then the second term of the factor is negative.
- Check to make sure that twice the product of the first and last terms equals the middle term.

EXAMPLES 12 and 13 **Factoring perfect square trinomials**

12 $x^2 + 6x + 9$

■ **SOLUTION**

$x^2 + 2(3)x + 3^2 = (x + 3)^2$

13 $a^2 - 8ab + 16b^2$

■ **SOLUTION**

$a^2 - 4(2)b + (4b)^2 = (a - 4b)^2$

Recall the rule for the product of the **difference of two squares.**

For all real numbers a and b: $(a - b)(a + b) = a^2 - b^2$

You can use what you know about the product of $(a - b)(a + b)$ to factor the difference of two squares. The steps are described below.

To Factor the Difference of 2 Squares

- Find the square root of each term.
- Write two binomials that are the sum and difference of those square roots.

Visit: PearsonSchool.com
Web Code: ayp-0282

EXAMPLES 14 and 15 **Factoring the difference of 2 squares**

14 $4x^4 - 9y^6$

■ **SOLUTION**

$(2x^2)^2 - (3y^3)^2 = (2x^2 - 3y^3)(2x^2 + 3y^3)$

15 $25a^2 - 49b^2$

■ **SOLUTION**

$(5a)^2 - (7b)^2 = (5a - 7b)(5a + 7b)$

You may be asked to determine the correctly factored form of a polynomial.

EXAMPLE 16 **Recognizing the correct factored form**

16 Which product is equivalent to $m^2 - 5m + 6$?

A. $(m + 3)(m - 2)$ **C.** $(m + 3)(m + 2)$
B. $(m - 3)(m - 2)$ **D.** $(m - 3)(m + 2)$

SOLUTION

Examine the choices.

A and D These products will each have a negative constant term.

C This product will have a positive constant term, but the coefficient of the linear term will also be positive.

B By a process of elimination, choice B must be the correct factorization. You can check any factorization by multiplying:

$$(m - 3)(m - 2) = m^2 - 2m - 3m + (-3)(-2) = m^2 - 5m + 6 \checkmark$$

The correct choice is B.

In some cases, factoring completely will involve two types of factorization. In general, you should always begin by looking for a common monomial factor.

EXAMPLES 17 and 18 **Factoring in two steps**

Factor each expression completely.

17 $5v^2 - 5$ **SOLUTION**

$5v^2 - 5$ ← The GCF of $5v^2$ and 5 is 5.
$5(v^2 - 1)$ ← $v^2 - 1$ is a difference of two squares.
$5(v + 1)(v - 1)$

18 $6h^3 + 9h^2 - 6h$ **SOLUTION**

$6h^3 + 9h^2 - 6h$ ← The GCF of $6h^3$, $9h^2$, and $6h$ is $3h$.
$3h(2h^2 + 3h - 2)$ ← $2h^2 + 3h - 2$ has two binomial factors.
$3h(2h - 1)(h + 2)$

Practice

Choose the letter preceding the word or expression that best completes the statement or answers the question.

1 What is the greatest common factor of $24c^2d$, $18c^2d^2$, and $12cd^2$?

A. $72c^2d^2$ **C.** $6cd$
B. $6c^2d$ **D.** $2c^2d$

2 Which is a perfect square trinomial?

A. $x^2 - 8x + 16x^2$ **C.** $x^2 - 8x + 16$
B. $x^2 + 8x - 16$ **D.** $x^2 - 8x - 16$

3 Which is not a true statement?

A. $a^2 + 2ab + b^2 = (a + b)^2$

B. $a^2 - 2ab + b^2 = (a - b)^2$

C. $a^2 + 2ab - b^2 = (b - a)^2$

D. $a^2 - b^2 = (a + b)(a - b)$

4 Which expression is a factor of $9m^2 - 9m - 10$?

A. $3m - 5$ **C.** $9m + 1$

B. $3m - 2$ **D.** $9m - 1$

5 Which is equivalent to $9r^2 - 16s^2$?

A. $(3r + 4s)(3r - 4s)$

B. $(3r - 4s)^2$

C. $(9r + 16s)(9r - 16s)$

D. $(9r - 16s)^2$

6 Which expression cannot be factored over the integers?

A. $z^2 + 7z + 6$ **C.** $z^2 + 5z - 6$

B. $z^2 + 7z - 6$ **D.** $z^2 + 5z + 6$

In Exercises 7–10, find the GCF.

7 $9t^2, 15t, 12$ **8** $2y^3, 10y^2, 20y$

9 $4r^2s^2, 12rs^2, 9r^2s$ **10** a^3b^3, a^2b^3, a^2b

In Exercises 11–54, factor each expression completely. If it is not possible to factor over the integers, write *cannot be factored.*

11 $8n - 72$ **12** $9b^2 + 17b$

13 $12r^2 + 18r$ **14** $8v^3 - 36v$

15 $v^6 + v^3 + v$ **16** $3x^5 - 15x^3 + 9x^2$

17 $16j^2k^2 - 40jk$ **18** $4cd^2 + 2c^2d - 6cd$

19 $c^2 + 14c + 45$ **20** $a^2 - 16a + 28$

21 $x^2 - x - 30$ **22** $q^2 + 2q - 63$

23 $y^2 - 16y + 48$ **24** $b^2 - 14b - 72$

25 $h^2 + h - 42$ **26** $s^2 - 10s + 9$

27 $3d^2 + 8d + 5$ **28** $5m^2 - 11m + 2$

29 $3t^2 - 7t - 6$ **30** $3j^2 + 7j - 10$

31 $6x^2 - 19x + 15$ **32** $4y^2 - 4y - 15$

33 $b^2 + 4b + 4$ **34** $n^2 - 24n + 144$

35 $w^2 - 10w + 25$ **36** $r^2 + 8r + 16$

37 $9z^2 + 30z + 25$ **38** $4c^2 - 60c + 225$

39 $4p^2 + 44p + 121$ **40** $16g^2 - 72g + 81$

41 $u^2 - 100$ **42** $9k^2 - 49$

43 $36a^2 - 1$ **44** $144c^2 - 25$

45 $4n^2 - 16$ **46** $12w^2 - 27$

47 $5z^2 + 25z + 30$ **48** $40d^2 - 10d - 15$

49 $50t^3 - 32t$ **50** $16y^3 + 48y^2 + 36y$

51 $k^6 - 9k^4$ **52** $b^4 - 1$

53 $9c^2 - 100d^2$ **54** $4r^2 + 2rs - 6s^2$

In Exercises 55–59, solve the problem. Clearly show all necessary work.

55 What are all the possible values of n that make $x^2 + nx - 10$ a factorable expression over the integers?

56 For what value(s) of m is $x^2 + 2x + m$ a perfect square trinomial?

57 For what value(s) of p is $x^2 + px + 81$ a perfect square trinomial?

58 Explain why there is no integer value of q for which $x^2 + 7x + q$ is a perfect square.

59 Selena says that $(a - b)^2$ and $(b - a)^2$ are equivalent expressions. Do you agree or disagree? Explain.

Chapter 5 Preparing for the ADP℠ Algebra I Exam

DIRECTIONS FOR QUESTIONS 1–26: For each of the questions below, select the answer choice that is best for each case.

1 What is the difference when $3r^2 + 5$ is subtracted from $3r^3 + 3r^2 + 2r$?

A. $-3r^2 - 2r + 5$ **B.** $3r^2 + 2r$

C. $3r^3 + 2r - 5$ **D.** $3r^3 + 6r^2 + 2r + 5$

2 Which is not equal to $5^2 \cdot 5^{-3}$?

A. 5^{2-3} **B.** 5^{-1}

C. $\frac{5^2}{5^3}$ **D.** $(5^2)^{-3}$

3 Which is equivalent to the expression $(4w - 2)(3w - 5)$?

A. $7w - 7$ **B.** $-2w - 5$

C. $7w^2 - 14w - 7$ **D.** $12w^2 - 26w + 10$

4 Which of the following is a cubic binomial?

A. $-6x^3$ **B.** $3x^2 + 3x$

C. $5x^3 - 2x$ **D.** $-7x^3 + 4x + x^2$

5 What is the result when $2c^2 - 3c + 6$ is subtracted from $c^2 + c - 2$?

A. $c^2 - 4c + 8$

B. $-c^2 - 2c + 4$

C. $c^2 - 4c + 8$

D. $-c^2 + 4c - 8$

6 Which of the following is the product of $(4x - 2)(5 - 3x)$?

A. $-12x^2 + 14x - 10$

B. $20x^2 + 12x - 10$

C. $-12x^2 + 26x - 10$

D. $-12x^2 + 20x$

7 Compare the degrees of the expressions $4x(x^2 + 5x)$ and $2x^2(4x + 10)$. Which has the greater degree?

A. The degree of $4x(x^2 + 5x)$ is greater.

B. The degree of $2x^2(4x + 10)$ is greater.

C. The two degrees are equal.

D. Cannot be determined

8 Which of the following are factors of $2x^2 - 5x - 12$?

A. $(2x + 3)(x - 4)$ **B.** $(2x - 3)(x + 4)$

C. $(2x - 5)(x - 7)$ **D.** $(2x - 2)(x - 6)$

9 Which is *not* equivalent to $-\frac{x + 5}{x - 1}$?

A. $\frac{-x + 5}{x - 1}$ **B.** $\frac{-x - 5}{x - 1}$

C. $\frac{x + 5}{1 - x}$ **D.** $\frac{x + 5}{-x + 1}$

10 What is equivalent to the expression $(6c^2 + 5c - 3) - (3c^2 + 8c - 1)$?

A. $3c^2 + 13c - 4$ **B.** $3c^2 - 3c - 4$

C. $3c^2 - 3c - 2$ **D.** $3c^2 + 13c - 2$

11 What is the product of $(-3x^3y^2)(5xy^5)$?

A. $-15x^4y^7$ **B.** $2x^4y^7$

C. $-15x^3y^{10}$ **D.** $2x^3y^{10}$

12 Which is equivalent to the expression $(3xy)(2x^2y)^3$?

A. $18x^6y^5$ **B.** $24x^7y^4$

C. $216x^9y^6$ **D.** $18x^6y^3$

ALGEBRA I

13 Which of the following expressions is equivalent to $\left(\frac{5x}{3y^2}\right)^{-1}$?

A. $\frac{3y^2}{5x}$ B. $\frac{3x}{5y^2}$ C. $-\frac{5x}{3y^2}$ D. $-\frac{3y^2}{5x}$

14 Simplify the expression $(w - 8) + 2(4w - 1)$.

A. $9w - 10$ B. $-23w + 6$

C. $9w - 9$ D. $10w - 18$

15 What is the product of $(2a - 5)(3a + 1)$?

A. $6a^2 - 5$ B. $5a - 4$

C. $6a^2 - 13a - 5$ D. $6a^2 - 17a - 5$

16 Which trinomial is equivalent to $(2r - 1)^2$?

A. $4r^2 + 1$ B. $4r^2 - 4r + 1$

C. $4r^2 + 4r + 1$ D. $4r - 2$

17 Solve the equation $-4n + 7 = (n - 1)(-3)$.

A. $n = 10$ B. $n = -\frac{10}{7}$

C. $n = 4$ D. $n = -4$

18 Which of the following is the solution for $5j - 3(2j - 1) = 3j + 8$?

A. 10 B. -3 C. $-\frac{5}{4}$ D. $-\frac{9}{4}$

19 Simplify the expression $(5j^2 + 3j) + (j^2 + 4j + 4) - (2j - 3)$.

A. $11j^2 - 1$ B. $6j^2 + 5j + 7$

C. $6j^2 + 5j - 1$ D. $11j^2 - 7$

20 Which of the following is equivalent to the expression $(2z^2 - 4) - (z^2 - 4) - (3z^2 - 2)$?

A. $4z^2 + 2$ B. $-2z^2 - 10$

C. $-2z^2 + 2$ D. $4z^2 - 10$

21 What is the GCF of the terms of the trinomial $3x^5 - 15x^3 + 9x^2$?

A. 3 B. x C. $3x$ D. $3x^2$

22 Which is the completely factored form of $5z^2 + 5z - 30$?

A. $(5z + 15)(z - 2)$ B. $5(z + 3)(z - 2)$

C. $(5z - 10)(z + 3)$ D. $5(z - 3)(z - 2)$

23 The length of the base of a triangular-shaped sail is represented by $2x + 5$, and the height is represented by $2x - 4$. Which expression represents the area of the sail?

A. $4x + 1$ B. $4x^2 - 20$

C. $2x^2 + x - 10$ D. $x^2 + x - 20$

24 The length of a rug is represented by $x + 6$, and the width is represented by $x - 2$. Which expression represents the area of the rug?

A. $2x + 42$ B. $x^2 + 4x - 12$

C. $x^2 - 12$ D. $x^2 - 8x - 12$

25 Two cars leave the same location at the same time. One car drives due east and the other travels south. The southbound car travels 12 mi less than the other. Which expression describes the distance between the two cars at that point?

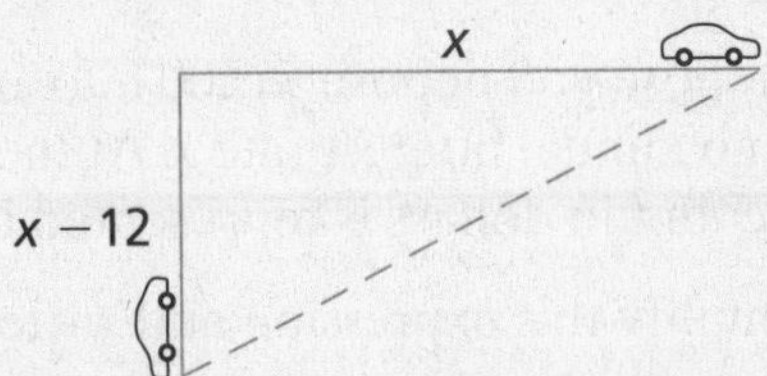

A. $\sqrt{2x - 12}$ B. $\sqrt{x^2 - 12x}$

C. $\sqrt{2x^2 + 144}$ D. $\sqrt{2x^2 - 24x + 144}$

26 Factor $2a^2 + 7a - 4$ completely.

A. $(2a + 1)(a - 4)$

B. $2(a + 4)(a - 1)$

C. $(a + 4)(2a - 1)$

D. $(2a + 4)(a - 1)$

DIRECTIONS FOR 27–29: Solve each problem. Show all your work or provide an explanation for your answer.

27 A rectangular pool is being constructed according to the plan shown below. The formula for the area A of a rectangle is $A = lw$, where l is the length of the rectangle and w is the width.

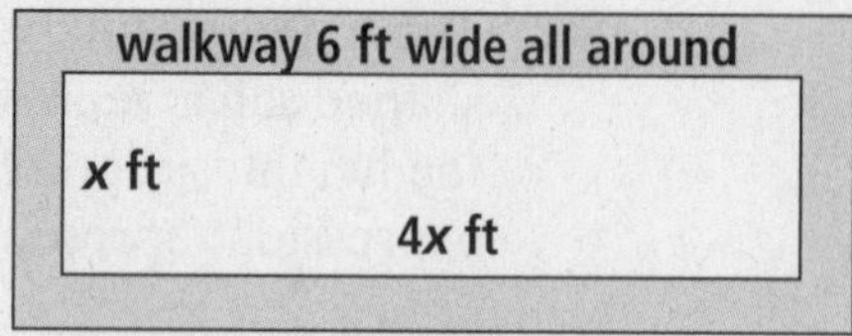

Write a simplified expression for the area in square feet of the pool and the walkway combined. Explain your work.

28 The volume V of a rectangular prism is given by the formula $V = lwh$, where l is the length of the prism, w is its width, and h is its height. The length of a certain rectangular prism is three times its width, and its height is 2 ft less than its width. Write a simplified expression that represents the volume of the prism in cubic feet.

Calculate the volume of the prism if the width w equals 6 ft.

29 Suppose you deposit \$1200 into an account that pays simple interest at an annual interest rate r. At the end of two years, the amount in the account in dollars is represented by the expression $1200(1 + r)^2$.

Simplify this expression and write the result in standard form.

Assuming no additional deposits or withdrawals, what is the total amount in the account after two years if r is 3%?

Assuming no additional deposits or withdrawals, what is the total amount in the account after two years if r is 3.5%?

Assuming no additional deposits or withdrawals, how much money is in the account after two years if r is 3.5% with an initial deposit of \$2000?

6 Quadratic Equations and Functions

Discovering Indiana

College Football Hall of Fame

The National Football Foundation was founded in 1947 to develop achievement in scholarship, citizenship, and athletics among American youth. Its most successful program is the College Football Hall of Fame, located in South Bend, Indiana.

The College Football Hall hosts over 200 events every year. Its premier event is the annual Enshrinement Festival. This event is a week-long festival that celebrates the history and traditions of college football. At the end of the week, new members are inducted into the Hall of Fame.

The first class of Hall of Famers was inducted in 1951. Today, the Hall of Fame includes over 1,000 players and coaches.

6.1 Solving Quadratic Equations Using Square Roots

ADP℠ Standards

N1.c Using quadratic models

N2.b Solve quadratic equations

A **quadratic equation** is any equation that can be written in the form

$$ax^2 + bx + c = 0, \text{ where } a, b, \text{ and } c \text{ are real numbers and } a \neq 0.$$

This is the **standard form of a quadratic equation** in x.

The following examples describe both quadratic and nonquadratic equations.

Equation	Description	Classification
$3x + 2 = 7x - 5$	Both $3x + 2$ and $7x - 5$ are linear polynomials in x.	not quadratic
$n^2 = 25$	The greatest power of n is 2.	quadratic not in standard form
$6x^2 + 5x - 7 = 0$	The greatest power of x is 2.	quadratic in standard form
$27a^3 = 9$	The equation contains a power of a greater than 2.	not quadratic

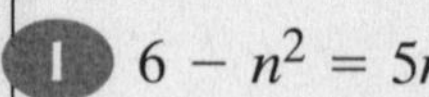

Writing quadratic equations in standard form

Write each quadratic equation in standard form.

1 $6 - n^2 = 5n$

■ **SOLUTION**

$$6 - n^2 = 5n$$
$$6 - n^2 - 5n = 5n - 5n$$
$$6 - n^2 - 5n = 0$$
$$-n^2 - 5n + 6 = 0$$

2 $5x^2 = 3x - 2$

■ **SOLUTION**

$$5x^2 = 3x - 2$$
$$5x^2 + 2 = 3x - 2 + 2$$
$$5x^2 + 2 = 3x$$
$$5x^2 + 2 - 3x = 0$$
$$5x^2 - 3x + 2 = 0$$

A **solution to a quadratic equation** in one variable is any number that makes the equation true. For example, if $b^2 + b = 6$, you can conclude that $b = 2$ and $b = -3$ are solutions since $(2)^2 + 2 = 4 + 2 = 6$ and $(-3)^2 + (-3) = 9 - 3 = 6$. Solutions are also called **roots.**

If the value of b (the coefficient of the x term in a quadratic equation) is zero, the equation can be written as $x^2 = k$. If $k \geq 0$, this equation can be solved by using square roots. There are no real solutions for the quadratic equation if k is negative ($k < 0$).

For example, you can solve the equation $x^2 = 64$ by finding the square root of each side of the equation. Therefore, $x = \pm\sqrt{64}$; $x = \pm 8$.

Go Online
PearsonSchool.com
Visit: PearsonSchool.com
Web Code: ayp-0294

EXAMPLES 3 through 8 Solving quadratic equations in one variable

Solve each of the following quadratic equations.

3 $x^2 = 9$

■ **SOLUTION**

$x^2 = 9$

$x = \pm\sqrt{9}$

$x = \pm 3$

4 $5s^2 = 125$

■ **SOLUTION**

$5s^2 = 125$

$\frac{5s^2}{5} = \frac{125}{5}$

$s^2 = 25$

$s = \pm\sqrt{25} = \pm 5$

5 $x^2 - 61 = 20$

■ **SOLUTION**

$x^2 - 61 = 20$

$x^2 = 81$

$x = \pm\sqrt{81} = \pm 9$

6 $3m^2 - 24 = 2m^2 + 40$

■ **SOLUTION**

$3m^2 - 24 = 2m^2 + 40$

$3m^2 = 2m^2 + 64$

$m^2 = 64$

$m = \pm\sqrt{64} = \pm 8$

7 $x^2 + 40 = 15$

■ **SOLUTION**

$x^2 + 40 = 15$

$x^2 = -25$

$x = \pm\sqrt{-25}$

no real solution

8 $3(h + 5)^2 = 48$

■ **SOLUTION**

$3(h + 5)^2 = 48$

$(h + 5)^2 = 16$

$\sqrt{(h + 5)^2} = \pm\sqrt{16}$

$h + 5 = \pm 4$

$h + 5 = 4$ *or* $h + 5 = -4$

$h = -1$ *or* $h = -9$

If the value of k in the equation $x^2 = k$ is not a perfect square, then the roots are irrational. You can use a calculator to approximate the root to the desired degree of accuracy.

EXAMPLES 9 through 11 Solving quadratic equations with irrational roots

Solve each of the following equations and round your answers to the nearest hundredth.

9 $12n^2 = 60$

■ **SOLUTION**

$12n^2 = 60$

$n^2 = 5$

$n = \pm\sqrt{5}$

$n = \pm 2.24$

10 $3y^2 - 144 = 30$

■ **SOLUTION**

$3y^2 - 144 = 30$

$3y^2 = 174$

$y^2 = 58$

$y = \pm\sqrt{58}$

$y = \pm 7.62$

11 $2(x - 5)^2 - 10 = 24$

■ **SOLUTION**

$2(x - 5)^2 - 10 = 24$

$2(x - 5)^2 = 34$

$(x - 5)^2 = 17$

$x - 5 = \pm\sqrt{17}$

$x - 5 = \pm 4.12$

$x = 4.12 + 5$ *or* $x = -4.12 + 5$

$x = 9.12$ *or* $x = 0.88$

Certain verbal problems translate to a quadratic equation. You can use what you know about quadratic equations to solve these types of equations.

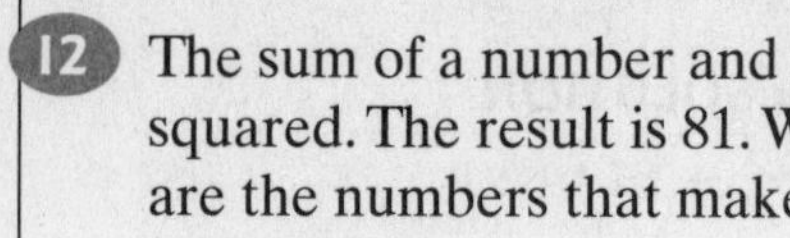

Using quadratic equations to solve verbal problems

Solve the following problems using a quadratic equation.

12 The sum of a number and 5 is squared. The result is 81. What are the numbers that make this statement true?

■ **SOLUTION**

Let n represent the number.

$(n + 5)^2 = 81$

$n + 5 = \pm\sqrt{81}$

$n + 5 = \pm 9$

$n + 5 = 9$ *or* $n + 5 = -9$

$n = 4$ *or* $n = -14$

13 Five times the square of the sum of two and a number is equal to 45. What are the numbers that make this statement true?

■ **SOLUTION**

Let n represent the number.

$5(n + 2)^2 = 45$

$n + 2 = \pm\sqrt{9}$

$n + 2 = \pm 3$

$n + 2 = 3$ *or* $n + 2 = -3$

$n = 1$ *or* $n = -5$

Quadratic equations can be used to describe the area of some shapes algebraically. You can use these equations to find side lengths and areas.

It is important to check the solutions of a quadratic equation with the information in the problem. Often a solution will be rejected because it does not make sense in the context of the problem. For example, if you are asked to find a side length, a negative solution does not make sense.

EXAMPLE 14 **Using a quadratic equation to solve an area problem**

Write an expression in x for the area of the shaded region. Find x such that the area of the shaded region equals 75% of the full square.

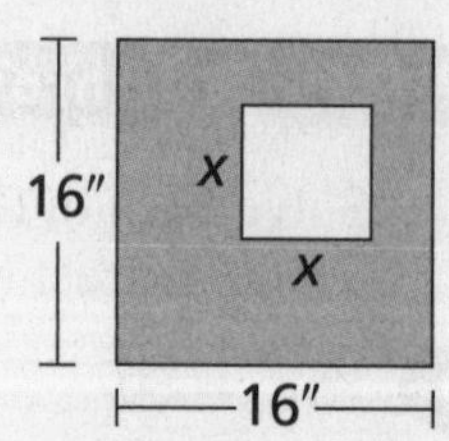

■ **SOLUTION**

area of full square − area of small square

$16^2 - x^2$

Since 75% = 0.75, solve $16^2 - x^2 = 0.75 \times 16^2$.

$16^2 - x^2 = 0.75 \times 256$

$256 - x^2 = 192$

$-x^2 = -64$ ← **Use the Addition Property of Equality.**

$x = \pm 8$

$x = 8$ ← **Reject the negative solution.**

The desired value of x is 8 inches.

Note

Because the length of a square must be a positive number, keep 8 as a solution and reject −8 as a possible solution.

Practice

Choose the letter preceding the word or expression that best completes the statement or answers the question.

1 Which is not a quadratic equation?

A. $x^2 = 81$

B. $3x^2 = 5x - 7$

C. $4x + 5 = 9 - 2x$

D. $5x - 7x^2 = 21$

2 Which equation has the same solutions as $2(b^2 - 5) = 18$?

A. $b^2 = 14$ **C.** $2b^2 = 23$

B. $b^2 = 8$ **D.** $b^2 = \frac{18}{2} - 5$

3 Which numbers are the solutions to $n^2 = 2.25$?

A. 0.15; −0.15 **C.** 1.5; −1.5

B. 0.05; −0.05 **D.** 1.125; −1.125

4 Suppose x represents a real number. Which statement is true?

A. $\sqrt{x^2} = x$ for all x

B. $\sqrt{x^2} = -x$ for all x

C. $\sqrt{x^2} = \frac{1}{2}x$ for all x

D. $\sqrt{x^2} = x$ for all x zero or more

In Exercises 5–14, solve each quadratic equation. Give exact solutions. If the equation has no solutions, so state.

5 $x^2 = 49$ **6** $-x^2 = -9$

7 $3a^2 = 48$ **8** $12x^2 = 3$

9 $3a^2 - 5 = 43$ **10** $12m^2 + 3 = 3$

11 $12m^2 - 23 = -11$

12 $5x^2 + 6x - 7 = 3x^2 + 6x - 5$

13 $5n^2 + n + 4 = 6n^2 + n - 5$

14 $5k^2 - 2k + 18 = 9k^2 - 2k - 82$

In Exercises 15–20, solve each quadratic equation. Give solutions rounded to the nearest hundredth. If the equation has no solutions, so state.

15 $-x^2 = -10$ **16** $-4t^2 = -48$

17 $3a^2 = 2a^2 + 2$ **18** $-3c^2 = 2c^2 - 10$

19 $3(x - 5)^2 = 120$

20 $5x^2 + x + 8 = 3x^2 + x + 30$

In Exercises 21–26, solve the problem. Clearly show all necessary work.

21 The ratio of 90 to some number is equal to the ratio of that number to 40. What is the number?

22 Suppose that you want to build a square garden whose area is to be 729 square feet. What should the length of one side be?

23 The area A of a circle with radius r is given by $A = \pi r^2$. If the area of a circular pond is 1156 square feet, what is the radius to the nearest tenth of a foot?

24 The length of a rectangular sign is three times its width. What are the dimensions of the sign if its area is 192 square feet?

25 Write an expression in m for the shaded region. For what m will the area of the shaded region be 175 square units?

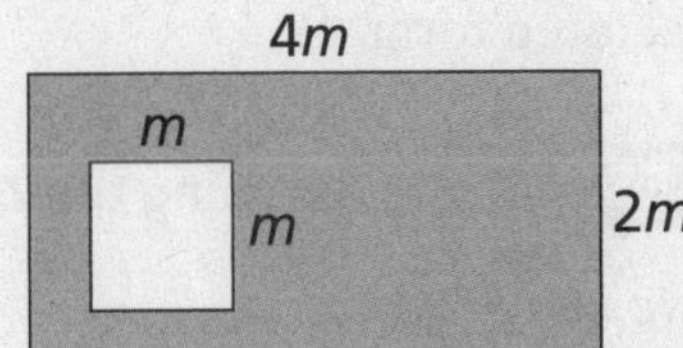

26 What are the lengths of the height and the base of this right triangle?

z

area:
162 square units

4z

6.2 Solving Quadratic Equations by Various Methods

ADP℠ Standards

N1.c Using quadratic models

N2.a Solve literal equations

N2.b Solve quadratic equations

Suppose that each card below has a number written on the reverse side. If you are told $ab = 0$, you must conclude that at least one of the cards has 0 written on it. For example, if card a has 2 written on it, then $2b = 0$. Therefore, b must equal 0.

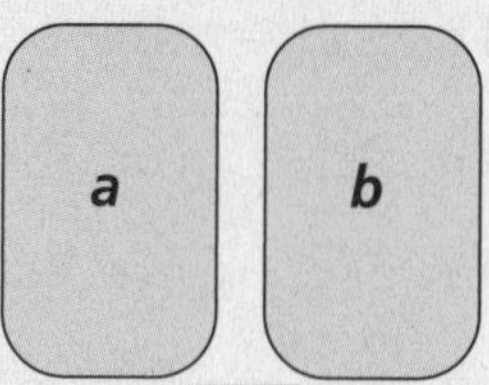

The *Zero-Product Property* is a generalization of the idea above.

Zero-Product Property

If a and b are real numbers and $ab = 0$, then either $a = 0$ or $b = 0$.

If $2x = 0$, then $x = 0$. If $-3(x - 5) = 0$, then $x - 5 = 0$. If $x(x - 2) = 0$, then $x = 0$ or $x - 2 = 0$.

EXAMPLE 1 Reading solutions from a product equal to 0

1 Which is true given that $(n - 5)(n + 4) = 0$?

A. $n - 5 = 0$ and $n + 4 = 0$

B. $n - 5 = 0$ and $n + 4 \neq 0$

C. $n - 5 = 0$ or $n + 4 = 0$

D. $n - 5 \neq 0$ and $n + 4 = 0$

■ SOLUTION

By the Zero-Product Property, one or the other factor in $(n - 5)(n + 4)$ equals 0. Therefore, $n - 5 = 0$ or $n + 4 = 0$. The correct choice is C.

You can use the Zero-Product Property to solve a quadratic equation written in factored form.

EXAMPLES 2 and 3 Using the Zero-Product Property with factored form

Solve each equation.

2 $3h(h + 7) = 0$

■ SOLUTION

$3h(h + 7) = 0$

$3h = 0$ or $h + 7 = 0$ ← **Apply the Zero-Product Property.**

$h = 0$ or $h = -7$

The solutions are 0 or -7.

3 $(x + 5)(x + 6) = 0$

■ SOLUTION

$(x + 5)(x + 6) = 0$

$x + 5 = 0$ or $x + 6 = 0$ ← **Apply the Zero-Product Property.**

$x = -5$ or $x = -6$

The solutions are -5 or -6.

You can use the Zero-Product Property to solve quadratic equations not written in factored form like those shown below.

$b^2 + 3b = 0 \qquad m^2 + m - 6 = 0 \qquad z^2 + 4z + 4 = 0$

You can use these steps to solve quadratic equations by factoring.

Solving a Quadratic Equation by Factoring

Step 1 Write the given quadratic equation in standard form, if it is not already.

Step 2 Factor the quadratic expression into a pair of linear expressions.

Step 3 Use the Zero-Product Property to write a pair of linear equations.

Step 4 Solve the linear equations.

Step 5 The solutions to the linear equations are the solutions to the given equation.

Visit: PearsonSchool.com
Web Code: ayp-0295

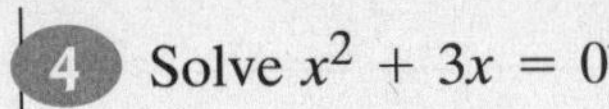

Solving a quadratic equation by factoring

4 Solve $x^2 + 3x = 0$.

■ **SOLUTION**

$x^2 + 3x = 0$

$x(x + 3) = 0$ ← Factor the quadratic expression.

$x = 0$ or $x = -3$ ← Apply the Zero-Product Property.

5 Solve $\frac{z}{2} = \frac{z - 2}{z + 6}$.

■ **SOLUTION**

$z(z + 6) = 2(z - 2)$ ← Cross multiply.

$z^2 + 6z = 2z - 4$

$z^2 + 4z + 4 = 0$

$(z + 2)(z + 2) = 0$ ← $z^2 + 4z + 4$ is a perfect square trinomial.

$z + 2 = 0$ or $z + 2 = 0$ ← Apply the Zero-Product Property.

$z = -2$ or $z = -2$ ← -2 is called a double root.

6 Solve $6w^2 - 28 = 13w$.

■ **SOLUTION**

$6w^2 - 28 = 13w$

$6w^2 - 13w - 28 = 0$ ← Write in standard form.

$(2w - 7)(3w + 4) = 0$ ← Apply the Zero-Product Property.

$2w - 7 = 0$ or $3w + 4 = 0$

$w = \frac{7}{2}$ or $w = -\frac{4}{3}$

Note

The quadratic must be equal to zero to use the Zero-Product Property.

Recall that quadratic equations can be used to solve area problems.

EXAMPLE 7 **Using factoring to solve an area problem**

The area of a rectangle is 220 square inches. The length of the rectangle is 12 inches more than its width. What are the dimensions of the rectangle?

■ SOLUTION

Step 1 Represent the given information in an equation.
Let w represent the width of the rectangle. Then $w + 12$ represents the length.

$(w + 12)w = 220$ ← **length × width = area**

Step 2 Solve the equation.

$w^2 + 12w - 220 = 0$ ← **Write in standard form.**

$(w + 22)(w - 10) = 0$ ← **Factor $w^2 + 12w - 220$.**

$w = -22$ or $w = 10$ ← **Use the Zero-Product Property.**

Step 3 Interpret the solution.
Because length must be positive, length cannot be −22 inches.
The rectangle has a width of 10 inches. So the length is 22 inches.

Another way to solve a quadratic equation is to use the **quadratic formula.** You can use it to find the roots of a quadratic equation.

Solving a Quadratic Equation by Using the Quadratic Formula

If $ax^2 + bx + c = 0$, a, b, and c are real numbers, and $a \neq 0$,

$$x = \frac{-b \pm \sqrt{b^2 - 4ac}}{2a}.$$

- If $b^2 - 4ac > 0$, there are two distinct real solutions.
- If $b^2 - 4ac = 0$, there is one real solution.
- If $b^2 - 4ac < 0$, there are no real solutions.

EXAMPLE 8 **Using the quadratic formula to solve an equation**

Go Online PearsonSchool.com
Visit: PearsonSchool.com
Web Code: ayp-0602

Solve $2x^2 + 7x - 15 = 0$.

■ SOLUTION

$2x^2 + 7x - 15 = 0$

$x = \frac{-7 \pm \sqrt{7^2 - 4(2)(-15)}}{2(2)}$ ← $a = 2, b = 7, c = -15$

$x = \frac{-7 + \sqrt{169}}{4} = \frac{6}{4} = \frac{3}{2}$ or $x = \frac{-7 - \sqrt{169}}{4} = -5$

You can use the quadratic formula to solve quadratic equations that can also be solved by factoring. Consider $6x^2 + x = 12$.

$6x^2 + x = 12$

$6x^2 + x - 12 = 0$

$(2x + 3)(3x - 4) = 0$

$x = -\frac{3}{2}$ or $x = \frac{4}{3}$

$6x^2 + x - 12 = 0$

$x = \frac{-1 \pm \sqrt{1^2 - 4(6)(-12)}}{2(6)}$

$x = \frac{-1 \pm 17}{12} = -\frac{3}{2}$ or $x = \frac{4}{3}$

When modeling real-world situations, perpendicular lines will often create situations involving right triangles. You can use the Pythagorean Theorem (or its converse) to determine the length of an unknown side of a right triangle.

EXAMPLES 9 through 11 Applying the Pythagorean Theorem

9 To alleviate traffic, the city decides to pave a new road that connects Route 19 to Main Street, as shown in the diagram below. The construction cost has been estimated at \$100 per foot. To the nearest dollar, estimate the cost for building the street. (Hint: 1 mile = 5,280 ft.)

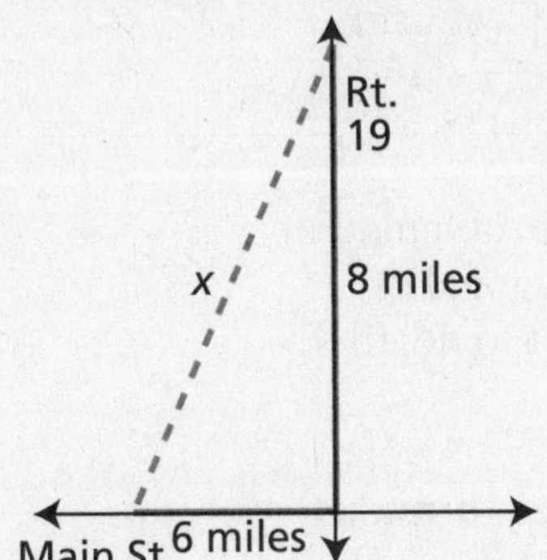

■ **SOLUTION**

Step 1

$x^2 = 8^2 + 6^2$

$x^2 = 64 + 36$

$x = \sqrt{100} = 10$ miles

Step 2

1 mile = 5,280 ft

10 miles = (10) · (5,280) = 52,800 ft

Find the cost of 52,800 ft at \$100 per foot

Total Cost = (52,800) · (100) = \$5,280,000

10 The locations of Chicago and San Diego are placed on the coordinate plane with Chicago at the point (6, 5) and San Diego at the point (2, 2). A major airline plans a route that will fly directly from Chicago to San Diego. What distance represents the flight path on the coordinate grid?

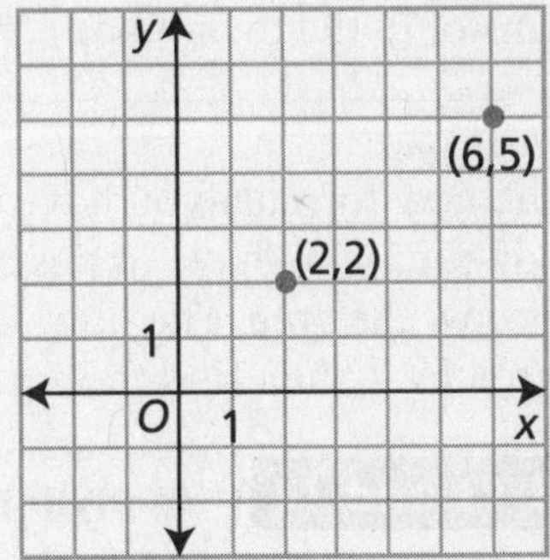

■ **SOLUTION**

You can use the Distance Formula to find the distance between the two cities.

$$d = \sqrt{(6 - 2)^2 + (5 - 2)^2}$$
$$= \sqrt{16 + 9} = \sqrt{25} = 5$$

Therefore, the distance that represents the flight path on the coordinate grid is 5 units.

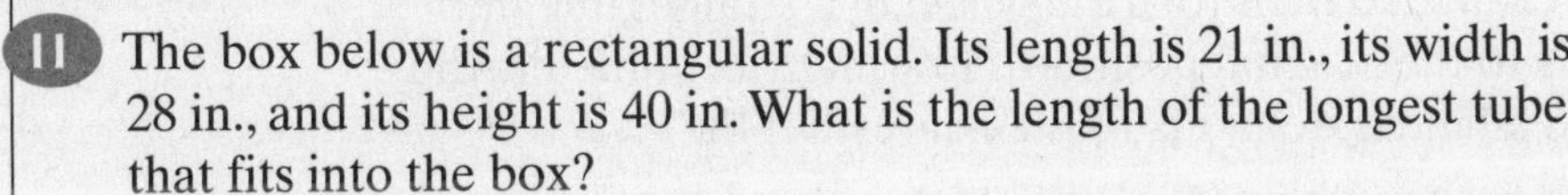

11 The box below is a rectangular solid. Its length is 21 in., its width is 28 in., and its height is 40 in. What is the length of the longest tube that fits into the box?

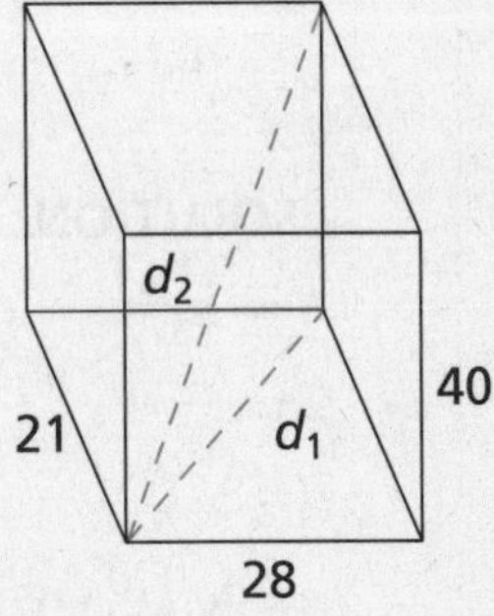

■ **SOLUTION**

The longest tube fits along the diagonal d_2 of the box. To find the length d_2, first find the length of a diagonal d_1 of the face.

Step 1

$d_1 = \sqrt{21^2 + 28^2}$

$= \sqrt{441 + 784} = \sqrt{1225} = 35$

Step 2

$d_2 = \sqrt{35^2 + 40^2}$

$= \sqrt{1224 + 1600}$

$= \sqrt{2835} = 53.1$ in.

The longest tube that can fit into the box has a length of 53.1 in.

A **literal equation** is commonly called a formula. You may find it helpful to rewrite a literal equation so that you are solving for a particular variable. Then you can plug in the values of the known variables and solve.

EXAMPLE 12 Rewriting literal equations

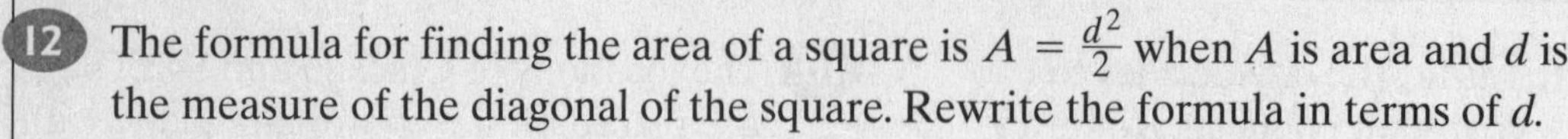

12 The formula for finding the area of a square is $A = \frac{d^2}{2}$ when A is area and d is the measure of the diagonal of the square. Rewrite the formula in terms of d.

■ SOLUTION

$A = \frac{d^2}{2}$ ← **Your goal is to isolate *d*.**

$2A = d^2$ ← **Multiply both sides by 2.**

$\sqrt{2A} = d$ ← **Take the square root of both sides.**

In terms of d, the formula for the area of a square is $d = \sqrt{2A}$.

You can use the new formula you have created to solve other problems. For example, imagine that you have to describe how to find the diagonal of a square if you know the area. The literal equation tells you what to do: first, multiply the area by 2, then find the square root.

EXAMPLES 13 and 14 Applying circumference and area formulas

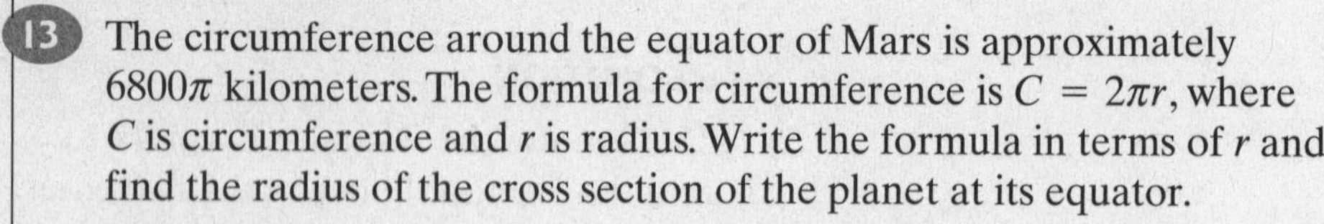

13 The circumference around the equator of Mars is approximately 6800π kilometers. The formula for circumference is $C = 2\pi r$, where C is circumference and r is radius. Write the formula in terms of r and find the radius of the cross section of the planet at its equator.

■ SOLUTION

$C = 2\pi r$ ← **Rewrite the formula in terms of *r*.**

$r = \frac{C}{2\pi}$

$r = \frac{C}{2\pi}$ ← **Substitute and solve for *r*.**

$r = \frac{6800\pi}{2\pi} = 3400$ km

Note

Remember, you can't distribute exponents. $(a + b)^2 \neq a^2 + b^2$

14 A wheel has an area of 100 cm^2. A team of students marks the side of the wheel with a piece of chalk and then rolls the wheel in a straight line until the chalk mark returns to the original position. How many centimeters did the wheel roll? Round all measurements to the nearest tenth.

Use the formulas: $A = \pi r^2$ where A = Area of a circle and r = radius.
$C = 2\pi r$ where C = Circumference of a circle and r = radius.

■ SOLUTION

$A = \pi r^2$ ← **Rewrite the area formula in terms of *r*.**

$\frac{A}{\pi} = r^2$

$r = \sqrt{\frac{A}{\pi}}$

$r = \sqrt{\frac{100}{3.14}} \approx 5.6$ cm ← **Substitute 100 for *A* and solve for *r*.**

$C = 2\pi r$ ← **Use the formula $C = 2\pi r$.**

$C = 2(3.14)(5.6) \approx 35.2$ cm ← **Substitute 5.6 for *r* and solve for *C*.**

Practice

Choose the letter preceding the word or expression that best completes the statement or answers the question.

1 The solutions to $(z + 1)(z + 2) = 0$ are

A. 1 and 2. **C.** −1 and −2.

B. 0 and −2. **D.** 0 and −1.

2 The solutions to $a^2 - 10a = 0$ are

A. 0 and −10. **C.** 1 and 10.

B. 0 and 10. **D.** 1 and −10.

3 The solutions to $n(n + 1)(n - 2) = 0$ are

A. 0, 1, and 2. **C.** −1 and −2.

B. 0 and −2. **D.** 0, −1, and 2.

In Exercises 4–12, solve each equation.

4 $x^2 + 5x + 6 = 0$ 5 $x^2 + 7x = 8$

6 $a^2 - 5a = 0$ 7 $x^2 - 64 = 0$

8 $x^2 = 20 - 8x$ 9 $2b^2 - b - 21 = 0$

10 $18d - 81 = d^2$ 11 $r^3 - 7r^2 - 18r = 0$

12 $4x^3 - 100x = 0$

In Exercises 13–20, solve the problem. Clearly show all necessary work.

13 The altitude of a model rocket is given by $h = -16t^2 + 160t$ where h is the altitude in feet and t is elapsed time in seconds. After how many seconds of flight will the rocket hit the ground?

14 The length and width of a rectangle are represented by consecutive even integers. The area of the rectangle is 224 square inches. What are the length and the width?

15 A positive number is 5 more than another. Their product is 36. What are the numbers?

16 A rectangle is 8 feet long and 6 feet wide. If each side is increased by the same amount, the area of the new rectangle is 72 square feet more than the area of the original rectangle. Find the length and width of the new rectangle in feet.

17 The volume of a rectangular solid is the product of its length, width, and height. The volume of this solid is 440 cubic feet. What are the dimensions of the base?

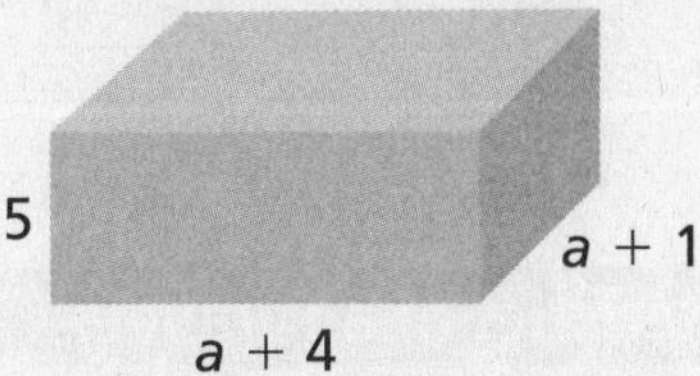

18 One number is 3 more than another. The sum of their squares is 89. What are the numbers?

19 The figure below shows a square inside a rectangle. If the area of the shaded region is 55 square units, determine the value of x.

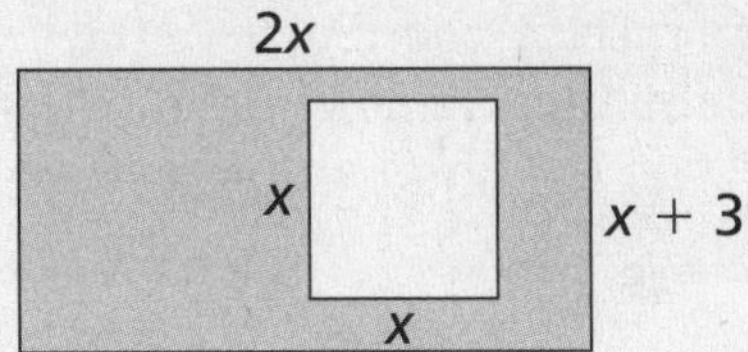

20 The product of two consecutive integers is 132. What is the sum of the numbers?

In Exercises 21–26, solve by using the quadratic formula. If the equation has no solutions, so state.

21 $5n^2 + 2n - 3 = 0$

22 $3p^2 + 5p - 2 = 0$

23 $-2h^2 + h + 1 = 0$

24 $2d^2 - 7d + 3 = 0$

25 $5z^2 + 2z = 3z^2 + 7z + 7$

26 $m^2 + 30m + 20 = -7m^2 + m - 2$

6.3 Quadratic Functions, Parabolas, and Circles

ADP℠ Standards

N1.a Represent quadratic functions

N1.b Distinguish between function types

Recall that the graph of a linear equation in two variables is a line. The equation $y = ax^2 + bx + c$, where a, b, and c are real numbers and $a \neq 0$, represents a **quadratic function.** Its graph is a **parabola,** a smooth and symmetric U-shape.

For example, a table of values for $y = x^2 - 2x - 4$ and its graph are shown here.

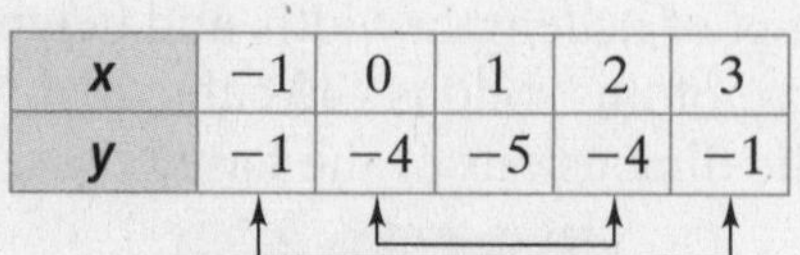

x	−1	0	1	2	3
y	−1	−4	−5	−4	−1

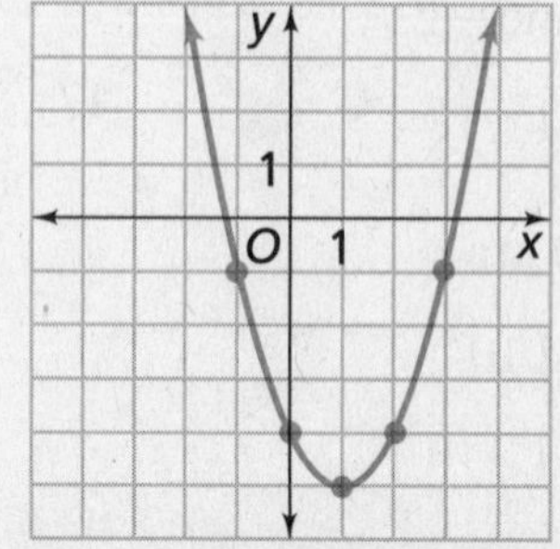

Characteristics of a Parabola

- The **axis of symmetry** is the line that divides the parabola into two matching parts. Its equation is $x = -\frac{b}{2a}$.
- The highest or lowest point on a parabola is called the **vertex** (also called a *turning point*). Its x-coordinate is the value of $-\frac{b}{2a}$.

If $a > 0$, the parabola opens upward. The vertex is the lowest point on the parabola. The y-coordinate of the vertex is the **minimum** value of the function.

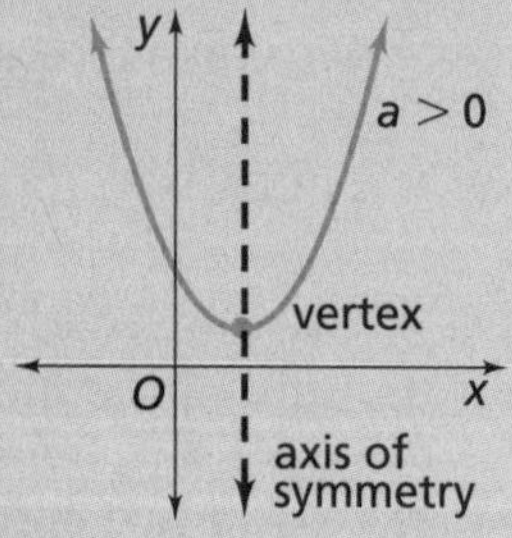

If $a < 0$, the parabola opens downward. The vertex is the highest point on the parabola. The y-coordinate of the vertex is the **maximum** value of the function.

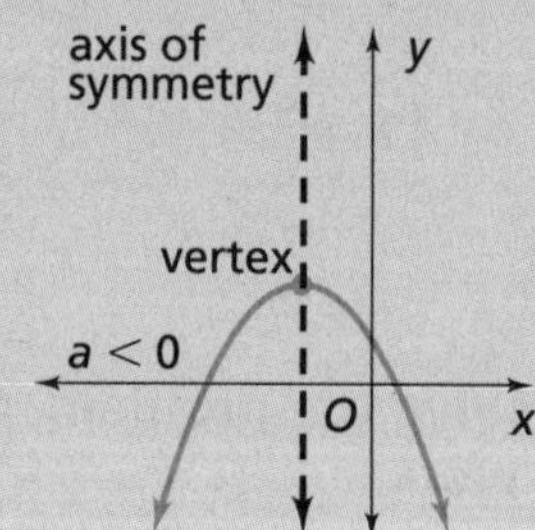

You can also identify the vertex from the graph of a parabola.

EXAMPLE 1 **Identifying the vertex of a parabola**

1 Find the vertex of the parabola shown.

■ **SOLUTION**

Because the vertex is either the lowest or highest point of a parabola, the vertex of this parabola is (−3, −5).

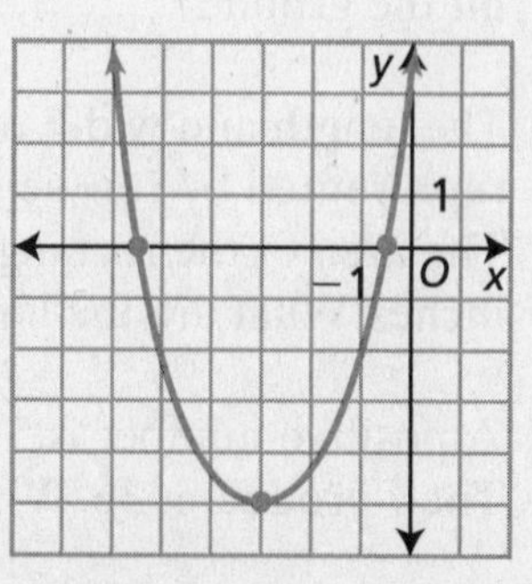

You can use the characteristics of a parabola to match an equation to its graph.

EXAMPLE 2 Recognizing an equation for a parabola

Which equation represents the graph shown here?

A. $y = -\frac{4}{3}x^2 + \frac{8}{3}x + 4$ **C.** $y = \frac{4}{3}x^2 - \frac{8}{3}x + 4$

B. $y = -\frac{4}{3}x^2 - \frac{8}{3}x - 4$ **D.** $y = \frac{4}{3}x^2 - \frac{8}{3}x - 4$

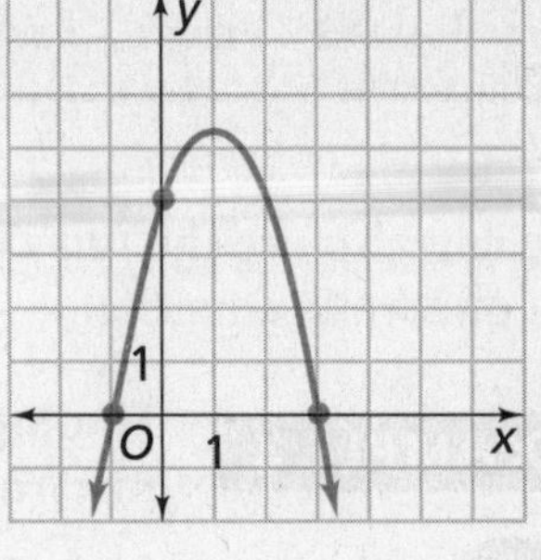

■ **SOLUTION**

Eliminate choices **C** and **D** because the graphs of these equations open upward. Because $y = 4$ when $x = 0$, the graph crosses the y-axis at $(0, 4)$. Eliminate choice **B.** The correct choice is A.

You can graph a quadratic function by making a table of values. Finding the coordinates of the vertex first can reduce the work involved.

EXAMPLE 3 Using the vertex to help sketch a parabola

Graph $y = -x^2 - 2x + 4$ using the vertex and a table of values. Label the axis of symmetry.

■ **SOLUTION**

Identify the values of a and b in $y = -x^2 - 2x + 4$. $\quad$ $\mathbf{a = -1}$ **and** $\mathbf{b = -2}$

Calculate the value of $-\frac{b}{2a}$ $\quad$ $-\frac{-2}{2(-1)} = -1$

An equation for the axis of symmetry is $x = -1$. Make a table containing five x-values with -1 being the third x-value.

x	−3	−2	−1	0	1
y	1	4	5	4	1

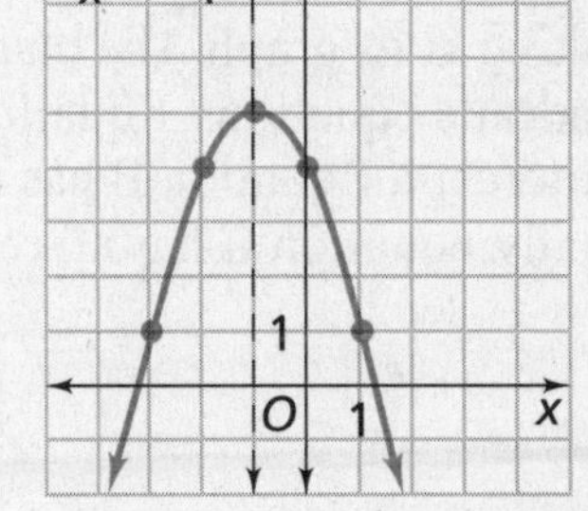

Graph the ordered pairs in the table as shown here. Draw a smooth curve through them. Notice that the parabola opens downward because $a < 0$.

Let's look at how the real-number solutions of $x^2 - 4 = 0$ are related to the x-intercepts of the graph of $y = x^2 - 4$.

$$x^2 - 4 = 0$$

$$(x + 2)(x - 2) = 0$$

$$x + 2 = 0 \text{ or } x - 2 = 0$$

$$x = -2 \text{ or } x = 2$$

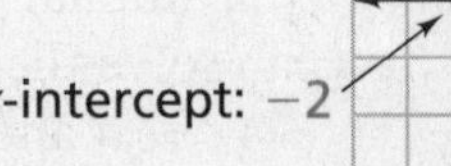

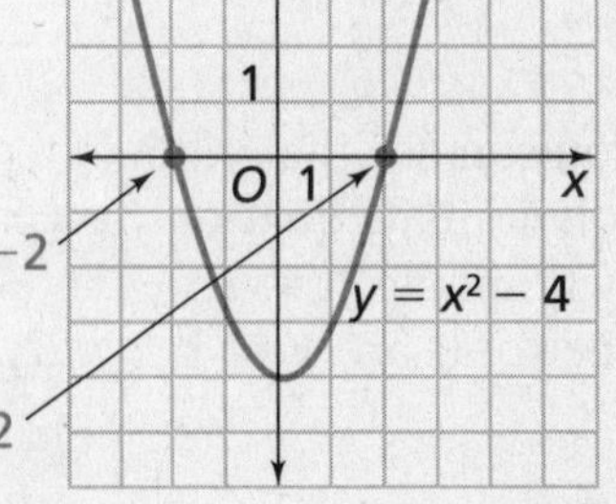

The real solutions to $x^2 - 4 = 0$ are **−2** and **2**.

In general, you can make the following statements relating solutions to quadratic equations and graphs of quadratic functions.

Solutions to Quadratic Equations and Graphs of Quadratic Functions

- The real numbers that are solutions to $ax^2 + bx + c = 0$ are the x-intercepts of the graph of $y = ax^2 + bx + c$.
- The x-intercepts of the graph of $y = ax^2 + bx + c$ are the real solutions to $ax^2 + bx + c = 0$.

You can also use the functions of a graphing calculator to find the solutions of a quadratic equation.

Visit: PearsonSchool.com
Web Code: ayp-0293

EXAMPLE 4 **Finding real solutions of a quadratic equation in x from a graph**

4 Solve $x^2 + 5x - 7 = 0$ graphically. Approximate the roots to the nearest tenth.

■ SOLUTION

Graph $y = x^2 + 5x - 7$.

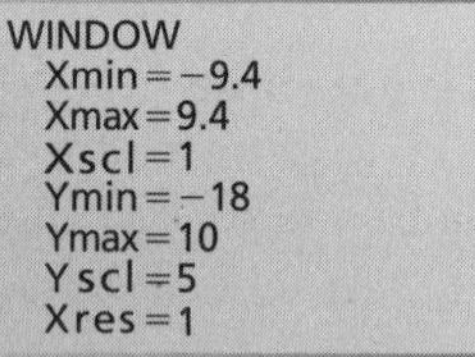

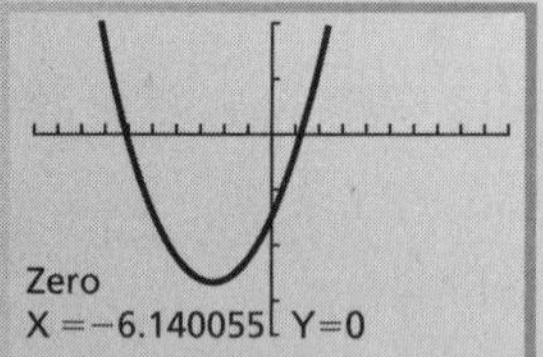

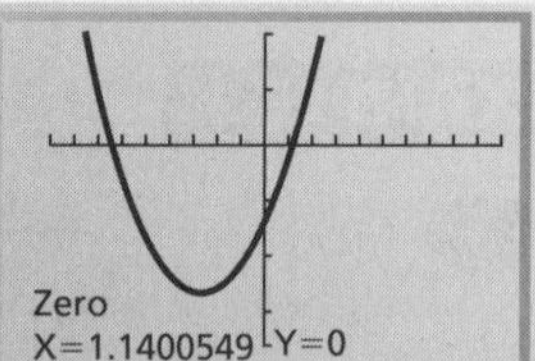

To the nearest tenth, the **roots are $x = -6.1$ and $x = 1.1$.**

The nature of the roots of a quadratic equation can be determined by looking at its graph. The diagram below shows the graphs of three different quadratic equations. Equation A has one real root because it has one x-intercept. Equation B has two real roots because it has two x-intercepts. Finally, equation C has no real roots because it never crosses the x-axis.

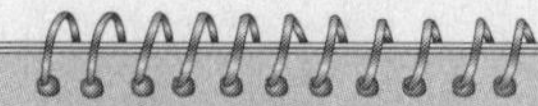

Note

The x-intercept is the point where the graph crosses the x-axis. A graph can have more than one x-intercept.

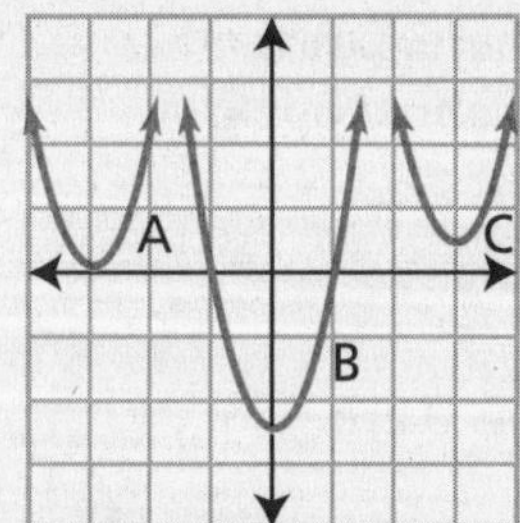

You can use the graph of a polynomial to determine the roots of a polynomial equation. You can solve the equation $x^3 - x^2 - 4x + 4 = 0$ by graphing $y = x^3 - x^2 - 4x + 4$ and determining the x-intercepts. The roots are $x = 1$, $x = 2$, and $x = -2$.

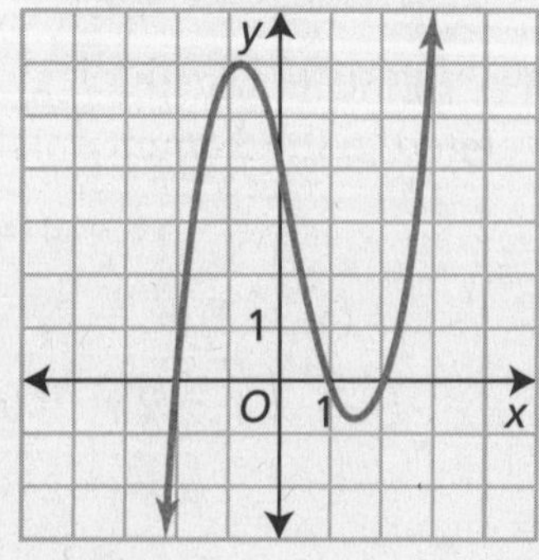

A quadratic equation in two variables is a special kind of *second-degree equation in two variables*. A circle is another kind of second-degree equation in two variables.

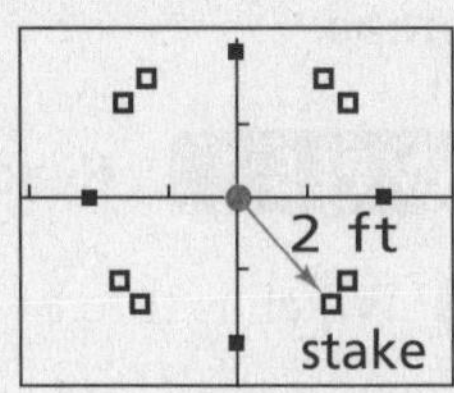

Suppose that a gardener marks a spot on the ground and then puts stakes in the ground at a distance of 2 feet from that point as shown. If the points are joined to make a continuous curve, the result will be a *circle*. The set of all points in the plane a fixed distance, the **radius,** from a fixed point in the same plane, the **center,** is called a **circle.**

Equation of a Circle

The set of all points a fixed distance r from a fixed point $P(h, k)$ in the coordinate plane can be represented by the equation below, called the **standard form for an equation of a circle.**

$$(x - h)^2 + (y - k)^2 = r^2$$

If the point $P(h, k)$ is the origin, then the equation becomes what is shown here.

$$x^2 + y^2 = r^2$$

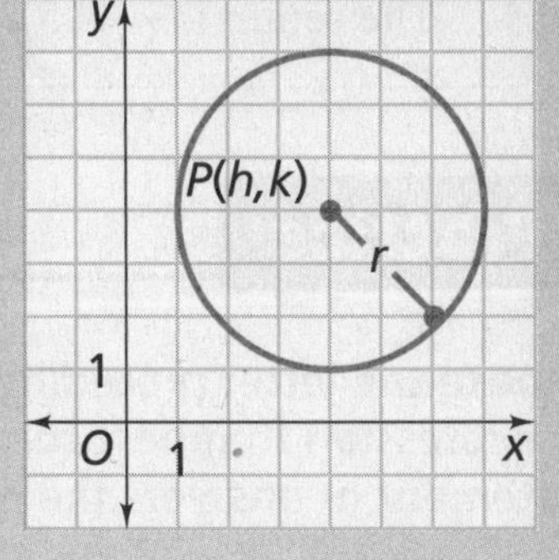

EXAMPLE 5 **Determining whether points lie on a circle from its equation**

5 Which points do not lie on the circle with equation $x^2 + y^2 = 5^2$?

A. (0, 5) and (5, 0) **B.** (5, 5) and (−5, 5) **C.** (0, −5) and (−5, 0) **D.** (3, 4) and (−4, 3)

▪ **SOLUTION**

A point lies on the circle if the ordered pair is a solution to the equation.

choice **A.**	(0, 5) and (5, 0) are 5 units from O.	(0, 5) and (5, 0) are on the circle.
choice **C.**	(0, −5) and (−5, 0) are 5 units from O.	(0, −5) and (−5, 0) are on the circle.
choice **D.**	$3^2 + 4^2 = 5^2$ and $(-4)^2 + 3^2 = 5^2$.	(3, 4) and (−4, 3) are on the circle.

The correct choice is B.

To sketch the graph of a circle, first determine its radius and center.

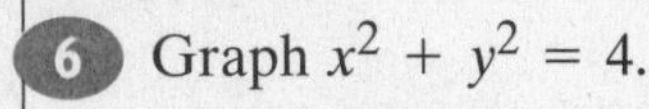

EXAMPLE 6 **Sketching a circle from an equation**

6 Graph $x^2 + y^2 = 4$.

▪ **SOLUTION**

The equation represents a circle with radius 2 and center at the origin. Graph the points where the circle intersects each axis.

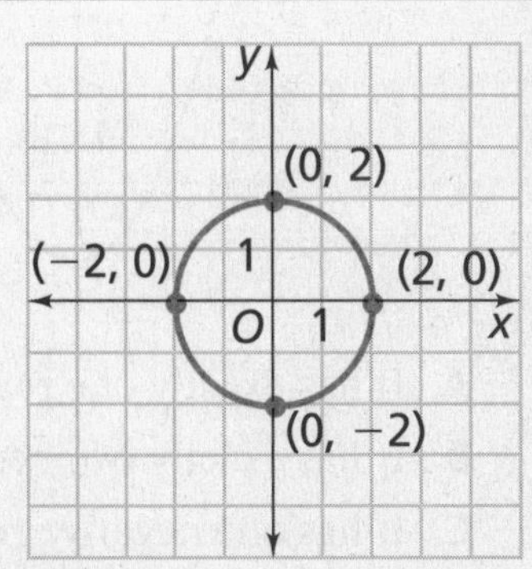

$x = 0$	$y = 0$
$0^2 + y^2 = 4$	$x^2 + 0^2 = 4$
So, $y = -2$ or 2.	So, $x = -2$ or 2.

Graph (0, −2), (0, 2), (−2, 0), and (2, 0). Sketch the circle as shown here.

The equation of a circle gives you information about the shape and position of its graph.

EXAMPLE 7 **Reading information about a circle from its equation**

7 Which is true of the circle with equation $(x + 3)^2 + (y - 5)^2 = 36$?

A. center (3, 5) and radius 6
B. center (3, −5) and radius 6
C. center (−3, −5) and radius 36
D. center (−3, 5) and radius 6

SOLUTION

Write $(x + 3)^2 + (y - 5)^2 = 36$ as $(x - (-3))^2 + (y - 5)^2 = 6^2$.
The center is (−3, 5). The correct choice is D.

Practice

Choose the letter preceding the word or expression that best completes the statement or answers the question.

1 The graph of an equation of the form $y = ax^2 + bx + c$ is shown. Which is true?

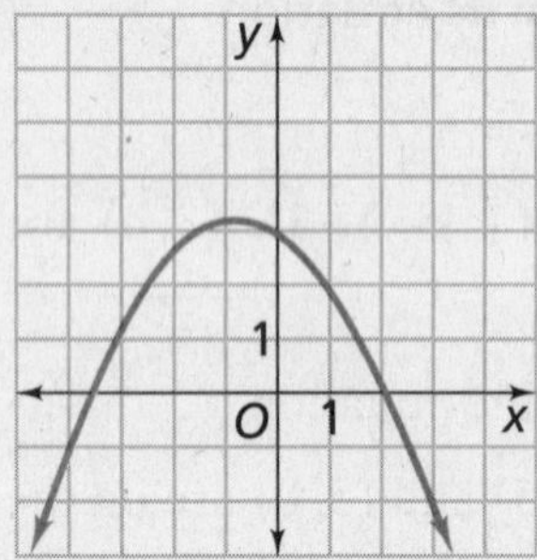

A. $a > 0$ and $c > 0$ **C.** $a < 0$ and $c < 0$
B. $a > 0$ and $c < 0$ **D.** $a < 0$ and $c > 0$

2 Which of the following statements is true of the equation graphed below?

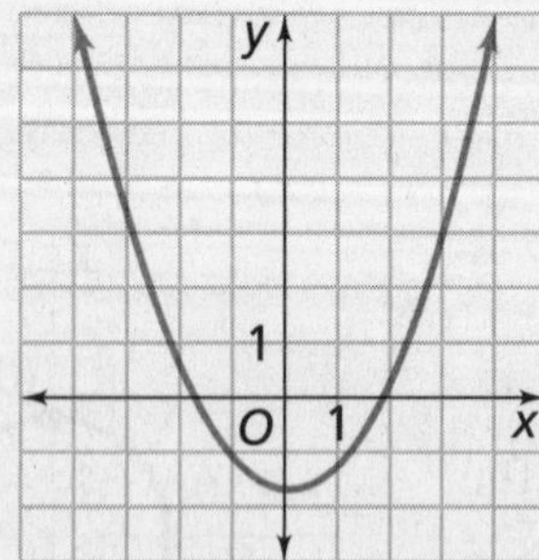

A. It has exactly one real root.
B. It has exactly two negative roots.
C. It has one negative root and one positive root.
D. It has no real roots.

3 Which represents the coordinates of the vertex of the graph of $y = x^2 - 6x - 10$?

A. (−6, 10) **C.** (3, −22)
B. (3, −19) **D.** (6, 10)

4 The graph of which equation has a maximum?

A. $y = \frac{1}{3}x^2 - 3x + 2$
B. $y = -5x + \frac{1}{2}x^2 - 5$
C. $y - \frac{1}{2}x^2 = 4x + 6$
D. $y = 6x - \frac{1}{3}x^2 + 2$

In Exercises 5–11, give the coordinates of the vertex. Tell whether the graph opens up or down and whether the vertex is the minimum or maximum of the graph.

5 $y = 2x^2$

6 $y = -2x^2$

7 $y = 5 - 3x^2$

8 $y = 1.5x^2 + 3x$

9 $y = \frac{1}{2}x^2 + 4x$

10 $y = 2x^2 + 4x - 5$

11 $y = -x^2 + 6x - 1$

In Exercises 12–14, the graph of a quadratic function, $y = ax^2 + bx + c$, is given. Find the solutions to the related equation $ax^2 + bx + c = 0$.

12 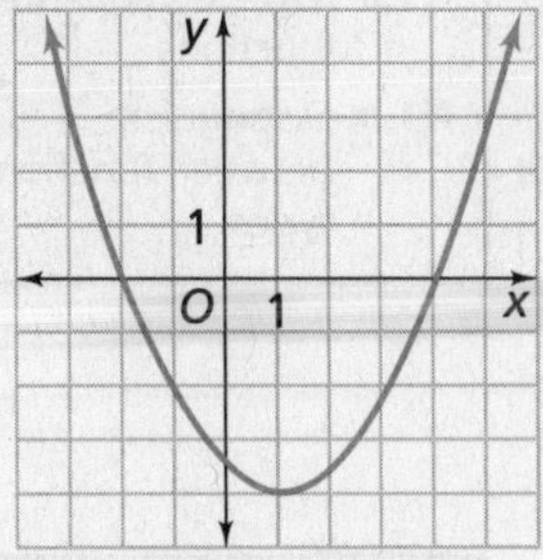

13 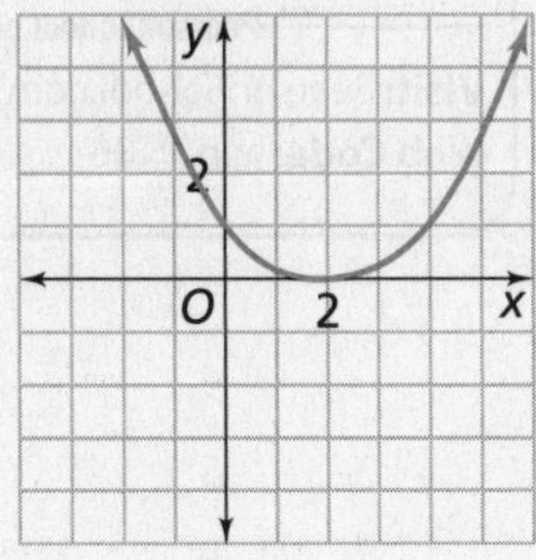

14 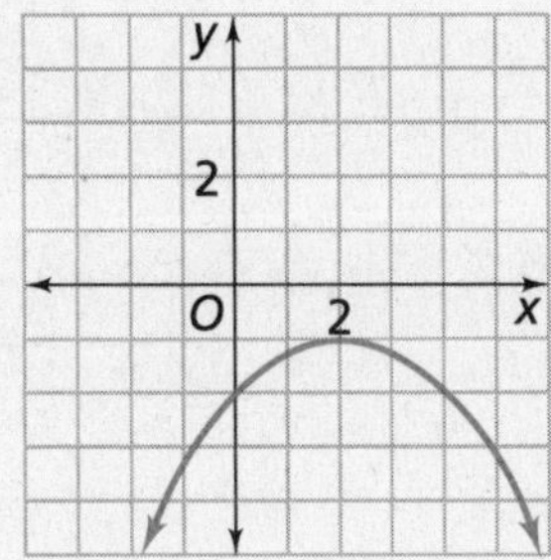

In Exercises 15–23, sketch each parabola or circle.

15 $y = x^2 - 3x$

16 $y = (x + 2)^2$

17 $y = x^2 - 2x + 2$

18 $y = 0.5x^2 - 4x$

19 $y = \frac{1}{3}x^2 - 2$

20 $y = x^2 - 3x + 2$

21 $x^2 + y^2 = 9$

22 $x^2 + y^2 = 16$

23 $(x + 2)^2 + (y - 2)^2 = 4$

In Exercises 24–30, solve the problem. Clearly show all necessary work.

24 Profit P in dollars made by a manufacturing company that makes w units of a product is given by $P = w^2 - 25w + 5000$. Determine the minimum profit for this company.

25 Write an equation of a parabola that has a y-intercept 6 and x-intercepts -3 and 4. Explain how you arrived at your answer.

26 The square shown below has sides 18 units in length. The shaded region has area 100π square units. Find the radius of the circle to the nearest tenth.

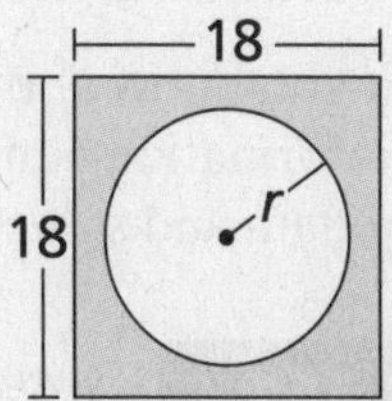

27 Write an equation in standard form for the set of all points that are in the coordinate plane and are 5 units from $P(-5, 2)$. Sketch that set of points.

28 Becky drops a coin into a well 64 feet deep. If the distance d in feet the coin falls is given by $d = 16t^2$, how many seconds t will it take the coin to hit the bottom?

29 Use a graph or an analysis of a graph to show that $x^2 + 5 = 4x$ has no real solutions.

30 Andre threw a ball into the air from the top of a building as shown. An equation for the altitude h of the ball in feet is given by $h = -16t^2 + 64t + 60$, where t is elapsed time in seconds. What is the maximum altitude of the ball?

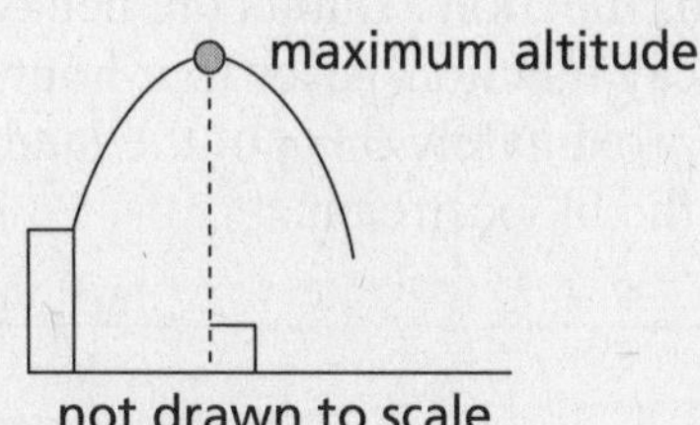

6.4 Applications of Linear and Nonlinear Functions

ADP℠ Standards

L1.d Model problems using linear functions

N1.a Represent quadratic functions

N1.b Distinguish between function types

You can interpret graphs of functions to solve problems. Characteristics of a graph, such as the intercepts or the slope of a line, can give you information needed to solve a problem. Suppose a concrete patio has a garden in the middle shaped like a square. The function $y = 25(15) - x(x) = 375 - x^2$ gives the area of the concrete area of the patio without garden.

Using the graph of the area function at the right, you can estimate the length of the garden that results in a patio area of 150 ft^2. By drawing a horizontal line at 150 and dropping a vertical line from the point of intersection with the parabola, the x-value can be found that results in a patio of 150 ft^2. It can be estimated that the length of the garden is 15 feet.

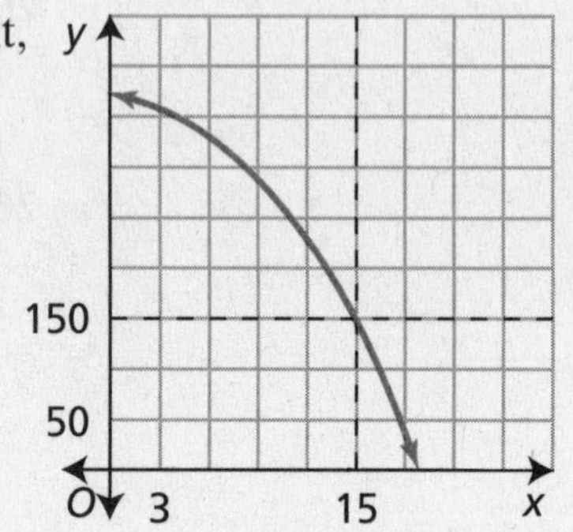

You can use what you know about interpreting the information contained in graphs to analyze data and solve problems.

EXAMPLES 1 and 2 Interpreting graphs

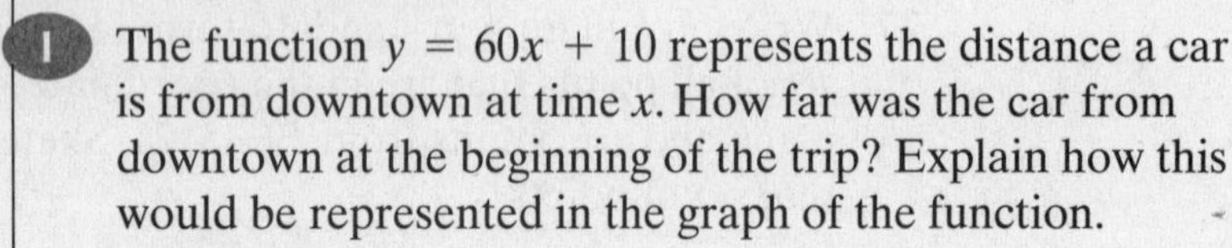

1 The function $y = 60x + 10$ represents the distance a car is from downtown at time x. How far was the car from downtown at the beginning of the trip? Explain how this would be represented in the graph of the function.

■ SOLUTION

At the beginning of the trip, $x = 0$. So the car was **(60)0 + 10 = 10 miles** from downtown. The function is linear, and the distance the car is from downtown is the point at which $x = 0$, which is also the y-intercept.

2 The accompanying graph shows the absorption of a particular medication in the bloodstream after a given amount of time. Describe this function and estimate the amount of the drug absorbed after 4 hours.

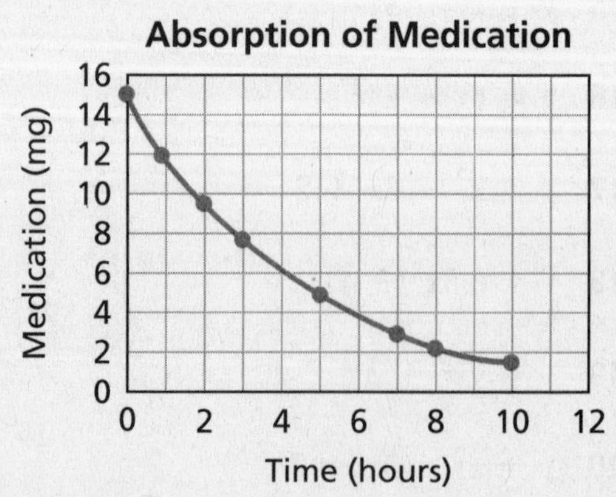

■ SOLUTION

This function exhibits the behavior of an exponential decay function. After four hours there will be approximately *6 mg* of the medication absorbed in the bloodstream.

You can use what you know about the vertex of the graph of a quadratic function to determine maximum or minimum values in problems.

EXAMPLE 3 Finding maximum areas

You have 28 yd of fencing for a rectangular-shaped garden. If x is the width of the garden, the area of the garden is given by $y = 14x - x^2$. What is the maximum area that can be enclosed by the fence?

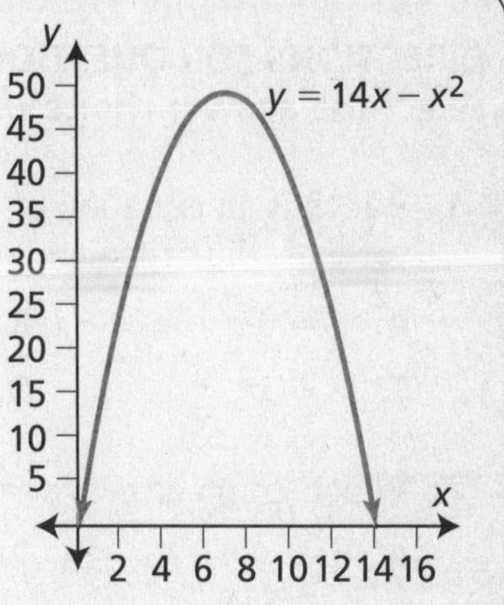

■ SOLUTION

The vertex of the graph is at $x = 7$. From the graph it appears that the maximum value is between 45 and 50. Substituting $x = 7$ into the equation for area, the maximum possible enclosed area is $y = 14(7) - (7)^2 = 49$.

Practice

Choose the letter preceding the word or expression that best completes the statement or answers the question.

1 The accompanying graph shows the profit in dollars from bicycle sales at the Wheels-a-Turning Bicycle Shop. How many bicycles must be sold to maximize profit?

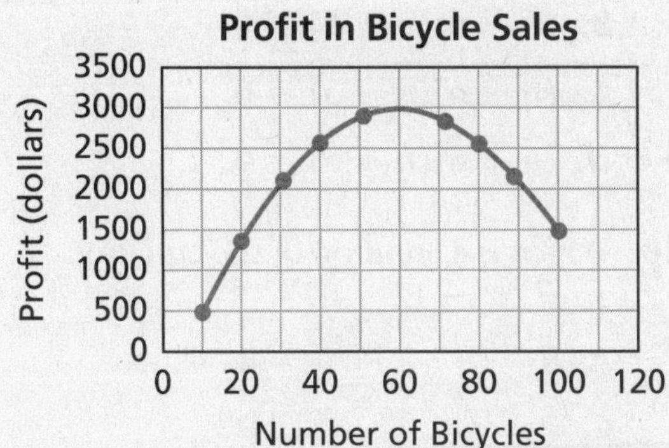

A. 60 **B.** 100 **C.** 500 **D.** 3000

2 A stone is dropped down a deep well. The graph shows the distance from the water at the bottom of the well after a given time. The x-intercept of this graph represents which of the following?

A. The depth of the well.

B. The speed of the stone.

C. The time it takes to hit the water.

D. The depth of the water in the well.

3 The function displayed in the graph for Exercise 2 is best described as

A. linear. **C.** exponential growth.

B. quadratic. **D.** exponential decay.

DIRECTIONS FOR 4–5: Solve each problem and show your work.

4 The height of a ball thrown in the air is represented by a parabola. Describe how the graph of the function would reflect at what time the ball hits the ground.

5 The table shows the 2006 United States rates for mailing a first class letter weighing up to 8 ounces. Graph the cost of mailing a letter as a function of the weight of the letter.

First-Class Mail Rates

Weight at most (ounces)	Rate
1	$0.39
2	$0.63
3	$0.87
4	$1.11
5	$1.35
6	$1.59
7	$1.83
8	$2.07

Chapter 6 Preparing for the ADP[SM] Algebra I Exam

DIRECTIONS FOR QUESTIONS 1–22: For each of the questions below, select the answer choice that is best for each case.

1 Which is an equation of a parabola whose vertex is the origin and opens down?

A. $y = 3x^2$ **B.** $y = -3x^2$

C. $y - x^2 = 1$ **D.** $y + 1 = x^2$

2 Which graph crosses $y = 0$ in two points?

A. $y = x^2 - 6x + 8$

B. $y = x^2 + 6x + 9$

C. $y = x^2 - 6x + 10$

D. $y = x^2 + 6x + 11$

3 The equation of a circle whose center is the origin and whose radius is $\sqrt{5}$ is

A. $x^2 + y^2 = \sqrt{5}$ **B.** $x^2 + y^2 = 5$

C. $x^2 + y^2 = 25$ **D.** $x^2 - y^2 = 5$

4 Which is equivalent to $6x^2 + 19x + 10 = 0$?

A. $(3x + 2)(2x + 5) = 0$

B. $(3x - 2)(2x - 5) = 0$

C. $(x + 2)(6x + 5) = 0$

D. $(6x - 5)(x - 2) = 0$

5 Which are the solutions to $19n = 4n^2 + 19n - 9$?

A. $\frac{3}{2}$ and $-\frac{3}{2}$ **B.** only $\frac{3}{2}$

C. $\frac{2}{3}$ and $-\frac{2}{3}$ **D.** no solution

6 Which is true of the graph of $y = -x^2 + 12x$?

A. The graph opens down and the axis of symmetry is $x = -12$.

B. The graph opens down and the axis of symmetry is $x = 12$.

C. The graph opens up and the axis of symmetry is $x = 6$.

D. The graph opens down and the axis of symmetry is $x = 6$.

7 Which equation does not have the same solutions as $3x^2 = 6x - 9$?

A. $3x^2 - 6x + 9 = 0$

B. $3x^2 - 6x = -9$

C. $3x^2 - 6x - 9 = 0$

D. $x^2 - 2x + 3 = 0$

8 Which equation has exactly one solution?

A. $(c - 3)^2 = 0$

B. $(c - 3)^2 = 5$

C. $(c - 3)^2 = -5$

D. $c - (2c^2 + 1) = -5$

9 Which is equivalent to $n^2 + n = 30$?

A. $(n + 6)(n - 5) = 0$

B. $(n - 6)(n + 5) = 0$

C. $(n - 6)(n - 5) = 0$

D. $(n + 6)(n + 5) = 0$

10 Which is a solution of the equation $x^2 - 4x - 12 = 0$?

A. 6 **B.** 4

C. 2 **D.** −3

11 Which does not represent a rectangle with length $m + 2$, width $m + 4$, and area 63?

A. $(m + 2)(m + 4) = 63$

B. $(m + 2)(m + 4) - 63 = 0$

C. $m^2 + 6m + 8 = 63$

D. $m^2 + 6m + 71 = 0$

12 The solutions to $s(s - 3)(s + 8) = 0$ are

A. 0, 3, and 8. **B.** −3 and 8.

C. 0, 3, and −8. **D.** 0, −3, and 8.

13 Which equation represents the circle with center at the origin and radius 6?

A. $x^2 - y^2 = 6$

B. $x^2 + y^2 = 36$

C. $x^2 - y^2 = 36$

D. $x^2 + y^2 = 6$

14 The roots of a quadratic are $x = -5$ and $x = 3$. Which of the following are possible factors of the quadratic?

A. $(x - 5)$ and $(x + 3)$

B. $(x + 5)$ and $(x - 3)$

C. $x = -5$ and $x = 3$

D. $(x - 5)$ and $(x - 3)$

In Exercises 15–17, solve the quadratic equation.

15 $4h^2 = 2h^2 + 32$

A. 8 and −8 **B.** 16

C. −4 and 4 **D.** 8

16 $4p^2 = -16$

A. 4 and −4 **B.** 2 and −2

C. −2 **D.** no real solutions

17 $2a^2 = 13a + 7$

A. -7 and $\frac{1}{2}$ **B.** 1 and $\frac{7}{2}$

C. $-\frac{1}{2}$ and 7 **D.** -1 and $\frac{7}{2}$

18 Which points are the zeros of the equation $x^2 - 2x - 15 = y$?

A. $(-3, 0)$ and $(5, 0)$

B. $(0, -3)$ and $(0, 5)$

C. $(3, 0)$ and $(-5, 0)$

D. $(0, -2)$ and $(0, -15)$

19 Which is not true of the parabola with equation $y = -3x^2 + 2x - 4$?

A. The parabola opens down.

B. The parabola has a minimum.

C. The parabola has vertex $\left(\frac{1}{3}, -\frac{11}{3}\right)$.

D. The y-intercept is $(0, -4)$.

20 The graph of which equation has a maximum?

A. $y = \frac{1}{2}x^2 - 6x + 5$

B. $y = -2x + \frac{3}{4}x^2 - 1$

C. $y = 3x - \frac{7}{8}x^2 + 2$

D. $y - \frac{2}{3}x^2 = 7x + 5$

21 The axis of symmetry for a parabola passes through

A. the y-intercept.

B. the vertex.

C. the x-intercept.

D. the origin.

22 A line given by $f(x)$ passes through the origin. Which could be the function shown in the graph?

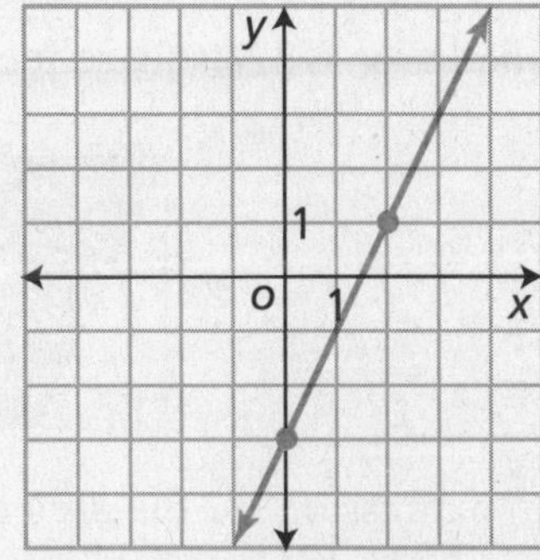

A. $f(x - 3)$ **B.** $f(x + 3)$

C. $f(x) - 3$ **D.** $f(x) + 3$

DIRECTIONS FOR 23–25: Solve each problem. Show your work or provide an explanation for your answer.

23 The graph of a parabola crosses the x-axis at $x = -5$ and $x = 2$, and crosses the y-axis at $y = 5$.

Write an equation for the parabola.

24 The altitude of an object in feet is given by $h = -16t^2 + 8t + 48$.

What is its maximum altitude?

After how many seconds t will it strike the ground?

25 The shaded area is 324 square feet.

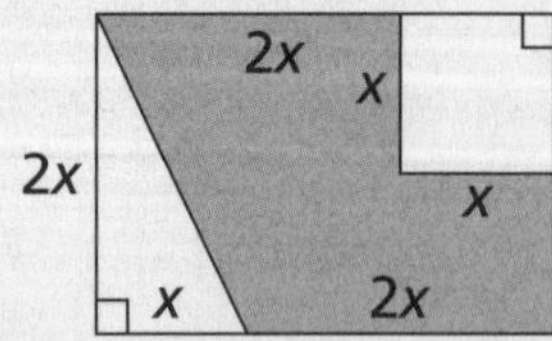

Write an expression for the area of the square shown.

Write an expression for the area of the right triangle shown.

Find x.

7 Rational and Radical Expressions and Equations

ALGEBRA I

Discovering Washington

Grand Coulee Dam

The Grand Coulee Dam on the Columbia River is the largest producer of hydroelectric power in the U.S. Construction of the Grand Coulee Dam began in 1933, and it was completed in 1942. It stands 550 feet tall and is 5,223 feet long. The dam was built using 11,975,521 cubic yards of concrete, making it one of the largest concrete structures in the world.

In addition to providing electric power, the Grand Coulee Dam serves several other important functions. It helps control flooding of the Columbia River. The Dam's reservoir, Franklin D. Roosevelt Lake, provides water for irrigating more than 600,000 acres in the Columbia River Basin. The lake's 600 miles of shoreline, designated as a National Recreation Area in 1948, provides many outdoor recreational activities.

7.1 Rational Expressions

ADP℠ Standards

O2.b Operate with polynomial expressions

O2.c Factor simple polynomial expressions

Recall that a rational number is any number that can be written in the form $\frac{a}{b}$, where a and b are integers and $b \neq 0$. It is necessary to exclude 0 because the fraction $\frac{a}{b}$ represents $a \div b$, and division by zero is undefined.

A **rational expression** is an expression that can be written in the form $\frac{P}{Q}$, where P and Q are polynomials and the value of Q is not zero. The following are some examples of rational expressions.

$$\frac{-3}{2} \qquad \frac{y^2 - 1}{4} \qquad \frac{5}{x + 2} \qquad \frac{t^2 + 5t + 6}{t + 3} \qquad \frac{ab^2}{c} \qquad \frac{m^2 - 3m}{m - n}$$

Like a rational number, a rational expression represents a division, and so the denominator cannot be 0. A rational expression is said to be *undefined* for any value of a variable that results in a denominator of zero.

Recall that the **domain** or **replacement set** is the set of all possible numbers that can be used to substitute for the variable in an algebraic expression. The domain for a rational expression will be **restricted** to all real numbers except those that make the denominator equal to zero.

EXAMPLES 1 through 4 **Recognizing when a rational expression is undefined**

Describe the circumstances, if any, in which the given expression is undefined.

1 $\frac{n}{6}$

▪ **SOLUTION** The denominator is 6, which is a constant. So the expression is defined for all real-number values of n.

2 $\frac{6}{n}$

▪ **SOLUTION** The denominator is n, which is a variable. So the expression is undefined when $n = 0$.

3 $\frac{6}{n + 1}$

▪ **SOLUTION** The denominator is $n + 1$. When $n = -1$, $n + 1 = 0$. So the expression is undefined when $n = -1$.

4 $\frac{6}{n^2 + 1}$

▪ **SOLUTION** The denominator is $n^2 + 1$, which is a variable expression. However, there is no real number n for which $n^2 + 1 = 0$. So the expression is defined for all real-number values of n.

Any value of a variable for which a rational expression is undefined is called an **excluded value** of the variable. It is said that the excluded values are *restricted from the domain* of that variable.

To find the excluded values of a variable, you can use what you learned about solving equations.

EXAMPLES 5 and 6 Finding values for which a rational expression is undefined

Note

Recall the Zero-Product Property: If a and b are real numbers and $ab = 0$, then either $a = 0$ or $b = 0$.

State any restrictions on the domain of the variable in each expression.

5 $\frac{w}{3w + 2}$

■ **SOLUTION**

Solve $3w + 2 = 0$.

$3w + 2 = 0$ ← **$3w + 2 = 0$ is a linear equation.**

$3w = -2$

$w = -\frac{2}{3}$

The only excluded value is $-\frac{2}{3}$.

You write: $w \neq -\frac{2}{3}$

6 $\frac{2b}{b^2 + 4b + 3}$

■ **SOLUTION**

Solve $b^2 + 4b + 3 = 0$.

$b^2 + 4b + 3 = 0$ ← **$b^2 + 4b + 3 = 0$ is a quadratic equation.**

$(b + 1)(b + 3) = 0$

$b = -1$ or $b = -3$

The excluded values are −1 and −3.

You write: $b \neq -1, b \neq -3$

Recall that an arithmetic fraction is in *lowest terms* if the GCF of its numerator and denominator is 1. You can rewrite a fraction in lowest terms by dividing both its numerator and denominator by their GCF.

$$\frac{16}{24} = \frac{16 \div 8}{24 \div 8} = \frac{2}{3}$$ ← **The GCF of 16 and 24 is 8.**

Similarly, a rational expression is in *simplest form* if the GCF of its numerator and denominator is 1. You can use the following procedure to simplify a rational expression.

Simplifying a Rational Expression

Step 1 Factor both the numerator and the denominator, if necessary.

Step 2 Divide both the numerator and the denominator by their GCF.

EXAMPLE 7 Simplifying a rational expression: monomial GCF

Simply the expression. State any restrictions on the domain of the variable.

7 $\frac{a^2b - ab}{a^2b}$

■ **SOLUTION**

$$\frac{a^2b - ab}{a^2b} = \frac{ab(a - 1)}{a^2b}$$ ← **Factor.**

$$= \frac{\overset{1}{\cancel{ab}}(a - 1)}{a \cdot \underset{1}{\cancel{ab}}}$$ ← **The GCF is ab.**

$$= \frac{1 \cdot (a - 1)}{a \cdot 1}$$

$$= \frac{a - 1}{a}$$

To find the restrictions on the domains of a and b, solve $a^2b = 0$.

$a^2b = 0$

$a^2 = 0$ or $b = 0$

$a = 0$ or $b = 0$

The simplest form is $\frac{a - 1}{a}$, with the restrictions $a \neq 0, b \neq 0$.

Notice that $\frac{a-1}{a}$ cannot be simplified further, even though the variable a appears in both the numerator and denominator. When simplifying, you must look for *factors* that are common to the numerator and denominator. In $\frac{a-1}{a}$, the a in the numerator is a term, not a factor.

Also notice that, although the variable b does not appear in the simplified expression in Example 7, there is a restriction on b. When determining restrictions on the variables, you must examine the original expression.

EXAMPLE 8 **Simplifying a rational expression: binomial GCF**

8 Simplify $\frac{d^2 - 9d + 18}{d^2 - 6d + 9}$. State any restrictions on the domain of the variable.

▪ **SOLUTION**

$$\frac{d^2 - 9d + 18}{d^2 - 6d + 9} = \frac{(d-3)(d-6)}{(d-3)(d-3)} \quad \leftarrow \text{Factor.}$$

$$= \frac{\overset{1}{\cancel{(d-3)}}(d-6)}{\underset{1}{\cancel{(d-3)}}(d-3)} \quad \leftarrow \text{The GCF is } (d-3).$$

$$= \frac{1 \cdot (d-6)}{1 \cdot (d-3)}$$

$$= \frac{d-6}{d-3}$$

To find the restrictions on the domain of d, solve $d^2 - 6d + 9 = 0$.

$$d^2 - 6d + 9 = 0$$
$$(d-3)^2 = 0$$
$$d = 3$$

So the simplest form is $\frac{d-6}{d-3}$, with the restriction $d \neq 3$.

Recall that we can reverse the signs of a polynomial by factoring -1 from every term. Therefore,

$$b - a = (-1)(-b + a) \text{ or } (-1)(a - b).$$

EXAMPLE 9 **Simplifying a rational expression: binomial factors that are opposites**

9 Simplify $\frac{w-4}{16-w^2}$. State any restrictions on the domain of the variable.

▪ **SOLUTION**

$$\frac{w-4}{16-w^2} = \frac{w-4}{(4-w)(4+w)} \quad \leftarrow \text{Factor.}$$

$$= \frac{w-4}{(-1)(w-4)(4+w)} \quad \leftarrow 4 - w = (-1)(w-4)$$

$$= \frac{\overset{1}{\cancel{w-4}}}{(-1)\underset{1}{\cancel{(w-4)}}(4+w)} \quad \leftarrow \text{The GCF is } (w-4).$$

$$= \frac{1}{(-1)(1)(4+w)}$$

$$= \frac{1}{-(4+w)}$$

$$= \frac{1}{-4-w} \text{ or } \frac{-1}{4+w}$$

To find the restrictions on the domain of w, solve $16 - w^2 = 0$.

$$16 - w^2 = 0$$
$$(4+w)(4-w) = 0$$
$$w = -4 \text{ or } w = 4$$

So the simplest form is $\frac{1}{-4-w}$, with the restrictions $w \neq -4$, $w \neq 4$.

Practice

Choose the letter preceding the word or expression that best completes the statement or answers the question.

1 Given the expression $\frac{3}{x^3 - 4x}$, what are the excluded values of x?

A. 2 and −2 **C.** −2, 0, and 2

B. 0 and 2 **D.** 0 and 4

2 If $a \neq b$, which is equivalent to $\frac{a^2 - b^2}{a - b}$?

A. $a - b$ **C.** 1

B. $a + b$ **D.** 0

3 Which expression is equivalent to −1 for all values of n for which it is defined?

A. $\frac{n - 2}{n^2 - 2}$ **C.** $\frac{(n - 2)^2}{n^2 - 4}$

B. $\frac{n^2 - 4}{4 - n^2}$ **D.** $\frac{n + 1}{n - 1}$

4 Which is $\frac{4a^2 - 20ab}{4a^2 - 100b^2}$ in simplest form?

A. $\frac{1 - 2ab}{1 - 10b^2}$

B. $\frac{a(a - 5b)}{(a - 5b)(a - 5b)}$

C. $\frac{4a(a - 5b)}{(2a - 10b)(2a + 10b)}$

D. $\frac{a}{a + 5b}$

5 Which best describes the restrictions on the variables in $\frac{a^2 - 10ab + 25b^2}{a^2 - 25b^2}$?

A. $a \neq 5b, a \neq -5b$

B. $a \neq 5b, b \neq 5a$

C. $a \neq 5, a \neq -5$

D. $a \neq 5, a \neq -5, b \neq 5, b \neq -5$

In Exercises 6–11, state any restrictions on the domains of the variables in each expression.

6 $\frac{5}{2x - 8}$ **7** $\frac{h^2 - 36}{h^2}$

8 $\frac{p^2 - 2p - 3}{p^2 - 9}$ **9** $\frac{m^2 - 4m + 4}{m^2 + 4}$

10 $\frac{s^2 + t^2}{s^2 - t^2}$ **11** $\frac{a^2 - ab + b^2}{a^2 - ab}$

In Exercises 12–31, simplify each expression. State any restrictions on the domains of the variables.

12 $\frac{3j - 9}{3j}$ **13** $\frac{5u}{5u + 10}$

14 $\frac{x^2 - 2x}{x}$ **15** $\frac{2t}{4t^2 - 2t}$

16 $\frac{6z - 9}{4z - 6}$ **17** $\frac{c + 3}{c^2 + 3c}$

18 $\frac{s^3 - 2s^2}{2s^2 - 4s}$ **19** $\frac{3w - 6w^2}{2w^3}$

20 $\frac{p^2 - p}{pq - p}$ **21** $\frac{x^2 - xy}{x^2 + xy}$

22 $\frac{n^2 - 5n + 6}{n - 3}$ **23** $\frac{v + 7}{v^2 - 49}$

24 $\frac{b^2 - 36}{b^2 + 4b - 12}$ **25** $\frac{r^2 - r - 6}{r^2 + r - 12}$

26 $\frac{6k - 15}{2k^2 - 3k - 5}$ **27** $\frac{4z^2 + 3z - 1}{8z - 2}$

28 $\frac{5d + 20}{16 - d^2}$ **29** $\frac{2g^2 + 3g - 9}{3 - 2g}$

30 $\frac{b^2 + 2b + 1}{1 - b^2}$ **31** $\frac{m^2 - mn}{n^2 - mn}$

In Exercises 32–33, use the expression given to solve the problem.

32 Given $\frac{c + 4}{c - 4}$, explain why 4 is excluded from the domain of c, but −4 is not.

33 Is the expression $\frac{3p^2 - 27q^2}{p^2 - 9q^2}$ defined when $p = 3$ and $q = -1$? Show your work.

7.2 Multiplication and Division with Rational Expressions

ADP℠ Standards

02.b Operate with polynomial expressions

02.c Factor simple polynomial expressions

When you multiply arithmetic fractions, you multiply the numerators and multiply the denominators. Then, if necessary, you simplify the result.

$$\frac{4}{5} \cdot \frac{15}{16} = \frac{4 \cdot 15}{5 \cdot 16} = \frac{60}{80} = \frac{60 \div 20}{80 \div 20} = \frac{3}{4}$$

The procedure for multiplying rational expressions is similar to the procedure for multiplying arithmetic fractions.

Multiplying Rational Expressions

If $\frac{P}{Q}$ and $\frac{R}{S}$ are rational expressions, and the values of Q and S are not zero, then:

$$\frac{P}{Q} \cdot \frac{R}{S} = \frac{PR}{QS}$$

When you are performing operations with rational expressions in this book, you may assume that the domain of each variable is restricted so that no denominator has a value of zero.

- You can multiply rational expressions by first multiplying the numerators and denominators and then reducing the resulting rational expression by the common monomial factor (the GCF) of both the numerator and denominator.
- You can also divide the numerators and denominators by the common factors first and then multiply the remaining factors.

EXAMPLE 1 **Multiplying $\frac{P}{Q} \cdot \frac{R}{S}$: monomial numerators and denominators**

1 Simplify $\frac{7x}{9} \cdot \frac{3}{4x^2}$.

■ SOLUTION 1

Multiply first.

$$\frac{7x}{9} \cdot \frac{3}{4x^2} = \frac{21x}{36x^2}$$

$$= \frac{21x \div 3x}{36x^2 \div 3x} \quad \leftarrow \textbf{Find the common factor.}$$

$$= \frac{7}{12x} \quad \leftarrow \textbf{Divide by the common factor.}$$

■ SOLUTION 2

Factor first.

$$\frac{7x}{9} \cdot \frac{3}{4x^2}$$

$$= \frac{7 \cdot x}{3 \cdot 3} \cdot \frac{3}{4 \cdot x \cdot x} \quad \leftarrow \textbf{Factor first.}$$

$$= \frac{7 \cdot 1 \cdot 1}{3 \cdot 4 \cdot x} = \frac{7}{12x}$$

You may use the second method if the rational expressions have polynomials in the numerator and denominator. Because both numerators and denominators are multiplied, the common factors can be removed from any numerator and denominator.

EXAMPLES 2 and 3 Multiplying polynomial expressions

Go Online
PearsonSchool.com
Visit: PearsonSchool.com
Web Code: ayp-0638

Simplify each expression.

2 $\frac{3v-6}{5v+25}\cdot\frac{v+5}{9v-18}$

■ SOLUTION

$$\frac{3v-6}{5v+25}\cdot\frac{v+5}{9v-18}$$
$$=\frac{3(v-2)}{5(v+5)}\cdot\frac{v+5}{9(v-2)}$$
$$=\frac{\overset{1}{\cancel{3}}\,\overset{1}{\cancel{(v-2)}}}{5\underset{1}{\cancel{(v+5)}}}\cdot\frac{\overset{1}{\cancel{(v+5)}}}{\underset{3}{\cancel{9}}\underset{1}{\cancel{(v-2)}}}$$
$$=\frac{1\cdot1\cdot1}{5\cdot1\cdot3\cdot1}$$
$$=\frac{1}{15}$$

3 $\frac{c^2+4c-12}{4c-6}\cdot\frac{8c^2-18}{5c+30}$

■ SOLUTION

$$\frac{c^2+4c-12}{4c-6}\cdot\frac{8c^2-18}{5c+30}$$
$$=\frac{(c+6)(c-2)}{2(2c-3)}\cdot\frac{2(2c+3)(2c-3)}{5(c+6)}$$
$$=\frac{\overset{1}{\cancel{(c+6)}}(c-2)}{\underset{1}{\cancel{2}}\underset{1}{\cancel{(2c-3)}}}\cdot\frac{\overset{1}{\cancel{2}}(2c+3)\overset{1}{\cancel{(2c-3)}}}{5\underset{1}{\cancel{(c+6)}}}$$
$$=\frac{1\cdot(c-2)\cdot1\cdot(2c+3)\cdot1}{1\cdot1\cdot5\cdot1}$$
$$=\frac{(c-2)(2c+3)}{5}\text{ or }\frac{2c^2-c-6}{5}$$

Recall that any whole number is a rational number whose denominator is 1. Therefore, you can multiply a rational expression by a polynomial by writing the polynomial as a rational expression with a denominator of 1, for example,

$$2x^2+3=\frac{2x^2+3}{1}.$$

EXAMPLE 4 Multiplying a rational expression by a polynominal

4 Simplify $\frac{5x+10}{x^2+7x+10}\cdot x^2+8x+15$.

■ SOLUTION

$$\frac{5x+10}{x^2+7x+10}\cdot x^2+8x+15=\frac{5(x+2)}{(x+5)(x+2)}\cdot\frac{(x+3)(x+5)}{1}=5(x+3)$$

When you divide two arithmetic fractions, you multiply the dividend by the reciprocal of the divisor and simplify the result.

$$\frac{3}{4}\div\frac{5}{6}=\frac{3}{4}\cdot\frac{6}{5}=\frac{3\cdot6}{4\cdot5}=\frac{18}{20}=\frac{18\div2}{20\div2}=\frac{9}{10}$$

The procedure for dividing rational expressions is similar.

Note

Recall that the reciprocal of any rational number $\frac{a}{b}$ is $\frac{b}{a}$, provided that $a\neq0$ and $b\neq0$.

Dividing Rational Expressions

If $\frac{P}{Q}$ and $\frac{R}{S}$ are rational expressions, and the values of Q, R, and S are not zero, then:

$$\frac{P}{Q}\div\frac{R}{S}=\frac{P}{Q}\cdot\frac{S}{R}=\frac{PS}{QR}$$

EXAMPLES 5 and 6 Dividing $\frac{P}{Q} \div \frac{R}{S}$: monomial numerators and denominators

Simplify each expression. Write each answer using positive exponents.

5 $\frac{9h^2}{35} \div \frac{h^3}{7}$

■ **SOLUTION**

$$\frac{9h^2}{35} \div \frac{h^3}{7} = \frac{9h^2}{35} \cdot \frac{7}{h^3}$$

$$= \frac{9\cancel{h^2}^{1}}{\cancel{35}_{5}} \cdot \frac{\cancel{7}^{1}}{\cancel{h^3}_{h}}$$

$$= \frac{9}{5h}$$

6 $\frac{6a}{5b} \div \frac{3b}{5a}$

■ **SOLUTION**

$$\frac{6a}{5b} \div \frac{3b}{5a} = \frac{6a}{5b} \cdot \frac{5a}{3b}$$

$$= \frac{\cancel{6}^{2}a}{\cancel{5}_{1}b} \cdot \frac{\cancel{5}^{1}a}{\cancel{3}_{1}b}$$

$$= \frac{2a^2}{b^2}$$

To divide a rational expression by a polynomial, you must multiply by the reciprocal of the polynomial. For example, to divide a rational expression by $2x + 3$, you would multiply by $\frac{1}{2x + 3}$.

Go Online
PearsonSchool.com
Visit: PearsonSchool.com
Web Code: ayp-0639

EXAMPLES 7 and 8 Dividing polynomial expressions

Simplify each expression.

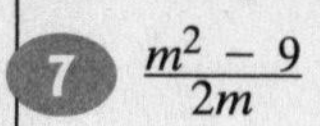

7 $\frac{m^2 - 9}{2m} \div \frac{m + 3}{m}$

■ **SOLUTION**

$$\frac{m^2 - 9}{2m} \div \frac{m + 3}{m}$$

$$= \frac{m^2 - 9}{2m} \cdot \frac{m}{m + 3}$$

$$= \frac{(m + 3)(m - 3)}{2m} \cdot \frac{m}{m + 3}$$

$$= \frac{\cancel{(m + 3)}^{1}(m - 3)}{2\cancel{m}_{1}} \cdot \frac{\cancel{m}^{1}}{\cancel{m + 3}_{1}}$$

$$= \frac{m - 3}{2}$$

8 $\frac{3y - 4}{5} \div \frac{6y - 8}{2}$

■ **SOLUTION**

$$\frac{3y - 4}{5} \div \frac{6y - 8}{2}$$

$$= \frac{3y - 4}{5} \cdot \frac{2}{6y - 8}$$

$$= \frac{3y - 4}{5} \cdot \frac{2}{2(3y - 4)}$$

$$= \frac{\cancel{3y - 4}^{1}}{5} \cdot \frac{\cancel{2}^{1}}{\cancel{2}_{1}\cancel{(3y - 4)}_{1}}$$

$$= \frac{1}{5}$$

When performing multiplications and divisions with rational expressions, you may need to work with binomial factors that are opposites of each other.

EXAMPLE 9 Dividing rational expressions when binomial factors are opposites

9 Simplify $\frac{z - 6}{5} \div \frac{6 - z}{2}$.

■ **SOLUTION**

$$\frac{z - 6}{5} \div \frac{6 - z}{2} = \frac{z - 6}{5} \cdot \frac{2}{6 - z} = \frac{z - 6}{5} \cdot \frac{2}{(-1)(z - 6)} = \frac{\cancel{z - 6}^{1}}{5} \cdot \frac{2}{(-1)\cancel{(z - 6)}_{1}} = \frac{2}{-5} = -\frac{2}{5}$$

Practice

Choose the letter preceding the word or expression that best completes the statement or answers the question.

1 Which is equivalent to $\frac{16r^2}{5s^2} \div \frac{4r^2}{5s}$?

A. $\frac{5s^2}{16r^2} \cdot \frac{4r^2}{5s}$

B. $\frac{16r^2}{5s^2} \cdot \frac{5s}{4r^2}$

C. $\frac{5s^2}{16r^2} \cdot \frac{5s}{4r^2}$

D. $\frac{4r^2}{5s} \div \frac{16r^2}{5s^2}$

2 Which is equivalent to $\frac{4}{n-6} \div \frac{n+6}{4}$?

A. $\frac{n+6}{n-6}$

B. $\frac{n-6}{n+6}$

C. $\frac{16}{n^2-36}$

D. $\frac{4n+24}{4n-24}$

3 Simplify $\frac{a+2}{a-2} \cdot \frac{2-a}{2+a}$.

A. -2

B. -1

C. 0

D. 1

4 Which is not equivalent to $\frac{b-1}{b} \cdot (1-b)$?

A. $\frac{b-1}{b} \cdot \frac{1-b}{1}$

B. $\frac{b-1}{b} \cdot \frac{-(b-1)}{1}$

C. $\frac{-(b-1)^2}{b}$

D. $-\frac{1}{b}$

In Exercises 5–30, simplify each expression. Write answers using positive exponents.

5 $\frac{9}{j} \cdot \frac{3}{j}$

6 $\frac{4}{t} \div \frac{16}{t}$

7 $\frac{2c^2}{7} \cdot \frac{21}{12c^3}$

8 $\frac{6}{5s} \cdot \frac{s^3}{8}$

9 $\frac{m^4}{9} \div \frac{3}{2m^2}$

10 $\frac{1}{10v^3} \div \frac{35}{v}$

11 $\frac{4y^2}{3} \cdot 12y$

12 $\frac{1}{d^3} \div 5d^2$

13 $\frac{3}{xy} \cdot \frac{5}{2xy}$

14 $\frac{7p}{2q^2} \cdot \frac{3p^2}{q}$

15 $\frac{2-t}{t} \cdot \frac{4}{4+t}$

16 $\frac{2x}{2x+8} \cdot \frac{x+4}{3x^2}$

17 $\frac{4}{2c-3} \div \frac{3}{4c-6}$

18 $\frac{6z+6}{z} \div \frac{z+1}{z^3}$

19 $\frac{3y+12}{y-4} \div \frac{3y}{2y-8}$

20 $\frac{4s}{s-5} \cdot \frac{4s-20}{s+4}$

21 $\frac{g}{g^2+6g-7} \cdot \frac{g^2+7g}{g^3}$

22 $\frac{6w^3}{w^2-3w} \div \frac{3w^2}{w^2-9}$

23 $\frac{b^2-b-6}{b^2-4b+4} \cdot \frac{b-2}{b-3}$

24 $\frac{q-9}{q+2} \div \frac{q^2-81}{q^2-2q-8}$

25 $\frac{n^2+6n+8}{n-1} \div \frac{n^2-4}{n-1}$

26 $\frac{u^2-3u-10}{u-2} \cdot \frac{u-5}{u^2-10u+25}$

27 $(6h-36) \cdot \frac{h^2+h-12}{h^2-2h-24}$

28 $\frac{t^2-6t-27}{t^2+2t-3} \cdot (t^2-1)$

29 $\frac{y^2+y-30}{y^2+3y-10} \div (y+6)$

30 $(m-4) \div \frac{m^2-16}{m^2+5m+4}$

7.3 Addition and Subtraction with Rational Expressions

ADP℠ Standards

O2.b Operate with polynomial expressions
O2.c Factor simple polynomial expressions

When you add or subtract arithmetic fractions with like denominators, you add or subtract the numerators. Then you place the sum or difference over the common denominator and simplify the result.

$$\frac{3}{7} + \frac{2}{7} = \frac{3+2}{7} = \frac{5}{7} \qquad \frac{3}{7} - \frac{2}{7} = \frac{3-2}{7} = \frac{1}{7}$$

The procedure for adding and subtracting rational expressions is similar.

Adding and Subtracting Rational Expressions

If $\frac{P}{Q}$ and $\frac{R}{Q}$ are rational expressions, and the value of Q is not zero, then:

$$\frac{P}{Q} + \frac{R}{Q} = \frac{P+R}{Q} \quad \text{and} \quad \frac{P}{Q} - \frac{R}{Q} = \frac{P-R}{Q}$$

EXAMPLES 1 through 4 Simplifying $\frac{P}{Q} + \frac{R}{Q}$ and $\frac{P}{Q} - \frac{R}{Q}$: monomial numerators

Simplify each expression.

1. $\frac{9}{4s} - \frac{1}{4s}$

■ SOLUTION $\frac{9}{4s} - \frac{1}{4s} = \frac{9-1}{4s} = \frac{8}{4s} = \frac{\overset{2}{\cancel{8}}}{\underset{1}{\cancel{4}}s} = \frac{2}{s}$

2. $\frac{2}{p-1} - \frac{7}{p-1}$

■ SOLUTION $\frac{2}{p-1} - \frac{7}{p-1} = \frac{2-7}{p-1} = \frac{-5}{p-1}$

3. $\frac{2a}{a+b} + \frac{6a}{a+b}$

■ SOLUTION $\frac{2a}{a+b} + \frac{6a}{a+b} = \frac{2a+6a}{a+b} = \frac{8a}{a+b}$

4. $\frac{m}{n+3} - \frac{3}{n+3}$

■ SOLUTION $\frac{m}{n+3} - \frac{3}{n+3} = \frac{m-3}{n+3}$

Often you must perform additions or subtractions in which the numerators are polynomials with more than one term. In such cases, you will need to apply what you have learned about adding and subtracting polynomials. When subtracting, be especially careful to use the rules for opposites of sums and differences that are summarized at the right.

$$-(a+b) = -a - b$$
$$-(a-b) = -a + b$$

EXAMPLES 5 and 6 Simplifying $\frac{P}{Q} + \frac{R}{Q}$ and $\frac{P}{Q} - \frac{R}{Q}$: polynomial numerators

Simplify each expression.

5. $\frac{c+2}{c-6} + \frac{c-3}{c-6}$

■ SOLUTION

$$\frac{c+2}{c-6} + \frac{c-3}{c-6} = \frac{(c+2)+(c-3)}{c-6}$$
$$= \frac{(c+c)+(2-3)}{c-6}$$
$$= \frac{2c-1}{c-6}$$

6. $\frac{5z}{2z+7} - \frac{z-1}{2z+7}$

■ SOLUTION

$$\frac{5z}{2z+7} - \frac{z-1}{2z+7} = \frac{5z-(z-1)}{2z+7}$$
$$= \frac{5z-z+1}{2z+7}$$
$$= \frac{4z+1}{2z+7}$$

To simplify some sums or differences, you may need to factor expressions in the numerator or denominator.

Go Online
PearsonSchool.com
Visit: PearsonSchool.com
Web Codes: ayp-0334
ayp-0335

EXAMPLES 7 and 8 Further simplifying $\frac{P}{Q} + \frac{R}{Q}$ and $\frac{P}{Q} - \frac{R}{Q}$

Simplify each expression.

7 $\frac{w+1}{3w+2} + \frac{5w+3}{3w+2}$

■ SOLUTION

$$\frac{w+1}{3w+2} + \frac{5w+3}{3w+2} = \frac{(w+1)+(5w+3)}{3w+2}$$
$$= \frac{6w+4}{3w+2}$$
$$= \frac{2(3w+2)}{3w+2}$$
$$= \frac{2\cancel{(3w+2)}^{1}}{\cancel{3w+2}_{1}}$$
$$= 2$$

8 $\frac{k^2+k}{k-1} - \frac{k+1}{k-1}$

■ SOLUTION

$$\frac{k^2+k}{k-1} - \frac{k+1}{k-1} = \frac{(k^2+k)-(k+1)}{k-1}$$
$$= \frac{k^2+k-k-1}{k-1}$$
$$= \frac{k^2-1}{k-1}$$
$$= \frac{(k+1)(k-1)}{k-1}$$
$$= \frac{(k+1)\cancel{(k-1)}^{1}}{\cancel{k-1}_{1}}$$
$$= k+1$$

In some additions and subtractions, the denominators are opposite binomials. You can use the basic relationship shown at the right to rewrite one of the expressions so that the denominators are like.

$$\frac{a}{-b} = \frac{-a}{b}$$

EXAMPLE 9 Working with binomial denominators that are opposites

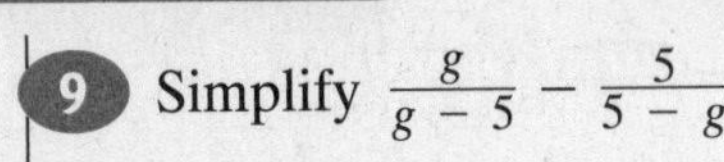

9 Simplify $\frac{g}{g-5} - \frac{5}{5-g}$.

■ SOLUTION

$$\frac{g}{g-5} - \frac{5}{5-g} = \frac{g}{g-5} - \frac{5}{-(g-5)} = \frac{g}{g-5} - \frac{-5}{g-5} = \frac{g-(-5)}{g-5} = \frac{g+5}{g-5}$$

When you add or subtract numeric fractions with unlike denominators, you first rewrite one or both fractions with their least common denominator (LCD).

$$\frac{1}{6} + \frac{4}{15} = \frac{1}{2 \cdot 3} + \frac{4}{3 \cdot 5} \quad \leftarrow \text{Find the prime factorization of 6 and of 15.}$$
$$= \frac{1 \cdot 5}{2 \cdot 3 \cdot 5} + \frac{2 \cdot 4}{2 \cdot 3 \cdot 5} \quad \leftarrow \text{The LCD is } 2 \cdot 3 \cdot 5\text{, or 30.}$$
$$= \frac{5}{30} + \frac{8}{30}$$
$$= \frac{5+8}{30}$$
$$= \frac{13}{30}$$

The procedure for adding and subtracting rational expressions with unlike denominators is similar. Although you can use any common denominator, your work generally is easier if you use the following method to find the LCD.

Go Online
PearsonSchool.com
Visit: PearsonSchool.com
Web Codes: ayp-0036
ayp-0037

Finding the LCD of Rational Expressions

Step 1 Factor each denominator completely, writing the prime factorization of any numerical factors.

Step 2 Write the product of the factors that appear in any of the denominators, using each factor the greatest number of times it appears.

EXAMPLES 10 through 15 Simplifying $\frac{P}{Q} + \frac{R}{S}$ and $\frac{P}{Q} - \frac{R}{S}$

Simplify each expression.

10 $\frac{3}{x} + \frac{4}{y}$

■ **SOLUTION**

$$\frac{3}{x} + \frac{4}{y} = \frac{3 \cdot y}{x \cdot y} + \frac{4 \cdot x}{x \cdot y} = \frac{3y + 4x}{xy}$$

11 $\frac{5}{8} + \frac{1}{6d}$

■ **SOLUTION**

$$\frac{5}{8} + \frac{1}{6d} = \frac{5 \cdot 3d}{8 \cdot 3d} + \frac{1 \cdot 4}{6d \cdot 4} = \frac{15d + 4}{24d}$$

12 $\frac{2}{a} - \frac{3}{a^2}$

■ **SOLUTION**

$$\frac{2}{a} - \frac{3}{a^2} = \frac{2}{a} - \frac{3}{a \cdot a}$$
$$= \frac{2 \cdot a}{a \cdot a} - \frac{3}{a \cdot a}$$
$$= \frac{2a - 3}{a^2}$$

13 $\frac{m}{5} - \frac{m + 1}{m}$

■ **SOLUTION**

$$\frac{m}{5} - \frac{m + 1}{m} = \frac{m \cdot m}{5 \cdot m} - \frac{5 \cdot (m + 1)}{5 \cdot m}$$
$$= \frac{m^2 - 5(m + 1)}{5m}$$
$$= \frac{m^2 - 5m - 5}{5m}$$

14 $\frac{4}{3h + 6} - \frac{3}{2h + 4}$

■ **SOLUTION**

$$\frac{4}{3h + 6} - \frac{3}{2h + 4}$$
$$= \frac{4}{3(h + 2)} - \frac{3}{2(h + 2)}$$
$$= \frac{2 \cdot 4}{2 \cdot 3 \cdot (h + 2)} - \frac{3 \cdot 3}{2 \cdot 3 \cdot (h + 2)}$$
$$= \frac{8}{6(h + 2)} - \frac{9}{6(h + 2)}$$
$$= \frac{8 - 9}{6(h + 2)}$$
$$= \frac{-1}{6(h + 2)} \text{ or } \frac{-1}{6h + 12}$$

15 $\frac{5}{r^2 - 4} - \frac{7}{r + 2}$

■ **SOLUTION**

$$\frac{5}{r^2 - 4} - \frac{7}{r + 2}$$
$$= \frac{5}{(r + 2)(r - 2)} - \frac{7}{(r + 2)}$$
$$= \frac{5}{(r + 2)(r - 2)} - \frac{7(r - 2)}{(r + 2)(r - 2)}$$
$$= \frac{5 - 7(r - 2)}{(r + 2)(r - 2)}$$
$$= \frac{5 - 7r + 14}{(r + 2)(r - 2)}$$
$$= \frac{-7r + 19}{(r + 2)(r - 2)} \text{ or } \frac{-7r + 19}{r^2 - 4}$$

Practice

Choose the letter preceding the word or expression that best completes the statement or answers the question.

1 In simplest form, $\frac{4x + 6}{3} + \frac{5x + 9}{3}$ is

A. $\frac{9x + 15}{3}$ **C.** $3x + 5$

B. $\frac{9x + 15}{6}$ **D.** $\frac{x + 3}{3}$

2 Simplify $\frac{1}{c - 1} - \frac{1}{1 - c}$.

A. 0 **C.** $\frac{2}{c - 1}$

B. 2 **D.** $\frac{2}{c^2 - 1}$

3 Which is equivalent to $\frac{1}{a + b} + \frac{1}{a}$?

A. $\frac{2}{a + b}$ **C.** $\frac{2}{a^2 + b}$

B. $\frac{2a + b}{a^2 + ab}$ **D.** $\frac{2}{a^2 + ab}$

4 Which is equivalent to $\frac{m}{n} - \frac{1}{3}$?

A. $\frac{m - 1}{n - 3}$ **C.** $\frac{3m - n}{n - 3}$

B. $\frac{m - 1}{3n}$ **D.** $\frac{3m - n}{3n}$

In Exercises 5–31, simplify each expression. Write answers using positive exponents.

5 $\frac{7}{g} + \frac{3}{g}$

6 $\frac{8}{j} + \frac{1}{k}$

7 $-\frac{4}{3r} - \frac{2}{3r}$

8 $\frac{1}{z^2} + \frac{1}{z}$

9 $\frac{6}{v} + \frac{3}{v}$

10 $\frac{3}{2x} + \frac{3}{4x^2}$

11 $\frac{2}{c} + \frac{1}{5}$

12 $\frac{2}{25b^3} - \frac{1}{5b^2}$

13 $\frac{2b}{2b + 6} - \frac{4b}{2b + 6}$

14 $\frac{x}{x - y} - \frac{2y}{x - y}$

15 $\frac{r}{5r + 5s} + \frac{s}{5r + 5s}$

16 $\frac{8m}{4m - n} - \frac{2n}{4m - n}$

17 $\frac{5a}{a - 4} - \frac{3a}{4 - a}$

18 $\frac{p}{3p - 3} + \frac{1}{3p - 3}$

19 $\frac{q}{q + 1} + \frac{q - 9}{q + 1}$

20 $\frac{3g - h}{2g - 3h} - \frac{h}{2g - 3h}$

21 $\frac{z - 1}{z - 3} + \frac{z - 7}{z - 3}$

22 $\frac{8m - 1}{2m + 5} - \frac{6m - 6}{2m + 5}$

23 $\frac{2}{k + 1} + \frac{1}{2k + 2}$

24 $\frac{d}{3d + 9} - \frac{5}{4d + 12}$

25 $\frac{1}{y - 4} + \frac{3}{4}$

26 $\frac{3}{3s - 6} - \frac{2}{s^2 - 2s}$

27 $\frac{2}{x + 2} + \frac{8}{x^2 - 4}$

28 $\frac{2v}{v^2 - 1} - \frac{3}{v + 1}$

29 $\frac{1}{a + b} + \frac{1}{a - b}$

30 $\frac{4}{2c + d} + \frac{3}{2c - d}$

31 $\frac{2a}{a - 4} - 7$

7.4 Solving Rational Equations

ADP℠ Standards

O2.b Operate with polynomial expressions

O2.c Factor simple polynomial expressions

A **rational equation** is an equation that contains one or more rational expressions. Rational equations are generally easier to solve if you first eliminate all denominators other than 1. You can solve rational equations by using the following procedure.

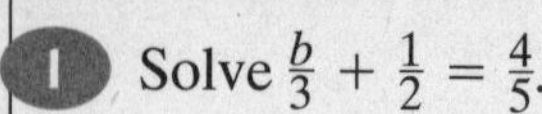

Solving a Rational Equation

Step 1 Find the LCD of all the denominators.

Step 2 Multiply all terms on each side of the equation by the LCD.

Step 3 Simplify the terms and solve the resulting equation.

EXAMPLES 1 and 2 **Solving rational equations by using the LCD: monomial denominators**

1 Solve $\frac{b}{3} + \frac{1}{2} = \frac{4}{5}$.

■ SOLUTION

$\frac{b}{3} + \frac{1}{2} = \frac{4}{5}$ ← **The denominators are 3, 2, and 5. The LCD is 30.**

$30\left(\frac{b}{3} + \frac{1}{2}\right) = 30\left(\frac{4}{5}\right)$ ← **Multiply each side by 30.**

$30\left(\frac{b}{3}\right) + 30\left(\frac{1}{2}\right) = 30\left(\frac{4}{5}\right)$ ← **Apply the Distributive Property.**

$10b + 15 = 24$ ← **Simplify each term.**

$10b = 9$ ← **Solve.**

$b = 0.9$

Check: $\frac{b}{3} + \frac{1}{2} = \frac{4}{5} \rightarrow \frac{0.9}{3} + \frac{1}{2} = \frac{4}{5}$

$0.3 + 0.5 = 0.8$ ✔

2 Solve $\frac{5}{4} + \frac{1}{2y} = \frac{7}{6}$.

■ SOLUTION

$\frac{5}{4} + \frac{1}{2y} = \frac{7}{6}$ ← **The denominators are 4, 2*y*, and 6. The LCD is 12*y*.**

$12y\left(\frac{5}{4} + \frac{1}{2y}\right) = 12y\left(\frac{7}{6}\right)$ ← **Multiply each side by 12*y*.**

$12y\left(\frac{5}{4}\right) + 12y\left(\frac{1}{2y}\right) = 12y\left(\frac{7}{6}\right)$ ← **Apply the Distributive Property.**

$15y + 6 = 14y$ ← **Simplify each term.**

$y + 6 = 0$ ← **Solve.**

$y = -6$

Check: $\frac{5}{4} + \frac{1}{2y} = \frac{7}{6} \rightarrow \frac{5}{4} + \frac{1}{2(-6)} = \frac{7}{6}$

$\frac{15}{12} + \frac{-1}{12} = \frac{14}{12}$ ✔

When checking a solution to any equation, you must check it in the *original equation,* not in any of the subsequent equations. This procedure is especially important with rational equations. You must make sure that no proposed solution results in a denominator of zero in the original equation.

EXAMPLE 3 Solving rational equations by using the LCD: polynomial denominators

Visit: PearsonSchool.com
Web Code: ayp-0338

3 Solve $\frac{1}{m-4} + \frac{1}{m+4} = \frac{8}{m^2-16}$.

■ SOLUTION

$$\frac{1}{m-4} + \frac{1}{m+4} = \frac{8}{m^2-16}$$

$$\frac{1}{m-4} + \frac{1}{m+4} = \frac{8}{(m+4)(m-4)}$$

$$(m+4)(m-4)\left[\frac{1}{m-4} + \frac{1}{m+4}\right] = (m+4)(m-4)\left[\frac{8}{(m+4)(m-4)}\right]$$

$$(m+4)(m-4)\left[\frac{1}{m-4}\right] + (m+4)(m-4)\left[\frac{1}{m+4}\right] = (m+4)(m-4)\left[\frac{8}{(m+4)(m-4)}\right]$$

$$(m+4) + (m-4) = 8$$

$$2m = 8$$

$$m = 4$$

Check 4:

$$\frac{1}{m-4} + \frac{1}{m+4} = \frac{8}{m^2-16} \rightarrow \frac{1}{4-4} + \frac{1}{4+4} = \frac{8}{4^2-16} \rightarrow \frac{8}{0}$$

Replacing m with 4 in the original equation results in denominators of zero. Therefore, the equation has *no solution*.

When each side of a rational equation is a single rational expression, you can solve the equation by using the cross products property of proportions.

Visit: PearsonSchool.com
Web Code: ayp-0340

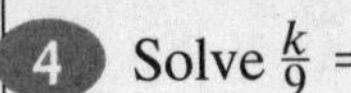

EXAMPLES 4 and 5 Solving rational equations by using cross products

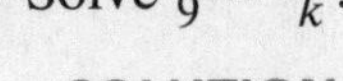

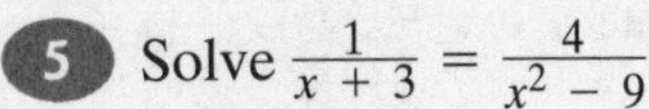

4 Solve $\frac{k}{9} = \frac{36}{k}$.

■ SOLUTION

$\frac{k}{9} = \frac{36}{k}$

$k \cdot k = 9 \cdot 36$ ← **Write the cross products.**

$k^2 = 324$

$k = 18$ *or* $k = -18$

Check 18:

$\frac{k}{9} = \frac{36}{k} \rightarrow \frac{18}{9} = \frac{36}{18}$ ✔

Check −18:

$\frac{k}{9} = \frac{36}{k} \rightarrow \frac{-18}{9} = \frac{36}{-18}$ ✔

Therefore, the solutions are 18 *and* −18.

5 Solve $\frac{1}{x+3} = \frac{4}{x^2-9}$.

■ SOLUTION

$\frac{1}{x+3} = \frac{4}{x^2-9}$

$1(x^2-9) = (x+3)(4)$ ← **Write the cross products.**

$x^2 - 9 = 4x + 12$ ← **Simplify each side.**

$x^2 - 4x - 21 = 0$ ← **Solve.**

$(x-7)(x+3) = 0$

$x = 7$ *or* $x = -3$

Check 7:

$\frac{1}{x+3} = \frac{4}{x^2-9} \rightarrow \frac{1}{7+3} = \frac{4}{7^2-9}$

$\frac{1}{10} = \frac{4}{40}$ ✔

Check −3:

$\frac{1}{x+3} = \frac{4}{x^2-9} \rightarrow \frac{1}{-3+3} = \frac{4}{(-3)^2-9}$

$\frac{1}{0} = \frac{4}{0}$

Replacing x with −3 in the original equation results in denominators of zero. Therefore, the only solution is 7.

You can use rational equations to solve word problems.

EXAMPLES 6 and 7 Using a rational equation to solve problems

6 One copy machine can complete a job in 25 minutes. This machine and a newer machine working together can complete the same job in 10 minutes. How long would it take the newer machine, working by itself, to complete the job?

■ **SOLUTION**

Let m represent the time in minutes for the newer machine to do the job. Then the following are the work rates.

The first machine does 1 job in 25 minutes, so it does $\frac{1}{25}$ of the job in 1 minute.

The newer machine does 1 job in m minutes, so it does $\frac{1}{m}$ of the job in 1 minute.

The two machines do 1 job in 10 minutes, so they do $\frac{1}{10}$ of the job in 1 minute.

Step 1

Translate the situation into an equation.

part of job done by first machine in one minute	plus	part of job done by newer machine in one minute	equals	part of job done by both machines in one minute
↓	↓	↓	↓	↓
$\frac{1}{25}$	$+$	$\frac{1}{m}$	$=$	$\frac{1}{10}$

Step 2

Solve the equation.

$$\frac{1}{25} + \frac{1}{m} = \frac{1}{10}$$
$$50m\left(\frac{1}{25} + \frac{1}{m}\right) = 50m\left(\frac{1}{10}\right)$$
$$50m\left(\frac{1}{25}\right) + 50m\left(\frac{1}{m}\right) = 50m\left(\frac{1}{10}\right)$$
$$2m + 50 = 5m$$
$$50 = 3m$$
$$\frac{50}{3} = m$$
$$m = \frac{50}{3}, \text{ or } 16\tfrac{2}{3}$$

Working by itself, the newer machine can do the job in $\frac{50}{3}$ minutes, or $16\frac{2}{3}$ minutes.

7 When $\frac{2}{3}$ is subtracted from the quotient of a number n divided by 3, the result equals the ratio of 1 to n. What is n?

■ **SOLUTION**

Step 1

Translate the situation into an equation.

The quotient of n divided by three	minus	two thirds	equals	the ratio of one to n
↓	↓	↓	↓	↓
$\frac{n}{3}$	$-$	$\frac{2}{3}$	$=$	$\frac{1}{n}$

Step 2

Solve the equation.

$$\frac{n}{3} - \frac{2}{3} = \frac{1}{n}$$
$$\frac{n-2}{3} = \frac{1}{n}$$
$$(n-2)n = 3(1)$$
$$n^2 - 2n = 3$$
$$n^2 - 2n - 3 = 0$$
$$(n-3)(n+1) = 0$$
$$n = 3 \text{ or } n = -1$$

The number n is either 3 or -1.

Practice

Choose the letter preceding the word or expression that best completes the statement or answers the question.

1 The solution set of $\frac{1}{r+1} = \frac{3}{r^2-1}$ consists of

A. 4 and -1 C. only -1

B. only 4 D. -4 and 1

2 Which equation is equivalent to $\frac{3}{a} - \frac{1}{a^2} = 2$?

A. $3 - a = 2a^2$

B. $2a^2 - 3a + 1 = 0$

C. $3a^2 - a = 2a^2$

D. $\frac{48}{a^2} = 2a$

3 Which equation has at least one solution?

A. $\frac{3}{m-1} = \frac{4}{m-1}$

B. $\frac{p}{5} = \frac{-5}{p}$

C. $\frac{7}{2x-5} = \frac{3}{2x-5}$

D. $\frac{3}{d+1} = \frac{d+1}{3}$

4 For which equation is 6 the only solution?

A. $\frac{s}{6} = \frac{6}{s}$ C. $\frac{s}{6} = \frac{36}{s}$

B. $\frac{s}{6} = \frac{-6}{s}$ D. $\frac{s}{s+2} = \frac{3}{4}$

In Exercises 5–22, solve each equation. If there is no solution, so state.

5 $\frac{w}{6} - \frac{1}{3} = \frac{1}{2}$

6 $\frac{1}{3} + \frac{d}{9} = \frac{5}{6}$

7 $\frac{3r}{8} + \frac{5}{2} = \frac{r}{3}$

8 $2 = \frac{5z}{8} - \frac{1}{2}$

9 $\frac{2}{a} + \frac{1}{2} = 3$

10 $\frac{3}{h} - \frac{3}{4} = 4$

11 $\frac{3}{5n} - \frac{3}{2} = \frac{2}{3}$

12 $\frac{1}{5} = \frac{3}{2y} + \frac{3}{10}$

13 $\frac{6}{j+1} = 1 + \frac{2}{j}$

14 $\frac{6}{t} - 1 = \frac{3}{t+2}$

15 $\frac{1}{n-1} + \frac{2}{n+1} = \frac{2n+1}{n^2-1}$

16 $\frac{4s}{s^2-25} = \frac{1}{s+5} - \frac{2}{s-5}$

17 $\frac{8}{q} = \frac{q}{8}$

18 $\frac{k}{4} = \frac{25}{k}$

19 $\frac{4}{m-1} = \frac{6}{m-5}$

20 $\frac{2}{z+2} = \frac{8}{z-1}$

21 $\frac{d-1}{d-4} = \frac{10}{d-2}$

22 $\frac{4}{b+5} = \frac{b-5}{4}$

In Exercises 23–26, solve the problem.

23 When a number is divided by 3 the quotient is the same as the quotient obtained when 27 is divided by the number. What is the number?

24 Paul can complete a plumbing job in 3 hours. If he and his friend Sam work together, they can complete the same job in 2 hours. How many hours would it take Sam, working alone, to complete this job?

25 Jessica can wash the family dog in 45 minutes. Her brother can wash the dog in just 30 minutes. How long would it take them, working together, to wash the dog?

26 Two pipes can fill a storage tank in 9 hours. The larger pipe fills the tank three times as fast as the smaller one. How long would it take the smaller pipe alone to fill the tank?

7.5 Radical Expressions and Equations

ADP℠ Standards

O1.d Use properties of radicals

O2.d Convert algebraic radical expressions

Recall that when solving eqations like $x^2 = 144$, $x = \pm 12$. However, when asked to evaluate or simplify a radical, we will consider only the positive or **principal square root.**

The square root $\sqrt{}$ symbol is also called a **radical sign.** An expression that involves a radical sign is called a **radical expression.** The expression under the radical is called the **radicand.**

$$\text{radical}\sqrt{16_{\text{radicand}}} = 4_{\text{root}}$$

You can simplify some radical expressions by using the definition of square root.

$$\sqrt{144} = 12 \text{ because } 12 \cdot 12 = 12^2 = 144.$$

$$\sqrt{\tfrac{1}{9}} = \tfrac{1}{3} \text{ because } \tfrac{1}{3} \cdot \tfrac{1}{3} = \left(\tfrac{1}{3}\right)^2 = \tfrac{1}{9}.$$

Visit: PearsonSchool.com
Web Code: ayp-0171

To simplify other radical expressions, you may need to apply one of the following properties of square roots.

Properties of Square Roots

Let a and b represent real numbers.

Product Property

If $a \geq 0$ and $b \geq 0$,

then $\sqrt{ab} = \sqrt{a} \cdot \sqrt{b}$.

Quotient Property

If $a \geq 0$ and $b > 0$,

then $\sqrt{\frac{a}{b}} = \frac{\sqrt{a}}{\sqrt{b}}$.

EXAMPLES 1 through 4 **Using the properties of square roots to simplify rational square roots**

Simplify each expression.

1. $\sqrt{1600}$

■ **SOLUTION**

$$\sqrt{1600} = \sqrt{16 . 100}$$
$$= \sqrt{16} \cdot \sqrt{100}$$
$$= 4 \cdot 10$$
$$= 40$$

2. $\sqrt{\frac{81}{64}}$

■ **SOLUTION**

$$\sqrt{\frac{81}{64}} = \frac{\sqrt{81}}{\sqrt{64}}$$
$$= \frac{9}{8}$$

3. $\sqrt{2916}$

■ **SOLUTION**

$$\sqrt{2916} = \sqrt{36 . 81}$$
$$= \sqrt{36} \cdot \sqrt{81}$$
$$= 6 \cdot 9$$
$$= 54$$

4. $\sqrt{\frac{16}{144}}$

■ **SOLUTION**

$$\sqrt{\frac{16}{144}} = \frac{\sqrt{16}}{\sqrt{144}}$$
$$= \frac{4}{12} \text{ or } \frac{1}{3}$$

When the square root of a number is rational, the number is a **perfect square.** In the set of whole numbers, the perfect squares less than or equal to 100 are 1, 4, 9, 16, 25, 36, 49, 64, 81, and 100. Most whole numbers are not perfect squares and do not have rational square roots. These non-perfect squares have *irrational* square roots.

Recall that an irrational number is a non-terminating, non-repeating decimal. Therefore, if you are trying to find the square root of a non-perfect square the closest decimal answer will be an approximation.

Some radical expressions containing non-perfect squares can also be simplified.

A radical expression is in simplest form if:

- the radicand contains no perfect-square factors other than 1;
- the radicand contains no fractions; and
- no denominator contains a radical.

Note

When you simplify a non-perfect square, your answer will still contain a square root.

To find the simplest form of an irrational square root, you can use the product and quotient properties of square roots.

EXAMPLES 5 through 8 **Using the product and quotient properties of square roots to simplify irrational square roots**

Simplify each expression.

5 $\sqrt{72}$

■ **SOLUTION**

$\sqrt{72} = \sqrt{36 \cdot 2}$

$= \sqrt{36} \cdot \sqrt{2}$ ← $\sqrt{ab} = \sqrt{a} \cdot \sqrt{b}$

$= 6\sqrt{2}$

6 $\sqrt{48}$

■ **SOLUTION**

$\sqrt{48} = \sqrt{2 \cdot 2 \cdot 2 \cdot 2 \cdot 3}$ ← **If at first you cannot identify a perfect-square factor, write the prime factors.**

$= \sqrt{2^2 \cdot 2^2 \cdot 3}$

$= \sqrt{2^2} \cdot \sqrt{2^2} \cdot \sqrt{3}$

$= 2 \cdot 2 \cdot \sqrt{3}$

$= 4\sqrt{3}$

7 $\sqrt{\frac{5}{49}}$

■ **SOLUTION**

$\sqrt{\frac{5}{49}} = \frac{\sqrt{5}}{\sqrt{49}}$ ← $\sqrt{\frac{a}{b}} = \frac{\sqrt{a}}{\sqrt{b}}$

$= \frac{\sqrt{5}}{7}$, or $\frac{1}{7}\sqrt{5}$

8 $\sqrt{\frac{8}{25}}$

■ **SOLUTION**

$\sqrt{\frac{8}{25}} = \frac{\sqrt{8}}{\sqrt{25}}$

$= \frac{\sqrt{8}}{5}$

$= \frac{\sqrt{4 \cdot 2}}{5}$

$= \frac{\sqrt{4} \cdot \sqrt{2}}{5}$

$= \frac{2\sqrt{2}}{5}$, or $\frac{2}{5}\sqrt{2}$

You can apply the product and quotient properties to simplify square roots that include variable expressions.

Go Online
PearsonSchool.com
Visit: PearsonSchool.com
Web Code: ayp-0304

EXAMPLES 9 and 10 **Using properties of square roots to simplify variable expressions**

Simplify each expression.

9 $\sqrt{24y^3}$

■ **SOLUTION**

$$\begin{aligned}\sqrt{24y^3} &= \sqrt{4 \cdot 6 \cdot y^2 \cdot y}\\ &= \sqrt{4} \cdot \sqrt{6} \cdot \sqrt{y^2} \cdot \sqrt{y}\\ &= 2 \cdot \sqrt{6} \cdot y \cdot \sqrt{y}\\ &= 2y\sqrt{6y}\end{aligned}$$

10 $\sqrt{\frac{a^7}{16}}$

■ **SOLUTION**

$$\begin{aligned}\sqrt{\frac{a^7}{16}} &= \frac{\sqrt{a^7}}{\sqrt{16}}\\ &= \frac{\sqrt{a^6 \cdot a}}{16}\\ &= \frac{\sqrt{a^6} \cdot \sqrt{a}}{\sqrt{16}}\\ &= \frac{a^3\sqrt{a}}{4}\end{aligned}$$

You also use the product and quotient properties of square roots when multiplying and dividing with radical expressions.

EXAMPLES 11 through 14 **Using properties of square roots to simplify products and quotients**

Simplify each expression.

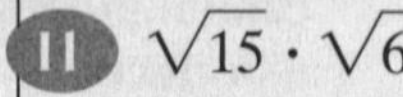

11 $\sqrt{15} \cdot \sqrt{6}$

■ **SOLUTION**

$$\begin{aligned}\sqrt{15} \cdot \sqrt{6} &= \sqrt{15 \cdot 6}\\ &= \sqrt{90}\\ &= \sqrt{9 \cdot 10}\\ &= \sqrt{9} \cdot \sqrt{10}\\ &= 3\sqrt{10}\end{aligned}$$

12 $5\sqrt{3s} \cdot \sqrt{18s^3}$

■ **SOLUTION**

$$\begin{aligned}5\sqrt{3s} \cdot \sqrt{18s^3} &= 5\sqrt{3s \cdot 18s^3}\\ &= 5\sqrt{54s^4}\\ &= 5\sqrt{9 \cdot 6 \cdot s^4}\\ &= 5 \cdot \sqrt{9} \cdot \sqrt{6} \cdot \sqrt{s^4}\\ &= 5 \cdot 3 \cdot \sqrt{6} \cdot s^2\\ &= 15s^2\sqrt{6}\end{aligned}$$

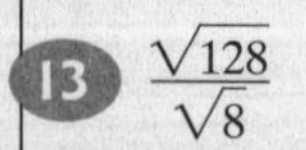

13 $\frac{\sqrt{128}}{\sqrt{8}}$

■ **SOLUTION**

$$\begin{aligned}\frac{\sqrt{128}}{\sqrt{8}} &= \sqrt{\frac{128}{8}}\\ &= \sqrt{16}\\ &= 4\end{aligned}$$

14 $\frac{\sqrt{48b^2}}{\sqrt{6b}}$

■ **SOLUTION**

$$\begin{aligned}\frac{\sqrt{48b^2}}{\sqrt{6b}} &= \sqrt{\frac{48b^2}{6b}}\\ &= \sqrt{8b}\\ &= \sqrt{4 \cdot 2 \cdot b}\\ &= \sqrt{4} \cdot \sqrt{2b}\\ &= 2\sqrt{2b}\end{aligned}$$

In a simplified radical expression, no denominator contains a radical. So if an expression has a radical in the denominator, and if that radical is not a perfect square, then you must *rationalize the denominator*. You do this by multiplying both numerator and denominator by the radical in the denominator.

Go Online PearsonSchool.com
Visit: PearsonSchool.com
Web Code: ayp-0307

EXAMPLES 15 and 16 Rationalizing the denominator

Simplify each expression.

15 $\sqrt{\frac{4}{3}}$

■ **SOLUTION**

$$\sqrt{\frac{4}{3}} = \frac{\sqrt{4}}{\sqrt{3}}$$
$$= \frac{2}{\sqrt{3}}$$
$$= \frac{2}{\sqrt{3}} \cdot \frac{\sqrt{3}}{\sqrt{3}} \quad \leftarrow \textbf{Multiply by } \frac{\sqrt{3}}{\sqrt{3}} = 1.$$
$$= \frac{2 \cdot \sqrt{3}}{\sqrt{3} \cdot \sqrt{3}}$$
$$= \frac{2\sqrt{3}}{3}, \text{ or } \frac{2}{3}\sqrt{3}$$

16 $\sqrt{\frac{5}{2n^3}}$

■ **SOLUTION**

$$\sqrt{\frac{5}{2n^3}} = \frac{\sqrt{5}}{\sqrt{2n^3}}$$
$$= \frac{\sqrt{5}}{n\sqrt{2n}}$$
$$= \frac{\sqrt{5}}{n\sqrt{2n}} \cdot \frac{\sqrt{2n}}{\sqrt{2n}}$$
$$= \frac{\sqrt{5 \cdot 2n}}{n\sqrt{2n \cdot 2n}}$$
$$= \frac{\sqrt{10n}}{n \cdot 2n} = \frac{\sqrt{10n}}{2n^2}$$

Radical expressions with exactly the same radicand are called **like radicals.**

Examples of like radicals	Examples of unlike radicals
$\sqrt{2}$ and $5\sqrt{2}$	$2\sqrt{3}$ and $2\sqrt{5}$
$4\sqrt{a}$ and $7\sqrt{a}$	$3\sqrt{m}$ and $3\sqrt{m^2}$

You add and subtract radical expressions in much the same way that you add and subtract variable expressions. That is, you can use the Distributive Property to combine like radicals.

EXAMPLES 17 and 18 Adding and subtracting radical expressions

Simplify each expression.

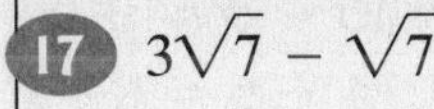

17 $3\sqrt{7} - \sqrt{7}$

■ **SOLUTION**

$$3\sqrt{7} - \sqrt{7}$$
$$= 3\sqrt{7} - 1\sqrt{7}$$
$$= (3 - 1)\sqrt{7}$$
$$= 2\sqrt{7}$$

18 $\sqrt{8} + \sqrt{50}$

■ **SOLUTION**

$$\sqrt{8} + \sqrt{50}$$
$$= \sqrt{4 \cdot 2} + \sqrt{25 \cdot 2} \quad \leftarrow \textbf{Rewrite unlike radicals.}$$
$$= 2\sqrt{2} + 5\sqrt{2} \quad \leftarrow \textbf{Simplify.}$$
$$= (2 + 5)\sqrt{2} \quad \leftarrow \textbf{Apply the Distributive Property.}$$
$$= 7\sqrt{2} \quad \leftarrow \textbf{Add.}$$

To simplify certain radical expressions, you must use the Distributive Property.

EXAMPLES 19 and 20 **Using the Distributive Property to simplify a product involving radical expressions**

Simplify each expression.

19 $\sqrt{2}(10 + 4\sqrt{7})$

■ **SOLUTION**

$$\begin{aligned}\sqrt{2}(10 + 4\sqrt{7}) &= \sqrt{2} \cdot 10 + \sqrt{2} \cdot 4\sqrt{7}\\ &= 10\sqrt{2} + 4\sqrt{2 \cdot 7}\\ &= 10\sqrt{2} + 4\sqrt{14}\end{aligned}$$

20 $\sqrt{3}(\sqrt{12} + 2\sqrt{15})$

■ **SOLUTION**

$$\begin{aligned}\sqrt{3}(\sqrt{12} + 2\sqrt{15}) &= \sqrt{3} \cdot \sqrt{12} + \sqrt{3} \cdot 2\sqrt{15}\\ &= \sqrt{3 \cdot 12} + 2\sqrt{3 \cdot 15}\\ &= \sqrt{36} + 2\sqrt{45}\\ &= 6 + 2\sqrt{5 \cdot 9}\\ &= 6 + 6\sqrt{5}\end{aligned}$$

A **radical equation** contains one or more radicals with variables in the radicand. To solve a radical equation, you can use the following procedure.

Solving a Radical Equation

Step 1 Isolate the radical on one side of the equation and simplify.

Step 2 Square each side of the equation to eliminate the radical.

Step 3 Solve the resulting equation.

EXAMPLES 21 and 22 **Solving radical equations**

Solve each equation.

21 $\sqrt{r} + 5 = 9$

■ **SOLUTION**

$$\begin{aligned}\sqrt{r} + 5 &= 9\\ \sqrt{r} + 5 - 5 &= 9 - 5 && \leftarrow \text{Subtract 5 from each side.}\\ \sqrt{r} &= 4 && \leftarrow \text{Simplify.}\\ (\sqrt{r})^2 &= (4)^2 && \leftarrow \text{Square each side.}\\ r &= 16\end{aligned}$$

Check 16:

$$\sqrt{r} + 5 = 9 \rightarrow \sqrt{16} + 5 = 9$$
$$4 + 5 = 9 \checkmark$$

Therefore, the solution is 16.

22 $\sqrt{a - 5} = 3$

■ **SOLUTION**

$$\begin{aligned}\sqrt{a - 5} &= 3 && \leftarrow \text{The radical is already isolated.}\\ (\sqrt{a - 5})^2 &= (3)^2 && \leftarrow \text{Square each side.}\\ a - 5 &= 9 && \leftarrow \text{Simplify.}\\ a &= 14 && \leftarrow \text{Solve.}\end{aligned}$$

Check 14:

$$\sqrt{a - 5} = 3 \rightarrow \sqrt{14 - 5} = 3$$
$$\sqrt{9} = 3 \checkmark$$

Therefore, the solution is 14.

Practice

Choose the letter preceding the word or expression that best completes the statement or answers the question.

1 Which statement is false?

A. $\sqrt{5} \cdot \sqrt{6} = \sqrt{30}$

B. $\sqrt{5} + \sqrt{6} = \sqrt{11}$

C. $(\sqrt{5})^2 = 5$

D. $\sqrt{5^2} = 5$

2 Which expression is in simplest form?

A. $\sqrt{12}$ **C.** $\sqrt{19}$

B. $\sqrt{\frac{1}{3}}$ **D.** $\frac{2}{\sqrt{5}}$

3 Which shows the expression $\sqrt{250}$ in simplest form?

A. $125\sqrt{2}$ **C.** $5\sqrt{10}$

B. $25\sqrt{10}$ **D.** $5\sqrt{5}$

4 Which expression is equivalent to $2\sqrt{72} - \sqrt{2}$?

A. $2\sqrt{70}$ **C.** $11\sqrt{2}$

B. $71\sqrt{2}$ **D.** 12

In Exercises 5–47, simplify each expression.

5 $\sqrt{324}$ **6** $\sqrt{1089}$ **7** $\sqrt{40{,}000}$

8 $\sqrt{\frac{1}{36}}$ **9** $\sqrt{\frac{169}{25}}$ **10** $\sqrt{\frac{441}{10{,}000}}$

11 $\sqrt{\frac{10}{9}}$ **12** $\sqrt{\frac{12}{49}}$ **13** $\sqrt{\frac{50}{81}}$

14 $\sqrt{64h^2}$ **15** $\sqrt{49w^6}$ **16** $\sqrt{100q^3}$

17 $\sqrt{x^2y^6}$ **18** $\sqrt{m^3n^5}$ **19** $\sqrt{abc^2}$

20 $\sqrt{\frac{y^6}{4}}$ **21** $\sqrt{\frac{16v^3}{25}}$ **22** $\sqrt{\frac{28v^5}{9}}$

23 $\sqrt{8} \cdot \sqrt{32}$ **24** $\sqrt{5} \cdot \sqrt{30}$

25 $\frac{\sqrt{120}}{\sqrt{15}}$ **26** $\frac{\sqrt{8}}{\sqrt{50}}$

27 $\sqrt{35t} \cdot \sqrt{5t}$ **28** $\sqrt{8a} \cdot \sqrt{22a^5}$

29 $\frac{\sqrt{32d^5}}{\sqrt{8d^2}}$ **30** $\frac{\sqrt{3z}}{\sqrt{75z^3}}$

31 $6\sqrt{11} - 2\sqrt{11}$ **32** $-8\sqrt{15} + 9\sqrt{15}$

33 $3\sqrt{2} + \sqrt{8}$ **34** $4\sqrt{3} - \sqrt{12}$

35 $\sqrt{75} - \sqrt{48}$ **36** $2\sqrt{20} + \sqrt{45}$

37 $\sqrt{2}(\sqrt{2} + \sqrt{3})$

38 $\sqrt{3}(\sqrt{6} - \sqrt{5})$

39 $\sqrt{5}(3\sqrt{5} - 2\sqrt{2})$

40 $2\sqrt{3}(7\sqrt{2} - \sqrt{6})$

41 $(\sqrt{2} + 1)(\sqrt{2} - 3)$

42 $(\sqrt{5} + 2)(2\sqrt{5} - 2)$

43 $(2\sqrt{3} + 3)(2\sqrt{3} - 3)$

44 $(2\sqrt{5} + 3)^2$

45 $\sqrt{27} - \sqrt{24} - \sqrt{54} + \sqrt{48}$

46 $2\sqrt{75} + 4\sqrt{12} - 2\sqrt{18}$

47 $\sqrt{16n + 32} + \sqrt{4n + 8}$

In Exercises 48–53, solve each equation.

48 $\sqrt{j} - 6 = 3$ **49** $4 + \sqrt{2x} = 10$

50 $\sqrt{s + 1} = 7$ **51** $2 = \sqrt{v - 8}$

52 $g = \sqrt{g + 12}$ **53** $\sqrt{2 - y} = y$

Chapter 7 Preparing for the ADP℠ Algebra I Exam

DIRECTIONS FOR QUESTIONS 1–21: For each of the questions below, select the answer choice that is best for each case.

1 In $\frac{1}{v^2 - 9}$, all excluded values of v are

A. 0 and 3.

B. −3, 0, and 3.

C. −3 and 3.

D. −9 and 9.

2 What is $\frac{1}{c} + \frac{c + 4}{c^2}$ as a single fraction?

A. $\frac{2c + 4}{c^2}$

B. $\frac{c + 5}{c^2}$

C. $\frac{c + 4}{c^3}$

D. $\frac{c + 5}{c^2 + c}$

3 If a, b, and z are positive numbers, simplify the expression $\sqrt{az} \cdot \sqrt{bz}$.

A. $\sqrt{abz}$

B. $z\sqrt{ab}$

C. $z\sqrt{a + b}$

D. $z^2\sqrt{ab}$

4 For which value of x is $\sqrt{3x - 5}$ a real number?

A. 1 **B.** 0 **C.** 2 **D.** −1

5 Simplify $\sqrt{\frac{49}{84}}$.

A. $\frac{7}{\sqrt{84}}$ **B.** $\frac{7}{2\sqrt{21}}$

C. $\frac{7\sqrt{21}}{2}$ **D.** $\frac{\sqrt{21}}{6}$

6 Approximate $\sqrt{93}$ to the nearest thousandth.

A. 9.644 **B.** 9.643

C. 0.964 **D.** 0.963

7 Find the value $-\sqrt{225}$.

A. 15 **B.** ±15

C. 15(−15) **D.** −15

8 Which of the following is irrational?

A. $\sqrt{\frac{9}{25}}$

B. $-\sqrt{625}$

C. $\sqrt{\frac{200}{50}}$

D. $\sqrt{0.90}$

9 Which expression is equivalent to $\sqrt{27} + \sqrt{48}$?

A. $7\sqrt{3}$ **B.** $\sqrt{75}$

C. $5\sqrt{3}$ **D.** $7\sqrt{6}$

10 Compare the values $16\sqrt{2}$ and $\frac{16\sqrt{8}}{2}$. Which statement is true?

A. The value of $16\sqrt{2}$ is greater than $\frac{16\sqrt{8}}{2}$.

B. The value of $\frac{16\sqrt{8}}{2}$ is greater than $16\sqrt{2}$.

C. The two values are equal.

D. Nothing can be determined.

11 What is $\sqrt{2} \cdot \sqrt{128}$ simplified?

A. $\sqrt{256}$ **B.** $8\sqrt{2}$

C. 16 **D.** $6\sqrt{2}$

12 Simplify $\frac{10x}{5x + 20}$.

A. $\frac{1}{10}$

B. $\frac{2}{x + 4}$

C. $\frac{x}{5x + 2}$

D. $\frac{2x}{x + 4}$

13 Divide. Express the answer in simplest form.

$$\frac{4x + 12}{x^2 + x - 30} \div \frac{3x^2 + 5x - 12}{3x^2 - 15x}$$

A. $\frac{3x^2 + 14x - 24}{12x}$

B. $\frac{12x}{3x^2 + 14x - 24}$

C. $\frac{14x^2 - 20x}{(x^2 + x - 30)(3x + 4)}$

D. $\frac{4}{3x^2 - 15x}$

14 Simplify $\frac{2m + 6}{3m^2 + 11m + 6}$.

A. $\frac{4m}{3m^2 + 11m}$

B. $\frac{4}{3m^2 + 11}$

C. $\frac{2}{3m + 2}$

D. $\frac{1}{3m}$

15 Which is the product of $\frac{3x^2}{8y} \cdot \frac{20}{9x}$ expressed in simplest form?

A. $\frac{5x}{6y}$ **B.** $\frac{20x}{24y}$

C. $\frac{23x^2}{17xy}$ **D.** $\frac{60x}{72y}$

16 Solve for m.

$$\frac{3}{m + 4} + 2 = \frac{5}{m}$$

A. −5 and 2

B. −2 and 5

C. 9

D. −9

17 Simplify $\sqrt{72x^5}$.

A. $3x\sqrt{8x^3}$ **B.** $3x^2\sqrt{8x}$

C. $6\sqrt{2x^5}$ **D.** $6x^2\sqrt{2x}$

18 Find the difference.

$$\frac{8x}{x - 9} - \frac{5x + 2}{x - 9}$$

A. $\frac{3x - 2}{-18}$ **B.** $\frac{3x + 2}{x - 9}$

C. $\frac{3x - 2}{x - 9}$ **D.** $\frac{x}{x - 9}$

19 Find the sum.

$$\frac{2n}{n + 3} + \frac{5}{n + 8}$$

A. $\frac{2n + 5}{n^2 + 11}$

B. $\frac{23n + 3}{n^2 + 11n + 24}$

C. $\frac{2n^2 + 5n + 11}{n^2 + 11n + 24}$

D. $\frac{2n^2 + 21n + 15}{n^2 + 11n + 24}$

20 The quotient of a number divided by 6 is subtracted from $\frac{3}{4}$. The result is $\frac{5}{12}$. What is the number?

A. 1 **B.** 2 **C.** 4 **D.** 5

21 Solve $\sqrt{r - 9} = 7$.

A. 10 **B.** 58 **C.** 100 **D.** 256

DIRECTIONS FOR 22–24: Solve each problem. Show your work or provide an explanation for your answer.

22 Jake can unload a delivery truck in 40 minutes, and Jennie can unload the same truck in 60 minutes. Write an equation of rational expressions to find how long it would take Jake and Jennie to unload the truck together.

How long would it take Jake and Jennie to unload the truck together?

23 Ed rode his bike for 2 more hours than Ann rode hers. Ed rode 24 miles, and Ann rode 6 miles. Write an equation that can be used to find how many hours Ed rode his bike if he rode at the same speed as Ann.

If they both rode at the same speed, how long did Ed ride his bike?

24 The motion of a pendulum is approximated by the equation $T = 2\pi\sqrt{\frac{L}{9.8}}$, where T is the time of one swing, and L is the length of the pendulum.

Find the time, approximated to the nearest tenth, of one swing of the pendulum if the length is 10 units.

Find the length of the pendulum, rounded to the nearest tenth, if it takes 2 seconds for each swing of the pendulum.

Does the time of one pendulum swing T increase or decrease as the length L increases? Explain your reasoning and justify your solution mathematically.

8 Probability

Discovering Minnesota

The Minnesota State Fish

The walleye (*Stizostedion vitreum*) is the state fish of Minnesota for good reason. The walleye is the most sought-after fish in Minnesota. About 3.5 million walleye are caught in Minnesota each year. The average walleye caught is about 14 inches long and weighs about 1 pound (the state record is over 17 pounds).

In order to protect this valuable resource, Minnesota's Department of Natural Resources regulates the number of walleye that can be caught, protects their natural habitat, and stocks lakes in order to meet the demand for this popular fish.

The walleye gets its name from the fact that its eyes have a pearly luster. A special pigment creates this luster, which allows walleye to see in dark and murky water.

8.1 Experimental and Theoretical Probability

ADP[SM] Standards

D2.b Determine probability

Probability is a measure of the likelihood that an event will occur. You can represent a probability by using a ratio or a percent. Some events will never occur, others will always occur, and the likelihood of many events is uncertain.

There are two types of probability: a priori, or theoretical probability, and experimental probability.

In general, you can define the probability of flipping heads as the ratio 1 out of 2, or $\frac{1}{2}$. This is called the **a priori,** or **theoretical probability,** of flipping heads.

Theoretical probability is a calculation of the ratio of the number of favorable outcomes to the total number of outcomes. You can express probability as a fraction, a percent, or a decimal.

Experimental probability is determined by collecting data from an *experiment.* The sum of the probabilities of all of the events of an experiment is always equal to 1. Suppose that you flip a coin and record the occurrence of heads.

Number of flips	10	10	10	10	10
Number of heads	4	5	5	6	5
Ratio	4 of 10	5 of 10	5 of 10	6 of 10	5 of 10

In each experiment, heads occur about 5 times in every 10 flips. You can say that the experimental or **empirical probability** of heads' occurring is about 1 out of 2 for this coin.

Theoretical Probability of an Event

If an event E contains m favorable outcomes in a sample space containing n outcomes, the **theoretical probability** of E, denoted $P(E)$, is found as follows.

$$P(E) = \frac{\text{number } m \text{ of favorable outcomes}}{\text{total number } n \text{ of outcomes}} = \frac{m}{n}$$

Note

"At random" means that the selection is made without any preference or bias for one outcome over another.

EXAMPLE 1 Calculating theoretical probabilities

In a local district, there are 1300 Democratic, 1100 Republican, and 400 Independent registered voters. If a voter is selected at random, what is the probability to the nearest whole percent that the voter selected is Republican?

■ **SOLUTION**

Calculate the total number of voters in the district. $1300 + 1100 + 400 = 2800$

$$P(\text{Republican}) = \frac{\text{number of Republicans}}{\text{total number of registered voters}} = \frac{1100}{2800} \approx 0.39$$

The probability of selecting a Republican is about 39%.

Go Online
PearsonSchool.com
Visit: PearsonSchool.com
Web Code: ayp-0871

A **sample space** is the set of all possible outcomes in a given situation. An **event** is any set of outcomes in the sample space. You can use a table or a tree diagram to identify a sample space.

EXAMPLE 2 Using a table or tree diagram to identify a sample space

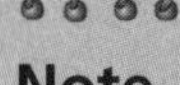

Note

There are four outcomes. H and T is different from T and H.

2 What is the sample space when two coins are flipped consecutively?

▪ **SOLUTION**

Determine all of the possible outcomes of flipping two coins consecutively.

coin 1 / coin 2	H	T
H	H H	H T
T	T H	T T

coin 1	coin 2	outcome
H	H	H and H
	T	H and T
T	H	T and H
	T	T and T

The sample space is HH, HT, TH, TT.

The table below shows all possible ordered pairs (cube X, cube Y) in the sample space for rolling two number cubes. Notice that there are 36 outcomes in all.

cube X/cube Y	1	2	3	4	5	6
1	(1, 1)	(1, 2)	(1, 3)	(1, 4)	(1, 5)	(1, 6)
2	(2, 1)	(2, 2)	(2, 3)	(2, 4)	(2, 5)	(2, 6)
3	(3, 1)	(3, 2)	(3, 3)	(3, 4)	(3, 5)	(3, 6)
4	(4, 1)	(4, 2)	(4, 3)	(4, 4)	(4, 5)	(4, 6)
5	(5, 1)	(5, 2)	(5, 3)	(5, 4)	(5, 5)	(5, 6)
6	(6, 1)	(6, 2)	(6, 3)	(6, 4)	(6, 5)	(6, 6)

If one cube shows 1, there are 6 possibilities for the second cube.

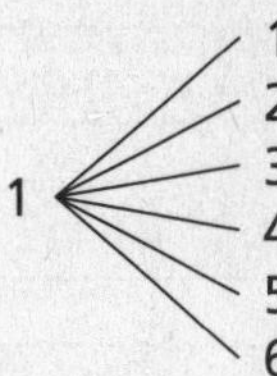

EXAMPLE 3 through 5 Using probability facts with ordered pairs

Find each of the following probabilities using the sample space for rolling a pair of number cubes. Write the probabilities as fractions in lowest terms.

3 P(sum equals 3)

▪ **SOLUTION**

The only ordered pairs whose numbers total 3 are (1, 2) and (2, 1). There are two favorable outcomes.

P(sum equals 3)

$= \frac{2}{36}$, or $\frac{1}{18}$

4 P(same number on each)

▪ **SOLUTION**

The six ordered pairs (1, 1), (2, 2), (3, 3), (4, 4), (5, 5), and (6, 6) are the only outcomes with identical numbers.

P(same number on each)

$= \frac{6}{36}$, or $\frac{1}{6}$

5 P(sum not equal to 12)

▪ **SOLUTION**

There is exactly one ordered pair whose numbers total 12. It is (6, 6).

P(sum not equal to 12)

$= 1 - P$(sum equal to 12)

$= 1 - \frac{1}{36} = \frac{35}{36}$

You can say the outcomes from rolling a single number cube are **equally likely.**

$P(1) = \frac{1}{6}$ $P(2) = \frac{1}{6}$ $P(3) = \frac{1}{6}$ $P(4) = \frac{1}{6}$ $P(5) = \frac{1}{6}$ $P(6) = \frac{1}{6}$

If you roll a pair of number cubes, the probability of rolling one sum is not necessarily equal to the probability of rolling another sum. You can say that the outcomes from rolling a pair of number cubes are *not equally likely.*

$$P(\text{sum } 2) = \frac{1}{36} \text{ but } P(\text{sum } 3) = \frac{2}{36}$$

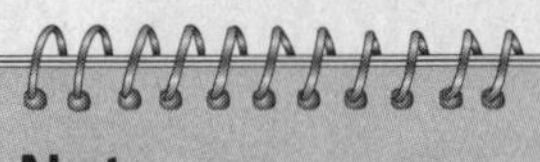

Note

Notice that not all probabilities are equal, but that the sum of the probabilities equals 1.

The possible sums from rolling a pair of number cubes are 2, 3, 4, 5, 6, 7, 8, 9, 10, 11, and 12. If x represents these numbers, you can say that x is a **random variable** and assign to it the probability of each sum. A **probability distribution** represents the values of the variable and corresponding probabilities.

x	2	3	4	5	6	7	8	9	10	11	12
$P(x)$	$\frac{1}{36}$	$\frac{2}{36}$	$\frac{3}{36}$	$\frac{4}{36}$	$\frac{5}{36}$	$\frac{6}{36}$	$\frac{5}{36}$	$\frac{4}{36}$	$\frac{3}{36}$	$\frac{2}{36}$	$\frac{1}{36}$

Go Online
PearsonSchool.com
Visit: PearsonSchool.com
Web Code: ayp-0675

EXAMPLE 6 Making a probability distribution

6 A bag contains marbles identical in every way but color. The bag contains 1 red, 2 blue, 3 green, and 4 orange marbles. Make a probability distribution that represents the probabilities of choosing each color of marble from the bag. Write the probabilities as fractions and as decimals.

■ SOLUTION

Find the total number of outcomes. $1 + 2 + 3 + 4 = 10$
Make a table of ratios as shown.

color	red	blue	green	orange
probability	$\frac{1}{10} = 0.1$	$\frac{2}{10} = 0.2$	$\frac{3}{10} = 0.3$	$\frac{4}{10} = 0.4$

The **complement** of an event E is the set of outcomes in the sample space *not* in E. You can find the probability of the complement by subtracting the $P(E)$ from 1. For example, there is a 25% chance that your birth month is January, February, or March, so the probability of the complement, that your birth month is *not* in January, February, or March, is $1 - 0.25 = 0.75$ or 75%.

Characteristics of Probabilities

If E is impossible, $P(E) = 0$.	The number of favorable outcomes equals 0.
If E is certain, $P(E) = 1$.	The number of favorable outcomes equals the total number of outcomes.
Otherwise, $0 < P(E) < 1$.	The number of favorable outcomes is less than the total number of outcomes.
$P(\text{not } E) = 1 - P(E)$	The number of favorable outcomes is the difference of the unfavorable outcomes and 1.
$\sum P(E) = 1$	The sum of the probabilities of all of the events of an experiment is equal to 1.

Practice

Choose the letter preceding the word or expression that best completes the statement or answers the question.

1 If the probability of an event is 0, then

A. it is certain.

B. it is impossible.

C. it is probable but not certain.

D. it is probable but not impossible.

2 Which completes this probability distribution?

B	4	2	6	8
P(B)	0.2	0.1	0.3	

A. 0.2 **B.** 0.05 **C.** 0.4 **D.** 0.6

3 The probability that the sun will set in the west is

A. 0 **B.** 1 **C.** −1 **D.** $\frac{1}{2}$

4 A box contains five cutouts of the same triangle differing only in color. If one cutout is drawn at random, what is the probability of choosing a specific color?

A. $\frac{1}{5}$ **B.** $\frac{5}{5}$ **C.** $\frac{2}{5}$ **D.** $\frac{3}{5}$

5 In a local district, there are 2,000 Democratic, 1,700 Republican, and 300 Independent voters registered. If a voter is selected at random, which is the probability that the voter selected is not an Independent?

A. $1 - \frac{3}{40}$ **C.** $\frac{17}{40}$

B. $1 - \frac{37}{40}$ **D.** $1 - \frac{17}{40}$

6 A bag contains 7 red, 6 green, and 7 white marbles, all identical but for color. The prob-ability of randomly choosing a red marble is

A. $\frac{7}{20}$ **B.** $\frac{13}{20}$ **C.** $\frac{3}{10}$ **D.** $1 - \frac{7}{20}$

In Exercises 7–10, solve the problem.

7 Which is more likely, an event with probability 0.36 or an event with probability 0.6?

8 In an algebra class, 5 students wear contact lenses, 4 students wear glasses, and 13 students wear neither contact lenses nor glasses. If a student is chosen at random, what is the probability that the student wears contact lenses?

9 A weather forecaster predicts that there is a 45% probability of snow today. What is the probability that it will not snow?

10 For the pair of spinners below, make a tree diagram showing all of the outcomes spinning the two spinners. Calculate the probability of having the pointer land on light gray in spinner 1 and on light blue in spinner 2.

spinner 1

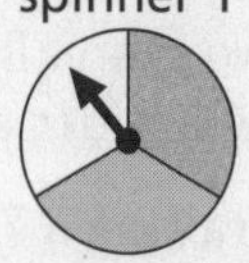

spinner 2

In Exercises 11–14, refer to the table of outcomes for rolling a pair of number cubes. Find each probability as a fraction in lowest terms.

11 P(sum equals 8) 12 P(numbers unequal)

13 P(sum equals 11) 14 P(sum equals 13)

In Exercises 15–16, use the given data to make a probability distribution for the selection of one object or person at random.

15 A bag contains 8 blue slips of paper, 9 brown slips of paper, and 8 green slips of paper, all identical but for color. The values of a random variable are 1 for blue, 2 for brown, and 3 for green.

16 The science club consists of 13 first-year students, 12 second-year students, 13 third-year students, and 10 fourth-year students. The values of the random variable are 1, 2, 3, and 4 for the class year.

8.2 Using Probability Formulas

ADP℠ Standards

D2.b Determine probability

There are situations when two events cannot occur at the same time. For example, the following statements about integers cannot both be true at the same time.

An integer is even. The same integer is odd.

You can say that these outcomes are *mutually exclusive.* Two events are **mutually exclusive** if there are no outcomes common to both events.

EXAMPLE 1 **Identifying mutually exclusive events**

1 Which events are mutually exclusive?

A. selecting a baseball card showing a Yankee and also a pitcher
B. scoring above 80 on a test and scoring above 90 on the same test
C. rolling a prime number that is also an even number
D. rolling a multiple of 2 that is also a divisor of 17

■ SOLUTION

Seventeen is not a multiple of 2, so the outcomes in choice **D** are mutually exclusive. The correct choice is D.

To find the probability of two mutually exclusive events, you add the probabilities of each event. Consider the following problem.

What is the probability of drawing a 7 or a queen when drawing a card from a standard deck of playing cards? There are 52 possible outcomes; four of them are 7s and four of them are queens. Since there is no card that is both a 7 and a queen, these events are mutually exclusive. Therefore,

$$P(7 \text{ or } Q) = P(7) + (Q) = \frac{4}{52} + \frac{4}{52} = \frac{8}{52} = \frac{2}{13}.$$

Note

A standard deck of 52 playing cards consists of 13 red hearts, 13 black clubs, 13 red diamonds, and 13 black spades. Each suit has an ace, a king, a queen, a jack, and the numbers 2 through 10.

Probability Involving Mutually Exclusive Events

If A and B are mutually exclusive events, then $P(A \text{ or } B) = P(A) + P(B)$.

Go Online
PearsonSchool.com
Visit: PearsonSchool.com
Web Code: ayp-0643

EXAMPLE 2 **Using the formula for the probability of mutually exclusive events**

2 Suppose you roll a pair of number cubes. Find the probability that the numbers showing are the same or that their sum is 11.

■ SOLUTION

The events are mutually exclusive since a sum of 11 cannot occur at the same time two number cubes are showing the same number.

Count the outcomes in which the numbers showing are equal. There are six.
Count the outcomes in which the sum of the numbers showing is 11. There are two.

$$P(\text{numbers equal or sum is } 11) = P(\text{numbers equal}) + P(\text{sum is } 11)$$
$$= \frac{6}{36} + \frac{2}{36} = \frac{8}{36}, \text{ or } \frac{2}{9}$$

There are also situations when two events can occur at the same time. These events are not mutually exclusive. Consider the following problem.

What is the probability of drawing a red card or a card showing a queen from a standard deck of 52 playing cards?

26 red cards	26 black cards
2 red queens	2 black queens

The diagram at the right shows that these events are not mutually exclusive because there are two cards that show queen and are also red.

You can calculate the probability P(red card or queen) as follows.

$$P(\text{red card or queen}) = \frac{26+2}{52} = \frac{28}{52}\ \frac{28}{52} = \underbrace{\frac{26}{52}}_{\text{number of red cards}} + \underbrace{\frac{4}{52}}_{\text{number of queens}} - \underbrace{\frac{2}{52}}_{\text{number of red queens}}$$

To determine the probability of events that are *not* mutually exclusive, you add the probabilities of each event and then subtract the probability of both occurring at the same time.

Note

If A and B are mutually exclusive, $P(A \text{ and } B) = 0$.

Probability of Events Involving Or

If A and B are events in a sample space, $P(A \text{ or } B) = P(A) + P(B) - P(A \text{ and } B)$.

EXAMPLES 3 and 4 Finding probability of events that are not mutually exclusive

3 Of the 200 seniors at Southside High School, 98 are boys, 34 are on the track team, and 20 are boys on the track team. Find the probability that a student chosen at random is a boy or is on the track team.

■ **SOLUTION**

Sketch a Venn diagram that shows the sets and relationships.

$$P(\text{boy or track}) = P(\text{boy}) + P(\text{track}) - P(\text{boy and track})$$
$$= \frac{98}{200} + \frac{34}{200} - \frac{20}{200}$$
$$= \frac{98 + 34 - 20}{200}$$
$$= \frac{112}{200}$$
$$= 0.56$$

boys and track
track
boys
200 seniors

The probability that a student chosen is a boy or is on the track team is 0.56, or 56%.

4 What is the probability that either of two number cubes tossed simultaneously shows a 3?

■ **SOLUTION**

$$P(3 \text{ or } 3) = P(3) + P(3) - P(\text{both cubes show } 3)$$
$$= \frac{6}{36} + \frac{6}{36} - \frac{1}{36}$$
$$= \frac{11}{36}$$

The probability that either of the two cubes shows a 3 is $\frac{11}{36}$.

You can use given information to solve many probability problems.

EXAMPLES 5 through 16 **Using probability formulas to solve problems**

In Examples 5 through 16, use the information about the Sun City Council. Each council member is identified by gender and party. Parties are indicated by D for Democrat, R for Republican, I for Independent, and C for Conservative. Find each probability that a council member fits the criteria specified.

Name	Gender	Party	Name	Gender	Party
B. Green	M	D	M. Adams	M	I
B. White	F	D	R. Jones	M	C
C. Washington	F	D	T. Black	M	D
S. Brown	F	R	D. Jackson	M	I
L. Smith	M	R	N. Goodman	F	R
R. Jackson	M	R			

5 $P(D)$

■ **SOLUTION**

$P(D) = \frac{4}{11}$ ← **four Democrats**

6 $P(\text{not } I)$

■ **SOLUTION**

$P(\text{not } I) = 1 - \frac{2}{11}$ ← **two Independents**

$= \frac{9}{11}$

7 $P(F \text{ or } R)$

■ **SOLUTION**

$P(F \text{ or } R) = \frac{4}{11} + \frac{4}{11} - \frac{2}{11}$ ← **two female Republicans**

$= \frac{6}{11}$

8 $P(D \text{ or } C)$

■ **SOLUTION**

$P(D \text{ or } C) = \frac{4}{11} + \frac{1}{11}$ ← **4 Democrats 1 Conservative**

$= \frac{5}{11}$

9 $P(R \text{ and } D)$

■ **SOLUTION**

$P(R \text{ and } D) = 0$ ← **impossible event**

10 $P(M \text{ or } D)$

■ **SOLUTION**

$P(M \text{ or } D) = \frac{7}{11} + \frac{4}{11} - \frac{2}{11}$

$= \frac{9}{11}$

11 $P(M \text{ or } I)$

■ **SOLUTION**

$P(M \text{ or } I) = \frac{7}{11} + \frac{2}{11} - \frac{2}{11}$

$= \frac{7}{11}$

12 $P(F \text{ or } C)$

■ **SOLUTION**

$P(F \text{ or } C) = \frac{4}{11} + \frac{1}{11} - \frac{0}{11}$

$= \frac{5}{11}$

13 $P(F \text{ and } C)$

■ **SOLUTION**

$P(F \text{ and } C) = 0$

14 $P(M \text{ and } D)$

■ **SOLUTION**

$P(M \text{ and } D) = \frac{2}{11}$

15 $P(I \text{ and } F)$

■ **SOLUTION**

$P(I \text{ and } F) = 0$

16 $P(I \text{ or } F)$

■ **SOLUTION**

$P(I \text{ or } F) = \frac{2}{11} + \frac{4}{11} - \frac{0}{11}$

$= \frac{6}{11}$

Practice

Choose the letter preceding the word or expression that best completes the statement or answers the question.

1 Two events, A and B, each having at least one outcome, are mutually exclusive. Which of these statements is true?

A. $P(A \text{ or } B) = 0$

B. $P(A) = 0$

C. $P(B) = 0$

D. $P(A \text{ and } B) = 0$

2 Which events are mutually exclusive?

A. Bill and Elizabeth both won when they played racquetball against one another.

B. Bill lost and Elizabeth won when they played racquetball against one another.

C. The national average age of high school seniors is 17 and for sophomores it is 16.

D. In one year, the Yankees won the World Series and the Mets won the National League Pennant.

3 A box contains cards, each having exactly one different number from 1 to 19 inclusive on it. Which gives the probability of drawing a card with an odd number on it or a multiple of 3 on it?

A. $P(\text{odd}) \times P(\text{multiple of } 3)$

B. $P(\text{odd}) + P(\text{multiple of } 3)$

C. $P(\text{odd}) + P(\text{multiple of } 3) - P(\text{odd multiple of } 3)$

D. $P(\text{odd}) \times P(\text{multiple of } 3) - P(\text{odd multiple of } 3)$

4 Mikki has 7 different shirts, 8 different pairs of pants, and 8 different pairs of shoes. How many outfits can she make?

A. $7 + 8 + 8$ **C.** $7 \times 8 \times 8$

B. $7^3 + 8^3 + 8^3$ **D.** $3(7 + 8 + 8)$

In Exercises 5–8, suppose you select a card at random from a standard deck of cards. Find each probability as a fraction in lowest terms.

5 P(queen or diamond)

6 P(king or black card)

7 P(heart or 5 of clubs)

8 P(even number or clubs)

In Exercises 9–12, suppose you roll a pair of number cubes. Find each probability as a fraction in lowest terms.

9 P(equal numbers or sum of 7)

10 P(equal numbers or even sum)

11 P(equal numbers or odd sum)

12 P(sum less than 4)

In Exercises 13–15, each card in a bag has exactly one of the numbers 3, $\frac{2}{3}$, −4, $\sqrt{25}$, π, $\sqrt{6}$, 15, 17, or 64 written on it. Find each probability as a fraction in lowest terms.

13 P(perfect square or even number)

14 P(irrational number or negative)

15 P(divisible by 3 or by 5)

16 In a certain area, 104 houses are for sale. Fifty-two houses have garages but not swimming pools, 13 houses have swimming pools but not garages, and 8 houses have both garages and swimming pools. Find the probability that a house for sale has a garage or swimming pool, but not both.

8.3 Independent and Dependent Events

ADP℠ Standards

D2.b Determine probability

Sometimes you need to determine the size of a rather large sample space. Suppose that Maggie has 5 pairs of jeans and 6 T-shirts. How many outfits consisting of one pair of jeans and one T-shirt does she have available to her? You could make a tree diagram to count the different outfits; however, there is a simpler way to find the answer.

Since Maggie has 5 choices for jeans and 6 T-shirt choices, she has 5×6, or 30 choices, altogether. You can generalize this discussion to state the *Fundamental Counting Principle*.

Fundamental Counting Principle

If there are m ways to make a selection and n ways to make a second selection, then there are mn ways to make the pair of selections.

If there are m ways to make a selection, n ways to make a second selection, and p ways to make a third selection, then there are mnp ways to make the three selections.

Visit: PearsonSchool.com
Web Code: ayp-0120

EXAMPLES 1 and 2 Applying the Fundamental Counting Principle

1 How many seven-digit telephone numbers are possible if the first three digits are 268 in that order, the fourth digit is not 0, and the seventh digit is not 9?

■ SOLUTION

Sketch a diagram showing how many digits are possible for each slot.

268 –	not 0	any digit	any digit	not 9
	↑	↑	↑	↑
	9 digits	10 digits	10 digits	9 digits

In all, there are $9 \times 10 \times 10 \times 9$, or *8,100*, possible telephone numbers.

2 Bag A contains 5 red marbles, 6 green marbles, and 7 purple marbles. Bag B contains 12 black marbles, 18 blue marbles, and 10 orange marbles. A marble is chosen at random from each bag. Find the probability of selecting a red marble from Bag A and a black marble from Bag B.

■ SOLUTION

There are 18×40, or 720, pairs of choices (Bag A, Bag B).

There are 5×12, or 60, pairs of choices (red, black).

$$P(\text{red, then black}) = \frac{60}{720}, \text{ or } \frac{1}{12}$$

Two events are **independent** if the occurrence of one event does not affect the occurrence of the other event.

EXAMPLES 3 and 4 **Identifying and finding probabilities of independent events**

3 For which is the occurrence of one event dependent on that of the other event?

A. flipping heads on a coin toss and rolling 6 on a number cube
B. drawing a jack from a standard deck of cards and rolling a 6 on a number cube
C. drawing a jack and, without replacing the card, drawing a second jack
D. drawing a jack and, after replacing the card, drawing a second jack

■ **SOLUTION**

In choice **C,** the card is not replaced. So, the sample space for the second draw has only 51 members. The second event is dependent on the first. The correct choice is C.

4 A card is drawn from a standard deck of playing cards, replaced, and a second card is drawn. What is the probability that the second card drawn is a spade?

■ **SOLUTION**

In this situation the probability of drawing the second spade is $\frac{13}{52}$ since after replacement there are still 13 spades out of 52 cards.

The counting principle for independent events says that if $P(A)$ is the probability of event A and $P(B)$ is the probability of event B, then you can find the probability of both A and B occurring by multiplying $P(A) \cdot P(B)$.

EXAMPLES 5 through 7 **Solving problems involving two independent events**

Suppose that you flip a coin and spin a spinner with a 50% red region, 25% blue region, and 25% green region. Find each probability.

5 P(heads and green)

■ **SOLUTION**

$$P(\text{heads and green}) = P(\text{heads}) \times P(\text{green})$$
$$= 0.5 \times 0.25 = 0.125$$

6 P(heads and not green)

■ **SOLUTION**

$$P(\text{heads and not green}) = P(\text{heads}) \times P(\text{not green})$$
$$= P(\text{heads}) \times (1 - P(\text{green}))$$
$$= 0.5 \times (1 - 0.25) = 0.375$$

7 P(tails and red)

■ **SOLUTION**

$$P(\text{tails and red}) = P(\text{tails}) \times P(\text{red})$$
$$= 0.5 \times 0.5 = 0.25$$

Consider this next example.

- A card is drawn from a standard deck of playing cards without replacement. Then a second card is drawn. What is the probability that the second card drawn is a spade?

In this situation the probability of drawing the second spade is $\frac{12}{51}$ since there are now 12 spades out of the remaining 51 cards.

The events of this situation are **dependent** because the occurrence of one event affects the probability of the other.

EXAMPLES 8 and 9 Finding probabilities of dependent events

A bag contains 3 red marbles and 5 blue marbles. Samuel draws a marble from the bag without looking, puts it into his pocket, and then draws a second marble without looking.

8 Find the probability that both marbles Samuel drew from the bag are red.

■ SOLUTION

Make a tree diagram showing the selections. Label the probabilities.

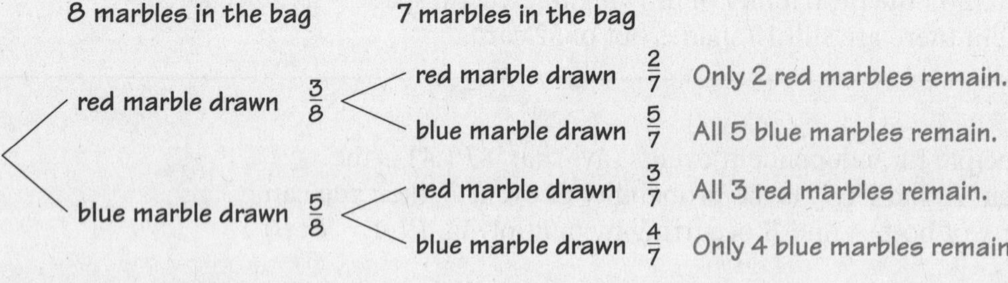

$P(\text{red, then red})\ \frac{3}{8} \cdot \frac{2}{7} = \frac{3}{28}$

9 Find the probability that both marbles that Samuel drew at random are the same color.

■ SOLUTION

Refer to the tree diagram in the solution to Example 8.

$$P(\text{both marbles the same color}) = P(\text{red, then red}) + P(\text{blue, then blue})$$

$$= \frac{3}{8} \cdot \frac{2}{7} + \frac{5}{8} \cdot \frac{4}{7}$$

$$P(\text{both marbles the same color}) = \frac{26}{56} = \frac{13}{28}$$

Independent and Dependent Events

If events A and B are independent, then $P(A, \text{then } B) = P(A) \cdot P(B)$.

If events A and B are dependent, then $P(A, \text{then } B) = P(A) \cdot P(B \text{ given } A)$.

EXAMPLES 10 and 11 Solving problems: independent and dependent events

Find each probability.

10 A spade is randomly drawn from a standard deck of playing cards on two successive draws, given that the card is replaced.

■ SOLUTION

Number of (spade, spade) cards → 13×13

Total number of cards → 52×52

$$P(\text{spade, then spade}) = \frac{13 \times 13}{52 \times 52}$$
$$= \frac{1}{4} \times \frac{1}{4} = \frac{1}{16}$$

11 A spade is randomly drawn from a standard deck of playing cards on two successive draws, given that the card is not replaced.

■ SOLUTION

Number of (spade, spade) cards → 13×12

Total number of cards → 52×51

$$P(\text{spade, then spade}) = \frac{13 \times 12}{52 \times 51}$$
$$= \frac{1}{17}$$

The probability of an event occurring given that some other event has already occurred is called **conditional probability.** The conditional probability that an event A occurs, given that event B occurs, can be denoted as $P(A|B)$.

EXAMPLE 12 Finding conditional probability

12 High school students were asked to identify their most likely after-school activity. The data is shown below.

Class	Sports Activity	Club Meetings	Homework	Watch TV	Total
Freshman	68	55	22	30	175
Sophomore	56	48	29	27	160
Junior	72	50	20	20	162
Senior	60	45	25	25	155
Total	256	198	96	102	652

Given that the student is a junior, what is the probability that the student's most likely after-school activity is a sports activity?

■ SOLUTION 1

Use the formula.

$$P(\text{sports} \mid \text{junior}) = \frac{P(\text{junior and chose sports})}{P(\text{junior})}$$
$$= \frac{\frac{72}{652}}{\frac{162}{652}} = \frac{72}{162} = 0.44$$

■ SOLUTION 2

Intuitively, the condition is that you are a junior, so our total sample space is now made up of just juniors (162). The probability that sports are a junior student's most likely after-school activity is

$$\frac{72}{162} = 0.44.$$

Conditional Probability

The conditional probability of event A, given event B, is

$$P(A|B) = \frac{P(A \text{ and } B)}{P(B)},\ P(B) \neq 0.$$

A coin is *fair* if the probability of heads is the same as the probability of tails. A coin is *unfair* if one of these probabilities does not equal the other. You can apply this to the coin problem in Example 13.

EXAMPLE 13 Finding probabilities involving successive independent events

13 A fair coin is tossed three times. Find *P*(heads, then heads, then heads).

■ SOLUTION

$P(\text{heads, heads, heads}) = \frac{1}{2} \cdot \frac{1}{2} \cdot \frac{1}{2} = \left(\frac{1}{2}\right)^3 = \frac{1}{8}$ ← three independent events with $P(\text{heads}) = \frac{1}{2}$

Just as one event can be dependent on a second event, a third event can be dependent on the two events preceding it.

EXAMPLE 14 Finding probabilities involving successive dependent events

14 A student council sends 4 boys and 6 girls to the local school board meeting. Three of the students will be interviewed. Find the probability that all three students interviewed are girls.

■ SOLUTION

Sketch a diagram showing the three successive selections.

first selection	second selection	third selection
6 girls of 10 students	5 girls of 9 students ← one student already selected; ↑ one girl already selected	4 girls of 8 students ← two students already selected; ↑ two girls already selected

$P(\text{girl, girl, girl}) = \frac{\cancel{6}^3}{\cancel{10}_5} \times \frac{5}{9} \times \frac{\cancel{4}^1}{\cancel{8}_2} = \frac{\cancel{3}^1}{\cancel{5}_1} \times \frac{\cancel{5}^1}{\cancel{9}_3} \times \frac{1}{2} = \frac{1}{6}$

Practice

Choose the letter preceding the word or expression that best completes the statement or answers the question.

1 A fair coin is flipped four times. If the coin lands heads up on the first three tosses, what is the probability that it will land heads up on the fourth toss?

A. $\frac{1}{2}$ C. $4 \cdot \frac{1}{2}$

B. $\left(\frac{1}{2}\right)^4$ D. $\frac{1}{4 \cdot 2}$

2 Which is the probability of a coin landing heads up each time on three tosses of a fair coin?

A. $\frac{1}{2}$ B. $\left(\frac{1}{2}\right)^3$ C. $3 \cdot \frac{1}{2}$ D. $\frac{1}{3 \cdot 2}$

3 A marble is randomly selected from among 5 red and 4 blue marbles, kept, and then a second marble is drawn at random. What is the probability that both marbles drawn will be red?

A. $\frac{5}{9} \cdot \frac{4}{9}$ B. $\frac{5}{9} + \frac{4}{9}$ C. $\frac{5}{9} \cdot \frac{4}{8}$ D. $\frac{5}{9} + \frac{3}{8}$

4 A marble is randomly selected from among 5 red and 4 blue marbles, replaced, and then a second marble is drawn at random. What is the probability of selecting red both times?

A. $\frac{5}{9} \cdot \frac{5}{9}$ B. $\frac{5}{9} + \frac{4}{9}$ C. $\frac{5}{9} \cdot \frac{3}{8}$ D. $\frac{5}{9} + \frac{3}{8}$

5 A coin is tossed and the arrow on the spinner shown here is spun. What is the probability of heads showing and the arrow landing in the light gray region?

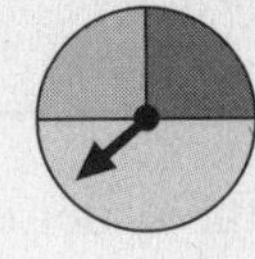

A. $\frac{1}{2} \cdot \frac{1}{4}$ **C.** $\frac{1}{2} \cdot \frac{1}{2}$

B. $\frac{1}{2} + \frac{1}{4}$ **D.** $\frac{1}{2} \cdot \left(1 - \frac{1}{4}\right)$

In Exercises 6–11, a bag contains 3 red, 4 blue, and 5 green marbles, identical but for color. Find each probability given the specified condition.

6 P(red, then red); with replacement

7 P(green, then blue); with replacement

8 P(red, then green); without replacement

9 P(blue, then blue); without replacement

10 P(neither is green); with replacement

11 P(neither is green); without replacement

In Exercises 12–15, find the probability that a family having three children has the indicated number of boys or girls. Use this tree diagram.

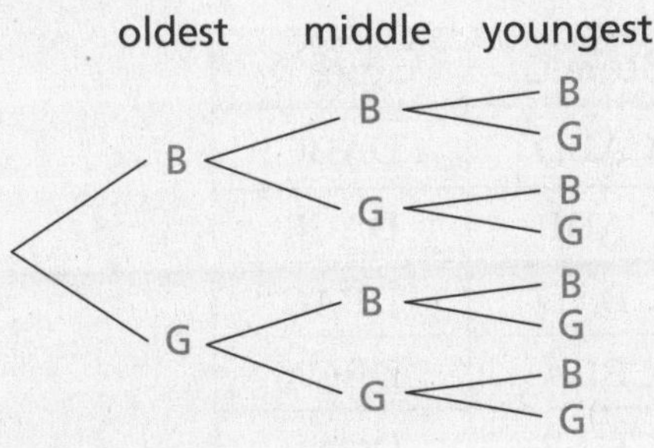

12 All three children are boys.

13 The family has one boy and two girls.

14 The family has at least one girl.

15 The youngest is a boy given that the oldest is a girl.

In Exercises 16–19, teachers send 7 boys and 8 girls to the local science fair. The first three students leaving the fair at lunch time are interviewed. Find each probability.

16 All students interviewed are boys.

17 Exactly two girls are interviewed.

18 A girl is interviewed, then a boy is interviewed, and then a girl is interviewed.

19 A boy is interviewed, given that a boy is interviewed first.

In Exercises 20–23, use the spinners below to find the probability of the situation described. Assume the spinners are fair.

spinner 1 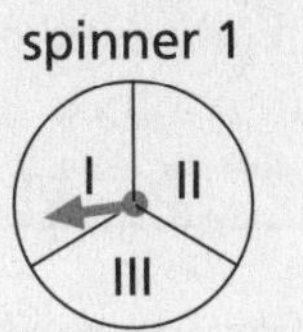

spinner 2 

spinner 3 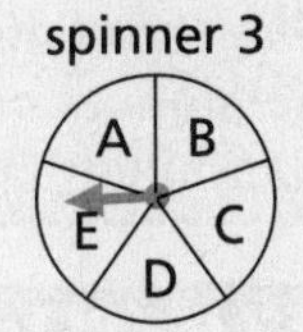

20 The arrow lands in region I, lands in the red region, and lands in region A.

21 The arrow lands in region I or II, lands in the tan region, and lands in region B.

22 The arrow lands in region III, lands in the tan or red region, and lands in region E.

23 The arrow lands in region II, lands in the blue region, and lands in regions A, B, or C.

In Exercise 24, solve the problem. Clearly show all necessary work.

24 Among Jan's 5 sweaters is a red one and a blue one. Among her 5 blouses is a white one and a yellow one. Among her 5 skirts is a green one and a black one. What is the probability that she chooses a red or blue sweater, a white or yellow blouse, and a green or black skirt?

8.4 Combinations

ADP℠ Standards

D2.a Use counting principles

A **combination** is an arrangement of objects in which the order of the objects is not important. A permutation is an arrangement of objects in which order does matter.

For example, both of the following sentences use the word *combination*:

- The fruit salad has a combination of apples, bananas, and cherries.
- The combination you need to open the lock is 24, 15, 17.

In the first sentence, the order of the objects does not matter. The fruits in the salad are a combination because the order does not matter. The salad is the same no matter what order you add the fruit.

However, in the second sentence, to open the lock, the numbers must be entered in a certain order. This is an example of a permutation. The lock will only open if the numbers 24, 15, 17 are entered in the right order.

> A **combination** is an arrangement of items in which the order of the items *does not matter*.
>
> A **permutation** is an arrangement of items in which the order of the items *does matter*. A combination to a lock is an example of a permutation.

EXAMPLE 1 **Solving permutation problems**

 James is the sales manager for four local stores. During his workday, he visits each of the stores (A, B, C, and D) exactly once. He tries to visit the stores in a different order every day. How many different ways are there? Is this an example of a permutation or combination?

■ SOLUTION

Since the order in which James visits the store matters, this is an example of a permutation. One way to solve the problem is to make an organized list.

Starting point →	Store A	Store B	Store C	Store D
Possible orders →	ABCD	BACD	CABD	DABC
	ABDC	BADC	CADB	DACB
	ACBD	BCAD	CBAD	DBAC
	ACDB	BCDA	CBDA	DBCA
	ADBC	BDAC	CDAB	DCAB
	ADCB	BDCA	CDBA	DCBA

There are 24 different arrangements.

You can also use multiplication to solve permutation problems.

When James starts his day, he has the choice of 4 stores to visit. After he visits the first store, there are 3 choices of stores left. Then there are 2 stores left, and finally 1.

$4 \times 3 \times 2 \times 1 = 24$ ← **Multiply the progression of choices.**

When you work with combinations, you have to make sure that you eliminate duplicate groupings. For instance, the groups ABC, ACB, BAC, BCA, CAB, and CBA are different permutations, but they are considered the same combination because they have the same three letters.

To solve a combination problem, you find the permutations and then reduce it by the number of duplicates that equal one combination.

Go Online
PearsonSchool.com
Visit: PearsonSchool.com
Web Code: ayp-0124

EXAMPLE 2 **Solving combination problems**

2 A school chess club has 10 members. Three students will be chosen at random to go to a tournament. Is this an example of a permutation or combination? How many different groups could be chosen?

■ **SOLUTION**

Since the order in which the names are selected does not matter, this is an example of a combination. Imagine selecting three names for the tournament. You would choose the first name from a group of 10, the second name from a group of 9, and the third name from a group of 8.

$10 \times 9 \times 8 = 720$ ← **Find the permutations for 3 members out of a group of 10.**

$3 \times 2 \times 1 = 6$ ← **Find out the permutations of 3 items equal 1 combination.**

$\frac{10 \times 9 \times 8}{3 \times 2 \times 1} = \frac{720}{6} = 120$ ← **Divide to find the number of unique combinations.**

There are 120 unique combinations of 3 students that can be chosen from a group of 10.

Practice

Choose the letter preceding the word or expression that best completes the sentence or answers the question.

1 Five friends are waiting in line together to buy tickets to a movie. If they stand in single file, how many different ways can they line up?

A. 24 **C.** 125

B. 120 **D.** 3125

2 A basketball team has 15 members. The coach wants to choose 2 members of the team to serve as team captains. How many different combinations of captains could the coach choose?

A. 105 **C.** 455

B. 210 **D.** 2730

3 Each student identification number begins with a 3-letter code chosen from the letters M, N, P, Q, R, S, and T. The code MNT is considered different from the code TNM. How many different codes can be formed if a letter can be used no more than twice?

4 Eight runners are in a race. How many possible ways could they finish first, second, and third place?

5 In a game, a player draws 4 cards from a deck of 20 different cards. How many possible 4-card hands could the player draw? Suppose you are the second player to draw 4 cards. How many possible hands could you draw?

8.5 Using Counting Methods with Probability

ADP℠ Standards

D2.a Use counting principles

Counting permutations and combinations plays an important role in solving many probability problems.

The chart below shows the permutations of the letters in the word MATH taken two letters at a time.

MA	MT	MH	AM	AT	AH
TM	TA	TH	HM	HA	HT

Notice that there are 12 in all. Now consider this probability question: If one of the permutations is chosen at random, what is the probability that it will start with M?

You can easily see that three of the permutations start with M, so the probability is 3 out of 12, or $\frac{3}{12} = \frac{1}{4}$.

You can see that probability problems can be solved by listing, counting, and comparing outcomes. However, you can solve these kinds of problems mathematically.

When solving probability problems involving permutations, begin by counting the number of favorable outcomes, and then divide by the total number of possible outcomes.

Visit: PearsonSchool.com
Web Code: ayp-0582

EXAMPLE 1 Solving probability problems using permutation

1 The student council at Bradville High School consists of the following students. Three members are to be chosen at random as president, secretary, and treasurer. Find the probability that A. Wilson is the president.

A. Wilson	J. Easler	J. Solis	S. Burnap	C. Wade
N. Vera	G. Baskin	S. Gage	J. Aaron	D. Hoyt

■ **SOLUTION**

Step 1 Count the favorable outcomes.
How many 3-member groups have A. Wilson as president?
There is 1 favorable choice for president. Then there are 9 choices left for secretary, and 8 choices left for treasurer.

$$1(9)(8) = 72 \text{ favorable outcomes}$$

Step 2 Count the total outcomes.
How many permutations of 3 can be formed from 10 students?

$$(10)(9)(8) = 720 \text{ favorable outcomes}$$

Step 3 Find the probability.

$$\frac{\text{favorable outcomes}}{\text{total outcomes}} = \frac{72}{720} = \frac{1}{10}$$

The key to solving a counting problem is to understand the information. Making a list or a sketch can help you process the facts in the problem.

EXAMPLE 2 **Solving probability problems using combinations**

2 Eight students are sitting around a circular table. A teacher chooses three students at random. What is the probability that the chosen students are sitting in consecutive seats?

SOLUTION

Step 1 Decide whether this problem is about permutations or combinations. The students must be sitting in a certain order at the table, so at first glance, order seems important. But think about it. The teacher can choose the 3 students in any order, so the order doesn't really matter. This problem is about combinations of students that happen to be in consecutive seats.

Step 2 Count the possible combinations the teacher could choose.

$\frac{8 \times 7 \times 6}{3 \times 2 \times 1} = 56$ There are 56 ways to select any 3 students.

Step 3 Count the number of favorable outcomes – the combinations that include 3 *consecutive* students. There are 8. Take a look at the sketch. Think of each student as the middle student in a group of 3. There is only one possible group where B is in the middle. Since there are 8 students, there are 8 groups of consecutive students.

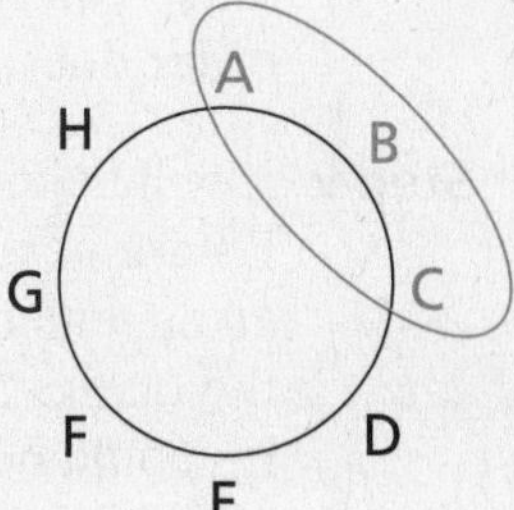

Step 4 Find the probability: $\frac{\text{favorable outcomes}}{\text{total outcomes}} = \frac{8}{56} = \frac{1}{7}$

The probability that the chosen students were sitting next to each other is $\frac{1}{7}$.

As you solve probability situations, pay close attention to the idea of **replacement.** For instance, in a certain lottery game, players try to predict the results of 3 balls drawn from a bin that contains 10 balls, numbered with the digits from 0 through 9. The number of total outcomes changes depending on whether each ball is replaced before the next one is drawn. Which of these games would you have the best chance of winning?

Game 1	**Game 2**
After a ball is chosen, it is replaced before the next one is selected.	A ball is not replaced before the next one is chosen.
Total outcomes: $10 \times 10 \times 10 = 1000$	Total outcomes: $10 \times 9 \times 8 = 720$

You have better chance of winning Game 2. Since there are fewer total outcomes for Game 2, you have a better chance of guessing correctly.

You may have noticed that most probability problems are actually counting problems. You have to use your knowledge of permutations and combinations to calculate the favorable and total outcomes and then compare the results.

Sometimes you can use your understanding of math to make this process easier. For example, sometimes it is easier to calculate the unfavorable outcomes. You can use the probability of something NOT happening to find the probability that it will happen. We call it **complementary counting** when you count the opposite of what you need.

Note

If the probability of an event occurring is P, then the probability of the event **NOT** *occurring is 1 − P.*

EXAMPLE 3 **Using complementary counting to find probability**

3 The letters of the name HILLARY are arranged randomly in a row. What is the probability that the 2 L's are NOT next to each other?

■ SOLUTION

Step 1 Count the total possible placements for the two L's given 7 different placements. The first L has 7 possible placements. The second L has 6 remaining placements. Since you can't tell the difference between the L's, their order doesn't matter.

$\frac{7 \times 6}{2 \times 1} = 21$

Step 2 It will be difficult to count all the placements where the L's are not next to each other. Instead, count the arrangements where they are together. Look at the blanks to the right. There are 6 placements where the L's could be next to each other: 1 and 2, 2 and 3, 3 and 4, 4 and 5, 5 and 6, and 6 and 7.

$\overline{1}\,\overline{2}\,\overline{3}\,\overline{4}\,\overline{5}\,\overline{6}\,\overline{7}$

Step 3 Find the probability that the 2 L's will be next to each other. $\frac{6}{21} = \frac{2}{7}$

Step 4 Find the probability that the 2 L's will NOT be next to each other. $1 - \frac{2}{7} = \frac{5}{7}$

There is a 5 out of 7 chance that the 2 L's will not be next to each other.

If you feel stuck when you are figuring out a counting or probability problem, try a simpler problem to check your thinking.

> You have 2 math books and 4 history books. All the books have different titles. How many ways could you stack the books so that there is a math book on the top and the bottom of the stack?

You decide that you should find the permutations of the 4 books in the middle and then multiply by 2, but you aren't sure it will work. Test your method using a smaller number of books in the middle.

Book (A) in the middle	M_1 A M_2 M_2 A M_1	2 arrangements
2 books (A and B) in the middle	M_1 A B M_2 M_2 A B M_1 M_1 B A M_2 M_2 B A M_1	4 arrangements

Your method makes sense. After you find the permutations of the books in the middle, you multiply by 2 because the math books can have 2 possible placements. If there are 4 books in the middle, there are $2(4 \times 3 \times 2 \times 1) = 48$ arrangements.

Practice

Choose the letter preceding the word or expression that best completes the sentence or answers the question.

1 Max has four shirts: brown, blue, red, and green. He has three pair of pants: brown, blue, and black. If he chooses an outfit at random, what is the probability that he will be wearing something blue?

A. $\frac{1}{12}$ **C.** $\frac{1}{2}$

B. $\frac{5}{12}$ **D.** $\frac{7}{12}$

2 Of the following students, three are chosen randomly to be officers in a school club. What is the probability that both John K. and Lana A. will be chosen?

John K.	Lana A.	Nita M.
Dave R.	Maya L.	Noah J.
Mark G.	Risa H.	Larry T.

A. $\frac{1}{12}$ **C.** $\frac{2}{9}$

B. $\frac{1}{7}$ **D.** $\frac{1}{3}$

3 A lock has a combination consisting of three randomly chosen one-digit numbers. What is the probability that a lock will have a combination with at least two of the same digit?

A. $\frac{2}{5}$ **C.** $\frac{3}{5}$

B. $\frac{7}{25}$ **D.** $\frac{18}{25}$

4 A computer program randomly generates all the permutations of the letters in the word FACTOR. If one of the permutations is chosen randomly, what is the probability that it will have a T in the second position?

A. $\frac{1}{6}$ **C.** $\frac{2}{5}$

B. $\frac{1}{5}$ **D.** $\frac{1}{3}$

5 A basketball coach has the following players on his team.

Max	Jay	Brad	Lynn
Howie	Jamal	Chris	Cliff
Steve	Ivan	Bob	Andy

He needs to choose five players to start the game. He will definitely start his two star players Max and Brad. If he chooses the rest of the starters randomly, what is the probably that he will choose Jamal, Bob, and Cliff?

A. $\frac{1}{1320}$ **C.** $\frac{1}{220}$

B. $\frac{1}{720}$ **D.** $\frac{1}{120}$

6 If five blocks with the letters A, B, C, D, and E are randomly arranged in a row, what is the probability that A and E are placed next to each other?

A. $\frac{1}{30}$ **C.** $\frac{1}{6}$

B. $\frac{1}{15}$ **D.** $\frac{2}{5}$

7 Of 1, 2, 3, 4, 5, 6, 7, and 8, two different numbers are chosen randomly and multiplied together. What is the probability that the product is an even number? (*Hint*: Use complementary counting.)

8 A box contains three red marbles and seven white marbles. If you draw one marble randomly, replace it, and draw another, what is the probability that both marbles will be red?

9 In a deck of cards, there are 4 suits, and each suit contains 13 cards, of which 3 are face cards. If you shuffle the cards and draw 2 without replacement, what is the probability that you will draw 2 face cards?

Chapter 8 Preparing for the ADP℠ Algebra I Exam

DIRECTIONS FOR QUESTIONS 1–25: For each of the questions below, select the answer choice that is best for each case.

1 Which represents the probability of randomly drawing a card showing 7 or a card showing 5 from a standard deck of 52 cards?

A. $\frac{4}{52} + \frac{4}{52}$ **B.** $1 - \left(\frac{4}{52} + \frac{4}{52}\right)$

C. $\frac{4}{52} \cdot \frac{4}{52}$ **D.** $\frac{5}{52} + \frac{7}{52}$

2 Which event is impossible?

A. choosing a number between 20 and 30 that is also a prime number

B. rolling a 6 on a number cube and flipping heads on a coin

C. choosing a rational number between 2.1 and 3.9 that is an even number

D. getting a perfect score on a mathematics test and passing that test

3 In how many ways can 5 books be placed on a shelf in any order?

A. 5 **B.** 25 **C.** 15 **D.** 120

4 A bag contains 7 red, 7 blue, and 7 green marbles. Which represents the probability that a red marble will be randomly drawn from the bag and then a green marble will be randomly drawn from the bag given that the first marble drawn is not replaced?

A. $\frac{7}{21} \cdot \frac{6}{20}$ **B.** $\frac{7}{21} \cdot \frac{7}{21}$

C. $\frac{7}{21} \cdot \frac{7}{20}$ **D.** $\frac{7}{21} \cdot \frac{6}{21}$

5 On a bookshelf, there are 5 red books, 7 green books, and 10 brown books. If a book is picked at random, to the nearest whole percent, what is the probability that it is green?

A. 7% **B.** 23% **C.** 32% **D.** 45%

6 A weather forecaster predicts that there is a 25% probability of rain today. What is the probability that it will not rain?

A. 65% **B.** 5%

C. 75% **D.** 45%

7 A container holds 6 red balls and 3 green balls. One green ball is drawn randomly and set aside. What is the probability the second ball drawn is green?

A. $\frac{1}{4}$ **B.** $\frac{2}{3}$

C. $\frac{1}{3}$ **D.** $\frac{3}{4}$

8 How many four-digit numbers can be made using only the even digits 0, 2, 4, 6, and 8, and with 0 not being the first digit?

A. 500 **B.** 120

C. 625 **D.** 20

In Exercises 9–12, refer to a table of outcomes for rolling a pair of number cubes. Find each probability to the nearest whole percent.

9 *P*(you roll two 5s)

A. 3% **B.** 17% **C.** 33% **D.** 6%

10 *P*(sum equals 1)

A. 31% **B.** 0% **C.** 3% **D.** 17%

11 *P*(sum is not 4)

A. 16% **B.** 8% **C.** 3% **D.** 92%

12 *P*(sum is even)

A. 25% **B.** 50%

C. 10% **D.** 75%

In Exercises 13–14, the Big Dipper Ice Cream Shop has 8 flavors of ice cream, 4 flavors of syrup, and 3 different toppings.

13 How many different ice cream dishes can be made with one flavor of ice cream, one syrup, and one topping?

A. 15 **B.** 3 **C.** 36 **D.** 96

14 If vanilla and chocolate are two of the available flavors of ice cream, what is the probability that vanilla or chocolate ice cream will be chosen at random?

A. $\frac{2}{15}$ **B.** $\frac{1}{3}$ **C.** $\frac{1}{8}$ **D.** $\frac{1}{4}$

15 Bag A contains 10 marbles and Bag B contains 24 marbles. If Bag A contains 2 red marbles and Bag B contains 2 red marbles, what is the probability of randomly drawing a red marble from each bag?

A. $\frac{17}{60}$ **B.** $\frac{1}{60}$ **C.** $\frac{1}{55}$ **D.** $\frac{1}{120}$

16 There are 3 up escalators and one elevator to take shoppers from the first floor to the second floor. There are 3 down escalators and the same elevator to take shoppers from the second floor to the first floor. In how many ways can a shopper go from the first floor to the second floor and back?

A. 4 **B.** 9 **C.** 16 **D.** 6

17 For which is the occurrence of one event not dependent on that of the other event?

A. Drawing a 6 out of a deck of cards, and then drawing an 8 without replacing the 6.

B. Flipping tails on one coin, and then flipping heads on a second coin.

C. Drawing a king out of a deck of cards, leaving the king out, and then drawing another king.

D. Randomly choosing a penny and then a nickel out of a bag of coins without replacing the first coin.

18 Find the probability of choosing two aces from a deck of cards on successive draws, given that the card is replaced.

A. $\frac{1}{169}$ **B.** $\frac{1}{26}$ **C.** $\frac{2}{13}$ **D.** $\frac{4}{13}$

In Exercises 19–21, a bag contains 4 white, 3 silver, and 9 red paper clips identical in size. Find the probability of drawing two paper clips given the specified conditions.

19 *P*(white, then silver); with replacement

A. $\frac{7}{16}$ **B.** $\frac{1}{12}$ **C.** $\frac{3}{64}$ **D.** $\frac{7}{12}$

20 *P*(red, then red); without replacement

A. $\frac{3}{10}$ **B.** $\frac{81}{256}$ **C.** $\frac{2}{9}$ **D.** $\frac{1}{72}$

21 *P*(neither is silver); without replacement

A. $\frac{2}{13}$ **B.** $\frac{169}{256}$ **C.** $\frac{1}{156}$ **D.** $\frac{13}{20}$

22 How many different arrangements of the letters in the word **GOAL** are there if all the letters are used exactly once?

A. 16 **B.** 24 **C.** 1 **D.** 10

23 Evaluate the expression $\frac{6!}{4!2!}$.

A. 1 **B.** 15 **C.** $\frac{21}{13}$ **D.** $\frac{1}{8}$

24 How many four-letter arrangements can be made from the letters in HERMIT?

A. 12

B. 30

C. 360

D. 720

25 A fair spinner has 8 sections numbered 1–8. If the spinner is spun once, what is the probability that it lands on 2?

A. $\frac{1}{8}$ **B.** $\frac{1}{2}$ **C.** $\frac{1}{4}$ **D.** $\frac{7}{8}$

DIRECTIONS FOR 26–28: Solve each problem. Show your work or provide an explanation for your answer.

26 The chart below lists the number of Democratic, Republican, and Independent voters there are in a local district. A voter from the district is selected at random. Use the information in the chart to help you answer the following questions.

Democratic	Republican	Independent
9,800	11,000	1,200

Find the probability that the voter is from any of the three parties.

Find the probability that the voter is a Democrat.

Find the probability that the voter is a Republican.

27 A mathematics teacher places an algebra book, a geometry book, and an algebra II book on a shelf. What is the probability that the geometry book is placed first?

28 A card is drawn from a standard deck of 52 cards and a number cube is rolled.

Find the probability that a spade is drawn and a 1 is rolled.

Find the probability that a king or a queen is drawn and a 6 is rolled.

Find the probability that a red card is drawn and a number greater than or equal to 3 is rolled.

9 Data Analysis

Discovering Kentucky

Kentucky Bluegrass

One of 50 species of bluegrass found in the United States, Kentucky bluegrass (*Poa pratensis*) is a cold-season grass that grows best in the fall, winter, and spring. The leaves of Kentucky bluegrass are narrow, ending in boat-shaped tips.

Kentucky bluegrass is a hardy plant native to Europe. Its tendency to form dense sod makes it popular in heavy-use areas, such as parks, golf courses, and ball fields. For the same reason, Kentucky bluegrass is used extensively as an erosion-control plant.

Despite its hardiness, Kentucky bluegrass is susceptible to diseases. In extremely dry conditions, it is vulnerable to Fusarium Blight, a disease that bleaches its leaves and causes its roots to rot.

9.1 Measures of Central Tendency

ADP℠ Standards

D1.b Use measures of center and spread

Statistics is the mathematical study of **data,** its gathering, organization, analysis, representation, and interpretation. You can consider the scores on a mathematics test recorded at the right as data. The entire class in this example is called the **population.** Any subset of the population is called a **sample** of the population.

The **arithmetic mean** (mean) or **average** of a set of values is the sum of all of the values divided by the number of values in the set. If the sum of 32 test scores is 2,543, then the average score, to the nearest tenth, is $\frac{2543}{32} \approx 79.5$.

56	97	97	96	95	92	90	89
81	80	78	78	76	75	74	73
89	89	86	85	85	84	83	83
72	70	70	68	67	65	62	58

EXAMPLE 1 **Calculating the mean of a data set**

Visit: PearsonSchool.com
Web Code: ayp-0796

1 Find the mean of the test scores below.

{84, 80, 78, 73, 71, 95, 74, 93}

■ **SOLUTION**

Step 1 Calculate the sum of the scores.

$$84 + 80 + 78 + 73 + 71 + 95 + 74 + 93 = 648$$

Step 2 Divide the total by 8.

$$\frac{648}{8} = 81$$

The mean of the test scores is 81. (A calculator solution is also shown.)

```
84+80+78+73+71+
95+74+93
                648
Ans/8
                 81
```

When values in a data set repeat, you can organize them in a *frequency table.* The **frequency** represents the number of times a particular value appears in the data set. The **range** of a set a data is the difference between the **minimum** data value and the **maximum** data value.

EXAMPLE 2 **Using data frequencies find the mean**

2 Find the mean of the data in this table.

Data value	3.5	3.4	3.7	3.8	4.0
Frequency	6	3	2	3	1

■ **SOLUTION**

Step 1 Calculate the sum of the products of data values and frequencies.

$$6(3.5) + 3(3.4) + 2(3.7) + 3(3.8) + 4.0 = 54$$

Step 2 Divide by the sum of the frequencies, which is 15.

$$\frac{54}{15} = 3.6$$

Sometimes it is helpful to write an equation to solve a problem involving the mean.

EXAMPLE 3 **Using an equation to solve a data problem with the mean**

3 Jasmine earns scores of 80, 78, 85, and 82 on four successive history tests. What score must she earn on her fifth test to have a mean (average) of 80?

■ **SOLUTION**

Let x represent the needed score. Solve the equation below.

$$\frac{\text{sum of scores}}{\text{number of scores}} \begin{matrix}\rightarrow \\ \rightarrow\end{matrix} \frac{80 + 78 + 85 + 82 + x}{5} = 80 \quad \leftarrow \text{mean}$$

$$325 + x = 400$$

$$x = 75$$

Jasmine needs to get a 75 to have a mean score of 80.

Check: $\frac{80 + 78 + 85 + 82 + 75}{5} = \frac{400}{5} = 80$ ✓

The **mode** of a set of data is the value that has the greatest frequency.

{2, 3, 4, 5, 4, 5, 7, 8, 5, 9} The value 5 occurs three times. It has the greatest frequency. The mode is 5.	{5, 3, 6, 4, **8**, 6, **8**, 9, 7, 10, 11} Both 6 and 8 occur twice. There are two modes, 6 and 8.

Note

Data sets with one mode, two modes, and three modes are called *unimodal, bimodal,* and *trimodal,* respectively.

If each data value has a frequency of 1 or if the frequencies of all of the data values are the same, then you can say that the data set has no mode.

The **median** of a data set is the middle value in an ordered data set. If there is an even number of data values, the median is the average of the two middle values.

EXAMPLES 4 and 5 **Finding the median of a data set**

Find the median of each data set.

4 {3, 6, 7, 2, 4, 8, 3}

■ **SOLUTION**

Arrange in order from least to greatest.
Identify the middle number.

2 3 3 4 6 7 8

↑ middle number (4)

The median is 4.

5 {3, 7, 8, 1, 3, 8, 4, 6}

■ **SOLUTION**

Arrange in order from least to greatest.
Identify the middle numbers.

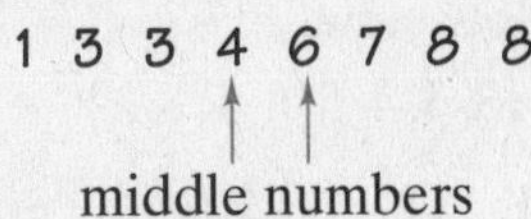

middle numbers (4 and 6)

The median is $\frac{4 + 6}{2}$, or 5.

The mean, median, and mode are referred to as the **measures of central tendency.** These statistics provide an idea of the value around which the set of data is centered.

Sometimes one measure of central tendency is more representative than another for describing the "center" of a data set. Although the values of the mode and median are not generally affected by the other data values, the mean can be significantly affected by extreme values in a data set. You can analyze the data along with the measures of central tendency to determine which measure is the most representative of the data.

EXAMPLES 6 and 7 **Finding the most appropriate measure of central tendency**

6 A real estate agent sells homes for $85,000, $93,000, $110,000, and $220,000. Which measure of central tendency best describes the cost of the homes sold? What would be the effect on the mean and median if the real estate agent sold a fifth home for $230,000? Explain your answer.

■ SOLUTION

The mean is $127,000, and the median is $101,500. The mean is not representative of the home prices because it is affected by the one higher-priced home. The median is a more representative measure of central tendency for this set of data because it seems to represent the data and is not affected by the higher-priced home. If the real estate agent sold another home for $230,000, both the mean and median would increase.

7 A head manager earns $250,000 each year. The department manager earns $55,000, and two assistant managers earn $40,000 each. Which is the most appropriate measure of the salaries associated with the managers of the business?

■ SOLUTION

The mean, $96,250, is not a representative measure of the typical manager's salary because it is significantly affected by the huge salary of the head manager. The mode is $40,000 and represents only the lowest-paid of the managers. The median is $47,500 and best represents the typical salary of the managers of this business.

Practice

Choose the letter preceding the word or expression that best completes the statement or answers the question.

1 Which value of x will make the mean of the data set below equal to 6?

$\{3, 3, 4, 5, 6, 7, 8, x\}$

A. 8 **B.** 12 **C.** 40 **D.** 48

2 Which value is the mean of the data set below?

$\{1, 4, 4, 5, 6, 7, 8, 9\}$

A. 4 **B.** 9 **C.** 1 **D.** 5.5

3 Which data set has 54 as its median?

A. $\{10, 30, 40, 45, 50, 58, 60, 65, 75, 90\}$

B. $\{25, 25, 30, 35, 50, 56, 65, 70, 75, 80\}$

C. $\{30, 40, 45, 47, 54, 55, 60, 65, 75, 85\}$

D. $\{10, 20, 30, 40, 50, 54, 60, 70, 80, 90\}$

4 Which expression does not represent the mean of the data set below?

$$\{2, 2, 5, 7, 8, 8, 8\}$$

A. $\frac{2(2) + 5 + 7 + 3(8)}{7}$

B. $\frac{2 + 2 + 5 + 7 + 8 + 8 + 8}{7}$

C. $\frac{40}{7}$

D. $\frac{7}{2 + 2 + 5 + 7 + 8 + 8 + 8}$

5 Which statement is always true?

A. The median is a value in the data set.

B. The median is also the maximum.

C. The median and the mean are the same.

D. Fifty percent of the data is at or below the median.

In Exercises 6–16, solve the following problems. Clearly show all necessary work.

6 Find the mean of the data set in this table.

Data Value	Frequency
6	//
4	////
8	///
11	/

7 Find the median of this data set.

Plant Height

9	3 6 7 8 9 9
8	2 4 6 8 9
7	4 6 8
6	2 5
5	3 6
4	4
3	3
2	1

Key: 2 | 1 means 2.1 cm

8 The mean of a number and 6 equals the mean of twice the number and 1. What is the number?

9 Which interval contains the median?

Interval	Frequency
14–16	2
17–19	6
20–22	9
23–25	8

10 Gina earns scores of 65, 78, 85, and 82 on four tests. What grade must she earn on the next test to have an average of 80?

11 If n represents the smallest of four consecutive integers, write an expression for the mean of the numbers.

12 For the data set {11, 13, 15, 15, 16, 17, 18, 19, 19, 20} which is greater, the mean or the median?

13 Boxes weighing 12.5 pounds, 12.4 pounds, 12.5 pounds, and 13.6 pounds have the same average weight as 3 packages of equal weight. How much does each of the equal packages weigh?

14 A set of data contains 200 elements. Explain how to find the median of the data.

15 For which value of a will 2, 3, 5, a, 10, and 12 arranged in order from least to greatest have a median of 5.5?

16 A survey taker forgot to write the frequency n for the data value 6 in the frequency table below, but noted a mean of 6.6. What was the frequency of the data value 6?

Data Value	Frequency
5	//
6	n
8	////

9.2 Data Types, Data Collection, and Bias

ADP℠ Standards

D1.c Evaluate the use of data in the media

Data may be of two general types, *qualitative* and *quantitative*. **Qualitative** data may be words or numbers. **Quantitative** data are represented by numerical values.

EXAMPLE 1 **Classifying data as qualitative or quantitative**

1 Classify the following data as qualitative or quantitative: favorite band, gender, age, hair color, weight, test grade, zip code.

■ **SOLUTION**

Qualitative data	Quantitative data
Favorite band	Age
Gender	Weight
Hair color	Test grade
Zip code	

Quantitative data can be classified as *discrete* or *continuous*. A **discrete** variable is one that can take on a finite number of values. **Continuous** variables can take on all the values of a continuous scale.

Visit: PearsonSchool.com
Web Code: ayp-0192

EXAMPLE 2 **Classifying quantitative data as discrete or continuous**

2 Classify the following quantitative data as discrete or continuous: time to complete homework, SAT score, blood pressure, weight, number of DVDs you own, height, number of children in a family.

■ **SOLUTION**

Quantitative Data

Discrete	Continuous
SAT score	Time to complete homework
Number of DVDs you own	Blood Pressure
Number of children in a family	Weight or Height

Univariate data are values collected for a single variable. For example, the age of the first 50 students to arrive at school would create a univariate data set where age is the variable. **Bivariate data** are values collected for two different variables. If you ask the first 50 students who arrive at school how much time they spend doing homework per week and their GPA, a bivariate data set would be created where time on homework is one variable and GPA is the second variable.

You can use data to give a statistical analysis of a population. Sometimes it is impossible or impractical to study an entire population, so only a sample of the population is considered. A sample must be representative of the entire population in order to gather reliable data and assume that the characteristics of the sample accurately reflect those of the entire population.

In order to collect reliable data, you have to determine what data to collect and how to collect it. Among the most common data collection methods, or sampling techniques, are *convenience sampling, voluntary response sampling,* and *random sampling*. **Convenience sampling** uses a sample because it is convenient. **Voluntary response sampling** depends on voluntary respondents to generate a sample of the population. **Random sampling** is usually the most representative of the populations since each member of the population has an equal chance of being part of the sample.

Some advantages and disadvantages of each sampling technique are described in the table below.

Sampling Techniques					
Convenience Sampling		Voluntary Response Sampling		Random Sampling	
Advantages	**Disadvantages**	**Advantages**	**Disadvantages**	**Advantages**	**Disadvantages**
Easy and convenient	Limited useful applications	Easy and convenient	More costly and time consuming	Most common	Expensive and not feasible for large population
Accurate results when the members of the population are the same	Sample not typically representative of target population, which leads to bias	Mail survey format is not intrusive and allows respondents to complete at their convenience	Only those who feel strongly may respond, while the majority of sample does not respond; this leads to strong bias of the data and unreliable data.	Each member of a population has an equal chance of being selected, a fact that eliminates or limits bias.	Supplementary information important to the population is not used to determine the sample; sample is completely random.
Inexpensive	Data unreliable	Familiar to population	Interviews "interrupt" lives of respondents	Analysis of this reliable data is well established.	Often impossible to identify every member of a population

You can use a *random sample* to gather data from a group that is representative of the target population. Remember that random sampling requires that each member of the population has an equal chance of being selected.

EXAMPLE 3 Choosing a random sample

You want to determine which prom is most popular among senior class members. There are 547 students in the senior class. Describe how you would determine a random sample of 60 seniors to poll.

SOLUTION

Step 1 Assign each senior student a distinct number from 1 to 547.

Step 2 Generate a random selection of 60 integers from 1 to 547. Use the *randInt* function on a graphing calculator to generate this list. The screen shows the first six random integers generated by the calculator.

```
randInt(1, 547)
                517
                497
                 81
                282
                222
                402
```

Step 3 Compile a list of the 60 students that correspond to the 60 integers generated in Step 2.

Bias is an influence that affects the reliability of a statistical measurement in some way. Biased samples result in unreliable data.

> **Note**
>
> A group is **random** if each member has the same chance of being in the group.

EXAMPLE 4 Analyzing biased data

Suppose that a basketball coach wants to determine the average weight of the members of his team. The players' weights, in pounds, are 125, 132, 128, 145, and 138. While the coach weighs each player, he inadvertently places his foot on the scale, resulting in his recording the following weights; 130, 137, 133, 150, and 143.

■ SOLUTION 1

$$\text{true mean} = \frac{125 + 132 + 128 + 145 + 138}{5} = 133.6 \text{ lbs}$$

$$\text{biased mean} = \frac{130 + 137 + 133 + 150 + 143}{5} = 138.6 \text{ lbs}$$

■ SOLUTION 2

You can use a graphing calculator to find the mean of a set of data.
Enter the data by pressing STAT and then choose 1: Edit.
Next, press STAT, CALC, 1: 1 − Var Stats.
The statistics will show on the screen. $\overline{x}$ is the mean.

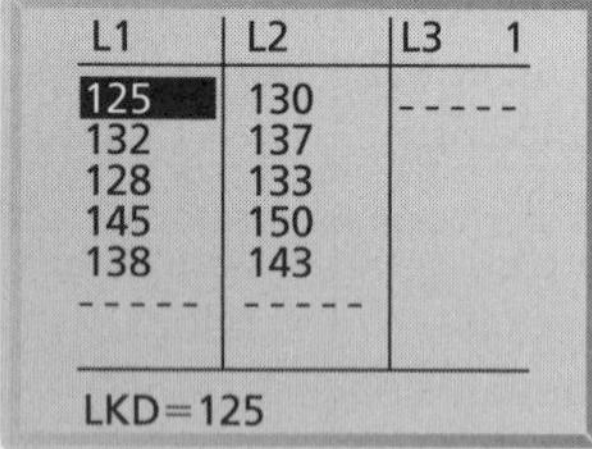

L1	L2	L3 1
125	130	-----
132	137	
128	133	
145	150	
138	143	
-----	-----	

LKD=125

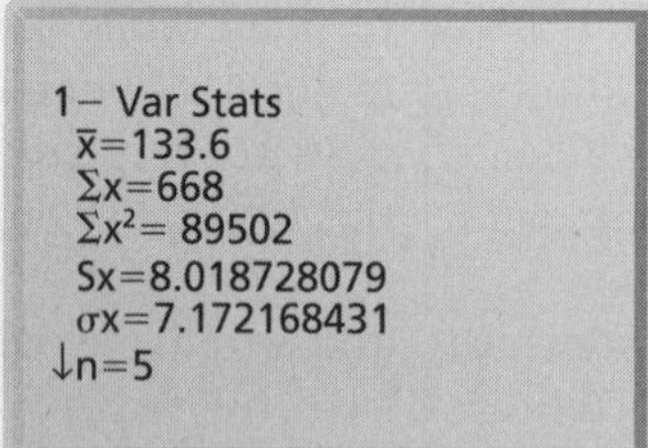

1−Var Stats
x=138.6
Σx=693
Σx²=96307
Sx=8.018728079
σx=7.172168431
↓n=5

This bias increases each of the weights by exactly 5 pounds and so increases the true mean by exactly 5 pounds also.

Samples that are not representative of the population are another common source of bias.

EXAMPLE 5 Classifying a sample as biased or unbiased

A researcher intends to gather data in order to determine the likelihood that the citizens of the city of Springwood will support a new indoor football team. Which of the following data collection methods would result in an unbiased sample?

A. Polling fans as they leave a big league football game
B. A telephone poll conducted every afternoon throughout the week
C. A written survey mailed to all Springwood residents
D. Polling every 5 shoppers at the local shopping mall

> **Note**
>
> You cannot detect bias after collecting data, so you must be careful to avoid bias in the data collection.

■ SOLUTION

Choice **A** is biased because it limits the sample to only football fans.
Choice **B** is biased because it limits the sample to residents who are at home and able to answer the telephone during the specified time.
Choice **C** is biased because it is a voluntary response sample.
Choice D is not biased to any specific population and so is the best choice for an unbiased sample.

Practice

In Exercises 1–4, identify the following components for the situations given, if possible

a. Population
b. Sample
c. The data of interest
d. Potential for bias

1 A sports magazine mailed a questionnaire to NFL players and received responses from 25% of the players. Those responding reported that they did not use steroids as part of their training.

2 Researchers waited outside a local library. The researchers stopped every tenth person who left the library and asked whether that person believed that reading to young children is important.

3 The Environmental Safety Organization took air samples at 20 locations in the school and checked for evidence of poor air quality. They found no readings that resulted in designating the air quality as poor.

4 The mayor wants to know whether the residents of Mytown support a tax imposed to raise money that will be used to update the city's parks and recreational areas. One hundred residents are surveyed as they enter the local parks.

In Exercises 5–7, clearly answer the questions asked.

5 The California poll sometimes conducts preelection surveys by telephone. Could this practice bias the results? How?

6 Suppose that a pollster asks, "What kind of sweet toppings do you like on fruit salad?" Is this question biased?

7 To determine whether the production process is satisfactory, a factory samples the first 30 items of each day's production. Is this a good sampling procedure?

In Exercises 8–13, determine whether the data is quantitative or qualitative. If it is quantitative, determine whether it is discrete or continuous.

8 The number of dollar bills in your wallet

9 Your favorite brand of jeans

10 Your waist size

11 Your area code

12 Number of students in each of your classes

13 Air pressure in your bike tire

In Exercises 14–17, determine whether the data being collected is univariate or bivariate.

14 A student's grade in mathematics

15 A car's weight and its miles per gallon rating

16 A person's age and the number of televisions in his or her home

17 A person's heart rate and the amount of calories being burned

In Exercises 18–21, identify the type of sample described and tell whether the sample is biased or unbiased.

18 A high school baseball coach asks coaches in the Mid-City League if they would prefer that, in their state, the baseball season be held during the fall rather than in the spring.

19 A local newspaper editor wants to know whether customers are satisfied with the newspaper's delivery service. A written survey is mailed to each customer.

20 A history teacher decides to determine the order of the class presentations by writing the names of the students on individual sheets of paper, placing them in a container, and randomly drawing the names.

21 Sam wants to learn how often high school students use the Internet as a tool when completing homework assignments. An Internet survey is sent to each person in Sam's address book.

In Exercise 22, solve the problem. Clearly show all necessary work.

22 You wish to determine the average age of all of the families with students attending your school. Describe how you would gather the data. Collect the data as you described and determine from your data the average age of a family with students attending your school.

9.3 Scatter Plots and Trend Lines

ADP℠ Standards

D1.a Interpret linear trends in data

D1.c Evaluate the use of data in the media

A **scatter plot** is a display of bivariate data. Each data value in one set of data is paired with a data value in the other set of data. These ordered pairs are plotted on a grid. After you have plotted all of the data pairs, look at the clustering of points to determine whether one set of data is related to another.

The line about which the data clusters is known as a **trend line.** This line indicates the tendency or behavior of the data.

If the points seem to cluster about a line sloping up to the right, you can say that there is a **positive correlation,** or relationship, between the variables.

If the points seem to cluster about a line sloping down to the right, you can say that there is a **negative correlation,** or relationship, between the data sets.

If the points are scattered and do not seem to cluster around a line, you can say that there is little or **no correlation** between the data sets.

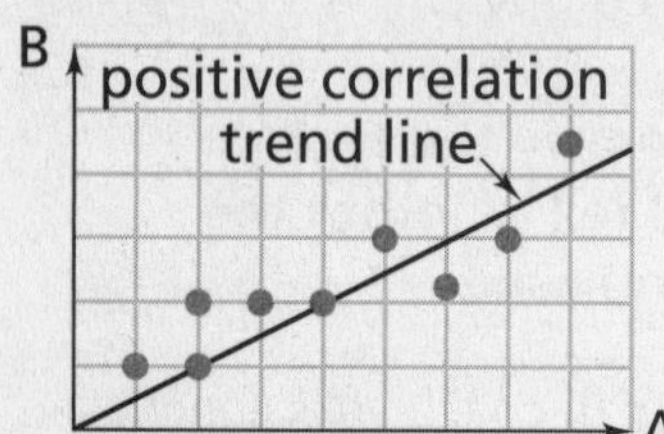

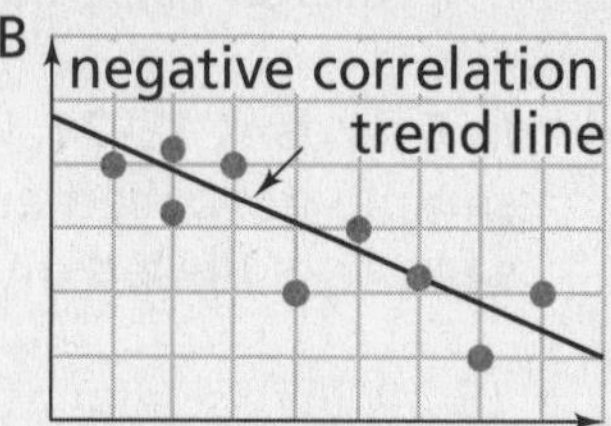

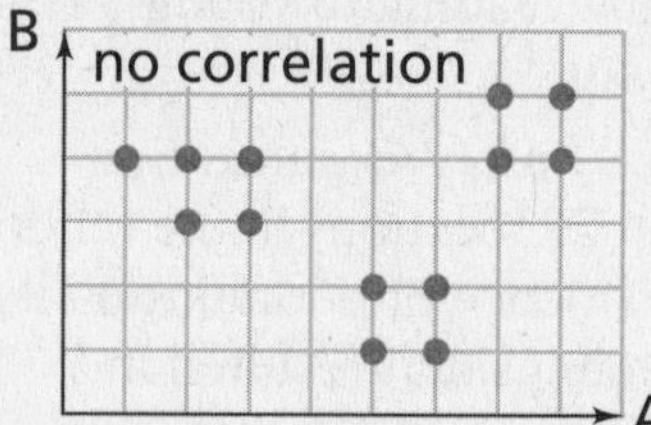

EXAMPLE 1 **Constructing a scatter plot**

Visit: PearsonSchool.com
Web Code: ayp-0920

1 A student asks 15 classmates how many hours they spent studying for a test and how many incorrect answers they gave.

Number of Hours	1	5	6	9	10	8	5	4	10	4	10	7	9	2	8
Incorrect Answers	8	5	3	1	0	3	6	6	2	8	1	4	2	7	2

Represent the relationship between the two variables in a scatter plot.

■ **SOLUTION**

Step 1 Number the horizontal axis from 1 to 10 to represent hours spent studying. Number the vertical axis from 1 to 8 to represent the numbers of incorrect answers.

Step 2 Plot the pairs of data points in the table. For example, for the student who spent 1 hour studying and gave 8 incorrect answers, plot the ordered pair (1, 8).

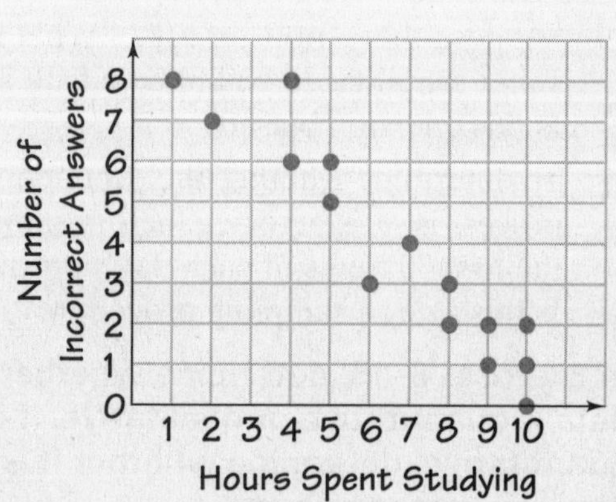

You can model the data displayed in a scatter plot by finding the equation of a trend line.

EXAMPLE 2 Finding the equation of a trend line

Use the data from Example 1 to determine an equation for a trend line.

■ **SOLUTION**

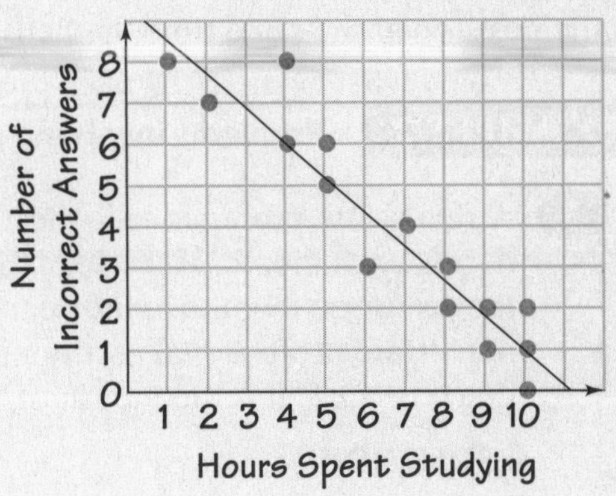

Step 1 Draw a line that includes as many points as possible.

Step 2 Choose 2 points on the line, (4, 6) and (10, 1), to find the slope.

$$m = \frac{(6-1)}{(4-10)} = -\frac{5}{6}$$

Step 3 Find the y-intercept of the line. Substitute the slope and the coordinates of a point in the equation $y = mx + b$.

$$6 = -\frac{5}{6}(4) + b$$

$$\frac{56}{6} = b$$

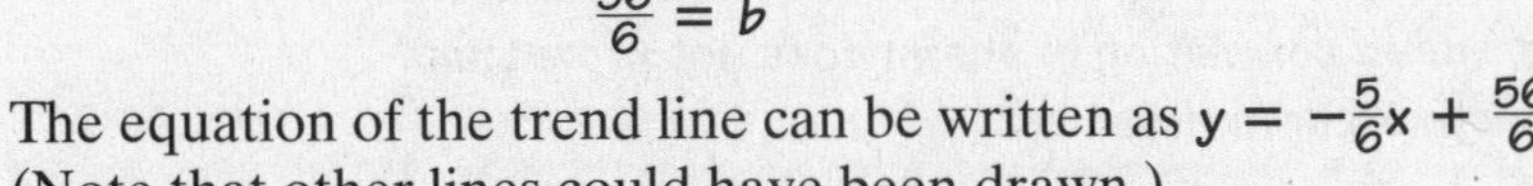

The equation of the trend line can be written as $y = -\frac{5}{6}x + \frac{56}{6}$. (Note that other lines could have been drawn.)

Using the trend line that you have drawn, you can make **predictions** about the data. You can predict the number of incorrect answers that a person who studied for 3 hours would give by substituting 3 for x in the equation.

$$y = -\frac{5}{6}(3) + \frac{56}{6} = \frac{41}{6} \approx 7$$

To the nearest integer, you can expect a student who studied for 3 hours to answer 7 questions incorrectly.

You can also find the trend line by using a calculator. By plotting the data with the window settings shown, you can determine a **manual** line of best fit. If you use the same two points as before, (4, 6) and (10, 1), your calculator result will be the same as the one you found by using hand calculations.

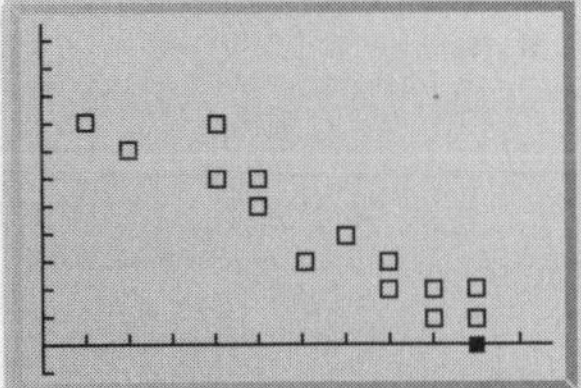

WINDOW
Xmin=0
Xmax=11.75
Xscl=1
Ymin=−1
Ymax=11.4
Yscl=1
Xres=1

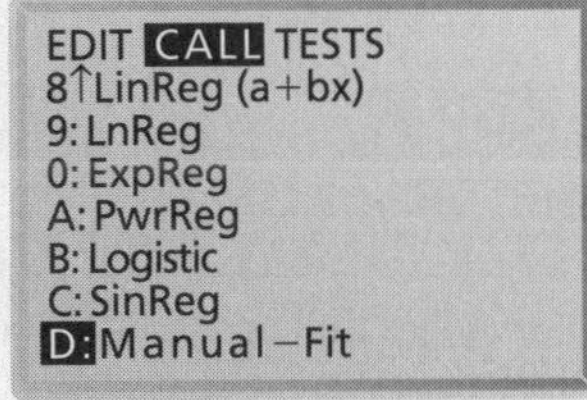

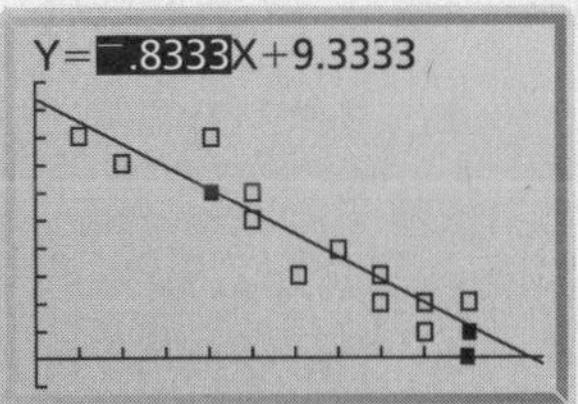

An outlier is a value that differs greatly from the rest of the values in the data set. Sometimes you can justify removing an extreme outlier. If you remove an outlier, the trendline will be affected and you will need to redraw it. The greater the distance between an outlier and the trendline, the greater the impact the outlier has on the trendline.

Note that two data sets or variables may show a correlation; however, this correlation does not necessarily mean that a cause-and-effect relationship exists between the two variables. Consider this example. *Correlation does not guarantee causation*. A man takes the bus to work each day. When he steps off the bus, he hears the bells in the town hall tower ring. If this happens every day, there is a strong positive correlation between the two events. However, you cannot say that stepping off the bus causes the bells to ring. It is more likely that the man takes the same bus to work each day, arriving at the bus stop at the same time the bells ring.

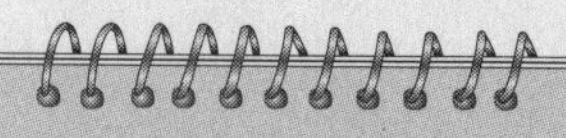

Note

Correlation measures association, but association is not the same as causation.

EXAMPLE 3 **Problems involving correlation and causation**

A real estate professional collects data on a number of home sales during each month of the year. He finds a negative correlation between the last three months of the year and the number of home sales. Can the real estate professional accurately conclude that home sales will be down because it is the month of November?

▪ **SOLUTION**

The real estate professional cannot accurately conclude that fewer homes will be sold in November. The fact that a correlation is shown does not prove that slowing of home sales will always occur in November.

Practice

Choose the letter preceding the word or expression that best completes the statement or answers the question.

1 Which of the following statements is true of the scatter plot below?

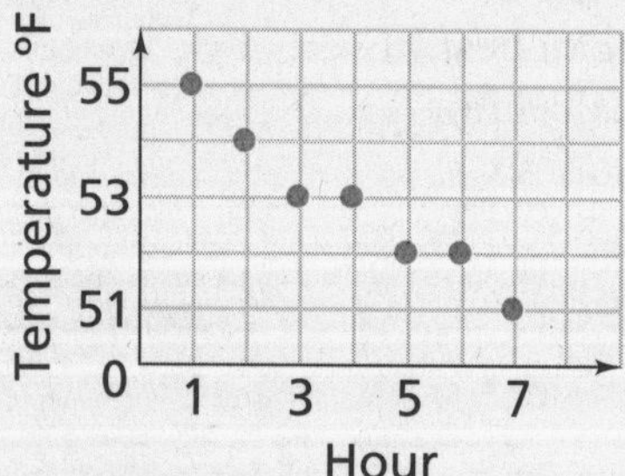

A. The data have a negative correlation.

B. The data have a positive correlation.

C. The data have no correlation.

D. The correlation cannot be determined.

2 Which of the following statements best describes the scatter plot below?

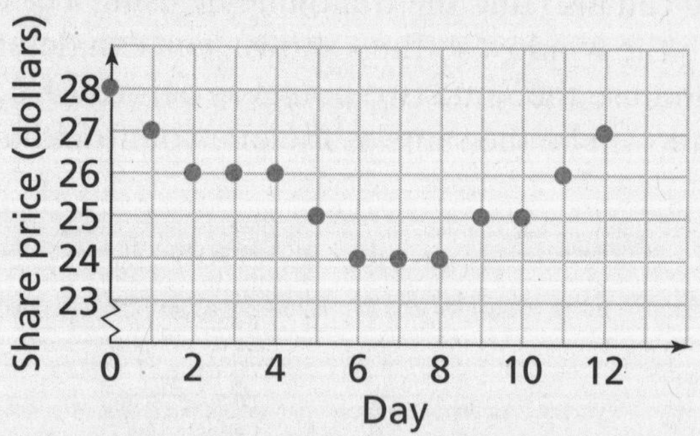

A. The data have a negative correlation.

B. The data have a positive correlation.

C. The data have no correlation.

D. The correlation cannot be determined.

3 Which data set is shown in the scatter plot below?

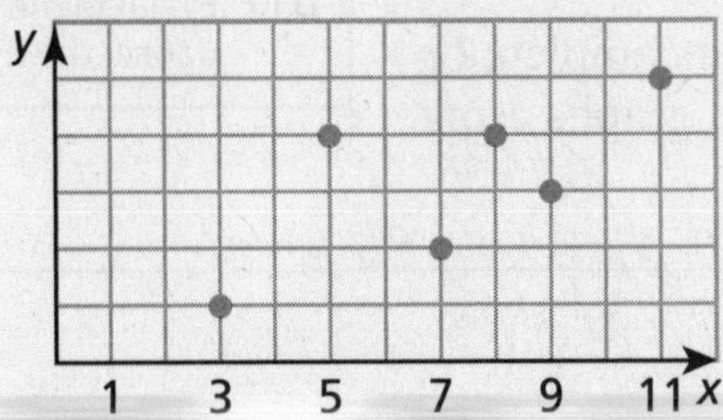

A.

x	3	5	7	8	9	11
y	1	4	2	4	3	5

B.

x	1	4	2	4	3	5
y	3	5	7	8	9	11

C.

x	1	5	2	8	3	11
y	3	4	7	4	9	5

D.

x	3	4	7	4	9	5
y	1	5	2	8	3	11

4 A math teacher records the number of hours a student sleeps the night before a test and the grade the student earns on the test. A scatter plot of the data shows a positive correlation between the hours of sleep and the test grade. Which of the following is a true statement?

A. A student sleeping more hours will earn a higher test grade.

B. A student sleeping fewer hours will earn a lower test grade.

C. A student who earns a higher test grade must sleep more hours than a student who earned a lower test grade.

D. A student may or may not earn a higher test grade by sleeping more hours the night before the test.

In Exercises 5–8, represent each relationship between *x* and *y* in a scatter plot with *x* on the horizontal axis and *y* on the vertical axis.

5

x	23	24	25	26	27	28
y	2.8	3.0	3.2	3.0	3.4	3.4

6

x	3	4	5	6	7	8
y	7	6	3	5	4	3

7

x	0	1	2	3	4	5
y	7	6	4	6	7	8

8

x	0	1	2	3	4	5
y	1	3	5	7	9	11

In Exercises 9–11, solve the following problems. Clearly show all necessary work.

9 The weight and fuel consumption of different vehicles are given in the accompanying table. Construct a scatter plot of these data and find an equation of a trend line for the data. Use the equation to predict the fuel consumption for a vehicle that weighs 4,800 pounds. Also, predict the weight of a vehicle that gets 18 miles per gallon (mpg).

Weight (in 100 lbs)	27	45	30	47	22	40	34	50
mpg	30	16	24	15	29	20	22	13

10 The table below shows the respiration and heart rates for adult males. Construct a scatter plot of these data and determine a trend line. Use the equation of the line to predict the heart rate of a man with a respiration of 32 breaths per minute.

Respiration (breaths/min)	50	30	25	20	18	16	14
Heart Rate (beats/min)	200	150	140	130	120	110	100

11 Using this scatter plot, find the mean temperature of those recorded between noon and 7:00 P.M.

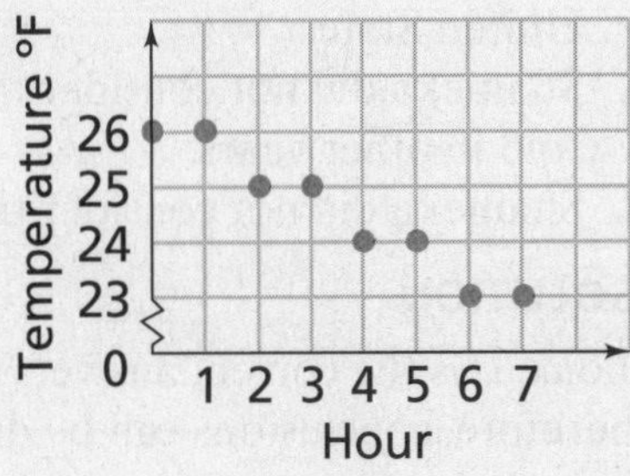

9.4 Misuse of Statistics

ADP℠ Standards

D1.c Evaluate the use of data in the media

You can use statistics to draw conclusions from data. However, incomplete or misleading data can lead to inaccurate conclusions. For example, graphs using different scales can depict data very differently.

The accompanying diagrams show the value of the Dow Jones Industrial Average over time. The first graph shows the average over the course of just one day. The many fluctuations indicate that the value changes dramatically and frequently, making investment seem unpredictable and risky.

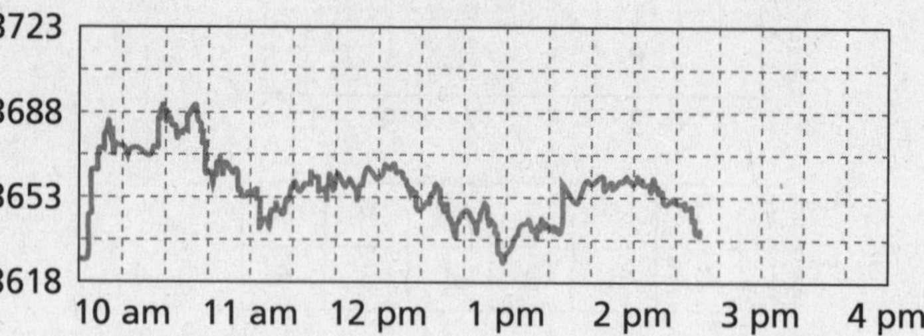

Now look at the average on a different scale. The second graph shows fluctuations in the average over a period of one year. Although this graph indicates some volatility in the stock market, it is clear that over this longer period of time, there is an overall increase in the value of the Dow Jones Industrial Average.

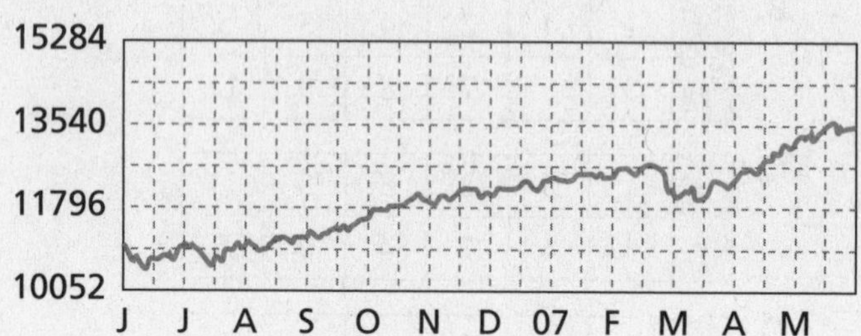

EXAMPLE 1 Analyzing the scale of a graph

 Examine the scale on the vertical axis in each of the two graphs above. Explain how this scale affects the information shown in the graphs.

■ SOLUTION

In the first graph the unit along the *y*-axis is 17.5 points and in the second the vertical unit is 872 points. ***A change in scale can increase or decrease the visual effect of the volatility of the Dow Jones average displayed by the graph.***

It is important to understand the sample space represented by the data. Sometimes it is easy to draw incorrect conclusions that are beyond what the data represents.

EXAMPLE 2 Incomplete data

 The table at the right lists the most frequently purchased cars in Chemung County for the year 2006. Shameka concludes that 24% of the cars purchased in Chemung County in 2006 were Chevy Impalas. Why is Shameka's conclusion wrong?

Most Frequently Purchased Cars in Chemung County in 2006

Rank	Make	Number
1	Toyota Camry	60
2	Ford Focus	48
3	Chevy Impala	36
4	Honda Accord	27

A. Shameka did not consider the top-selling trucks.
B. Shameka did not consider the total sales in the United States.
C. Shameka did not consider the cars most frequently sold in other years.
D. Shameka did not consider that other makes were sold in 2006.

■ SOLUTION

Choice D is the correct answer. This table only includes four makes of autos. Therefore, conclusions can be drawn only about those four.

The choice of statistics used to analyze data influence greatly the interpretation of the data. In general, it is best to consider all of the statistics that apply to a data set, such as the mean, median, range, and mode.

EXAMPLE 3 Mean versus median

3 Five workers for Smooth Road Paving Company have requested a wage increase. The owner believes that an increase is unnecessary because the average salary for company employees is over $44,000. What is misleading about the owner's claim?

Salaries for Employees of Smooth Road Paving Co.	
Owner	$100,000
Foreman	$60,000
Laborer	$30,000

■ **SOLUTION**

Although the mean salary for this company's employees is approximately $44,285, only two people, the owner and the foreman, make more than the average. The median of $30,000 is a better indicator of the "middle" salary earned at this company.

When presenting data, the visual impact of a graph can have a greater impression than only the raw data.

EXAMPLE 4 Analyzing misleading graphs

4 In a metropolitan area, each of 37 paper carriers has a route that includes fewer than 100 customers. Another 55 have routes that include between 100 and 150 customers, and 28 have routes that include more than 150 customers. Both a pictograph and bar graph are used to present the data. Describe why either representation may be misleading and which better displays the data.

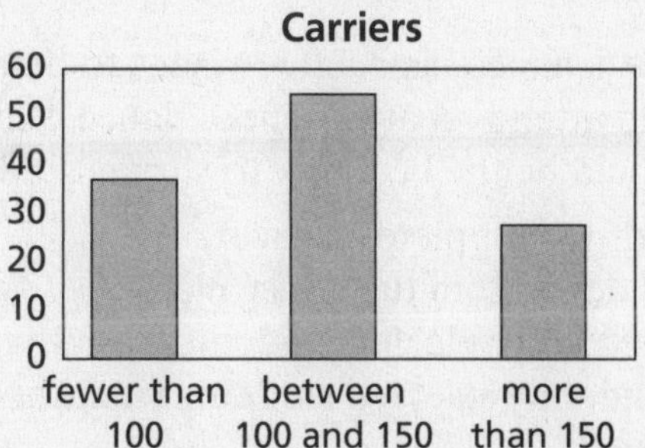

■ **SOLUTION**

The pictograph shows that most carriers have between 100 and 150 customers. The information shows that approximately twice as many carriers have from 100 to 150 customers as have over 150 customers. However, to magnify the figure and avoid distortion, the artist must increase both the height and width of the figure. As a result, the center figure is almost four times as large as the figure on the right. Because the artist's rendering is misleading, a bar graph would better represent these data.

Statistics are important for analyzing trends in data. It is important, however, not to extrapolate too far beyond the range of the sample space.

EXAMPLE 5 **Analyzing trends in data**

The data in the table show the number of boat registrations and the number of manatee deaths for a region of Florida.

Year	1992	1993	1994	1995	1996	1997	1998	1999	2000	2001	2002
Boat Registrations	4980	5130	5120	5260	5590	5850	6140	6450	6750	7110	7190
Manatee Deaths	16	24	20	15	34	33	33	39	43	50	47

A least squares linear regression results in a line of best fit represented by the equation $y = .014x - 51.923$. Use the data and equation given to predict the number of manatee deaths in the year 2020. Is this estimate reliable? Explain your reasoning.

■ **SOLUTION**

It is expected that in 2020, 15,000 boats will be registered. Using the equation of the line, you can predict manatee deaths represented by $y = 0.014(15{,}000) - 51.923 \approx 158$. However, the year 2020 is too far in the future for the range of data represented in the table. There is no guarantee that this linear model will continue to be followed that far into the future.

A common error that results in faulty information is *sampling bias*. If not collected carefully, sample data have little value. Samples collected for convenience, self-selected samples, systematic samples, or any nonrandom samples should be avoided. Simple random samples can usually be trusted.

Visit: PearsonSchool.com
Web Code: ayp-0927

EXAMPLE 6 **Sampling bias**

Ms. Lightfoote, a dance instructor, wishes to determine whether students would attend an after-school dance. Which of the following techniques would be the best way to survey students about the dance?

A. Ask 50 girls to complete a survey.
B. Ask 50 students from the dance class.
C. Ask 50 randomly selected students from the school.
D. Ask 50 randomly selected students from those who attended the last dance.

■ **SOLUTION**

Choices **A, B,** and **D** indicate some type of sampling bias. Choice *C* is the correct choice because simple random samples are usually reliable and unbiased.

Practice

Choose the letter preceding the word or expression that best completes the statement or answers the question.

1 The graphs below show the number of students who were selected for all-conference teams from two schools with comparable student bodies. The principal of school B uses the graphs to claim a greater increase in the number of all-conference students in school B than in school A from 2001 to 2004.

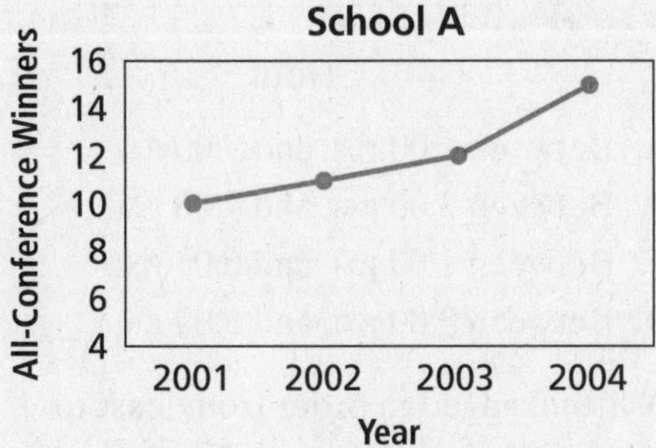

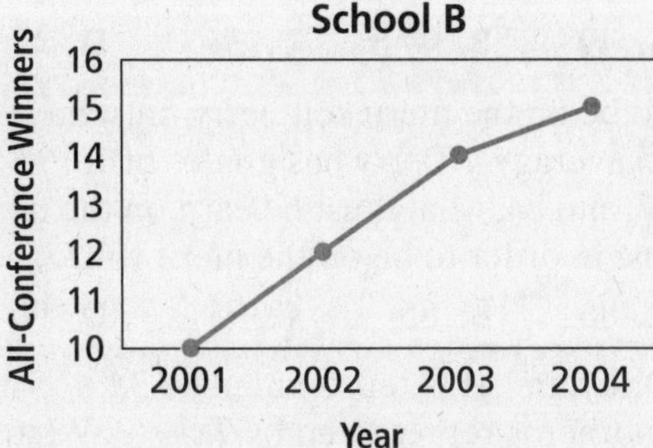

According to the information given, which of these statements explains why the graphs are misleading?

A. The time periods are different.

B. The population of the schools are different.

C. The types of data are different.

D. The vertical scales are different.

2 Dominic has learned that 85 percent of the students in his math class own a graphing calculator. Therefore, he estimates that of the 1000 students in the school, 850 of them own graphing calculators. Which of the following describes why Dominic's conclusion is faulty?

A. incorrect mathematics computation

B. use of opinion to influence a prediction

C. biased sampling

D. inappropriate use of the mean

In Exercises 3–5, solve the following problems. Clearly show all necessary work.

3 During the campaign season in a particular city, the incumbent mayor claimed that the number of people employed had increased. His challenger claimed that unemployment was up. How can both claims be true?

4 Two algebra classes are compared after the first exam of the semester. Class A has a mean score of 76.25 and a median score of 75. Class B has a mean score of 73.2 and a median score of 75. Knowing this information, the students conclude that the classes are performing similarly. Is their conclusion justified?

5 The accompanying pictograph shows that the cost of building a new home has doubled from 1995 to 2002. Why might this representation be misleading?

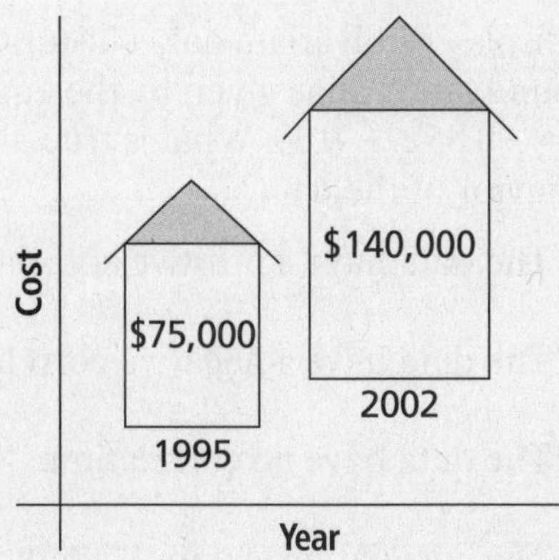

Chapter 9 Preparing for the ADP[SM] Algebra I Exam

DIRECTIONS FOR QUESTIONS 1–17: For each of the questions below, select the answer choice that is best for each case.

1 What is the mean of the data set below?

{4, 4, 5, 3, 4, 8, 6, 4, 8, 7, 9, 10, 2, 1, 9}

A. 4 **B.** 5.6 **C.** 15 **D.** 84

2 Which statement is always true for a given data set?

A. The mean is greater than the median.

B. The mode is greater than the mean.

C. Fifty percent of the data is at or above the median.

D. The mean and the median are equal.

3 Which of the following represents the mean of the data?

Data Value	Frequency
5	4
6	7
8	3

A. $4 + 7 + 3$

B. $\frac{5 + 6 + 8}{4 + 7 + 3}$

C. $4(5) + 7(6) + 3(8)$

D. $\frac{4(5) + 7(6) + 3(8)}{4 + 7 + 3}$

4 A display of bivariate data clusters around a trendline given by the equation $y = -0.85x + 9.39$. What is true about the behavior of the data?

A. The data have a positive correlation.

B. The data have a negative correlation.

C. The data have no correlation.

D. The correlation cannot be determined.

5 The data were recorded between 1:00 P.M. and 7:00 P.M. Over what period of time was the temperature at or below 53°F?

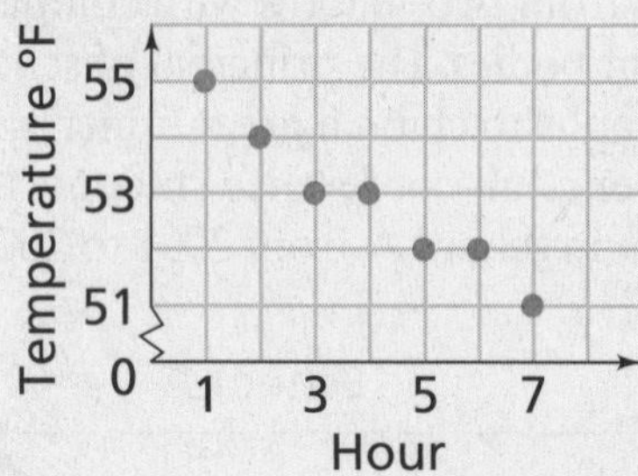

A. Between 1:00 P.M. and 7:00 P.M.

B. Between 3:00 P.M. and 7:00 P.M.

C. Between 1:00 P.M. and 6:00 P.M.

D. Between 3:00 P.M. and 5:00 P.M.

6 A list arranged in order from least to greatest is 25, 30, 44, x, 51, 60, 75, 80. If the median is 50, what does x equal?

A. 49 **B.** 47.5 **C.** 35 **D.** 47

7 To be on the merit roll, Jerry must have an 85 average. If Jerry has grades of 78, 93, 88, 77, and 84, what must he earn on the next test in order to be on the merit roll?

A. 86 **B.** 85 **C.** 95 **D.** 90

8 One number is represented by $3x + 5$ and another is represented by $7x - 3$. What is the average of these numbers in terms of x?

A. $10x + 1$ **B.** $\frac{10x + 8}{2}$

C. $5x + 1$ **D.** $5x$

9 Find the mean temperature of those recorded between 3:00 A.M. and 10:00 A.M.

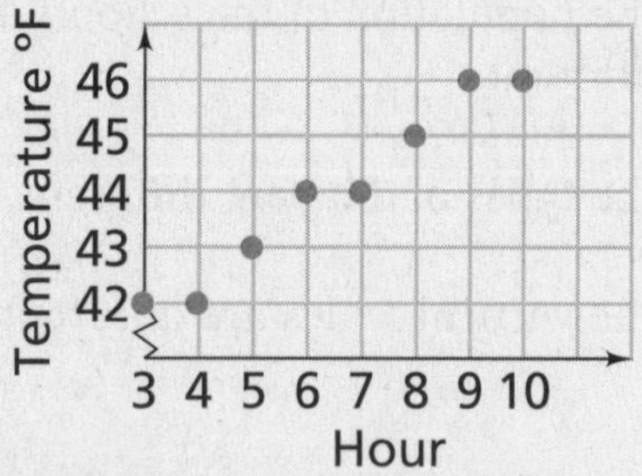

A. 46°F **B.** 44°F **C.** 42°F **D.** 45.5°F

10 Given the set of data shown below, which point, if removed, would have the **greatest** impact on the trendline?

$(1,1), (1,6), (3,1), (3,2), (4,1), (5,2), (6,1), (6,3)$

A. $(6,1)$

B. $(5,2)$

C. $(1,6)$

D. $(1,1)$

11 To the nearest cent, find the mean share price over the period of time shown in this graph.

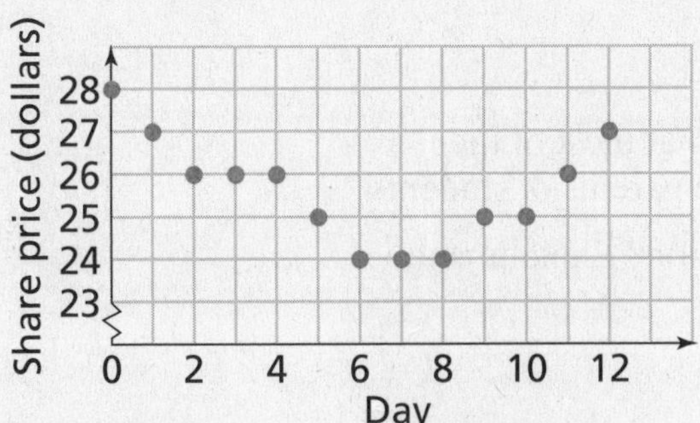

A. \$26.00 **B.** \$26.50

C. \$25.62 **D.** \$27.75

12 Which of the following can be used to predict the value of a variable?

A. mean

B. median

C. trend line

D. scatter plot

13 Grocery bags weighing 3.5 pounds, 4.2 pounds, 1.8 pounds, 2.7 pounds, and 3.3 pounds have the same average weight as two grocery bags of equal weight. To the nearest tenth of a pound, what do each of the equal grocery bags weigh?

A. 3.3 pounds **B.** 3.1 pounds

C. 1.8 pounds **D.** 3.0 pounds

14 Find the mean of the data in this table to the nearest hundredth.

Data Value	Frequency
3	////
−2	/
6	//
10	///
−1	////

A. 3.43 **B.** 6.00 **C.** 3.20 **D.** 3.00

15 Which set of data has a median of 58?

A. $\{10, 20, 30, 40, 50, 60, 70, 80, 90, 100\}$

B. $\{5, 20, 25, 34, 53, 55, 65, 69, 75, 90\}$

C. $\{10, 20, 30, 44, 50, 58, 62, 66, 74, 85\}$

D. $\{25, 34, 46, 50, 54, 62, 70, 80, 80, 95\}$

16 Shameka recorded the daily temperatures for the past week. Her records show 72°, 78°, 80°, 85°, 80°, 73°, and 77°. Which of the following statements is true for these data?

A. The mean is greater than the mode.

B. The mode is less than the median.

C. The mean is greater than the median.

D. The mode is greater than the mean.

17 The combined weight of the luggage in an elevator is 224 pounds. What is the weight of the suitcase with frequency 3?

Weight (pounds)	Frequency
w	///
22	//
50	/
15	/
20	//

A. 25 pounds **B.** 117 pounds

C. 21 pounds **D.** 27 pounds

DIRECTIONS FOR 18–20: Solve each problem. Show your work or provide an explanation for your answer.

18 The ages of the first 50 people to come to a high-school basketball game are shown.

Age	Frequency
0–9	10
10–19	9
20–29	8
30–39	13
40–49	5
50–59	3
60–69	2

The local paper quoted the athletic director, saying that most of the people who attend the school's basketball games are parents of students.

Does the data support the athletic director's conclusion? Explain your reasoning.

19 A restaurant wants to estimate how many customers they would have if they began to serve breakfast. They ask all of the customers at lunch one day if they would consider coming to the restaurant for breakfast.

Is this sample biased? Explain your reasoning.

20 The following table shows the salaries of employees in an office.

$25,500	$45,500	$46,800	$32,300
$34,000	$45,500	$56,000	$42,250
$52,000	$48,900	$44,600	$51,700

What is the mean salary?

What is the median salary?

If each salary is increased by $1,000, how does this affect the mean and the median?

Glossary

GLOSSARY

Abscissa The value of the x-coordinate in an ordered pair.

Absolute value The distance that a number is from zero on a number line. The symbol for the absolute value of a number n is $|n|$.

Acute angle An angle whose measure is greater than 0° and less than 90°.

Acute triangle A triangle that has three acute angles.

Addend One of a set of numbers to be added. In the expression $a + b$, a and b are the addends.

Addition-multiplication method A method used to solve a system of equations in which the equations are added to eliminate one of the variables. In some cases, one or more of the equations must be multiplied by a nonzero constant before the addition can occur. Also called the *elimination method*.

Addition property of equality For all real numbers a, b, and c, if $a = b$, then $a + c = b + c$.

Addition property of inequality For all real numbers a, b, and c,

- If $a < b$, then $a + c < b + c$; and
- If $a > b$, then $a + c > b + c$.

Additive identity Zero. When 0 is added to any given number, the sum is identical to the given number. See also *identity property of addition*.

Additive inverse See *inverse property of addition*.

Adjacent angles Two coplanar angles that share a common side and a common vertex, but have no interior points in common.

Algebraic expression See *variable expression*.

Alternate exterior angles A pair of nonadjacent exterior angles on opposite sides of a transversal.

Alternate Exterior Angles Theorem If two parallel lines are cut by a transversal, then alternate exterior angles are congruent.

Alternate interior angles A pair of nonadjacent interior angles on opposite sides of a transversal.

Alternate Interior Angles Theorem If two parallel lines are cut by a transversal, then alternate interior angles are congruent.

Altitude of a triangle A perpendicular segment from a vertex to the line containing the opposite side.

Angle The figure formed by two rays with a common endpoint.

Angle Addition Postulate If point B is in the interior of $\angle AOC$, then $m\angle AOB + m\angle BOC = m\angle AOC$.

Angle-Angle-Side (AAS) Congruence Theorem If two angles and the nonincluded side of one triangle are congruent to two angles and the nonincluded side of another triangle, then the triangles are congruent.

Angle-Angle (AA) Similarity Postulate If two angles of one triangle are congruent to two angles of another triangle, then the triangles are similar.

Angle bisector The ray that divides a given angle into two congruent angles.

Angle of a convex polygon See *interior angle of a convex polygon*.

Angle of depression An angle whose vertex and horizontal side are level with an observer's eye and whose other side slopes downward from an observer's eye level to an object below.

Angle of elevation An angle whose vertex and horizontal side are level with an observer's eye and whose other side slopes upward from an observer's eye level to an object above.

Angle-Side-Angle (ASA) Congruence Postulate If two angles and the included side of one triangle are congruent to two angles and the included side of another triangle, then the triangles are congruent.

Antecedent See *hypothesis*.

Apothem In a regular polygon, the segment, or the length of the segment, drawn from the center to the midpoint of a side.

Arc An unbroken part of a circle.

Area of a plane figure The number of nonoverlapping square units contained in its interior.

Arithmetic sequence A sequence in which each term differs by a common difference.

Associative property of addition For all real numbers a, b, and c, $a + b + c = (a + b) + c = a + (b + c)$.

Associative property of multiplication For all real numbers a, b, and c, $a \cdot b \cdot c = (a \cdot b) \cdot c = a \cdot (b \cdot c)$.

Average See *mean*.

Axis of symmetry of a parabola The line that divides the parabola into two matching parts. For a parabola with equation $y = ax^2 + bx + c, a \neq 0$, the equation of the axis of symmetry is $x = -\frac{b}{2a}$.

Bar graph A statistical display in which data are represented by bars that are determined by two axes; one of these axes is labeled with categories of data, and the other is labeled with a numerical scale.

Base angles See *isosceles triangle, trapezoid*.

Base of an isosceles triangle See *isosceles triangle*.

Base of a plane figure See *triangle, trapezoid, parallelogram*.

Base of a power When a number is written in the exponential form x^n, the number x is the base.

Base of a three-dimensional figure See *prism, cylinder, pyramid, cone*.

Between On a number line, point C is between point A and point B if the coordinate of point C is between the coordinates of points A and B.

Biconditional statement The conjunction of a conditional statement and its converse. The biconditional *If p, then q and If q, then p* is written in abbreviated form as *p if, and only if, q*.

Binomial A polynomial with exactly two terms.

Boundary of a half-plane See *open half-plane*.

Box-and-whisker plot A display of numerical data in which a *box* represents the data from the first to third quartiles, a vertical segment crosses the box at the median, and horizontal *whiskers* extend from the left and right of the box to represent the rest of the data.

Broken-line graph See *line graph*.

Center of a circle See *circle*.

Center of a regular polygon The point that is equidistant from all the vertices of the polygon.

Center of rotation See *rotation*.

Center of a sphere See *sphere*.

Center of symmetry See *rotational symmetry*.

Chord of a circle Any line segment that has endpoints on the circle.

Circle The set of all points in a plane that are a fixed distance from a fixed point in the plane. The fixed point is called the *center of the circle*. The fixed distance is called the *radius of the circle*.

Circle graph A statistical display in which a data set is represented by a circle, and distinct categories of the data are represented by distinct "slices" of the circle; the percent of the circle allotted to each slice is equal to the percent of the data set within that category.

Circuit A path that begins and ends at the same point.

Circumference of a circle The distance around the circle.

Closed half-plane The union of an open half-plane and its boundary.

Closed statement A statement that is either true or false.

Closure property of addition For all real numbers a and b, $a + b$ is a unique real number.

Closure property of multiplication For all real numbers a and b, $a \cdot b$ is a unique real number.

Coefficient of a term The numerical part of a term that contains variables. Also called the *numerical coefficient of a term*.

Collinear points Points that lie on the same line. Points that do not lie on the same line are called *noncollinear points*.

Column matrix An $n \cdot 1$ matrix, meaning there are n number of rows with only one element in each.

Combination A selection of objects from a set without regard to order.

Common difference A fixed number by which all the terms in an arithmetic sequence will differ.

Common ratio A fixed number by which all the terms in a geometric sequence will vary.

Commutative property of addition For all real numbers a and b, $a + b = b + a$.

Commutative property of multiplication For all real numbers a and b, $a \cdot b = b \cdot a$.

Compatible matrices A row matrix and a column matrix having an equal number of elements.

Complement of an event The difference between the set of possible outcomes and the set of actual outcomes of an event.

Complement of a set If E is a subset of a set X, then the set of all members of X that are not in E is the *complement* of E.

Complementary angles Two angles whose measures equal a sum of 90°. Each angle is the *complement* of the other.

Composite number A natural number greater than 1 that has more than two factors.

Composition When multiple transformations are applied to a figure.

Compound inequality Two inequalities joined by the word *and* or the word *or*.

Compound statement A statement formed by linking two or more simple statements.

Concave polygon A polygon in which at least one diagonal contains a point in the exterior of the polygon.

Conclusion In a conditional statement, the part that follows *then*. Also called *consequent*.

Conditional probability The probability of an event occurring given that some other event has already occurred.

Conditional statement A statement formed by connecting two statements with the words *if* and *then*.

Cone A three-dimensional figure that consists of a face bounded by a circle, called its *base*; a point called the *vertex* that is outside the plane of the base; and a *lateral surface* that connects the vertex to each point on the boundary of the base. The *height* of a cone is the length of a perpendicular segment drawn from the vertex to the plane of the base.

Congruent angles Angles that are equal in measure.

Congruent figures Figures that have the same shape and the same size.

Congruent polygons Polygons whose sides and angles can be placed in a correspondence so that corresponding sides are congruent and corresponding angles are congruent.

Congruent segments Segments that are equal in length.

Conjunction A compound statement that is formed by linking simple statements with the word *and*.

GLOSSARY

Consecutive angles of a polygon Two angles whose vertices are consecutive vertices of the polygon.

Consecutive integers Integers that differ by 1.

Consecutive sides of a polygon Two sides that have a common endpoint.

Consecutive vertices of a polygon Two vertices that are endpoints of the same side.

Consequent See *conclusion.*

Constant term A term that has no variable part. Also called a *constant*.

Constant of variation See *direct variation.*

Continued ratio A ratio that relates more than two numbers. Also called *extended ratio*.

Continuous data set A set of data that involves measurements such as length, weight, or temperature in which there is always another data value between any two given data values. The graph of a continuous data set is a line or a smooth curve with no holes or breaks.

Contrapositive of a conditional statement The statement that results when the hypothesis and conclusion are interchanged, then both negated.

Converse of a conditional statement The statement that results when the hypothesis and conclusion are interchanged.

Conversion factor A ratio of two measurements that is equal to one.

Convex polygon A polygon in which no diagonal contains a point in the exterior of the polygon.

Coordinate plane A number plane formed by a horizontal number line and a vertical number line that intersect at their origins.

Coordinate(s) of a point The real number or numbers that correspond to the point. On a number line, the coordinate of each point is a single number. On a coordinate plane, each point has an ordered pair (x, y) of coordinates. The first number of the ordered pair is called the *x-coordinate* of the point, and the second is called the *y-coordinate*. See also *Ruler Postulate*.

Coplanar figures Figures that lie on the same plane. Figures that do not lie on the same plane are called *noncoplanar figures*.

Corollary A theorem that follows directly from a previously proved theorem.

Correlation A measure of the relationship between two sets of numerical data. If both sets of data generally increase or decrease together, there is a *positive correlation*. If one set generally increases as the other decreases, there is a *negative correlation*. If there is no apparent relationship, there is *no correlation*.

Corresponding angles A pair of nonadjacent angles, one interior and one exterior, that are on the same side of a transversal.

Corresponding Angles Postulate If two parallel lines are cut by a transversal, then corresponding angles are congruent.

Corresponding Parts of Congruent Triangles Are Congruent Postulate If two triangles are congruent, then the corresponding sides and angles of the two triangles must also be congruent.

Cosine of an angle The cosine of an acute angle of a right triangle is the ratio of the length of the leg adjacent to the angle to the length of the hypotenuse. The symbol for the cosine of an angle A is $\cos A$.

Counterexample A particular instance that shows a general statement is not true for all values in the replacement set.

Counting number See *natural number.*

Cross products property of proportions For real numbers a, b, c and d, where $b \neq 0$ and $d \neq 0$, if $\frac{a}{b} = \frac{c}{d}$, then $ad = bc$. Also stated as *In a proportion, the product of the means equals the product of the extremes.*

Cube A prism whose faces are bounded by six congruent squares.

Cubic polynomial A polynomial of degree three.

Cumulative frequency histogram A histogram that displays the data from a cumulative frequency table.

Cumulative frequency table A summary of a data set in which each data value is paired with the sum of the frequencies of all values less than or equal to it.

Cylinder A three-dimensional figure that consists of two parallel *bases* bounded by congruent circles and a *lateral surface* that connects the circles. The *height* of a cylinder is the length of any perpendicular segment drawn from a point on one base to the plane containing the other base.

Data A collection of information, usually numerical.

Decagon A polygon that has exactly ten sides.

Definition A statement of the meaning of a word or phrase.

Degree measure of an angle A unique real number from 0 to 180 that is paired with the angle.

Degree of a polynomial The greatest degree of any of its terms after it has been simplified.

Degree of a term of a polynomial The sum of the exponents of all the variables in the term. For a polynomial in one variable, the degree of each term is the exponent of the variable in that term. The degree of a constant term is 0.

Degree of a vertex The number of edges that meet at a vertex in a vertex–edge graph.

Denominator In the fraction $\frac{a}{b}$, the number b is the denominator.

Dependent events Two events are dependent if the occurrence of one affects the occurrence of the other.

Dependent system of equations A system that has infinitely many solutions.

Dependent variable A variable whose value is affected by the value of another variable.

Diagonal of a polygon A segment whose endpoints are nonconsecutive vertices of the polygon.

Diameter of a circle A segment, or the length of the segment, whose endpoints are points of the circle and that contains the center of the circle.

Difference The result of a subtraction.

Difference of two squares The product that results from multiplying two binomials that are the sum and difference of the same two terms. Algebraically, $(a + b)(a - b) = a^2 - b^2$.

Dihedral tiling A tessellation made up of two different congruent figures.

Dilation A dilation with center O and *scale factor n*, where $n > 0$, is a transformation in which the image of a point A is a point A' such that point A' is on $\overrightarrow{OA}$ and $OA' = n \cdot OA$. The image of point O is point O. If $n > 1$, the dilation is an *enlargement*. If $0 < n < 1$, it is a *reduction*. A dilation is also called a *similarity transformation*.

Dimensional analysis A method for converting a measurement from one unit of measure to another by multiplying by a ratio representing the relationship between the units. The ratio is called a *conversion factor*.

Direct measurement See *indirect measurement*.

Direct variation A relationship described by an equation of the form $y = kx$, where k is a constant nonzero real number. The number k is called the *constant of variation*.

Discrete data set A set of data that involves a count, such as numbers of people or objects. The graph of a discrete data set consists of points that are not connected.

Discriminant of a quadratic equation For a quadratic equation of the form $ax^2 + bx + c = 0$, the discriminant is the expression $b^2 - 4ac$.

Disjunction A compound statement that is formed by linking simple statements with the word *or*.

Distance between a line and a point not on the line The length of the perpendicular segment from the line to the point.

Distance between two parallel lines The distance between one line and a point on the other line.

Distance between two points (number line) The absolute value of the difference of the coordinates of the points. See also *Ruler Postulate*.

Distance formula (coordinate plane) The distance PQ between $P(x_1, y_1)$ and $Q(x_2, y_2)$ is given by the formula $PQ = \sqrt{(x_2 - x_1)^2 + (y_2 - y_1)^2}$.

Distributive property For all real numbers a, b, and c, $a \cdot (b + c) = a \cdot b + a \cdot c$ and $(b + c) \cdot a = b \cdot a + c \cdot a$.

Dividend In a division, the number that is being divided. In the expression $a \div b$, a is the dividend.

Divisible One number is divisible by another if the second number divides the first with remainder 0.

Division property of equality For all real numbers a and b and all nonzero real numbers c, if $a = b$, then $\frac{a}{c} = \frac{b}{c}$.

Division property of inequality For all real numbers a, b, and c,

1. If $a < b$ and $c > 0$, then $\frac{a}{c} < \frac{b}{c}$;

   If $a < b$ and $c < 0$, then $\frac{a}{c} > \frac{b}{c}$; and

2. If $a > b$ and $c > 0$, then $\frac{a}{c} > \frac{b}{c}$;

   If $a > b$ and $c < 0$, then $\frac{a}{c} < \frac{b}{c}$.

Divisor In a division, the number by which you divide. In the expression $a \div b$, b is the divisor.

Dodecagon A polygon with exactly twelve sides.

Domain of a function See *function*.

Domain of a relation See *relation*.

Domain of a variable See *replacement set*.

Dot product The sum of the products of the corresponding elements of a row matrix and a column matrix.

E

Edge A line segment that joins two vertices.

Edge of a polyhedron A segment that is the intersection of two faces.

Element of a set See *member of a set*.

Elimination method See *addition-multiplication method*.

Empirical probability See *experimental probability*.

Endpoint See *segment* and *ray*.

Endpoint of a kite The common endpoint of a pair of congruent sides.

Enlargement See *dilation*.

Equally likely outcomes In a sample space, those outcomes that have the same probability.

Equation A statement that two mathematical expressions are equal.

Equiangular polygon A polygon whose angles are all congruent.

Equiangular triangle A triangle that has three congruent angles.

Equilateral polygon A polygon whose sides are all congruent.

Equilateral triangle A triangle that has three congruent sides.

Equivalent equations Equations that have the same solution set.

GLOSSARY

Equivalent expressions Expressions that name the same number.

Equivalent inequalities Inequalities that have the same solution set.

Equivalent systems Systems that have the same solution set.

Euler circuit An Euler path that begins and ends at the same vertex.

Euler path A path that traverses each edge of a vertex–edge graph exactly once.

Evaluate a variable expression To replace each variable in the expression with a value from its replacement set, then simplify the resulting numerical expression.

Even number A member of the set $\{\ldots, -4, -2, 0, 2, 4, \ldots\}$.

Event In probability, any set of outcomes that are in the sample space.

Excluded value Any value excluded from the domain of a variable because that value would result in a denominator of zero. The excluded values are said to be *restricted from the domain* of the variable.

Expected value The average of the possible outcomes in a sample space.

Experimental probability A probability determined by collecting data from an experiment. Also called *empirical probability*.

Explicit sequence A sequence of terms in which subsequent terms are defined in relation to the number of the term without regard to the value of the preceding term or terms.

Exponent When a number is written in the exponential form x^n, the number n is the exponent.

Exponential form The expression x^n is the exponential form of the nth power of x. When n is a natural number, $x^n = x \cdot x \cdot x \cdot \ldots \cdot x$, with n factors of x.

Exponential function A function in the form $y = ab^x$ where the variable is an exponent.

Extended ratio See *continued ratio*.

Exterior angle of a convex polygon An angle that forms a linear pair with one of the polygon's interior angles.

Extremes of a proportion In the proportion $\frac{a}{b} = \frac{c}{d}$, a and d are the extremes.

Face of a polyhedron One of its flat surfaces.

Factor of a multiplication One of a set of numbers to be multiplied. In the expression ab, a and b are the factors.

Factor a polynomial completely To express the polynomial as a product of one or more polynomials that cannot be factored further.

Factor of a whole number A natural number that divides the number with a remainder of 0.

Factorial notation The notation $n!$, which is read as "n factorial" and which represents the product $n \times (n-1) \times (n-2) \times \ldots \times 2 \times 1$. The value of 0! is defined to be 1.

Figure In geometry, any set of points.

First quartile In a numerical data set, the median of the data values that are less than the median of the entire set.

Fixed point A point that is its own image under a transformation.

FOIL method A procedure for multiplying two binomials: The product of two binomials is the sum of the product of the First terms within the parentheses, plus the product of the Outer terms, plus the product of the Inner terms, plus the product of the Last terms. Algebraically, $(a + b)(c + d) = ac + ad + bc + bd$.

Formula A literal equation in which each variable represents a quantity.

Foundation or base drawing A drawing which shows the base of a structure and the height of each part.

Frequency of a data value The number of times the value occurs in the data set.

Frequency table A summary of a set of data in which each data value is matched with its frequency.

Function A relationship in which every member of one set, called the *domain*, is assigned exactly one member of a second set, called the *range*.

Geometric construction A drawing that is made using only an unmarked *straightedge* and a *compass*. The straightedge is used to draw segments, rays, and lines. The compass is used to draw arcs and circles.

Geometric sequence When each term of the sequence varies by a constant quotient.

Graph of an equation or inequality in two variables The set of all points in the coordinate plane that correspond to solutions to the equation or inequality.

Graph of an inequality (number line) The set of the graphs of all solutions to the inequality.

Graph of a number The point that corresponds to the number on a number line.

Graph of an ordered pair The point that corresponds to the ordered pair on a coordinate plane.

Great circle Any circle in the plane that contains the center of the sphere.

Greatest common factor (GCF) of monomials The product of the greatest common factor of their numerical coefficients and the greatest common factor of their variable parts.

Greatest common factor (GCF) of natural numbers The greatest number that is a factor of each number in a set of two or more natural numbers.

Greatest integer function A step function that assigns to each real number the greatest integer that is less than or equal to that number.

Greatest possible error In a measurement, half the smallest unit on the measuring instrument.

Grouping symbol In a numerical or variable expression, a device that indicates certain operations are to be done before others. Common grouping symbols are parentheses, brackets, braces, fraction bars, radical signs, and absolute-value bars.

Half-turn A rotation of exactly 180°.

Height of a plane figure See *triangle, trapezoid, parallelogram.*

Height of a three-dimensional figure See *prism, cylinder, pyramid, cone.*

Hexagon A polygon that has exactly six sides.

Histogram A vertical bar graph of a frequency distribution. The bars represent equal intervals of the data, and there is no space between the bars.

Hypotenuse The side of a right triangle that is opposite the right angle.

Hypotenuse-Leg (HL) Congruence Theorem If the hypotenuse and one leg of a right triangle are congruent to the hypotenuse and one leg of another right triangle, then the triangles are congruent.

Hypothesis In a conditional statement, the part that follows *if.* Also called the *antecedent.*

Identity An equation that is true for all values of the variable(s).

Identity matrix A square matrix with the elements of the main diagonal equal to 1 and all other elements equal to 0.

Identity property of addition For all real numbers a, $a + 0 = a$ and $0 + a = a$. See also *additive identity.*

Identity property of multiplication For all real numbers a, $a \cdot 1 = a$ and $1 \cdot a = a$. See also *multiplicative identity.*

Image See *transformation.*

Inconsistent system of equations A system that has no solution.

Independent events Two events are independent if the occurrence of one does not affect the occurrence of the other.

Independent system of equations A system that has exactly one solution.

Independent variable A variable whose value is not affected by the value of another variable.

Indirect measurement Determining an unknown measurement by using mathematical relationships among known measurements rather than using a *direct measurement* tool such as a ruler or protractor.

Inequality A statement that consists of two expressions joined by an inequality symbol. Commonly used inequality symbols are $<, \leq, >, \geq$, and $\neq$.

Inscribed angle An angle inside a circle that is formed by three points that lie on the circle.

Integer A member of the set $\{\ldots, -3, -2, -1, 0, 1, 2, 3, \ldots\}$.

Intercepted arc The section of a circle that is between the endpoints of an inscribed angle.

Interior angle of a convex polygon An angle determined by two consecutive sides of the polygon. Also called an *angle of the polygon.*

Interquartile range The difference when the first quartile of a data set is subtracted from the third quartile.

Intersection of figures The set of all points common to two or more figures. The figures are said to *intersect* in these points.

Inverse of a conditional statement The statement that results when the hypothesis and conclusion are both negated.

Inverse matrix The matrix multiplied by a given, the product of which is an identity matrix.

Inverse property of addition For every real number a, there is a unique real number $-a$ such that $a + (-a) = 0$ and $-a + a = 0$; $-a$ is the *additive inverse* of a, or the *opposite* of a.

Inverse property of multiplication For every nonzero real number a, there is a unique real number $\frac{1}{a}$ such that $a \cdot \frac{1}{a} = 1$ and $\frac{1}{a} \cdot a = 1$; $\frac{1}{a}$ is the *multiplicative inverse* of a, or the *reciprocal* of a.

Inverse variation When two quantities are related such that a change in one produces the opposite type of change in the other.

Irrational number A number represented by a decimal that does not terminate and does not repeat.

Isometry A transformation in which a figure and its image are congruent.

Isosceles trapezoid A trapezoid whose legs are congruent.

Isosceles triangle A triangle that has at least two congruent sides, called the *legs.* The third side is the *base.* The angles opposite the congruent sides are called the *base angles.* The third angle is the *vertex angle.*

Isosceles Triangle Bisectors Theorem The bisector of the vertex angle of an isosceles triangle is the perpendicular bisector of the base.

Isosceles Triangle Theorem If two sides of a triangle are congruent, then the angles opposite those sides are congruent. Also stated as: *Base angles of an isosceles triangle are congruent.*

Kite A convex quadrilateral in which two distinct pairs of consecutive sides are congruent.

Lateral area of a prism or pyramid The sum of the areas of the lateral faces.

Lateral face See *prism*, *pyramid*.

Lateral surface See *cylinder*, *cone*.

Law of large numbers When an experiment is repeated many times, the proportion of each possible outcome will be close to its theoretical probability.

Leading coefficient of a polynomial The coefficient of the leading term.

Leading term of a polynomial In a polynomial in one variable, the term with the greatest degree.

Least common denominator (LCD) The least common multiple of the denominators of a set of fractions.

Least common multiple (LCM) of numbers The least number that is a multiple of each number in a set of two or more numbers.

Legs of an isosceles triangle See *isosceles triangle*.

Legs of a right triangle The sides opposite the acute angles.

Legs of a trapezoid The nonparallel sides.

Length of a segment The distance between the endpoints of the segment.

Like radicals Radical expressions with exactly the same radicand.

Like terms Terms that have exactly the same variable parts.

Line A set of points that extends in two opposite directions without end. This is one of the basic *undefined terms* of geometry.

Line graph A statistical display in which paired data are represented by points, the position of the points being determined by two axes labeled with numerical scales; the points are then connected in order with segments. Also called a *broken-line graph*.

Line Intersection Postulate If two lines intersect, then they intersect in exactly one point.

Line segment See *segment*.

Line symmetry A plane figure that has line symmetry is its own image after reflection across some line in the plane. The line is called a *line of symmetry* for the figure.

Linear equation in two variables For the variables x and y, any equation that can be written in the form $ax + by = c$, where a, b, and c are real numbers and a and b are not both 0. The equation $ax + by = c$ is called the *standard form* of a linear equation in two variables.

Linear inequality in two variables For the variables x and y, any inequality that can be written in the form $ax + by \geq c$, $ax + by > c$, $ax + by \leq c$, or $ax + by < c$, where a, b, and c are real numbers and a and b are not both 0.

Linear pair Adjacent angles whose noncommon sides are opposite rays.

Linear Pair Postulate If two angles form a linear pair, then they are supplementary.

Linear polynomial A polynomial of degree one.

Literal equation An equation that contains two or more variables.

Locus The set of all points that satisfy specified conditions. The plural of locus is *loci*.

Logically equivalent statements Statements that have the same truth values.

Lowest terms A fraction is in lowest terms if the GCF of its numerator and denominator is 1.

Matrix A rectangular array of numbers.

Maximum data value The greatest data value in a set of numerical data.

Maximum value of a quadratic function The y-coordinate of the vertex of the graph of a quadratic function described by $y = ax^2 + bx + c$, where $a < 0$.

Mean The sum of the data values in a numerical set of data, divided by the number of data values in the set. Also called *average*.

Means of a proportion In the proportion $\frac{a}{b} = \frac{c}{d}$, b and c are the means.

Measure of an angle See *degree measure of an angle*.

Measure of central tendency A statistic that is in some way representative or typical of a set of data. Commonly used measures of central tendency are the *mean*, the *median*, and the *mode*.

Median of a data set The middle data value in a set of data that has been arranged in numerical order. If the number of data values in the set is even, then the median is the average of the *two* middle data values.

Median of a triangle A segment whose endpoints are a vertex of the triangle and the midpoint of the opposite side.

Member of a set Any object in the set. Also called *element of a set*.

Midpoint of a segment The point that divides the segment into two congruent segments.

Midpoint formula The coordinates of the midpoint of the segment with endpoints $P(x_1, y_1)$ and $Q(x_2, y_2)$ are $\left(\frac{x_1 + x_2}{2}, \frac{y_1 + y_2}{2}\right)$.

Minimum data value The least data value in a set of numerical data.

Minimum value of a quadratic function The *y*-coordinate of the vertex of the graph of a quadratic function described by $y = ax^2 + bx + c$, where $a > 0$.

Mode In a data set, the data value(s) with the greatest frequency.

Monohedral tiling A tessellation made up of congruent copies of one figure.

Monomial A number, a variable, or a product of a number and one or more variables with nonnegative exponents.

Multiple of a number The result when the number is multiplied by a whole number.

Multiplication counting principle If there are *m* ways to make a selection and *n* ways to make a second selection, then there are *mn* ways to make the pair of selections. If there are *p* ways to make a third selection, then there are *mnp* ways to make the three selections.

Multiplication property of equality For all real numbers *a*, *b*, and *c*, if $a = b$, then $ac = bc$.

Multiplication property of inequality For all real numbers *a*, *b*, and *c*,

1. If $a < b$ and $c > 0$, then $ac < bc$;
   If $a < b$ and $c < 0$, then $ac > bc$; and
2. If $a > b$ and $c > 0$, then $ac > bc$;
   If $a > b$ and $c < 0$, then $ac < bc$.

Multiplicative identity One. When any given number is multiplied by 1, the product is identical to the given number. See also *identity property of multiplication*.

Multiplicative inverse See *inverse property of multiplication*.

Mutually exclusive events Events that have no outcomes in common.

Natural number A member of the set $\{1, 2, 3, 4, 5, 6, \ldots\}$. Also called *counting number*.

Negation of a statement The statement formed when the word *not* is inserted into or removed from a statement. The negation of a true statement is always false. The negation of a false statement is always true.

Negative correlation See *correlation*.

Negative number On a number line, a number that corresponds to a point on the negative side of zero. If the numbers increase in order from left to right, the negative side is to the left of zero.

Net A 2-dimensional model of a 3-dimensional figure.

Network See *Vertex-edge graph*.

***n*-gon** A polygon that has exactly *n* sides.

Nonagon A polygon that has exactly nine sides.

Number line A line whose points have been placed in one-to-one correspondence with the set of real numbers.

Numerator In the fraction $\frac{a}{b}$, the number *a* is the numerator.

Numerical coefficient See *coefficient of a term*.

Numerical expression A name for a number.

Obtuse angle An angle whose measure is greater than 90° and less than 180°.

Obtuse triangle A triangle that has one obtuse angle.

Octagon A polygon that has exactly eight sides.

Odd number A member of the set $\{\ldots, -5, -3, -1, 1, 3, 5, \ldots\}$.

Open half-plane Either of two regions into which a line separates a coordinate plane. The line is called the *boundary* of each half-plane.

Open statement A statement that contains one or more variables.

Opposite(s) Numbers that are the same distance from zero on a number line, but on opposite sides of zero. The symbol for the opposite of a number *n* is $-n$. See also *inverse property of addition*.

Opposite angles of a quadrilateral Two angles that are not consecutive.

Opposite rays On a line, if point *B* is between points *A* and *C*, then $\overrightarrow{BA}$ and $\overrightarrow{BC}$ are opposite rays.

Opposite sides of a quadrilateral Two sides that are not consecutive.

Ordered pair In a coordinate plane, the pair of real numbers (x, y) that corresponds to a point.

Ordinate The value of the *y*-coordinate in an ordered pair.

Origin of a coordinate plane The point where the axes intersect.

Origin of a number line The point that corresponds to the number zero.

Orthographic drawing A drawing that shows a top view, a front view, and a right view.

Overlapping figures Figures that have interior points in common.

Parabola The U-shaped curve that is the graph of a quadratic function.

Parallel lines Coplanar lines that do not intersect. The symbol for parallel is $\|$.

Parallel Postulate Through a point not on a line, there is exactly one line parallel to the given line.

Parallelogram A quadrilateral that has two pairs of parallel sides. To calculate area, any of the sides may be considered the *base*, and the length of that side is also called the base. The *height* is then the length of any perpendicular segment drawn from a point on the side opposite the base to the line containing the base.

Pascal's triangle An array of numbers arranged in rows beginning with 1 such that the terms in each subsequent row are the sum of the two terms in the previous row.

Path The sequence of connections between vertices.

Pentagon A polygon that has exactly five sides.

Percent Percent means "per 100," "out of 100," or "divided by 100". The symbol for percent is %.

Percent of change The percent an amount changes from an original amount. The change may be a *percent of increase* or a *percent of decrease*.

Percentile rank If n percent of the data values in a set are less than or equal to a given data value, then n is the percentile rank of that data value.

Perfect square A number whose square roots are rational numbers.

Perfect square trinomial A trinomial that results from squaring a binomial. The form of the square of a binomial sum is $(a + b)^2 = a^2 + 2ab + b^2$. For a binomial difference, $(a - b)^2 = a^2 - 2ab + b^2$.

Perimeter of a plane figure The distance around the figure. The perimeter of a polygon is the sum of the lengths of its sides.

Period The interval over which a periodic function repeats itself.

Periodic function A function whose graph repeats itself over and over on an interval of a fixed length.

Permutation An arrangement of some or all objects from a set in a specific order.

Perpendicular bisector of a segment Any line, ray, or segment that is perpendicular to the segment at its midpoint.

Perpendicular lines Lines that intersect to form right angles. The symbol for perpendicular is $\perp$.

Perpendicular Transversal Theorem If a transversal is perpendicular to one of two parallel lines, then it is perpendicular to the other.

Plane A set of points that extends along a flat surface in every direction without end. This is one of the basic *undefined terms* of geometry.

Plane figure A figure whose points all lie in the same plane.

Plane Intersection Postulate If two planes intersect, then they intersect in a line.

Point A location. This one of the basic *undefined terms* of geometry.

Point-slope form of an equation of a line For an equation in the variables x and y, the point-slope form is $y - y_1 = m(x - x_1)$, where $P(x_1, y_1)$ is a point on the line and m is the slope of the line.

Point symmetry A plane figure that has point symmetry is its own image after a half-turn in the plane.

Polygon A plane figure formed by three or more segments such that each segment intersects exactly two others, one at each endpoint, and no two segments with a common endpoint are collinear. Each segment is a *side* of the polygon. The common endpoint of two sides is a *vertex* of the polygon. A polygon completely encloses a region of the plane, called its *interior*.

Polygon Exterior Angle-Sum Theorem The sum of the measures of the exterior angles of a convex polygon, one at each vertex, is 360°.

Polygon Interior Angle-Sum Theorem The sum of the measures of the interior angles of a convex polygon that has n sides is $(n - 2)180°$.

Polyhedron A three-dimensional figure formed by flat surfaces that are bounded by polygons joined in pairs along their sides.

Polynomial A monomial or a sum of monomials.

Population In a statistical study, the set of all individuals or objects being studied.

Positive correlation See *correlation*.

Positive number On a number line, a number that corresponds to a point on the positive side of zero. If the numbers increase in order from left to right, the positive side is to the right of zero.

Postulate A statement whose truth is accepted without proof.

Power The simplified form of x^n. For example, since $2^5 = 32$, 32 is the fifth power of 2.

Power of a power property of exponents For all integers m and n and all nonzero real numbers a, $(a^m)^n = a^{mn}$.

Power of a product property of exponents For all integers m and all nonzero real numbers a and b, $(ab)^m = a^m b^m$.

Power of a quotient property of exponents For all integers m and all nonzero real numbers a and b, $\left(\frac{a}{b}\right)^m = \frac{a^m}{b^m}$.

Precision The level of accuracy of a measurement.

Preimage See *transformation*.

Prime factorization An expression that shows a natural number as a product of prime numbers.

Prime number A natural number greater than 1 that has exactly two factors, 1 and the number itself.

Principal square root The positive square root of a number.

Prism A polyhedron with two parallel faces, called its *bases*, that are bounded by congruent polygons; and with *lateral faces* that are bounded by parallelograms connecting corresponding sides of the bases. The *height* of a prism is the length of any perpendicular segment drawn from a point on one base to the plane containing the other base.

Probability A number from 0 to 1, inclusive, that represents the likelihood an event will occur. If an event is *impossible*, its probability is 0. If an event is *certain*, its probability is 1. Events that are *possible but not certain* are assigned probabilities between 0 and 1.

Probability distribution For a given sample space, a table that pairs each value of the random variable with its probability.

Product The result of a multiplication.

Product of powers property of exponents For all integers m and n and all nonzero real numbers a, $a^m \cdot a^n = a^{m+n}$.

Product property of square roots If a and b are real numbers with $a \geq 0$ and $b \geq 0$, then $\sqrt{ab} = \sqrt{a} \cdot \sqrt{b}$.

Proportion A statement that two ratios are equal. The proportion that equates the ratios "a to b" and "c to d" can be written in three ways:

a is to b as c is to d $\quad a : b = c : d \quad \frac{a}{b} = \frac{c}{d}$

Protractor Postulate Let $\overrightarrow{OA}$ and $\overrightarrow{OB}$ be opposite rays. Consider $\overrightarrow{OA}, \overrightarrow{OB}$, and all the rays with endpoint O that can be drawn in a plane on one side of $\overleftrightarrow{AB}$. These rays can be paired with the real numbers from 0 to 180, one-to-one, in such a way that:

- $\overrightarrow{OA}$ is paired with 0 and $\overrightarrow{OB}$ is paired with 180.
- If $\overrightarrow{OP}$ is paired with x and $\overrightarrow{OQ}$ is paired with y, then the number paired with $\angle POQ$ is $|x - y|$. This is called the *measure*, or the *degree measure*, of $\angle POQ$.

Pyramid A polyhedron that consists of a face bounded by a polygon, called its *base*; a point called the *vertex* that is outside the plane of the base; and triangular *lateral faces* that connect the vertex to each side of the base. The *height* of a pyramid is the length of the perpendicular segment drawn from the vertex to the plane of the base.

Pythagorean Theorem If a triangle is a right triangle with legs of lengths a and b and hypotenuse of length c, then $a^2 + b^2 = c^2$.

Pythagorean triple Any set of three positive integers that satisfy the relationship $a^2 + b^2 = c^2$.

Quadrant One of the four regions into which a coordinate plane is divided by the x- and y-axes.

Quadratic equation An equation that can be written in the form $ax^2 + bx + c = 0$, where a, b, and c are real numbers and $a \neq 0$. The equation $ax^2 + bx + c = 0$ is called the *standard form* of a quadratic equation in x.

Quadratic formula A method for determining the solution set of a quadratic equation in one variable. If $ax^2 + bx + c = 0$, and a, b, and c are real numbers with $a \neq 0$, then $x = \frac{-b \pm \sqrt{b^2 - 4ac}}{2a}$.

Quadratic function A function that can be represented by an equation of the form $y = ax^2 + bx + c$, where a, b, and c are real numbers and $a \neq 0$.

Quadratic polynomial A polynomial of degree two.

Quadrilateral A polygon that has exactly four sides.

Quadrilateral Angle-Sum Theorem The sum of the measures of the interior angles of a quadrilateral is 360°.

Quartile See *first quartile, third quartile.*

Quotient The result of dividing one number by another.

Quotient of powers property of exponents For all integers m and n and all nonzero real numbers a, $\frac{a^m}{a^n} = a^{m-n}$.

Quotient property of square roots If a and b are real numbers with $a \geq 0$ and $b > 0$, then $\sqrt{\frac{a}{b}} = \frac{\sqrt{a}}{\sqrt{b}}$.

Radical equation An equation that contains one or more radical expressions with variables in the radicand.

Radical expression An expression that contains a radical sign. The square root symbol, $\sqrt{}$, is an example of a radical sign.

Radicand An expression under a radical sign.

Radius of a circle A segment, or the length of the segment, whose endpoints are the center of the circle and a point of the circle. See also *circle.*

Radius of a sphere See *sphere.*

Random variable In probability, a variable that represents the outcomes in a sample space.

Range of a data set In a set of numerical data, the difference when the minimum data value is subtracted from the maximum data value.

Range of a function See *function.*

Range of a relation See *relation.*

Rate A ratio that compares two different types of measures.

Ratio A comparison of two numbers by division. *The ratio of a to b* can be written in three ways:

a to $b \qquad a : b \qquad \frac{a}{b}$

Rational equation An equation that contains one or more rational expressions.

Rational expression An expression that can be written in the form $\frac{P}{Q}$, where P and Q are polynomials and the value of Q is not zero.

Rational number A number that can be expressed in the form $\frac{a}{b}$, where a and b are integers and $b \neq 0$.

Ray Part of a line that begins at one point and extends without end in one direction. The point is called the *endpoint of the ray.*

Real number A number that is either a rational number or an irrational number.

Reciprocal Two numbers are reciprocals if their product is 1. See also *inverse property of multiplication.*

GLOSSARY

Rectangle A quadrilateral that has four right angles.

Recursive formula An algorithm used to identify terms in a recursive sequence.

Recursive sequence A sequence of terms in which subsequent terms are defined in relation to the preceding term or terms in the sequence.

Reduction See *dilation*.

Reflection in a line A reflection in line m is a transformation such that, if point A is on line m, then the image of point A is point A; and if point B is not on line m, then its image B' is the point such that line m is the perpendicular bisector of $\overline{BB'}$. Line m is called the *line of reflection*.

Reflection in a point A reflection in point P is a transformation such that the image of point P is point P; and the image of any other point Q is the point Q' such that point P is the midpoint of $\overline{QQ'}$. Point P is called the *point of reflection*.

Reflexive property of equality For all real numbers a, $a = a$.

Regular polygon A polygon that is both equilateral and equiangular.

Regular polyhedron All of the faces of a polyhedron are regular polygons that are congruent to each other.

Regular pyramid A pyramid whose base is bounded by a regular polygon and in which the segment joining the center of the base to the vertex is perpendicular to the plane of the base. The lateral faces of a regular pyramid are congruent isosceles triangles.

Relation Any correspondence between two sets, called the *domain* and *range* of the relation.

Relatively prime Two natural numbers are relatively prime if their greatest common factor is 1.

Remote interior angles For each exterior angle of a triangle, the two nonadjacent interior angles are called remote interior angles.

Repeating decimal A decimal in which a digit or a block of digits repeats without end. The symbol for a repeating decimal is a bar over the repeating digit(s).

Replacement set The set of numbers that a variable may represent. Also called the *domain of a variable*.

Rhombus A quadrilateral that has four congruent sides.

Right angle An angle whose measure is 90°.

Right cone A cone in which the segment joining the center of the base to the vertex is perpendicular to the plane of the base. If a cone is not a right cone, then it is called *oblique*.

Right cylinder A cylinder in which the segment joining the centers of the bases is perpendicular to the planes of the bases. If a cylinder is not a right cylinder, then it is called *oblique*.

Right prism A prism in which the segments that connect corresponding vertices of the bases are perpendicular to the planes of the bases. The lateral faces of a right prism are bounded by rectangles. If a prism is not a right prism, then it is called *oblique*.

Right triangle A triangle with one right angle.

Root A solution to a quadratic equation.

Rotation A rotation of $x°$ about point O is a transformation such that the image of point O is point O; and for any other point P, its image is the point P' such that $\overline{OP} = \overline{OP'}$ and $m\angle POP' = x°$. Point O is called the *center of rotation*. The direction of rotation is specified as *clockwise* or *counterclockwise*.

Rotational symmetry A plane figure that has rotational symmetry is its own image after a rotation of 180° or less around some point in the plane. The point is called the *center of symmetry* for the figure.

Row matrix A $1 \times n$ matrix, meaning there is only one row with n number of elements.

Ruler Postulate The points of a line can be paired with the real numbers, one-to-one, so that any point corresponds to 0 and any other point corresponds to 1. The real number that corresponds to a point is the *coordinate* of that point. The *distance* between two points is equal to the absolute value of the difference of their coordinates.

Same-Side Interior Angles Theorem If two parallel lines are cut by a transversal, then interior angles on the same side of the transversal are supplementary.

Sample In a statistical study, a subset of the population being studied.

Sample space The set of all possible outcomes in a given situation.

Scalar A number by which a matrix is multiplied.

Scale drawing A two-dimensional drawing that is similar to the object it represents. The ratio of the size of the drawing to the actual size of the object is the *scale* of the drawing.

Scale factor See *similarity ratio*, *dilation*.

Scalene triangle A triangle that has no congruent sides.

Scatter plot A statistical display of the relationship between two sets of data in which ordered pairs of the data are represented by points, the position of the points being determined by two axes labeled with numerical scales. See also *correlation*.

Scientific notation A number is written in scientific notation when it is written in the form $a \times 10^n$, where $1 \le a < 10$ and n is an integer.

Secant A line, ray, or segment, that intersects a circle at 2 points.

Sector of a circle The part of a circle formed by two radii and the arc they intercept.

Segment Part of a line that begins at one point and ends at another. The points are called the *endpoints of the segment.* Also called *line segment.*

Segment Addition Postulate If point C is between point A and point B, then $AC + CB = AB$.

Segment bisector Any line, ray, or segment that intersects a given segment at its midpoint.

Semicircle Half of a circle.

Set A group of objects.

Side of an angle One of the two rays that form the angle.

Side of an equation One of two mathematical expressions that are joined by an equals sign.

Side of an inequality One of two mathematical expressions that are joined by an inequality symbol.

Side of a polygon See *polygon.*

Side-Angle-Side (SAS) Congruence Postulate If two sides and the included angle of one triangle are congruent to two sides and the included angle of another triangle, then the triangles are congruent.

Side-Angle-Side (SAS) Similarity Theorem If an angle of one triangle is congruent to an angle of another triangle, and the lengths of the sides including these angles are in proportion, then the triangles are similar.

Side-Side-Side (SSS) Congruence Postulate If three sides of one triangle are congruent to three sides of another triangle, then the triangles are congruent.

Side-Side-Side (SSS) Similarity Theorem If corresponding sides of two triangles are in proportion, then the triangles are similar.

Side-Splitter Theorem If a line is parallel to one side of a triangle and intersects the other two sides at distinct points, then it divides those two sides proportionally.

Signed numbers Positive and negative numbers.

Significant digits Numbers that make a contribution to a value.

Similar figures Figures that have the same shape, but not necessarily the same size.

Similar polygons Polygons whose sides and angles can be placed in a correspondence so that corresponding angles are congruent and corresponding sides are in proportion.

Similarity ratio The ratio of the lengths of corresponding sides of similar polygons. Also called the *scale factor.*

Similarity transformation See *dilation.*

Simplest form of a radical expression The form of the expression in which the radicand contains no perfect-square factors other than 1; the radicand contains no fractions; and no denominator contains a radical.

Simplify a numerical expression To give the most common name for the number the expression represents.

Simplify a variable expression To perform as many of the indicated operations as possible.

Sine of an angle The sine of an acute angle of a right triangle is the ratio of the length of the leg opposite the angle to the length of the hypotenuse. The symbol for the sine of an angle A is $\sin A$.

Skew lines Lines that are noncoplanar.

Slant height of a regular pyramid The height of a lateral face.

Slant height of a right cone The distance between the vertex of the cone and any point on the boundary of the base.

Slope On a coordinate plane, the steepness of a nonvertical line, described informally as $\frac{\text{rise}}{\text{run}}$. Formally, if $P(x_1, y_1)$ and $Q(x_2, y_2)$ lie on $\overleftrightarrow{PQ}$, and $x_1 \neq x_2$, then the slope m of $\overleftrightarrow{PQ}$ is defined by $m = \frac{y_2 - y_1}{x_2 - x_1}$.

Slope-intercept form of an equation of a line For an equation in the variables x and y, $y = mx + b$, where m is the slope of the graph and b is the y-intercept.

Solution to an equation or inequality in two variables For an equation or inequality in the variables x and y, any ordered pair of numbers (x, y) that together make the equation or inequality a true statement.

Solution to an open statement Any value of the variable(s) that makes the statement true.

Solution set of an open statement The set of all solutions to the open statement.

Solution to a system of equations or inequalities in two variables For a system in the variables x and y, any ordered pair (x, y) that is a solution to each equation or inequality in the system.

Solve an equation or inequality To find the solution set of the equation or inequality.

Space In geometry, the set of all points.

Space figure A figure whose points extend beyond a single plane into space. Also called a *three-dimensional figure.*

Sphere The set of all points in space that are a fixed distance from a fixed point. The fixed point is called the *center of the sphere.* The fixed distance is called the *radius of the sphere.*

Square A quadrilateral that has four congruent sides and four right angles.

Square of a number The second power of the number.

Square root If $a^2 = b$, then a is a square root of b. The positive square root is denoted $\sqrt{b}$. The negative square root is denoted $-\sqrt{b}$.

Standard form of an equation of a circle For a circle with center $P(h, k)$ and radius r, the equation is $(x - h)^2 + (y - k)^2 = r^2$. If P is the origin, the equation becomes $x^2 + y^2 = r^2$.

Standard form of a linear equation in two variables See *linear equation in two variables.*

GLOSSARY

Standard form of a polynomial A polynomial in one variable is in standard form when it has no like terms and the terms are written in descending order.

Standard form of a quadratic equation See *quadratic equation.*

Statement Any mathematical sentence.

Statistics The branch of mathematics that deals with the gathering, organization, analysis, representation, and interpretation of data.

Stem-and-leaf plot A display of data in which digits with higher place values are listed in a column as *stems*; digits with lower place values are listed in rows as *leaves* extending from the corresponding stems.

Step function Functions that result in graphs that are not continuous.

Straight angle An angle whose measure is 180°.

Substitution method A method used to solve a system of equations in which one equation is solved for one variable in terms of the other. Then this expression is substituted for that variable in the other equation.

Substitution principle If $a = b$, then a may be replaced by b in any expression.

Subtraction property of equality For all real numbers a, b, and c, if $a = b$, then $a - c = b - c$.

Subtraction property of inequality For all real numbers a, b, and c,

- If $a < b$, then $a - c < b - c$; and
- If $a > b$, then $a - c > b - c$.

Sum The result of an addition.

Supplementary angles Two angles whose measures have a sum of 180°. Each angle is the *supplement* of the other.

Surface area The total area of all surfaces of a three-dimensional figure.

Symmetric property of equality For all real numbers a and b, if $a = b$, then $b = a$.

System of equations or inequalities in two variables A set of equations or inequalities in the same two variables.

Tangent of an angle The tangent of an acute angle of a right triangle is the ratio of the length of the leg opposite the angle to the length of the leg adjacent to it. The symbol for the tangent of an angle A is tan A.

Term of an expression A number, a variable, or a product or quotient of numbers and variables.

Terminating decimal A decimal that stops, or terminates.

Terms of a proportion The numbers that form the proportion. In $\frac{a}{b} = \frac{c}{d}$, a, b, c, and d are the terms.

Tessellation or tiling A covering of the plane with congruent copies of the same region with no holes and no overlaps.

Theorem A statement that can be proved true.

Theoretical probability If an event E contains m favorable outcomes in a sample space that consists of n outcomes, then the theoretical probability of E, denoted $P(E)$, is given by the formula $P(E) = \frac{m}{n}$.

Third quartile In a numerical data set, the median of the data values that are greater than the median of the entire set.

Three-dimensional figure See *space figure.*

Transformation A correspondence between one figure, called a *preimage*, and a second figure, called its *image*, such that each point of the image is paired with exactly one point of the preimage, and each point of the preimage is paired with exactly one point of the image.

Transitive property of equality For all real numbers a, b, and c, if $a = b$ and $b = c$, then $a = c$.

Transitive property of inequality For all real numbers a, b, and c,

1. If $a < b$ and $b < c$, then $a < c$; and
2. If $a > b$ and $b > c$, then $a > c$.

Transitivity of Parallelism Theorem If two lines are parallel to a third line, then the lines are parallel to each other.

Translation A transformation in which the image is the figure that would result if each point of the preimage were moved the same distance and in the same direction.

Transversal A line that intersects two or more coplanar lines at different points.

Trapezoid A quadrilateral that has exactly one pair of parallel sides. The parallel sides, and the lengths of the parallel sides, are called the *bases*. Two angles of the trapezoid whose vertices are the endpoints of a single base are a pair of *base angles*. The *height* is the length of any perpendicular segment drawn from a point on one base to the line containing the other base.

Traversable A graph is said to be traversable if a path can connect each vertex of the graph to at least one other vertex without traveling the same path twice.

Tree diagram A visual method of displaying all the outcomes in a sample space by using a network of "branches" that together resemble a tree.

Trend line On a scatter plot, a line around which the data points seem to cluster. The trend line can be used to analyze the correlation between the data sets.

Triangle A polygon that has exactly three sides. To calculate area, any of the sides may be considered the *base*, and the length of that side is also called the base. The *height* is then the length of the altitude drawn to the base from the opposite vertex.

Triangle Angle-Sum Theorem The sum of the measures of the angles of a triangle is 180°.

Triangle Exterior-Angle Theorem The measure of each exterior angle of a triangle is equal to the sum of the measures of the remote interior angles.

Triangle Inequality Theorem The sum of the lengths of any two sides of a triangle is greater than the length of the third side.

Trinomial A polynomial with exactly three terms.

Truth value A closed statement is either *true* or *false*. These are its possible truth values.

Turning point of a parabola See *vertex of a parabola*.

Two Perpendiculars Theorem If two coplanar lines are perpendicular to a third line, then the lines are parallel.

Two-point form of an equation of a line For an equation in the variables x and y, $y - y_1 = \frac{y_2 - y_1}{x_2 - x_1}(x - x_1)$ where $P(x_1, y_1)$ and $Q(x_2, y_2)$ lie on a nonvertical line.

Undefined term A term that is used without a specific mathematical definition. In geometry, the three undefined terms are *point*, *line*, and *plane*.

Unequal Angles Theorem If two angles of a triangle are not congruent, then the side opposite the larger of the two angles is longer than the side opposite the smaller angle.

Unequal Sides Theorem If two sides of a triangle are not congruent, then the angle opposite the longer of the two sides is larger than the angle opposite the shorter side.

Unique Line Postulate Through any two points there is exactly one line. Also stated as: *Two points determine a line.*

Unique Plane Postulate Through any three noncollinear points there is exactly one plane. Also stated as: *Three noncollinear points determine a plane.*

Unit rate A rate per one unit of a measure. An example of a familiar unit rate is *miles per hour*.

Value of a function A member of the range of the function.

Value of a variable Any number in the replacement set of the variable.

Variable A letter that represents a number.

Variable expression An expression that contains at least one variable. Also called *algebraic expression*.

Vector A quantity that has magnitude and direction.

Venn diagram A diagram in which a rectangle represents all members of a set, with circles within it showing selected subsets and relationships among them.

Vertex angle of an isosceles triangle The angle opposite the base of an isosceles triangle. See *isosceles triangle*.

Vertex of an angle The common endpoint of the sides.

Vertex of a cone See *cone*.

Vertex-edge graph A graph in which the vertices are connected by edges to form a path.

Vertex of a parabola For a parabola that opens upward, its vertex is its lowest point. For a parabola that opens downward, its vertex is its highest point. Also called the *turning point* of the parabola.

Vertex of a polygon See *polygon*.

Vertex of a polyhedron A point that is the intersection of three or more edges.

Vertex of a pyramid See *pyramid*.

Vertical angles Two angles whose sides form two pairs of opposite rays.

Vertical Angles Theorem If two angles are vertical angles, then they are congruent.

Vertical-line test If every vertical line that intersects a graph intersects that graph in exactly one point, then the graph represents a function.

Volume of a three-dimensional figure The amount of space the figure encloses, measured by the number of nonoverlapping cubic units in its interior.

Whole number A member of the set $\{0, 1, 2, 3, 4, 5, 6, \ldots\}$.

x-axis The horizontal number line in a coordinate plane.

x-coordinate See *coordinate(s) of a point*.

x-intercept of a graph The x-coordinate of any point where the graph intersects the x-axis.

y-axis The vertical number line in a coordinate plane.

y-coordinate See *coordinate(s) of a point*.

y-intercept of a graph The y-coordinate of any point where the graph intersects the y-axis.

Zero-product property If a and b are real numbers and $ab = 0$, then either $a = 0$ or $b = 0$.

Algebra I Sample Test I

Part I

DIRECTIONS FOR QUESTIONS 1–28: Solve the following items. For multiple-choice items, select the best answer choice. For all other items, show your work and clearly explain your answer. Calculators may NOT be used in Part 1.

1 Which of the following expressions has a positive value?

A. $-6(5 - 2)$ **B.** $-6(2 - 5)$

C. $6(2 - 5)$ **D.** $6(-5 - 2)$

2 Find the value of $\frac{2(a - 4b + c)}{b^2 - 5a}$ for $a = 2$, $b = -5$, and $c = 8$.

A. -4 **B.** $-\frac{12}{7}$ **C.** $-\frac{4}{3}$ **D.** 4

3 Based on the examples $4^2 = 16$ and $(-4)^2 = 16$, David reached the following conclusion: "The square of a number is always greater than the number." Is David correct? If yes, justify your answer. If no, provide a counterexample.

4 After working for two weeks, Nita put 11% of her income in savings. Her friend Pat saved 8% of her income during the same time period. If each put \$22 in savings, how much more did Pat earn than Nita?

A. \$34 **B.** \$66 **C.** \$75 **D.** \$733

5 The graph matches the solution set of which of the following inequalities?

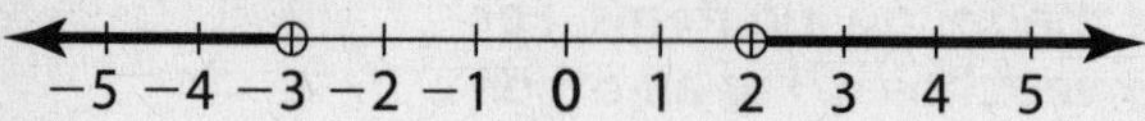

A. $|x| > 2$ **B.** $|x| + 1 > 4$

C. $|x + 3| > 5$ **D.** $|2x + 1| > 5$

6 A soccer team won $\frac{3}{8}$ of its games. If it lost 8 more games than it won, how many games did the team play?

A. 20 **B.** 32 **C.** 44 **D.** 64

7 A line with slope $-\frac{1}{4}$ passes through points $A(1, -2)$ and $B(-2, n)$. What is the y-coordinate of point B?

A. $-\frac{5}{4}$ **B.** $-\frac{4}{5}$ **C.** $\frac{4}{5}$ **D.** $\frac{5}{4}$

8 The domain of $f(x) = x^2 - 1$ is $\{-3, -2, 0, 1, 3\}$. What is the range?

A. $\{-8, -3, -1, 0, 1, 3, 8\}$ **B.** $\{-8, -3, -1, 1, 8\}$

C. $\{-1, 0, 3, 8\}$ **D.** the set of all real numbers

9 The vertex of the graph of $y = |x|$ is $(0, 0)$. Which of the following changes to the equation moves the vertex of the graph to $(2, 3)$?

A. $y = |x - 2| + 3$ **B.** $y = |x + 2| + 3$

C. $y = |x - 3| + 2$ **D.** $y = |x + 3| + 2$

10 Which of the following is the equation of a line that is perpendicular to the line shown on the graph?

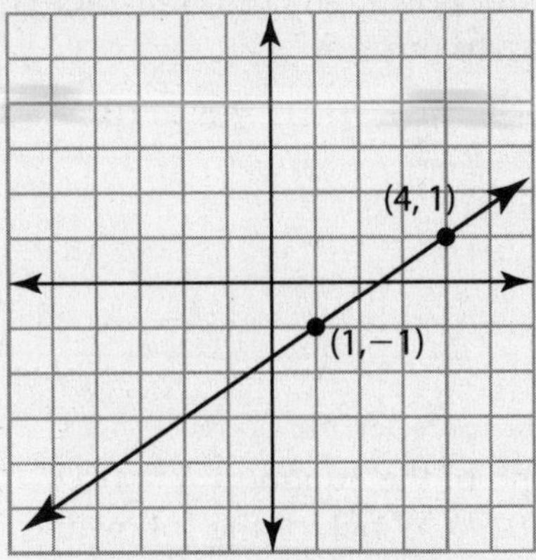

A. $y = \frac{2}{3}x - \frac{5}{3}$

B. $y = -\frac{2}{3}x - \frac{5}{3}$

C. $y = \frac{2}{3}x + \frac{3}{5}$

D. $y = -\frac{3}{2}x + \frac{3}{5}$

11 Sujean and Jeni are having a conversation about their weekly earnings. Sujean says, "The sum of your pay and twice mine is $840." Jeni says, "The sum of your pay and twice mine is $900." Based on their statements, how much do Sujean and Jeni earn together each week?

A. $420 **B.** $560 **C.** $580 **D.** $600

12 A boat took 2 hours to make a trip down a river. The same boat took 10 hours to make the return trip upstream. The river current is moving at a constant rate of 8 miles per hour. What is the average speed of the boat in still water?

A. 8 miles per hour

B. 10 miles per hour

C. 12 miles per hour

D. 14 miles per hour

13 Which of the following simplifies the expression $\frac{a^{-2}b^{-5}c}{a^4b^{-2}c^{-3}}$ using only positive exponents?

A. $\frac{a^8b^{10}}{c^3}$ **B.** $\frac{a^2c^2}{b^7}$ **C.** $\frac{b^{10}}{a^8b^3}$ **D.** $\frac{c^4}{a^6b^3}$

14 Large distances are measured in light years. The distance to the Andromeda Galaxy is 2.3×10^6 light years while the distance to our own sun is only 1.6×10^{-5} light years. About how many times farther is the distance to the Andromeda Galaxy than to our sun?

A. 1.4×10^{11} **B.** 7.0×10^{10} **C.** 1.4×10^1 **D.** 3.6×10^{-30}

15 The calculator screen below displays a graph of the equation: $y = 0.5^x$. Suppose the equation is changed to $y = 4(0.5^x)$. Which of the following best describes how the graph would change?

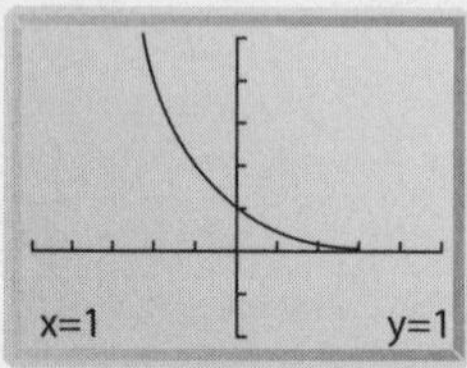

A. The graph would be steeper and intercept the y-axis at a higher point.

B. The graph would be less steep and intercept the y-axis at a lower point.

C. The graph would be steeper, rise from left to right, and intercept the y-axis at a higher point.

D. The graph would be less steep, rise from left to right, and intercept the y-axis at a lower point.

16 If you take a certain number and decrease it by 3, and then square the result, you will have 16. There are two different numbers that will work in this situation. What are they?

A. -7 and -1 **B.** -4 and 7 **C.** -1 and 1 **D.** -1 and 7

17 Simplify the following:

$$(-3x^2y + 2xy - 8) - (-2x^2y + 5xy - 4x + 5)$$

A. $5x^2y + 3xy - 4x - 3$

B. $x^2y - 3xy + 4x - 3$

C. $x^2y - 3xy + 4x - 13$

D. $-x^2y - 3xy + 4x - 13$

18 The area of a rectangular frame can be represented by the expression $2x^2 + 7x - 15$. If the width can be expressed as $x + 5$, which of the following expressions represents the length of the frame?

A. $2x + 3$ **B.** $2x - 3$ **C.** $4x - 3$ **D.** $6x + 3$

19 **Part A** For the quadratic equation below, determine the vertex of the parabola and whether the graph of the equation will open upwards or downward. Explain your reasoning.

$$y = -3x^2 - 12x - 5$$

Part B Determine points on both sides of the vertex and graph the parabola. Show all your work.

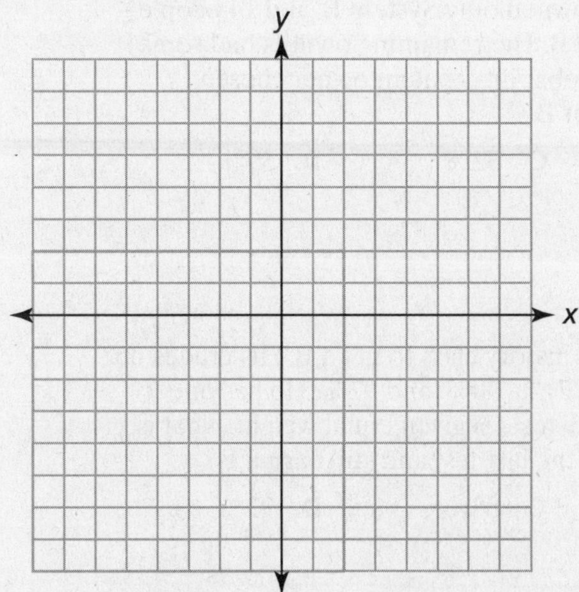

20 The equation of circle P is $(x + 2)^2 + (y - 6)^2 = 25$. Describe the circle by finding its center and its radius.

21 Joan is making sack lunches for a shelter. Working by herself, she estimates that it will take her 4 hours to make the lunches. If Peter helps her, she should be able to finish in $2\frac{1}{2}$ hours. How many hours would it take Peter to make the lunches by himself?

A. $1\frac{1}{2}$ **B.** $3\frac{2}{3}$ **C.** 5 **D.** $6\frac{2}{3}$

22 A projectile is launched upward from a platform 60 feet in the air. If its initial velocity is 68 feet per second, its distance above its starting point t seconds after it is launched can be modeled using the quadratic equation: $d(t) = -16t^2 + 68t + 60$. After how many seconds does the projectile hit the ground?

A. 8 **B.** 5 **C.** 4 **D.** 1

23 In a survey of 200 game system owners, a magazine finds that 76 people owned only System A, 60 people owned only System B, and 14 people owned both System A and System B. The remaining owners had some other game system. What is the probability that an owner chosen randomly does not own either A or B?

A. 22% **B.** 25% **C.** 32% **D.** 39%

24 Tony needs an 82% average in his history class to get a B. His grades on the first five tests were 76%, 75%, 71%, 90%, and 92%. He has one more test left to take. If each of the tests is given equal weight, what is the minimum grade he can get on the last test and still earn a B?

A. 83% **B.** 85% **C.** 88% **D.** 92%

25 Which of the following equations has no real number solution?

A. $\frac{2}{x} = \frac{x}{2}$

B. $\frac{x + 4}{6} = \frac{2}{x}$

C. $\frac{x}{-4} = \frac{4}{x}$

D. $\frac{5}{x} = \frac{x}{25}$

26 Find the sum. Write your answer in simplified form using positive exponents. Show all your work.

$$\frac{1}{c + d} + \frac{1}{c - d}$$

27 Sharon, Nita, and Diane are in student government. The principal plans to choose 3 school officers to attend a conference at the state capital. If there are 5 school officers in all, what is the probability that Sharon, Nita, and Diane will be selected?

A. $\frac{1}{20}$ **B.** $\frac{1}{10}$ **C.** $\frac{3}{10}$ **D.** $\frac{3}{5}$

28 A teacher gives the same 20-point quiz to two different classes. Then she finds the mean, median, and mode for each class. Her results are shown below.

Class A		Class B	
Mean:	14.2	Mean:	15.5
Median:	16	Median:	16
Mode:	17	Mode:	16

From the data, the teacher concludes that Class B has a greater number of high-achieving students. Do you agree with the teacher's conclusion? Support your argument.

Part 2

DIRECTIONS FOR QUESTIONS 29–57: Solve the following items. For multiple-choice items, select the best answer choice. For all other items, show your work and clearly explain your answer. Calculators may be used in Part 2.

29 Which choice lists the following values in order from least to greatest?

$$4.\overline{3} \quad -\tfrac{9}{2} \quad -2.1^2 \quad \tfrac{3}{10}$$

A. $-\frac{9}{2}, \frac{3}{10}, 4.\overline{3}, -2.1^2$

B. $-2.1^2, -\frac{9}{2}, \frac{3}{10}, 4.\overline{3}$

C. $-\frac{9}{2}, \frac{3}{10}, -2.1^2, 4.\overline{3}$

D. $-\frac{9}{2}, -2.1^2, \frac{3}{10}, 4.\overline{3}$

30 Which of the following equations could be used to find the *n*th term in the arithmetic sequence 14, 8, 2, −4, ... ?

A. $a_n = 14 - 8(n - 1)$

B. $a_n = 14 + (n - 1)6$

C. $a_n = 14 - 6(n - 1)$

D. $a_n = 14 - 6 + 8(n - 1)$

31 Jamie has 2 packages of pencils plus 4 extra pencils. Amber had 3 packages of pencils, but she gave away 2 pencils from one of the packages. If there are *x* pencils in each package, which of the following expressions represents the total pencils they have together?

A. $5x + 2$ **B.** $7x$

C. $6x + 6$ **D.** $8x + 6$

32 The formula for finding the area of a trapezoid can be written $A = \frac{1}{2}h(B + b)$. Which of the following is an equivalent formula that solves for B?

A. $B = \frac{A}{2h} - b$ **B.** $B = \frac{2A}{h} - b$

C. $B = 2A - hb$ **D.** $B = \frac{2A - b}{h}$

33 Two cars begin driving from the same point in opposite directions. The first car travels at an average rate of 58 miles per hour. The second car drives 67 miles per hour. How many minutes will it take for the cars to be 100 miles apart.

A. 40 **B.** 48 **C.** 76 **D.** 125

34 Sandy has a bag full of dimes and nickels. There are three times as many nickels as there are dimes. If the value of the coins is $4.75, how many dimes are in the bag?

A. 19 **B.** 23 **C.** 31 **D.** 57

35 Ron is buying chess sets for a school club. Chess World charges $8 for shipping and $12 for each set. Ron can spend up to $110. Which of the following inequalities could Ron solve to find the greatest number of chess sets s he could buy without going over budget?

A. $12s \geq 110$ **B.** $12s \leq 110$

C. $12s + 8 \geq 110$ **D.** $12s + 8 \leq 110$

36 Determine whether points $D(-4, -4)$, $E(2, -1)$, and $F(1, 4)$ lie on the same line. Prove your answer algebraically. Show all your work.

37 Which of the following relations is NOT a function?

A. $\{(-3,-6),(-2,-4),(-1,-2),(0,0)\}$

B. $\{(1,5),(2,10),(3,15),(4,20)\}$

C. $\{(-2,1),(-2,-1),(2,1),(2,-1)\}$

D. $\{(10,1),(8,2),(6,3),(4,4)\}$

38 Which of these points lies on the line shown in the graph?

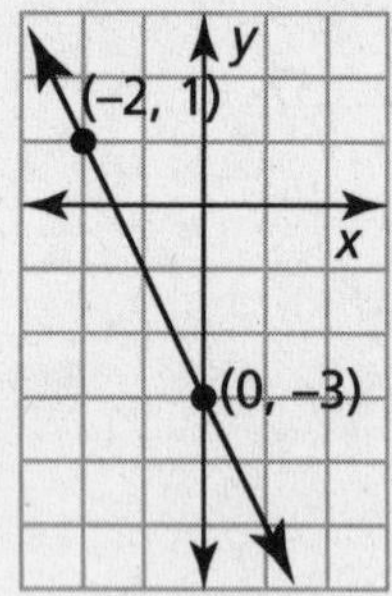

A. $(-12,-21)$

B. $(-11,19)$

C. $(-5,-7)$

D. $(4,11)$

39 Which is a true statement regarding the following system of equations?

$$\begin{cases} -3x + y = 5 \\ x - \frac{1}{3}y = 2 \end{cases}$$

A. The system has exactly one solution.

B. The system has exactly two solutions.

C. The system has an infinite number of solutions.

D. The system has no solution.

40 Which of the systems of inequalities is represented by the shaded region of the graph below?

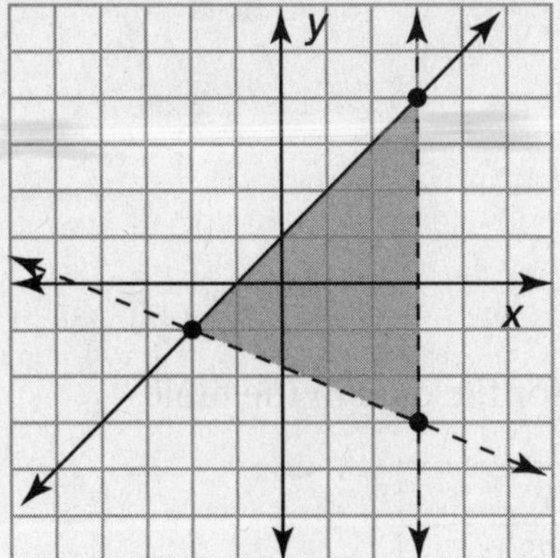

A. $\begin{cases} x < 3 \\ 2x + 5y > -9 \\ -x + y \leq 1 \end{cases}$

B. $\begin{cases} x > 3 \\ 2x + 5y < -9 \\ -x + y \leq 1 \end{cases}$

C. $\begin{cases} x < 3 \\ 2x + 5y < -9 \\ -x + y < 1 \end{cases}$

D. $\begin{cases} x < 3 \\ 2x + 5y < -9 \\ -x + y \geq 1 \end{cases}$

41 A school sold 600 tickets to a varsity basketball game. Ticket prices were \$5 for students and children and \$9 for adults. The total ticket receipts for the game were \$3,632.

Part A Let a represent the number of adult tickets sold and s represent the number of student tickets sold. Write a system of equations to model the situation.

Part B How many adult tickets were sold? Show all your work.

Algebra I Sample Test I

42 What is the product of $(x^2yz^4)^3$ and $(4x^2y^3)^2$?

A. $16x^9y^8z^7$ **B.** $16x^{10}y^9z^{12}$

C. $8x^9y^8z^7$ **D.** $8x^{10}y^9z^{12}$

43 Which of the equations is the best model for the data in the table?

x	*y*
−2	128
−1	32
0	8
1	2
2	0.5
3	0.125
4	0.3125

A. $y = 4(0.5)^x$ **B.** $y = 8(0.25)^x$ **C.** $y = 8(0.4)^x$ **D.** $y = (2)^x$

44 Which is equivalent to $-\frac{4 - x}{x - 2}$?

A. $\frac{x + 4}{x - 2}$ **B.** $\frac{4 - x}{2 - x}$

C. $\frac{x - 4}{2 - x}$ **D.** $\frac{-x - 4}{2 - x}$

45 Which of the following is the complete factorization of the polynomial $6x^3 - 3x^2 - 108x$?

A. $3x(2x - 9)(x + 4)$

B. $3x(2x + 4)(x - 9)$

C. $3x(2x - 4)(x + 9)$

D. $3(x^2 + 4)(2x - 9)$

46 What are the solutions to the equation: $a(6a + 13) = 5$?

A. 0 and $-\frac{13}{2}$

B. 0 and $-\frac{5}{2}$

C. $-\frac{13}{2}$ and $\frac{1}{3}$

D. $-\frac{5}{2}$ and $\frac{1}{3}$

47 What restrictions are there on the domain of the variable in the expression $\frac{x^2 + x - 6}{x^2 - x - 12}$?

A. $x \neq 4$ or $x \neq -3$

B. $x \neq 2$ or $x \neq -3$

C. $x \neq 0$ or $x \neq 4$

D. $x \neq 3$ or $x \neq -4$

48 Divide: $\frac{a}{a - b} \div \frac{a^2}{a^2 - b^2}$. What is the quotient in simplified form?

A. $\frac{a}{a - b}$

B. $\frac{a + b}{a}$

C. $\frac{b}{a - b}$

D. $\frac{a + b}{b}$

49 What is the measure of a side of a square whose diagonal is 4 inches longer than its side? Round your answer to the nearest tenth. Show all your work.

50 Which of the following is the simplified form of the radical $\sqrt{\frac{8}{5}}$?

A. $\sqrt{5}$ **B.** $2\sqrt{2}$

C. $\frac{2\sqrt{10}}{5}$ **D.** $\frac{4\sqrt{10}}{5}$

51 A spinner has ten equal sections labeled with the numbers from 1 through 10. If you spin the spinner twice, what is the probability that you will get numbers less than or equal to 4 on both spins? State the probability as a percent. Show all your work.

52 A solution is 20% acid and 80% water. What is the ratio of acid to water in the solution?

A. 1 : 4

B. 2 : 10

C. 8 : 10

D. 4 : 1

53 James has removed 12 cards from a regular deck of playing cards. Of those, 7 are hearts and are marked with the symbol ♥. He shuffles these cards and then deals two cards face down on a table. What is the probability that the cards on the table are both hearts?

A. $\frac{7}{24}$ **B.** $\frac{7}{22}$

C. $\frac{3}{11}$ **D.** $\frac{1}{12}$

54 Michi has 3 different math books and 4 different history books. In how many unique orders can Michi arrange the books on a shelf if the three math books must remain next to each other?

A. 144

B. 576

C. 720

D. 5,040

55 The letters A, B, C, D, E, and F are written on cards. One card is selected at random and then replaced. A second card is then selected. What is the probability that the letter C is NOT drawn both times?

A. $\frac{5}{6}$

B. $\frac{17}{18}$

C. $\frac{35}{36}$

D. $\frac{359}{360}$

56 An airline samples the weight of carry-on luggage for 9 passengers. The passengers are chosen randomly. The weights (in pounds) are 9, 14, 15, 15, 16, 17, 20, 22, and 34 pounds. Which of the following is NOT a true statement about the data?

A. The median is less than the mean.

B. The mean is closer to 9 than to 34.

C. The mode is less than the mean.

D. The mode and the median are equal.

57 A teacher is investigating the connection between attendance and grades in her class. She selects 12 students randomly and gathers the following data.

Average Grade	68%	90%	85%	88%	95%	63%
Absences	3	0	1	2	5	6

Average Grade	87%	92%	62%	77%	72%	70%
Absences	1	0	4	3	4	5

Part A Describe how you could use the data to determine whether a relationship exists between absences and grade.

Part B Analyze the data according to your plan presented in Part A. Describe any correlation you see in the data. Identify outliers.

Part C Discuss any problems with this investigation that may affect the validity of your conclusions. How would you improve this study?

Part I

DIRECTIONS FOR QUESTIONS 1–28: Solve the following items. For multiple-choice items, select the best answer choice. For all other items, show your work and clearly explain your answer. Calculators may NOT be used in Part 1.

1 What expression must be subtracted from $3a - 2b - c$ to get a difference of $4a - 3b$?

A. $a - b + c$ **B.** $-a + b - c$

C. $7a - 5b - c$ **D.** $-7a + 5b + c$

2 What is the sum of $\frac{2c^2 - 6c}{5c - 15} + \frac{2d^2 + 2d}{4d + 4}$ in simplest terms?

A. $\frac{-4c + d}{5c + 5cd - 15d - 15}$

B. $\frac{2c^2 - 6c + 2d^2 + 2d}{20cd + 20c - 60d - 60}$

C. $\frac{4cd}{20}$

D. $\frac{4c + 5d}{10}$

3 Two years ago, Stuart was 7 times as old as Paige. Now Stuart is 5 times as old as Paige. Write a system of equations to find out how old Stuart is now. Show all your work.

4 A game store owner pays \$36 for a video game. He prices the game so that during a 25% off sale he can still earn a profit of 20%. What is the selling price of the game?

A. \$57.60 **B.** \$56.25 **C.** \$54.00 **D.** \$47.00

5 Which graph shows the solution set for the following system of inequalities?

$$\begin{cases} 2x - y \leq -3 \\ x - 3y \geq 9 \end{cases}$$

A.

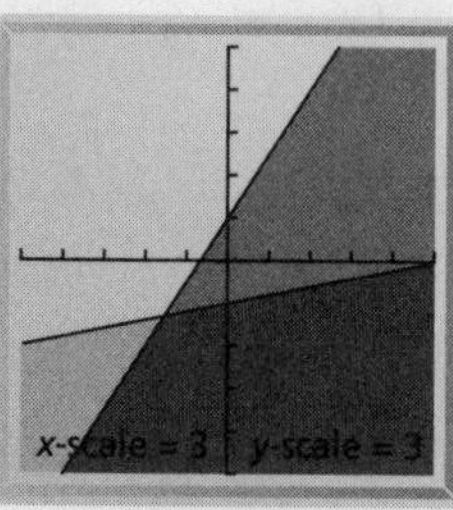

B.

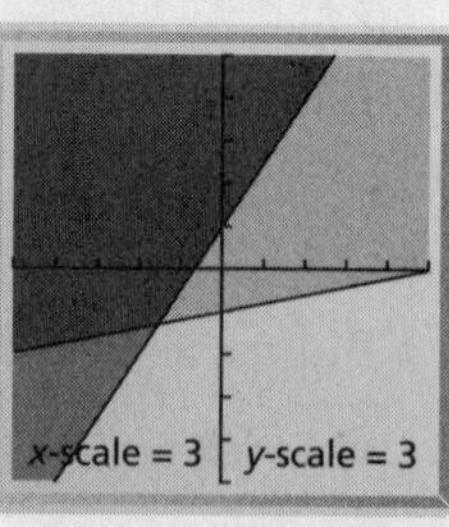

C.

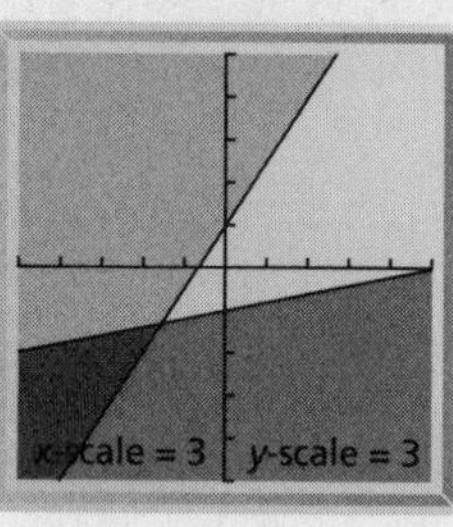

D.

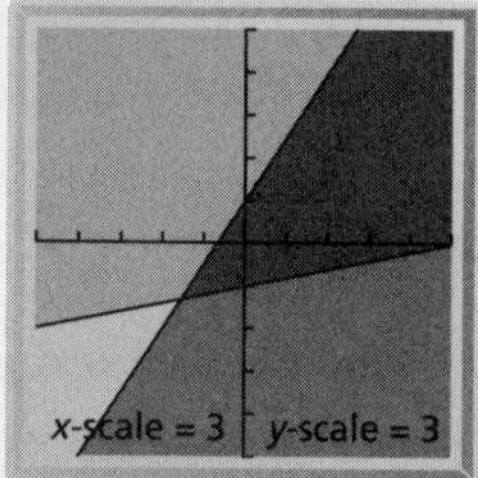

6 At the performance of a play, the ratio of full seats to empty seats was 4 to 3. If there were 135 empty seats, how many seats are in the theater?

A. 180 **B.** 315 **C.** 540 **D.** 945

7 Dylan and Oscar are talking about their tips for the week. Dylan says, "Twice my tips is $108 more than your tips." Oscar says, "Twice my tips is $39 more than your tips." Based on their statements, what is the total amount that Dylan and Oscar earned in tips this week?

A. $69 **B.** $147 **C.** $186 **D.** $294

8 Solve for x in the following equation: $\sqrt[3]{x-8} = \sqrt[3]{4-x}$. Show all your work. Justify each step.

9 A line with slope $-\frac{3}{4}$ passes through points $C(-6, 1)$ and $D(2, n)$. What is the y-coordinate of point D?

A. -10 **B.** -7 **C.** 0 **D.** -5

10 The domain of $f(x) = y^2 - 2y$ is $\{-5, -3, -1, 1, 3, 5\}$. What is the range?

A. $\{35, 15, 3, -3, -15, -35\}$

B. $\{35, 15, 3, -1\}$

C. $\{15, 3, -1\}$

D. the set of all real numbers

11 Which of the following is the equation of a line that is parallel to the line shown on the graph?

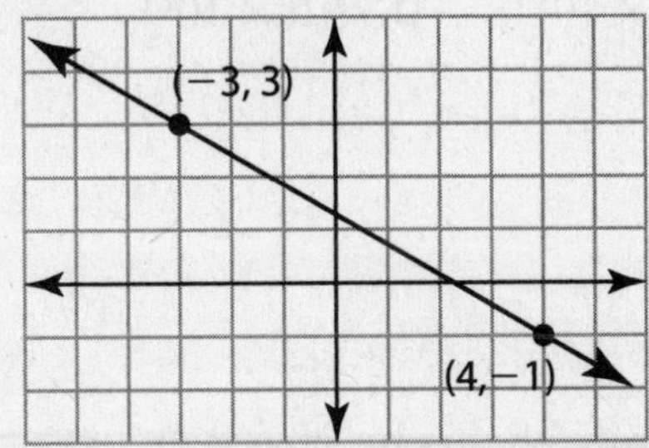

A. $-4x + 7y = -14$ **B.** $-7x + 4y = -20$

C. $4x + 7y = -35$ **D.** $7x + 4y = -12$

12 The vertex of the graph of $y = |x + 2|$ is $(-2, 0)$. Which of the following changes to the equation moves the vertex of the graph to $(4, -3)$?

A. $y = |x + 2 - 6| - 3$ **B.** $y = |x + 2 - 3| - 4$

C. $y = |x + 2 - 6| + 3$ **D.** $y = |x + 2 - 3| + 4$

13 A freight train is $\frac{1}{2}$ mile long. The last car of the train exits a tunnel exactly 2 minutes after the front of the train entered the tunnel. If the train is traveling 40 miles per hour, what is the length of the tunnel in miles?

A. $\frac{2}{3}$ **B.** $\frac{5}{6}$ **C.** $1\frac{1}{3}$ **D.** $1\frac{5}{6}$

14 Which of the following simplifies the expression $\frac{x^3y^{-1}z^{-2}}{x^{-2}y^{-4}z^0}$ using positive exponents?

A. $\frac{y^4}{x^6}$ **B.** $\frac{xy^5}{z^2}$ **C.** $\frac{x}{y^3z^2}$ **D.** $\frac{x^5y^3}{z^2}$

15 The smallest unit of a certain substance has a mass of 2.4×10^{-15} grams. How many units of this substance would be needed to make 4.8×10^5 grams of the substance?

A. 2.0×10^{-3} **B.** 2.0×10^{20} **C.** 5.0×10^{19} **D.** 5.0×10^{21}

16 A tank can be filled in 10 hours by Pipe A or in 5 hours by Pipe B. It takes 20 hours to drain the tank. If the tank is empty and the drain is open, how long will it take to fill the tank using both Pipes A and B?

A. 10 hours **B.** 8 hours **C.** 5 hours **D.** 4 hours

17 Find the sum. Write your answer in simplified form using positive exponents. Show all your work.

$$\frac{a^2}{a-4} + \frac{16}{4-a}$$

18 The calculator screen below displays a graph of the equation: $y = -\frac{1}{2}x^2$. Suppose the equation is changed to $y = \frac{3}{2}x^2$. Which of the following best describes how the graph would change?

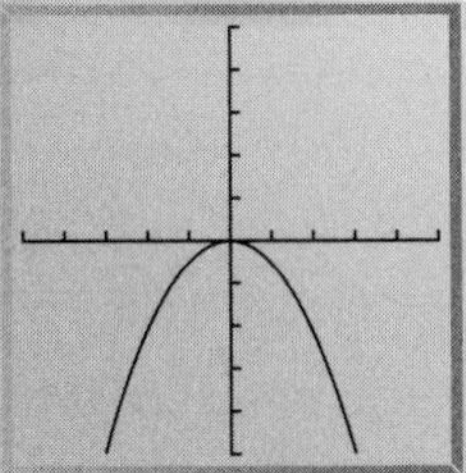

A. The parabola would widen and the vertex would move 3 units higher on the y-axis.

B. The parabola would narrow and the vertex would move 3 units higher on the y-axis.

C. The parabola would narrow and open upward. The vertex would not change.

D. The parabola would widen and open upward. The vertex would not change.

19 **Part A** Graph the function: $f(x) = |x| - 3$

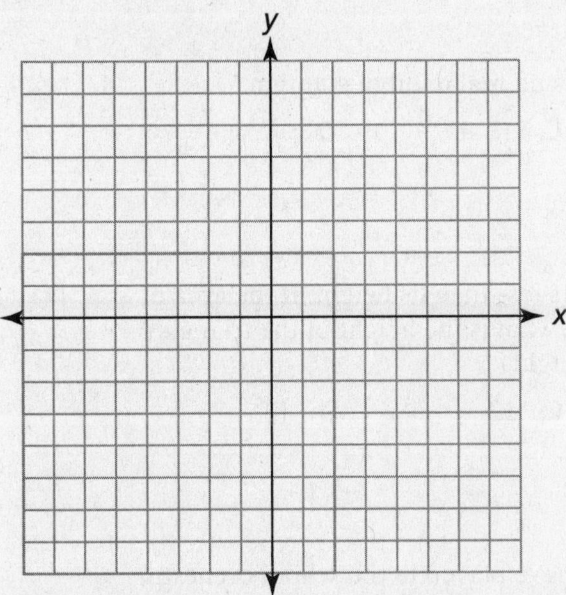

Part B State the domain and range of the function. Why are some values in the domain excluded from the range?

Algebra I Sample Test 2

20 Simplify the following:

$$-2x(3y - x) - 4(6xy - x^2)$$

A. $6x(x - 5y)$ **B.** $6x(x + 3y)$
C. $2x(x - 15y)$ **D.** $-2x(x + 15y)$

21 The area of a rectangle is represented by the expression $6x^2 + 11xy - 10y^2$. If the length of the rectangle can be expressed as $3x - 2y$, which of the following represents its width?

A. $2x + 5y$ **B.** $2x - 5y$ **C.** $3x + 8y$ **D.** $3x - 8y$

22 What are the possible solutions to the following equation?

$$-28a^3 - 18a = -71a^2$$

A. 2, 4, 7, and 9 **B.** 0
C. $0, \frac{2}{7}$, and $\frac{9}{4}$ **D.** There are no solutions.

23 Which of the following equations has no real number solution?

A. $\frac{9}{x} = \frac{x}{7}$ **B.** $\frac{x + 5}{8} = \frac{2}{x}$ **C.** $\frac{2x}{25} = \frac{-2}{x}$ **D.** $\frac{-4}{3x} = \frac{5x}{-30}$

24 In a triangle, the base is 7 centimeters less than its height. If the area of the triangle is 60 square centimeters, what is the height of the triangle? (Area of a triangle $= \frac{1}{2} \times$ base $\times$ height)

A. 7.5 **B.** 8 **C.** 12 **D.** 15

25 Of 180 students in a senior class, 80 have played in the school orchestra and 50 have sung in the school choir. Thirty students have been in both the choir and the orchestra. If a student is chosen randomly from the senior class, what is the probability that the student did NOT participate in either orchestra or choir?

A. $\frac{1}{9}$ **B.** $\frac{4}{9}$ **C.** $\frac{5}{9}$ **D.** $\frac{8}{9}$

26 Gina, Kent, and Larry enter a contest. If there are 7 other people who also enter the contest and all have an equal chance of winning, what is the probability that Gina will win first place and either Kent or Larry will win second place?

A. $\frac{1}{90}$ **B.** $\frac{1}{45}$ **C.** $\frac{3}{100}$ **D.** $\frac{1}{30}$

27 Stan's biology teacher gives 5 tests during one grading period. Each test is worth 120 points. Stan needs an average grade of 95 points on each test to get an A in the class. His points earned for the first 4 tests are shown below. What is the least number of points that Stan can earn on the last test and still get an A in the class?

Test	1	2	3	4	5
Points	78	105	102	90	?

A. 95 **B.** 97 **C.** 100 **D.** 115

28 A math teacher wants to find out whether there is a correlation between how many questions a student misses on a quiz and how many hours of sleep that student got the night before the quiz. She gathers the following data from 15 students.

Hours of Sleep	8	7	8	6	6	8	7	9	6	7	6	6	8	6	6
Missed Items	0	1	1	3	0	1	1	1	3	2	2	4	0	4	5

Part A Describe in detail how you would use the data to help the teacher reach a conclusion.

Part B Do you think the data will demonstrate a correlation? Justify your thinking.

Part 2

DIRECTIONS FOR QUESTIONS 29–57: Solve the following items. For multiple-choice items, select the best answer choice. For all other items, show your work and clearly explain your answer. Calculators may be used in Part 2.

29 For $x = -3$, which choice lists the following expressions in order from greatest to least value?

$$4x^0 \qquad x^2 + 1 \qquad \frac{x^2}{-x} \qquad \frac{1}{x^{-2}}$$

A. $x^2 + 1, 4x^0, \frac{x^2}{-x}, \frac{1}{x^{-2}}$

B. $x^2 + 1, \frac{1}{x^{-2}}, 4x^0, \frac{x^2}{-x}$

C. $\frac{1}{x^{-2}}, x^2 + 1, 4x^0, \frac{x^2}{-x}$

D. $\frac{1}{x^{-2}}, x^2 + 1, \frac{x^2}{-x}, 4x^0$

30 Which of the following equations could be used to find the nth term in the arithmetic sequence $-11, -6, -1, 4, \dots$?

A. $a_n = 5 - 11(n - 1)$

B. $a_n = -11 - 5(n - 1)$

C. $a_n = -11 + 5(n - 1)$

D. $a_n = -11 - 5(n + 1)$

31 There are two consecutive odd integers such that the first integer is 4 more than the product of the second integer and 3. Let x represent the first integer. Which of the following equations could be used to find the integers?

A. $x = 4 + 3(x + 2)$

B. $x + 2 = 4 + 3x$

C. $x = 3(x + 4)$

D. $x - 2 = 3x + 4$

32 Which of the following solves the equation $\frac{1}{a} + \frac{1}{b} = \frac{1}{c}$ for a in terms of b and c?

A. $a = \frac{b - c}{bc}$

B. $a = \frac{c - b}{bc}$

C. $a = \frac{bc}{b - c}$

D. $a = \frac{bc}{c - b}$

33 Tom is painting the set for a school play. Working alone, he could finish the job in 12 hours. His friend Brad could paint the set in 8 hours. Tom and Brad begin working together, but after 3 hours, Brad leaves. How many more hours will Tom need to work to finish the set?

A. $1\frac{1}{8}$

B. $4\frac{1}{2}$

C. 5

D. $7\frac{1}{2}$

34 Colin has a bag of nickels and pennies. He knows that there are 300 coins in the bag. He puts the coins on a metric scale and finds that the coins have a total weight of 1,212.5 grams. If each nickel weighs 5 grams and each penny weighs 2.5 grams, what is the total value of the coins?

A. $4.85

B. $5.75

C. $9.00

D. $10.40

35 Val is having custom shirts printed for a school event. The T-shirt design company charges $28 to create the design and $9 per shirt. Val can spend up to $275. Which of the following inequalities could Val use to find the greatest number of shirts, x, he could order without going over budget?

A. $9(x - 28) \leq 275$

B. $9(x + 28) \leq 275$

C. $9x + 28 \geq 275$

D. $9x + 28 \leq 275$

36 The vertices of a triangle are located at points $A(-3, -4)$, $B(5, 0)$, and $C(-1, -2)$. Is triangle ABC a right triangle? Use your knowledge of slope to prove your answer. Show all your work.

37 Which of the following relations is NOT a function?

A. $\{(-3,9),(-2,6),(-1,3),(0,0)\}$

B. $\{(0,1),(10,3),(20,5),(30,7)\}$

C. $\{(2,\frac{1}{2}),(4,\frac{1}{2}),(6,\frac{1}{2}),(8,\frac{1}{2})\}$

D. $\{(4,10),(4,-10),(3,9),(3,-9)\}$

38 Which of these points lies on the line shown in the graph?

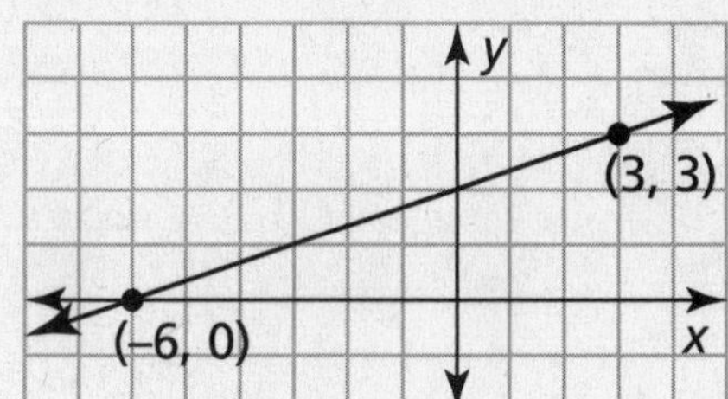

A. $(-12,-2)$

B. $(-4,10)$

C. $(-3,-3)$

D. $(4,5)$

39 Which is a true statement regarding the following system of equations?

$$\begin{cases} -\frac{2}{5}x - 1 = y \\ -2x - 5y = 5 \end{cases}$$

A. The system has exactly one solution.

B. The system has exactly two solutions.

C. The system has an infinite number of solutions.

D. The system has no solution.

40 Which choice shows the result of rationalizing the denominator and simplifying the following expression?

$$\frac{\sqrt{10} + \sqrt{5}}{\sqrt{10} - \sqrt{5}}$$

A. $\frac{2\sqrt{5}}{5}$

B. $3 + 2\sqrt{2}$

C. $\sqrt{3}$

D. -1

41 The length of a rectangle is 4 inches less than twice the width of the rectangle. The perimeter of the rectangle is 58 inches.

Part A Let L represent the length and W the width of the rectangle. Write a system of equations to model the information in the problem.

Part B What are the dimensions of the rectangle? Show all your work.

42 What is the product of $(3^2ab^3)^2$ and $(3a^4b)^{-3}$?

A. a^3b^2 **B.** $\frac{1}{a^5b^4}$

C. $\frac{3b^3}{a^{10}}$ **D.** $3ab^2$

43 Which of the equations is the best model for the data in the table?

x	y
−3	375
−2	75
−1	15
0	3
1	0.6
2	0.12
3	0.024

A. $6(0.1)^x$ **B.** $3(0.25)^x$ **C.** $5(0.15)^x$ **D.** $3(0.2)^x$

44 Which is equivalent to $-\frac{a+3}{5-a}$?

A. $\frac{-a+3}{-a-5}$ **B.** $\frac{3+a}{a-5}$

C. $\frac{a+3}{-a-5}$ **D.** $\frac{3-a}{5-a}$

45 Which of the following is the complete factorization of the polynomial $24a^3 + 2a^2 - 2a$?

A. $2a(4a + 1)(3a - 1)$ **B.** $2a(4a - 1)(3a + 1)$

C. $a(6a - 2)(4a + 1)$ **D.** $a(6a + 2)(4a - 1)$

Algebra I Sample Test 2

46 What are the solutions to the equation: $2x(5x - 12) = 18$?

A. 0 and $\frac{12}{5}$ **B.** $\frac{1}{3}$ and $\frac{3}{5}$

C. $\frac{1}{2}$ and $\frac{12}{5}$ **D.** 3 and $-\frac{3}{5}$

47 What restrictions are there on the domain of the variable in the expression $\frac{x^3 - 16x}{3x^2 - 13x - 10}$?

A. $x \neq 0$ or $-\frac{3}{2}$ **B.** $x \neq 0, 4,$ or -4

C. $x \neq 5$ or $-\frac{2}{3}$ **D.** $x \neq -5$ or -3

48 Divide: $\frac{x - y}{x} \div \frac{x^2 - y^2}{x^3}$. What is the quotient in simplified form?

A. $\frac{x - y}{x + y}$ **B.** $\frac{x + y}{x - y}$

C. $\frac{x^2}{x + y}$ **D.** $\frac{x^2}{x - y}$

49 One integer is 8 less than 4 times another integer. The product of the two integers is 60. What are the two integers? Solve the problem algebraically. Show all your work.

50 Which is the solution to the equation $\sqrt{4x + 5} + 1 = 0$?

A. 1 **B.** 0

C. -1 **D.** There is no real solution.

51 A bag has 5 red marbles, 8 blue marbles, and 3 green marbles. Suppose you draw 1 marble from the bag without looking and put it in your pocket. What is the probability that the marble in your pocket is blue? State the probability as a fraction. Show all your work.

52 The Cougars just finished their softball season. They won 75% of their first 20 games. They won only 50% of their games for the rest of the season. At the end of the season, they had won 60% of their games. How many games did they win during the season?

A. 20 **B.** 30 **C.** 50 **D.** 60

53 Two number cubes, each numbered from 1 through 6, are rolled. What is the probability that the sum of the numbers rolled are greater than 6?

A. $\frac{4}{9}$ **B.** $\frac{5}{12}$ **C.** $\frac{7}{12}$ **D.** $\frac{3}{5}$

54 A family has 5 children. Two of the children are twin boys named Nick and James. The boys always sit next to each other, with Nick on the left side of James. In how many different orders could the children sit in a row of 5 chairs if the twins always sit next to each other?

A. 24 **B.** 48 **C.** 60 **D.** 120

55 Ten students belong to a school club. Five of the members are juniors. If 2 students are chosen at random to serve as club officers, what is the probability that the officers will both be juniors?

A. $\frac{1}{5}$ **B.** $\frac{2}{9}$ **C.** $\frac{5}{18}$ **D.** $\frac{2}{5}$

56 A newspaper reporter is investigating how much money the average adult spends on fast food each week. He goes to the city library and surveys the first 20 adults who enter the library. He asks, "To the nearest $10, how much money did you spend on fast food last week?"

He gathers the following data:

$30	$50	$10	$20	$20
$60	$30	$20	$20	$40
$120	$20	$40	$30	$20
$40	$50	$30	$20	$10

Part A Find the mean, median, and mode of the data.

Part B Which measure of central tendency from Part A best answers the reporter's question? Explain your reasoning.

Part C Identify any factors that may cause the results to be misleading.

57 Eleven boys are playing in a youth basketball league. The boys are all 8 years old. Their heights are 52, 52, 54, 55, 56, 56, 57, 60, 60, 60, and 65 inches. Which of the following is NOT a true statement about the data?

A. The median is less than the mean.

B. The mean is closer to 65 than to 52.

C. The mode is greater than the mean.

D. The median is closer to 52 than to 65.

Diagnostic Test

Chapter 1

1 A **3** C **5** A **7** D **9** D

Chapter 2

1 B **3** D **5** B **7** C **9** A

Chapter 3

1 B **3** D **5** A **7** B **9** A

Chapter 4

1 B **3** A **5** C **7** B **9** C

Chapter 5

1 D **3** C **5** B **7** A **9** D

Chapter 6

1 C **3** B **5** C **7** A **9** A

Chapter 7

1 B **3** A **5** D **7** A **9** D

Chapter 8

1 C **3** D **5** D **7** B **9** C

Chapter 9

1 C **3** B **5** A **7** C **9** B

Chapter 1

Lesson 1.1

1 C **3** C **5** D **7** C **9** B
11 $0.42 = \frac{42}{100}$ **13** $0 = \frac{0}{n}$ for any nonzero integer n.
For example, $0 = \frac{0}{1}$. **15** > **17** < **19** >
21 > **23** < **25** $-\frac{8}{9}, -\frac{13}{15}, -\frac{5}{6}$
27 −1.101, −1.1, −1.01, −0.1001

Lesson 1.2

1 C **3** C **5** B **7** 0.6 **9** −7
11 $-\frac{3}{2}$ or $-1\frac{1}{2}$ **13** −7.28 **15** −2 **17** $\frac{49}{60}$
19 Commutative Property of Multiplication
21 Distributive Property **23** Commutative Property of Addition **25** 9 **27** 2 **29** <
31 0 **33** Yes, since you can add odd numbers in any order and the sum is the same.

Lesson 1.3

1 B **3** B **5** D **7** C **9** 121 **11** 1
13 8,000 **15** 0.000031 **17** 4×10^6
19 3.409×10^1 **21** 6.5×10^7 **23** 8 **25** −1.2
27 5 and 6 **29** 3 and 4 **31** 1.73 **33** −2.2
35 0.97 **37** −17 **39** 8 **41** 2 **43** Answers will vary. Sample answer: $0.5^2 = 0.25$, and $0.25 < 0.5$.
45 $(4 \times 3 + 12) \div 3$, because $(4 \times 3 + 12) \div 3 = (12 + 12) \div 3 = 24 \div 3 = 8$.

Lesson 1.4

1 B **3** A **5** arithmetic **7** geometric
9 20; 29 **11** −27; −45 **13** 45; 405 **15** 45; 405
17 −5; −20, −25 **19** −4; −4, −8
21 0.5; 2.25, 1.125 **23** −4; −576, 2304
25 $a_n = 7 + (n - 1)7$ **27** $a_n = -252\left(\frac{1}{6}\right)^{n-1}$
29 $a_n = 4 + (n - 1)(5)$ **31** $a_n = -8\left(\frac{1}{2}\right)^{n-1}$

Lesson 1.5

1 D **3** D **5** C **7** C **9** −20 **11** $\frac{11}{2}$ or $5\frac{1}{2}$ **13** 12 **15** $-5r + 5s$ **17** $-3x - 36$
19 $-11v + 77$ **21** $18t$ **23** $c - 17$
25 $2(y + 9)$ **27** $\frac{a+b}{ab}$ **29** the square root of the quotient of $3a$ squared and $5b$ to the 4th **31** $-2n - 6$ **33** $m + 30$

Chapter 1: Preparing for the ADP[SM] Algebra I Exam

1 A **3** C **5** D **7** B **9** C **11** C
13 A **15** B **17** C **19** B **21** D
23 D **25** C **27** A
29 • $\frac{2d}{c}$
• $187.16
31 • Tuesday
• 3.75
• $17\frac{7}{12}$

Chapter 2

Lesson 2.1

1 B **3** D **5** D **7** 37 **9** 21 **11** −100
13 −21 **15** $-\frac{45}{4}$ or $-11\frac{1}{4}$ **17** 40 **19** −1

SELECTED ANSWERS

21 $\frac{30}{11}$ or $2\frac{8}{11}$ **23** 10 **25** $p = \frac{q+r}{2}$
27 $y = \frac{z}{x}$ **29** $t = \frac{d}{r}$ **31** $\frac{24}{5}, -\frac{24}{5}$ **33** $\frac{2}{3}, \frac{10}{3}$
35 No, Daneesha's statement is incorrect. If $3t = -3t$, it follows from the Addition Property of Equality that $6t = 0$; so $t = 0$. Therefore, the equation does have a solution, $t = 0$.

Lesson 2.2

1 C **3** C **5** C **7** 38° **9** −1

Lesson 2.3

1 B **3** C **5** C **7** B

Lesson 2.4

1 C **3** C **5** B **7** 72% **9** 12
11 28%; decrease **13** 150%; increase
15 17 **17** \$13.26 **19** 19.2 minutes **21** 1440

Lesson 2.5

1 A **3** D **5** B **7** $x < -1$
9 $x < -2$ or $x \geq 4$
11 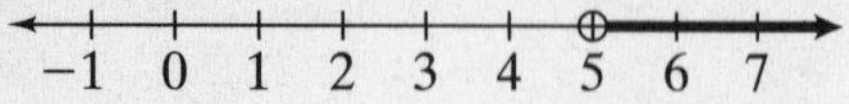
−1 0 1 2 3 4 5 6 7
13 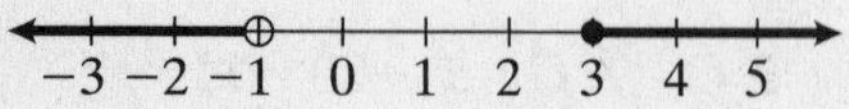
−3 −2 −1 0 1 2 3 4 5
15 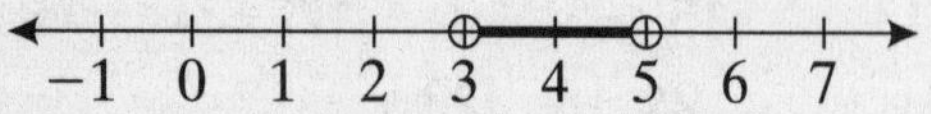
−1 0 1 2 3 4 5 6 7
17 
−1 0 1 2 3 4 5 6 7 8 9 10 11 12
19 $n > -8$ 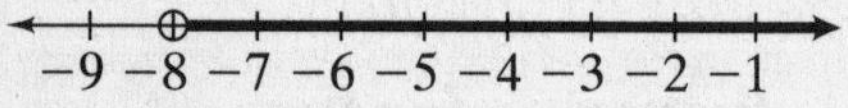
−9 −8 −7 −6 −5 −4 −3 −2 −1
21 $a \leq -18$ 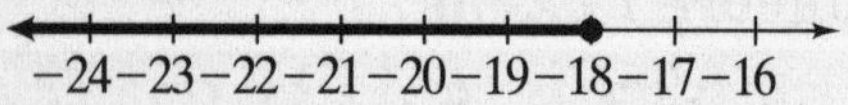
−24 −23 −22 −21 −20 −19 −18 −17 −16
23 $w \geq 3$ 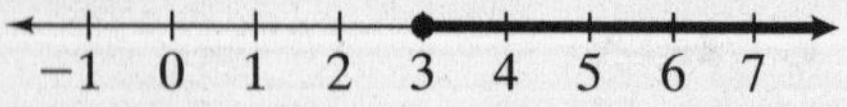
−1 0 1 2 3 4 5 6 7
25 $z > -9$ 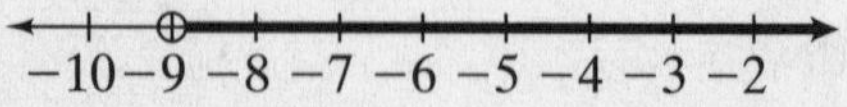
−10 −9 −8 −7 −6 −5 −4 −3 −2
27 $c \leq 4$ 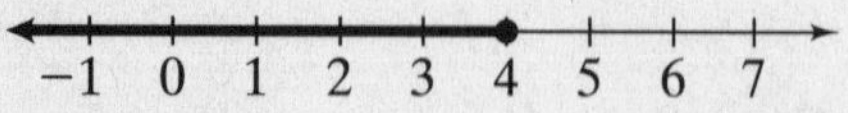
−1 0 1 2 3 4 5 6 7
29 $1 < x \leq 4$
−2 0 2 4 6 8 10 12 14
31 10, 11, 12, . . .
4 5 6 7 8 9 10 11 12 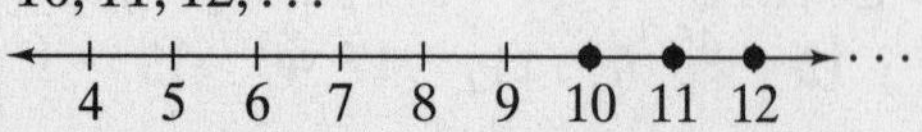
33 −4, −3, −2, −1, 0, 1, 2 
−5 −4 −3 −2 −1 0 1 2 3
35 $h < -2$ or $h > 2$ 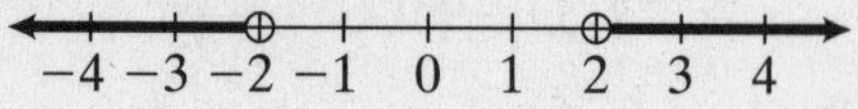
−4 −3 −2 −1 0 1 2 3 4
37 $-2 < t < 1$
−5 −4 −3 −2 −1 0 1 2 3
39 *true*; Explanations may vary. Sample explanation: $2q + 5 \leq 3$ is equivalent to $q \leq -1$. There are no real numbers satisfying $q \leq -1$ and $q > 0$.

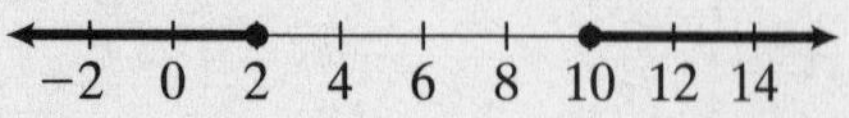

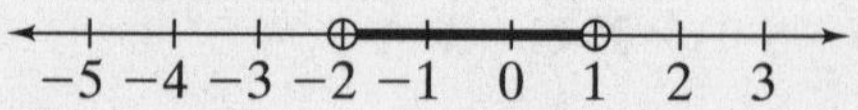

Lesson 2.6

1 B **3** B **5** D **7** 0, 1, and 2 **9** 4
11 at least \$2500 **13** no more than 20
15 any whole number of meters from 1 through 14, inclusive **17** The lesser partner receives at least \$800 but no more than \$1600. The greater partner receives at least \$1000 but no more than \$2000.

Chapter 2: Preparing for the ADP℠ Algebra I Exam

1 A **3** C **5** B **7** B **9** D **11** A
13 D **15** A **17** A **19** B **21** D
23
- 30 miles
- 1:50 pm
- 45 miles
- $1\frac{1}{3}$ hours or 80 minutes

23
- \$510
- \$51
- No, because the current sale price of the sofa is \$459, and the cost of the sofa at 25% off is \$450.

Chapter 3

Lesson 3.1

1 B **3** C **5** triangle **7** $\frac{5}{3}$ **9** $-\frac{5}{3}$
11 no slope **13** $-\frac{2}{5}$ **15** B(−3, −4)
17 P(6, 12) **19** $F(9, 6.5)$ **21** 54 miles per hour

Lesson 3.2

1 C **3** B **5** C **7** B **9** A **11** Answers may vary. Sample answer: No, because it does not pass the vertical-line test. **13** $G(T) = 9T$ (domain: 0

$\leq T \leq 3200$; range: $0 \leq G \leq 28{,}800$ and G and T are integers) **15** $p(f) = 2f$ (domain: $f \geq 0$; range: $p \geq 0$ and f and p are integers)

17

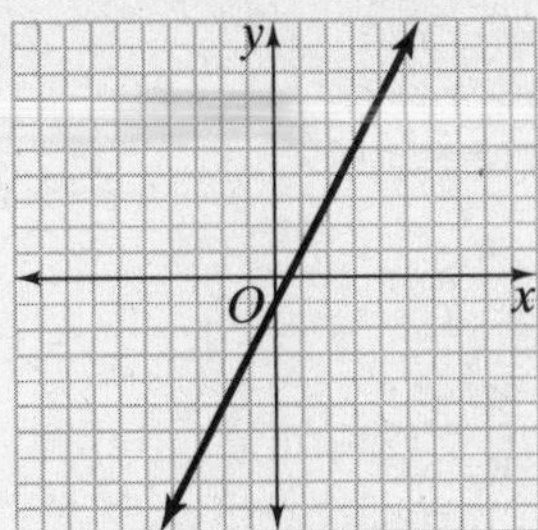

domain and range: {all real numbers}

19

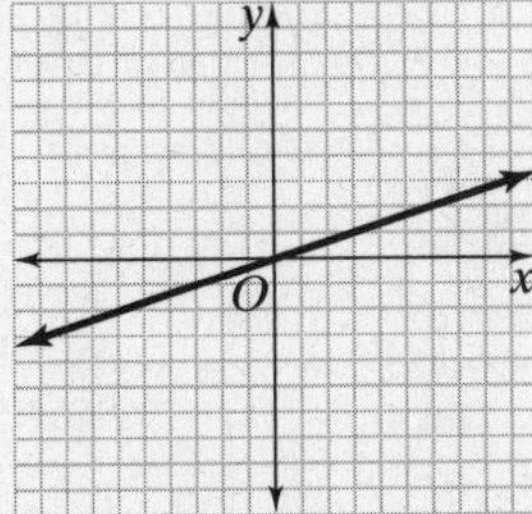

domain and range: {all real numbers}

21

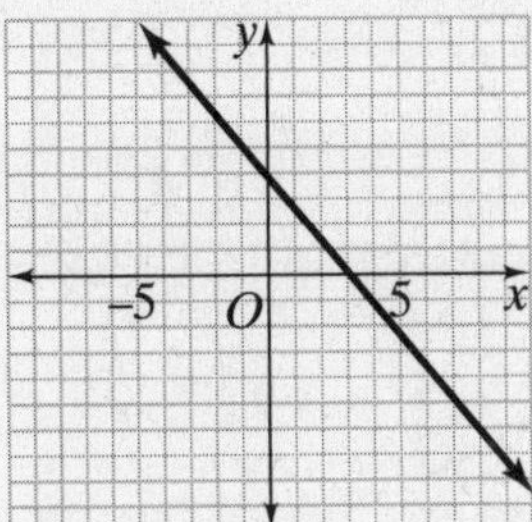

domain and range: {all real numbers}

23

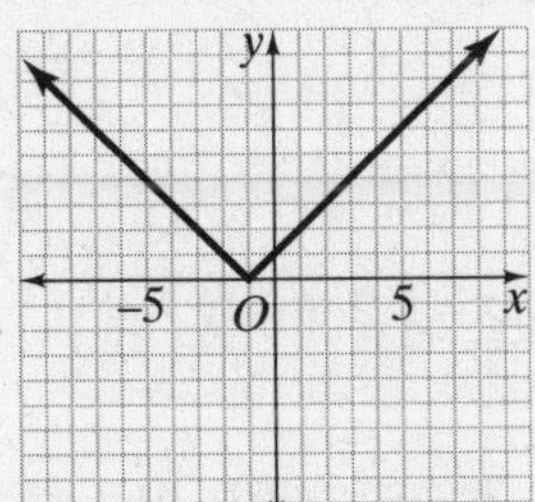

domain and range: {all real numbers}, range: $\{f(x) \geq 0\}$

25

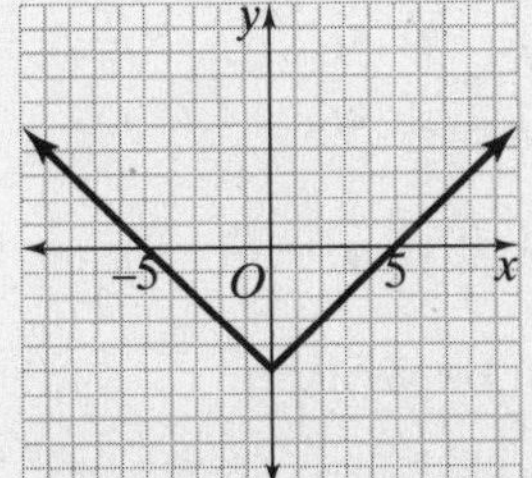

domain and range: {all real numbers}, range: $\{f(x) \geq -5\}$

Lesson 3.3

1 C **3** D **5** 48.2°F **7** −17.8°C **9** 5 **11** −4.5 **13** domain: all real numbers; range: all real numbers **15** domain: all real numbers; range: all real numbers greater than or equal to −1

17

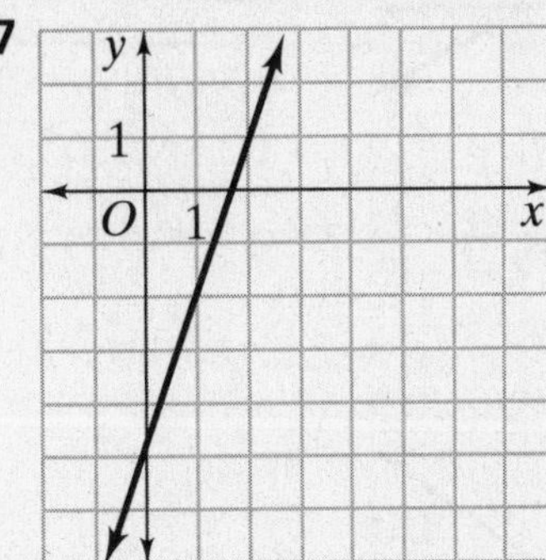

19

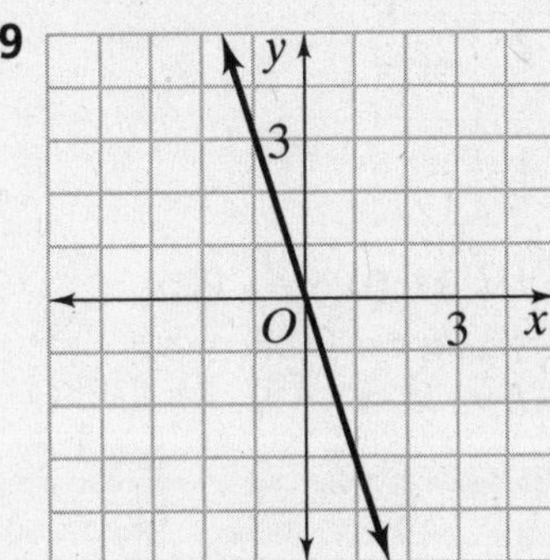

21

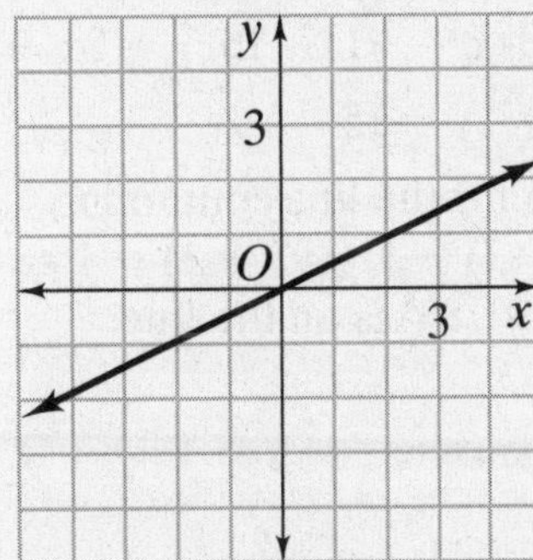

23

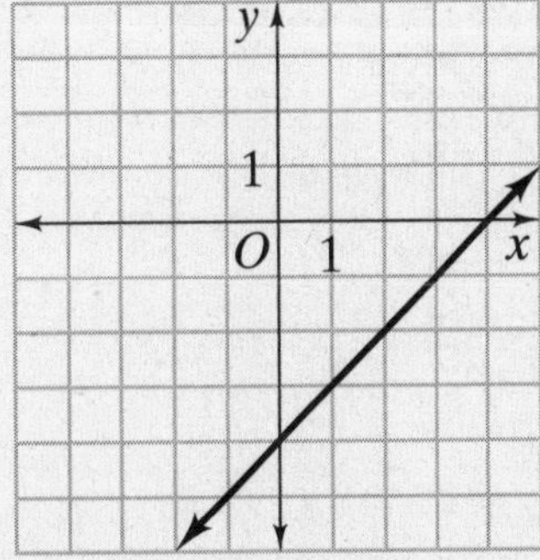

25

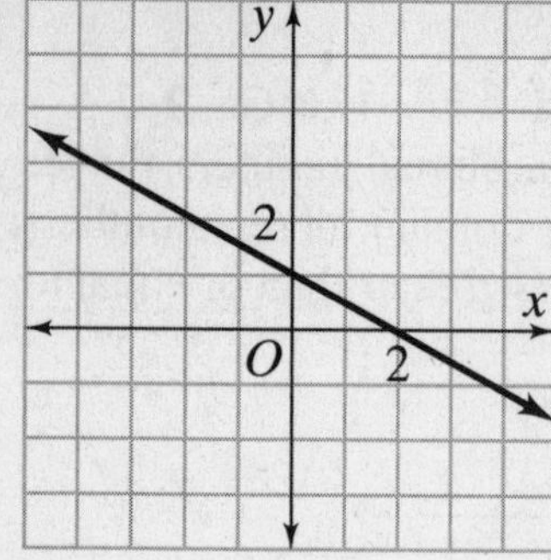

27

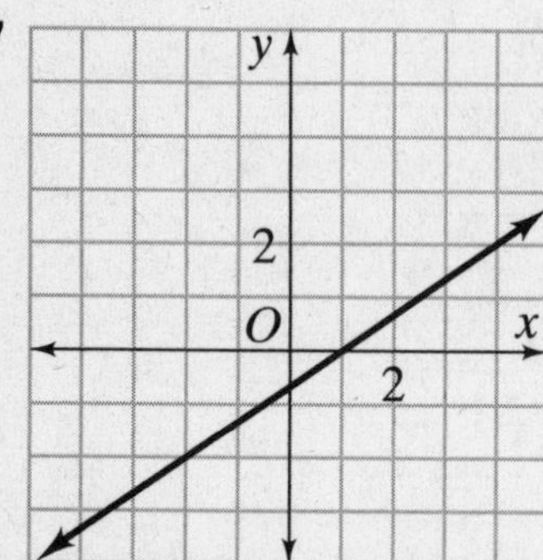

29 $0.05n + 0.1d = 1.20$ **31** $0.05n + 0.1d = 2.45$ **33** $r + b + 35 = 185; r = 70, b = 80; r = 90, b = 60; r = 75, b = 75$

Lesson 3.4

1 B **3** A **5** C **7** B **9** $y = -2x - 1$ **11** $y = -\frac{3}{5}x + \frac{2}{5}$ **13** $x = -11$ **15** $y = 2x + 2$ **17** $\left(0, \frac{13}{8}\right)$ **19** $3x + 5y = 15$

21 Yes; An equation for the line containing P and Q is $y = \frac{7}{8}(x + 3) - 1$; $\frac{7}{8}(93 + 3) - 1 = 7(12) - 1 = 83$. So, $(93, 83)$ is on the line.

Lesson 3.5

1 B **3** D **5** D

7

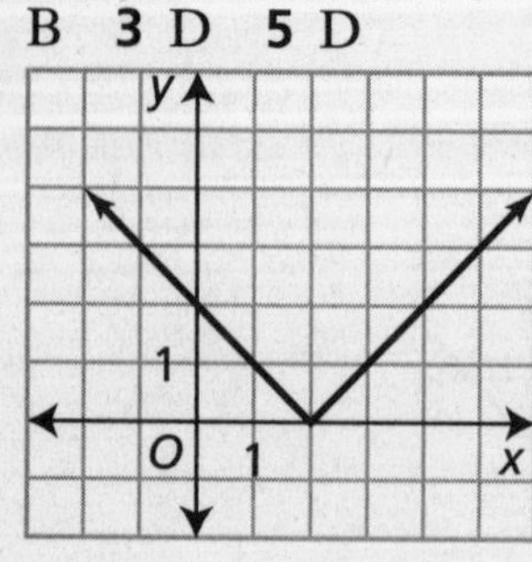

$(2, 0)$

9

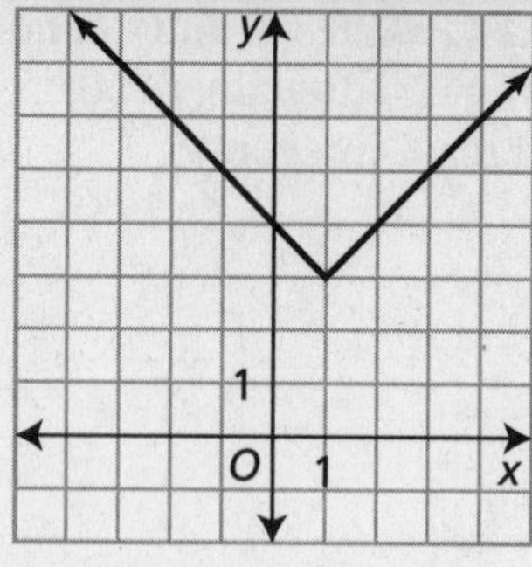

$(1, 3)$

11

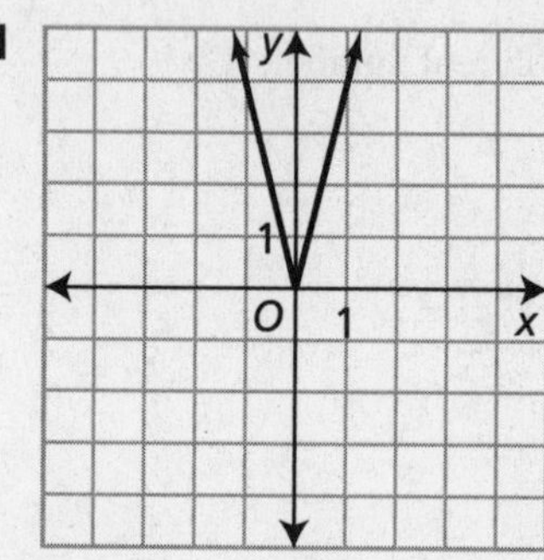

$(0, 0)$

13

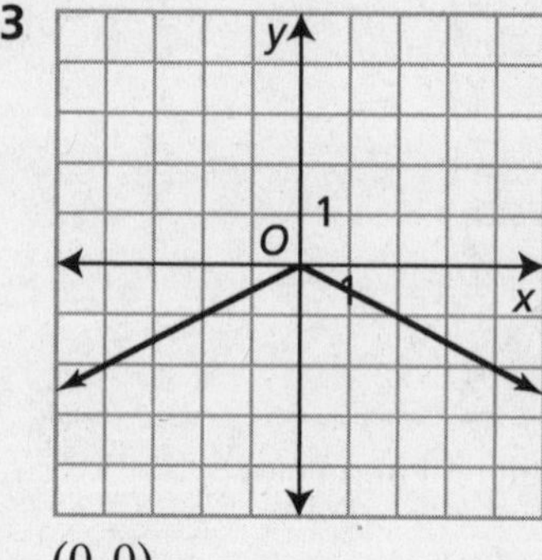

$(0, 0)$

15 $y = |x| - 6$ **17** $y = |x + 0.5|$ **19** $y = -|x| - 2$

21 Sample answer; $y = |x| + 3$ and $y = |x - 3|$

Lesson 3.6

1 D **3** A **5** $(-2, 1)$ **7** $(-5, -5)$ **9** Let m represent the number of months a person is a member and c represent the cost of membership.; $\begin{cases} c = 20m + 50 \\ c = 15m + 80 \end{cases}$

11 $\begin{cases} y = 2x \\ y + x = 21 \end{cases}$ **13** $(4, 3)$

15 The given system can be written $\begin{cases} y = 3x + 5 \\ y = 3x + 5 \end{cases}$. The graphs coincide. The system is dependent.

Lesson 3.7

1 D **3** D **5** $(-1, 1)$ **7** $\left(-\frac{8}{5}, -\frac{11}{5}\right)$
9 $(2, -1)$ **11** $(3, -6)$ **13** 55° and 125°
15 47 and 23 **17** 90 boys and 160 girls **19** 11 nickels, 6 dimes, and 7 quarters **21** If $k = 2$ then the lines are parallel and have no solution.

23 Solve $\begin{Bmatrix} 3x - 5y = 4 \\ 4x + 7y = 19 \end{Bmatrix}$ The solution is $(3, 1)$.
Thus, the graphs intersect at the point $(3, 1)$. **25** 3

Lesson 3.8

1 D **3** A **5** A **7** D

9

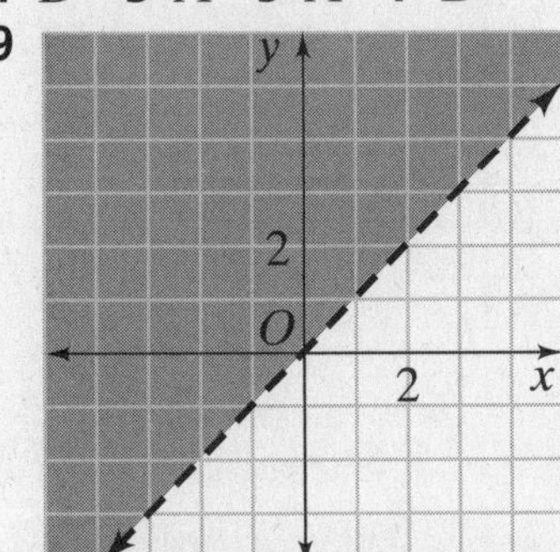

11

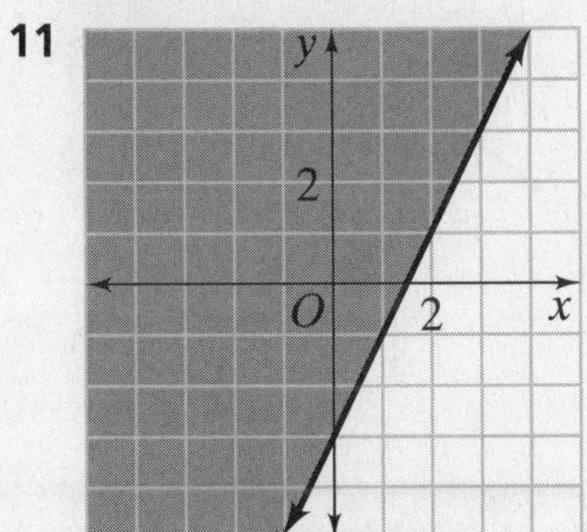

13

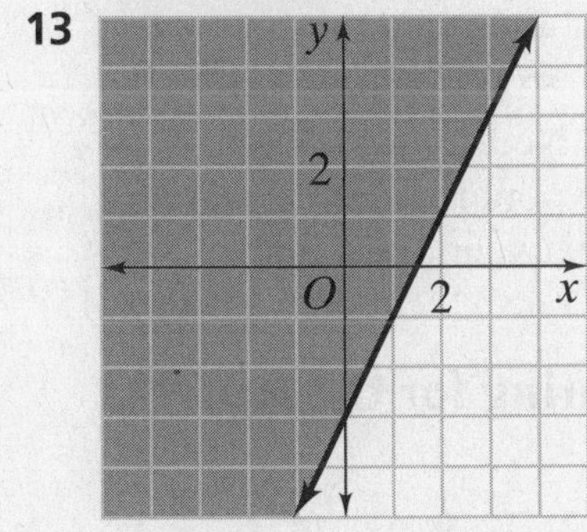

15

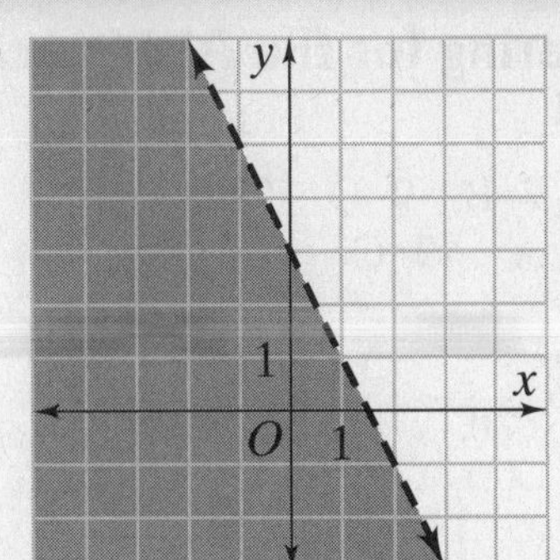

17

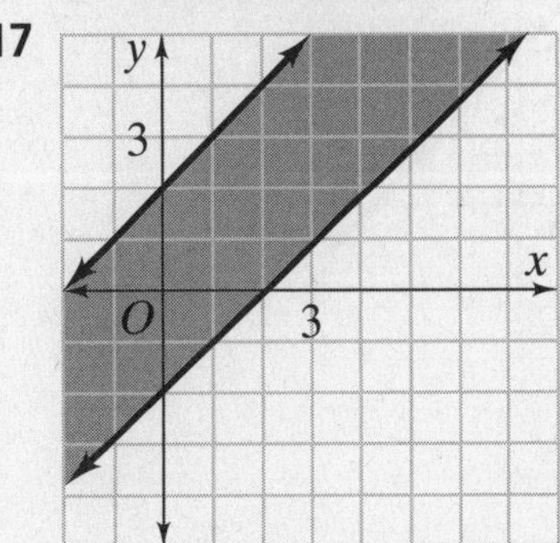

19

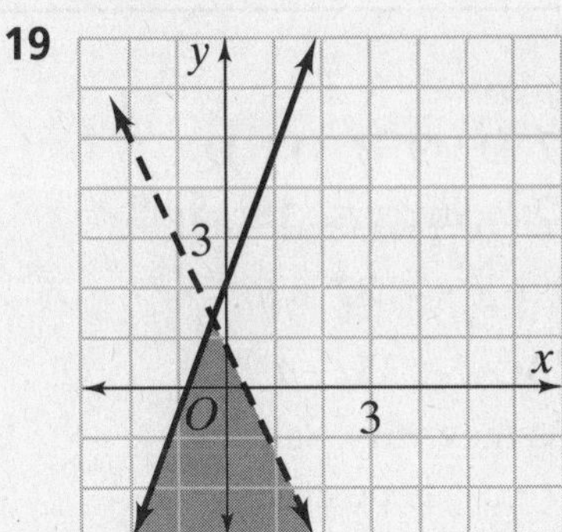

21 Jessica: 9, 10, 11, 12, 13, 14; Melissa: 11, 12, 13, 14, 15, 16, respectively
23 A triangle and its interior.

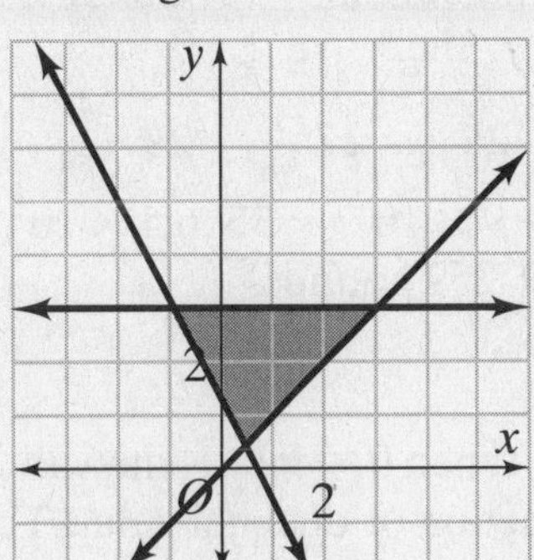

SELECTED ANSWERS

Chapter 3 Preparing for the ADP[SM] Algebra I Exam

1 B **3** A **5** B **7** B **9** D **11** B
13 C **15** D **17** A **19** C
21 • $y = 4x - 1$
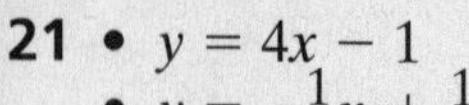
• $y = -\frac{1}{4}x + \frac{13}{4}$
23 • $x + y \le 50, 7 \le 0.1x + 0.25y \le 9$

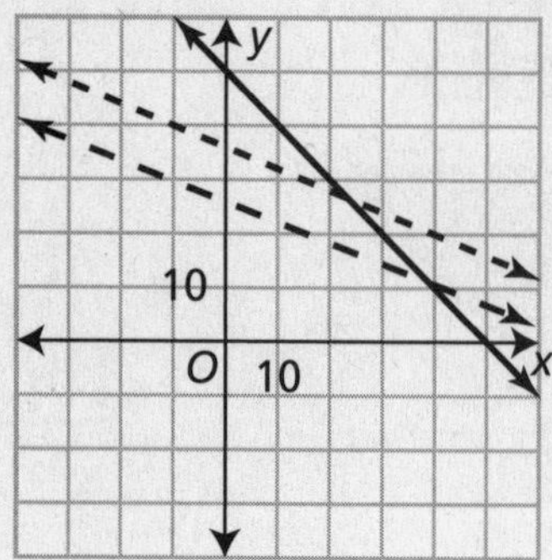

Chapter 4

Lesson 4.1

1 C **3** A **5** C **7** D **9** B **11** D
13 243 **15** $-\frac{1}{8}$ **17** $-96x^7yz$ **19** x^8y^{16}
21 $\frac{vw}{3}$ **23** $\frac{x^6}{y^{14}}$ **25** $-\frac{8y^{15}}{27x^9}$ **27** $5ab^4$
29 $-4n^4$ **31** 4 **33** −2 **35** −4
37 No; Explanations may vary. Sample: -5^2 is negative but $(-5)^2$ is positive.

Lesson 4.2

1 C **3** A **5** D **7** C **9** A **11** 5.15×10^{14} square meters. **13** about 2.8×10^4 dollars = $28,000 **15** k^3 **17** $2^{10}a^5$ **19** $\frac{1}{a}$
21 c^4d^{12} **23** −6 **25** $\frac{1}{8}$ **27** $\frac{n^6}{m^4}$ **29** $\frac{3j^2}{2k^2}$
31 7.8×10^{-7} **33** 9×10^{-8} **35** 6.4×10^5
37 3.01×10^{27} **39** 259 pounds

Lesson 4.3

1 D **3** C **5** fall; When 0 < b < 1, the value of the power is a fraction or decimal value. This value multiplied by the original number will cause a decrease in values over time.
7 {0.16, 0.4, 1, 2.5, 6.25, 15.625} increase
9 $\{\frac{9}{4}, \frac{3}{2}, 1, \frac{2}{3}, \frac{4}{9}, \frac{8}{27}\}$ decrease **11** $y = 1$; increasing **13** $y = 5$; increasing

15 $y = 0.5^x$

x	0.5^x
−2	4
−1	2
0	1
1	0.5
2	0.25

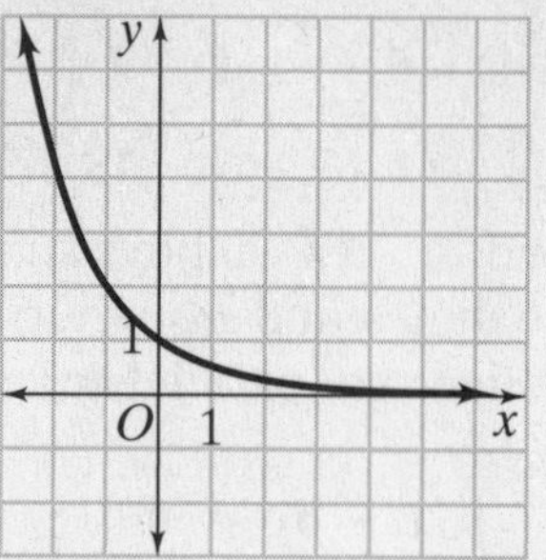

17 $y = \left(\frac{1}{3}\right)^x$

x	$\left(\frac{1}{3}\right)^x$
−2	9
−1	3
0	1
1	$\frac{1}{3}$
2	$\frac{1}{9}$

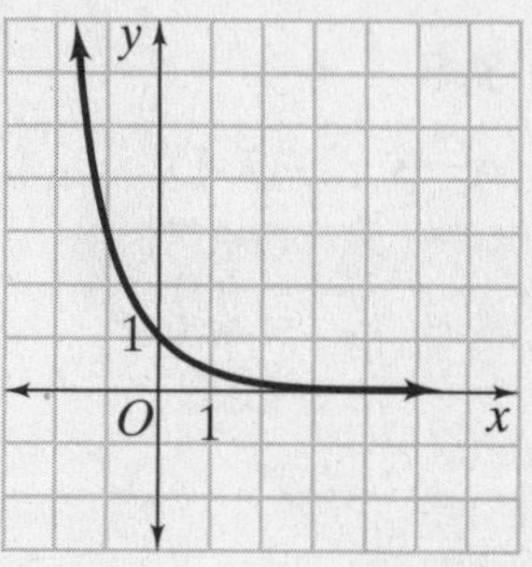

19 $y = -\frac{3}{4}^x$

x	$-\left(\frac{3}{4}\right)^x$
−2	$-\frac{16}{9}$
−1	$-\frac{4}{3}$
0	−1
1	$-\frac{3}{4}$
2	$-\frac{9}{16}$

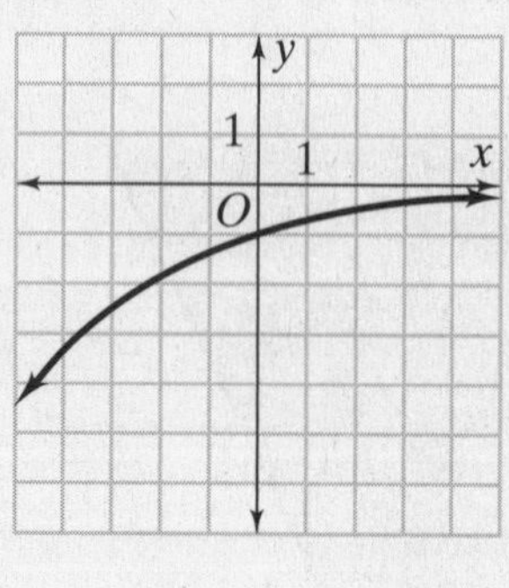

Lesson 4.4

1 C **3** 1.025 **1** $y = 75{,}000(1.025)^x$
7 8,000,000 **9** $y = 8{,}000{,}000(0.9825)^x$
11 $10,648.93 **13** Neither **15** Linear
17 Neither **19** Exponential, because there is a common ratio between the values.
21 12.5 grams **23** 2,187 **25** $y = 21{,}000(0.815)^t$

Chapter 4 Preparing for the ADP[SM] Algebra I Exam

1 C **3** D **5** C **7** B **9** A **11** C
13 B **15** A **17** C **19** C
21 • 6.2×10^7
• 5.9×10^7

- 5.1×10^{-1}
- 4.9×10^{-1}

23 Exponential; The data are modeled by $y = 3x$.

Chapter 5

Lesson 5.1

1 B **3** C **5** C **7** $5m^2n^2 + 3mn^2 - 9m^2n$ **9** $c^4 + 2c^2d + 3cd^2 - 13d$ **11** $4b^3 + 9b^2 - b + 1$ **13** $-3v^3 + v$ **15** $6w^3 - 3w^2 + 4w - 7$ **17** quadratic trinomial **19** linear binomial **21** linear monomial **23** $8s - 7$ **25** $4a^3 + a^2 + 5a - 15$ **27** $-2r^3 - 3r^2 - 3r + 2$ **29** $-9x^3 + 3z - 4$ **31** $-2a^3 - a^2 + 14a - 3$ **33** $-2w^4 - 8w^3 + 11w^2 + 8w - 9$ **35** $6j^2 + 5j + 7$ **37** $4z^2 + 2$ **39** No; the expression contains a negative power of x. **41** $3t - 16$

Lesson 5.2

1 D **3** B **5** C **7** $24a - 12$ **9** $2y^2 - y - 6$ **11** $6w^2 - w - 35$ **13** $9q^2 + 24q + 16$ **15** $2k + 5$ **17** $-5p^4 - 10p^3 - 5p^2$ **19** $2n^3 - 9n^2 + 13n - 21$ **21** $3z^2 - 5z - 4$ **23** $-\frac{13}{2}$

Lesson 5.3

1 C **3** C **5** A **7** 3 **9** rs **11** $8(n - 9)$ **13** $6r(2r + 3)$ **15** $v(v^5 + v^2 + 1)$ **17** $8jk(2jk - 5)$ **19** $(c + 5)(c + 9)$ **21** $(x - 6)(x + 5)$ **23** $(y - 4)(y - 12)$ **25** $(h + 7)(h - 6)$ **27** $(d + 1)(3d + 5)$ **29** $(t - 3)(3t + 2)$ **31** $(2x - 3)(3x - 5)$ **33** $(b + 2)^2$ **35** $(w - 5)^2$ **37** $(3z + 5)^2$ **39** $(2p + 11)^2$ **41** $(u + 10)(u - 10)$ **43** $(6a + 1)(6a - 1)$ **45** $4(n + 2)(n - 2)$ **47** $5(z + 3)(z + 2)$ **49** $2t(5t - 4)(5t + 4)$ **51** $k^4(k + 3)(k - 3)$ **53** $(3c - 10d)(3c + 10d)$ **55** $-9, -3, 3$, and 9 **57** -18 and 18 **59** Agree. Explanation:

$(a - b)^2 = a^2 - ab - ab + b^2 = a^2 - 2ab + b^2$
$(b - a)^2 = b^2 - ab - ab + a^2 = a^2 - 2ab + b^2$

Chapter 5 Preparing for the ADP[SM] Algebra I Exam

1 C **3** D **5** D **7** C **9** A **11** A **13** A **15** C **17** C **19** B **21** D **23** C **25** D **27** $4x^2 + 60x + 144$ ft^2 **29**
- $1200r^2 + 2400r + 1200$
- \$1273.08
- \$1285.47
- \$2142.45

Chapter 6

Lesson 6.1

1 C **3** C **5** 7 or −7 **7** 4 or −4 **9** 4 or −4 **11** 1 or −1 **13** 3 or −3 **15** 3.16 or −3.16 **17** 1.41 or −1.41 **19** −1.32 or 11.32 **21** 60 or −60 **23** 19.2 feet **25** $7m^2$; 5

Lesson 6.2

1 C **3** D **5** −8 and 1 **7** −8 and 8 **9** −3 and $\frac{7}{2}$ **11** −2, 0, and 9 **13** 10 **15** 4 and 9 **17** 8 feet and 11 feet **19** 5 **21** $\frac{3}{5}$ and −1 **23** 1.0 and −0.5 **25** −1 and $\frac{7}{2}$

Lesson 6.3

1 D **3** A **5** vertex (0, 0), up, minimum **7** vertex (0, 0), down, maximum **9** vertex (0, 5), down, maximum **11** vertex (3, 8), down, maximum **13** 2

15

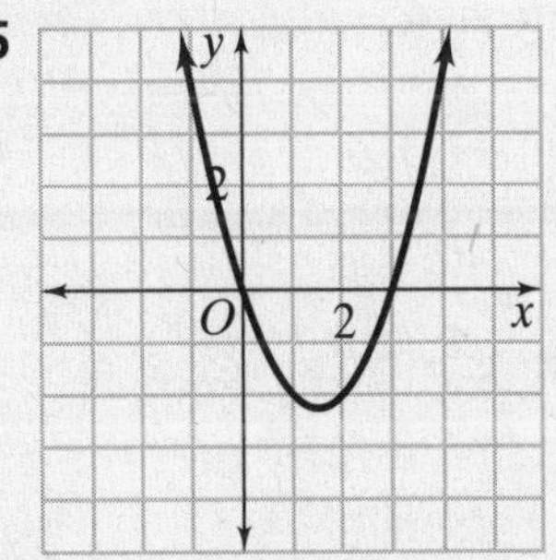

17

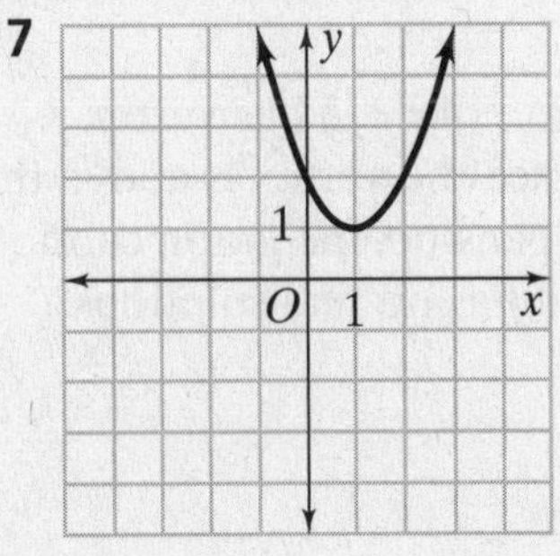

19

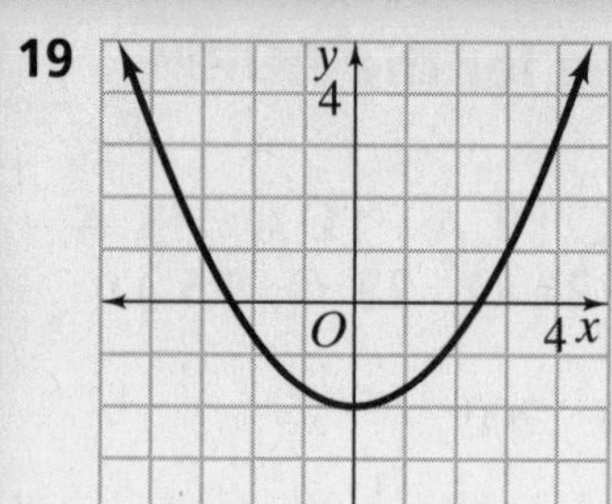

21

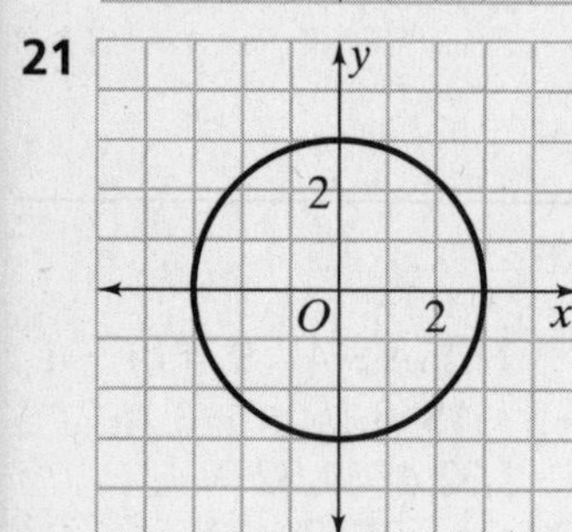

23

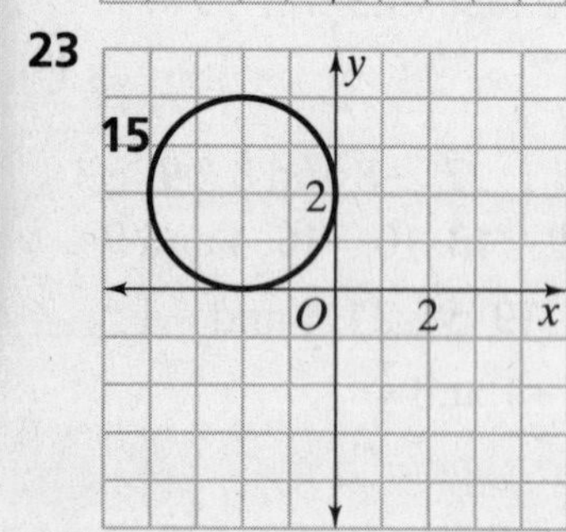

25 $y = a(x + 3)(x - 4)$ for some nonzero real number a. If $y = 6$ when $x = 0$, then $6 = a(-12)$. Thus, $a = -\frac{1}{2}$. Therefore, $y = -\frac{1}{2}x^2 + \frac{1}{2}x + 6$.

27 $(x + 5)^2 + (y - 2)^2 = 5^2$

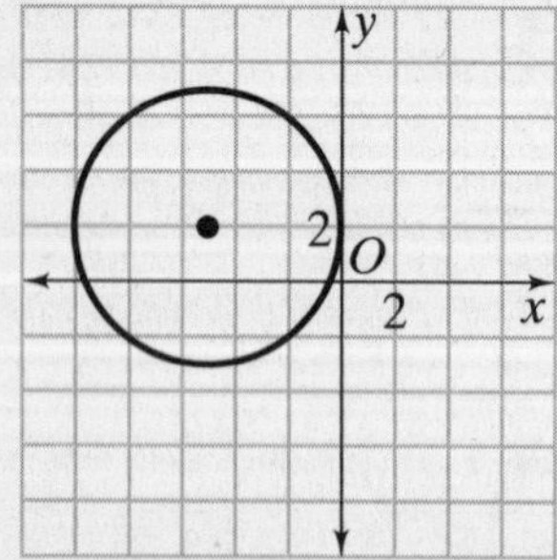

29 The graph of $y = x^2 - 4x + 5$ has vertex $(2, 1)$ and opens up. Since the vertex is above the x-axis and the graph opens up, the graph cannot cross the x-axis. Thus, it has no real solutions.

Lesson 6.4

1 A 3 B

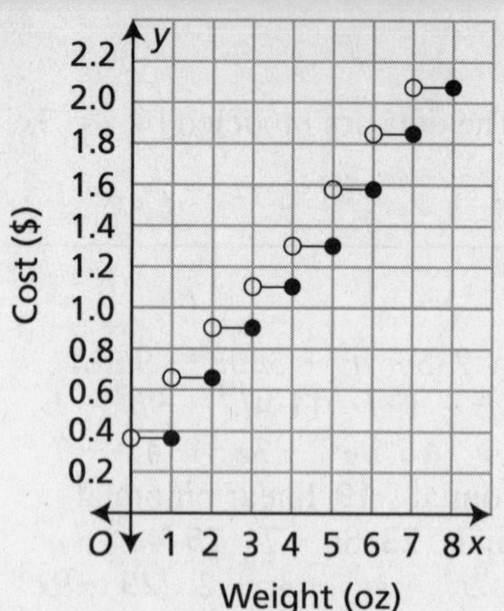

Chapter 6 Preparing for the ADP[SM] Algebra I Exam

1 B 3 B 5 A 7 C 9 A 11 D 13 B 15 C 17 C 19 B 21 B

23 $-\frac{1}{2}x^2 - \frac{3}{2}x + 5 = y$

25 • x^2
• x^2
• 9 feet

Chapter 7

Lesson 7.1

1 C 3 B 5 A 7 $h \neq 0$ 9 none

11 $a \neq 0, a \neq b$ 13 $\frac{u}{u + 2}, u \neq -2$

15 $\frac{1}{2t - 1}, t \neq 0, t \neq \frac{1}{2}$ 17 $\frac{1}{c}, c \neq 0, c \neq -3$

19 $\frac{3 - 6w}{2w^2}, w \neq 0$ 21 $\frac{x - y}{x + y}, x \neq 0, x \neq -y$

23 $\frac{1}{v - 7}, v \neq 7, v \neq -7$ 25 $\frac{r + 2}{r + 4}, r \neq -4, r \neq 3$

27 $\frac{z + 1}{2}, z \neq \frac{1}{4}$ 29 $-g - 3, g \neq \frac{3}{2}$

31 $-\frac{m}{n}, n \neq 0, n \neq m$ 33 No; When $p = 3$ and $q = -1$, $p^2 - 9q^2 = (3)^2 - 9(-1)^2 = 0$.

Lesson 7.2

1 B 3 B 5 $\frac{27}{j^2}$ 7 $\frac{1}{2c}$ 9 $\frac{2m^6}{27}$ 11 $16y^3$

13 $\frac{15}{2x^2y^2}$ 15 $\frac{4(2 - t)}{t(4 + t)}$, or $\frac{8 - 4t}{4t + t^2}$ 17 $\frac{8}{3}$

19 $\frac{2(y + 4)}{y}$, or $\frac{2y + 8}{y}$

21 $\frac{1}{g(g-1)}$, or $\frac{1}{g^2-g}$ **23** $\frac{b+2}{b-2}$

25 $\frac{n+4}{n-2}$ **27** $6(h-3)$, or $6h-18$

29 $\frac{y-5}{(y+5)(y-2)}$, or $\frac{y-5}{y^2+3y-10}$

Lesson 7.3

1 C **3** B **5** $\frac{10}{g}$ **7** $-\frac{2}{r}$ **9** $\frac{9}{v}$ **11** $\frac{c+10}{5c}$

13 $-\frac{b}{b+3}$ **15** $\frac{1}{5}$ **17** $\frac{8a}{a-4}$ **19** $\frac{2q-9}{q+1}$

21 $\frac{2z-8}{z-3}$ **23** $\frac{5}{2(k+1)}$, or $\frac{5}{2k+2}$

25 $\frac{3y-8}{4(y-4)}$, or $\frac{3y-8}{4y-16}$ **27** $\frac{2}{x-2}$

29 $\frac{2a}{(a-b)(a+b)}$, or $\frac{2a}{a^2-b^2}$

31 $\frac{-5a+28}{a-4}$

Lesson 7.4

1 B **3** D **5** 5 **7** −60 **9** 0.8 **11** $\frac{18}{65}$
13 1 and 2 **15** 2 **17** ±8 **19** −7
21 6 and 7 **23** ±9 **25** 18 minutes

Lesson 7.5

1 B **3** C **5** 18 **7** 200 **9** $\frac{13}{5}$ **11** $\frac{\sqrt{10}}{3}$

13 $\frac{5\sqrt{2}}{9}$ **15** $7w^3$ **17** xy^3 **19** $c\sqrt{ab}$

21 $\frac{4v\sqrt{v}}{5}$ **23** 16 **25** $2\sqrt{2}$ **27** $5t\sqrt{7}$

29 $2d\sqrt{d}$ **31** $4\sqrt{11}$ **33** $5\sqrt{2}$ **35** $\sqrt{3}$

37 $2+\sqrt{6}$ **39** $15-2\sqrt{10}$ **41** $-1-2\sqrt{2}$

43 3 **45** $7\sqrt{3}-5\sqrt{6}$ **47** $\sqrt{16(n+2)}+\sqrt{4(n+2)}=4\sqrt{n+2}+2\sqrt{n+2}=6\sqrt{n+2}$ **49** $x=18$ **51** $v=12$

53 $y=1$

Chapter 7 Preparing for the ADP[SM] Algebra I Exam

1 C **3** B **5** D **7** D **9** A **11** C

13 B **15** A **17** D **19** D **21** B

23 • $\frac{x+2}{24}=\frac{x}{6}$
• 2 hours 40 minutes

Chapter 8

Lesson 8.1

1 B **3** B **5** A **7** The event with probability 0.6. **9** 55% **11** $\frac{5}{36}$ **13** $\frac{1}{18}$

15

1	2	3
$\frac{8}{25}$	$\frac{9}{25}$	$\frac{8}{25}$

Lesson 8.2

1 D **3** C **5** $\frac{4}{13}$ **7** $\frac{7}{26}$ **9** $\frac{1}{3}$ **11** $\frac{2}{3}$

13 $\frac{2}{9}$ **15** $\frac{1}{3}$

Lesson 8.3

1 A **3** C **5** A **7** $\frac{5}{36}$ **9** $\frac{1}{11}$ **11** $\frac{7}{22}$

13 $\frac{3}{8}$ **15** $\frac{1}{2}$ **17** $\frac{28}{65}$ **19** $\frac{3}{7}$ **21** $\frac{1}{30}$ **23** $\frac{1}{20}$

Lesson 8.4

1 B **3** 210 **5** 4,745; 1,820

Lesson 8.5

1 C **3** B **5** D **7** $\frac{11}{14}$ **9** $\frac{11}{221}$

Chapter 8 Preparing for the ADP[SM] Algebra I Exam

1 A **3** D **5** C **7** A **9** A **11** D **13** D
15 B **17** B **19** C **21** D **23** B **25** A
27 • *P*(geometry book is placed first) = $\frac{1}{3}$

Chapter 9

Lesson 9.1

1 B **3** A **5** D 7 8.2 9 20–22

11 $\frac{4n+6}{4}$ **13** 12.75 15 6

Lesson 9.2

1 a. Population − NFL players b. Sample − 25% that responded c. The variable of interest − Use of steroids in training
d. Potential for bias − Nonresponse. Difficult to generalize because who responds is related to the question asked. Users of steroids probably will not respond to the survey. **3** a. Population − Air in the school b. Sample − **20** air samples

c. The variable of interest – quality of air, d. Potential for bias – Where were the samples taken? Were the locations randomly selected? Were all sections of the school represented in the sample? **5** Yes. Telephone subscribers are probably different from nonsubscribers. For example, some people have only a cell phone and do not subscribe to regular phone service. Others screen their calls and may not answer survey calls. **7** No, the process may deteriorate after the first 30 items. Sampling randomly throughout the day would be preferred. **9** Qualitative **11** Qualitative **13** Quantitative, continuous **15** Bivariate **17** Bivariate **19** Voluntary response sample 2 unbiased **21** Convenience and voluntary response sample – biased

Lesson 9.3

1 A **3** A

5

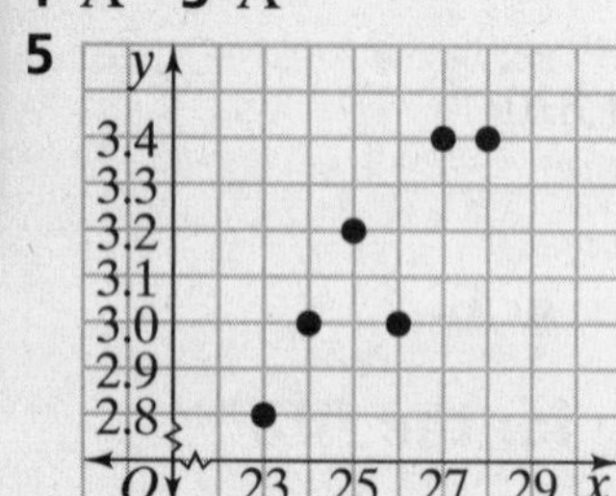

7

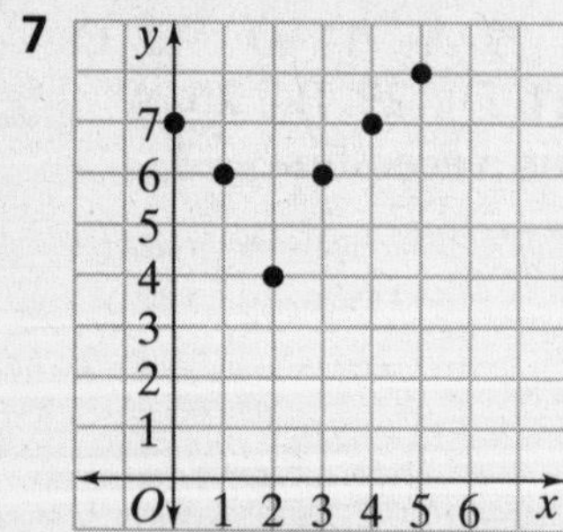

9

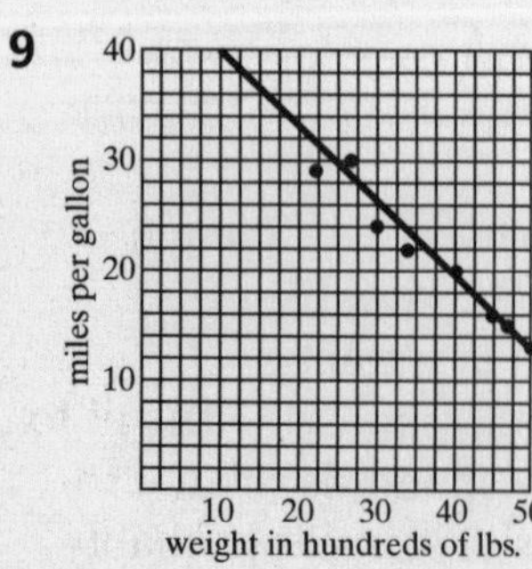

Approximately 14 miles per gallon; about 4250 lbs. 11 24.5°F

Lesson 9.4

1 D **3** During the specified period of time, the population increased, and the number of people who were employed and the number of people who were unemployed had both increased. **5** Although the dimensions of the large house are twice the smaller, the area is four times as large. This gives the impression that the increase is greater than it actually is. The graphs are not aligned at the bottom.

Chapter 9 Preparing for the ADP[SM] Algebra I Exam

1 B **3** D **5** B **7** D **9** B **11** C **13** B **15** D **17** A **19** The sample is biased because the population is made up of only people who already frequent the restaurant at lunchtime.

ADP[SM] Algebra I Sample Test I

1 B **3** No. $\left(\frac{1}{2}\right)^2 = \frac{1}{4}$ and $\frac{1}{4} < \frac{1}{2}$ **5** D **7** A **9** A **11** C **13** D **15** A **17** D

19 The vertex is located at (–2, 7) and the parabola opens downward.

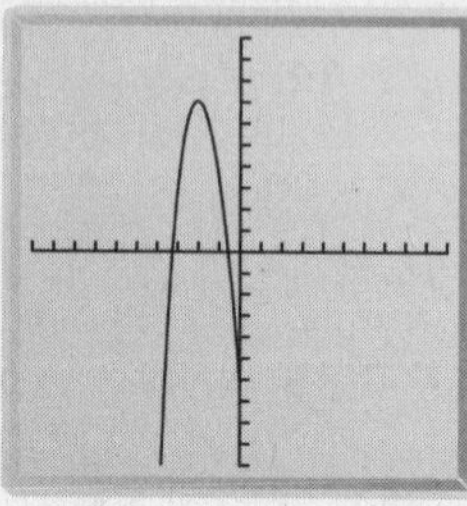

x-scale = 1 *y*-scale = 1

21 D **23** D **25** C **27** B **29** D **31** A **33** B **35** D **37** C **39** D

41 $\begin{cases} s + a = 600 \\ 5s + 9a = 3632 \end{cases}$; $a = 158$ tickets

43 B **45** A

47 A **49** Each side measures about 9.7 inches.

51 16% $\frac{4}{10} \times \frac{4}{10} = \frac{16}{100}$ **53** B **55** C

57 **Part A.** Answers will vary.
Part B. There is a negative correlation meaning that more absences are connected to lower grades. There is one significant outlier: a student with 95% and 5 absences.

Part C. The data sampling is small. Also, reasons for absences are not considered. Other factors that could affect correlation are whether the absences are consecutive.

ADP[SM] Algebra I Sample Test 2

1 B **3** 30; $\begin{cases} s - 2 = 7(p - 2) \\ s = 5p \end{cases}$ **5** C **7** B **9** D

11 C **13** B **15** B **17** $a - 4$

19 Part A

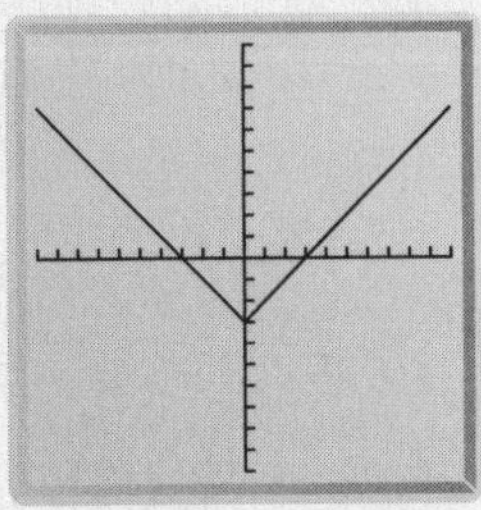

x-scale = 1 y-scale = 1

Part B Domain: all real numbers; Range: $\{y(2x) \,|\, y(2x) \geq -3\}$ **21** A **23** C **25** B **27** C **29** B **31** A **33** B **35** D **37** D **39** C

41 $\begin{cases} L = 2W - 4 \\ 2L + 2W = 58 \end{cases}$;
length = 18 inches;
width = 11 inches
43 D **45** B **47** C

49 12 and 5 **51** $\frac{1}{2}$ **53** C **55** B **57** B

INDEX

A

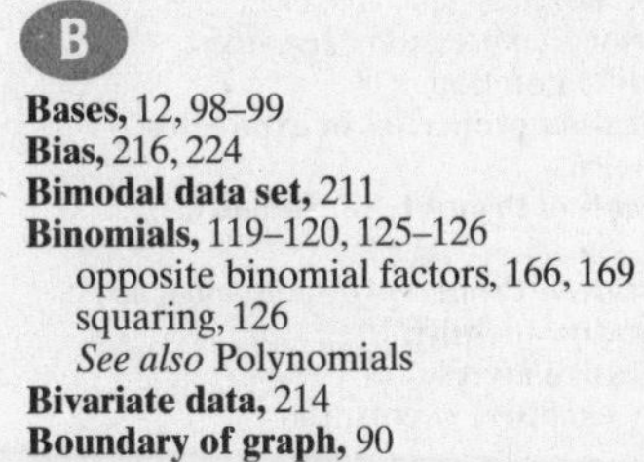

INDEX

INDEX

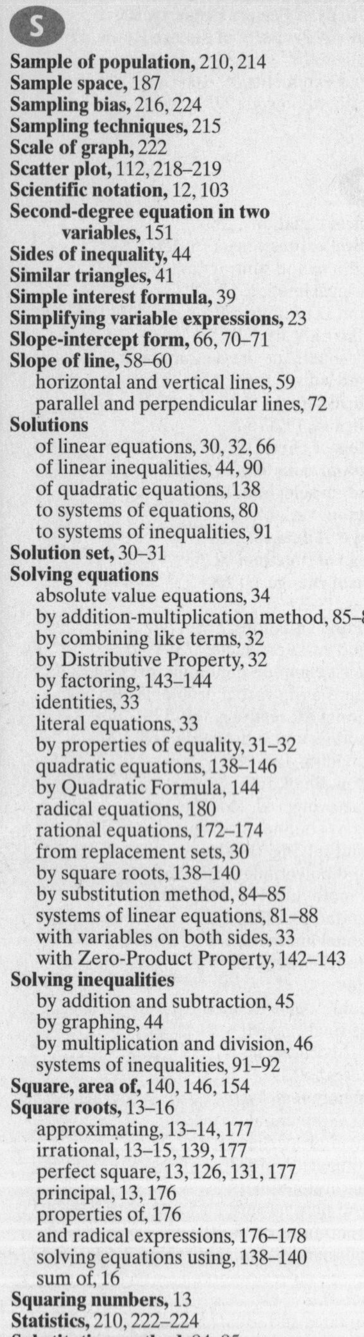

ACKNOWLEDGMENTS

Staff Credits:

The people who make up the ***ADP Algebra I Brief Review*** team—representing design, editorial, educational technology, marketing, production services, and publication processes—are listed below. Boldface type denotes the core team members.

Jane Breen, Stacey Clark, **Jennifer Creane**, **Glen Dixon**, **Linda D. Johnson**, Courtney Marsh

Additional Credits:

The Quarasan Group, Inc.: Chicago, IL;
Bob Burnham, Kathy Osmus

Lapiz Digital Services: Chennai, India
Lapiz, Inc.: Boston, MA

Cover Image:

Shutterstock/Steve Degenhardt